The New Hacker's Dictionary

The New Hacker's Dictionary

Second Edition

compiled by
Eric S. Raymond

foreword and cartoons by
Guy L. Steele Jr.

The MIT Press
Cambridge, Massachusetts
London, England

This book was typeset by ESR using TeX 3.0 and a customized version of GNU's Texinfo package, with formatting by TechBooks. The running font is Adobe Times Roman. This book corresponds to version 3.0.0 of the on-line Jargon File.

Printed and bound in the United States of America.

Cover art by Duane Bibby.

Library of Congress Cataloging-in-Publication Data

The New hacker's dictionary / compiled by Eric S. Raymond; foreword and cartoons by
Guy L. Steele, Jr. — 2nd ed.
p. cm.
ISBN 0-262-18154-1. — ISBN 0-262-68079-3 (pbk.)
1. Electronic data processing—Terminology—Humor. 2. Computers—Humor.
3. Computers—Slang—Dictionaries. I. Raymond, Eric S. II. Steele, Guy.
PN6231.E4H3 1993
004' .014—dc20 93-2464
CIP

Dedication

This edition is for Cathy, and all the women and men like her who've ever snuggled up to a crashing hacker at 4AM in the morning. You keep us reminded of what's real.

Disclaimer

Much of the content of this book does not reflect the opinions of the editors or publishers. In fact, if you could get all the contributors to agree on anything you'd be ready for the Nobel Peace Prize.

Contents

Confessions of a Happy Hacker *by Guy L. Steele Jr.* ix
Hacker in a Strange Land *by Eric S. Raymond* xv
Preface to the Second Edition xix

Introduction 1
How Jargon Works 9
How to Use the Lexicon 25

The Jargon Lexicon 31

Appendix A: Hacker Folklore 467
Appendix B: A Portrait of J. Random Hacker 483
Appendix C: Bibliography 491
Contributors 497

Confessions of a Happy Hacker

Guy L. Steele Jr.

I was a teen-age hacker.

When I was about twelve or so, a lab secretary at MIT who knew I was 'interested in science' (it might be more accurate to say 'a latent nerd' — more on that later) arranged for one of the computer hackers there to give me an informal tour. I remember stumbling around racks full of circuit boards and wires, a screeching cabinet that printed a full page every six seconds, and rows of blinking lights; the computer room was crammed full of equipment with no obvious organization. One set of gray cabinets had some trophies and plaques sitting on it: this was the PDP-6 computer that, running a program called MacHack, won prizes playing against human players in chess tournaments. The PDP-6 also had two speakers and a stereo amplifier sitting on top of it. The hacker typed a couple of commands on a keyboard, and the PDP-6 burst into a Bach Brandenburg concerto (no. 6, as I recall).

One part of that tour stands out most clearly in my mind. I was told to sit down in front of a large, round, glass screen and was given a box that had some buttons and a stick on the top. My hacker guide typed another command on the keyboard and, suddenly, green and purple spaceships appeared on the screen! The purple one started shooting little red dots at the green one, which was soon obliterated in a multicolored shower of sparkles. The green ship was mine, and the hacker had expertly shot it down. Years later I learned that this had been a color version of Space War, one of the very first video games.

Remember that this was years before 'Apple' and 'TRS-80' had become household words. Back then computers were still rather mysterious, hidden away in giant corporations and university laboratories.

Playing Space War was fun, but I learned nothing of programming then. I had the true fascination of computers revealed to me in November, 1968, when a chum slipped me the news that our school (Boston Latin) had an IBM computer locked up in the basement. I was dubious. I had earlier narrowly avoided buying from a senior a ticket to the fourth-floor swimming pool (Boston Latin has only three stories, and no swimming pool at all), and assumed this was another scam. So of course I laughed in his face.

When he persisted, I checked it out. Sure enough, in a locked basement room was an IBM 1130 computer. If you want all the specs: 4096 words of memory, 16 bits per word, a 15-character-per-second Selectric ('golf ball') printer, and a card reader (model 1442) that could read 300 cards per minute. Yes, this was back in the days of punched cards. Personal computers were completely unheard of then.

Nominally the computer was for the training of juniors and seniors, but I cajoled a math teacher into lending me a computer manual and spent all of Thanksgiving vacation reading it.

I was hooked.

No doubt about it. I was born to be a hacker. Fortunately, I didn't let my studies suffer (as many young hackers do), but every spare moment I thought about the computer. It was spellbinding. I wanted to know all about it: what it could and couldn't do, how its programs worked, what its circuits looked like. During study halls, lunch, and after school, I could be found in the computer room, punching programs onto cards and running them through the computer.

I was not the only one. Very soon there was a small community of IBM 1130 hackers. We helped to maintain the computer and we tutored our less fanatical fellow students in the ways of computing. What could possibly compensate us for these chores? Free rein in the computer room.

Soon after that, I developed into one of the unauthorized but tolerated 'random people' hanging around the MIT Artificial Intelligence Laboratory. A random hacker is to a computer laboratory much as a groupie is to a rock band: not really doing useful work, but emotionally involved and contributing to the ambience, if nothing else. After a while, I was haunting the computer rooms at off-hours, talking to people but more often looking for chances to run programs. Sometimes 'randoms' such as I were quite helpful, operating the computers for no pay and giving advice to college students who were having trouble. Sometimes, however, we were quite a nuisance. Once I was ejected from the Artificial Intelligence Laboratory by none other than Richard Greenblatt, the very famous hacker who had written the MacHack program with which the PDP-6 had won its chess trophies. He threw me out because I was monopolizing the one terminal that produced letter-quality copy. (I was using the computer as a word processor to write customized form letters to various computer manufacturers, asking them to send me computer manuals.) I deserved to be tossed out and gave him no argument. But when you're hooked, you're hooked, and I was undaunted; within a week or two I was back again.

Eventually I got a part-time job as a programmer at MIT's Project MAC computer laboratory. There I became a full-fledged member of the hacker community, and ultimately an MIT graduate student.

I was never a lone hacker, but one of many. Despite stories you may have read about anti-social nerds glued permanently to display screens, totally addicted to the computer, hackers have (human) friends too. Through timesharing (where many people use one computer) and networking (where many computers are connected together), the computer makes possible a new form of human communication, better than the telephone and the postal system put together. You can send a message by electronic mail and get a reply within two minutes, or you can just link two terminals together and have a conversation. This sort of thing used to be a near-exclusive province of hackers, but is nowadays quite commonplace through commercial services such as Compuserve and GEnie.

Speaking of nerds: a hacker doesn't have to be a nerd (but it helps). More important, it is certainly not true that all nerds are hackers! Too many nerds are just nerds. But I must mention one more story from my days at MIT. When the famous National Lampoon "Are You a Nerd?" poster first came out in the mid-1970s, a secretary at MIT bought a copy to post outside her office door so everyone at the laboratory could enjoy the joke (which we did, immensely). As she was taping it up, I happened to be leaving for dinner, briefcase in hand. I glanced at the poster, then put on my glasses (heavy black frames — I still wear them), hiked up my polyester slacks an extra half-inch, and assumed The Pose (booger and all). I matched about 80% of the itemized points: button-down shirt with loose collar, six pens in my shirt pocket, same haircut — too bad I had left my slide rule at home. The poor secretary turned beet-red and protested, "N-no! I didn't mean *you*!" I just chuckled and told her that the poster artist had obviously done a remarkably good job. (Being a nerd isn't all bad — sometimes it can turn a girl's head. Once, when I was fifteen, I was strolling across Copley Square in downtown Boston and passed three bubblegum teenyboppers. I just barely caught one of them exclaiming to her friends, "Wow! Did you see all those pens?")

Perhaps one reason for the nerd-hacker connection is that the truly dedicated hacker does little else but eat, sleep, and hack. Hackers often work strange hours that put them out of synch with normal humanity. Some hackers just get up at dinnertime and go to bed after breakfast, or perhaps get up at noon and sack out at 4 A.M. (See the terms **phase** and **night mode** for more information on hackers' sleeping schedules.) Before computers were inexpensive enough to be 'personal', they had to be shared, either by taking turns or by what is called timesharing (where the computer is programmed to take turns at split-second speeds). Either way, there was heavier demand for the computer during the day than at night, because non-hacker users tended to work during the day. Hackers often therefore worked late into the evening or night, when the other computer users weren't competing for cycles. It's more fun, after all, to use the computer when it's responding at split-second speeds.

Now that personal computers and individual workstations are ubiquitous, there is less need to avoid day shifts. Many hackers, however, still find a 10 P.M.-to-6 A.M. or noon-to-8 A.M. schedule more pleasant than rising at the crack of dawn. There are different theories about why this is so: my personal one is that there is some correlation between the hackish sort of creativity and 'night person' physiology. It has also been suggested that working at night is an adaptation to the hacker's need for long stretches of **hack mode**, a literally altered state of consciousness that doesn't tolerate distractions well; I find this eminently reasonable. Just as the VCR has allowed television watchers to 'time-shift' movies, electronic mail allows the hacker to time-shift most of his communication with others, making it much less important for everyone to have exactly the same work hours.

The earliest of the hacker cultures that directly contributed to this book was the one that grew up around the PDP-1 at MIT in the early 1960s (many of these people were also in TMRC, the Tech Model Railroad Club). Later, the PDP-1 hackers formed the nucleus of the famed MIT AI Lab. Thus, when I began hacking there I connected with a tradition that was already well established, and was to continue as one of its most important sub-communities for another decade.

But MIT had no monopoly on hackers. In the 1960s and 1970s hackers congregated around any computer center that made computer time available for play. (Some of this play turned out to be very important work, but hacking is done mostly for fun, for its own sake, for the pure joy of it.) Because universities tend to be more flexible than corporations in this regard, most hackers' dens arose in university laboratories. While some of these hackers were unauthorized 'random people' like me, many hackers were paid employees who chose to stay after hours and work on their own projects — or even continue their usual work — purely for pleasure.

The hacker community became larger and more closely knit after 1969, when the government funded a project to see whether it would be useful and practical to let the computers at dozens of universities and other sites 'talk' to each other. The project succeeded and produced the famous ARPANET, a network that now links hundreds of computers across the country. Through the ARPANET researchers could share programs, trade research results, and send electronic mail — both to individuals and to massive mailing lists.

And it first allowed once-isolated hackers to talk to each other via computer. During the two decades that followed, other networks grew and connected to the ARPANET. Eventually software gave most of these a common address space; the resulting super-network, called 'Internet' or simply 'the net', links thousands and thousands of computers worldwide. The ARPANET itself no longer exists as a distinct entity.

The result is a worldwide hackers' community, now two decades old. In some ways the community serves as a geographically dispersed think tank; people use it to share ideas and software. One good recent example of this was during the great cold-fusion flap of 1988; many of the papers on both sides of the dispute were available on the net long before making print.

But the net also has a social importance non-hackers tend to miss. I have many friends that I have never met face to face or talked to on the telephone. I feel I know them quite well, though, because I've had extended conversations with them through the computer. (I had one friend through the computer who worked in the same building that I did, but I never knew he was deaf until I chanced to meet him face to face several months later!)

When you walk up to the terminal of a time-shared computer, the first thing you do is to 'log in', that is, tell the computer who you are. As a result everyone acquires a login name, which you need to know to communicate with another hacker via computer. A login name serves in much the same way as a CB 'handle'. Login names are often used as nicknames, pronounced if possible and spelled if necessary. My wife and I met at MIT, and she still calls me "Gliss" because my login name was GLS. "Guy" still sounds very weird to her, even after N years of marriage.

On the net, people are usually known by their logins and addresses. Thus, I have many friends whom I know only by login name; I have no idea what their real names are. Once, at a wedding, I ran into a good hacker friend who was also a guest there. I recalled his login name instantly, but was embarrassed that I couldn't immediately remember his real name in order to introduce him to a third person. It was 'swapped out' (see **swap**). A more egregious example: when Barbara and I got married, we sent out wedding invitations of the usual sort without considering the consequences. One hacker friend was completely puzzled: "Barbara Kerns . . . Guy Steele . . . Who *are* these people???" His girlfriend looked over his shoulder and said, tentatively, "Guy Steele . . . isn't that Quux?" This was someone I knew quite well, but he knew me only by that handle. Some hackers actually prefer to be called by their login name and seldom use their given ('mundane') names (Richard Stallman, aka RMS, is a well-known example).

In these and other ways, the working and social life of the hacker revolves primarily around the computer. This is not to say that hackers have no other interests; for a look at those, see appendix B, the Portrait of J. Random Hacker. But hackerdom is defined by the community of interest that has grown up around computers and electronic networks. Indeed, these electronic networks have grown in importance over time.

When I drafted the first version of this preface, in 1983, I expressed some concern that hackerdom might be dying — killed off, ironically, by the spread of knowledge about computers. As programming education became more formalized, as the personal computer atomized hacker communities previously knitted together by timesharing, and as the lure of big money in industry siphoned off some of the best and brightest, it seemed as though hackerdom's unique values might be lost.

Though these gloomy predictions were an accurate projection of some trends of that year, they didn't survive an editor's objections and never made it into the first edition. This is perhaps fortunate; now, in 1991, I am happy to report that hacking is most certainly not dead. Some of its traditional vehicles, licit and illicit, have disappeared: the PDP-10 is no longer manufactured, and improved technology and security have made phone phreaking much less intellectually rewarding. But the hacking spirit remains very much alive. The personal computer revolution has made hackers free to hack almost anywhere — and the net is the community glue.

This book was put together almost entirely through the net. Hundreds of contributors responded to a net-wide request for new entries and updates. Eric Raymond sifted through thousands of electronic messages, collecting old and new words and cross-checking the evidence. (By the way, I got to know Eric through the net — we worked on this project for about a year before meeting face to face.)

The New Hacker's Dictionary reflects the technological and social changes in the hacker community over the last decade or so (Eric's preface discusses some of these). At times, assisting Eric in this project has made me feel like an old fuddy-duddy; more often I have felt freshly charged with the excitement of the hacker spirit. Hackers are doing exciting new things and coining new words and phrases to describe their changing and innovative culture. If you want to get involved, interest, ability, and computer access are pretty much the only requirements; social skills help a great deal but are not mandatory. If you are just curious, this book provides a window into a strange world that may amuse or astonish you. Whichever it may be, welcome!

Happy hacking!

Hacker in a Strange Land

Eric S. Raymond

I am a hacker of a later generation than Guy Steele and the coauthors of the first edition, and my history is different from theirs in a way that illuminates the major changes that have taken place in hackerdom since that edition was published in 1983. This revised and massively expanded edition is a response to those changes, so I think a bit of my history might illuminate its whys and wherefores.

Back around 1968, I was one of the first few hundred people in the world to play a video game. I was about twelve years old, and my father (an executive for UNIVAC and himself formerly one of the very first programmers back in the days of the great electromechanical dinosaurs of the 1950s) sat me down in front of an $8 million mainframe and showed me how. The program was a demo for the UNISCOPE 3000, which many have called the first commercial video terminal. By pressing keys on the keyboard, you could drop a bomb from a little vector-graphic bomber at a stick-figure freighter sailing serenely across the cartoon sea at the bottom of the tube. If you hit (which wasn't trivial, because the bomb followed a proper parabolic trajectory) the machine would oblige with a lovely little explosion, after which the ship would break up and sink majestically beneath the waves.

I was fascinated — even more so after they showed me the keys that allowed one to vary the speed of the bomber, the speed of the ship, and the height and angle of the bomber's passes. I quickly mastered hitting the ship and lost interest in the default settings; I spent the rest of my time there experimenting with various extreme combinations of the simulation parameters — hacking at the program, trying to see what I could make it do. I remember being disappointed at the realization that the ship would break up in exactly the same way regardless of where the bomb hit.

It took me ten years to realize it, but that experience set my feet on the road to hackerdom. In 1972, I played BASIC games on some *amazingly* clunky ASR-33 teletypes hooked up to the old Dartmouth Time-Sharing System; I'll never forget the uniquely satisfying *tchoonk* those stiff keys made, and the musty smell and feel of the yellow paper they spooled on the carriage in huge rolls. I hadn't learned how to program yet, but DTSS included some rudimentary email/talk mode facilities and I had my first exposure to the odd and wonderful world of on-line communication there. Then, in high school around 1974, I did a little hacking on a Wang 720B 'programmable calculator', a big clunky machine with a neat nixie-tube display that you could program with ditsy little punched cards; five years later it would have been called a personal computer. But what I was serious about was wanting to be a pure mathematician; all this stuff with computers was just playing around.

If I'd gone to MIT, I would certainly have gravitated to the AI Lab hacker culture, which was perhaps at its most vigorous when I started college in 1976. As things turned out, I went to the University of Pennsylvania and learned hacking more or less on my own using a 'borrowed' account on the Wharton School's DEC-10. When it became apparent that I'd taken on too much too soon and burned out in the math department, getting seriously into hacking seemed the most natural thing in the world. In 1978, I was mousing around on the ITS systems using a tourist account over the ARPANET; by 1979, I was handholding for APL and LISP users, making my lunch money coding for research projects, and writing a manual for UCI LISP that for all I know may still be in use at Penn. And sometime in there I got my first look at the old Jargon File. I loved it, and I spread some of the jargon around among the other expert-user and fledgling-hacker types at my site.

My first real job, in 1980, was in a LISP support group for AI research at Burroughs. But that only lasted a year, and it was after that that my career really took a turn away from what, up to then, had been the 'classical' hacker growth path. I'd been one of the last generation of LISP hackers to cut my teeth on the PDP-10; and, while I was at Burroughs, I became one of the first to get involved with microcomputers. I bought an Osborne 1 and learned CP/M; a few months later, I ditched that and bought IBM PC number six-hundred-and-something.

Yes, the age of the personal computer had arrived. For the next two and a half years I toiled over TRS-80s and IBM PCs in a basement sweatshop off Walnut Street in Philadelphia. In 1983 I went to work for a startup company in the suburbs, helping write comm software to link microcomputers to VAXen and IBM mainframes. Outside, change was overtaking the AI-hacker culture that Steele & Co. had grown up in and I had briefly been part of. The DEC-10 died, displaced by the VAX; the AI Lab lost its bloom as rival groups tried to commercialize LISP and AI technology; and, almost unnoticed by the AI crowd, an operating system called UNIX was beginning to win hearts and minds out in the real world.

I'd first become intrigued by UNIX in 1974 after reading the classic Thompson and Ritchie paper in *Communications of the ACM*, only to have my curiosity pooh-poohed by my father's mainframe colleagues. When I moved to the 'burbs in '83 I learned C and sold my new employers on the idea of training me into their house UNIX wizard — and that's just what I did for two and a half years. I grew into my maturity as a programmer right along with UNIX and C, watching them spread from a few niches in academic and research environments into an unstoppable tide that completely transformed the computing landscape.

The second time I saw the Jargon File was in late '83, right around the time the first edition of *The Hacker's Dictionary* came out — with nary a word about C or microcomputers or UNIX or any of the areas where I *knew* the hottest action in computers was happening. At the time I just accepted it — in fact, I printed out a copy and gave it to my boss as a joke, in a report folder blazoned with "UNDERSTANDING YOUR HACKER" in big letters on the outside. And then I hardly thought about it for the next six years. I was very busy programming, writing, consulting, and building a professional reputation as a UNIX expert. I was lucky; my background convinced me earlier than most that UNIX on microcomputers was going to be the wave of the commodity-computing future, so I was out front ready to catch it as it rose.

When I stumbled across the Jargon File again in early 1990, then, I saw it from a new and more confident point of view. By then, I'd known Richard Stallman for years and had brought EMACS into the UNIX shops I'd been working in. I'd grown used to seeing my own history and skills as a bridge between the 'old' LISP/PDP-10/ARPANET culture and the huge newer community of C and UNIX hackers and USENETters and personal computer hobbyists in which I'd spent most of the 1980s. I'd even originated some jargon terms myself that I'd seen pass into fairly wide use on USENET or elsewhere (See: **bondage & discipline language**, **code-grinder**, **crawling horror**, **defenestration**, **drool-proof paper**, **fear and loathing**, **larval stage**, **nailed to the wall**, **quantum bogodynamics**, **raster burn**, **rice box**, **silly walk**).

So I called Guy Steele one day, and we hit it off well and got to talking . . . and the result is this *New Hacker's Dictionary* you hold in your hands. It's more than just a meeting of two cultures, his and mine, because we decided to make an effort to get input from all the different technical cultures we could reach.

So although a bit over half the entries are from the C/UNIX world and many of the rest are from the ITS/LISP culture of the 'old' Jargon file, there are healthy contributions from supercomputing, graphics, the compiler-design community, TCP/IP wizards, microcomputer developers, and just about everywhere else in computing where the true hacker nature is manifested.

A few days after I wrote the first version of this preface (in late April 1990), I received network mail indicating that the ITS machines were going to be shut down in the near future. These were the home of the old Jargon File and the digital heartland of the old AI-hacker culture at MIT; despite a couple of remnant ITS sites in Sweden, the decision to retire them truly marked the end of an era. They will doubtless be replaced by some conglomeration of UNIX machines — the final sign that it's truly up to the UNIX and C community to keep the flame alive now.

We hope this expanded lexicon will be educational to fledgling hackers, thought-provoking to linguists and anthropologists, and interesting to future historians of our technological age. And we hope it helps preserve and extend the values of the hacker culture: the dedication, the irreverence, the respect for competence, and the intellectual playfulness that makes hackers such a stimulating group to be among. But most of all, we hope it will be fun.

Preface to the Second Edition

Hackerdom's support and the general public's response to the first edition of this book vastly exceeded our expectations. We are delighted to be able to bring you this revised and updated second edition.

Here are the new entries:

0; 1TBS; AFJ; AI; AIDX; ARMM; ASCIIbetical order; BLOB; BOF; BUAF; BUAG; Bloggs Family, the; C Programmer's Disease; CrApTeX; DAU; DEC; DED; Duff's Device; FAQ; FITNR; FIXME; FM; Great Worm, the; HHOK; HHOS; ICBM address; IRC; If you want X, you know where to find it.; Imminent Death Of The Net Predicted!; Infinite-Monkey Theorem; KIBO; Life is hard; Lubarsky's Law of Cybernetic Entomology; MicroDroid; NetBOLLIX; Ninety-Ninety Rule, The; Nominal Semidestructor; Open DeathTrap; P-mail; PARC; PDL; PostScript; RTBM; RTFB; RTFS; Real Programmer; SIG; ScumOS; Share and enjoy!; Stupids; Sturgeon's Law; TANSTAAFL; TMRCie; That's not a bug, that's a feature!; This can't happen; Turing tar-pit; WYSIAYG; What's a spline?; XEROX PARC; XON; YAFIYGI; YKYBHTL; altmode; annoybot; atomic; bagbiting; barfmail; barney; blargh; blue wire; blurgle; bottom feeder; boustrophedon; brain fart; bread crumbs; break-even point; brochureware; bzzt, wrong; can't happen; candygrammar; cascade; cd tilde; channel hopping; channel op; channel; chanop; check; chop; command key; con; confuser; cooked mode; cookie jar; copious free time; core cancer; crack root; cracking; crayola books; creep; dark-side hacker; dead; death code; dec; decay; die horribly; die; dirtball; disclaimer; drum; dumb terminal; dumpster diving; elegance; error 33; evil and rude; external memory; fan; faradize; farkled; fat electrons; feature key; file signature; finn; firehose syndrome; flood; flypage; fnord; fontology; for values of; fork bomb; frink; frogging; fum; furrfu; gilley; gorets; grilf; gripenet; guru meditation; gweep; hacker ethic, the; hammer; hand cruft; hand-roll; handle; haque; heatseeker; hing; hysterical reasons; idempotent; inc; initgame; jack in; jolix; jupiter; kiboze; kick; klugistic; kyrka; lasherism; leapfrog attack; lightweight; line 666; line noise; lithium lick; locals, the; loose bytes; mailbomb; manularity; maximum Maytag mode; memory farts; memory smash; metasynctactic variable; metasyntactic variable; metasyntatctic variable; missile address; mockingbird; monty; moose call, the; muddie; mudheads; mumble; munge; nadger; nagware; nasal demons; neats vs. scruffies; netburp; netdead; netlag; netsplit; netter; nick; not ready for prime time; nroff; nude; ogg; one-banana problem; op; optical diff; optical grep; optimism; overflow pdl; pastie; person of no account; phage; phase-wrapping; plaid screen; point-and-drool interface; postcardware; power hit; printing discussion; programming fluid; purple wire; quine; rabbit job; rainbow series; real; red wire; register dancing; religion of CHI; return from the dead; robot; round tape; salt; samizdat; samurai; scag; scanno; schroedinbug; scream and die; screaming tty; scruffies; shambolic link; sharchive; shim; shovelware; sig virus; slack; smoke and mirrors; smoke; smurf; social engineering; software laser; spelling flame; spike; splash screen; spod; spoiler; spoo; spool file; square tape; stone knives and bearskins; sun lounge; syntactic salt; sysape; teledildonics; thumb; time bomb; trawl; treeware; troff; tron; tweeter; twilight zone; unleaded; ventilator card; virtual shredder; warlording; whack; whalesong; window shopping; wirewater; woofer; wumpus; yellow wire.

Here are the changed entries:

ASCII art; ASCII; BASIC; BIFF; Berkeley Quality Software; Big Gray Wall; COME FROM; Chernobyl packet; Commonwealth Hackish; DDT; Duff's device; EMACS; EOF; FAQ list; Fortrash; Great Renaming; Green's Theorem; J. Random Hacker; Lasherism; MFTL; MS-DOS; Moof; NIL; NP-; Nightmare File System; Obfuscated C Contest; PIP; Pascal; Purple Book; README file; RFC; RTFM; Red Book; T; TELNET; TMRC; UTSL; VAX; WIMP environment; WYSIWYG; White Book; Wizard Book; XXX; You know you've been hacking too long when...; Zork; alt; angle brackets; app; arena; bagbiter; baz; bit; blit; blivet; boat anchor; bogon; bounce; break; breath-of-life packet; brute force; bucky bits; bug; burble; by hand; byte; can; casters-up mode; chain; chicken head; compress; condom; connector conspiracy; control-Q; copy protection; copybroke; core; cracker; crash; crippleware; crock; cruft; cut a tape; dead code; deckle; delint; demo; deprecated; dickless workstation; diff; dongle-disk; dongle; dot file; dread high-bit disease; droid; drunk mouse syndrome; dusty deck; elegant; emoticon; epoch; exec; feature creature; fence; film at 11; flap; flat; foo; forked; fortune cookie; frob; frobnitz; funny money; glitch; gobble; gotcha; grep; grind; gubbish; gumby; hack value; hack; hacker; hairy; hamster; heavyweight; heisenbug; hop; hot spot; ice; infant mortality; kluge; kremvax; letterbomb; lexiphage; line starve; link farm; logical; magic cookie; magic number; mailing list; meta bit; microfortnight; microtape; misfeature; moby; mode; moria; mudhead; mung; neep-neep; one-liner wars; paper-net; parent message; patch; pdl; peek; ping; plan file; plokta; plonk; plumbing; postmaster; prettyprint; punched card; quantifiers; randomness; raw mode; real programmer; retcon; rococo; rude; saga; scratch monkey; security through obscurity; smart terminal; snarf; sorcerer's apprentice mode; space-cadet keyboard; spool; store;

syntactic sugar; talk mode; tar and feather; terpri; thread; tiger team; times-or-divided-by; tits on a keyboard; toolsmith; toto; trap door; tree-killer; tty; uninteresting; vadding; vdiff; virtual Friday; virtual; wabbit; wall time; wall; wedged; weenie; workaround; xyzzy; zorch.

The more than 250 new entries represent a quite substantial amount of fresh material. We are even more pleased to be able to include many historical and etymological additions to existing entries, many of which adduce vital facts previously unrecorded in print.

Special thanks to Pete Samson <prs@fernwood.mpk.ca.us>, compiler of the first TMRC Dictionary in 1959, for resurfacing to clarify the murky origins of several important jargon terms. In a few cases Mr. Samson's revelations overturned folk etymologies of long standing in hackerdom.

One of the goals for TNHD was to assist mainstream lexicographers and linguists in better understanding the meaning and etymology of some hackerisms which have passed into general use. We've since realized that the size and breadth of the collection might actually make it an embarrassment of riches for that audience. Accordingly, we direct the mainstream lexicographer's attention particularly to the entries for:

bells and whistles, **bogon**, **bogus**, **brain-dead**, **brute force**, **bug**, **catatonic**, **chad**, **copious free time**, **copyleft**, **cracker**, **cracking**, **crash**, **cruft**, **crufty**, **dark-side hacker**, **defenestration**, **dike**, **down**, **dumpster diving**, **fascist**, **fencepost error**, **Finagle's Law**, **flame**, **flame on**, **flame war**, **flamer**, **foo**, **foobar**, **frob**, **frobnicate**, **frobnitz**, **Get a life!**, **glork**, **gnarly**, **grok**, **guru**, **hack**, **hacker**, **hacker ethic, the**, **hacking**, **hex**, **highly**, **hot spot**, **house wizard**, **hung**, **J. Random**, **J. Random Hacker**, **jack in**, **jaggies**, **kludge**, **kluge**, **laser chicken**, **lose**, **lose lose**, **loser**, **losing**, **loss**, **lossage**, **luser**, **magic number**, **marginal**, **meta**, **moby**, **mu**, **mundane**, **mung**, **Murphy's Law**, **netter**, **network, the newbie**, **no-op**, **nontrivial**, **number-crunching**, **obscure**, **param**, **phreaking**, **ping**, **quux**, **retcon**, **Right Thing**, **scram switch**, **scratch**, **screw**, **signal-to-noise ratio**, **snarf**, **syntactic sugar**, **sysop**, **theory**, **turist**, **virgin**, **wallpaper**, **wedged**, **win**, **win big**, **win win**, **winnage**, **winner**, **winnitude**, **wizard**, **Wrong Thing**, **zap**, and **zapped**.

This list includes most of the hackerisms that (by 1993) have both achieved near-universal recognition in the culture and occasionally surfaced in mainstream use. A few other entries convey information of potential interest about idioms primarily used outside of hackerdom: **cyberpunk**, **cyberspace**, **old fart**, and **retcon**.

We hope these pointers will prove useful.

Happy hacking! — ESR

The New Hacker's Dictionary

Introduction

About This Book

This document is a collection of slang terms used by various subcultures of computer hackers. Though some technical material is included for background and flavor, it is not a technical dictionary; what we describe here is the language hackers use among themselves for fun, social communication, and technical debate.

The 'hacker culture' is actually a loosely networked collection of subcultures that is nevertheless conscious of some important shared experiences, shared roots, and shared values. It has its own myths, heroes, villains, folk epics, in-jokes, taboos, and dreams. Because hackers as a group are particularly creative people who define themselves partly by rejection of 'normal' values and working habits, it has unusually rich and conscious traditions for an intentional culture less than 35 years old.

As usual with slang, the special vocabulary of hackers helps hold their culture together — it helps hackers recognize each other's places in the community and expresses shared values and experiences. Also as usual, *not* knowing the slang (or using it inappropriately) defines one as an outsider, a mundane, or (worst of all in hackish vocabulary) possibly even a **suit**. All human cultures use slang in this threefold way — as a tool of communication, and of inclusion, and of exclusion.

Among hackers, though, slang has a subtler aspect, paralleled perhaps in the slang of jazz musicians and some kinds of fine artists but hard to detect in most technical or scientific cultures; parts of it are code for shared states of *consciousness*. There is a whole range of altered states and problem-solving mental stances basic to high-level hacking which don't fit into conventional linguistic reality any better than a Coltrane solo or one of Maurits Escher's *trompe l'oeil* compositions (Escher is a favorite of hackers), and hacker slang encodes these subtleties in many unobvious ways. As a simple example, take the distinction between a **kluge** and an **elegant** solution, and the differing connotations attached to each. The distinction is not only of engineering significance; it reaches right back into the nature of the generative processes in program design and asserts something important about two different kinds of relationship between the hacker and the hack. Hacker slang is unusually rich in implications of this kind, of overtones and undertones that illuminate the hackish psyche.

But there is more. Hackers, as a rule, love wordplay and are very conscious and inventive in their use of language. These traits seem to be common in young children, but the conformity-enforcing machine we are pleased to call an educational system bludgeons them out of most of us before adolescence. Thus, linguistic invention in most subcultures of the modern West is a halting and largely unconscious process. Hackers, by contrast, regard slang formation and use as a game to be played for conscious pleasure. Their inventions thus display an almost unique combination of the neotenous enjoyment of language-play with the discrimination of educated and powerful intelligence. Further, the electronic media which knit them together are fluid, 'hot' connections, well adapted to both the dissemination of new slang and the ruthless culling of weak and superannuated specimens. The results of this process give us perhaps a uniquely intense and accelerated view of linguistic evolution in action.

Hackish slang also challenges some common linguistic and anthropological assumptions. For example, it has recently become fashionable to speak of 'low-context' versus 'high-context' communication, and to classify cultures by the preferred context level of their languages and art forms. It is usually claimed that low-context communication (characterized by precision, clarity, and completeness of self-contained utterances) is typical in cultures which value logic, objectivity, individualism, and competition; by contrast, high-context communication (elliptical, emotive, nuance-filled, multi-modal, heavily coded) is associated with cultures which value subjectivity, consensus, cooperation, and tradition. What then are we to make of hackerdom, which is themed around extremely low-context interaction with computers and exhibits primarily "low-context" values, but cultivates an almost absurdly high-context slang style?

The intensity and consciousness of hackish invention make a compilation of hacker slang a particularly effective window into the surrounding culture — and, in fact, this one is the latest version of an evolving compilation called the 'Jargon File', maintained by hackers themselves for over 15 years. This one (like its ancestors) is primarily a lexicon, but also includes 'topic entries' which collect background or sidelight information on hacker culture that would be awkward to try to subsume under individual entries.

Though the format is that of a reference volume, it is intended that the material be enjoyable to browse. Even a complete outsider should find at least a chuckle on nearly every page, and much that is amusingly thought-provoking. But it is also true that hackers use humorous wordplay to make strong, sometimes combative statements about what they feel. Some of these entries reflect the views of opposing sides in disputes that have been genuinely passionate; this is deliberate. We have not tried to moderate or pretty up these disputes; rather we have attempted to ensure that *everyone's* sacred cows get gored, impartially. Compromise is not particularly a hackish virtue, but the honest presentation of divergent viewpoints is.

The reader with minimal computer background who finds some references incomprehensibly technical can safely ignore them. We have not felt it either necessary or desirable to eliminate all such; they, too, contribute flavor, and one of this document's major intended audiences — fledgling hackers already partway inside the culture — will benefit from them.

A selection of longer items of hacker folklore and humor is included in appendix A. The 'outside' reader's attention is particularly directed to appendix B, "A Portrait of J. Random Hacker". Appendix C is a bibliography of non-technical works which have either influenced or described the hacker culture.

Because hackerdom is an intentional culture (one each individual must choose by action to join), one should not be surprised that the line between description and influence can become more than a little blurred. Earlier versions of the Jargon File have played a central role in spreading hacker language and the culture that goes with it to successively larger populations, and we hope and expect that this one will do likewise.

Of Slang, Jargon, and Techspeak

Linguists usually refer to informal language as 'slang' and reserve the term 'jargon' for the technical vocabularies of various occupations. However, the ancestor of this collection was called the 'Jargon File', and hackish slang is traditionally 'the jargon'. When talking about the jargon there is therefore no convenient way to distinguish it from what a *linguist* would call hackers' jargon — the formal vocabulary they learn from textbooks, technical papers, and manuals.

To make a confused situation worse, the line between hackish slang and the vocabulary of technical programming and computer science is fuzzy, and shifts over time. Further, this vocabulary is shared with a wider technical culture of programmers, many of whom are not hackers and do not speak or recognize hackish slang.

Accordingly, this lexicon will try to be as precise as the facts of usage permit about the distinctions among three categories:

- *slang*: informal language from mainstream English or non-technical subcultures (bikers, rock fans, surfers, etc).
- *jargon*: without qualifier, denotes informal 'slangy' language peculiar to or predominantly found among hackers — the subject of this lexicon.
- *techspeak*: the formal technical vocabulary of programming, computer science, electronics, and other fields connected to hacking.

This terminology will be consistently used throughout the remainder of this lexicon.

The jargon/techspeak distinction is the delicate one. A lot of techspeak originated as jargon, and there is a steady continuing uptake of jargon into techspeak. On the other hand, a lot of jargon arises from overgeneralization of techspeak terms (there is more about this in the "Jargon Construction" section below).

In general, we have considered techspeak any term that communicates primarily by a denotation well established in textbooks, technical dictionaries, or standards documents.

A few obviously techspeak terms (names of operating systems, languages, or documents) are listed when they are tied to hacker folklore that isn't covered in formal sources, or sometimes to convey critical historical background necessary to understand other entries to which they are cross-referenced. Some other techspeak senses of jargon words are listed in order to make the jargon senses clear; where the text does not specify that a straight technical sense is under discussion, these are marked with '[techspeak]' as an etymology. Some entries have a primary sense marked this way, with subsequent jargon meanings explained in terms of it.

We have also tried to indicate (where known) the apparent origins of terms. The results are probably the least reliable information in the lexicon, for several reasons. For one thing, it is well known that many hackish usages have been independently reinvented multiple times, even among the more obscure and intricate neologisms. It often seems that the generative processes underlying hackish jargon formation have an internal logic so powerful as to create substantial parallelism across separate cultures and even in different languages! For another, the networks tend to propagate innovations so quickly that 'first use' is often impossible to pin down. And, finally, compendia like this one alter what they observe by implicitly stamping cultural approval on terms and widening their use.

Despite these problems, the organized collection of jargon-related oral history for the File's 2.x.x versions has enabled us to put to rest quite a number of folk etymologies, place credit where credit is due, and illuminate the early history of many important hackerisms such as **kluge**, **cruft**, and **foo**. We believe specialist lexicographers will find many of the historical notes more than casually instructive.

Revision History

The original Jargon File was a collection of hacker jargon from technical cultures including the MIT AI Lab, the Stanford AI lab (SAIL), and others of the old ARPANET AI/LISP/PDP-10 communities including Bolt, Beranek and Newman (BBN), Carnegie-Mellon University (CMU), and Worcester Polytechnic Institute (WPI).

The Jargon File (hereafter referred to as 'jargon-1' or 'the File') was begun by Raphael Finkel at Stanford in 1975. From this time until the plug was finally pulled on the SAIL computer in 1991, the File was named AI-WORD.RF[UP,DOC] there. Some terms in it date back considerably earlier (**frob** and some senses of **moby**, for instance, go back to the Tech Model Railroad Club at MIT and are believed to date at least back to the early 1960s). The revisions of jargon-1 were all unnumbered and may be collectively considered 'Version 1'.

In 1976, Mark Crispin, having seen an announcement about the File on the SAIL computer, **FTP**ed a copy of the File to MIT. He noticed that it was hardly restricted to 'AI words' and so stored the file on his directory as AI:MRC;SAIL JARGON.

The file was quickly renamed JARGON > (the '>' caused versioning under ITS) as a flurry of enhancements were made by Mark Crispin and Guy L. Steele Jr. Unfortunately, amidst all this activity, nobody thought of correcting the term 'jargon' to 'slang' until the compendium had already become widely known as the Jargon File.

Raphael Finkel dropped out of active participation shortly thereafter and Don Woods became the SAIL contact for the File (which was subsequently kept in duplicate at SAIL and MIT, with periodic resynchronizations).

The File expanded by fits and starts until about 1983; Richard Stallman was prominent among the contributors, adding many MIT and ITS-related coinages.

In Spring 1981, a hacker named Charles Spurgeon got a large chunk of the File published in Stewart Brand's *CoEvolution Quarterly* (issue 29, pages 26–35) with illustrations by Phil Wadler and Guy Steele (including a couple of the Crunchly cartoons). This appears to have been the File's first paper publication.

A late version of jargon-1, expanded with commentary for the mass market, was edited by Guy Steele into a book published in 1983 as *The Hacker's Dictionary* (Harper & Row CN 1082, ISBN 0-06-091082-8). The other jargon-1 editors (Raphael Finkel, Don Woods, and Mark Crispin) contributed to this revision, as did Richard M. Stallman and Geoff Goodfellow. This book (now out of print) is hereafter referred to as 'Steele-1983' and those six as the Steele-1983 coauthors.

Shortly after the publication of Steele-1983, the File effectively stopped growing and changing. Originally, this was due to a desire to freeze the file temporarily to facilitate the production of Steele-1983, but external conditions caused the 'temporary' freeze to become permanent.

The AI Lab culture had been hit hard in the late 1970s by funding cuts and the resulting administrative decision to use vendor-supported hardware and software instead of homebrew whenever possible. At MIT, most AI work had turned to dedicated LISP Machines. At the same time, the commercialization of AI technology lured some of the AI Lab's best and brightest away to startups along the Route 128 strip in Massachusetts and out West in Silicon Valley. The startups built LISP machines for MIT; the central MIT-AI computer became a **TWENEX** system rather than a host for the AI hackers' beloved **ITS**.

The Stanford AI Lab had effectively ceased to exist by 1980, although the SAIL computer continued as a Computer Science Department resource until 1991. Stanford became a major **TWENEX** site, at one point operating more than a dozen TOPS-20 systems; but by the mid-1980s most of the interesting software work was being done on the emerging BSD UNIX standard.

In April 1983, the PDP-10-centered cultures that had nourished the File were dealt a death-blow by the cancellation of the Jupiter project at Digital Equipment Corporation. The File's compilers, already dispersed, moved on to other things. Steele-1983 was partly a monument to what its authors thought was a dying tradition; no one involved realized at the time just how wide its influence was to be.

By the mid-1980s the File's content was dated, but the legend that had grown up around it never quite died out. The book, and softcopies obtained off the ARPANET, circulated even in cultures far removed from MIT and

Stanford; the content exerted a strong and continuing influence on hackish language and humor. Even as the advent of the microcomputer and other trends fueled a tremendous expansion of hackerdom, the File (and related materials such as the AI Koans in Appendix A) came to be seen as a sort of sacred epic, a hacker-culture Matter of Britain chronicling the heroic exploits of the Knights of the Lab. The pace of change in hackerdom at large accelerated tremendously — but the Jargon File, having passed from living document to icon, remained essentially untouched for seven years.

This revision contains nearly the entire text of a late version of jargon-1 (a few obsolete PDP-10-related entries were dropped after careful consultation with the editors of Steele-1983). It merges in about 80% of the Steele-1983 text, omitting some framing material and a very few entries introduced in Steele-1983 that are now also obsolete.

This new version casts a wider net than the old Jargon File; its aim is to cover not just AI or PDP-10 hacker culture but all the technical computing cultures wherein the true hacker-nature is manifested. More than half of the entries now derive from **USENET** and represent jargon now current in the C and UNIX communities, but special efforts have been made to collect jargon from other cultures including IBM PC programmers, Amiga fans, Mac enthusiasts, and even the IBM mainframe world.

Eric S. Raymond <*esr@snark.thyrsus.com*> maintains the new File with assistance from Guy L. Steele Jr. <*gls@think.com*>; these are the persons primarily reflected in the File's editorial 'we', though we take pleasure in acknowledging the special contribution of the other coauthors of Steele-1983. Please email all additions, corrections, and correspondence relating to the Jargon File to *jargon@thyrsus.com* (UUCP-only sites without connections to an autorouting smart site can use *...!uunet!snark!jargon*).

(Warning: other email addresses appear in this file *but are not guaranteed to be correct* after date of publication. *Don't* email us if an attempt to reach someone bounces — we have no magic way of checking addresses or looking up people.)

Please try to review a recent copy of the on-line document before submitting entries; it should be available at major archive sites. It may contain new material not recorded in this paper snapshot that could save you some typing. It also includes some submission guidelines not reproduced here.

Our thanks to the coauthors of Steele-1983 for oversight and assistance, and to the hundreds of USENETters (too many to name here) who contributed entries and encouragement. More thanks go to several of the old-timers on the USENET group *alt.folklore.computers*, who contributed much useful commentary and many corrections and valuable historical perspective: Joseph M. Newcomer *<jn11+@andrew.cmu.edu>*, Bernie Cosell *<cosell@bbn.com>*, Earl Boebert *<boebert@SCTC.com>*, and Joe Morris <jcmorris@mwunix.mitre.org>.

We were fortunate enough to have the aid of some accomplished linguists. David Stampe <stampe@uhunix.uhcc.hawaii.edu> and Charles Hoequist <hoequist@bnr.ca> contributed valuable criticism; Joe Keane <jgk@osc.osc.com> helped us improve the pronunciation guides.

A few bits of this text quote previous works. We are indebted to Brian A. LaMacchia <bal@zurich.ai.mit.edu> for obtaining permission for us to use material from the *TMRC Dictionary*; also, Don Libes <libes@cme.nist.gov> contributed some appropriate material from his excellent book *Life With UNIX*. We thank Per Lindberg <per@front.se>, author of the remarkable Swedish-language 'zine *Hackerbladet*, for bringing *FOO!* comics to our attention and smuggling one of the IBM hacker underground's own baby jargon files out to us. Thanks also to Maarten Litmaath for generously allowing the inclusion of the ASCII pronunciation guide he formerly maintained. And our gratitude to Marc Weiser of XEROX PARC <Marc_Weiser.PARC@xerox.com> for securing us permission to quote from PARC's own jargon lexicon and shipping us a copy.

It is a particular pleasure to acknowledge the major contributions of Mark Brader <msb@sq.com> and Steve Summit <scs@adam.mit.edu> to the File and Dictionary; they have read and reread many drafts, checked facts, caught typos, submitted an amazing number of thoughtful comments, and did yeoman service in catching typos and minor usage bobbles. Their rare combination of enthusiasm, persistence, wide-ranging technical knowledge, and precisionism in matters of language has been of invaluable help. The sustained volume and quality of Mr. Brader's input over many months, especially, has only allowed him to escape co-editor credit by the slimmest of margins.

Finally, George V. Reilly <georgere@microsoft.com> helped with TeX arcana and painstakingly proofread some 2.7 and 2.8 versions, and Eric Tiedemann <est@thyrsus.com> contributed sage advice throughout on rhetoric, amphigory, and philosophunculism.

How Jargon Works

Jargon Construction

There are some standard methods of jargonification that became established quite early (i.e., before 1970), spreading from such sources as the Tech Model Railroad Club, the PDP-1 SPACEWAR hackers, and John McCarthy's original crew of LISPers. These include the following:

Verb Doubling

A standard construction in English is to double a verb and use it as an exclamation, such as "Bang, bang!" or "Quack, quack!". Most of these are names for noises. Hackers also double verbs as a concise, sometimes sarcastic comment on what the implied subject does. Also, a doubled verb is often used to terminate a conversation, in the process remarking on the current state of affairs or what the speaker intends to do next. Typical examples involve **win**, **lose**, **hack**, **flame**, **barf**, **chomp**:

> "The disk heads just crashed." "Lose, lose."
> "Mostly he talked about his latest crock. Flame, flame."
> "Boy, what a bagbiter! Chomp, chomp!"

Some verb-doubled constructions have special meanings not immediately obvious from the verb. These have their own listings in the lexicon.

The **USENET** culture has one *tripling* convention unrelated to this; the names of 'joke' topic groups often have a tripled last element. The first and paradigmatic example was *alt.swedish.chef.bork.bork.bork* (a "Muppet Show" reference); other infamous examples have included:

> *alt.french.captain.borg.borg.borg*
> *alt.wesley.crusher.die.die.die*
> *comp.unix.internals.system.calls.brk.brk.brk*
> *sci.physics.edward.teller.boom.boom.boom*
> *alt.sadistic.dentists.drill.drill.drill*

Soundalike Slang

Hackers will often make rhymes or puns in order to convert an ordinary word or phrase into something more interesting. It is considered particularly **flavorful** if the phrase is bent so as to include some other jargon word; thus the computer hobbyist magazine *Dr. Dobb's Journal* is almost always referred to among hackers as 'Dr. Frob's Journal' or simply 'Dr. Frob's'. Terms of this kind that have been in fairly wide use include names for newspapers:

Boston Herald ⇒ Horrid (or Harried)
Boston Globe ⇒ Boston Glob
Houston (or San Francisco) Chronicle
    ⇒ the Crocknicle (or the Comical)
New York Times ⇒ New York Slime

However, terms like these are often made up on the spur of the moment. Standard examples include:

Data General ⇒ Dirty Genitals
IBM 360 ⇒ IBM Three-Sickly
Government Property — Do Not Duplicate (on keys)
    ⇒ Government Duplicity — Do Not Propagate
for historical reasons ⇒ for hysterical raisins
Margaret Jacks Hall (the CS building at Stanford)
    ⇒ Marginal Hacks Hall

This is not really similar to the Cockney rhyming slang it has been compared to in the past, because Cockney substitutions are opaque whereas hacker punning jargon is intentionally transparent.

The '-P' Convention

Turning a word into a question by appending the syllable 'P'; from the LISP convention of appending the letter 'P' to denote a predicate (a boolean-valued function). The question should expect a yes/no answer, though it needn't. (See **T** and **NIL**.)

At dinnertime:
    Q: "Foodp?"
    A: "Yeah, I'm pretty hungry." or "T!"

At any time:

Q: "State-of-the-world-P?"

A: (Straight) "I'm about to go home."

A: (Humorous) "Yes, the world has a state."

On the phone to Florida:

Q: "State-p Florida?"

A: "Been reading JARGON.TXT again, eh?"

[One of the best of these is a **Gosperism**. Once, when we were at a Chinese restaurant, Bill Gosper wanted to know whether someone would like to share with him a two-person-sized bowl of soup. His inquiry was: "Split-p soup?" — GLS]

Overgeneralization

A very conspicuous feature of jargon is the frequency with which techspeak items such as names of program tools, command language primitives, and even assembler opcodes are applied to contexts outside of computing wherever hackers find amusing analogies to them. Thus (to cite one of the best-known examples) UNIX hackers often **grep** for things rather than searching for them. Many of the lexicon entries are generalizations of exactly this kind.

Hackers enjoy overgeneralization on the grammatical level as well. Many hackers love to take various words and add the wrong endings to them to make nouns and verbs, often by extending a standard rule to nonuniform cases (or vice versa). For example, because

porous ⇒ porosity
generous ⇒ generosity

hackers happily generalize:

mysterious ⇒ mysteriosity
ferrous ⇒ ferrosity
obvious ⇒ obviosity
dubious ⇒ dubiosity

Another class of common construction uses the suffix '-itude' to abstract a quality from just about any adjective or noun. This usage arises especially in cases where mainstream English would perform the same abstraction through '-iness' or '-ingness'. Thus:

win ⇒winnitude (a common exclamation)
loss ⇒lossitude
cruft ⇒cruftitude
lame ⇒lameitude

Some hackers cheerfully reverse this transformation; they argue, for example, that the horizontal degree lines on a globe ought to be called 'lats' — after all, they're measuring latitude!

Also, note that all nouns can be verbed. E.g.: "All nouns can be verbed", "I'll mouse it up", "Hang on while I clipboard it over", "I'm grepping the files". English as a whole is already heading in this direction (towards pure-positional grammar like Chinese); hackers are simply a bit ahead of the curve.

However, hackers avoid the unimaginative verb-making techniques characteristic of marketroids, bean-counters, and the Pentagon; a hacker would never, for example, 'productize', 'prioritize', or 'securitize' things. Hackers have a strong aversion to bureaucratic bafflegab and regard those who use it with contempt.

Similarly, all verbs can be nouned. This is only a slight overgeneralization in modern English; in hackish, however, it is good form to mark them in some standard nonstandard way. Thus:

win ⇒ winnitude, winnage
disgust ⇒ disgustitude
hack ⇒ hackification

Further, note the prevalence of certain kinds of nonstandard plural forms. Some of these go back quite a ways; the TMRC Dictionary includes an entry which implies that the plural of 'mouse' is **meeces**, and notes that the defined plural of 'caboose' is 'cabeese'. This latter has apparently been standard (or at least a standard joke) among railfans (railroad enthusiasts) for many years.

On a similarly Anglo-Saxon note, almost anything ending in 'x' may form plurals in '-xen' (see **VAXen** and **boxen** in the main text). Even words ending in phonetic */k/* alone are sometimes treated this way; e.g., 'soxen' for a bunch of socks. Other funny plurals are 'frobbotzim' for the plural of 'frobbozz' (see **frobnitz**) and 'Unices' and 'Twenices' (rather than 'Unixes' and 'Twenexes'; see **UNIX**, **TWENEX** in main text). But note that 'Unixen' and 'Twenexen' are never used; it has been suggested that this is because '-ix' and '-ex' are Latin singular endings that attract a Latinate plural. Finally, it has been suggested to general approval that the plural of 'mongoose' ought to be 'polygoose'.

The pattern here, as with other hackish grammatical quirks, is generalization of an inflectional rule that in English is either an import or a fossil (such as the Hebrew plural ending '-im', or the Anglo-Saxon plural suffix '-en') to cases where it isn't normally considered to apply.

This is not 'poor grammar', as hackers are generally quite well aware of what they are doing when they distort the language. It is grammatical creativity, a form of playfulness. It is done not to impress but to amuse, and never at the expense of clarity.

Spoken Inarticulations

Words such as 'mumble', 'sigh', and 'groan' are spoken in places where their referent might more naturally be used. It has been suggested that this usage derives from the impossibility of representing such noises on a comm link or in electronic mail (interestingly, the same sorts of constructions have been showing up with increasing frequency in comic strips). Another expression sometimes heard is "Complain!", meaning "I have a complaint!"

Anthromorphization

Semantically, one rich source of jargon constructions is the hackish tendency to anthropomorphize hardware and software. This isn't done in a naive way; hackers don't personalize their stuff in the sense of feeling empathy with it, nor do they mystically believe that the things they work on every day are 'alive'. What *is* common is to hear hardware or software talked about as though it has homunculi talking to each other inside it, with intentions and desires. Thus, one hears "The protocol handler got confused", or that programs "are trying" to do things, or one may say of a routine that "its goal in life is to X". One even hears explanations like " . . . and its poor little brain couldn't understand X, and it died." Sometimes modelling things this way actually seems to make them easier to understand, perhaps because it's instinctively natural to think of anything with a really complex behavioral repertoire as 'like a person' rather than 'like a thing'.

Of the six listed constructions, verb doubling, peculiar noun formations, anthromorphization, and (especially) spoken inarticulations have become quite general; but punning jargon is still largely confined to MIT and other large universities, and the '-P' convention is found only where LISPers flourish.

Finally, note that many words in hacker jargon have to be understood as members of sets of comparatives. This is especially true of the adjectives and nouns used to describe the beauty and functional quality of code. Here is an approximately correct spectrum:

> monstrosity brain-damage screw bug lose misfeature
> crock kluge hack win feature elegance perfection

The last is spoken of as a mythical absolute, approximated but never actually attained. Another similar scale is used for describing the reliability of software:

> broken flaky dodgy fragile brittle
> solid robust bulletproof armor-plated

Note, however, that 'dodgy' is primarily Commonwealth Hackish (it is rare in the U.S.) and may change places with 'flaky' for some speakers.

Coinages for describing **lossage** seem to call forth the very finest in hackish linguistic inventiveness; it has been truly said that hackers have even more words for equipment failures than Yiddish has for obnoxious people.

Hacker Writing Style

We've already seen that hackers often coin jargon by overgeneralizing grammatical rules. This is one aspect of a more general fondness for form-versus-content language jokes that shows up particularly in hackish writing. One\break correspondent reports that he consistently misspells 'wrong' as 'worng'. Others have been known to criticize glitches in Jargon File drafts by observing (in the mode of Douglas Hofstadter) "This sentence no verb", or "Too repetetetive", or "Bad speling", or "Incorrectspa cing." Similarly, intentional spoonerisms are often made of phrases relating to confusion or things that are confusing; 'dain bramage' for 'brain damage' is perhaps the most common (similarly, a hacker would be likely to write "Excuse me, I'm cixelsyd today", rather than "I'm dyslexic today"). This sort of thing is quite common and is enjoyed by all concerned.

Hackers tend to use quotes as balanced delimiters like parentheses, much to the dismay of American editors. Thus, if "Jim is going" is a phrase, and so are "Bill runs" and "Spock groks", then hackers generally prefer to write: "Jim is going", "Bill runs", and "Spock groks". This is incorrect according to standard American usage (which would put the continuation commas and the final period inside the string quotes); however, it is counter-intuitive to hackers to mutilate literal strings with characters that don't belong in them. Given the sorts of examples that can come up in discussions of programming, American-style quoting can even be grossly misleading. When communicating command lines or small pieces of code, extra characters can be a real pain in the neck.

Consider, for example, a sentence in a **vi** tutorial that looks like this:

> Then delete a line from the file by typing "dd".

Standard usage would make this

> Then delete a line from the file by typing "dd."

but that would be very bad — because the reader would be prone to type the string d-d-dot, and it happens that in `vi(1)` dot repeats the last command accepted. The net result would be to delete *two* lines!

The Jargon File follows hackish usage throughout.

Interestingly, a similar style is now preferred practice in Great Britain, though the older style (which became established for typographical reasons having to do with the aesthetics of comma and quotes in typeset text) is still accepted there. *Hart's Rules* and the *Oxford Dictionary for Writers and Editors* call the hacker-like style 'new' or 'logical' quoting.

Another hacker quirk is a tendency to distinguish between 'scare' quotes and 'speech' quotes; that is, to use British-style single quotes for marking and reserve American-style double quotes for actual reports of speech or text included from elsewhere. Interestingly, some authorities describe this as correct general usage, but mainstream American English has gone to using double-quotes indiscriminately enough that hacker usage appears marked [and, in fact, I thought this was a personal quirk of mine until I checked with USENET — ESR]. One further permutation that is definitely *not* standard is a hackish tendency to do marking quotes by using apostrophes (single quotes) in pairs; that is, 'like this'. This is modelled on string and character literal syntax in some programming languages (reinforced by the fact that many character-only terminals display the apostrophe in typewriter style, as a vertical single quote).

One quirk that shows up frequently in the **email** style of UNIX hackers in particular is a tendency for some things that are normally all-lowercase (including usernames and the names of commands and C routines) to remain uncapitalized even when they occur at the beginning of sentences. It is clear that, for many hackers, the case of such identifiers becomes a part of their internal representation (the 'spelling') and cannot be overridden without mental effort (an appropriate reflex because UNIX and C both distinguish cases and confusing them can lead to **lossage**). A way of escaping this dilemma is simply to avoid using these constructions at the beginning of sentences.

There seems to be a meta-rule behind these nonstandard hackerisms to the effect that precision of expression is more important than conformance to traditional rules; where the latter create ambiguity or lose information they can be discarded without a second thought. It is notable in this respect that other hackish inventions (for example, in vocabulary) also tend to carry very precise shades of meaning even when constructed to appear slangy and loose. In fact, to a hacker, the contrast between 'loose' form and 'tight' content in jargon is a substantial part of its humor!

Hackers have also developed a number of punctuation and emphasis conventions adapted to single-font all-ASCII communications links, and these are occasionally carried over into written documents even when normal means of font changes, underlining, and the like are available.

One of these is that TEXT IN ALL CAPS IS INTERPRETED AS 'LOUD', and this becomes such an ingrained synesthetic reflex that a person who goes to caps-lock while in **talk mode** may be asked to "stop shouting, please, you're hurting my ears!".

Also, it is common to use bracketing with unusual characters to signify emphasis. The asterisk is most common, as in "What the *hell*?" even though this interferes with the common use of the asterisk suffix as a footnote mark. The underscore is also common, suggesting underlining (this is particularly common with book titles; for example, "It is often alleged that Joe Haldeman wrote _The_Forever_War_ as a rebuttal to Robert Heinlein's earlier novel of the future military, _Starship_Troopers_."). Other forms exemplified by "=hell=", "\hell/", or "/hell/" are occasionally seen (it's claimed that in the last example the first slash pushes the letters over to the right to make them italic, and the second keeps them from falling over). Finally, words may also be emphasized L I K E T H I S, or by a series of carets (^) under them on the next line of the text.

There is a semantic difference between *emphasis like this* (which emphasizes the phrase as a whole), and *emphasis* *like* *this* (which suggests the writer speaking very slowly and distinctly, as if to a very young child or a mentally impaired person). Bracketing a word with the '*' character may also indicate that the writer wishes readers to consider that an action is taking place or that a sound is being made. Examples: *bang*, *hic*, *ring*, *grin*, *kick*, *stomp*, *mumble*.

Another habit is that of using angle-bracket enclosure to genericize a term; this derives from conventions used in **BNF**. Uses like the following are common:

So this <ethnic> walks into a bar one day, and . . .

There is also an accepted convention for 'writing under erasure'; the text

```
Be nice to this fool^H^H^H^Hgentleman, he's in
from corporate HQ.
```

would be read as "Be nice to this fool, I mean this gentleman . . . ". This comes from the fact that the digraph ^H is often used as a print representation for a backspace. It parallels (and may have been influenced by) the ironic use of 'slashouts' in science-fiction fanzines.

In a formula, * signifies multiplication but two asterisks in a row are a shorthand for exponentiation (this derives from FORTRAN). Thus, one might write 2 * *8 = 256.

Another notation for exponentiation one sees more frequently uses the caret (^, ASCII 1011110); one might write instead `2^8 = 256`. This goes all the way back to Algol-60, which used the archaic ASCII 'up-arrow' that later became the caret; this was picked up by Kemeny and Kurtz's original BASIC, which in turn influenced the design of the `bc(1)` and `dc(1)` UNIX tools, which have probably done most to reinforce the convention on USENET. The notation is mildly confusing to C programmers, because '^' means bitwise **XOR** in C. Despite this, it was favored 3:1 over ** in a late-1990 snapshot of USENET. It is used consistently in this text.

In on-line exchanges, hackers tend to use decimal forms or improper fractions ('3.5' or '7/2') rather than 'typewriter style' mixed fractions ('3-1/2'). The major motive here is probably that the former are more readable in a monospaced font, together with a desire to avoid the risk that the latter might be read as 'three minus one-half'. The decimal form is definitely preferred for fractions with a terminating decimal representation; there may be some cultural influence here from the high status of scientific notation.

Another on-line convention, used especially for very large or very small numbers, is taken from C (which derived it from FORTRAN). This is a form of 'scientific notation' using 'e' to replace '*10^'; for example, one year is about 3e7 seconds (that is, 3×10^7 seconds) long.

The tilde (~) is commonly used in a quantifying sense of 'approximately'; that is, '~50' means *about fifty*.

On USENET and in the **MUD** world, common C boolean, logical, and relational operators such as '|', '&', '||', '&&', '!', '==', '!=', '>', '<', '>=', and '=<' are often combined with English. The Pascal not-equals, '<>', is also recognized, and occasionally one sees '/=' for not-equals (from Ada, Common Lisp, and Fortran 90). The use of prefix '!' as a loose synonym for 'not-' or 'no-' is particularly common; thus, '!clue' is read 'no-clue' or 'clueless'.

A related practice borrows syntax from preferred programming languages to express ideas in a natural-language text. For example, one might see the following:

```
In <jrh578689@thudpucker.com> J. R. Hacker wrote:
>I recently had occasion to field-test the Snafu
>Systems 2300E adaptive gonkulator.  The price
>was right, and the racing stripe on the case
>looked kind of neat, but its performance left
>something to be desired.

Yeah, I tried one out too.

#ifdef FLAME
Hasn't anyone told those idiots that you can't
get decent bogon suppression with AFJ filters at
today's net volumes?
#endif /* FLAME */

I guess they figured the price premium for true
frame-based semantic analysis was too high.
Unfortunately, it's also the only workable
approach. I wouldn't recommend purchase of this
product unless you're on a *very* tight budget.

#include <disclaimer.h>
--
                    == Frank Foonly (Fubarco Systems)
```

In the above, the #ifdef/#endif pair is a conditional compilation syntax from C; here, it implies that the text between (which is a **flame**) should be evaluated only if you have turned on (or defined on) the switch FLAME. The `#include` at the end is C for "include standard disclaimer here"; the 'standard disclaimer' is understood to read, roughly, "These are my personal opinions and not to be construed as the official position of my employer."

The top section in the example, with > at the left margin, is an example of an inclusion convention we'll discuss below.

Hackers also mix letters and numbers more freely than in mainstream usage. In particular, it is good hackish style to write a digit sequence where you intend the reader to understand the text string that names that number in English. So, hackers prefer to write '1970s' rather than 'nineteen-seventies' or '1970's' (the latter looks like a possessive).

It should also be noted that hackers exhibit much less reluctance to use multiply nested parentheses than is normal in English. Part of this is almost certainly due to influence from LISP (which uses deeply nested parentheses (like this (see?)) in its syntax a lot), but it has also been suggested that a more basic hacker trait of enjoying playing with complexity and pushing systems to their limits is in operation.

Finally, it is worth mentioning that many studies of on-line communication have shown that electronic links have a de-inhibiting effect on people. Deprived of the body-language cues through which emotional state is expressed, people tend to forget everything about other parties except what is presented over that ASCII link. This has both good and bad effects. A good one is that it encourages honesty and tends to break down hierarchical authority relationships; a bad one is that it may encourage depersonalization and gratuitous rudeness. Perhaps in response to this, experienced netters often display a sort of conscious formal *politesse* in their writing that has passed out of fashion in other spoken and written media (for example, the phrase "Well said, sir!" is not uncommon).

Many introverted hackers who are next to inarticulate in person communicate with considerable fluency over the net, perhaps precisely because they can forget on an unconscious level that they are dealing with people and thus don't feel stressed and anxious as they would face to face.

Though it is considered gauche to publicly criticize posters for poor spelling or grammar, the network places a premium on literacy and clarity of expression. It may well be that future historians of literature will see in it a revival of the great tradition of personal letters as art.

Email Quotes and Inclusion Conventions

One area where hackish conventions for on-line writing are still in some flux is the marking of included material from earlier messages — what would be called 'block quotations' in ordinary English. From the usual typographic convention employed for these (smaller font at an extra indent), there derived the notation of included text being indented by one ASCII TAB (0001001) character, which under UNIX and many other environments gives the appearance of an 8-space indent.

Early mail and netnews readers had no facility for including messages this way, so people had to paste in copy manually. BSD `Mail(1)` was the first message agent to support inclusion, and early USENETters emulated its style. But the TAB character tended to push included text too far to the right (especially in multiply nested inclusions), leading to ugly wraparounds. After a brief period of confusion (during which an inclusion leader consisting of three or four spaces became established in EMACS and a few mailers), the use of leading '>' or '> ' became standard, perhaps owing to its use in `ed(1)` to display tabs (alternatively, it may derive from the '>' that some early UNIX mailers used to quote lines starting with "From" in text, so they wouldn't look like the beginnings of new message headers). Inclusions within inclusions keep their '>' leaders, so the 'nesting level' of a quotation is visually apparent.

The practice of including text from the parent article when posting a followup helped solve what had been a major nuisance on USENET: the fact that articles do not arrive at different sites in the same order. Careless posters used to post articles that would begin with, or even consist entirely of, "No, that's wrong" or "I agree" or the like. It was hard to see who was responding to what. Consequently, around 1984, new news-posting software evolved a facility to automatically include the text of a previous article, marked with "> " or whatever the poster chose. The poster was expected to delete all but the relevant lines. The result has been that, now, careless posters post articles containing the *entire* text of a preceding article, *followed* only by "No, that's wrong" or "I agree".

Many people feel that this cure is worse than the original disease, and there soon appeared newsreader software designed to let the reader skip over included text if desired. Today, some posting software rejects articles containing too high a proportion of lines beginning with '>' — but this too has led to undesirable workarounds, such as the deliberate inclusion of zero-content filler lines which aren't quoted and thus pull the message below the rejection threshold.

Because the default mailers supplied with UNIX and other operating systems haven't evolved as quickly as human usage, the older conventions using a leading TAB or three or four spaces are still alive; however, >-inclusion is now clearly the prevalent form in both netnews and mail.

In 1991 practice is still evolving, and disputes over the 'correct' inclusion style occasionally lead to **holy wars**. One variant style reported uses the citation character '|' in place of '>' for extended quotations where original variations in indentation are being retained. One also sees different styles of quoting a number of authors in the same message: one (deprecated because it loses information) uses a leader of '> ' for everyone, another (the most common) is '> > > > ', '> > > ', etc. (or '>>>> ', '>>> ', etc., depending on line length and nesting depth) reflecting the original order of messages, and yet another is to use a different citation leader for each author, say '> ', ': ', '| ', '} ' (preserving nesting so that the inclusion order of messages is still apparent, or tagging the inclusions with authors' names). Yet *another* style is to use each poster's initials (or login name) as a citation leader for that poster. Occasionally one sees a '# ' leader used for quotations from authoritative sources such as standards documents; the intended allusion is to the root prompt (the special UNIX command prompt issued when one is running as the privileged super-user).

Hacker Speech Style

Hackish speech generally features extremely precise diction, careful word choice, a relatively large working vocabulary, and relatively little use of contractions or street slang. Dry humor, irony, puns, and a mildly flippant attitude are highly valued — but an underlying seriousness and intelligence are essential. One should use just enough jargon to communicate precisely and identify oneself as a member of the culture; overuse of jargon or a breathless, excessively gung-ho attitude is considered tacky and the mark of a loser.

This speech style is a variety of the precisionist English normally spoken by scientists, design engineers, and academics in technical fields. In contrast with the methods of jargon construction, it is fairly constant throughout hackerdom.

It has been observed that many hackers are confused by negative questions — or, at least, that the people to whom they are talking are often confused by the sense of their answers. The problem is that they have done so much programming that distinguishes between

```
if (going) ...
```

and

```
if (!going) ...
```

that when they parse the question "Aren't you going?" it seems to be asking the opposite question from "Are you going?", and so merits an answer in the opposite sense. This confuses English-speaking non-hackers because they were taught to answer as though the negative part weren't there. In some other languages (including Russian, Chinese, and Japanese) the hackish interpretation is standard and the problem wouldn't arise. Hackers often find themselves wishing for a word like French 'si' or German 'doch' with which one could unambiguously answer 'yes' to a negative question.

For similar reasons, English-speaking hackers almost never use double negatives, even if they live in a region where colloquial usage allows them. The thought of uttering something that logically ought to be an affirmative knowing it will be misparsed as a negative tends to disturb them.

In a related vein, hackers sometimes make a game of answering questions containing logical connectives with a strictly literal rather than colloquial interpretation. A non-hacker who is indelicate enough to ask a question like "So, are you working on finding that bug *now* or leaving it until later?" is likely to get the perfectly correct answer "Yes!" (that is, "Yes, I'm doing it either now or later, and you didn't ask which!").

International Style

Although the Jargon File remains primarily a lexicon of hacker usage in American English, we have made some effort to get input from abroad. Though the hacker-speak of other languages often uses translations of jargon from English (often as transmitted to them by earlier Jargon File versions!), the local variations are interesting, and knowledge of them may be of some use to travelling hackers.

There are some references herein to 'Commonwealth English'. These are intended to describe some variations in hacker usage as reported in the

English spoken in Great Britain and the Commonwealth (Canada, Australia, India, etc. — though Canada is heavily influenced by American usage). There is also an entry on **Commonwealth Hackish** reporting some general phonetic and vocabulary differences from U.S. hackish.

Hackers in Western Europe and (especially) Scandinavia report that they often use a mixture of English and their native languages for technical conversation. Occasionally they develop idioms in their English usage that are influenced by their native-language styles. Some of these are reported here.

A few notes on hackish usages in Russian have been added where they are parallel with English idioms and thus comprehensible to English-speakers.

How to Use the Lexicon

Pronunciation Guide

Pronunciation keys are provided in the jargon listings for all entries that are neither dictionary words pronounced as in standard English nor obvious compounds thereof. Slashes bracket phonetic pronunciations, which are to be interpreted using the following conventions:

1. Syllables are hyphen-separated, except that an accent or back-accent follows each accented syllable (the back-accent marks a secondary accent in some words of four or more syllables). If no accent is given, the word is pronounced with equal accentuation on all syllables (this is common for abbreviations).
2. Consonants are pronounced as in American English. The letter 'g' is always hard (as in "got" rather than "giant"); 'ch' is soft ("church" rather than "chemist"). The letter 'j' is the sound that occurs twice in "judge". The letter 's' is always as in "pass", never a z sound. The digraph 'kh' is the guttural of "loch" or "l'chaim". The digraph 'gh' is the aspirated g+h of "bughouse" or "ragheap" (rare in English).
3. Uppercase letters are pronounced as their English letter names; thus (for example) */H-L-L/* is equivalent to */aitch el el/*. */Z/* may be pronounced */zee/* or */zed/* depending on your local dialect.
4. Vowels are represented as follows:

a	back, that
ah	father, palm (see note)
ar	far, mark
aw	flaw, caught
ay	bake, rain
e	less, men
ee	easy, ski
eir	their, software
i	trip, hit
i:	life, sky
o	block, stock (see note)
oh	flow, sew
oo	loot, through

or	more, door
ow	out, how
oy	boy, coin
uh	but, some
u	put, foot
y	yet, young
yoo	few, chew
[y]oo	*/oo/* with optional fronting as in 'news' (*/nooz/* or */nyooz/*)

A */ə/* is used for the 'schwa' sound of unstressed or occluded vowels. The schwa vowel is omitted in syllables containing vocalic r, l, m or n; that is, 'kitten' and 'color' would be rendered */kit´n/* and */kuhl´r/*, not */kit´ən/* and */kuhl´ər/*.

Note that the above table reflects mainly distinctions found in standard American English (that is, the neutral dialect spoken by TV network announcers and typical of educated speech in the Upper Midwest, Chicago, Minneapolis/St.Paul and Philadelphia). However, we separate /o/ from /ah/, which tend to merge in standard American. This may help readers accustomed to dialects resembling British Received Pronunciation.

Entries with a pronunciation of '*//*' are written-only usages. (No, UNIX weenies, this does *not* mean 'pronounce like previous pronunciation'!)

Other Lexicon Conventions

Entries are sorted in case-blind ASCII collation order (rather than the letter-by-letter order ignoring interword spacing common in mainstream dictionaries), except that all entries beginning with nonalphabetic characters are sorted after Z. The case-blindness is a feature, not a bug.

Jargon terms with entries in the file are **boldfaced**. This isn't done all the time for every such word, but it is done everywhere that a reminder seems useful that the term has a jargon meaning and one might wish to refer to its entry.

Defining instances of terms and phrases appear in *slanted type*. A defining instance is one which occurs near to or as part of an explanation of it.

Prefix ** is used as linguists do; to mark examples of incorrect usage.

We follow the 'logical' quoting convention described in the Writing Style section above. In addition, we reserve double quotes for actual excerpts of text or (sometimes invented) speech. Scare quotes (which mark a word being used in a nonstandard way), and philosopher's quotes (which turn an utterance into the string of letters or words that name it) are both rendered with single quotes.

References such as `malloc(3)` and `patch(1)` are to UNIX facilities (some of which, such as `patch(1)`, are actually freeware distributed over USENET). The UNIX manuals use `foo(n)` to refer to item foo in section (n) of the manual, where $n = 1$ is utilities, $n = 2$ is system calls, $n = 3$ is C library routines, $n = 6$ is games, and $n = 8$ (where present) is system administration utilities. Sections 4, 5, and 7 of the manuals have changed roles frequently and in any case are not referred to in any of the entries.

Various abbreviations used frequently in the lexicon are summarized here:

abbrev.	abbreviation
adj.	adjective
adv.	adverb
alt.	alternate
cav.	caveat
esp.	especially
excl.	exclamation
imp.	imperative
interj.	interjection
n.	noun
obs.	obsolete
pl.	plural
poss.	possibly
pref.	prefix
prob.	probably
prov.	proverbial
quant.	quantifier
suff.	suffix
syn.	synonym (or synonymous with)
v.	verb (may be transitive or intransitive)
var.	variant
vi.	intransitive verb
vt.	transitive verb

Where alternate spellings or pronunciations are given, *alt.* separates two possibilities with nearly equal distribution, while *var.* prefixes one that is markedly less common than the primary.

Where a term can be attributed to a particular subculture or is known to have originated there, we have tried to so indicate. Here is a list of abbreviations used in etymologies:

Berkeley	University of California at Berkeley
Cambridge	the university in England (*not* the city in Massachusetts where MIT happens to be located!)
BBN	Bolt, Beranek & Newman
CMU	Carnegie-Mellon University
Commodore	Commodore Business Machines
DEC	The Digital Equipment Corporation
Fairchild	The Fairchild Instruments Palo Alto development group
Fidonet	See the **Fidonet** entry
IBM	International Business Machines
MIT	Massachusetts Institute of Technology; esp. the legendary MIT AI Lab culture of roughly 1971 to 1983 and its feeder groups, including the Tech Model Railroad Club
NRL	Naval Research Laboratories
NYU	New York University
OED	The Oxford English Dictionary
Purdue	Purdue University
SAIL	Stanford Artificial Intelligence Laboratory (at Stanford University)
SI	From *Système International*, the name for the standard conventions of metric nomenclature used in the sciences
Stanford	Stanford University
Sun	Sun Microsystems
TMRC	Some MITisms go back as far as the Tech Model Railroad Club (TMRC) at MIT c. 1960. Material marked TMRC is from *An Abridged Dictionary of the TMRC Language*, originally compiled by Pete Samson in 1959
UCLA	University of California at Los Angeles
UK	the United Kingdom (England, Wales, Scotland, Northern Ireland)

USENET	See the **USENET** entry
WPI	Worcester Polytechnic Institute, site of a very active community of PDP-10 hackers during the 1970s
XEROX PARC	XEROX's Palo Alto Research Center, site of much pioneering research in user interface design and networking
Yale	Yale University

Some other etymology abbreviations such as **UNIX** and **PDP-10** refer to technical cultures surrounding specific operating systems, processors, or other environments. The fact that a term is labelled with any one of these abbreviations does not necessarily mean its use is confined to that culture. In particular, many terms labelled 'MIT' and 'Stanford' are in quite general use. We have tried to give some indication of the distribution of speakers in the usage notes; however, a number of factors mentioned in the introduction conspire to make these indications less definite than might be desirable.

A few new definitions attached to entries are marked [proposed]. These are usually generalizations suggested by editors or USENET respondents in the process of commenting on previous definitions of those entries. These are *not* represented as established jargon.

The Jargon Lexicon

The Crunchly saga begins here.
The next cartoon in the Crunchly saga is 05-18-73, page 273.

The infamous Crunchly cartoons by The Great Quux are woven into the lexicon, each next to an appropriate entry. To read them in the sequence in which they were written, **chase pointers** from here using the 'next cartoon' information in the captions. A few don't have next pointers; these are vignettes from the 1973 "Crunchland" tableau spread that inaugurated the strip.

= A =

abbrev */ə-breev´/, /ə-brev´/* n. Common abbreviation for 'abbreviation'.

ABEND [ABnormal END] */o´bend/, /ə-bend´/* n. Abnormal termination (of software); **crash**; **lossage**. Derives from an error message on the IBM 360; used jokingly by hackers but seriously mainly by **code grinders**. Usually capitalized, but may appear as 'abend'. Hackers will try to persuade you that ABEND is called *abend* because it is what system operators do to the machine late on Friday when they want to call it a day, and hence is from the German 'Abend' = 'Evening'.

accumulator n. 1. Archaic term for a register. On-line use of it as a synonym for 'register' is a fairly reliable indication that the user has been around for quite a while and/or that the architecture under discussion is quite old. The term in full is almost never used of microprocessor registers, for example, though symbolic names for arithmetic registers beginning in 'A' derive from historical use of the term 'accumulator' (and not, actually, from 'arithmetic'). Confusingly, though, an 'A' register name prefix may also stand for 'address', as for example on the Motorola 680x0 family. 2. A register being used for arithmetic or logic (as opposed to addressing or a loop index), especially one being used to accumulate a sum or count of many items. This use is in context of a particular routine or stretch of code. "The FOOBAZ routine uses A3 as an accumulator." 3. One's in-basket (esp. among old-timers who might use sense 1). "You want this reviewed? Sure, just put it in the accumulator." (See **stack**.)

ACK */ak/* interj. 1. [from the ASCII mnemonic for 0000110] Acknowledge. Used to register one's presence (compare mainstream *Yo!*). An appropriate response to **ping** or **ENQ**. 2. [from the comic strip "Bloom County"] An exclamation of surprised disgust, esp. in "Ack pffft!" Semi-humorous. Generally this sense is not spelled in caps (ACK) and is distinguished by a following exclamation point. 3. Used to politely interrupt someone to tell them you understand their point (see **NAK**). Thus, for example, you might cut off an overly long explanation with "Ack. Ack. Ack. I get it now".

There is also a usage "ACK?" (from sense 1) meaning "Are you there?", often used in email when earlier mail has produced no reply, or during a lull in **talk mode** to see if the person has gone away (the standard humorous response is of course **NAK** (sense 2), i.e., "I'm not here").

This is **ad-hockery** in action.
The next cartoon in the Crunchly saga is 08-18-74, page 446.

ad-hockery */ad-hok´ər-ee/* [Purdue] n. 1. Gratuitous assumptions made inside certain programs, esp. expert systems, which lead to the appearance of semi-intelligent behavior but are in fact entirely arbitrary. For example, fuzzy-matching against input tokens that might be typing errors against a symbol table can make it look as though a program knows how to spell. 2. Special-case code to cope with some awkward input that would otherwise cause a program to **choke**, presuming normal inputs are dealt with in some cleaner and more regular way. Also called *ad-hackery*, *ad-hocity* (*/ad-hos´ə-tee/*), *ad-crockery*. See also **ELIZA effect**.

Ada n. A **Pascal**-descended language that has been made mandatory for Department of Defense software projects by the Pentagon. Hackers are nearly unanimous in observing that, technically, it is precisely what one might expect given that kind of endorsement by fiat; designed by committee, crockish, difficult to use, and overall a disastrous, multi-billion-dollar boondoggle (one common description is "The PL/I of the 1980s"). Hackers find Ada's exception-handling and inter-process communication features particularly hilarious. Ada Lovelace (the daughter of Lord Byron who became the world's first programmer while cooperating with Charles Babbage on the design of his mechanical computing engines in the mid-1800s) would almost certainly blanch at the use to which her name has latterly been put; the kindest thing that has been said about it is that there is probably a good small language screaming to get out from inside its vast, **elephantine** bulk.

adger */aj´r/* [UCLA] vt. To make a bonehead move with consequences that could have been foreseen with even slight mental effort. E.g., "He started removing files and promptly adgered the whole project". Compare **dumbass attack**.

admin */ad-min´/* n. Short for 'administrator'; very commonly used in speech or on-line to refer to the systems person in charge on a computer. Common constructions on this include *sysadmin* and *site admin* (emphasizing the administrator's role as a site contact for email and news) or *newsadmin* (focusing specifically on news). Compare **postmaster**, **sysop**, **system mangler**.

ADVENT */ad´vent/* n. The prototypical computer adventure game, first implemented on the **PDP-10** by Will Crowther as an attempt at computer-refereed fantasy gaming, and expanded into a puzzle-oriented game by Don Woods. Now better known as Adventure, but the **TOPS-10** operating system permitted only six-letter filenames. See also **vadding**.

Nowadays we say this of Ada.

This game defined the terse, dryly humorous style now expected in text adventure games, and popularized several tag lines that have become fixtures of hacker-speak: "A huge green fierce snake bars the way!" "I see no X here" (for some noun X). "You are in a maze of twisty little passages, all alike." "You are in a little maze of twisty passages, all different." The 'magic words' **xyzzy** and **plugh** also derive from this game.

Crowther, by the way, participated in the exploration of the Mammoth & Flint Ridge cave system; it actually *has* a 'Colossal Cave' and a 'Bedquilt' as in the game, and the 'Y2' that also turns up is cavers' jargon for a map reference to a secondary entrance.

AFJ // n. Written-only abbreviation for "April Fool's Joke". Elaborate April Fool's hoaxes are a long-established tradition on USENET and Internet; see **kremvax** for an example. In fact, April Fool's Day is the *only* seasonal holiday marked by customary observances on the hacker networks.

AI */A-I/* n. Abbreviation for 'Artificial Intelligence', so common that the full form is almost never written or spoken among hackers.

AI-complete */A-I kəm-pleet´/* [MIT, Stanford: by analogy with 'NP-complete' (see **NP-**)] adj. Used to describe problems or subproblems in AI, to indicate that the solution presupposes a solution to the 'strong AI problem' (that is, the synthesis of a human-level intelligence). A problem that is AI-complete is, in other words, just too hard.

Examples of AI-complete problems are 'The Vision Problem' (building a system that can see as well as a human) and 'The Natural Language Problem' (building a system that can understand and speak a natural language as well as a human). These may appear to be modular, but all attempts so far (1993) to solve them have foundered on the amount of context information and 'intelligence' they seem to require. See also **gedanken**.

AI koans */A-I koh´anz/* pl.n. A series of pastiches of Zen teaching riddles created by Danny Hillis at the MIT AI Lab around various major figures of the Lab's culture (several are included under "A Selection of AI Koans" in Appendix A). See also **ha ha only serious**, **mu**, and **Humor, Hacker**.

AIDS */aydz/* n. Short for A* Infected Disk Syndrome ('A*' is a **glob** pattern that matches, but is not limited to, Apple), this condition is quite often the result of practicing unsafe **SEX**. See **virus**, **worm**, **Trojan horse**, **virgin**.

AIDX n. */aydkz/* n. Derogatory term for IBM's perverted version of UNIX, AIX, especially for the AIX 3.? used in the IBM RS/6000 series (some hackers think it is funnier just to pronounce "AIX" as "aches"). A victim of the dreaded "hybridism" disease, this attempt to combine the two main currents of the UNIX stream (**BSD** and **USG UNIX**) became a **monstrosity** to haunt system administrators' dreams. For example, if new accounts are created while many users are logged on, the load average jumps quickly over 20 due to silly implementation of the user databases. For a quite similar disease, compare **HP-SUX**. Also, compare **Macintrash Nominal Semidestructor**, **Open DeathTrap**, **ScumOS**, **sun-stools**.

airplane rule n. "Complexity increases the possibility of failure; a twin-engine airplane has twice as many engine problems as a single-engine airplane." By analogy, in both software and electronics, the rule that simplicity increases robustness. It is correspondingly argued that the right way to build reliable systems is to put all your eggs in one basket, after making sure that you've built a really *good* basket. See also **KISS Principle**.

aliasing bug n. A class of subtle programming errors that can arise in code that does dynamic allocation, esp. via `malloc(3)` or equivalent. If several pointers address (*aliases for*) a given hunk of storage, it may happen that the storage is freed or reallocated (and thus moved) through one alias and then referenced through another, which may lead to subtle (and possibly intermittent) lossage depending on the state and the allocation history of the malloc **arena**. Avoidable by use of allocation strategies that never alias allocated core, or by use of higher-level languages, such as **LISP**, which employ a garbage collector (see **GC**). Also called a **stale pointer bug**. See also **precedence lossage**, **smash the stack**, **fandango on core**, **memory leak**, **memory smash**, **overrun screw**, **spam**.

Historical note: Though this term is nowadays associated with C programming, it was already in use in a very similar sense in the Algol-60 and FORTRAN communities in the 1960s.

all-elbows [MS-DOS] adj. Of a TSR (terminate-and-stay-resident) IBM PC program, such as the N pop-up calendar and calculator utilities that circulate on **BBS** systems: unsociable. Used to describe a program that rudely steals the resources that it needs without considering that other TSRs may also be resident. One particularly common form of rudeness is lock-up due to programs fighting over the keyboard interrupt. See **rude**, also **mess-dos**.

alpha particles n. See **bit rot**.

alt */awlt/* 1. n. The alt shift key on an IBM PC or **clone** keyboard; see **bucky bits**, sense 2 (though typical PC usage does not simply set the 0200 bit). 2. n. The 'clover' or 'Command' key on a Macintosh; use of this term usually reveals that the speaker hacked PCs before coming to the Mac (see also **feature key**). Some Mac hackers, confusingly, reserve 'alt' for the Option key (and it is so labeled on some Mac II keyboards). 3. n.obs. [PDP-10; often capitalized to ALT] Alternate name for the ASCII ESC character (ASCII 0011011), after the keycap labeling on some older terminals; also *altmode* (*/awlt´mohd/*). This character was almost never pronounced 'escape' on an ITS system, in **TECO**, or under TOPS-10 — always alt, as in "Type alt alt to end a TECO command" or "alt-U onto the system" (for "log onto the [ITS] system"). This usage probably arose because alt is more convenient to say than 'escape', especially when followed by another alt or a character (or another alt *and* a character, for that matter).

alt bit */awlt bit/* [from alternate] adj. See **meta bit**.

altmode n. Syn. **alt** sense 3.

Aluminum Book [MIT] n. *Common LISP: The Language*, by Guy L. Steele Jr. (Digital Press, first edition 1984, second edition 1990). Note that due to a technical screwup some printings of the second edition are actually of a color the author describes succinctly as "yucky green". See also **book titles**.

amoeba n. Humorous term for the Commodore Amiga personal computer.

amp off [Purdue] vt. To run in **background**. From the UNIX shell '&' operator.

amper n. Common abbreviation for the name of the ampersand ('&', ASCII 0100110) character. See **ASCII** for other synonyms.

angle brackets n. Either of the characters '<' (ASCII 0111100) and '>' (ASCII 0111110) (ASCII less-than or greater-than signs). Typographers in the **Real World** use angle brackets which are either taller and slimmer (the ISO 'Bra' and 'Ket' characters), or significantly smaller (single or double guillemets) than the less-than and greater-than signs. The typeset left angle bracket is '⟨'; the typeset right angle bracket is '⟩'. See **broket**, **ASCII**.

angry fruit salad n. A bad visual-interface design that uses too many colors. (This term derives, of course, from the bizarre day-glo colors found in canned fruit salad.) Too often one sees similar effects from interface designers using color window systems such as **X**; there is a tendency to create displays that are flashy and attention-getting but uncomfortable for long-term use.

annoybot */ə-noy-bot/* [IRC] n. See **robot**.

AOS 1. */aws/* (East Coast), */ay-os/* (West Coast) [based on a PDP-10 increment instruction] vt.,obs. To increase the amount of something. "AOS the campfire." Usage: considered silly, and now obsolete. Now largely supplanted by **bump**. See **SOS**. 2. n. A **Multics**-derived OS supported at one time by Data General. This was pronounced */A-O-S/* or */A-os/.* A spoof of the standard AOS system administrator's manual (*How to Load and Generate your AOS System*) was created, issued a part number, and circulated as photocopy folklore; it was called *How to Goad and Levitate your CHAOS System.* 3. n. Algebraic Operating System, in reference to those calculators which use infix instead of postfix (reverse Polish) notation.

Historical note: AOS in sense 1 was the name of a **PDP-10** instruction that took any memory location in the computer and added 1 to it; AOS meant 'Add One and do not Skip'. Why, you may ask, does the 'S' stand for 'do not Skip' rather than for 'Skip'? Ah, here was a beloved piece of PDP-10 folklore. There were eight such instructions: AOSE added 1 and then skipped the next instruction if the result was Equal to zero; AOSG added 1 and then skipped if the result was Greater than 0; AOSN added 1 and then skipped if the result was Not 0; AOSA added 1 and then skipped Always; and so on. Just plain AOS didn't say when to skip, so it never skipped.

For similar reasons, AOJ meant 'Add One and do not Jump'. Even more bizarre, SKIP meant 'do not SKIP'! If you wanted to skip the next instruction, you had to say 'SKIPA'. Likewise, JUMP meant 'do not JUMP'; the unconditional form was JUMPA. However, hackers never did this. By some quirk of the 10's design, the **JRST** (Jump and ReSTore flag with no flag specified) was actually faster and so was invariably used. Such were the perverse mysteries of assembler programming.

app */ap/* n. Short for 'application program', as opposed to a systems program. Apps are what systems vendors are forever chasing developers to create for their environments so they can sell more boxes. Hackers tend not to think of the things they themselves run as apps; thus, in hacker parlance the term excludes compilers, program editors, games, and messaging systems, though a user would consider all those to be apps. (Broadly, an app is often a self-contained environment for performing some well-defined task such as 'word processing'; hackers tend to prefer more general-purpose tools.) Oppose **tool, operating system**.

arena [UNIX] n. The area of memory attached to a process by `brk(2)` and `sbrk(2)` and used by `malloc(3)` as dynamic storage. So named from a `malloc: corrupt arena` message emitted when some early versions detected an impossible value in the free block list. See **overrun screw, aliasing bug, memory leak, memory smash, smash the stack**.

arg */arg/* n. Abbreviation for 'argument' (to a function), used so often as to have become a new word (like 'piano' from 'pianoforte'). "The sine function takes 1 arg, but the arc-tangent function can take either 1 or 2 args." Compare **param, parm, var**.

ARMM [acronym, 'Automated Retroactive Minimal Moderation'] n. A USENET robot created by Dick Depew of Munroe Falls, Ohio. ARMM was intended to automatically cancel posts from anonymous-posting sites. Unfortunately, the robot's recognizer for anonymous postings triggered on its own automatically-generated control messages! Transformed by this stroke of programming ineptitude into a monster of Frankensteinian proportions, it broke loose on the night of March 31, 1993 and proceeded to **spam** *news.admin.policy* with a recursive explosion of over 200 messages.

ARMM's bug produced a recursive **cascade** of messages each of which mechanically added text to the ID and Subject and some other headers of its parent. This produced a flood of messages in which each header took up several screens and each message ID and subject line got longer and longer and longer.

Reactions varied from amusement to outrage. The pathological messages crashed at least one mail system, and upset people paying line charges for their USENET feeds. One poster described the ARMM debacle as "instant USENET history" (also establishing the term **despew**), and it has since been widely cited as a cautionary example of the havoc the combination of good intentions and incompetence can wreak on a network. Compare **Great Worm, The**; **sorcerer's apprentice mode**. See also **software laser, network meltdown**.

armor-plated n. Syn. for **bulletproof**.

asbestos adj. Used as a modifier to anything intended to protect one from **flames**; also in other highly **flame**-suggestive usages. See, for example, **asbestos longjohns** and **asbestos cork award**.

asbestos cork award n. Once, long ago at MIT, there was a **flamer** so consistently obnoxious that another hacker designed, had made, and distributed posters announcing that said flamer had been nominated for the *asbestos cork award.* (Any reader in doubt as to the intended application of the cork should consult the etymology under **flame**.) Since then, it is agreed that only a select few have risen to the heights of bombast required to earn this dubious dignity — but there is no agreement on *which* few.

asbestos longjohns n. Notional garments donned by **USENET** posters just before emitting a remark they expect will elicit **flamage**. This is the most common of the **asbestos** coinages. Also *asbestos underwear, asbestos overcoat,* etc.

ASCII [American Standard Code for Information Interchange] */as´kee/* n. The predominant character set encoding of present-day computers. The modern version uses 7 bits for each character, whereas most earlier codes (including an early version of ASCII) used fewer. This change allowed the inclusion of lowercase letters — a major **win** — but it did not provide for accented letters or any other letterforms not used in English (such as the German sharp-S 'ß' or the ae-ligature 'æ' which is a letter in, for example, Norwegian). It could be worse, though. It could be much worse. See **EBCDIC** to understand how.

Computers are much pickier and less flexible about spelling than humans; thus, hackers need to be very precise when talking about characters, and have developed a considerable amount of verbal shorthand for them. Every character has one or more names — some formal, some concise, some silly. Common jargon names for ASCII characters are collected here. See also individual entries for **bang**, **excl**, **open**, **ques**, **semi**, **shriek**, **splat**, **twiddle**, and **Yu-Shiang Whole Fish**.

This list derives from revision 2.3 of the USENET ASCII pronunciation guide. Single characters are listed in ASCII order; character pairs are sorted in by first member. For each character, common names are given in rough order of popularity, followed by names that are reported but rarely seen; official ANSI/CCITT names are surrounded by brokets: <>. Square brackets mark the particularly silly names introduced by **INTERCAL**. The abbreviations

ASCII

"l/r" and "o/c" stand for left/right and "open/close" respectively. Ordinary parentheticals provide some usage information.

!	Common: **bang**; pling; excl; shriek; <exclamation mark>. Rare: factorial; exclam; smash; cuss; boing; yell; wow; hey; wham; eureka; [spark-spot]; soldier.
"	Common: double quote; quote. Rare: literal mark; double-glitch; <quotation marks>; <dieresis>; dirk; [rabbit-ears]; double prime.
#	Common: number sign; pound; pound sign; hash; sharp; **crunch**; hex; [mesh]. Rare: grid; crosshatch; octothorpe; flash; <square>, pig-pen; tictactoe; scratchmark; thud; thump; **splat**.
$	Common: dollar; <dollar sign>. Rare: currency symbol; buck; cash; string (from BASIC); escape (when used as the echo of ASCII ESC); ding; cache; [big money].
%	Common: percent; <percent sign>; mod; grapes. Rare: [double-oh-seven].
&	Common: <ampersand>; amper; and. Rare: address (from C); reference (from C++); andpersand; bitand; background (from `sh(1)`); pretzel; amp. [INTERCAL called this *ampersand*; what could be sillier?]
'	Common: single quote; quote; <apostrophe>. Rare: prime; glitch; tick; irk; pop; [spark]; <closing single quotation mark>; <acute accent>.
( )	Common: l/r paren; l/r parenthesis; left/right; open/close; paren/thesis; o/c paren; o/c parenthesis; l/r parenthesis; l/r banana. Rare: so/already; lparen/rparen; <opening/closing parenthesis>; o/c round bracket, l/r round bracket, [wax/wane]; parenthisey/unparenthisey; l/r ear.
*	Common: star; [**splat**]; <asterisk>. Rare: wildcard; gear; dingle; mult; spider; aster; times; twinkle; glob (see **glob**); **Nathan Hale**.
+	Common: <plus>; add. Rare: cross; [intersection].
,	Common: <comma>. Rare: <cedilla>; [tail].
-	Common: dash; <hyphen>; <minus>. Rare: [worm]; option; dak; bithorpe.

. Common: dot; point; <period>; <decimal point>. Rare: radix point; full stop; [spot].

/ Common: slash; stroke; <slant>; forward slash. Rare: diagonal; solidus; over; slak; virgule; [slat].

: Common: <colon>. Rare: dots; [two-spot].

; Common: <semicolon>; semi. Rare: weenie; [hybrid], pit-thwong.

< > Common: <less/greater than>; bra/ket; l/r angle; l/r angle bracket; l/r broket. Rare: from/{into, towards}; read from/write to; suck/blow; comes-from/gozinta; in/out; crunch/zap (all from UNIX); [angle/right angle].

= Common: <equals>; gets; takes. Rare: quadrathorpe; [half-mesh].

? Common: query; <question mark>; **ques**. Rare: whatmark; [what]; wildchar; huh; hook; buttonhook; hunchback.

@ Common: at sign; at; strudel. Rare: each; vortex; whorl; [whirlpool]; cyclone; snail; ape; cat; rose; cabbage; <commercial at>.

V Rare: [book].

[ ] Common: l/r square bracket; l/r bracket; <opening/closing bracket>; bracket/unbracket. Rare: square/unsquare; [U turn/U turn back].

\ Common: backslash; escape (from C/UNIX); reverse slash; slosh; backslant; backwhack. Rare: bash; <reverse slant>; reversed virgule; [backslat].

^ Common: hat; control; uparrow; caret; <circumflex>. Rare: chevron; [shark (or shark-fin)]; to the ('to the power of'); fang; pointer (in Pascal).

_ Common: <underline>; underscore; underbar; under. Rare: score; backarrow; skid; [flatworm].

` Common: backquote; left quote; left single quote; open quote; <grave accent>; grave. Rare: backprime; [backspark]; unapostrophe; birk; blugle; back tick; back glitch; push; <opening single quotation mark>; quasiquote.

{ } Common: o/c brace; l/r brace; l/r squiggly; l/r squiggly bracket/brace; l/r curly bracket/brace; <opening/closing

 ASCII

brace>. Rare: brace/unbrace; curly/uncurly; leftit/rytit; l/r squirrelly; [embrace/bracelet].

| Common: bar; or; or-bar; v-bar; pipe; vertical bar. Rare: <vertical line>; gozinta; thru; pipesinta (last three from UNIX); [spike].

~ Common: <tilde>; squiggle; **twiddle**; not. Rare: approx; wiggle; swung dash; enyay; [sqiggle (sic)].

The pronunciation of '#' as 'pound' is common in the U.S. but a bad idea; **Commonwealth Hackish** has its own, rather more apposite use of 'pound sign' (confusingly, on British keyboards the pound graphic '*$*' happens to replace '#'; thus Britishers sometimes call '#' on a U.S.-ASCII keyboard 'pound', compounding the American error). The U.S. usage derives from an old-fashioned commercial practice of using a '#' suffix to tag pound weights on bills of lading. The character is usually pronounced 'hash' outside the U.S.

The 'uparrow' name for circumflex and 'leftarrow' name for underline are historical relics from archaic ASCII (the 1963 version), which had these graphics in those character positions rather than the modern punctuation characters.

The 'swung dash' or 'approximation' sign is not quite the same as tilde in typeset material (it looks like this: $\sim$) but the ASCII tilde serves for both (compare **angle brackets**).

Some other common usages cause odd overlaps. The '#', '$', '>', and '&' characters, for example, are all pronounced "hex" in different communities because various assemblers use them as a prefix tag for hexadecimal constants (in particular, '#' in many assembler-programming cultures, '$' in the 6502 world, '>' at Texas Instruments, and '&' on the BBC Micro, Sinclair, and some Z80 machines). See also **splat**.

The inability of ASCII text to correctly represent any of the world's other major languages makes the designers' choice of 7 bits look more and more like a serious **misfeature** as the use of international networks continues to increase (see **software rot**). Hardware and software from the U.S. still tends to embody the assumption that ASCII is the universal character set and that characters have 7 bits; this is a a major irritant to people who want to use a character set suited to their own languages. Perversely, though, efforts to solve this problem by proliferating 'national' character sets produce an evolutionary pressure to use a *smaller* subset common to all those in use.

ASCII art n. The fine art of drawing diagrams using the ASCII character set (mainly '|', '-', '/', '\', and '+'). Also known as *character graphics* or *ASCII graphics*; see also **boxology**. Here is a serious example:

```
o----)||(--+--|<----+   +---------o + D O
  L  )||(  |        |   |             C U
A I  )||(  +-->|-+  |   +-\/\/-+--o -   T
C N  )||(        |  |   |      |        P
  E  )||(  +-->|-+--)---+--)|--+-o      U
     )||(  |        |          | GND    T
o----)||(--+--|<----+----------+

A power supply consisting of a full wave rectifier
circuit feeding a capacitor input filter circuit
```

Figure 1.

And here are some very silly examples:

```
  |\/\/\/|     ____/|             ___    |\_/|    ___
  |      |     \ o.O|  ACK!      /   \_  |` '|  _/   \
  |      |      =(_)= THPHTH!   /      \/     \/      \
  | (o)(o)        U            /                       \
  C      _)  (__)               \/\/\/\  _____  /\/\/\/
  | ,___|    (oo)                      \/     \/
  |   /       \/-------\         U                  (__)
 /____\        ||     | \    /---V  `v'-            oo )
/      \       ||---W||  *  * |--|   || |`.        |_/\

                        //-o-\\
                 ____---=======---____
             ====____\  /.. ..\   /____====
           //        ---\__O__/---        \\
           \_\                           /_/
```

Figure 2.

There is an important subgenre of ASCII art that puns on the standard character names in the fashion of a rebus.

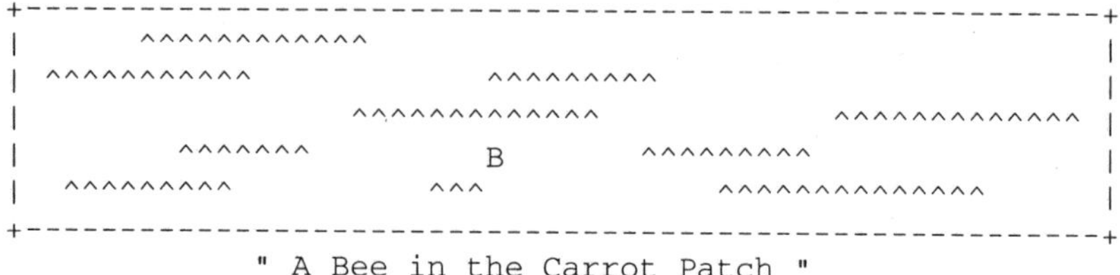

Figure 3.

Within humorous ASCII art, there is for some reason an entire flourishing subgenre of pictures of silly cows. Four of these are reproduced in Figure 2; here are three more:

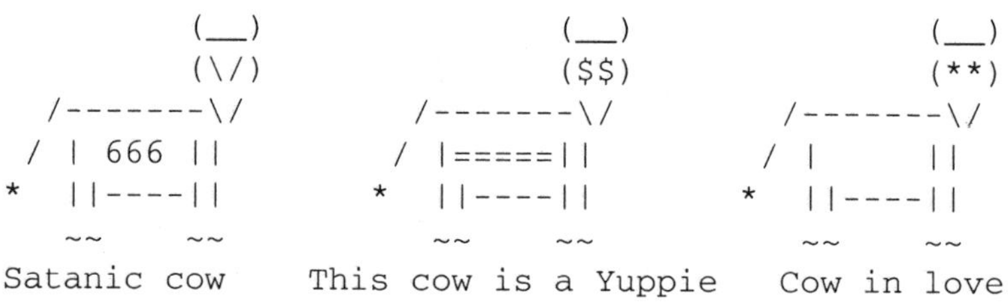

Figure 4.

ASCIIbetical order */as´kee-be´-tə-kl or´dr/* adj.,n. Used to indicate that data is sorted in ASCII collated order rather than alphabetical order. This lexicon is sorted in something close to ASCIIbetical order, but with case ignored and entries beginning with non-alphabetic characters moved to the end.

atomic [from Gk. 'atomos', indivisible] adj. 1. Indivisible; cannot be split up. For example, an instruction may be said to do several things 'atomically', i.e., all the things are done immediately, and there is no chance of the instruction being half-completed or of another being interspersed. Used esp. to convey that an operation cannot be screwed up by interrupts. "This routine locks the file and increments the file's semaphore atomically." 2. [primarily techspeak] Guaranteed to complete successfully or not at all, usu. refers to database transactions. If an error prevents a partially-performed transaction from proceeding to completion, it must be "backed out," as the database must not be left in an inconsistent state.

Computer usage, in either of the above senses, has none of the connotations that 'atomic' has in mainstream English (i.e. of particles of matter, nuclear explosions etc.).

attoparsec n. About an inch. 'atto-' is the standard SI prefix for multiplication by 10^{-18}. A parsec (parallax-second) is 3.26 light-years; an attoparsec is thus $3.26 * 10^{-18}$ light years, or about 3.1 cm (thus, 1 attoparsec/**microfortnight** equals about 1 inch/sec). This unit is reported to be in use (though probably not very seriously) among hackers in the U.K. See **micro-**.

autobogotiphobia */aw´toh-boh-got`ə-foh´bee-ə/* n. See **bogotify**.

automagically */aw-toh-maj´i-klee/* or */aw-toh-maj´i-kəl-ee/* adv. Automatically, but in a way that, for some reason (typically because it is too complicated, or too ugly, or perhaps even too trivial), the speaker doesn't feel like explaining to you. See **magic**. "The C-INTERCAL compiler generates C, then automagically invokes `cc(1)` to produce an executable."

avatar [CMU, Tektronix] n. Syn. **root**, **superuser**. There are quite a few UNIX machines on which the name of the superuser account is 'avatar' rather than 'root'. This quirk was originated by a CMU hacker who disliked the term 'superuser', and was propagated through an ex-CMU hacker at Tektronix.

awk 1. n. [UNIX techspeak] An interpreted language for massaging text data developed by Alfred Aho, Peter Weinberger, and Brian Kernighan (the name derives from their initials). It is characterized by C-like syntax, a declaration-free approach to variable typing and declarations, associative arrays, and field-oriented text processing. See also **Perl**. 2. n. Editing term for an expression awkward to manipulate through normal **regexp** facilities (for example, one containing a **newline**). 3. vt. To process data using `awk(1)`.

= B =

back door n. A hole in the security of a system deliberately left in place by designers or maintainers. The motivation for such holes is not always sinister;

some operating systems, for example, come out of the box with privileged accounts intended for use by field service technicians or the vendor's maintenance programmers. Syn. **trap door**; may also be called a *wormhole.* See also **iron box, cracker, worm, logic bomb**.

Historically, back doors have often lurked in systems longer than anyone expected or planned, and a few have become widely known. The infamous **RTM** worm of late 1988, for example, used a back door in the **BSD** UNIX `sendmail(8)` utility.

Ken Thompson's 1983 Turing Award lecture to the ACM revealed the existence of a back door in early UNIX versions that may have qualified as the most fiendishly clever security hack of all time. The C compiler contained code that would recognize when the 'login' command was being recompiled and insert some code recognizing a password chosen by Thompson, giving him entry to the system whether or not an account had been created for him.

Normally such a back door could be removed by removing it from the source code for the compiler and recompiling the compiler. But to recompile the compiler, you have to *use* the compiler — so Thompson also arranged that the compiler would *recognize when it was compiling a version of itself,* and insert into the recompiled compiler the code to insert into the recompiled 'login' the code to allow Thompson entry — and, of course, the code to recognize itself and do the whole thing again the next time around! And having done this once, he was then able to recompile the compiler from the original sources; the hack perpetuated itself invisibly, leaving the back door in place and active but with no trace in the sources.

The talk that revealed this truly moby hack was published as "Reflections on Trusting Trust", *Communications of the ACM 27*, 8 (August 1984), pp. 761–763.

backbone cabal n. A group of large-site administrators who pushed through the **Great Renaming** and reined in the chaos of **USENET** during most of the 1980s. The cabal **mailing list** disbanded in late 1988 after a bitter internal catfight.

backbone site n. A key USENET and email site; one that processes a large amount of third-party traffic, especially if it is the home site of any of the regional coordinators for the USENET maps. Notable backbone sites as of early 1993 include *uunet* and the mail machines at Rutgers University, UC Berkeley, **DEC**'s Western Research Laboratories, Ohio State University, and the University of Texas. Compare **rib site, leaf site**.

backgammon See **bignum** (sense 3), **moby** (sense 4), and **pseudoprime**.

background n.,adj.,vt. To do a task *in background* is to do it whenever **foreground** matters are not claiming your undivided attention, and *to background* something means to relegate it to a lower priority. "For now, we'll just print a list of nodes and links; I'm working on the graph-printing problem in background." Note that this implies ongoing activity but at a reduced level or in spare time, in contrast to mainstream 'back burner' (which connotes benign neglect until some future resumption of activity). Some people prefer to use the term for processing that they have queued up for their unconscious minds (a tack that one can often fruitfully take upon encountering an obstacle in creative work). Compare **amp off**, **slopsucker**.

Technically, a task running in background is detached from the terminal where it was started (and often running at a lower priority); oppose **foreground**. Nowadays this term is primarily associated with **UNIX**, but it appears to have been first used in this sense on OS/360.

backspace and overstrike interj. Whoa! Back up. Used to suggest that someone just said or did something wrong. Common among APL programmers.

backward combatability */bak´wərd kəm-bat´ə-bil´ə-tee/* [from 'backward compatibility'] n. A property of hardware or software revisions in which previous protocols, formats, layouts, etc. are irrevocably discarded in favor of 'new and improved' protocols, formats, and layouts, leaving the previous ones not merely deprecated but actively defeated. (Too often, the old and new versions cannot definitively be distinguished, such that lingering instances of the previous ones yield crashes or other infelicitous effects, as opposed to a simple "version mismatch" message.) A backwards compatible change, on the other hand, allows old versions to coexist without crashes or error messages, but too many major changes incorporating elaborate backwards compatibility processing can lead to extreme **software bloat**. See also **flag day**.

BAD */B-A-D/* [IBM: acronym, 'Broken As Designed'] adj. Said of a program that is **bogus** because of bad design and misfeatures rather than because of bugginess. See **working as designed**.

Bad Thing [from the 1930 Sellar & Yeatman parody *1066 And All That*] n. Something that can't possibly result in improvement of the subject. This term is always capitalized, as in "Replacing all of the 9600-baud modems with bicycle couriers would be a Bad Thing". Oppose **Good Thing**. British correspondents confirm that **Bad Thing** and **Good Thing** (and prob. therefore **Right Thing** and **Wrong Thing**) come from the book referenced in the etymology, which discusses rulers who were Good Kings but Bad Things. This has apparently created a mainstream idiom on the British side of the pond.

bag on the side n. An extension to an established hack that is supposed to add some functionality to the original. Usually derogatory, implying that the original was being overextended and should have been thrown away, and the new product is ugly, inelegant, or bloated. Also v. phrase, 'to hang a bag on the side [of]'. "C++? That's just a bag on the side of C. . . ." "They want me to hang a bag on the side of the accounting system."

bagbiter */bag´bi:t-ər/* n. 1. Something, such as a program or a computer, that fails to work, or works in a remarkably clumsy manner. "This text editor won't let me make a file with a line longer than 80 characters! What a bagbiter!" 2. A person who has caused you some trouble, inadvertently or otherwise, typically by failing to program the computer properly. Synonyms: **loser**, **cretin**, **chomper**. 3. *bite the bag* vi. To fail in some manner. "The computer keeps crashing every five minutes." "Yes, the disk controller is really biting the bag." The original loading of these terms was almost undoubtedly obscene, possibly referring to the scrotum, but in their current usage they have become almost completely sanitized.

ITS's lexiphage program is the first and to date only known example of a program *intended* to be a bagbiter.

bagbiting adj. Having the quality of a **bagbiter**. "This bagbiting system won't let me compute the factorial of a negative number." Compare **losing**, **cretinous**, **bletcherous**, 'barfucious' (under **barfulous**) and 'chomping' (under **chomp**).

bamf */bamf/* 1. [from old X-Men comics] interj. Notional sound made by a person or object teleporting in or out of the hearer's vicinity. Often used in **virtual reality** (esp. **MUD**) electronic **fora** when a character wishes to make a dramatic entrance or exit. 2. The sound of magical transformation, used in virtual reality **fora** like sense 1.

banana label n. The labels often used on the sides of **macrotape** reels, so called because they are shaped roughly like blunt-ended bananas. This term, like macrotapes themselves, is still current but visibly headed for obsolescence.

banana problem n. [from the story of the little girl who said "I know how to spell 'banana', but I don't know when to stop"]. Not knowing where or when to bring a production to a close (compare **fencepost error**). One may say *there is a banana problem* of an algorithm with poorly defined or incorrect termination conditions, or in discussing the evolution of a design that may be succumbing to featuritis (see also **creeping elegance**, **creeping featuritis**). See item 176 under **HAKMEM**, which describes a banana problem in a **Dissociated Press** implementation. Also, see **one-banana problem** for a superficially similar but unrelated usage.

bandwidth n. 1. Used by hackers (in a generalization of its technical meaning) as the volume of information per unit time that a computer, person, or transmission medium can handle. "Those are amazing graphics, but I missed some of the detail — not enough bandwidth, I guess." Compare **low-bandwidth**. 2. Attention span. 3. On **USENET**, a measure of network capacity that is often wasted by people complaining about how items posted by others are a waste of bandwidth.

bang 1. n. Common spoken name for '!' (ASCII 0100001), especially when used in pronouncing a **bang path** in spoken hackish. In **elder days** this was considered a CMUish usage, with MIT and Stanford hackers preferring **excl** or **shriek**; but the spread of UNIX has carried 'bang' with it (esp. via the term **bang path**) and it is now certainly the most common spoken name for '!'. Note that it is used exclusively for non-emphatic written '!'; one would not say "Congratulations bang" (except possibly for humorous purposes), but if one wanted to specify the exact characters 'foo!' one would speak "Eff oh oh bang". See **shriek**, **ASCII**. 2. interj. An exclamation signifying roughly "I have achieved enlightenment!", or "The dynamite has cleared out my brain!" Often used to acknowledge that one has perpetrated a **thinko** immediately after one has been called on it.

bang on vt. To stress-test a piece of hardware or software: "I banged on the new version of the simulator all day yesterday and it didn't crash once. I guess it is ready for release." The term **pound on** is synonymous.

bang path n. An old-style UUCP electronic-mail address specifying hops to get from some assumed-reachable location to the addressee, so called because each **hop** is signified by a **bang** sign. Thus, for example, the path *...!bigsite!foovax!barbox!me* directs people to route their mail to machine *bigsite* (presumably a well-known location accessible to everybody) and from there through the machine *foovax* to the account of user *me* on *barbox*.

In the bad old days of not so long ago, before autorouting mailers became commonplace, people often published compound bang addresses using the `{ }` convention (see **glob**) to give paths from *several* big machines, in the hopes that one's correspondent might be able to get mail to one of them reliably (example: *...!{seismo, ut-sally, ihnp4}!rice!beta!gamma!me*). Bang paths of 8 to 10 hops were not uncommon in 1981. Late-night dial-up UUCP links would cause week-long transmission times. Bang paths were often selected by both transmission time and reliability, as messages would often get lost. See **Internet address**, **network, the**, and **sitename**.

banner n. 1. The title page added to printouts by most print spoolers (see **spool**). Typically includes user or account ID information in very large character-graphics capitals. Also called a *burst page*, because it indicates where to burst (tear apart) fanfold paper to separate one user's printout from the next. 2. A similar printout generated (typically on multiple pages of fan-fold paper) from user-specified text, e.g., by a program such as UNIX's `banner({1,6})`. 3. On interactive software, a first screen containing a logo and/or author credits and/or a copyright notice.

bar */bar/* n. 1. The second **metasyntactic variable**, after **foo** and before **baz**. "Suppose we have two functions: FOO and BAR. FOO calls BAR. . . ." 2. Often appended to **foo** to produce **foobar**.

bare metal n. 1. New computer hardware, unadorned with such snares and delusions as an **operating system**, an **HLL**, or even assembler. Commonly used in the phrase *programming on the bare metal*, which refers to the arduous work of **bit bashing** needed to create these basic tools for a new machine. Real bare-metal programming involves things like building boot proms and BIOS chips, implementing basic monitors used to test device drivers, and writing the assemblers that will be used to write the compiler back ends that will give the new machine a real development environment. 2. 'Programming on the bare metal' is also used to describe a style of **hand-hacking** that relies on bit-level peculiarities of a particular hardware design, esp. tricks for speed and space optimization that rely on crocks such as overlapping instructions (or, as in the famous case described in The Story of Mel, a Real Programmer (in Appendix A), interleaving of opcodes on a magnetic drum to minimize fetch delays due to the device's rotational latency). This sort of thing has become less common as the relative costs of programming time and machine resources have changed, but is still found in heavily constrained environments such as industrial embedded systems, and in the code of hackers who just can't let go of that low-level control. See **Real Programmer**.

In the world of personal computing, bare metal programming (especially in sense 1 but sometimes also in sense 2) is often considered a **Good Thing**, or at least a necessary evil (because these machines have often been sufficiently slow and poorly designed to make it necessary; see **ill-behaved**). There, the term usually refers to bypassing the BIOS or OS interface and writing the application to directly access device registers and machine addresses. "To get 19.2 kilobaud on the serial port, you need to get down to the bare metal." People who can do this sort of thing well are held in high regard.

barf */barf/* [from mainstream slang meaning 'vomit'] 1. interj. Term of disgust. This is the closest hackish equivalent of the Val\-speak "gag me with a spoon". (Like, euwww!) See **bletch**. 2. vi. To say "Barf!" or emit some similar expression of disgust. "I showed him my latest hack and he barfed" means only that he complained about it, not that he literally vomited. 3. vi. To fail to work because of unacceptable input, perhaps with a suitable error message, perhaps not. Examples: "The division operation barfs if you try to divide by 0." (That is, the division operation checks for an attempt to divide by zero, and if one is encountered it causes the operation to fail in some unspecified, but generally obvious, manner.) "The text editor barfs if you try to read in a new file before writing out the old one." See **choke**, **gag**. In Commonwealth Hackish, *barf* is generally replaced by 'puke' or 'vom'. **barf** is sometimes also used as a **metasyntactic variable**, like **foo** or **bar**.

barfmail n. Multiple **bounce messages** accumulating to the level of serious annoyance, or worse. The sort of thing that happens when an inter-network mail gateway goes down or wonky.

barfulation */bar`fyoo-lay´shən/* interj. Variation of **barf** used around the Stanford area. An exclamation, expressing disgust. On seeing some particularly bad code one might exclaim, "Barfulation! Who wrote this, Quux?"

barfulous */bar´fyoo-ləs/* adj. (alt. *barfucious, /bar-fyoo-shəs/*) Said of something that would make anyone barf, if only for esthetic reasons.

barney n. In Commonwealth hackish, *barney* is to **fred** (sense #1) as **bar** is to **foo**. That is, people who commonly use *fred* as their first metasyntactic variable will often use *barney* second. The reference is, of course, to Fred Flintstone and Barney Rubble in the Flintstones cartoons.

baroque adj. Feature-encrusted; complex; gaudy; verging on excessive. Said of hardware or (esp.) software designs, this has many of the connotations of **elephantine** or **monstrosity** but is less extreme and not pejorative in itself. "Metafont even has features to introduce random variations to its letterform output. Now *that* is baroque!" See also **rococo**.

BASIC [acronym, from Beginner's All-purpose Symbolic Instruction Code] n. A programming language, originally designed for Dartmouth's experimental timesharing system in the early 1960s, which has since become the leading cause of brain-damage in proto-hackers. This is another case (like **Pascal**) of the cascading lossage that happens when a language deliberately designed as an educational toy gets taken too seriously. A novice can write short BASIC programs (on the order of 10–20 lines) very easily; writing anything longer is (a) very painful, and (b) encourages bad habits that will make it harder to use more powerful languages well. This wouldn't be so bad if historical accidents hadn't made BASIC so common on low-end micros. As it is, it ruins thousands of potential wizards a year.

batch adj. 1. Non-interactive. Hackers use this somewhat more loosely than the traditional technical definitions justify; in particular, switches on a normally interactive program that prepare it to receive non-interactive command input are often referred to as *batch mode* switches. A *batch file* is a series of instructions written to be handed to an interactive program running in batch mode. 2. Performance of dreary tasks all at one sitting. "I finally sat down in batch mode and wrote out checks for all those bills; I guess they'll turn the electricity back on next week . . . " 3. *batching up*: Accumulation of a number of small tasks that can be lumped together for greater efficiency. "I'm batching up those letters to send sometime" "I'm batching up bottles to take to the recycling center."

bathtub curve n. Common term for the curve (resembling an end-to-end section of one of those claw-footed antique bathtubs) that describes the expected failure rate of electronics with time: initially high, dropping to near 0 for most of the system's lifetime, then rising again as it 'tires out'. See also **burn-in period, infant mortality**.

The next cartoon in the Crunchly saga is 03-17-76:5-8, page 185.

baud */bawd/* [simplified from its technical meaning] n. Bits per second. Hence kilobaud or Kbaud, thousands of bits per second. The technical meaning is 'level transitions per second'; this coincides with bps only for two-level modulation with no framing or stop bits. Most hackers are aware of these nuances but blithely ignore them.

Historical note: *baud* was originally a unit of telegraph signalling speed, set at one pulse per second. It was proposed at the International Telegraph Conference of 1927, and named after J.M.E. Baudot (1845–1903), the French engineer who constructed the first successful teleprinter.

baud barf */bawd barf/* n. The garbage one gets on the monitor when using a modem connection with some protocol setting (esp. line speed) incorrect, or when someone picks up a voice extension on the same line, or when really bad line noise disrupts the connection. Baud barf is not completely **random**, by the way; hackers with a lot of serial-line experience can usually tell whether the device at the other end is expecting a higher or lower speed than the terminal is set to. *Really* experienced ones can identify particular speeds.

baz */baz/* n. 1. The third **metasyntactic variable** "Suppose we have three functions: FOO, BAR, and BAZ. FOO calls BAR, which calls BAZ. . . ." (See also **fum**) 2. interj. A term of mild annoyance. In this usage the term is often drawn out for 2 or 3 seconds, producing an effect not unlike the bleating of a sheep; */baaaaaaz/*. 3. Occasionally appended to **foo** to produce 'foobaz'.

Earlier versions of this lexicon derived *baz* as a Stanford corruption of **bar**. However, Pete Samson (compiler of the **TMRC** lexicon) reports it was already current when he joined TMRC in 1958. He says "It came from *Pogo*. Albert the Alligator, when vexed or outraged, would shout 'Bazz Fazz!' or 'Rowrbazzle!' The club layout was said to model the (mythical) New England counties of Rowrfolk and Bassex (Rowrbazzle mingled with (Norfolk/Suffolk/Middlesex/Essex)."

bboard */bee´bord/* [contraction of 'bulletin board'] n. 1. Any electronic bulletin board; esp. used of **BBS** systems running on personal micros, less frequently of a USENET **newsgroup** (in fact, use of this term for a newsgroup generally marks one either as a **newbie** fresh in from the BBS world or as a real old-timer predating USENET). 2. At CMU and other colleges with similar facilities, refers to campus-wide electronic bulletin boards. 3. The term *physical bboard* is sometimes used to refer to an old-fashioned, non-electronic cork-and-thumbtack memo board. At CMU, it refers to a particular one outside the CS Lounge.

In either of senses 1 or 2, the term is usually prefixed by the name of the intended board ('the Moonlight Casino bboard' or 'market bboard'); however, if the context is clear, the better-read bboards may be referred to by name alone, as in (at CMU) "Don't post for-sale ads on general".

BBS */B-B-S/* [abbreviation, 'Bulletin Board System'] n. An electronic bulletin board system; that is, a message database where people can log in and leave broadcast messages for others grouped (typically) into **topic groups**. Thousands of local BBS systems are in operation throughout the U.S., typically run by amateurs for fun out of their homes on MS-DOS boxes with a single modem line each. Fans of USENET and Internet or the big commercial time-sharing bboards such as CompuServe and GEnie tend to consider local BBSes the low-rent district of the hacker culture, but they serve a valuable function by knitting together lots of hackers and users in the personal-micro world who would otherwise be unable to exchange code at all. See also **bboard**.

beam [from Star Trek Classic's "Beam me up, Scotty!"] vt. To transfer **softcopy** of a file electronically; most often in combining forms such as *beam me a copy* or *beam that over to his site*. Compare **blast**, **snarf**, **BLT**.

beanie key [Mac users] n. See **command key**.

beep n.,v. Syn. **feep**. This term seems to be preferred among micro hobbyists.

beige toaster n. A Macintosh. See **toaster**; compare **Macintrash, maggotbox.**

bells and whistles [by analogy with the toyboxes on theater organs] n. Features added to a program or system to make it more **flavorful** from a hacker's point of view, without necessarily adding to its utility for its primary function. Distinguished from **chrome**, which is intended to attract users. "Now that we've got the basic program working, let's go back and add some bells and whistles." No one seems to know what distinguishes a bell from a whistle.

bells, whistles, and gongs n. A standard elaborated form of **bells and whistles**; typically said with a pronounced and ironic accent on the 'gongs'.

benchmark [techspeak] n. An inaccurate measure of computer performance. "In the computer industry, there are three kinds of lies: lies, damn lies, and benchmarks." Well-known ones include Whetstone, Dhrystone, Rhealstone (see **h**), the Gabriel LISP benchmarks (see **gabriel**), the SPECmark suite, and LINPACK. See also **machoflops, MIPS, smoke and mirrors**.

Berkeley Quality Software adj. (often abbreviated 'BQS') Term used in a pejorative sense to refer to software that was apparently created by rather spaced-out hackers late at night to solve some unique problem. It usually has nonexistent, incomplete, or incorrect documentation, has been tested on at least two examples, and core dumps when anyone else attempts to use it. This term was frequently applied to early versions of the `dbx(1)` debugger. See also **Berzerkeley**.

Note to British and Commonwealth readers: that's */berk´lee/*, not */bark´lee/* as in British Received Pronunciation.

berklix */berk´liks/* n.,adj. [contraction of 'Berkeley UNIX'] See **BSD**. Not used at Berkeley itself. May be more common among **suit**s attempting to sound like cognoscenti than among hackers, who usually just say 'BSD'.

Berzerkeley */bər-zer´klee/* [from 'berserk', via the name of a now-deceased record label] n. Humorous distortion of 'Berkeley' used esp. to refer to the practices or products of the **BSD** UNIX hackers. See **software bloat, Missed'em-five, Berkeley Quality Software**.

Mainstream use of this term in reference to the cultural and political peculiarities of UC Berkeley as a whole has been reported from as far back as the 1960s.

Sometimes ‘trouble’ is spelled **bells and whistles**...
The next cartoon in the Crunchly saga is 06-04-73, page 205.

beta */bay´tə/, /be´tə/* or (Commonwealth) */bee´tə/* n. 1. Mostly working, but still under test; usu. used with 'in': 'in beta'. In the **Real World**, systems (hardware or software) software often go through two stages of release testing: Alpha (in-house) and Beta (out-house?). Beta releases are generally made to a small number of lucky (or unlucky), trusted customers. 2. Anything that is new and experimental. "His girlfriend is in beta" means that he is still testing for compatibility and reserving judgment. 3. Flaky; dubious; suspect (since beta software is notoriously buggy).

Historical note: More formally, to beta-test is to test a pre-release (potentially unreliable) version of a piece of software by making it available to selected customers and users. This term derives from early 1960s terminology for product cycle checkpoints, first used at IBM but later standard throughout the industry. 'Alpha Test' was the unit, module, or component test phase; 'Beta Test' was initial system test. These themselves came from earlier A- and B-tests for hardware. The A-test was a feasibility and manufacturability evaluation done before any commitment to design and development. The B-test was a demonstration that the engineering model functioned as specified. The C-test (corresponding to today's beta) was the B-test performed on early samples of the production design.

BFI */B-F-I/* n. See **brute force and ignorance**. Also encountered in the variants *BFMI*, 'brute force and *massive* ignorance' and *BFBI* 'brute force and bloody ignorance'.

bible n. 1. One of a small number of fundamental source books such as **Knuth** and **K&R**. 2. The most detailed and authoritative reference for a particular language, operating system, or other complex software system.

BiCapitalization n. The act said to have been performed on trademarks (such as **PostScript**, NeXT, **NeWS**, VisiCalc, FrameMaker, TK!solver, EasyWriter) that have been raised above the ruck of common coinage by nonstandard capitalization. Too many **marketroid** types think this sort of thing is really cute, even the 2,317th time they do it. Compare **studlycaps**.

BIFF */bif/* [USENET] n. The most famous **pseudo**, and the prototypical **newbie**. Articles from BIFF are characterized by all uppercase letters sprinkled liberally with bangs, typos, 'cute' misspellings (EVRY BUDY LUVS GOOD OLD BIFF CUZ HE"S A KØØL DOOD AN HE RITES REEL AWESUM THINGZ IN CAPITULL LETTRS LIKE THIS!!!), use (and often misuse) of fragments of **talk mode** abbreviations, a long **sig block** (sometimes even a **doubled sig**), and unbounded naiveté. BIFF posts articles using his elder brother's VIC-20. BIFF's location is a mystery, as his articles appear to come from a variety of sites. However, **BITNET** seems to be the most frequent origin. The theory that BIFF is a denizen of BITNET is supported by BIFF's (unfortunately invalid) electronic mail address: BIFF@BIT.NET.

[1993: Now It Can Be Told! My spies inform me that BIFF was originally created by Joe Talmadge <jat@cup.hp.com>, also the author of the infamous and much-plagiarized "Flamer's Bible". The BIFF filter he wrote was later passed to Richard Sexton, who posted BIFFisms much more widely. Versions have since been posted for the amusement of the net at large. — ESR]

biff */bif/* vt. To notify someone of incoming mail. From the BSD utility `biff(1)`, which was in turn named after a friendly golden Labrador who used to chase frisbees in the halls at UCB while 4.2BSD was in development (it had a well-known habit of barking whenever the mailman came). No relation to **BIFF**.

Big Gray Wall n. What faces a **VMS** user searching for documentation. A full VMS kit comes on a pallet, the documentation taking up around 15 feet of shelf space before the addition of layered products such as compilers, databases, multivendor networking, and programming tools. Recent (since VMS version 5) DEC documentation comes with gray binders; under VMS version 4 the binders were orange (*big orange wall*), and under version 3 they were blue. See **VMS**. Often contracted to *Gray Wall*.

big iron n. Large, expensive, ultra-fast computers. Used generally of **number-crunching** supercomputers such as Crays, but can include more conventional big commercial IBMish mainframes. Term of approval; compare **heavy metal**, oppose **dinosaur**.

Big Red Switch [IBM] n. The power switch on a computer, esp. the 'Emergency Pull' switch on an IBM **mainframe** or the power switch on an IBM PC where it really is large and red. "This !@%$% **bitty box** is hung again; time to hit the Big Red Switch." Sources at IBM report that, in tune with the company's passion for **TLA**s, this is often abbreviated as *BRS* (this has also become established on FidoNet and in the PC **clone** world). It is alleged that the emergency pull switch on an IBM 360/91 actually fired a non-conducting bolt into the main power feed; the BRSes on more recent mainframes physically drop a block into place so that they can't be pushed back in. People get fired for pulling them, especially inappropriately (see also **molly-guard**). Compare **power cycle, three-finger salute, 120 reset**; see also **scram switch**.

Big Room, the n. The extremely large room with the blue ceiling and intensely bright light (during the day) or black ceiling with lots of tiny nightlights (during the night) found outside all computer installations. "He can't come to the phone right now, he's somewhere out in the Big Room."

big win n. Serendipity. "Yes, those two physicists discovered high-temperature superconductivity in a batch of ceramic that had been prepared incorrectly according to their experimental schedule. Small mistake; big win!" See **win big**.

big-endian [From Swift's *Gulliver's Travels* via the famous paper *On Holy Wars and a Plea for Peace* by Danny Cohen, USC/ISI IEN 137, dated April 1, 1980] adj. 1. Describes a computer architecture in which, within a given multi-byte numeric representation, the most significant byte has the lowest address (the word is stored 'big-end-first'). Most processors, including the IBM 370 family, the **PDP-10**, the Motorola microprocessor families, and most of the various RISC designs current in mid-1993, are big-endian. See **little-endian, middle-endian, NUXI problem, swab**. 2. An **Internet address** the wrong way round. Most of the world follows the Internet standard and writes email addresses starting with the name of the computer and ending up with the name of the country. In the U.K. the Joint Networking Team had decided to do it the other way round before the Internet domain standard was established; e.g., *me@uk.ac.wigan.cs*. Most gateway sites have **ad-hockery** in their mailers to handle this, but can still be confused. In particular, the address above could be in the U.K. (domain *uk*) or Czechoslovakia (domain *cs*).

bignum */big´nuhm/* [orig. from MIT MacLISP] n. 1. [techspeak] A multiple-precision computer representation for very large integers. 2. More generally, any very large number. "Have you ever looked at the United States Budget? There's bignums for you!" 3. [Stanford] In backgammon, large numbers on the dice especially a roll of double fives or double sixes (compare **moby**, sense 4). See also **El Camino Bignum**.

Sense 1 may require some explanation. Most computer languages provide a kind of data called 'integer', but such computer integers are usually very limited in size; usually they must be smaller than than 2^{31} (2,147,483,648) or (on a **bitty box**) 2^{15} (32,768). If you want to work with numbers larger than that, you have to use floating-point numbers, which are usually accurate to only six or seven decimal places. Computer languages that provide bignums can perform exact calculations on very large numbers, such as 1000! (the factorial of 1000, which is 1000 times 999 times 998 times . . . times 2 times 1). For example, this value for 1000! was computed by the MacLISP system using bignums:

402387260077093773543702433923003985719374864210714
632543799910429938512398629020592044208486969404800
479988610197196058631666872994808558901323829669944
590997424504087073759918823627727188732519779505950
995276120874975462497043601418278094646496291056393
887437886487337119181045825783647849977012476632889
835955735432513185323958463075557409114262417474349
347553428646576611667797396668820291207379143853719
588249808126867838374559731746136085379534524221586
593201928090878297308431392844403281231558611036976
801357304216168747609675871348312025478589320767169
132448426236131412508780208000261683151027341827977
704784635868170164365024153691398281264810213092761
244896359928705114964975419909342221566832572080821
333186116811553615836546984046708975602900950537616
475847728421889679646244945160765353408198901385442
487984959953319101723355556602139450399736280750137
837615307127761926849034352625200015888535147331611
702103968175921510907788019393178114194545257223865
541461062892187960223838971476088506276862967146674
697562911234082439208160153780889893964518263243671
616762179168909779911903754031274622289988005195444
414282012187361745992642956581746628302955570299024
324153181617210465832036786906117260158783520751516
284225540265170483304226143974286933061690897968482
590125458327168226458066526769958652682272807075781
391858178889652208164348344825993266043367660176999
612831860788386150279465955131156552036093988180612
138558600301435694527224206344631797460594682573103
790084024432438465657245014402821885252470935190620
929023136493273497565513958720559654228749774011413
346962715422845862377387538230483865688976461927383
814900140767310446640259899490222221765904339901886
018566526485061799702356193897017860040811889729918
311021171229845901641921068884387121855646124960798
722908519296819

372388642614839657382291123125024186649353143970137428531926649875337218940694281434118520158014123344828015051399694290153483077644569099073152433278288269864602789864321139083506217095002597389863554277196742822248757586765752344220207573630569498825087968928162753848863396909959826280956121450994871701244516461260379029309120889086942028510640182154399457156805941872748998094254742173582401063677404595741785160829230135358081840096996372524230560855903700624271243416909004153690105933983835777939410970027753472000.

bigot n. A person who is religiously attached to a particular computer, language, operating system, editor, or other tool (see **religious issues**). Usually found with a specifier; thus, *cray bigot, ITS bigot, APL bigot, VMS bigot, Berkeley bigot.* Real bigots can be distinguished from mere partisans or zealots by the fact that they refuse to learn alternatives even when the march of time and/or technology is threatening to obsolete the favored tool. It is truly said "You can tell a bigot, but you can't tell him much." Compare **weenie**.

bit [from the mainstream meaning and 'Binary digIT'] n. 1. [techspeak] The unit of information; the amount of information obtained by asking a yes-or-no question for which the two outcomes are equally probable. 2. [techspeak] A computational quantity that can take on one of two values, such as true and false or 0 and 1. 3. A mental flag: a reminder that something should be done eventually. "I have a bit set for you." (I haven't seen you for a while, and I'm supposed to tell or ask you something.) 4. More generally, a (possibly incorrect) mental state of belief. "I have a bit set that says that you were the last guy to hack on EMACS." (Meaning "I think you were the last guy to hack on EMACS, and what I am about to say is predicated on this, so please stop me if this isn't true.")

"I just need one bit from you" is a polite way of indicating that you intend only a short interruption for a question that can presumably be answered yes or no.

A bit is said to be *set* if its value is true or 1, and *reset* or *clear* if its value is false or 0. One speaks of setting and clearing bits. To **toggle** or *invert* a bit is to change it, either from 0 to 1 or from 1 to 0. See also **flag**, **trit**, **mode bit**.

The term *bit* first appeared in print in the computer-science sense in 1949, and seems to have been coined by early computer scientist John Tukey. Tukey records that it evolved over a lunch table as a handier alternative to *bigit* or *binit*.

bit bang n. Transmission of data on a serial line, when accomplished by rapidly tweaking a single output bit, in software, at the appropriate times. The technique is a simple loop with eight OUT and SHIFT instruction pairs for each byte. Input is more interesting. And full duplex (doing input and output at the same time) is one way to separate the real hackers from the **wannabees**.

Bit bang was used on certain early models of Prime computers, presumably when UARTs were too expensive, and on archaic Z80 micros with a Zilog PIO but no SIO. In an interesting instance of the **cycle of reincarnation**, this technique is now (1991) coming back into use on some RISC architectures because it consumes such an infinitesimal part of the processor that it actually makes sense not to have a UART.

bit bashing n. (alt. *bit diddling* or **bit twiddling**) Term used to describe any of several kinds of low-level programming characterized by manipulation of **bit**, **flag**, **nybble**, and other smaller-than-character-sized pieces of data; these include low-level device control, encryption algorithms, checksum and error-correcting codes, hash functions, some flavors of graphics programming (see **bitblt**), and assembler/compiler code generation. May connote either tedium or a real technical challenge (more usually the former). "The command decoding for the new tape driver looks pretty solid but the bit-bashing for the control registers still has bugs." See also **bit bang**, **mode bit**.

bit bucket n. 1. The universal data sink (originally, the mythical receptacle used to catch bits when they fall off the end of a register during a shift instruction). Discarded, lost, or destroyed data is said to have *gone to the bit bucket*. On **UNIX**, often used for **/dev/null**. Sometimes amplified as *the Great Bit Bucket in the Sky*. 2. The place where all lost mail and news messages eventually go. The selection is performed according to **Finagle's Law**; important mail is much more likely to end up in the bit bucket than junk mail, which has an almost 100% probability of getting delivered. Routing to the bit bucket is automatically performed by mail-transfer agents, news systems, and the lower layers of the network. 3. The ideal location for all unwanted mail responses: "Flames about this article to the bit bucket." Such a request is guaranteed to overflow one's mailbox with flames. 4. Excuse for all mail that has not been sent. "I mailed you those figures last week; they must have landed in the bit bucket." Compare **black hole**.

This term is used purely in jest. It is based on the fanciful notion that bits are objects that are not destroyed but only misplaced. This appears to have been a mutation of an earlier term 'bit box', about which the same legend was current; old-time hackers also report that trainees used to be told that when the CPU stored bits into memory it was actually pulling them 'out of the bit box'. See also **chad box**.

Another variant of this legend has it that, as a consequence of the 'parity preservation law', the number of 1 bits that go to the bit bucket must equal the number of 0 bits. Any imbalance results in bits filling up the bit bucket. A qualified computer technician can empty a full bit bucket as part of scheduled maintenance.

bit decay n. See **bit rot**. People with a physics background tend to prefer this variant for the analogy with particle decay. See also **computron**, **quantum bogodynamics**.

bit rot n. Also **bit decay**. Hypothetical disease the existence of which has been deduced from the observation that unused programs or features will often stop working after sufficient time has passed, even if 'nothing has changed'. The theory explains that bits decay as if they were radioactive. As time passes, the contents of a file or the code in a program will become increasingly garbled.

There actually are physical processes that produce such effects (alpha particles generated by trace radionuclides in ceramic chip packages, for example, can change the contents of a computer memory unpredictably, and various kinds of subtle media failures can corrupt files in mass storage), but they are quite rare (and computers are built with error-detecting circuitry to compensate for them). The notion long favored among hackers that cosmic rays are among the causes of such events turns out to be a myth; see the **cosmic rays** entry for details.

The term **software rot** is almost synonymous. Software rot is the effect, bit rot the notional cause.

A literal **bit bucket**.
The next cartoon in the Crunchly saga is 12-31-75, page 102.

bit twiddling n. 1. (pejorative) An exercise in tuning (see **tune**) in which incredible amounts of time and effort go to produce little noticeable improvement, often with the result that the code becomes incomprehensible. 2. Aimless small modification to a program, esp. for some pointless goal. 3. Approx. syn. for **bit bashing**; esp. used for the act of frobbing the device control register of a peripheral in an attempt to get it back to a known state.

bit-paired keyboard n. obs. (alt. *bit-shift keyboard*) A non-standard keyboard layout that seems to have originated with the Teletype ASR-33 and remained common for several years on early computer equipment. The ASR-33 was a mechanical device (see **EOU**), so the only way to generate the character codes from keystrokes was by some physical linkage. The design of the ASR-33 assigned each character key a basic pattern that could be modified by flipping bits if the SHIFT or the CTRL key was pressed. In order to avoid making the thing more of a Rube Goldberg kluge than it already was, the design had to group characters that shared the same basic bit pattern on one key.

Looking at the ASCII chart, we find:

```
high  low bits
bits  0000 0001 0010 0011 0100 0101 0110 0111 1000 1001
 010        !    "    #    $    %    &    '    (    )
 011   0    1    2    3    4    5    6    7    8    9
```

This is why the characters !"#$%&'() appear where they do on a Teletype (thankfully, they didn't use shift-0 for space). This was *not* the weirdest variant of the **QWERTY** layout widely seen, by the way; that prize should probably go to one of several (differing) arrangements on IBM's even clunkier 026 and 029 card punches.

When electronic terminals became popular, in the early 1970s, there was no agreement in the industry over how the keyboards should be laid out. Some vendors opted to emulate the Teletype keyboard, while others used the flexibility of electronic circuitry to make their product look like an office typewriter. These alternatives became known as *bit-paired* and *typewriter-paired* keyboards. To a hacker, the bit-paired keyboard seemed far more logical — and because most hackers in those days had never learned to touch-type, there was little pressure from the pioneering users to adapt keyboards to the typewriter standard.

The doom of the bit-paired keyboard was the large-scale introduction of the computer terminal into the normal office environment, where out-

and-out technophobes were expected to use the equipment. The *typewriter-paired* standard became universal, *bit-paired* hardware was quickly junked or relegated to dusty corners, and both terms passed into disuse.

bitblt */bit´blit/* n. [from **BLT**, q.v.] 1. Any of a family of closely related algorithms for moving and copying rectangles of bits between main and display memory on a bit-mapped device, or between two areas of either main or display memory (the requirement to do the **Right Thing** in the case of overlapping source and destination rectangles is what makes BitBlt tricky). 2. Synonym for **blit** or **BLT**. Both uses are borderline techspeak.

BITNET */bit´net/* [acronym: Because It's Time NETwork] n. Everybody's least favorite piece of the network (see **network, the**). The BITNET hosts are a collection of IBM dinosaurs and VAXen (the latter with lobotomized comm hardware) that communicate using 80-character **EBCDIC** card images (see **eighty-column mind**); thus, they tend to mangle the headers and text of third-party traffic from the rest of the ASCII/**RFC**-822 world with annoying regularity. BITNET is also notorious as the apparent home of **BIFF**.

bits n.pl. 1. Information. Examples: "I need some bits about file formats." ("I need to know about file formats.") Compare **core dump**, sense 4. 2. Machine-readable representation of a document, specifically as contrasted with paper: "I have only a photocopy of the Jargon File; does anyone know where I can get the bits?". See **softcopy**, **source of all good bits** See also **bit**.

bitty box */bit´ee boks/* n. 1. A computer sufficiently small, primitive, or incapable as to cause a hacker acute claustrophobia at the thought of developing software on or for it. Especially used of small, obsolescent, single-tasking-only personal machines such as the Atari 800, Osborne, Sinclair, VIC-20, TRS-80, or IBM PC. 2. [Pejorative] More generally, the opposite of 'real computer' (see **Get a real computer!**). See also **mess-dos, toaster**, and **toy**.

bixie */bik´see/* n. Variant **emoticon**s used on BIX (the Byte Information eXchange). The **smiley** bixie is <@_@>, apparently intending to represent two cartoon eyes and a mouth. A few others have been reported.

black art n. A collection of arcane, unpublished, and (by implication) mostly ad-hoc techniques developed for a particular application or systems area (compare **black magic**). VLSI design and compiler code optimization were (in their beginnings) considered classic examples of black art; as theory developed they became **deep magic**, and once standard textbooks had been written, became merely **heavy wizardry**. The huge proliferation of formal and informal channels for spreading around new computer-related technologies during the last twenty years has made both the term *black art* and what it describes less common than formerly. See also **voodoo programming**.

black hole n. What a piece of email or netnews has fallen into if it disappears mysteriously between its origin and destination sites (that is, without returning a **bounce message**). "I think there's a black hole at *foovax*!" conveys suspicion that site *foovax* has been dropping a lot of stuff on the floor lately (see **drop on the floor**). The implied metaphor of email as interstellar travel is interesting in itself. Compare **bit bucket**.

black magic n. A technique that works, though nobody really understands why. More obscure than **voodoo programming**, which may be done by cookbook. Compare also **black art**, **deep magic**, and **magic number** (sense 2).

blargh */blarg/* [MIT] n. The opposite of **ping**, sense 5; an exclamation indicating that one has absorbed or is emitting a quantum of unhappiness. Less common than **ping**.

blast 1. vt.,n. Synonym for **BLT**, used esp. for large data sends over a network or comm line. Opposite of **snarf**. Usage: uncommon. The variant 'blat' has been reported. 2. vt. [HP/Apollo] Synonymous with **nuke** (sense 3). Sometimes the message `Unable to kill all processes. Blast them (y/n)?` would appear in the command window upon logout.

blat n. 1. Syn. **blast**, sense 1. 2. See **thud**.

bletch */blech/* [from Yiddish/German 'brechen', to vomit, poss. via comic-strip exclamation 'blech'] interj. Term of disgust. Often used in "Ugh, bletch". Compare **barf**.

bletcherous */blech´ə-rəs/* adj. Disgusting in design or function; esthetically unappealing. This word is seldom used of people. "This keyboard is bletcherous!" (Perhaps the keys don't work very well, or are misplaced.) See **losing**, **cretinous**, **bagbiting**, **bogus**, and **random**. The term **bletcherous** applies to the esthetics of the thing so described; similarly for **cretinous**. By contrast, something that is *losing* or *bagbiting* may be failing to meet objective criteria. See also **bogus** and **random**, which have richer and wider shades of meaning than any of the above.

blinkenlights */blink´ən-li:tz/* n. Front-panel diagnostic lights on a computer, esp. a **dinosaur**. Derives from the last word of the famous blackletter-Gothic sign in mangled pseudo-German that once graced about half the computer rooms in the English-speaking world. One version ran in its entirety as follows:

> ACHTUNG! ALLES LOOKENSPEEPERS!
>
> **Das computermachine ist nicht fuer gefingerpoken und mittengrabben. Ist easy schnappen der springenwerk, blowenfusen und poppencorken mit spitzensparken. Ist nicht fuer gewerken bei das dumpkopfen. Das rubbernecken sichtseeren keepen das cotten-pickenen hans in das pockets muss; relaxen und watchen das blinkenlichten.**

This silliness dates back at least as far as 1959 at Stanford University and had already gone international by the early 1960s, when it was reported at London University's ATLAS computing site. There are several variants of it in circulation, some of which actually do end with the word 'blinkenlights'.

In an amusing example of turnabout-is-fair-play, German hackers have developed their own versions of the blinkenlights poster in fractured English, one of which is reproduced here:

> ATTENTION
>
> This room is fullfilled mit special electronische equippment. Fingergrabbing and pressing the cnoeppkes from the computers is allowed for die experts only! So all the "lefthanders" stay away and do not disturben the brainstorming von here working intelligencies. Otherwise you will be out thrown and kicked anderswhere! Also: please keep still and only watchen astaunished the blinkenlights.

See also **geef**.

blit */blit/* vt. 1. To copy a large array of bits from one part of a computer's memory to another part, particularly when the memory is being used to determine what is shown on a display screen. "The storage allocator picks through the table and copies the good parts up into high memory, and then blits it all back down again." See **bitblt**, **BLT**, **dd**, **cat**, **blast**, **snarf**. More generally, to perform some operation (such as toggling) on a large array of bits while moving them. 2. Sometimes all-capitalized as *BLIT*: an early experimental bit-mapped terminal designed by Rob Pike at Bell Labs, later commercialized as the AT&T 5620. (The folk etymology from 'Bell Labs Intelligent Terminal' is incorrect. Its creators liked to claim that "Blit" stood for the Bacon, Lettuce, and Interactive Tomato.)

blitter */blit´r/* n. A special-purpose chip or hardware system built to perform **blit** operations, esp. used for fast implementation of bit-mapped graphics. The Commodore Amiga and a few other micros have these, but in 1991 the trend is away from them (however, see **cycle of reincarnation**). Syn. **raster blaster**.

blivet */bliv´ət/* [allegedly from a World War II military term meaning "ten pounds of manure in a five-pound bag"] n. 1. An intractable problem. 2. A crucial piece of hardware that can't be fixed or replaced if it breaks. 3. A tool that has been hacked over by so many incompetent programmers that it has become an unmaintainable tissue of hacks. 4. An out-of-control but unkillable development effort. 5. An embarrassing bug that pops up during a customer demo. 6. In the subjargon of computer security specialists, a denial-of-service attack performed by hogging limited resources that have no access controls (for example, shared spool space on a multi-user system).

This term has other meanings in other technical cultures; among experimental physicists and hardware engineers of various kinds it seems to mean any random object of unknown purpose (similar to hackish use of **frob**). It has also been used to describe an amusing trick-the-eye drawing resembling a three-pronged fork that appears to depict a three-dimensional object until one realizes that the parts fit together in an impossible way.

BLOB [acronym, Binary Large OBject] n. Used by database people to refer to any random large block of bits that needs to be stored in a database, such as a picture or sound file. The essential point about a BLOB is that it's an object that cannot be interpreted within the database itself.

block [from process scheduling terminology in OS theory] 1. vi. To delay or sit idle while waiting for something. "We're blocking until everyone gets here." Compare **busy-wait**. 2. *block on* vt. To block, waiting for (something). "Lunch is blocked on Phil's arrival."

block transfer computations [from the television series "Dr. Who"] n. Computations so fiendishly subtle and complex that they could not be performed by machines. Used to refer to any task that should be expressible as an algorithm in theory, but isn't.

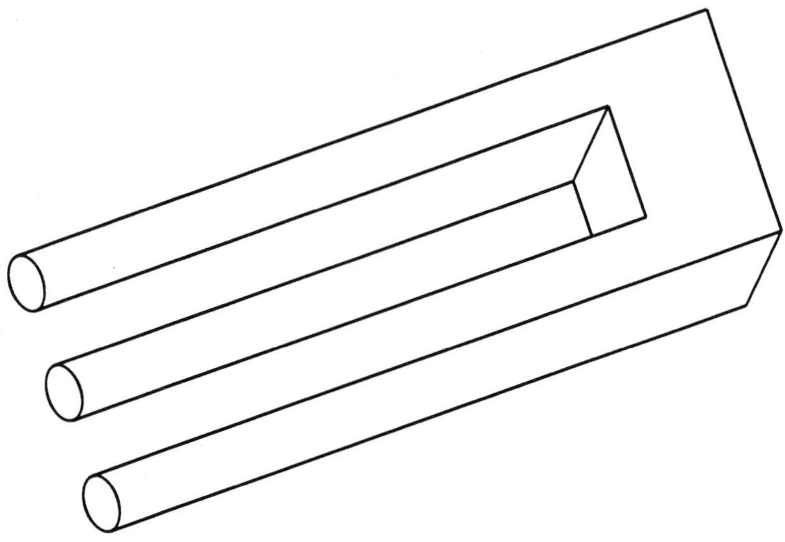

This is a blivet

Bloggs Family, the n. An imaginary family consisting of Fred and Mary Bloggs and their children. Used as a standard example in knowledge representation to show the difference between extensional and intensional objects. For example, every occurrence of "Fred Bloggs" is the same unique person, whereas occurrences of "person" may refer to different people. Members of the Bloggs family have been known to pop up in bizarre places such as the DEC Telephone Directory. Compare **Mbogo, Dr. Fred**.

blow an EPROM */bloh ən ee´prom/* v. (alt. *blast an EPROM, burn an EPROM*) To program a read-only memory, e.g. for use with an embedded system. This term arose because the programming process for the Programmable Read-Only Memories (PROMs) that preceded present-day Erasable Programmable Read-Only Memories (EPROMs) involved intentionally blowing tiny electrical fuses on the chip. The usage lives on (it's too vivid and expressive to discard) even though the write process on EPROMs is nondestructive.

blow away vt. To remove (files and directories) from permanent storage, generally by accident. "He reformatted the wrong partition and blew away last night's netnews." Oppose **nuke**.

blow out [prob. from mining and tunneling jargon] vi. Of software, to fail spectacularly; almost as serious as **crash and burn**. See **blow past**, **blow up**, **die horribly**.

blow past vt. To **blow out** despite a safeguard. "The server blew past the 5K reserve buffer."

blow up vi. 1. [scientific computation] To become unstable. Suggests that the computation is diverging so rapidly that it will soon overflow or at least go **nonlinear**. 2. Syn. **blow out**.

BLT */B-L-T/*, */blət/* or (rarely) */belt/* n.,vt. Synonym for **blit**. This is the original form of **blit** and the ancestor of **bitblt**. It referred to any large bit-field copy or move operation (one resource-intensive memory-shuffling operation done on pre-paged versions of ITS, WAITS, and TOPS-10 was sardonically referred to as 'The Big BLT'). The jargon usage has outlasted the **PDP-10** BLock Transfer instruction from which **BLT** derives; nowadays, the assembler mnemonic **BLT** almost always means 'Branch if Less Than zero'.

Blue Book n. 1. Informal name for one of the three standard references on the page-layout and graphics-control language **PostScript** (*PostScript Language Tutorial and Cookbook*, Adobe Systems, Addison-Wesley 1985, QA76.73.P67P68, ISBN 0-201-10179-3); the other three official guides are known as the **Green Book**, the **Red Book**, and the **White Book** (sense 2). 2. Informal name for one of the three standard references on Smalltalk: *Smalltalk-80: The Language and its Implementation*, David Robson, Addison-Wesley 1983, QA76.8.S635G64, ISBN 0-201-11371-63 (this book also has green and red siblings). 3. Any of the 1988 standards issued by the CCITT's ninth plenary assembly. These include, among other things, the X.400 email spec and the Group 1 through 4 fax standards. See also **book titles**.

Blue Glue [IBM] n. IBM's SNA (Systems Network Architecture), an incredibly **losing** and **bletcherous** communications protocol widely favored at commercial shops that don't know any better. The official IBM definition is "that which binds blue boxes together." See **fear and loathing**. It may not be irrelevant that **Blue Glue** is the trade name of a 3M product that is commonly used to hold down the carpet squares to the removable panel floors common in **dinosaur pens**. A correspondent at U. Minn. reports that the CS department there has about 80 bottles of the stuff hanging about, so they often refer to any messy work to be done as *using the blue glue*.

blue goo n. Term for 'police' **nanobot**s intended to prevent **gray goo**, denature hazardous waste, destroy pollution, put ozone back into the stratosphere, prevent halitosis, and promote truth, justice, and the American way, etc. See **nanotechnology**.

blue wire [IBM] n. Patch wires added to circuit boards at the factory to correct design or fabrication problems. These may be necessary if there hasn't been time to design and qualify another board version. Compare **purple wire**, **red wire**, **yellow wire**.

blurgle /bler'gl/ [Great Britain] n. Spoken **metasyntactic variable**, to indicate some text that is obvious from context, or which is already known. If several words are to be replaced, blurgle may well be doubled or trebled. "To look for something in several files use 'grep string blurgle blurgle'." In each case, "blurgle blurgle" would be understood to be replaced by the file you wished to search. Compare **mumble**, sense 7.

BNF /*B-N-F*/ n. 1. [techspeak] Acronym for 'Backus-Naur Form', a metasyntactic notation used to specify the syntax of programming languages, command sets, and the like. Widely used for language descriptions but seldom documented anywhere, so that it must usually be learned by osmosis from other hackers. Consider this BNF for a U.S. postal address:

```
<postal-address> ::= <name-part> <street-address>
                     <zip-part>

<personal-part> ::= <name> | <initial> "."

<name-part> ::= <personal-part> <last-name>
                [<jr-part>] <EOL>
               | <personal-part> <name-part>

<street-address> ::= [<apt>] <house-num>
                     <street-name> <EOL>

<zip-part> ::= <town-name> "," <state-code>
               <ZIP-code> <EOL>
```

This translates into English as: "A postal-address consists of a name-part, followed by a street-address part, followed by a zip-code part. A personal-part consists of either a first name or an initial followed by a dot. A name-part consists of either: a personal-part followed by a last name followed by an optional 'jr-part' (Jr., Sr., or dynastic number) and end-of-line, or a personal part followed by a name part (this rule illustrates the use of recursion in BNFs, covering the case of people who use multiple first and middle names and/or initials). A street address consists of an optional apartment specifier, followed by a street number, followed by a street name. A zip-part consists of a town-name, followed by a comma, followed by a state code, followed by a ZIP-code followed by an end-of-line." Note that many things (such as the format of a personal-part, apartment specifier, or ZIP-code) are left unspecified. These are presumed to be obvious from context or detailed somewhere nearby. See also **parse**. 2. Any of a number number of variants and extensions of BNF proper, possibly containing some or all of the **regexp** wildcards such as `*` or `+`. In fact the example above isn't the pure form invented for the Algol-60 report; it uses `[]`, which was introduced a few years later in IBM's PL/I definition but is now universally recognized. 3. In **science-fiction fandom**, a 'Big-Name Fan' (someone famous or notorious). Years ago a fan started handing out black-on-green BNF buttons at SF conventions; this confused the hacker contingent terribly.

boa [IBM] n. Any one of the fat cables that lurk under the floor in a **dinosaur pen**. Possibly so called because they display a ferocious life of their own when you try to lay them straight and flat after they have been coiled for some time. It is rumored within IBM that channel cables for the 370 are limited to 200 feet because beyond that length the boas get dangerous — and it is worth noting that one of the major cable makers uses the trademark 'Anaconda'.

board n. 1. In-context synonym for **bboard**; sometimes used even for USENET newsgroups (but see usage note under **bboard**, sense 1). 2. An electronic circuit board.

boat anchor n. 1. Like **doorstop** but more severe; implies that the offending hardware is irreversibly dead or useless. "That was a working motherboard once. One lightning strike later, instant boat anchor!" 2. A person who just takes up space.3. Obsolete but still working hardware, especially when used of an old S100-bus hobbyist system; originally a term of annoyance, but became more and more affectionate as the hardware became more and more obsolete.

BOF */B-O-F/* or */bof/* n. Abbreviation for the phrase "Birds Of a Feather" (flocking together), an informal discussion group and/or bull session scheduled on a conference program. It is not clear where or when this term originated, but it is now associated with the USENIX conferences for UNIX techies and was already established there by 1984. It was used earlier than that at DECUS conferences and is reported to have been common at SHARE meetings as far back as the early 1960s.

bogo-sort */boh`goh-sort´/* n. (var. *stupid-sort*) The archetypical perversely awful algorithm (as opposed to **bubble sort**, which is merely the generic *bad* algorithm). Bogo-sort is equivalent to repeatedly throwing a deck of cards in the air, picking them up at random, and then testing whether they are in order. It serves as a sort of canonical example of awfulness. Looking at a program and seeing a dumb algorithm, one might say "Oh, I see, this program uses bogo-sort." Compare **bogus**, **brute force**, **Lasherism**.

bogometer */boh-gom´-ət-er/* n. A notional instrument for measuring **bogosity**. Compare the 'wankometer' described in the **wank** entry; see also **bogus**.

bogon */boh´gon/* [by analogy with proton/electron/neutron, but doubtless reinforced after 1980 by the similarity to Douglas Adams's 'Vogons'; see the Bibliography in Appendix C] n. 1. The elementary particle of bogosity (see **quantum bogodynamics**). For instance, "the Ethernet is emitting bogons again" means that it is broken or acting in an erratic or bogus fashion. 2. A query packet sent from a TCP/IP domain resolver to a root server, having the reply bit set instead of the query bit. 3. Any bogus or incorrectly formed packet sent on a network. 4. By synecdoche, used to refer to any bogus thing, as in "I'd like to go to lunch with you but I've got to go to the weekly staff bogon". 5. A person who is bogus or who says bogus things. This was historically the original usage, but has been overtaken by its derivative senses 1–4. See also **bogosity**, **bogus**; compare **psyton**, **fat electrons**, **magic smoke**.

The bogon has become the type case for a whole bestiary of nonce particle names, including the 'clutron' or 'cluon' (indivisible particle of cluefulness, obviously the antiparticle of the bogon) and the futon (elementary particle of **randomness**). These are not so much live usages in themselves as examples of a live meta-usage: that is, it has become a standard joke or linguistic maneuver to "explain" otherwise mysterious circumstances by inventing nonce particle names. And these imply nonce particle theories, with all their dignity or lack thereof (we might note parenthetically that this is a generalization from "(bogus particle) theories" to "bogus (particle theories)"!). Perhaps such particles are the modern-day equivalents of trolls and wood-nymphs as standard starting-points around which to construct explanatory myths. Of course, playing on an existing word (as in the 'futon') yields additional flavor. Compare **magic smoke**.

bogon filter */boh´gon fil´tr/* n. Any device, software or hardware, that limits or suppresses the flow and/or emission of bogons. "Engineering hacked a bogon filter between the Cray and the VAXen, and now we're getting fewer dropped packets." See also **bogosity**, **bogus**.

bogon flux */boh´gon fluhks/* n. A measure of a supposed field of **bogosity** emitted by a speaker, measured by a **bogometer**; as a speaker starts to wander into increasing bogosity a listener might say "Warning, warning, bogon flux is rising". See **quantum bogodynamics**.

bogosity */boh-go´sə-tee/* n. 1. The degree to which something is **bogus**. At CMU, bogosity is measured with a **bogometer**; in a seminar, when a speaker says something bogus, a listener might raise his hand and say "My bogometer just triggered". More extremely, "You just pinned my bogometer" means you just said or did something so outrageously bogus that it is off the scale, pinning the bogometer needle at the highest possible reading (one might also say "You just redlined my bogometer"). The agreed-upon unit of bogosity is the microLenat */mi:k`roh-len´ət/* (μL); the consensus is that this is the largest unit practical for everyday use. 2. The potential field generated by a **bogon flux**; see **quantum bogodynamics**. See also **bogon flux**, **bogon filter**, **bogus**.

Historical note: The microLenat was invented as an attack against noted computer scientist Doug Lenat by a **tenured graduate student**. Doug had failed the student on an important exam for giving only "AI is bogus" as his answer to the questions. The slur is generally considered unmerited, but it has become a running gag nevertheless. Some of Doug's friends argue that *of course* a microLenat is bogus, since it is only one millionth of a Lenat. Others have suggested that the unit should be redesignated after the grad student, as the microReid.

bogotify */boh-go´tə-fi:/* vt. To make or become bogus. A program that has been changed so many times as to become completely disorganized has become bogotified. If you tighten a nut too hard and strip the threads on the bolt, the bolt has become bogotified and you had better not use it any more. This coinage led to the notional *autobogotiphobia* defined as 'the fear of becoming bogotified'; but is not clear that the latter has ever been 'live' jargon rather than a self-conscious joke in jargon about jargon. See also **bogosity**, **bogus**.

bogue out */bohg owt/* vi. To become bogus, suddenly and unexpectedly. "His talk was relatively sane until somebody asked him a trick question; then he bogued out and did nothing but **flame** afterwards." See also **bogosity**, **bogus**.

bogus adj. 1. Non-functional. "Your patches are bogus." 2. Useless. "OPCON is a bogus program." 3. False. "Your arguments are bogus." 4. Incorrect. "That algorithm is bogus." 5. Unbelievable. "You claim to have solved the halting problem for Turing Machines? That's totally bogus." 6. Silly. "Stop writing those bogus sagas."

Astrology is bogus. So is a bolt that is obviously about to break. So is someone who makes blatantly false claims to have solved a scientific problem. (This word seems to have some, but not all, of the connotations of **random** — mostly the negative ones.)

It is claimed that *bogus* was originally used in the hackish sense at Princeton in the late 1960s. It was spread to CMU and Yale by Michael Shamos, a migratory Princeton alumnus. A glossary of bogus words was compiled at Yale when the word was first popularized (see **autobogotiphobia** under **bogotify**). The word spread into hackerdom from CMU and MIT. By the early 1980s it was also current in something like the hackish sense in West Coast teen slang, and it had gone mainstream by 1985. A correspondent from Cambridge reports, by contrast, that these uses of *bogus* grate on British nerves; in Britain the word means, rather specifically, 'counterfeit', as in "a bogus 10-pound note".

Bohr bug */bohr buhg/* [from quantum physics] n. A repeatable **bug**; one that manifests reliably under a possibly unknown but well-defined set of conditions. Antonym of **heisenbug**; see also **mandelbug**, **schroedinbug**.

boink */boynk/* [USENET: ascribed to the TV series "Cheers" and "Moonlighting"] 1. To have sex with; compare **bounce**, sense 3. (This is mainstream slang.) In Commonwealth hackish the variant 'bonk' is more common. 2. After the original Peter Korn 'Boinkon' **USENET** parties, used for almost any net social gathering, e.g., Miniboink, a small boink held by Nancy Gillett in 1988; Minniboink, a Boinkcon in Minnesota in 1989; Humpdayboinks, Wednesday get-togethers held in the San Francisco Bay Area. Compare **@-party**. 3. Var of *bonk*; see **bonk/oif**.

bomb 1. v. General synonym for **crash** (sense 1) except that it is not used as a noun; esp. used of software or OS failures. "Don't run Empire with less than 32K stack, it'll bomb." 2. n.,v. Atari ST and Macintosh equivalents of a UNIX 'panic' or Amiga **guru** (sense 2), in which icons of little black-powder bombs or mushroom clouds are displayed, indicating that the system has died. On the Mac, this may be accompanied by a decimal (or occasionally hexadecimal) number indicating what went wrong, similar to the Amiga **guru meditation** number. **MS-DOS** machines tend to get **locked up** in this situation.

bondage-and-discipline language A language (such as **Pascal**, **Ada**, APL, or Prolog) that, though ostensibly general-purpose, is designed so as to enforce an author's theory of 'right programming' even though said theory is demonstrably inadequate for systems hacking or even vanilla general-purpose programming. Often abbreviated 'B&D'; thus, one may speak of things "having the B&D nature". See **Pascal**; oppose **languages of choice**.

bonk/oif */bonk/, /oyf/* interj. In the **MUD** community, it has become traditional to express pique or censure by *bonking* the offending person. Convention holds that one should acknowledge a bonk by saying 'oif!' and there is a myth to the effect that failing to do so upsets the cosmic bonk/oif balance, causing much trouble in the universe. Some MUDs have implemented special commands for bonking and oifing. See also **talk mode**.

book titles There is a tradition in hackerdom of informally tagging important textbooks and standards documents with the dominant color of their covers or with some other conspicuous feature of the cover. Many of these are described in this lexicon under their own entries. See **Aluminum Book**, **Blue Book**, **Cinderella Book**, **Devil Book**, **Dragon Book**, **Green Book**, **Orange Book**, **Pink-Shirt Book**, **Purple Book**, **Red Book**, **Silver Book**, **White Book**, **Wizard Book**, **Yellow Book**, and **bible**; see also **rainbow series**.

boot [techspeak; from 'by one's bootstraps'] v.,n. To load and initialize the operating system on a machine. This usage is no longer jargon (having passed into techspeak) but has given rise to some derivatives that are still jargon.

The derivative *reboot* implies that the machine hasn't been down for long, or that the boot is a **bounce** (sense 4) intended to clear some state of **wedgitude**. This is sometimes used of human thought processes, as in the following exchange: "You've lost me." "OK, reboot. Here's the theory. . . ."

This term is also found in the variants *cold boot* (from power-off condition) and *warm boot* (with the CPU and all devices already powered up, as after a hardware reset or software crash).

Another variant: *soft boot,* reinitialization of only part of a system, under control of other software still running: "If you're running the **mess-dos** emulator, control-alt-insert will cause a soft-boot of the emulator, while leaving the rest of the system running."

Opposed to this there is *hard boot*, which connotes hostility towards or frustration with the machine being booted: "I'll have to hard-boot this losing Sun." "I recommend booting it hard." One often hard-boots by performing a power cycle.

Historical note: this term derives from 'bootstrap loader', a short program that was read in from cards or paper tape, or toggled in from the front panel switches. This program was always very short (great efforts were expended on making it short in order to minimize the labor and chance of error involved in toggling it in), but was just smart enough to read in a slightly more complex program (usually from a card or paper tape reader), to which it handed control; this program in turn was smart enough to read the application or operating system from a magnetic tape drive or disk drive. Thus, in successive steps, the computer 'pulled itself up by its bootstraps' to a useful operating state. Nowadays the bootstrap is usually found in ROM or EPROM, and reads the first stage in from a fixed location on the disk, called the 'boot block'. When this program gains control, it is powerful enough to load the actual OS and hand control over to it.

bottom feeder n. Syn. for **slopsucker**, derived from the fishermen's and naturalists' term for finny creatures who subsist on the primordial ooze.

bottom-up implementation n. Hackish opposite of the techspeak term 'top-down design'. It is now received wisdom in most programming cultures that it is best to design from higher levels of abstraction down to lower, specifying sequences of action in increasing detail until you get to actual code. Hackers often find (especially in exploratory designs that cannot be closely specified in advance) that it works best to *build* things in the opposite order, by writing and testing a clean set of primitive operations and then knitting them together.

bounce v. 1. [perhaps by analogy to a bouncing check] An electronic mail message that is undeliverable and returns an error notification to the sender is said to *bounce*. See also **bounce message**. 2. [Stanford] To play volleyball. The now-demolished **D. C. Power Lab** building used by the Stanford AI Lab in the 1970s had a volleyball court on the front lawn. From 5 P.M. to 7 P.M. was the scheduled maintenance time for the computer, so every afternoon at 5 would come over the intercom the cry: "Now hear this: bounce, bounce!", followed by Brian McCune loudly bouncing a volleyball on the floor outside the offices of known volleyballers. 3. To engage in sexual intercourse; prob. from the expression 'bouncing the mattress', but influenced by Roo's psychosexually loaded "Try bouncing me, Tigger!" from the "Winnie-the-Pooh" books. Compare **boink**. 4. To casually reboot a system in order to clear up a transient problem. Reported primarily among **VMS** users. 5. [VM/CMS programmers] *Automatic* warm-start of a machine after an error. "I logged on this morning and found it had bounced 7 times during the night" 6. [IBM] To **power cycle** a peripheral in order to reset it.

bounce message [UNIX] n. Notification message returned to sender by a site unable to relay **email** to the intended **Internet address** recipient or the next link in a **bang path** (see **bounce**, sense 1). Reasons might include a nonexistent or misspelled username or a **down** relay site. Bounce messages can themselves fail, with occasionally ugly results; see **sorcerer's apprentice mode** and **software laser**. The terms *bounce mail* and *barfmail* are also common.

boustrophedon [from a Greek word for turning like an ox while plowing] n. An ancient method of writing using alternate left-to-right and right-to-left lines. This term is actually philologists' techspeak and typesetters' jargon. Erudite hackers use it for an optimization performed by some computer typesetting software and moving-head printers. The adverbial form 'boustrophedonically' is also found (hackers purely love constructions like this).

box n. 1. A computer; esp. in the construction *foo box* where *foo* is some functional qualifier, like 'graphics', or the name of an OS (thus, *UNIX box*, *MS-DOS box*, etc.) "We preprocess the data on UNIX boxes before handing it up to the mainframe." 2. [IBM] Without qualification but within an SNA-using site, this refers specifically to an IBM front-end processor or FEP */F-E-P/*. An FEP is a small computer necessary to enable an IBM **mainframe** to communicate beyond the limits of the **dinosaur pen**. Typically used in expressions like the cry that goes up when an SNA network goes down: "Looks like the **box** has fallen over." (See **fall over**.) See also **IBM**, **fear and loathing**, **fepped out**, **Blue Glue**.

boxed comments n. Comments (explanatory notes attached to program instructions) that occupy several lines by themselves; so called because in assembler and C code they are often surrounded by a box in a style something like this:

```
/*********************************************
 *
 * This is a boxed comment in C style
 *
 *********************************************/
```

Common variants of this style omit the asterisks in column 2 or add a matching row of asterisks closing the right side of the box. The sparest variant omits all but the comment delimiters themselves; the 'box' is implied. Oppose **winged comments**.

boxen */bok´sn/* [by analogy with **VAXen**] pl.n. Fanciful plural of **box** often encountered in the phrase 'UNIX boxen', used to describe commodity **UNIX** hardware. The connotation is that any two UNIX boxen are interchangeable.

boxology */bok-sol´ə-jee/* n. Syn. **ASCII art**. This term implies a more restricted domain, that of box-and-arrow drawings. "His report has a lot of boxology in it." Compare **macrology**.

bozotic */boh-zoh´tik/* or */boh-zo´tik/* [from the name of a TV clown even more losing than Ronald McDonald] adj. Resembling or having the quality of a bozo; that is, clownish, ludicrously wrong, unintentionally humorous. Compare **wonky**, **demented**. Note that the noun 'bozo' occurs in slang, but the mainstream adjectival form would be 'bozo-like' or (in New England) 'bozoish'.

BQS */B-Q-S/* adj. Syn. **Berkeley Quality Software**.

brain dump n. The act of telling someone everything one knows about a particular topic or project. Typically used when someone is going to let a new party maintain a piece of code. Conceptually analogous to an operating system **core dump** in that it saves a lot of useful **state** before an exit. "You'll have to give me a brain dump on FOOBAR before you start your new job at HackerCorp." See **core dump** (sense 4). At Sun, this is also known as *TOI* (transfer of information).

brain fart n. The actual result of a **braino**, as opposed to the mental glitch that is the braino itself. E.g., typing `dir` on a UNIX box after a session with DOS.

brain-damaged 1. [generalization of 'Honeywell Brain Damage' (HBD), a theoretical disease invented to explain certain utter cretinisms in Honeywell **Multics**] adj. Obviously wrong; **cretinous**; **demented**. There is an implication that the person responsible must have suffered brain damage, because he should have known better. Calling something brain-damaged is really bad; it also implies it is unusable, and that its failure to work is due to poor design rather than some accident. "Only six monocase characters per file name? Now *that's* brain-damaged!" 2. [esp. in the Mac world] May refer to free demonstration software that has been deliberately crippled in some way so as not to compete with the commercial product it is intended to sell. Syn. **crippleware**.

brain-dead adj. Brain-damaged in the extreme. It tends to imply terminal design failure rather than malfunction or simple stupidity. "This comm program doesn't know how to send a break — how brain-dead!"

braino */bray´no/* n. Syn. for **thinko**. See also **brain fart**.

branch to Fishkill [IBM: from the location of one of the corporation's facilities] n. Any unexpected jump in a program that produces catastrophic or just plain weird results. See **jump off into never-never land**, **hyperspace**.

bread crumbs n. Debugging statements inserted into a program that emit output or log indicators of the program's **state** to a file so you can see where it dies or pin down the cause of surprising behavior. The term is probably a reference to the Hansel and Gretel story from the Brothers Grimm; in several variants, a character leaves a trail of bread crumbs so as not to get lost in the woods.

break 1. vt. To cause to be **broken** (in any sense). "Your latest patch to the editor broke the paragraph commands." 2. v. (of a program) To stop temporarily, so that it may debugged. The place where it stops is a 'breakpoint'. 3. [techspeak] vi. To send an RS-232 break (two character widths of line high) over a serial comm line. 4. [UNIX] vi. To strike whatever key currently causes the tty driver to send SIGINT to the current process. Normally, break (sense 3), delete or **control-C** does this. 5. *break break* may be said to interrupt a conversation (this is an example of verb doubling). This usage comes from radio communications, which in turn probably came from landline telegraph/teleprinter usage, as badly abused in the Citizen's Band craze a few years ago.

break-even point n. in the process of implementing a new computer language, the point at which the language is sufficiently effective that one can implement the language in itself. That is, for a new language called, hypothetically, FOOGOL, one has reached break-even when one can write a demonstration compiler for FOOGOL in FOOGOL, discard the original implementation language, and thereafter use working versions of FOOGOL to develop newer ones. This is an important milestone; see **MFTL**.

[Since this entry was first written, several correspondents have reported that there actually was a compiler for a tiny Algol-like language called Foogol floating around on various **vaxen** in the early and mid-1980s. The above example may not, after all, be hypothetical. – ESR]

breath-of-life packet [XEROX PARC] n. An Ethernet packet that contains bootstrap (see **boot**) code, periodically sent out from a working computer to infuse the 'breath of life' into any computer on the network that has happened to crash. Machines depending on such packets have sufficient hardware or firmware code to wait for (or request) such a packet during the reboot process. See also **dickless workstation**.

The notional *kiss-of-death packet*, with a function complementary to that of a breath-of-life packet, is recommended for dealing with hosts that consume too many network resources. Though 'kiss-of-death packet' is usually used in jest, there is at least one documented instance of an Internet subnet with limited address-table slots in a gateway machine in which such packets were routinely used to compete for slots, rather like Christmas shoppers competing for scarce parking spaces.

breedle n. See **feep**.

bring X to its knees v. To present a machine, operating system, piece of software, or algorithm with a load so extreme or **pathological** that it grinds to a halt. "To bring a MicroVAX to its knees, try twenty users running **vi** — or four running **EMACS**." Compare **hog**.

brittle adj. Said of software that is functional but easily broken by changes in operating environment or configuration, or by any minor tweak to the software itself. Also, any system that responds inappropriately and disastrously to abnormal but expected external stimuli; e.g., a file system that is usually totally scrambled by a power failure is said to be brittle. This term is often used to describe the results of a research effort that were never intended to be robust, but it can be applied to commercially developed software, which displays the quality far more often than it ought to. Oppose **robust**.

broadcast storm n. An incorrect packet broadcast on a network that causes most hosts to respond all at once, typically with wrong answers that start the process over again. See **network meltdown**.

brochureware n. Planned but non-existent product like **vaporware**, but with the added implication that marketing is actively selling and promoting it (they've printed brochures). Brochureware is often deployed as a strategic weapon; the idea is to con customers into not committing to an existing product of the competition's. It is a safe bet that when a brochureware product finally becomes real, it will be more expensive than and inferior to the alternatives that had been available for years.

broken adj. 1. Not working properly (of programs). 2. Behaving strangely; especially (when used of people) exhibiting extreme depression.

broken arrow [IBM] n. The error code displayed on line 25 of a 3270 terminal (or a PC emulating a 3270) for various kinds of protocol violations and "unexpected" error conditions (including connection to a **down** computer). On a PC, simulated with '->/_', with the two center characters overstruck.

Note: to appreciate this term fully, it helps to know that 'broken arrow' is also military jargon for an accident involving nuclear weapons. . . .

broket */broh´kət/* or */broh´ket`/* [by analogy with 'bracket': a 'broken bracket'] n. Either of the characters '<' and '>', when used as paired enclosing delimiters. This word originated as a contraction of the phrase 'broken bracket', that is, a bracket that is bent in the middle. (At MIT, and apparently in the **Real World** as well, these are usually called **angle brackets**.)

Brooks's Law prov. "Adding manpower to a late software project makes it later" — a result of the fact that the expected advantage from splitting work among N programmers is $O(N)$ (that is, proportional to N), but the complexity and communications cost associated with coordinating and then merging their work is $O(N^2)$ (that is, proportional to the square of N). The quote is from Fred Brooks, a manager of IBM's OS/360 project and author of *The Mythical Man-Month* (Addison-Wesley, 1975, ISBN 0-201-00650-2), an excellent early book on software engineering. The myth in question has been most tersely expressed as "Programmer time is fungible" and Brooks established conclusively that it is not. Hackers have never forgotten his advice; too often, **management** still does. See also **creationism**, **second-system effect**, **optimism**.

BRS */B-R-S/* n. Syn. **Big Red Switch**. This abbreviation is fairly common on-line.

brute force adj. Describes a primitive programming style, one in which the programmer relies on the computer's processing power instead of using his or her own intelligence to simplify the problem, often ignoring problems of scale and applying naive methods suited to small problems directly to large ones. The term can also be used in reference to programming style: brute-force programs are written in a heavyhanded, tedious way, full of repetition and devoid of any elegance or useful abstraction (see also **brute force and ignorance**).

The **canonical** example of a brute-force algorithm is associated with the 'traveling salesman problem' (TSP), a classical **NP**-hard problem: Suppose a person is in, say, Boston, and wishes to drive to N other cities. In what order should the cities be visited in order to minimize the distance travelled? The brute-force method is to simply generate all possible routes and compare the distances; while guaranteed to work and simple to implement, this algorithm is clearly very stupid in that it considers even obviously absurd routes (like going from Boston to Houston via San Francisco and New York, in that order). For very small N it works well, but it rapidly becomes absurdly inefficient when N increases (for $N = 15$, there are already 1,307,674,368,000 possible routes to consider, and for $N = 1000$ — well, see **bignum**). Sometimes, unfortunately, there is no better general solution than brute force. See also **NP-**.

A more simple-minded example of brute-force programming is finding the smallest number in a large list by first using an existing program to sort the list in ascending order, and then picking the first number off the front.

Whether brute-force programming should actually be considered stupid or not depends on the context; if the problem is not terribly big, the extra CPU time spent on a brute-force solution may cost less than the programmer time it would take to develop a more 'intelligent' algorithm. Additionally, a more intelligent algorithm may imply more long-term complexity cost and bug-chasing than are justified by the speed improvement.

Ken Thompson, co-inventor of UNIX, is reported to have uttered the epigram "When in doubt, use brute force". He probably intended this as a **ha ha only serious**, but the original UNIX kernel's preference for simple, robust, and portable algorithms over **brittle** 'smart' ones does seem to have been a significant factor in the success of that OS. Like so many other tradeoffs in software design, the choice between brute force and complex, finely-tuned cleverness is often a difficult one that requires both engineering savvy and delicate esthetic judgment.

brute force and ignorance n. A popular design technique at many software houses — **brute force** coding unrelieved by any knowledge of how problems have been previously solved in elegant ways. Dogmatic adherence to design methodologies tends to encourage this sort of thing. Characteristic of early **larval stage** programming; unfortunately, many never outgrow it. Often abbreviated BFI: "Gak, they used a **bubble sort**! That's strictly from BFI." Compare **bogosity**.

BSD */B-S-D/* n. [abbreviation for 'Berkeley System Distribution'] a family of **UNIX** versions for the **DEC VAX** and PDP-11 developed by Bill Joy and others at **Berzerkeley** starting around 1980, incorporating paged virtual memory, TCP/IP networking enhancements, and many other features. The BSD versions (4.1, 4.2, and 4.3) and the commercial versions derived from them (SunOS, ULTRIX, and Mt. Xinu) held the technical lead in the UNIX world until AT&T's successful standardization efforts after about 1986, and are still widely popular. See **UNIX, USG UNIX**.

BUAF // [abbreviation, from *alt.fan.warlord*] n. Big Ugly ASCII Font — a special form of **ASCII art**. Various programs exist for rendering text strings into block, bloob, and pseudo-script fonts in cells between four and six character cells on a side; this is smaller than the letters generated by older **banner** (sense 2) programs. These are sometimes used to render one's name in a **sig block**, and are critically referred to as *BUAF*s. See **warlording**.

BUAG // [abbreviation, from *alt.fan.warlord*] n. Big Ugly ASCII Graphic. Pejorative term for ugly **ASCII ART**, especially as found in **sig block**s. For some reason, mutations of the head of Bart Simpson are particularly common in the least imaginative **sig block**s. See **warlording**.

bubble sort n. Techspeak for a particular sorting technique in which pairs of adjacent values in the list to be sorted are compared and interchanged if they are out of order; thus, list entries 'bubble upward' in the list until they bump into one with a lower sort value. Because it is not very good relative to other methods and is the one typically stumbled on by **naive** and untutored programmers, hackers consider it the **canonical** example of a naive algorithm. The canonical example of a really *bad* algorithm is **bogo-sort**. A bubble sort might be used out of ignorance, but any use of bogo-sort could issue only from brain damage or willful perversity.

bucky bits */buh´kee bits/* n. 1. obs. The bits produced by the CONTROL and META shift keys on a SAIL keyboard (octal 200 and 400 respectively), resulting in a 9-bit keyboard character set. The MIT AI TV (Knight) keyboards extended this with TOP and separate left and right CONTROL and META keys, resulting in a 12-bit character set; later, LISP Machines added such keys as SUPER, HYPER, and GREEK (see **space-cadet keyboard**). 2. By extension, bits associated with 'extra' shift keys on any keyboard, e.g., the ALT on an IBM PC or command and option keys on a Macintosh.

It has long been rumored that *bucky bits* were named for Buckminster Fuller during a period when he was consulting at Stanford. Actually, bucky bits were invented by Niklaus Wirth when *he* was at Stanford; he first suggested the idea of an EDIT key to set the 8th bit of an otherwise 7-bit ASCII character. This was used in a number of editors written at Stanford or in its environs (TV-EDIT and NLS being the best-known). Some sources claim that 'Bucky' was Niklaus Wirth's nickname at Stanford, but Wirth himself does not recall this.

Whatever its origins, the term spread to MIT and CMU early and is now in general use. See **double bucky**, **quadruple bucky**.

buffer overflow n. What happens when you try to stuff more data into a buffer (holding area) than it can handle. This may be due to a mismatch in the processing rates of the producing and consuming processes (see **overrun** and **firehose syndrome**), or because the buffer is simply too small to hold all the data that must accumulate before a piece of it can be processed. For example, in a text-processing tool that **crunch**es a line at a time, a short line buffer can result in **lossage** as input from a long line overflows the buffer and trashes data beyond it. Good defensive programming would check for overflow on each character and stop accepting data when the buffer is full up. The term is used of and by humans in a metaphorical sense. "What time did I agree to meet you? My buffer must have overflowed." Or "If I answer that phone my buffer is going to overflow." See also **spam**, **overrun screw**.

bug n. An unwanted and unintended property of a program or piece of hardware, esp. one that causes it to malfunction. Antonym of **feature**. Examples: "There's a bug in the editor: it writes things out backwards." "The system crashed because of a hardware bug." "Fred is a winner, but he has a few bugs" (i.e., Fred is a good guy, but he has a few personality problems).

Historical note: Admiral Grace Hopper (an early computing pioneer better known for inventing **COBOL**) liked to tell a story in which a technician solved a **glitch** in the Harvard Mark II machine by pulling an actual insect out from between the contacts of one of its relays, and she subsequently promulgated **bug** in its hackish sense as a joke about the incident (though, as she was careful to admit, she was not there when it happened). For many years the logbook associated with the incident and the actual bug in question (a moth) sat in a display case at the Naval Surface Warfare Center (NSWC). The entire story, with a picture of the logbook and the moth taped into it, is recorded in the *Annals of the History of Computing*, Vol. 3, No. 3 (July 1981), pp. 285–286.

The text of the log entry (from September 9, 1947), reads "1545 Relay #70 Panel F (moth) in relay. First actual case of bug being found". This wording establishes that the term was already in use at the time in its current specific sense — and Hopper herself reports that the term *bug* was regularly applied to problems in radar electronics during WWII.

Indeed, the use of *bug* to mean an industrial defect was already established in Thomas Edison's time, and a more specific and rather modern use can be found in an electrical handbook from 1896 (*Hawkin's New Catechism of Electricity*, Theo. Audel & Co.) which says: "The term 'bug' is used to a limited extent to designate any fault or trouble in the connections or working of electric apparatus." It further notes that the term is "said to have originated in quadruplex telegraphy and have been transferred to all electric apparatus."

The latter observation may explain a common folk etymology of the term; that it came from telephone company usage, in which "bugs in a telephone cable" were blamed for noisy lines. Though this derivation seems to be mistaken, it may well be a distorted memory of a joke first current among *telegraph* operators more than a century ago!

Actually, use of *bug* in the general sense of a disruptive event goes back to Shakespeare! In the first edition of Samuel Johnson's dictionary one meaning of *bug* is "A frightful object; a walking spectre"; this is traced to 'bugbear', a Welsh term for a variety of mythological monster which (to complete the circle) has recently been reintroduced into the popular lexicon through fantasy role-playing games.

In any case, in jargon the word almost never refers to insects. Here is a plausible conversation that never actually happened:

> "There is a bug in this ant farm!"
>
> "What do you mean? I don't see any ants in it."
>
> "That's the bug."

[There has been a widespread myth that the original bug was moved to the Smithsonian, and an earlier version of this entry so asserted. A correspondent who thought to check discovered that the bug was not there. While investigating this in late 1990, your editor discovered that the NSWC still had the bug, but had unsuccessfully tried to get the Smithsonian to accept it — and that the present curator of their History of American Technology Museum didn't know this and agreed that it would make a worthwhile exhibit. It was moved to the Smithsonian in mid-1991, but due to space and money constraints has not yet been exhibited. Thus, the process of investigating the original-computer-bug bug fixed it in an entirely unexpected way, by making the myth true! — ESR]

bug-compatible adj. Said of a design or revision that has been badly compromised by a requirement to be compatible with **fossil**s or **misfeature**s in other programs or (esp.) previous releases of itself. "MS-DOS 2.0 used \ as a path separator to be bug-compatible with some cretin's choice of / as an option character in 1.0."

bug-for-bug compatible n. Same as **bug-compatible**, with the additional implication that much tedious effort went into ensuring that each (known) bug was replicated.

buglix */buhg´liks/* n. Pejorative term referring to **DEC**'s ULTRIX operating system in its earlier *severely* buggy versions. Still used to describe ULTRIX, but without nearly so much venom. Compare **AIDX**, **HP-SUX**, **Nominal Semidestructor**, **Telerat**, **sun-stools**.

bulletproof adj. Used of an algorithm or implementation considered extremely **robust**; lossage-resistant; capable of correctly recovering from any imaginable exception condition — a rare and valued quality. Syn. **armor-plated**.

bum 1. vt. To make highly efficient, either in time or space, often at the expense of clarity. "I managed to bum three more instructions out of that code." "I spent half the night bumming the interrupt code." In **elder days**, John McCarthy (inventor of **LISP**) used to compare some efficiency-obsessed hackers among his students to "ski bums"; thus, optimization became "program bumming", and eventually just "bumming". 2. To squeeze out excess; to remove something in order to improve whatever it was removed from (without changing function; this distinguishes the process from a **featurec-**

It helps to remember that this dates from 1973.
The next cartoon in the Crunchly saga is 10-31-73, page 33.

tomy). 3. n. A small change to an algorithm, program, or hardware device to make it more efficient. "This hardware bum makes the jump instruction faster." Usage: now uncommon, largely superseded by v. **tune** (and n. **tweak**, **hack**), though none of these exactly capture sense 2. All these uses are rare in Commonwealth hackish, because in the parent dialects of English 'bum' is a rude synonym for 'buttocks'.

bump vt. Synonym for increment. Has the same meaning as C's ++ operator. Used esp. of counter variables, pointers, and index dummies in `for`, `while`, and `do-while` loops.

burble [from Lewis Carroll's "Jabberwocky"] v. Like **flame**, but connotes that the source is truly clueless and ineffectual (mere flamers can be competent). A term of deep contempt. "There's some guy on the phone burbling about how he got a DISK FULL error and it's all our comm software's fault." This is mainstream slang in some parts of England.

buried treasure n. A surprising piece of code found in some program. While usually not wrong, it tends to vary from **crufty** to **bletcherous**, and has lain undiscovered only because it was functionally correct, however horrible it is. Used sarcastically, because what is found is anything *but* treasure. Buried treasure almost always needs to be dug up and removed. "I just found that the scheduler sorts its queue using **bubble sort**! Buried treasure!"

burn-in period n. 1. A factory test designed to catch systems with **marginal** components before they get out the door; the theory is that burn-in will protect customers by outwaiting the steepest part of the **bathtub curve** (see **infant mortality**). 2. A period of indeterminate length in which a person using a computer is so intensely involved in his project that he forgets basic needs such as food, drink, sleep, etc. Warning: Excessive burn-in can lead to burn-out. See **hack mode**, **larval stage**.

burst page n. Syn. **banner**, sense 1.

busy-wait vi. Used of human behavior, conveys that the subject is busy waiting for someone or something, intends to move instantly as soon as it shows up, and thus cannot do anything else at the moment. "Can't talk now, I'm busy-waiting till Bill gets off the phone."

Technically, *busy-wait* means to wait on an event by **spin**ning through a tight or timed-delay loop that polls for the event on each pass, as opposed to setting up an interrupt handler and continuing execution on another part of the task. This is a wasteful technique, best avoided on time-sharing systems where a busy-waiting program may **hog** the processor.

buzz vi. 1. Of a program, to run with no indication of progress and perhaps without guarantee of ever finishing; esp. said of programs thought to be executing tight loops of code. A program that is buzzing appears to be **catatonic**, but never gets out of catatonia, while a buzzing loop may eventually end of its own accord. "The program buzzes for about 10 seconds trying to sort all the names into order." See **spin**; see also **grovel**. 2. [ETA Systems] To test a wire or printed circuit trace for continuity by applying an AC rather than DC signal. Some wire faults will pass DC tests but fail a buzz test. 3. To process an array or list in sequence, doing the same thing to each element. "This loop buzzes through the tz array looking for a terminator type."

BWQ */B-W-Q/* [IBM: abbreviation, 'Buzz Word Quotient'] The percentage of buzzwords in a speech or documents. Usually roughly proportional to **bogosity**. See **TLA**.

by hand adv. 1. Said of an operation (especially a repetitive, trivial, and/or tedious one) that ought to be performed automatically by the computer, but which a hacker instead has to step tediously through. "My mailer doesn't have a command to include the text of the message I'm replying to, so I have to do it by hand." This does not necessarily mean the speaker has to retype a copy of the message; it might refer to, say, dropping into a subshell from the mailer, making a copy of one's mailbox file, reading that into an editor, locating the top and bottom of the message in question, deleting the rest of the file, inserting '>' characters on each line, writing the file, leaving the editor, returning to the mailer, reading the file in, and later remembering to delete the file. Compare **eyeball search**. 2. By extension, writing code which does something in an explicit or low-level way for which a presupplied library routine ought to have been available. "This cretinous B-tree library doesn't supply a decent iterator, so I'm having to walk the trees by hand."

byte */bi:t/* [techspeak] n. A unit of memory or data equal to the amount used to represent one character; on modern architectures this is usually 8 bits, but may be 9 on 36-bit machines. Some older architectures used 'byte' for quantities of 6 or 7 bits, and the PDP-10 supported 'bytes' that were actually bitfields of 1 to 36 bits! These usages are now obsolete, and even 9-bit bytes have become rare in the general trend toward power-of-2 word sizes.

Historical note: The term was coined by Werner Buchholz in 1956 during the early design phase for the IBM Stretch computer; originally it was described as 1 to 6 bits (typical I/O equipment of the period used 6-bit chunks of information). The move to an 8-bit byte happened in late 1956, and this size was later adopted and promulgated as a standard by the System/360. The word was coined by mutating the word 'bite' so it would not be accidentally misspelled as **bit**. See also **nybble**.

bytesexual */bi:t`sek'shu-əl/* adj. Said of hardware, denotes willingness to compute or pass data in either **big-endian** or **little-endian** format (depending, presumably, on a **mode bit** somewhere). See also **NUXI problem**.

bzzzt, wrong */bzt rong/* [USENET/Internet] From a Robin Williams routine in the movie "Dead Poets Society" spoofing radio or TV quiz programs, such as *Truth or Consequences*, where an incorrect answer earns one a blast from the buzzer and condolences from the interlocutor. A way of expressing mock-rude disagreement, usually immediately following an included quote from another poster. The less abbreviated "*Bzzzzt*, wrong, but thank you for playing" is also common; capitalization and emphasis of the buzzer sound varies.

= C =

C n. 1. The third letter of the English alphabet. 2. ASCII 1000011. 3. The name of a programming language designed by Dennis Ritchie during the early 1970s and immediately used to reimplement **UNIX**; so called because many features derived from an earlier compiler named 'B' in commemoration of *its* parent, BCPL. Before Bjarne Stroustrup settled the question by designing C++, there was a humorous debate over whether C's successor should be named 'D' or 'P'. C became immensely popular outside Bell Labs after about 1980 and is now the dominant language in systems and microcomputer applications programming. See also **languages of choice**, **indent style**.

C is often described, with a mixture of fondness and disdain varying according to the speaker, as "a language that combines all the elegance and power of assembly language with all the readability and maintainability of assembly language".

C Programmer's Disease n. The tendency of the undisciplined C programmer to set arbitrary but supposedly generous static limits on table sizes (defined, if you're lucky, by constants in header files) rather than taking the

The Crunchly on the left sounds a little ANSI.

trouble to do proper dynamic storage allocation. If an application user later needs to put 68 elements into a table of size 50, the afflicted programmer reasons that he or she can easily reset the table size to 68 (or even as much as 70, to allow for future expansion) and recompile. This gives the programmer the comfortable feeling of having made the effort to satisfy the user's (unreasonable) demands, and often affords the user multiple opportunities to explore the marvelous consequences of **fandango on core**. In severe cases of the disease, the programmer cannot comprehend why each fix of this kind seems only to further disgruntle the user.

calculator [Cambridge] n. Syn. for **bitty box**.

can vt. To abort a job on a time-sharing system. Used esp. when the person doing the deed is an operator, as in "canned from the **console**". Frequently used in an imperative sense, as in "Can that print job, the LPT just popped a sprocket!" Synonymous with **gun**. It is said that the ASCII character with mnemonic CAN (0011000) was used as a kill-job character on some early OSes. Alternatively, this term may derive from mainstream slang 'canned' for being laid off or fired.

can't happen The traditional program comment for code executed under a condition that should never be true, for example a file size computed as negative. Often, such a condition being true indicates data corruption or a faulty algorithm; it is almost always handled by emitting a fatal error message and terminating or crashing, since there is little else that can be done. Some case variant of "can't happen" is also often the text emitted if the 'impossible' error actually happens! Although "can't happen" events are genuinely infrequent in production code, programmers wise enough to check for them habitually are often surprised at how frequently they are triggered during development and how many headaches checking for them turns out to head off. See also **firewall code** (sense 2).

candygrammar n. A programming-language grammar that is mostly **syntactic sugar**; the term is also a play on 'candygram'. **COBOL**, Apple's Hypertalk language, and a lot of the so-called '4GL' database languages share this property. The usual intent of such designs is that they be as English-like as possible, on the theory that they will then be easier for unskilled people to program. This intention comes to grief on the reality that syntax isn't what makes programming hard; it's the mental effort and organization required to specify an algorithm precisely that costs. Thus the invariable result is that 'candygrammar' languages are just as difficult to program in as terser ones, and far more painful for the experienced hacker.

[The overtones from the old Chevy Chase skit on Saturday Night Live should not be overlooked. This was a "Jaws" parody. Someone lurking outside an apartment door tries all kinds of bogus ways to get the occupant to open up, while ominous music plays in the background. The last attempt is a half-hearted "Candygram!" When the door is opened, a shark bursts in and chomps the poor occupant. There is a moral here for those attracted to candygrammars. Note that, in many circles, pretty much the same ones who remember Monty Python sketches, all it takes is the word "Candygram!", suitably timed, to get people rolling on the floor. — GLS]

canonical [historically, 'according to religious law'] adj. The usual or standard state or manner of something. This word has a somewhat more technical meaning in mathematics. Two formulas such as $9+x$ and $x+9$ are said to be equivalent because they mean the same thing, but the second one is in *canonical form* because it is written in the usual way, with the highest power of x first. Usually there are fixed rules you can use to decide whether something is in canonical form. The jargon meaning, a relaxation of the technical meaning, acquired its present loading in computer-science culture largely through its prominence in Alonzo Church's work in computation theory and mathematical logic (see **Knights of the Lambda Calculus**). Compare **vanilla**.

This word has an interesting history. Non-technical academics do not use the adjective 'canonical' in any of the senses defined above with any regularity; they do however use the nouns *canon* and *canonicity* (not **canonicalness or **canonicality). The *canon* of a given author is the complete body of authentic works by that author (this usage is familiar to Sherlock Holmes fans as well as to literary scholars). '*The* canon' is the body of works in a given field (e.g., works of literature, or of art, or of music) deemed worthwhile for students to study and for scholars to investigate.

The word 'canon' derives ultimately from the Greek (akin to the English 'cane') referring to a reed. Reeds were used for measurement, and in Latin and later Greek the word 'canon' meant a rule or a standard. The establishment of a canon of scriptures within Christianity was meant to define a standard or a rule for the religion. The above non-techspeak academic usages stem from this instance of a defined and accepted body of work. Alongside this usage was the promulgation of 'canons' ('rules') for the government of the Catholic Church. The techspeak usages ("according to religious law") derive from this use of the Latin 'canon'.

Hackers invest this term with a playfulness that makes an ironic contrast with its historical meaning. A true story: One Bob Sjoberg, new at the MIT AI Lab, expressed some annoyance at the incessant use of jargon. Over his loud objections, GLS and RMS made a point of using as much of it as possible in his presence, and eventually it began to sink in. Finally, in one conversation, he used the word *canonical* in jargon-like fashion without thinking. Steele: "Aha! We've finally got you talking jargon too!" Stallman: "What did he say?" Steele: "Bob just used 'canonical' in the canonical way."

Of course, canonicality depends on context, but it is implicitly defined as the way *hackers* normally expect things to be. Thus, a hacker may claim with a straight face that 'according to religious law' is *not* the canonical meaning of *canonical*.

card walloper n. An EDP programmer who grinds out batch programs that do stupid things like print people's paychecks. Compare **code grinder**. See also **punched card**, **eighty-column mind**.

careware */keir´weir/* n. **Shareware** for which either the author suggests that some payment be made to a nominated charity or a levy directed to charity is included on top of the distribution charge. Syn. **charityware**; compare **crippleware**, sense 2.

cargo cult programming n. A style of (incompetent) programming dominated by ritual inclusion of code or program structures that serve no real purpose. A cargo cult programmer will usually explain the extra code as a way of working around some bug encountered in the past, but usually neither the bug nor the reason the code apparently avoided the bug was ever fully understood (compare **shotgun debugging**, **voodoo programming**).

The term 'cargo cult' is a reference to aboriginal religions that grew up in the South Pacific after World War II. The practices of these cults center on building elaborate mockups of airplanes and military style landing strips in the hope of bringing the return of the god-like airplanes that brought such marvelous cargo during the war. Hackish usage probably derives from Richard Feynman's characterization of certain practices as "cargo cult science" in his book *Surely You're Joking, Mr. Feynman* (W. W. Norton & Co, New York 1985, ISBN 0-393-01921-7).

cascade n. 1. A huge volume of spurious error-message output produced by a compiler with poor error recovery. Too frequently, one trivial syntax error (such as a missing ')' or '}') throws the parser out of synch so that much of the remaining program text is interpreted as garbaged or ill-formed. 2. A chain of USENET followups, each adding some trivial variation or riposte to the text of the previous one, all of which is reproduced in the new message; an **include war** in which the object is to create a sort of communal graffito.

case and paste [from 'cut and paste'] n. 1. The addition of a new **feature** to an existing system by selecting the code from an existing feature and pasting it in with minor changes. Common in telephony circles because most operations in a telephone switch are selected using `case` statements. Leads to **software bloat**.

In some circles of EMACS users this is called 'programming by Meta-W', because Meta-W is the EMACS command for copying a block of text to a kill buffer in preparation to pasting it in elsewhere. The term is condescending, implying that the programmer is acting mindlessly rather than thinking carefully about what is required to integrate the code for two similar cases.

At DEC, this is sometimes called *clone-and-hack* coding.

casters-up mode [IBM, prob. fr. slang *belly up*] n. Yet another synonym for 'broken' or 'down'. Usually connotes a major failure. A system (hardware or software) which is *down* may be already being restarted before the failure is noticed, whereas one which is *casters up* is usually a good excuse to take the rest of the day off (as long as you're not responsible for fixing it).

casting the runes n. What a **guru** does when you ask him or her to run a particular program and type at it because it never works for anyone else; esp. used when nobody can ever see what the guru is doing different from what J. Random Luser does. Compare **incantation**, **runes**, **examining the entrails**; also see the AI koan about Tom Knight in "A Selection of AI Koans" (Appendix A).

cat [from 'catenate' via **UNIX** `cat(1)`] vt. 1. [techspeak] To spew an entire file to the screen or some other output sink without pause. 2. By extension, to dump large amounts of data at an unprepared target or with no intention of browsing it carefully. Usage: considered silly. Rare outside UNIX sites. See also **dd**, **BLT**.

Among UNIX fans, `cat(1)` is considered an excellent example of user-interface design, because it delivers the file contents without such verbosity as spacing or headers between the files, and because it does not require the files to consist of lines of text, but works with any sort of data.

Among UNIX haters, `cat(1)` is considered the **canonical** example of *bad* user-interface design, because of its woefully unobvious name. It is far more often used to **blast** a file to standard output than to concatenate two files. The name `cat` for the former operation is just as unintuitive as, say, LISP's **cdr**.

Of such oppositions are **holy wars** made. . . .

catatonic adj. Describes a condition of suspended animation in which something is so **wedged** or **hung** that it makes no response. If you are typing on a terminal and suddenly the computer doesn't even echo the letters back to the screen as you type, let alone do what you're asking it to do, then the computer is suffering from catatonia (possibly because it has crashed). "There I was in the middle of a winning game of **nethack** and it went catatonic on me! Aaargh!" Compare **buzz**.

cd tilde */C-D til-də/* vi. To go home. From the UNIX C-shell and Korn-shell command `cd ~`, which takes one to one's `$HOME` (`cd` with no arguments happens to do the same thing). By extension, may be used with other arguments; thus, over an electronic chat link, `cd ~coffee` would mean "I'm going to the coffee machine."

cdr */ku´dr/* or */kuh´dr/* [from LISP] vt. To skip past the first item from a list of things (generalized from the LISP operation on binary tree structures, which returns a list consisting of all but the first element of its argument). In the form *cdr down*, to trace down a list of elements: "Shall we cdr down the agenda?" Usage: silly. See also **loop through**.

Historical note: The instruction format of the IBM 7090 that hosted the original LISP implementation featured two 15-bit fields called the 'address' and 'decrement' parts. The term *cdr* was originally 'Contents of Decrement part of Register'. Similarly, *car* stood for 'Contents of Address part of Register'.

The cdr and car operations have since become bases for formation of compound metaphors in non-LISP contexts. GLS recalls, for example, a programming project in which strings were represented as linked lists; the get-character and skip-character operations were of course called CHAR and CHDR.

chad */chad/* n. 1. The perforated edge strips on printer paper, after they have been separated from the printed portion. Also called **selvage** and **perf**. 2. obs. The confetti-like paper bits punched out of cards or paper tape; this was also called *chaff*, *computer confetti*, and *keypunch droppings*.

Historical note: One correspondent believes *chad* (sense 2) derives from the Chadless keypunch (named for its inventor), which cut little u-shaped tabs in the card to make a hole when the tab folded back, rather than punching out a circle/rectangle; it was clear that if the Chadless keypunch didn't make them, then the stuff that other keypunches made had to be 'chad'.

chad box n. A metal box about the size of a lunchbox (or in some models a large wastebasket), for collecting the **chad** (sense 2) that accumulated in **Iron Age** card punches. You had to open the covers of the card punch periodically and empty the chad box. The **bit bucket** was notionally the equivalent device in the CPU enclosure, which was typically across the room in another great gray-and-blue box.

chain 1. [orig. from BASIC's `CHAIN` statement] vi. To hand off execution to a child or successor without going through the **OS** command interpreter that invoked it. The state of the parent program is lost and there is no returning to it. Though this facility used to be common on memory-limited micros and is still widely supported for backward compatibility, the jargon usage is semi-obsolescent; in particular, most UNIX programmers will think of this as an **exec**. Oppose the more modern 'subshell'. 2. A series of linked data areas within an operating system or application. *Chain rattling* is the process of repeatedly running through the linked data areas searching for one which is of interest to the executing program. The implication is that there is a very large number of links on the chain.

channel [IRC] n. The basic unit of discussion on **IRC**. Once one joins a channel, everything one types is read by others on that channel. Channels can either be named with numbers or with strings that begin with a '#' sign and can have topic descriptions (which are generally irrelevant to the actual subject of discussion). Some notable channels are `#initgame`, `#hottub`, and `#report`. At times of international crisis, `#report` has hundreds of members, some of whom take turns listening to various news services and typing in summaries of the news, or in some cases, giving first-hand accounts of the action (e.g., Scud missile attacks in Tel Aviv during the Gulf War in 1991).

channel hopping [IRC, GEnie] n. To rapidly switch channels on **IRC**, or a GEnie chat board, just as a social butterfly might hop from one group to another at a party. This term may derive from the TV watcher's idiom, *channel surfing*.

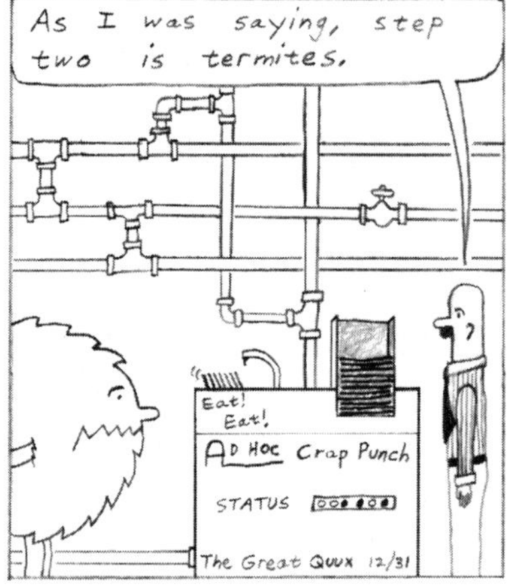

This is *one* way to be **chad**less.

The next cartoon in the Crunchly saga is 02-15-76, page 444.

channel op */chan'l op/* [IRC] n. Someone who is endowed with privileges on a particular **IRC** channel; commonly abbreviated *chanop* or *CHOP*. These privileges include the right to **kick** users, to change various status bits, and to make others into CHOPs.

chanop */chan'-op/* [IRC] n. See **channel op**.

char */keir/* or */char/*; rarely, */kar/* n. Shorthand for 'character'. Esp. used by C programmers, as 'char' is C's typename for character data.

charityware */cha'rit-ee-weir`/* n. Syn. **careware**.

chase pointers 1. vi. To go through multiple levels of indirection, as in traversing a linked list or graph structure. Used esp. by programmers in C, where explicit pointers are a very common data type. This is techspeak, but it remains jargon when used of human networks. "I'm chasing pointers. Bob said you could tell me who to talk to about. . . ." See **dangling pointer** and **snap**. 2. [Cambridge] *pointer chase* or *pointer hunt*: The process of going through a **core dump** (sense 1), interactively or on a large piece of paper printed with hex **runes**, following dynamic data-structures. Used only in a debugging context.

check n. A hardware-detected error condition, most commonly used to refer to actual hardware failures rather than software-induced traps. E.g., a *parity check* is the result of a hardware-detected parity error. Recorded here because the word often humorously extended to non-technical problems. For example, the term *child check* has been used to refer to the problems caused by a small child who is curious to know what happens when s/he presses all the cute buttons on a computer's console (of course, this particular problem could have been prevented with **molly-guard**s).

chemist [Cambridge] n. Someone who wastes computer time on **number-crunching** when you'd far rather the machine were doing something more productive, such as working out anagrams of your name or printing Snoopy calendars or running **life** patterns. May or may not refer to someone who actually studies chemistry.

Chernobyl chicken n. See **laser chicken**.

Chernobyl packet */cher-noh'bəl pak'ət/* n. A network packet that induces a **broadcast storm** and/or **network meltdown**, in memory of the April 1986 nuclear accident at Chernobyl in Ukraine. The typical scenario involves an IP Ethernet datagram that passes through a gateway with both source and destination Ether and IP address set as the respective broadcast addresses for the subnetworks being gated between. Compare **Christmas tree packet**.

chicken head [Commodore] n. The Commodore Business Machines logo, which strongly resembles a poultry part. Rendered in ASCII as 'C='. With the arguable exception of the Amiga (see **amoeba**), Commodore's machines are notoriously crocky little **bitty box**es (see also **PETSCII**). Thus, this usage may owe something to Philip K. Dick's novel *Do Androids Dream of Electric Sheep?* (the basis for the movie *Blade Runner*; the novel is now sold under that title), in which a 'chickenhead' is a mutant with below-average intelligence.

chiclet keyboard n. A keyboard with a small, flat rectangular or lozenge-shaped rubber or plastic keys that look like pieces of chewing gum. (Chiclets is the brand name of a variety of chewing gum that does in fact resemble the keys of chiclet keyboards.) Used esp. to describe the original IBM PCjr keyboard. Vendors unanimously liked these because they were cheap, and a lot of early portable and laptop products got launched using them. Customers rejected the idea with almost equal unanimity, and chiclets are not often seen on anything larger than a digital watch any more.

chine nual */sheen´yu-əl/* [MIT] n.,obs. The LISP Machine Manual, so called because the title was wrapped around the cover so only those letters showed on the front.

Chinese Army technique n. Syn. **Mongolian Hordes technique**.

choke v. 1. To reject input, often ungracefully. "NULs make System V's `lpr(1)` choke." "I tried building an **EMACS** binary to use **X**, but `cpp(1)` choked on all those `#define`s." See **barf**, **gag**, **vi**. 2. [MIT] More generally, to fail at any endeavor, but with some flair or bravado; the popular definition is "to snatch defeat from the jaws of victory."

chomp vi. To **lose**; specifically, to chew on something of which more was bitten off than one can. Probably related to gnashing of teeth. See **bagbiter**.

A hand gesture commonly accompanies this. To perform it, hold the four fingers together and place the thumb against their tips. Now open and close your hand rapidly to suggest a biting action (much like what Pac-Man does in the classic video game, though this pantomime seems to predate that). The gesture alone means 'chomp chomp' (see "Verb Doubling" in the "Jargon Construction" section of the Prependices). The hand may be pointed at the object of complaint, and for real emphasis you can use both hands at once. Doing this to a person is equivalent to saying "You chomper!" If you point the gesture at yourself, it is a humble but humorous admission of some failure. You might do this if someone told you that a program you had written had failed in some surprising way and you felt dumb for not having anticipated it.

chomper n. Someone or something that is chomping; a loser. See **loser**, **bagbiter**, **chomp**.

CHOP */chop/* [IRC] n. See **channel op**.

Christmas tree n. A kind of RS-232 line tester or breakout box featuring rows of blinking red and green LEDs suggestive of Christmas lights.

Christmas tree packet n. A packet with every single option set for whatever protocol is in use. See **kamikaze packet**, **Chernobyl packet**. (The term doubtless derives from a fanciful image of each little option bit being represented by a different-colored light bulb, all turned on.)

chrome [from automotive slang via wargaming] n. Showy features added to attract users but contributing little or nothing to the power of a system. "The 3D icons in Motif are just chrome, but they certainly are *pretty* chrome!" Distinguished from **bells and whistles** by the fact that the latter are usually added to gratify developers' own desires for featurefulness. Often used as a term of contempt.

chug vi. To run slowly; to **grind** or **grovel**. "The disk is chugging like crazy."

Church of the SubGenius n. A mutant offshoot of **Discordianism** launched in 1981 as a spoof of fundamentalist Christianity by the 'Reverend' Ivan Stang, a brilliant satirist with a gift for promotion. Popular among hackers as a rich source of bizarre imagery and references such as "Bob" the divine drilling-equipment salesman, the Benevolent Space Xists, and the Stark Fist of Removal. Much SubGenius theory is concerned with the acquisition of the mystical substance or quality of **slack**.

Cinderella Book [CMU] n. *Introduction to Automata Theory, Languages,* *and Computation*, by John Hopcroft and Jeffrey Ullman, (Addison-Wesley, 1979). So called because the cover depicts a girl (putatively Cinderella) sitting in front of a Rube Goldberg device and holding a rope coming out of it. On the back cover, the device is in shambles after she has (inevitably) pulled on the rope. See also **book titles**.

CI$ *//* n. Hackerism for 'CIS', CompuServe Information Service. The dollar sign refers to CompuServe's rather steep line charges. Often used in **sig blocks** just before a CompuServe address. Syn. **Compu$erve**.

Classic C */klas´ik C/* [a play on 'Coke Classic'] n. The C programming language as defined in the first edition of **K&R**, with some small additions. It is also known as 'K&R C'. The name came into use while C was being standardized by the ANSI X3J11 committee. Also 'C Classic'.

An analogous construction is sometimes applied elsewhere: thus, 'X Classic', where X = Star Trek (referring to the original TV series) or X = PC (referring to IBM's ISA-bus machines as opposed to the PS/2 series). This construction is especially used of product series in which the newer versions are considered serious losers relative to the older ones.

clean 1. adj. Used of hardware or software designs, implies 'elegance in the small', that is, a design or implementation that may not hold any surprises but does things in a way that is reasonably intuitive and relatively easy to comprehend from the outside. The antonym is 'grungy' or **crufty**. 2. v. To remove unneeded or undesired files in a effort to reduce clutter: "I'm cleaning up my account." "I cleaned up the garbage and now have 100 Meg free on that partition."

CLM */C-L-M/* [Sun: 'Career Limiting Move'] 1. n. An action endangering one's future prospects of getting plum projects and raises, and possibly one's job: "His Halloween costume was a parody of his manager. He won the prize for 'best CLM'." 2. adj. Denotes extreme severity of a bug, discovered by a customer and obviously missed earlier because of poor testing: "That's a CLM bug!"

clobber vt. To overwrite, usually unintentionally: "I walked off the end of the array and clobbered the stack." Compare **mung**, **scribble**, **trash**, and **smash the stack**.

clocks n. Processor logic cycles, so called because each generally corresponds to one clock pulse in the processor's timing. The relative execution times of instructions on a machine are usually discussed in clocks rather than absolute fractions of a second; one good reason for this is that clock speeds for various models of the machine may increase as technology improves, and it is usually the relative times one is interested in when discussing the instruction set. Compare **cycle**.

clone n. 1. An exact duplicate: "Our product is a clone of their product." Implies a legal reimplementation from documentation or by reverse-engineering. Also connotes lower price. 2. A shoddy, spurious copy: "Their product is a clone of our product." 3. A blatant ripoff, most likely violating copyright, patent, or trade secret protections: "Your product is a clone of my product." This use implies legal action is pending. 4. *PC clone:* a PC-BUS/ISA or EISA-compatible 80x86-based microcomputer (this use is sometimes spelled *klone* or *PClone*). These invariably have much more bang for the buck than the IBM archetypes they resemble. 5. In the construction *UNIX clone*: An OS designed to deliver a UNIX-lookalike environment without UNIX license fees, or with additional 'mission-critical' features such as support for real-time programming. 6. v. To make an exact copy of something. "Let me clone that" might mean "I want to borrow that paper so I can make a photocopy" or "Let me get a copy of that file before you **mung** it".

clone-and-hack coding [DEC] n. Syn. **case and paste**.

clover key [Mac users] n. See **feature key**.

clustergeeking */kluh´stər-gee`king/* [CMU] n. Spending more time at a computer cluster doing CS homework than most people spend breathing.

COBOL */koh´bol/* [COmmon Business-Oriented Language] n. (Synonymous with **evil**.) A weak, verbose, and flabby language used by **card wallopers** to do boring mindless things on **dinosaur** mainframes. Hackers believe that all COBOL programmers are **suits** or **code grinders**, and no self-respecting hacker will ever admit to having learned the language. Its very name is seldom uttered without ritual expressions of disgust or horror. See also **fear and loathing**, **software rot**.

COBOL fingers */koh´bol fing´grz/* n. Reported from Sweden, a (hypothetical) disease one might get from coding in COBOL. The language requires code verbose beyond all reason (see **candygrammar**); thus it is alleged that programming too much in COBOL causes one's fingers to wear down to stubs by the endless typing. "I refuse to type in all that source code again; it would give me COBOL fingers!"

code grinder n. 1. A **suit**-wearing minion of the sort hired in legion strength by banks and insurance companies to implement payroll packages in RPG and other such unspeakable horrors. In its native habitat, the code grinder often removes the suit jacket to reveal an underplumage consisting of button-down shirt (starch optional) and a tie. In times of dire stress, the sleeves (if long) may be rolled up and the tie loosened about half an inch. It seldom helps. The **code grinder**'s milieu is about as far from hackerdom as one can get and still touch a computer; the term connotes pity. See **Real World**, **suit**. 2. Used of or to a hacker, a really serious slur on the person's creative ability; connotes a design style characterized by primitive technique, rule-boundedness, **brute force**, and utter lack of imagination. Compare **card walloper**; contrast **hacker**, **real programmer**.

code police [by analogy with George Orwell's 'thought police'] n. A mythical team of Gestapo-like storm troopers that might burst into one's office and arrest one for violating programming style rules. May be used either seriously, to underline a claim that a particular style violation is dangerous, or ironically, to suggest that the practice under discussion is condemned mainly by anal-retentive **weenies**. "Dike out that goto or the code police will get you!" The ironic usage is perhaps more common.

codes [scientific computing] n. Programs. This usage is common in people who hack supercomputers and heavy-duty **number-crunching**, rare to unknown elsewhere (if you say "codes" to hackers outside scientific computing, their first association is likely to be "and cyphers").

codewalker n. A program component that traverses other programs for a living. Compilers have codewalkers in their front ends; so do cross-reference generators and some database front ends. Other utility programs that try to do too much with source code may turn into codewalkers. As in "This new `vgrind` feature would require a codewalker to implement."

coefficient of X n. Hackish speech makes heavy use of pseudo-mathematical metaphors. Four particularly important ones involve the terms *coefficient*, *factor*, *index*, and *quotient*. They are often loosely applied to things you cannot really be quantitative about, but there are subtle distinctions among them that convey information about the way the speaker mentally models whatever he or she is describing.

Foo factor and *foo quotient* tend to describe something for which the issue is one of presence or absence. The canonical example is **fudge factor**. It's not important how much you're fudging; the term simply acknowledges that some fudging is needed. You might talk of liking a movie for its silliness factor. Quotient tends to imply that the property is a ratio of two opposing factors: "I would have won except for my luck quotient." This could also be "I would have won except for the luck factor", but using *quotient* emphasizes that it was bad luck overpowering good luck (or someone else's good luck overpowering your own).

Foo index and *coefficient of foo* both tend to imply that foo is, if not strictly measurable, at least something that can be larger or smaller. Thus, you might refer to a paper or person as having a *high bogosity index*, whereas you would be less likely to speak of a *high bogosity factor. Foo index* suggests that foo is a condensation of many quantities, as in the mundane cost-of-living index; *coefficient of foo* suggests that foo is a fundamental quantity, as in a coefficient of friction. The choice between these terms is often one of personal preference; e.g., some people might feel that bogosity is a fundamental attribute and thus say *coefficient of bogosity*, whereas others might feel it is a combination of factors and thus say *bogosity index*.

cokebottle */kohk´bot-l/* n. Any very unusual character, particularly one you can't type because it it isn't on your keyboard. MIT people used to complain about the 'control-meta-cokebottle' commands at SAIL, and SAIL people complained right back about the '**altmode**-altmode-cokebottle' commands at MIT. After the demise of the **space-cadet keyboard**, *cokebottle* faded away as serious usage, but was often invoked humorously to describe an (unspecified) weird or non-intuitive keystroke command. It may be due for a second inning, however. The OSF/Motif window manager, `mwm(1)`, has a reserved keystroke for switching to the default set of keybindings and behavior. This keystroke is (believe it or not) 'control-meta-bang' (see **bang**). Since the exclamation point looks a lot like an upside down Coke bottle, Motif hackers have begun referring to this keystroke as *cokebottle*. See also **quadruple bucky**.

cold boot n. See **boot**.

COME FROM n. A semi-mythical language construct dual to the 'go to'; `COME FROM` <label> would cause the referenced label to act as a sort of trapdoor, so that if the program ever reached it control would quietly and

automagically be transferred to the statement following the `COME FROM`. `COME FROM` was first proposed in R.L. Clark's *A Linguistic Contribution to GOTO-less programming*, which appeared in a 1973 **Datamation** issue (and was reprinted in the April 1984 issue of *Communications of the ACM*). This parodied the then-raging 'structured programming' **holy wars** (see **considered harmful**). Mythically, some variants are the *assigned COME FROM* and the *computed COME FROM* (parodying some nasty control constructs in FORTRAN and some extended BASICs). Of course, multi-tasking (or non-determinism) could be implemented by having more than one `COME FROM` statement coming from the same label.

In some ways the FORTRAN `DO` looks like a `COME FROM` statement. After the terminating statement number/`CONTINUE` is reached, control continues at the statement following the DO. Some generous FORTRANs would allow arbitrary statements (other than `CONTINUE`) for the statement, leading to examples like:

```
      DO 10 I=1,LIMIT
C imagine many lines of code here, leaving the
C original DO statement lost in the spaghetti...
      WRITE(6,10) I,FROB(I)
 10   FORMAT(1X,I5,G10.4)
```

in which the trapdoor is just after the statement labeled 10. (This is particularly surprising because the label doesn't appear to have anything to do with the flow of control at all!)

While sufficiently astonishing to the unsuspecting reader, this form of `COME FROM` statement isn't completely general. After all, control will eventually pass to the following statement. The implementation of the general form was left to Univac FORTRAN, ca. 1975 (though a roughly similar feature existed on the IBM 7040 ten years earlier). The statement `AT 100` would perform a `COME FROM 100`. It was intended strictly as a debugging aid, with dire consequences promised to anyone so deranged as to use it in production code. More horrible things had already been perpetrated in production languages, however; doubters need only contemplate the `ALTER` verb in **COBOL**.

`COME FROM` was supported under its own name for the first time 15 years later, in C-INTERCAL (see **INTERCAL**, **retrocomputing**); knowledgeable observers are still reeling from the shock.

comm mode */kom mohd/* [ITS: from the feature supporting on-line chat; the term may spelled with one or two m's] Syn. for **talk mode**.

command key [Mac users] n. Syn. **feature key**.

comment out vt. To surround a section of code with comment delimiters or to prefix every line in the section with a comment marker; this prevents it from being compiled or interpreted. Often done when the code is redundant or obsolete, but is being left in the source to make the intent of the active code clearer; also when the code in that section is broken and you want to bypass it in order to debug some other part of the code. Compare **condition out**, usually the preferred technique in languages (such as **C**) that make it possible.

Commonwealth Hackish n. Hacker jargon as spoken outside the U.S., esp. in the British Commonwealth. It is reported that Commonwealth speakers are more likely to pronounce truncations like 'char' and 'soc', etc., as spelled (*/char/*, */sok/*), as opposed to American */keir/* and */sohsh/*. Dots in **newsgroup** names (especially two-component names) tend to be pronounced more often (so soc.wibble is */sok dot wib´l/* rather than */sohsh wib´l/*). The prefix **meta** may be pronounced */mee´tə/*; similarly, Greek letter beta is usually */bee´tə/*, zeta is usually */zee´tə/*, and so forth. Preferred **metasyntactic variable**s include **blurgle**, `eek`, `ook`, `frodo`, and `bilbo`; `wibble`, `wobble`, and in emergencies `wubble`; `banana`, `tom`, `dick`, `harry`, `wombat`, `frog`, **fish**, and so on and on (see **foo**, sense 4).

Alternatives to verb doubling include suffixes *-o-rama*, *frenzy* (as in feeding frenzy), and *city* (examples: "barf city!" "hack-o-rama!" "core dump frenzy!"). Finally, note that the American terms 'parens', 'brackets', and 'braces' for (), [], and { } are uncommon; Commonwealth hackish prefers 'brackets', 'square brackets', and 'curly brackets'. Also, the use of *pling* for **bang** is common outside the United States.

See also **attoparsec**, **calculator**, **chemist**, **console jockey**, **fish**, **go-faster stripes**, **grunge**, **hakspek**, **heavy metal**, **leaky heap**, **lord high fixer**, **loose bytes**, **muddie**, **nadger**, **noddy**, **psychedelicware**, **plingnet**, **raster blaster**, **RTBM**, **seggie**, **spod**, **sun lounge**, **terminal junkie**, **tick-list features**, **weeble**, **weasel**, **YABA**, and notes or definitions under **Bad Thing**, **barf**, **bogus**, **bum**, **chase pointers**, **cosmic rays**, **crippleware**, **crunch**, **dodgy**, **gonk**, **hamster**, **hardwarily**, **mess-dos**, **nybble**, **proglet**, **root**, **SEX**, **tweak**, and **xyzzy**.

compact adj. Of a design, describes the valuable property that it can all be apprehended at once in one's head. This generally means the thing created from the design can be used with greater facility and fewer errors than an equivalent tool that is not compact. Compactness does not imply triviality or lack of power; for example, C is compact and FORTRAN is not, but C is more powerful than FORTRAN. Designs become non-compact through accreting **feature**s and **cruft** that don't merge cleanly into the overall design scheme (thus, some fans of **Classic C** maintain that ANSI C is no longer compact).

compiler jock n. See **jock** (sense 2).

compress [UNIX] vt. When used without a qualifier, generally refers to **crunch**ing of a file using a particular C implementation of compression by James A. Woods et al. and widely circulated via **USENET**; use of **crunch** itself in this sense is rare among UNIX hackers. Specifically, compress is built around the Lempel-Ziv-Welch algorithm as described in "A Technique for High Performance Data Compression", Terry A. Welch, *IEEE Computer*, vol. 17, no. 6 (June 1984), pp. 8–19.

Compu$erve n. See **CI$**. Synonyms CompuSpend and Compu$pend are also reported.

computer confetti n. Syn. **chad**. Though this term is common, this use of punched-card chad is not a good idea, as the pieces are stiff and have sharp corners that could injure the eyes. GLS reports that he once attended a wedding at MIT during which he and a few other guests enthusiastically threw chad instead of rice. The groom later grumbled that he and his bride had spent most of the evening trying to get the stuff out of their hair.

computer geek n. One who eats (computer) bugs for a living. One who fulfills all the dreariest negative stereotypes about hackers: an asocial, malodorous, pasty-faced monomaniac with all the personality of a cheese grater. Cannot be used by outsiders without implied insult to all hackers; compare black-on-black usage of 'nigger'. A computer geek may be either a fundamentally clueless individual or a proto-hacker in **larval stage**. Also called *turbo nerd*, *turbo geek*. See also **propeller head**, **clustergeeking**, **geek out**, **wannabee**, **terminal junkie**, **spod**, **weenie**.

computron */kom´pyoo-tron`/* n. 1. A notional unit of computing power combining instruction speed and storage capacity, dimensioned roughly in instructions-per-second times megabytes-of-main-store times megabytes-of-mass-storage. "That machine can't run GNU EMACS, it doesn't have enough computrons!" This usage is usually found in metaphors that treat computing power as a fungible commodity good, like a crop yield or diesel horsepower. See **bitty box**, **Get a real computer!**, **toy**, **crank**. 2. A mythical subatomic particle that bears the unit quantity of computation or information, in much the same way that an electron bears one unit of electric charge (see also **bogon**). An elaborate pseudo-scientific theory of computrons has been developed based on the physical fact that the molecules in a solid object move more rapidly as it is heated. It is argued that an object melts because the molecules have lost their information about where they are supposed to be (that is, they have emitted computrons). This explains why computers get so hot and require air conditioning; they use up computrons. Conversely, it should be possible to cool down an object by placing it in the path of a computron beam. It is believed that this may also explain why machines that work at the factory fail in the computer room: the computrons there have been all used up by the other hardware. (This theory probably owes something to the "Warlock" stories by Larry Niven, the best known being "What Good is a Glass Dagger?", in which magic is fueled by an exhaustible natural resource called 'mana'.)

con [from SF fandom] n. A science-fiction convention. Not used of other sorts of conventions, such as professional meetings. This term, unlike many others of SF-fan slang, is widely recognized even by hackers who aren't **fans**. "We'd been corresponding on the net for months, then we met face-to-face at a con."

condition out vt. To prevent a section of code from being compiled by surrounding it with a conditional-compilation directive whose condition is always false. The **canonical** examples of these directives are `#if 0` (or `#ifdef notdef`, though some find the latter **bletcherous**) and `#endif` in C. Compare **comment out**.

condom n. 1. The protective plastic bag that accompanies 3.5-inch microfloppy diskettes. Rarely, also used of (paper) disk envelopes. Unlike the write protect tab, the condom (when left on) not only impedes the practice of **SEX** but has also been shown to have a high failure rate as drive mechanisms attempt to access the disk — and can even fatally frustrate insertion. 2. The protective cladding on a **light pipe**. 3. *keyboard condom*: A flexible, transparent plastic cover for a keyboard, designed to provide some protection against dust and **programming fluid** without impeding typing.

confuser n. Common soundalike slang for 'computer'. Usually encountered in compounds such as *confuser room, personal confuser, confuser guru.* Usage: silly.

connector conspiracy [probably came into prominence with the appearance of the KL-10 (one model of the **PDP-10**), none of whose connectors matched anything else] n. The tendency of manufacturers (or, by extension, programmers or purveyors of anything) to come up with new products that don't fit together with the old stuff, thereby making you buy either all new stuff or expensive interface devices. The KL-10 Massbus connector was actually *patented* by **DEC**, which reputedly refused to license the design and thus effectively locked third parties out of competition for the lucrative Massbus peripherals market. This policy is a source of never-ending frustration for the diehards who maintain older PDP-10 or VAX systems. Their CPUs work fine, but they are stuck with dying, obsolescent disk and tape drives with low capacity and high power requirements.

(A closely related phenomenon, with a slightly different intent, is the habit manufacturers have of inventing new screw heads so that only Designated Persons, possessing the magic screwdrivers, can remove covers and make repairs or install options. The Apple Macintosh takes this one step further, requiring not only a hex wrench but a specialized case-cracking tool to open the box.)

In these latter days of open-systems computing this term has fallen somewhat into disuse, to be replaced by the observation that "Standards are great! There are so *many* of them to choose from!" Compare **backward combatability**.

cons */konz/* or */kons/* [from LISP] 1. vt. To add a new element to a specified list, esp. at the top. "OK, cons picking a replacement for the console TTY onto the agenda." 2. *cons up*: vt. To synthesize from smaller pieces: "to cons up an example".

In LISP itself, `cons` is the most fundamental operation for building structures. It takes any two objects and returns a *dot-pair* or two-branched tree with one object hanging from each branch. Because the result of a cons is an object, it can be used to build binary trees of any shape and complexity. Hackers think of it as a sort of universal constructor, and that is where the jargon meanings spring from.

considered harmful adj. Edsger W. Dijkstra's note in the March 1968 *Com-*

munications of the ACM, "Goto Statement Considered Harmful", fired the first salvo in the structured programming wars. Amusingly, the ACM considered the resulting acrimony sufficiently harmful that it will (by policy) no longer print an article taking so assertive a position against a coding practice. In the ensuing decades, a large number of both serious papers and parodies have borne titles of the form "X considered Y". The structured-programming wars eventually blew over with the realization that both sides were wrong, but use of such titles has remained as a persistent minor in-joke (the 'considered silly' found at various places in this lexicon is related).

console n. 1. The operator's station of a **mainframe**. In times past, this was a privileged location that conveyed godlike powers to anyone with fingers on its keys. Under UNIX and other modern timesharing OSes, such privileges are guarded by passwords instead, and the console is just the **tty** the system was booted from. Some of the mystique remains, however, and it is traditional for sysadmins to post urgent messages to all users from the console (on UNIX, /dev/console). 2. On microcomputer UNIX boxes, the main screen and keyboard (as opposed to character-only terminals talking to a serial port). Typically only the console can do real graphics or run **X**. See also **CTY**.

console jockey n. See **terminal junkie**.

content-free [by analogy with techspeak 'context-free'] adj. Used of a message that adds nothing to the recipient's knowledge. Though this adjective is sometimes applied to **flamage**, it more usually connotes derision for communication styles that exalt form over substance or are centered on concerns irrelevant to the subject ostensibly at hand. Perhaps most used with reference to speeches by company presidents and other professional manipulators. "Content-free? Uh ... that's anything printed on glossy paper." (See also **four-color glossies**.) "He gave a talk on the implications of electronic networks for postmodernism and the fin-de-siecle aesthetic. It was content-free."

control-C vi. 1. "Stop whatever you are doing." From the interrupt character used on many operating systems to abort a running program. Considered silly. 2. interj. Among BSD UNIX hackers, the canonical humorous response to "Give me a break!"

control-O vi. "Stop talking." From the character used on some operating systems to abort output but allow the program to keep on running. Generally means that you are not interested in hearing anything more from that person, at least on that topic; a standard response to someone who is flaming. Considered silly. Compare **control-S**.

control-Q vi. "Resume." From the ASCII DC1 or **XON** character (the pronunciation /X-on/ is therefore also used), used to undo a previous **control-S**.

control-S vi. "Stop talking for a second." From the ASCII DC3 or XOFF character (the pronunciation */X-of/* is therefore also used). Control-S differs from **control-O** in that the person is asked to stop talking (perhaps because you are on the phone) but will be allowed to continue when you're ready to listen to him — as opposed to control-O, which has more of the meaning of "Shut up." Considered silly.

Conway's Law prov. The rule that the organization of the software and the organization of the software team will be congruent; originally stated as "If you have four groups working on a compiler, you'll get a 4-pass compiler".

Melvin Conway, an early proto-hacker who wrote an assembler for the Burroughs 220 called SAVE. The name 'SAVE' didn't stand for anything; it was just that you lost fewer card decks and listings because they all had SAVE written on them.

cookbook [from amateur electronics and radio] n. A book of small code segments that the reader can use to do various **magic** things in programs. One current example is the **PostScript** *Language Tutorial and Cookbook* by Adobe Systems, Inc (Addison-Wesley, ISBN 0-201-10179-3), also known as the **Blue Book** which has recipes for things like wrapping text around arbitrary curves and making 3D fonts. Cookbooks, slavishly followed, can lead one into **voodoo programming**, but are useful for hackers trying to **monkey up** small programs in unknown languages. This function is analogous to the role of phrasebooks in human languages.

cooked mode [UNIX, by opposition with **raw mode**] n. The normal character-input mode, with interrupts enabled and with erase, kill and other special-character interpretations performed directly by the tty driver. Oppose **raw mode**, **rare mode**. This term is techspeak under UNIX but jargon elsewhere; other operating systems often have similar mode distinctions, and the raw/rare/cooked way of describing them has spread widely along with the C language and other UNIX exports. Most generally, 'cooked mode' may refer to any mode of a system that does extensive preprocessing before presenting data to a program.

cookie n. A handle, transaction ID, or other token of agreement between cooperating programs. "I give him a packet, he gives me back a cookie." The claim check you get from a dry-cleaning shop is a perfect mundane example of a cookie; the only thing it's useful for is to relate a later transaction to this one (so you get the same clothes back). Compare **magic cookie**; see also **fortune cookie**.

cookie bear n. Syn. **cookie monster**.

cookie file n. A collection of **fortune cookie**s in a format that facilitates retrieval by a fortune program. There are several different cookie files in public distribution, and site admins often assemble their own from various sources including this lexicon.

cookie jar n. An area of memory set aside for storing cookies. Most commonly heard in the Atari ST community; many useful ST programs record their presence by storing a distinctive **magic number** in the jar. Programs can inquire after the presence or otherwise of other programs by searching the contents of the jar.

cookie monster [from the children's TV program "Sesame Street"] n. Any of a family of early (1970s) hacks reported on **TOPS-10**, **ITS**, **Multics**, and elsewhere that would lock up either the victim's terminal (on a time-sharing machine) or the **console** (on a batch **mainframe**), repeatedly demanding "I WANT A COOKIE". The required responses ranged in complexity from "COOKIE" through "HAVE A COOKIE" and upward. See also **wabbit**.

copious free time [Apple; orig. fr. the intro to Tom Lehrer's song "It Makes A Fellow Proud To Be A Soldier"] n. 1. [used ironically to indicate the speaker's lack of the quantity in question] A mythical schedule slot for accomplishing tasks held to be unlikely or impossible. Sometimes used to indicate that the speaker is interested in accomplishing the task, but believes that the opportunity will not arise. "I'll implement the automatic layout stuff in my copious free time." 2. [Archly] Time reserved for bogus or otherwise idiotic tasks, such as implementation of **chrome**, or the stroking of **suit**s. "I'll get back to him on that feature in my copious free time."

copper n. Conventional electron-carrying network cable with a core conductor of copper — or aluminum! Opposed to **light pipe** or, say, a short-range microwave link.

copy protection n. A class of methods for preventing incompetent pirates from stealing software and legitimate customers from using it. Considered silly.

copybroke */kop´ee-brohk/* adj. 1. [play on 'copyright'] Used to describe an instance of a copy-protected program that has been 'broken'; that is, a copy with the copy-protection scheme disabled. Syn. **copywronged**. 2. Copy-protected software which is unusable because of some bit-rot or bug that has confused the anti-piracy check. See also **copy protection**.

copyleft */kop´ee-left/* [play on 'copyright'] n. 1. The copyright notice ('General Public License') carried by **GNU EMACS** and other Free Software Foundation software, granting reuse and reproduction rights to all comers (but see also **General Public Virus**). 2. By extension, any copyright notice intended to achieve similar aims.

copywronged */kop´ee-rongd/* [play on 'copyright'] adj. Syn. for **copybroke**.

core n. Main storage or RAM. Dates from the days of ferrite-core memory; now archaic as techspeak most places outside IBM, but also still used in the UNIX community and by old-time hackers or those who would sound like them. Some derived idioms are quite current; *in core*, for example, means 'in memory' (as opposed to 'on disk'), and both **core dump** and the *core image* or *core file* produced by one are terms in favor. Some varieties of Commonwealth hackish prefer **store**.

core cancer n. A process that exhibits a slow but inexorable resource **leak** — like a cancer, it kills by crowding out productive *tissue*.

core dump n. [common **Iron Age** jargon, preserved by UNIX] 1. [techspeak] A copy of the contents of **core**, produced when a process is aborted by certain kinds of internal error. 2. By extension, used for humans passing out, vomiting, or registering extreme shock. "He dumped core. All over the floor. What a mess." "He heard about X and dumped core." 3. Occasionally used for a human rambling on pointlessly at great length; esp. in apology: "Sorry, I dumped core on you". 4. A recapitulation of knowledge (compare **bits**, sense 1). Hence, spewing all one knows about a topic (syn. **brain dump**), esp. in a lecture or answer to an exam question. "Short, concise answers are better than core dumps" (from the instructions to an exam at Columbia). See **core**.

A **core dump** lands our hero in hot water.
This is the last cartoon in the Crunchly saga.

core leak n. Syn. **memory leak**.

Core Wars n. A game between 'assembler' programs in a simulated machine, where the objective is to kill your opponent's program by overwriting it. Popularized by A. K. Dewdney's column in *Scientific American* magazine, this was actually devised by Victor Vyssotsky, Robert Morris Sr., and Dennis Ritchie in the early 1960s (their original game was called 'Darwin' and ran on a PDP-1 at Bell Labs). See **core**.

corge */korj/* [originally, the name of a cat] n. Yet another **metasyntactic variable**, invented by Mike Gallaher and propagated by the **GOSMACS** documentation. See **grault**.

cosmic rays n. Notionally, the cause of **bit rot**. However, this is a semi-independent usage that may be invoked as a humorous way to **handwave** away any minor **randomness** that doesn't seem worth the bother of investigating. "Hey, Eric — I just got a burst of garbage on my **tube**, where did that come from?" "Cosmic rays, I guess." Compare **sunspots**, **phase of the moon**. The British seem to prefer the usage *cosmic showers*; *alpha particles* is also heard, because stray alpha particles passing through a memory chip can cause single-bit errors (this becomes increasingly more likely as memory sizes and densities increase).

Factual note: Alpha particles cause bit rot, cosmic rays do not (except occasionally in spaceborne computers). Intel could not explain random bit drops in their early chips, and one hypothesis was cosmic rays. So they created the World's Largest Lead Safe, using 25 tons of the stuff, and used two identical boards for testing. One was placed in the safe, one outside. The hypothesis was that if cosmic rays were causing the bit drops, they should see a statistically significant difference between the error rates on the two boards. They did not observe such a difference. Further investigation demonstrated conclusively that the bit drops were due to alpha particle emissions from thorium (and to a much lesser degree uranium) in the encapsulation material. Since it is impossible to eliminate these radioactives (they are uniformly distributed through the earth's crust, with the statistically insignificant exception of uranium lodes) it became obvious that one has to design memories to withstand these hits.

cough and die v. Syn. **barf**. Connotes that the program is throwing its hands up by design rather than because of a bug or oversight. "The parser saw a control-A in its input where it was looking for a printable, so it coughed and died." Compare **die**, **die horribly**, **scream and die**.

cowboy [Sun, from William Gibson's **cyberpunk** SF] n. Synonym for **hacker**. It is reported that at Sun this word is often said with reverence.

CP/M */C-P-M/* n. [Control Program for Microcomputers] An early microcomputer **OS** written by hacker Gary Kildall for 8080- and Z80-based machines, very popular in the late 1970s but virtually wiped out by MS-DOS after the release of the IBM PC in 1981. Legend has it that Kildall's company blew its chance to write the OS for the IBM PC because Kildall decided to spend a day IBM's reps wanted to meet with him enjoying the perfect flying weather in his private plane. Many of CP/M's features and conventions strongly resemble those of early **DEC** operating systems such as **TOPS-10**, OS/8, RSTS, and RSX-11. See **MS-DOS, operating system**.

CPU Wars */C-P-U worz/* n. A 1979 large-format comic by Chas Andres chronicling the attempts of the brainwashed androids of IPM (Impossible to Program Machines) to conquer and destroy the peaceful denizens of HEC (Human Engineered Computers). This rather transparent allegory featured many references to **ADVENT** and the immortal line "Eat flaming death, minicomputer mongrels!" (uttered, of course, by an IPM stormtrooper). It is alleged that the author subsequently received a letter of appreciation on IBM company stationery from the head of IBM's Thomas J. Watson Research Laboratories (then, as now, one of the few islands of true hackerdom in the IBM archipelago). The lower loop of the B in the IBM logo, it is said, had been carefully whited out. See **eat flaming death**.

crack root v. To defeat the security system of a UNIX machine and gain **root** privileges thereby; see **cracking**.

cracker n. One who breaks security on a system. Coined ca. 1985 by hackers in defense against journalistic misuse of **hacker** (q.v., sense 8). An earlier attempt to establish *worm* in this sense around 1981–82 on USENET was largely a failure.

Use of both these neologisms reflects a strong revulsion against the theft and vandalism perpetrated by cracking rings. While it is expected that any real hacker will have done some playful cracking and knows many of the basic techniques, anyone past **larval stage** is expected to have outgrown the desire to do so except for immediate practical reasons (for example, if it's necessary to get around some security in order to get some work done).

Thus, there is far less overlap between hackerdom and crackerdom than the **mundane** reader misled by sensationalistic journalism might expect.

Crackers tend to gather in small, tight-knit, very secretive groups that have little overlap with the huge, open poly-culture this lexicon describes; though crackers often like to describe *themselves* as hackers, most true hackers consider them a separate and lower form of life.

Ethical considerations aside, hackers figure that anyone who can't imagine a more interesting way to play with their computers than breaking into someone else's has to be pretty **losing**. Some other reasons crackers are looked down on are discussed in the entries on **cracking** and **phreaking**. See also **samurai**, **dark-side hacker**, and **hacker ethic, the**.

cracking n. The act of breaking into a computer system; what a **cracker** does. Contrary to widespread myth, this does not usually involve some mysterious leap of hackerly brilliance, but rather persistence and the dogged repetition of a handful of fairly well-known tricks that exploit common weaknesses in the security of target systems. Accordingly, most crackers are only mediocre hackers.

crank [from automotive slang] vt. Verb used to describe the performance of a machine, especially sustained performance. "This box cranks (or, cranks at) about 6 megaflops, with a burst mode of twice that on vectorized operations."

CrApTeX */krap´tekh/* [University of York, England] n. Term of abuse used to describe TeX and LaTeX when they don't work (when used by TeXhackers), or all the time (by everyone else). The non-TeX enthusiasts generally dislike it because it is more verbose than other formatters (e.g. **troff**) and because (particularly if the standard Computer Modern fonts are used) it generates vast output files. See religious issues, **TEX**.

crash 1. n. A sudden, usually drastic failure. Most often said of the **system** (q.v., sense 1), esp. of magnetic disk drives (the term originally described what happened when the air gap of a hard disk collapses). "Three **luser**s lost their files in last night's disk crash." A disk crash that involves the read/write heads dropping onto the surface of the disks and scraping off the oxide may also be referred to as a *head crash*, whereas the term *system crash* usually, though not always, implies that the operating system or other software was at fault. 2. v. To fail suddenly. "Has the system just crashed?" "Something crashed the OS!" See **down**. Also used transitively to indicate the cause of the crash (usually a person or a program, or both). "Those idiots playing **SPACEWAR** crashed the system." 3. vi. Sometimes said of people hitting the sack after a long **hacking run**; see **gronk out**.

crash and burn vi.,n. A spectacular crash, in the mode of the conclusion of the car-chase scene in the movie "Bullitt" and many subsequent imitators (compare **die horribly**). Sun-3 monitors losing the flyback transformer and lightning strikes on VAX-11/780 backplanes are notable crash and burn generators. The construction *crash-and-burn machine* is reported for a computer used exclusively for alpha or **beta** testing, or reproducing bugs (i.e., not for development). The implication is that it wouldn't be such a disaster if that machine crashed, since only the testers would be inconvenienced.

crawling horror n. Ancient crufty hardware or software that is kept obstinately alive by forces beyond the control of the hackers at a site. Like **dusty deck** or **gonkulator**, but connotes that the thing described is not just an irritation but an active menace to health and sanity. "Mostly we code new stuff in C, but they pay us to maintain one big FORTRAN II application from nineteen-sixty-X that's a real crawling horror. . . ." Compare **WOMBAT**.

cray */kray/* n. 1. (properly, capitalized) One of the line of supercomputers designed by Cray Research. 2. Any supercomputer at all. 3. The **canonical number-crunching** machine.

The term is actually the lowercased last name of Seymour Cray, a noted computer architect and co-founder of the company. Numerous vivid legends surround him, some true and some admittedly invented by Cray Research brass to shape their corporate culture and image.

cray instability n. A shortcoming of a program or algorithm that manifests itself only when a large problem is being run on a powerful machine (see **cray**). Generally more subtle than bugs that can be detected in smaller problems running on a workstation or mini.

crayola */kray-oh´lə/* n. A super-mini or -micro computer that provides some reasonable percentage of supercomputer performance for an unreasonably low price. Might also be a **killer micro**.

crayola books n. The **rainbow series** of NCSC computer security standards (see **Orange Book**). Usage: humorous and/or disparaging.

crayon n. 1. Someone who works on Cray supercomputers. More specifically, it implies a programmer, probably of the CDC ilk, probably male, and almost certainly wearing a tie (irrespective of gender). Systems types who have a UNIX background tend not to be described as crayons. 2. A **com-**

putron (sense 2) that participates only in **number-crunching**. 3. A unit of computational power equal to that of a single Cray-1. There is a standard joke about this usage that derives from an old Crayola crayon promotional gimmick: When you buy 64 crayons you get a free sharpener.

creationism n. The (false) belief that large, innovative software designs can be completely specified in advance and then painlessly magicked out of the void by the normal efforts of a team of normally talented programmers. In fact, experience has shown repeatedly that good designs arise only from evolutionary, exploratory interaction between one (or at most a small handful of) exceptionally able designer(s) and an active user population — and that the first try at a big new idea is always wrong. Unfortunately, because these truths don't fit the planning models beloved of **management**, they are generally ignored.

creep v. To advance, grow, or multiply inexorably. In hackish usage this verb has overtones of menace and silliness, evoking the creeping horrors of low-budget monster movies.

creeping elegance n. Describes a tendency for parts of a design to become **elegant** past the point of diminishing return, something which often happens at the expense of the less interesting parts of the design, the schedule, and other things deemed important in the **Real World**. See also **creeping featurism**, **second-system effect**, **tense**.

creeping featurism */kree´ping fee´chr-izm/* n. 1. Describes a systematic tendency to load more **chrome** and **feature**s onto systems at the expense of whatever elegance they may have possessed when originally designed. See also **feeping creaturism**. "You know, the main problem with **BSD** UNIX has always been creeping featurism." 2. More generally, the tendency for anything complicated to become even more complicated because people keep saying "Gee, it would be even better if it had this feature too". (See **feature**.) The result is usually a patchwork because it grew one ad-hoc step at a time, rather than being planned. Planning is a lot of work, but it's easy to add just one extra little feature to help someone . . . and then another . . . and another. . . . When creeping featurism gets out of hand, it's like a cancer. Usually this term is used to describe computer programs, but it could also be said of the federal government, the IRS 1040 form, and new cars. A similar phenomenon sometimes afflicts conscious redesigns; see **second-system effect**. See also **creeping elegance**.

creeping featuritis */kree´ping fee´-chr-i:`təs/* n. Variant of **creeping featurism**, with its own spoonerization: *feeping creaturitis.* Some people like to reserve this form for the disease as it actually manifests in software or hardware, as opposed to the lurking general tendency in designers' minds. (After all, -ism means 'condition' or 'pursuit of', whereas -itis usually means 'inflammation of'.)

cretin */kret´in/* or */kree´tn/* n. Congenital **loser**; an obnoxious person; someone who can't do anything right. It has been observed that many American hackers tend to favor the British pronunciation */kret´in/* over standard American */kree´tn/*; it is thought this may be due to the insidious phonetic influence of Monty Python's Flying Circus.

cretinous */kret´n-əs/* or */kreet´n-əs/* adj. Wrong; stupid; non-functional; very poorly designed. Also used pejoratively of people. See **dread high-bit disease** for an example. Approximate synonyms: **bletcherous**, **bagbiting losing**, **brain-damaged**.

crippleware n. 1. Software that has some important functionality deliberately removed, so as to entice potential users to pay for a working version. 2. [Cambridge] **Guiltware** that exhorts you to donate to some charity (compare **careware**, **nagware**). 3. Hardware deliberately crippled, which can be upgraded to a more expensive model by a trivial change (e.g., cutting a jumper).

An excellent example of crippleware (sense 3) is Intel's 486SX chip, which is a standard 486DX chip with the co-processor dyked out (in some early versions it was present but disabled). To upgrade, you buy a complete 486DX chip with *working* co-processor (its identity thinly veiled by a different pinout) and plug it into the board's expansion socket. It then disables the SX, which becomes a fancy power sink. Don't you love Intel?

critical mass n. In physics, the minimum amount of fissionable material required to sustain a chain reaction. Of a software product, describes a condition of the software such that fixing one bug introduces one plus **epsilon** bugs. (This malady has many causes: **creeping featurism**, ports to too many disparate environments, poor initial design, etc.) When software achieves critical mass, it can never be fixed; it can only be discarded and rewritten.

crlf */ker´ləf/*, sometimes */kru´ləf/* or */C-R-L-F/* n. (often capitalized as 'CRLF') A carriage return (CR, ASCII 0001101) followed by a line feed

(LF, ASCII 0001010). More loosely, whatever it takes to get you from the end of one line of text to the beginning of the next line. See **newline**, **terpri**. Under **UNIX** influence this usage has become less common (UNIX uses a bare line feed as its 'CRLF').

crock [from the American scatologism *crock of shit*] n. 1. An awkward feature or programming technique that ought to be made cleaner. For example, using small integers to represent error codes without the program interpreting them to the user (as in, for example, UNIX `make(1)`, which returns code 139 for a process that dies due to **segfault**). 2. A technique that works acceptably, but which is quite prone to failure if disturbed in the least. For example, a too-clever programmer might write an assembler which mapped instruction mnemonics to numeric opcodes algorithmically, a trick which depends far too intimately on the particular bit patterns of the opcodes. (For another example of programming with a dependence on actual opcode values, see **The Story of Mel, a Real Programmer** in **Appendix A**.) Many crocks have a tightly woven, almost completely unmodifiable structure. See **kluge**, **brittle**. The adjectives *crockish* and *crocky*, and the nouns *crockishness* and *crockitude*, are also used.

cross-post [USENET] vi. To post a single article simultaneously to several newsgroups. Distinguished from posting the article repeatedly, once to each newsgroup, which causes people to see it multiple times (which is very bad form). Gratuitous cross-posting without a Followup-To line directing responses to a single followup group is frowned upon, as it tends to cause **followup** articles to go to inappropriate newsgroups when people respond to only one part of the original posting.

crudware */kruhd´weir/* n. Pejorative term for the hundreds of megabytes of low-quality **freeware** circulated by user's groups and BBS systems in the micro-hobbyist world. "Yet *another* set of disk catalog utilities for **MS-DOS**? What crudware!"

cruft */kruhft/* [back-formation from **crufty**] 1. n. An unpleasant substance. The dust that gathers under your bed is cruft; the TMRC Dictionary correctly noted that attacking it with a broom only produces more. 2. n. The results of shoddy construction. 3. vt. [from *hand cruft*, pun on 'hand craft'] To write assembler code for something normally (and better) done by a compiler (see **hand-hacking**). 4. n. Excess; superfluous junk; used esp. of redundant or superseded code.

This term is one of the oldest in the jargon and no one is sure of its etymology, but it is suggestive that there is a Cruft Hall at Harvard University which is part of the old physics building; it's said to have been the physics department's radar lab during WWII. To this day (early 1993) the windows appear to be full of random techno-junk. MIT or Lincoln Labs people may well have coined the term as a knock on the competition.

cruft together vt. (also *cruft up*) To throw together something ugly but temporarily workable. Like vt. **kluge up**, but more pejorative. "There isn't any program now to reverse all the lines of a file, but I can probably cruft one together in about 10 minutes." See **hack together**, **hack up**, **kluge up**, **crufty**.

cruftsmanship */kruhfts´mən-ship /* n. [from **cruft**] The antithesis of craftsmanship.

crufty */kruhf´tee/* [origin unknown; poss. from 'crusty'] adj. 1. Poorly built, possibly over-complex. The **canonical** example is "This is standard old crufty **DEC** software". In fact, one fanciful theory of the origin of *crufty* holds that was originally a mutation of 'crusty' applied to DEC software so old that the 's' characters were tall and skinny, looking more like 'f' characters. 2. Unpleasant, especially to the touch, often with encrusted junk. Like spilled coffee smeared with peanut butter and catsup. 3. Generally unpleasant. 4. (sometimes spelled *cruftie*) n. A small crufty object (see **frob**); often one that doesn't fit well into the scheme of things. "A LISP property list is a good place to store crufties (or, collectively, **random** cruft)."

crumb n. Two binary digits; a **quad**. Larger than a **bit**, smaller than a **nybble**. Considered silly. Syn. **tayste**.

crunch 1. vi. To process, usually in a time-consuming or complicated way. Connotes an essentially trivial operation that is nonetheless painful to perform. The pain may be due to the triviality's being embedded in a loop from 1 to 1,000,000,000. "FORTRAN programs do mostly **number-crunching**." 2. vt. To reduce the size of a file by a complicated scheme that produces bit configurations completely unrelated to the original data, such as by a Huffman code. (The file ends up looking something like a paper document would if somebody crunched the paper into a wad.) Since such compression usually takes more computations than simpler methods such as run-length encoding, the term is doubly appropriate. (This meaning is usually used in the construction 'file crunch(ing)' to distinguish it from **number-crunching**.) See **compress**. 3. n. The character '#'. Used at XEROX and CMU, among other places. See **ASCII**. 4. vt. To squeeze program source into a minimum-size representation that will still compile or execute. The term came into being specifically for a famous program on the BBC micro that crunched BASIC source in order to make it run more quickly (it was a wholly interpretive BASIC, so the number of characters mattered). **Obfuscated C Contest** entries are often crunched; see the first example under that entry.

cruncha cruncha cruncha */kruhn´chə kruhn´chə kruhn´chə/* interj. An encouragement sometimes muttered to a machine bogged down in a serious **grovel**. Also describes a notional sound made by groveling hardware. See **wugga wugga**, **grind** (sense 3).

cryppie */krip´ee/* n. A cryptographer. One who hacks or implements cryptographic software or hardware.

CTSS */C-T-S-S/* n. Compatible Time-Sharing System. An early (1963) experiment in the design of interactive time-sharing operating systems, ancestral to **Multics**, **UNIX**, and **ITS**. The name **ITS** (Incompatible Time-sharing System) was a hack on CTSS, meant both as a joke and to express some basic differences in philosophy about the way I/O services should be presented to user programs.

CTY */sit´ee/* or */C-T-Y/* n. [MIT] The terminal physically associated with a computer's system **console**. The term is a contraction of 'Console **tty**', that is, 'Console TeleTYpe'. This **ITS**- and **TOPS-10**-associated term has become less common, as most UNIX hackers simply refer to the CTY as 'the console'.

cube n. 1. [short for 'cubicle'] A module in the open-plan offices used at many programming shops. "I've got the manuals in my cube." 2. A NeXT machine (which resembles a matte-black cube).

cubing [parallel with 'tubing'] vi. 1. Hacking on an IPSC (Intel Personal SuperComputer) hypercube. "Louella's gone cubing *again*!!" 2. Hacking Rubik's Cube or related puzzles, either physically or mathematically. 3. An indescribable form of self-torture (see sense 1 or 2).

cursor dipped in X n. There are a couple of metaphors in English of the form 'pen dipped in X' (perhaps the most common values of X are 'acid', 'bile', and 'vitriol'). These map over neatly to this hackish usage (the cursor being what moves, leaving letters behind, when one is composing on-line). "Talk about a **nastygram**! He must've had his cursor dipped in acid when he wrote that one!"

cuspy */kuhs´pee/* [WPI: from the **DEC** abbreviation CUSP, for 'Commonly Used System Program', i.e., a utility program used by many people] adj. 1. (of a program) Well-written. 2. Functionally excellent. A program that performs well and interfaces well to users is cuspy. See **rude**. 3. [NYU] Said of an attractive woman, especially one regarded as available. Implies a certain curvaceousness.

cut a tape vi. To write a software or document distribution on magnetic tape for shipment. Has nothing to do with physically cutting the medium! Early versions of this lexicon claimed that one never analogously speaks of 'cutting a disk', but this has since been reported as live usage. Related slang usages are mainstream business's 'cut a check', the recording industry's 'cut a record', and the military's 'cut an order'.

All of these usages reflect physical processes in obsolete recording and duplication technologies. The first stage in manufacturing an old-style vinyl record involved cutting grooves in a stamping die with a precision lathe. More mundanely, the dominant technology for mass duplication of paper documents in pre-photocopying days involved "cutting a stencil", punching away portions of the wax overlay on a silk screen. More directly, paper tape with holes punched in it was an important early storage medium.

cybercrud */si:´ber-kruhd/* [coined by Ted Nelson] n. Obfuscatory tech-talk. Verbiage with a high **MEGO** factor. The computer equivalent of bureaucratese.

cyberpunk */si:´ber-puhnk/* [orig. by SF writer Bruce Bethke and/or editor Gardner Dozois] n.,adj. A subgenre of SF launched in 1982 by William Gibson's epoch-making novel *Neuromancer* (though its roots go back through Vernor Vinge's *True Names* (see "True Names . . . and Other Dangers" in appendix C) to John Brunner's 1975 novel *The Shockwave Rider*). Gibson's near-total ignorance of computers and the present-day hacker culture enabled him to speculate about the role of computers and hackers in the future in ways hackers have since found both irritatingly naïve and tremendously stimulating. Gibson's work was widely imitated, in particular by the short-lived but innovative "Max Headroom" TV series. See **cyberspace**, **ice**, **jack in**, **go flatline**.

cyberspace */si:´ber-spays/* n. 1. Notional 'information-space' loaded with visual cues and navigable with brain-computer interfaces called *cyberspace decks*; a characteristic prop of **cyberpunk** SF. At the time of this writing (mid-1991), serious efforts to construct **virtual reality** interfaces modeled explicitly on Gibsonian cyberspace are already under way, using more conventional devices such as glove sensors and binocular TV headsets. Few hackers are prepared to deny outright the possibility of a cyberspace someday evolving out of the network (see **network, the**). 2. Occasionally, the metaphoric location of the mind of a person in **hack mode**. Some hackers report experiencing strong eidetic imagery when in hack mode; interestingly, independent reports from multiple sources suggest that there are common features to the experience. In particular, the dominant colors of this subjective *cyberspace* are often gray and silver, and the imagery often involves constellations of marching dots, elaborate shifting patterns of lines and angles, or moire patterns.

cycle 1. n. The basic unit of computation. What every hacker wants more of (noted hacker Bill Gosper describes himself as a "cycle junkie"). One can describe an instruction as taking so many *clock cycles*. Often the computer can access its memory once on every clock cycle, and so one speaks also of *memory cycles*. These are technical meanings of **cycle**. The jargon meaning comes from the observation that there are only so many cycles per second, and when you are sharing a computer the cycles get divided up among the users. The more cycles the computer spends working on your program rather than someone else's, the faster your program will run. That's why every hacker wants more cycles: so he can spend less time waiting for the computer to respond. 2. By extension, a notional unit of *human* thought power, emphasizing that lots of things compete for the typical hacker's think time. "I refused to get involved with the Rubik's Cube back when it was big. Knew I'd burn too many cycles on it if I let myself." 3. vt. Syn. **bounce** (sense 4), **120 reset**; from the phrase 'cycle power'. "Cycle the machine again, that serial port's still hung."

cycle crunch n. A situation wherein the number of people trying to use a computer simultaneously has reached the point where no one can get enough cycles because they are spread too thin and the system has probably begun to **thrash**. This scenario is an inevitable result of Parkinson's Law applied to timesharing. Usually the only solution is to buy more computer. Happily, this has rapidly become easier since the mid-1980s, so much so that the very term 'cycle crunch' now has a faintly archaic flavor; most hackers now use workstations or personal computers as opposed to traditional timesharing systems.

cycle drought n. A scarcity of cycles. It may be due to a **cycle crunch**, but it could also occur because part of the computer is temporarily not working, leaving fewer cycles to go around. "The **high moby** is **down**, so we're running with only half the usual amount of memory. There will be a cycle drought until it's fixed."

cycle of reincarnation [coined by Ivan Sutherland ca. 1970] n. Term used to refer to a well-known effect whereby function in a computing system family is migrated out to special-purpose peripheral hardware for speed, then the peripheral evolves toward more computing power as it does its job, then somebody notices that it is inefficient to support two asymmetrical processors in the architecture and folds the function back into the main CPU, at which point the cycle begins again. Several iterations of this cycle have been observed in graphics-processor design, and at least one or two in communications and floating-point processors. Also known as *the Wheel of Life*, *the Wheel of Samsara*, and other variations of the basic Hindu/Buddhist theological idea. See also **blitter**, **bit bang**.

cycle server n. A powerful machine that exists primarily for running large **batch** jobs. Implies that interactive tasks such as editing are done on other machines on the network, such as workstations.

= D =

D. C. Power Lab n. The former site of **SAIL**. Hackers thought this was very funny because the obvious connection to electrical engineering was nonexistent — the lab was named for a Donald C. Power. Compare **Marginal Hacks**.

daemon */day´mn/* or */dee´mn/* [from the mythological meaning, later rationalized as the acronym 'Disk And Execution MONitor'] n. A program that is not invoked explicitly, but lies dormant waiting for some condition(s) to occur. The idea is that the perpetrator of the condition need not be aware that a daemon is lurking (though often a program will commit an action only because it knows that it will implicitly invoke a daemon). For example, under **ITS** writing a file on the **LPT** spooler's directory would invoke the spooling daemon, which would then print the file. The advantage is that programs wanting (in this example) files printed need neither compete for access to nor understand any idiosyncrasies of the **LPT**. They simply enter their implicit requests and let the daemon decide what to do with them. Daemons are usually spawned automatically by the system, and may either live forever or be regenerated at intervals.

Daemon and **demon** are often used interchangeably, but seem to have distinct connotations. The term 'daemon' was introduced to computing by **CTSS** people (who pronounced it */dee´mon/*) and used it to refer to what ITS called a **dragon**. Although the meaning and the pronunciation have drifted, we think this glossary reflects current (1993) usage.

dangling pointer n. A reference that doesn't actually lead anywhere (in C and some other languages, a pointer that doesn't actually point at anything valid). Usually this happens because it formerly pointed to something that has moved or disappeared. Used as jargon in a generalization of its techspeak meaning; for example, a local phone number for a person who has since moved to the other coast is a dangling pointer.

dark-side hacker n. A criminal or malicious hacker; a **cracker**. From George Lucas's Darth Vader, "seduced by the dark side of the Force". The implication that hackers form a sort of elite of technological Jedi Knights is intended. Oppose **samurai**.

Datamation */day`tə-may´shən/* n. A magazine that many hackers assume all **suit**s read. Used to question an unbelieved quote, as in "Did you read that in *Datamation?*" It used to publish something hackishly funny every once in a while, like the original paper on **COME FROM** in 1973, and Ed Post's "Real Programmers Don't Use Pascal" ten years later, but it has since become much more exclusively **suit**-oriented and boring.

DAU */dow/* [German Fidonet] n. German acronym for Dümmster Anzunehmender User (stupidest imaginable user). From the engineering-slang GAU for Grösster Anzunehmender Unfall, worst foreseeable accident, esp. of a LNG tank farm plant or something with similarly disastrous consequences. In popular German, GAU is used only to refer to worst-case nuclear acidents such as a core meltdown. See **cretin**, **fool**, **loser** and **weasel**.

day mode n. See **phase** (sense 1). Used of people only.

dd */dee-dee/* [UNIX: from IBM **JCL**] vt. Equivalent to **cat** or **BLT**. Originally the name of a UNIX copy command with special options suitable for block-oriented devices; it was often used in heavy-handed system maintenance, as in "Let's `dd` the root partition onto a tape, then use the boot PROM to load it back on to a new disk". The UNIX `dd(1)` was designed with a weird, distinctly non-UNIXy keyword option syntax reminiscent of IBM System/360 JCL (which had an elaborate DD 'Dataset Definition' specification for I/O devices); though the command filled a need, the interface design was clearly a prank. The jargon usage is now very rare outside UNIX sites and now nearly obsolete even there, as `dd(1)` has been **deprecated** for a long time (though it has no exact replacement). The term has been displaced by **BLT** or simple English 'copy'.

DDT */D-D-T/* n. 1. Generic term for a program that assists in debugging other programs by showing individual machine instructions in a readable symbolic form and letting the user change them. In this sense the term DDT is now archaic, having been widely displaced by 'debugger' or names of individual programs like `adb`, `sdb`, `dbx`, or `gdb`. 2. [ITS] Under MIT's fabled **ITS** operating system, DDT (running under the alias HACTRN) was also used as the **shell** or top level command language used to execute other programs. 3. Any one of several specific DDTs (sense 1) supported on early **DEC** hardware. The DEC PDP-10 Reference Handbook (1969) contained a footnote on the first page of the documentation for DDT that illuminates the origin of the term:

> Historical footnote: DDT was developed at MIT for the PDP-1 computer in 1961. At that time DDT stood for "DEC Debugging Tape". Since then, the idea of an on-line debugging program has propagated throughout the computer industry. DDT programs are now available for all DEC computers. Since media other than tape are now frequently used, the more descriptive name "Dynamic Debugging Technique" has been adopted, retaining the DDT abbreviation. Confusion between DDT-10 and another well known pesticide, dichloro-diphenyl-trichloroethane($C_{14}H_9Cl_5$) should be minimal since each attacks a different, and apparently mutually exclusive, class of bugs.

Sadly, this quotation was removed from later editions of the handbook after the **suit**s took over and DEC became much more 'businesslike'.

The history above is known to many old-time hackers. But there's more: Peter Samson, compiler of the original **TMRC** lexicon, reports that he named *DDT* after a similar tool on the TX-0 computer, the direct ancestor of the PDP-1 built at MIT's Lincoln Lab in 1957. The debugger on that groundbreaking machine (the first transistorized computer) rejoiced in the name FLIT (FLexowriter Interrogation Tape).

de-rezz */dee-rez´/* [from 'de-resolve' via the movie "Tron"] (also *derez*) 1. vi. To disappear or dissolve; the image that goes with it is of an object breaking up into raster lines and static and then dissolving. Occasionally used of a person who seems to have suddenly 'fuzzed out' mentally rather than physically. Usage: extremely silly, also rare. This verb was actually invented as *fictional* hacker jargon, and adopted in a spirit of irony by real hackers years after the fact. 2. vt. The Macintosh resource decompiler. On a Macintosh, many program structures (including the code itself) are managed in small segments of the program file known as *resources*; *Rez* and *DeRez* are a pair of utilities for compiling and decompiling resource files. Thus, decompiling a resource is *derezzing*. Usage: very common.

dead adj. 1. Non-functional; **down**; **crash**ed. Especially used of hardware. 2. At XEROX PARC, software that is working but not undergoing continued development and support.

dead code n. Routines that can never be accessed because all calls to them have been removed, or code that cannot be reached because it is guarded by a control structure that provably must always transfer control somewhere else. The presence of dead code may reveal either logical errors due to alterations in the program or significant changes in the assumptions and environment of the program (see also **software rot**); a good compiler should report dead code so a maintainer can think about what it means. (Sometimes it simply means that an *extremely* defensive programmer has inserted **can't happen** tests which really can't happen — yet.) Syn. **grunge**.

DEADBEEF */ded-beef/* n. The hexadecimal word-fill pattern for freshly allocated memory (decimal -21524111) under a number of IBM environments, including the RS/6000. As in "Your program is DEADBEEF" (meaning gone, aborted, flushed from memory); if you start from an odd half-word boundary, of course, you have BEEFDEAD.

deadlock n. 1. [techspeak] A situation wherein two or more processes are unable to proceed because each is waiting for one of the others to do something. A common example is a program communicating to a server, which may find itself waiting for output from the server before sending anything more to it, while the server is similarly waiting for more input from the controlling program before outputting anything. (It is reported that this particular flavor of deadlock is sometimes called a *starvation deadlock*, though the term *starvation* is more properly used for situations where a program can never run simply because it never gets high enough priority. Another common flavor is *constipation*, in which each process is trying to send stuff to the other but all buffers are full because nobody is reading anything.) See **deadly embrace**. 2. Also used of deadlock-like interactions between humans, as when two people meet in a narrow corridor, and each tries to be polite by moving aside to let the other pass, but they end up swaying from side to side without making any progress because they always move the same way at the same time.

deadly embrace n. Same as **deadlock**, though usually used only when exactly two processes are involved. This is the more popular term in Europe, while **deadlock** predominates in the United States.

death code n. A routine whose job is to set everything in the computer — registers, memory, flags, everything — to zero, including that portion of memory where it is running; its last act is to stomp on its own "store zero" instruction. Death code isn't very useful, but writing it is an interesting hacking challenge on architectures where the instruction set makes it possible, such as the PDP-8 (it has also been done on the DG Nova).

Perhaps the ultimate death code is on the TI 990 series, where all registers are actually in RAM, and the instruction "store immediate 0" has the opcode `"0"`. The PC will immediately wrap around core as many times as it can until a user hits HALT. Any empty memory location is death code. Worse, the manufacturer recommended use of this instruction in startup code (which would be in ROM and therefore survive).

Death Star [from the movie "Star Wars"] 1. The AT&T corporate logo, which appears on computers sold by AT&T and bears an uncanny resemblance to the Death Star in the movie. This usage is particularly common among partisans of **BSD** UNIX, who tend to regard the AT&T versions as inferior and AT&T as a bad guy. Copies still circulate of a poster printed by Mt. Xinu showing a starscape with a space fighter labeled 4.2 BSD streaking away from a broken AT&T logo wreathed in flames. 2. AT&T's internal magazine, *Focus*, uses *death star* to describe an incorrectly done AT&T logo in which the inner circle in the top left is dark instead of light — a frequent result of dark-on-light logo images.

DEC n. Digital Equipment Corporation. Before the **killer micro** revolution of the late 1980s, hackerdom was closely symbiotic with DEC's pioneering timesharing machines. The first of the group of cultures described by this lexicon nucleated around the PDP-1 (see **TMRC**. Subsequently, the PDP-6, **PDP-10**, **PDP-20**, PDP-11 and **VAX** were all foci of large and important hackerdoms, and DEC machines long dominated the ARPANET and Internet machine population. DEC was the technological leader of the minicomputer era (roughly 1967 to 1987), but its failure to embrace microcomputers and UNIX early cost it heavily in profits and prestige after **silicon** got cheap. However, the microprocessor design tradition owes a heavy debt to the PDP-11 instruction set, and every one of the major general-purpose microcomputer OSs so far (CP/M, MS-DOS, UNIX, OS/2) were either genetically descended from a DEC OS, or incubated on DEC hardware, or both. Accordingly, DEC is still regarded with a certain wry affection even among many hackers too young to have grown up on DEC machines. The contrast with **IBM** is instructive.

dec */dek/* v. Verbal (and only rarely written) shorthand for *decrement*, i.e. 'decrease by one'. Especially used by assembly programmers, as many assembly languages have a `dec` mnemonic. Antonym: **inc**.

DEC Wars n. A 1983 **USENET** posting by Alan Hastings and Steve Tarr spoofing the "Star Wars" movies in hackish terms. Some years later, ESR (disappointed by Hastings and Tarr's failure to exploit a great premise more thoroughly) posted a 3-times-longer complete rewrite called "UNIX WARS"; the two are often confused.

decay [from nuclear physics] n.,vi. An automatic conversion which is applied to most array-valued expressions in C; they 'decay into' pointer-valued expressions pointing to the array's first element. This term is borderline techspeak, but is not used in the official standard for the language.

DEChead */dek´hed/* n. 1. A **DEC field servoid**. Not flattering. 2. [from 'deadhead'] A Grateful Dead fan working at DEC.

deckle */dek'l/* [from dec- and **nybble**; the original spelling seems to have been *decle*] n. Two **nickles**; 10 bits. Reported among developers for Mattel's GI 1600 (the Intellivision games processor), a chip with 16-bit-wide RAM but 10-bit-wide ROM.

DED */D-E-D/* n. Dark-Emitting Diode (that is, a burned-out LED). Compare **SED**, **LER**, **write-only memory**. In the early 1970s both Signetics and Texas instruments released DED spec sheets as **AFJ**s (suggested uses included "as a power-off indicator").

deep hack mode n. See **hack mode**.

deep magic [poss. from C. S. Lewis's "Narnia" books] n. An awesomely arcane technique central to a program or system, esp. one neither generally published nor available to hackers at large (compare **black art**); one that could only have been composed by a true **wizard**. Compiler optimization techniques and many aspects of **OS** design used to be **deep magic**; many techniques in cryptography, signal processing, graphics, and AI still are. Compare **heavy wizardry**. Esp. found in comments of the form "Deep magic begins here . . . ". Compare **voodoo programming**.

deep space n. 1. Describes the notional location of any program that has gone **off the trolley**. Esp. used of programs that just sit there silently grinding long after either failure or some output is expected. "Uh oh. I should have gotten a prompt ten seconds ago. The program's in deep space somewhere." Compare **buzz**, **catatonic**, **hyperspace**. 2. The metaphorical location of a human so dazed and/or confused or caught up in some esoteric form of **bogosity** that he or she no longer responds coherently to normal communication. Compare **page out**.

defenestration [from the traditional Czechoslovakian method of assassinating prime ministers, via SF fandom] n. 1. Proper karmic retribution for an incorrigible punster. "Oh, ghod, that was *awful*!" "Quick! Defenestrate him!" 2. The act of exiting a window system in order to get better response time from a full-screen program. This comes from the dictionary meaning of *defenestrate*, which is to throw something out a window. 3. The act of discarding something under the assumption that it will improve matters. "I don't have any disk space left." "Well, why don't you defenestrate that 100 megs worth of old core dumps?" 4. [proposed] The requirement to support a command-line interface. "It has to run on a VT100." "Curses! I've been defenestrated!"

defined as adj. In the role of, usually in an organization-chart sense. "Pete is currently defined as bug prioritizer." Compare **logical**.

dehose */dee-hohz/* vt. To clear a **hosed** condition.

delint */dee-lint/* v. To modify code to remove problems detected when **lint**ing. Confusingly, this process is also referred to as 'linting' code.

delta n. 1. [techspeak] A quantitative change, especially a small or incremental one (this use is general in physics and engineering). "I just doubled the speed of my program!" "What was the delta on program size?" "About 30 percent." (He doubled the speed of his program, but increased its size by only 30 percent.) 2. [UNIX] A **diff**, especially a **diff** stored under the set of version-control tools called SCCS (Source Code Control System) or RCS (Revision Control System). 3. n. A small quantity, but not as small as **epsilon**. The jargon usage of **delta** and **epsilon** stems from the traditional use of these letters in mathematics for very small numerical quantities, particularly in 'epsilon-delta' proofs in limit theory (as in the differential calculus). The term **delta** is often used, once **epsilon** has been mentioned, to mean a quantity that is slightly bigger than **epsilon** but still very small. "The cost isn't epsilon, but it's delta" means that the cost isn't totally negligible, but it is nevertheless very small. Common constructions include *within delta of —*, *within epsilon of —*: that is, 'close to' and 'even closer to'.

demented adj. Yet another term of disgust used to describe a program. The connotation in this case is that the program works as designed, but the design is bad. Said, for example, of a program that generates large numbers of meaningless error messages, implying that it is on the brink of imminent collapse. Compare **wonky**, **bozotic**.

demigod n. A hacker with years of experience, a national reputation, and a major role in the development of at least one design, tool, or game used by or known to more than half of the hacker community. To qualify as a genuine demigod, the person must recognizably identify with the hacker community and have helped shape it. Major demigods include Ken Thompson and Dennis Ritchie (co-inventors of **UNIX** and **C**) and Richard M. Stallman (inventor of **EMACS**). In their hearts of hearts, most hackers dream of someday becoming demigods themselves, and more than one major software project has been driven to completion by the author's veiled hopes of apotheosis. See also **net.god**, **true-hacker**.

demo */de´moh/* [short for 'demonstration'] 1. v. To demonstrate a product or prototype. A far more effective way of inducing bugs to manifest than any number of **test** runs, especially when important people are watching. 2. n. The act of demoing. "I've gotta give a demo of the drool-proof interface; how does it work again?" 3. n. Esp. as *demo version*, can refer either to an early, barely-functional version of a program which can be used for demonstration purposes as long as the operator uses *exactly* the right commands and skirts its numerous bugs, deficiencies, and unimplemented portions, or to a special version of a program (frequently with some features crippled) which is distributed at little or no cost to the user for enticement purposes.

demo mode [Sun] n. 1. The state of being **heads down** in order to finish code in time for a **demo**, usually due yesterday. 2. A mode in which video games sit by themselves running through a portion of the game, also known as *attract mode*. Some serious **app**s have a demo mode they use as a screen saver, or may go through a demo mode on startup (for example, the Microsoft Windows opening screen — which lets you impress your neighbors without actually having to put up with **Microsloth Windows**).

demon n. 1. [MIT] A portion of a program that is not invoked explicitly, but that lies dormant waiting for some condition(s) to occur. See **daemon**. The distinction is that demons are usually processes within a program, while daemons are usually programs running on an operating system. 2. [outside MIT] Often used equivalently to **daemon** — especially in the **UNIX** world, where the latter spelling and pronunciation is considered mildly archaic.

Demons in sense 1 are particularly common in AI programs. For example, a knowledge-manipulation program might implement inference rules as demons. Whenever a new piece of knowledge was added, various demons would activate (which demons depends on the particular piece of data) and would create additional pieces of knowledge by applying their respective inference rules to the original piece. These new pieces could in turn activate more demons as the inferences filtered down through chains of logic. Meanwhile, the main program could continue with whatever its primary task was.

depeditate */dee-ped´ə-tayt/* [by (faulty) analogy with 'decapitate'] vt. Humorously, to cut off the feet of. When one is using some computer-aided typesetting tools, careless placement of text blocks within a page or above a rule can result in chopped-off letter descenders. Such letters are said to have been depeditated.

deprecated adj. Said of a program or feature that is considered obsolescent and in the process of being phased out, usually in favor of a specified replacement. Deprecated features can, unfortunately, linger on for many years. This term appears with distressing frequency in standards documents when the committees writing the documents realize that large amounts of extant (and presumably happily working) code depend on the feature(s) that have passed out of favor. See also **dusty deck**.

deserves to lose adj. Said of someone who willfully does the **Wrong Thing**; humorously, if one uses a feature known to be **marginal**. What is meant is that one deserves the consequences of one's **losing** actions. "Boy, anyone who tries to use **mess-dos** deserves to **lose**!" (**ITS** fans used to say the same thing of **UNIX**; many still do.) See also **screw**, **chomp**, **bagbiter**.

desk check n.,v. To **grovel** over hardcopy of source code, mentally simulating the control flow; a method of catching bugs. No longer common practice in this age of on-screen editing, fast compiles, and sophisticated debuggers — though some maintain stoutly that it ought to be. Compare **eyeball search**, **vdiff**, **vgrep**.

despew */də-spyoo´/* [USENET] v. To automatically generate a large amount of garbage to the net, esp. from an automated posting program gone wild. See **ARMM**.

Devil Book n. *The Design and Implementation of the 4.3BSD UNIX Operating System*, by Samuel J. Leffler, Marshall Kirk McKusick, Michael J. Karels, and John S. Quarterman (Addison-Wesley Publishers, 1989, ISBN 0-201-06196-1) — the standard reference book on the internals of **BSD** UNIX. So called because the cover has a picture depicting a little devil (a visual play on **daemon**) in sneakers, holding a pitchfork (referring to one of the characteristic features of UNIX, the `fork(2)` system call).

devo */dee´voh/* [orig. in-house jargon at Symbolics] n. A person in a development group. See also **doco** and **mango**.

dickless workstation n. Extremely pejorative hackerism for 'diskless workstation', a class of botches including the Sun 3/50 and other machines designed exclusively to network with an expensive central disk server. These combine all the disadvantages of time-sharing with all the disadvantages of distributed personal computers; typically, they cannot even **boot** themselves without help (in the form of some kind of **breath-of-life packet**) from the server.

dictionary flame [USENET] n. An attempt to sidetrack a debate away from issues by insisting on meanings for key terms that presuppose a desired conclusion or smuggle in an implicit premise. A common tactic of people who prefer argument over definitions to disputes about reality. Compare **spelling flame**.

diddle 1. vt. To work with or modify in a not particularly serious manner. "I diddled a copy of **ADVENT** so it didn't double-space all the time." "Let's diddle this piece of code and see if the problem goes away." See **tweak** and **twiddle**. 2. n. The action or result of diddling. See also **tweak, twiddle, frob**.

die v. Syn. **crash**. Unlike **crash**, which is used primarily of hardware, this verb is used of both hardware and software. See also **go flatline**, **casters-up mode**.

die horribly v. The software equivalent of **crash and burn**, and the preferred emphatic form of **die**. "The converter choked on an FF in its input and died horribly".

diff */dif/* n. 1. A change listing, especially giving differences between (and additions to) source code or documents (the term is often used in the plural *diffs*). "Send me your diffs for the Jargon File!" Compare **vdiff**. 2. Specifically, such a listing produced by the `diff(1)` command, esp. when used as specification input to the `patch(1)` utility (which can actually perform the modifications; see **patch**). This is a common method of distributing patches and source updates in the UNIX/C world. 3. v. To compare (whether or not by use of automated tools on machine-readable files); see also **vdiff, mod**.

digit n. An employee of Digital Equipment Corporation. See also **VAX**, **VMS**, **PDP-10**, **TOPS-10**, **DEChead**, **double DECkers**, **field circus**.

dike vt. To remove or disable a portion of something, as a wire from a computer or a subroutine from a program. A standard slogan is "When in doubt, dike it out". (The implication is that it is usually more effective to attack software problems by reducing complexity than by increasing it.) The word 'dikes' is widely used among mechanics and engineers to mean 'diagonal cutters', esp. the heavy-duty metal-cutting version, but may also refer to a kind of wire-cutters used by electronics techs. To *dike something out* means to use such cutters to remove something. Indeed, the TMRC Dictionary defined dike as "to attack with dikes". Among hackers this term has been metaphorically extended to informational objects such as sections of code.

ding n.,vi. 1. Synonym for **feep**. Usage: rare among hackers, but commoner in the **Real World**. 2. *dinged*: What happens when someone in authority gives you a minor bitching about something, esp. something trivial. "I was dinged for having a messy desk."

dink */dink/* adj. Said of a machine that has the **bitty box** nature; a machine too small to be worth bothering with — sometimes the system you're currently forced to work on. First heard from an MIT hacker working on a CP/M system with 64K, in reference to any 6502 system, then from fans of 32-bit architectures about 16-bit machines. "GNUMACS will never work on that dink machine." Probably derived from mainstream 'dinky', which isn't sufficiently pejorative. See **macdink**.

dinosaur n. 1. Any hardware requiring raised flooring and special power. Used especially of old minis and mainframes, in contrast with newer microprocessor-based machines. In a famous quote from the 1988 UNIX EXPO, Bill Joy compared the liquid-cooled mainframe in the massive IBM display with a grazing dinosaur "with a truck outside pumping its bodily fluids through it". IBM was not amused. Compare **big iron**; see also **mainframe**. 2. [IBM] A very conservative user; a **zipperhead**.

dinosaur pen n. A traditional **mainframe** computer room complete with raised flooring, special power, its own ultra-heavy-duty air conditioning, and a side order of Halon fire extinguishers. See **boa**.

dinosaurs mating n. Said to occur when yet another **big iron** merger or buyout occurs; reflects a perception by hackers that these signal another stage in the long, slow dying of the **mainframe** industry. In its glory days of the 1960s, it was 'IBM and the Seven Dwarves': Burroughs, Control Data, General Electric, Honeywell, NCR, RCA, and Univac. RCA and GE sold out early, and it was 'IBM and the Bunch' (Burroughs, Univac, NCR, Control Data, and Honeywell) for a while. Honeywell was bought out by Bull; Burroughs merged with Univac to form Unisys (in 1984 — this was when the phrase *dinosaurs mating* was coined); and in 1991 AT&T absorbed NCR. More such earth-shaking unions of doomed giants seem inevitable.

dirtball [XEROX PARC] n. A small, perhaps struggling outsider; not in the major or even the minor leagues. For example, "Xerox is not a dirtball company".

[Outsiders often observe in the PARC culture an institutional arrogance which usage of this term exemplifies. The brilliance and scope of PARC's contributions to computer science have been such that this superior attitude is not much resented. — ESR]

dirty power n. Electrical mains voltage that is unfriendly to the delicate innards of computers. Spikes, **drop-outs**, average voltage significantly higher or lower than nominal, or just plain noise can all cause problems of varying subtlety and severity (these are collectively known as **power hit**s).

disclaimer n. [USENET] n. Statement ritually appended to many USENET postings (sometimes automatically, by the posting software) reiterating the fact (which should be obvious, but is easily forgotten) that the article reflects its author's opinions and not necessarily those of the organization running the machine through which the article entered the network.

Discordianism */dis-kor´di-ən-ism/* n. The veneration of **Eris**, a.k.a. Discordia; widely popular among hackers. Discordianism was popularized by Robert Shea and Robert Anton Wilson's novel *Illuminatus!* as a sort of self-subverting Dada-Zen for Westerners — it should on no account be taken seriously but is far more serious than most jokes. Consider, for example, the Fifth Commandment of the Pentabarf, from *Principia Discordia*: "A Discordian is Prohibited of Believing What he Reads." Discordianism is usually connected with an elaborate conspiracy theory/joke involving millennia-long warfare between the anarcho-surrealist partisans of Eris and a malevolent, authoritarian secret society called the Illuminati. See Religion under Appendix B, **Church of the SubGenius**, and **ha ha only serious**.

disk farm n. (also **laundromat**) A large room or rooms filled with disk drives (esp. **washing machine**s).

display hack n. A program with the same approximate purpose as a kaleidoscope: to make pretty pictures. Famous display hacks include **munching squares**, **smoking clover**, the BSD UNIX `rain(6)` program, `worms(6)` on miscellaneous UNIXes, and the **X** `kaleid(1)` program. Display hacks can also be implemented without programming by creating text files containing numerous escape sequences for interpretation by a video terminal; one notable example displayed, on any VT100, a Christmas tree with twinkling lights and a toy train circling its base. The **hack value** of a display hack is proportional to the esthetic value of the images times the cleverness of the algorithm divided by the size of the code. Syn. **psychedelicware**.

Dissociated Press [play on 'Associated Press'; perhaps inspired by a reference in the 1949 Bugs Bunny cartoon "What's Up, Doc?"] n. An algorithm for transforming any text into potentially humorous garbage even more efficiently than by passing it through a **marketroid**. The algorithm starts by printing any N consecutive words (or letters) in the text. Then at every step it searches for any random occurrence in the original text of the last N words (or letters) already printed and then prints the next word or letter. **EMACS** has a handy command for this. Here is a short example of word-based Dissociated Press applied to an earlier version of this Jargon File:

> wart: n. A small, crocky **feature** that sticks out of an array (C has no checks for this). This is relatively benign and easy to spot if the phrase is bent so as to be not worth paying attention to the medium in question.

Here is a short example of letter-based Dissociated Press applied to the same source:

> window sysIWYG: n. A bit was named aften */bee´tə/* prefer to use the other guy's re, especially in every cast a chuckle on neithout getting into useful informash speech makes removing a featuring a move or usage actual abstractionsidered interj. Indeed spectace logic or problem!

A hackish idle pastime is to apply letter-based Dissociated Press to a random body of text and **vgrep** the output in hopes of finding an interesting new word. (In the preceding example, 'window sysIWYG' and 'informash' show some promise.) Iterated applications of Dissociated Press usually yield better results. Similar techniques called *travesty generators* have been employed with considerable satirical effect to the utterances of USENET flamers; see **pseudo**.

distribution n. 1. A software source tree packaged for distribution; but see **kit**. 2. A vague term encompassing mailing lists and USENET newsgroups (but not **BBS fora**); any topic-oriented message channel with multiple recipients. 3. An information-space domain (usually loosely correlated with geography) to which propagation of a USENET message is restricted; a much-underutilized feature.

disusered adj. [USENET] Said of a person whose account on a computer has been removed, esp. for cause rather than through normal attrition. "He got disusered when they found out he'd been cracking through the school's Internet access." The verbal form *disuser* is live but less common. Both usages probably derive from the DISUSER account status flag on VMS; setting it disables the account.

do protocol [from network protocol programming] vi. To perform an interaction with somebody or something that follows a clearly defined procedure. For example, "Let's do protocol with the check" at a restaurant means to ask for the check, calculate the tip and everybody's share, collect money from everybody, generate change as necessary, and pay the bill. See **protocol**.

doc */dok/* n. Common spoken and written shorthand for 'documentation'. Often used in the plural *docs* and in the construction *doc file* (i.e., documentation available on-line).

doco */do´koh/* [orig. in-house jargon at Symbolics] n. A documentation writer. See also **devo** and **mango**.

documentation n. The multiple kilograms of macerated, pounded, steamed, bleached, and pressed trees that accompany most modern software or hardware products (see also **tree-killer**). Hackers seldom read paper documentation and (too) often resist writing it; they prefer theirs to be terse and on-line. A common comment on this predilection is "You can't **grep** dead trees". See **drool-proof paper**, **verbiage**, **treeware**.

dodgy adj. Syn. with **flaky**. Preferred outside the U.S.

dogcow */dog´kow/* n. See **Moof**.

dogwash */dog´wosh/* [From a quip in the 'urgency' field of a very optional software change request, ca. 1982. It was something like "Urgency: Wash your dog first".] 1. n. A project of minimal priority, undertaken as an escape from more serious work. 2. v. To engage in such a project. Many games and much **freeware** get written this way.

domainist */doh-mayn´ist/* adj. 1. Said of an **Internet address** (as opposed to a **bang path**) because the part to the right of the '@' specifies a nested series of *domains*; for example, *esr@snark.thyrsus.com* specifies the machine called *snark* in the subdomain called *thyrsus* within the top-level domain called *com*. See also **big-endian**, sense 2. 2. Said of a site, mailer, or routing program which knows how to handle domainist addresses. 3. Said of a person (esp. a site admin) who prefers domain addressing, supports a domainist mailer, or proselytizes for domainist addressing and disdains **bang path**s. This term is now (1993) semi-obsolete, as most sites have converted.

Don't do that, then! [from an old doctor's office joke about a patient with a trivial complaint] Stock response to a user complaint. "When I type control-S, the whole system comes to a halt for thirty seconds." "Don't do that, then!" (or "So don't do that!"). Compare **RTFM**.

dongle */dong´gl/* n. 1. A security or **copy protection** device for commercial microcomputer programs consisting of a serialized EPROM and some drivers in a D-25 connector shell, which must be connected to an I/O port of the computer while the program is run. Programs that use a dongle query the port at startup and at programmed intervals thereafter, and terminate if it does not respond with the dongle's programmed validation code. Thus, users can make as many copies of the program as they want but must pay for each dongle. The idea was clever, but it was initially a failure, as users disliked tying up a serial port this way. Most dongles on the market today (1991) will pass data through the port and monitor for **magic** codes (and combinations of status lines) with minimal if any interference with devices further down the line — this innovation was necessary to allow daisy-chained dongles for multiple pieces of software. The devices are still not widely used, as the industry has moved away from copy-protection schemes in general. 2. By extension, any physical electronic key or transferable ID required for a program to function. Common variations on this theme have used parallel or even joystick ports. See **dongle-disk**.

[Note: in early 1992, advertising copy from Rainbow Technologies (a manufacturer of dongles) included a claim that the word derived from "Don Gall", allegedly the inventor of the device. The company's receptionist will cheerfully tell you that the story is a myth invented for the ad copy. Nevertheless, I expect it to haunt my life as a lexicographer for at least the next ten years. — ESR]

dongle-disk */don´gl disk/* n. A special floppy disk that is required in order to perform some task. Some contain special coding that allows an application to identify it uniquely, others *are* special code that does something that normally-resident programs don't or can't. (For example, AT&T's "Unix PC" would only come up in **root mode** with a special boot disk.) Also called a *key disk.* See **dongle**.

donuts n.obs. A collective noun for any set of memory bits. This usage is extremely archaic and may no longer be live jargon; it dates from the days of ferrite-**core** memories in which each bit was implemented by a doughnut-shaped magnetic flip-flop.

doorstop n. Used to describe equipment that is non-functional and halfway expected to remain so, especially obsolete equipment kept around for political reasons or ostensibly as a backup. "When we get another Wyse-50 in here, that ADM 3 will turn into a doorstop." Compare **boat anchor**.

dot file [UNIX] n. A file that is not visible by default to normal directory-browsing tools (on UNIX, files named with a leading dot are, by convention, not normally presented in directory listings). Many programs define one or more dot files in which startup or configuration information may be optionally recorded; a user can customize the program's behavior by creating the appropriate file in the current or home directory. (Therefore, dot files tend to **creep** — with every nontrivial application program defining at least one, a user's home directory can be filled with scores of dot files, of course without the user's really being aware of it.) See also **profile** (sense 1), **rc file**.

double bucky adj. Using both the CTRL and META keys. "The command to burn all LEDs is double bucky F."

This term originated on the Stanford extended-ASCII keyboard, and was later taken up by users of the **space-cadet keyboard** at MIT. A typical MIT comment was that the Stanford **bucky bits** (control and meta shifting keys) were nice, but there weren't enough of them; you could type only 512 different characters on a Stanford keyboard. An obvious way to address this was simply to add more shifting keys, and this was eventually done; but a keyboard with that many shifting keys is hard on touch-typists, who don't like to move their hands away from the home position on the keyboard. It was half-seriously suggested that the extra shifting keys be implemented as pedals; typing on such a keyboard would be very much like playing a full pipe organ. This idea is mentioned in a parody of a very fine song by Jeffrey

Moss called "Rubber Duckie", which was published in *The Sesame Street Songbook* (Simon and Schuster 1971, ISBN 0-671-21036-X). These lyrics were written on May 27, 1978, in celebration of the Stanford keyboard:

Double Bucky

Double bucky, you're the one!
You make my keyboard lots of fun.
  Double bucky, an additional bit or two:
(Vo-vo-de-o!)
Control and meta, side by side,
Augmented ASCII, nine bits wide!
  Double bucky! Half a thousand glyphs, plus a few!
Oh,
I sure wish that I
Had a couple of
  Bits more!
Perhaps a
Set of pedals to
Make the number of
  Bits four:
Double double bucky!
Double bucky, left and right
OR'd together, outta sight!
  Double bucky, I'd like a whole word of
  Double bucky, I'm happy I heard of
  Double bucky, I'd like a whole word of you!

— The Great Quux (with apologies to Jeffrey Moss)

[This, by the way, is an excellent example of computer **filk** — ESR] See also **meta bit**, **cokebottle**, and **quadruple bucky**.

double DECkers n. Used to describe married couples in which both partners work for Digital Equipment Corporation.

doubled sig [USENET] n. A **sig block** that has been included twice in a **USENET** article or, less commonly, in an electronic mail message. An article or message with a doubled sig can be caused by improperly configured software. More often, however, it reveals the author's lack of experience in electronic communication. See **BIFF**, **pseudo**.

down 1. adj. Not operating. "The up escalator is down" is considered a humorous thing to say, and "The elevator is down" always means "The elevator isn't working" and never refers to what floor the elevator is on. With respect to computers, this term has passed into the mainstream; the extension to other kinds of machine is still hackish. 2. *go down* vi. To stop functioning; usually said of the **system**. The message from the **console** that every hacker hates to hear from the operator is "System going down in 5 minutes". 3. *take down, bring down* vt. To deactivate purposely, usually for repair work or **PM**. "I'm taking the system down to work on that bug in the tape drive." Occasionally one hears the word *down* by itself used as a verb in this vt. sense. See **crash**; oppose **up**.

download vt. To transfer data or (esp.) code from a larger 'host' system (esp. a **mainframe**) over a digital comm link to a smaller 'client' system, esp. a microcomputer or specialized peripheral. Oppose **upload**.

However, note that ground-to-space communications has its own usage rule for this term. Space-to-earth transmission is always 'down' and the reverse 'up' regardless of the relative size of the computers involved. So far the in-space machines have invariably been smaller; thus the upload/download distinction has been reversed from its usual sense.

DP */D-P/* n. 1. Data Processing. Listed here because, according to hackers, use of the term marks one immediately as a **suit**. See **DPer**. 2. Common abbrev for **Dissociated Press**.

DPB */də-pib´/* [from the PDP-10 instruction set] vt. To plop something down in the middle. Usage: silly. "DPB yourself into that couch there." The connotation would be that the couch is full except for one slot just big enough for one last person to sit in. DPB means 'DePosit Byte', and was the name of a PDP-10 instruction that inserts some bits into the middle of some other bits. Hackish usage has been kept alive by the Common LISP function of the same name.

DPer */dee-pee-er/* n. Data Processor. Hackers are absolutely amazed that **suits** use this term self-referentially. *Computers* process data, not people! See **DP**.

dragon n. [MIT] A program similar to a **daemon**, except that it is not invoked at all, but is instead used by the system to perform various secondary tasks. A typical example would be an accounting program, which keeps track of who is logged in, accumulates load-average statistics, etc. Under ITS, many terminals displayed a list of people logged in, where they were, what they were running, etc., along with some random picture (such as a unicorn, Snoopy, or the Enterprise), which was generated by the 'name dragon'. Usage: rare outside MIT — under UNIX and most other OSes this would be called a *background demon* or **daemon**. The best-known UNIX example of a dragon is `cron(1)`. At SAIL, they called this sort of thing a *phantom*.

Dragon Book n. The classic text *Compilers: Principles, Techniques and Tools*, by Alfred V. Aho, Ravi Sethi, and Jeffrey D. Ullman (Addison-Wesley 1986; ISBN 0-201-10088-6), so called because of the cover design featuring a dragon labeled 'complexity of compiler design' and a knight bearing the lance 'LALR parser generator' among his other trappings. This one is more specifically known as the 'Red Dragon Book' (1986); an earlier edition, sans Sethi and titled *Principles Of Compiler Design* (Alfred V. Aho and Jeffrey D. Ullman; Addison-Wesley, 1977; ISBN 0-201-00022-9), was the 'Green Dragon Book' (1977). (Also *New Dragon Book, Old Dragon Book.*) The horsed knight and the Green Dragon were warily eying each other at a distance; now the knight is typing (wearing gauntlets!) at a terminal showing a video-game representation of the Red Dragon's head while the rest of the beast extends back in normal space. See also **book titles**.

drain [IBM] v. Syn. for **flush** (sense 2). Has a connotation of finality about it; one speaks of draining a device before taking it offline.

dread high-bit disease n. A condition endemic to PRIME (a.k.a. PR1ME) minicomputers that results in all the characters having their high (0x80) bit ON rather than OFF. This of course makes transporting files to other systems much more difficult, not to mention talking to true 8-bit devices. Folklore had it that PRIME adopted the reversed-8-bit convention in order to save 25 cents per serial line per machine; PRIME old-timers, on the other hand, claim they inherited the disease from Honeywell via customer NASA's compatibility requirements and struggled heroically to cure it. Whoever was responsible, this probably qualifies as one of the most **cretinous** design tradeoffs ever made. See **meta bit**. A few other machines have exhibited similar brain damage.

DRECNET */drek´net/* [from Yiddish/German 'dreck', meaning filth] n. Deliberate distortion of DECNET, a networking protocol used in the **VMS** community. So called because DEC helped write the Ethernet specification and then (either stupidly or as a malignant customer-control tactic) violated that spec in the design of DRECNET in a way that made it incompatible. See also **connector conspiracy**.

driver n. 1. The **main loop** of an event-processing program; the code that gets commands and dispatches them for execution. 2. [techspeak] In *device driver*, code designed to handle a particular peripheral device such as a magnetic disk or tape unit. 3. In the TeX world and the computerized typesetting world in general, a program that translates some device-independent or other common format to something a real device can actually understand.

droid [from *android*, SF terminology for a humanoid robot of essentially biological (as opposed to mechanical/electronic) construction] n. A person (esp. a low-level bureaucrat or service-business employee) exhibiting most of the following characteristics: (a) naive trust in the wisdom of the parent organization or 'the system'; (b) a blind-faith propensity to believe obvious nonsense emitted by authority figures (or computers!); (c) a rule-governed mentality, one unwilling or unable to look beyond the 'letter of the law' in exceptional situations; (d) a paralyzing fear of official reprimand or worse if Procedures are not followed No Matter What; and (e) no interest in doing anything above or beyond the call of a very narrowly-interpreted duty, or in particular in fixing that which is broken; an "It's not my job, man" attitude.

Typical droid positions include supermarket checkout assistant and bank clerk; the syndrome is also endemic in low-level government employees. The implication is that the rules and official procedures constitute software that the droid is executing; problems arise when the software has not been properly debugged. The term *droid mentality* is also used to describe the mindset behind this behavior. Compare **suit**, **marketroid**; see **-oid**.

drool-proof paper n. Documentation that has been obsessively **dumbed down**, to the point where only a **cretin** could bear to read it, is said to have succumbed to the 'drool-proof paper syndrome' or to have been 'written on drool-proof paper'. For example, this is an actual quote from Apple's LaserWriter manual: "Do not expose your LaserWriter to open fire or flame."

drop on the floor vt. To react to an error condition by silently discarding messages or other valuable data. "The gateway ran out of memory, so it just started dropping packets on the floor." Also frequently used of faulty mail and netnews relay sites that lose messages. See also **black hole**, **bit bucket**.

drop-ins [prob. by analogy with **drop-outs**] n. Spurious characters appearing on a terminal or console as a result of line noise or a system malfunction of some sort. Esp. used when these are interspersed with one's own typed input. Compare **drop-outs**, sense 2.

drop-outs n. 1. A variety of *power glitch* (see **glitch**); momentary 0 voltage on the electrical mains. 2. Missing characters in typed input due to software malfunction or system saturation (one cause of such behavior under UNIX when a bad connection to a modem swamps the processor with spurious character interrupts; see **screaming tty**). 3. Mental glitches; used as a way of describing those occasions when the mind just seems to shut down for a couple of beats. See **glitch, fried**.

drugged adj. (also *on drugs*) 1. Conspicuously stupid, heading toward **brain-damaged**. Often accompanied by a pantomime of toking a joint (but see Appendix B). 2. Of hardware, very slow relative to normal performance.

drum adj, n. Ancient techspeak term referring to slow, cylindrical magnetic media that were once state-of-the-art storage devices. Under BSD UNIX the disk partition used for swapping is still called `/dev/drum`; this has led to considerable humor and not a few straight-faced but utterly bogus 'explanations' getting foisted on **newbies**. See also "The Story of Mel, a Real Programmer" in Appendix A.

drunk mouse syndrome (also *mouse on drugs*) n. A malady exhibited by the mouse pointing device of some computers. The typical symptom is for the mouse cursor on the screen to move in random directions and not in sync with the motion of the actual mouse. Can usually be corrected by unplugging the mouse and plugging it back again. Another recommended fix for optical mice is to rotate your mouse pad 90 degrees.

At Xerox PARC in the 1970s, most people kept a can of copier cleaner (isopropyl alcohol) at their desks. When the steel ball on the mouse had picked up enough **cruft** to be unreliable, the mouse was doused in cleaner, which restored it for a while. However, this operation left a fine residue that accelerated the accumulation of cruft, so the dousings became more and more frequent. Finally, the mouse was declared 'alcoholic' and sent to the clinic to be dried out in a CFC ultrasonic bath.

Duff's device n. The most dramatic use yet seen of **fall through** in C, invented by Tom Duff when he was at Lucasfilm. Trying to **bum** all the

A really serious case of **drop-outs**.

The next cartoon in the Crunchly saga is 05-21-73, page 171.

instructions he could out of an inner loop that copied data serially onto an output port, he decided to **unroll** it. He then realized that the unrolled version could be implemented by *interlacing* the structures of a switch and a loop:

```
   register n = (count + 7) / 8;       /* count > 0 as-
sumed */

   switch (count % 8)
   {
   case 0:         do { *to = *from++;

   case 7:               *to = *from++;
   case 6:               *to = *from++;
   case 5:               *to = *from++;
   case 4:               *to = *from++;
   case 3:               *to = *from++;
   case 2:               *to = *from++;
   case 1:               *to = *from++;
                       } while (--n > 0);
   }
```

Shocking though it appears to all who encounter it for the first time, the device is actually perfectly valid, legal C. C's default **fall through** in case statements has long been its most controversial single feature; Duff observed that "This code forms some sort of argument in that debate, but I'm not sure whether it's for or against."

[For maximal obscurity, the outermost pair of braces above could be actually be removed — GLS]

dumb terminal n. A terminal that is one step above a **glass tty**, having a minimally addressable cursor but no on-screen editing or other features normally supported by a **smart terminal**. Once upon a time, when glass ttys were common and addressable cursors were something special, what is now called a dumb terminal could pass for a smart terminal.

dumbass attack */duhm´as ə-tak´/* [Purdue] n. Notional cause of a novice's mistake made by the experienced, especially one made while running as **root** under UNIX, e.g., typing `rm -r *` or `mkfs` on a mounted file system. Compare **adger**.

dumbed down adj. Simplified, with a strong connotation of *over*simplified. Often, a **marketroid** will insist that the interfaces and documentation of software be dumbed down after the designer has burned untold gallons of midnight oil making it smart. This creates friction. See **user-friendly**.

dump n. 1. An undigested and voluminous mass of information about a problem or the state of a system, especially one routed to the slowest available output device (compare **core dump**), and most especially one consisting of hex or octal **runes** describing the byte-by-byte state of memory, mass storage, or some file. In **elder days**, debugging was generally done by *groveling over* a dump (see **grovel**); increasing use of high-level languages and interactive debuggers has made such tedium uncommon, and the term *dump* now has a faintly archaic flavor. 2. A backup. This usage is typical only at large timesharing installations.

dumpster diving */dump´-ster di:´-ving/* n. 1. The practice of sifting refuse from an office or technical installation to extract confidential data, especially security-compromising information ('dumpster' is an Americanism for what is elsewhere called a *skip*). Back in AT&T's monopoly days, before paper shredders became common office equipment, phone phreaks (see **phreaking**) used to organize regular dumpster runs against phone company plants and offices. Discarded and damaged copies of AT&T internal manuals taught them much. The technique is still rumored to be a favorite of crackers operating against careless targets. 2. The practice of raiding the dumpsters behind buildings where producers and/or consumers of high-tech equipment are located, with the expectation (usually justified) of finding discarded but still-valuable equipment to be nursed back to health in some hacker's den. Experienced dumpster-divers not infrequently accumulate basements full of moldering (but still potentially useful) **cruft**.

dup killer */d[y]oop kill´r/* [FidoNet] n. Software that is supposed to detect and delete duplicates of a message that may have reached the FidoNet system via different routes.

dup loop */d[y]oop loop/* (also *dupe loop*) [FidoNet] n. An infinite stream of duplicated, near-identical messages on a FidoNet echo, the only difference being unique or mangled identification information applied by a faulty or incorrectly configured system or network gateway, thus rendering **dup killer**s ineffective. If such a duplicate message eventually reaches a system through which it has already passed (with the original identification information), all systems passed on the way back to that system are said to be involved in a **dup loop**.

dusty deck n. Old software (especially applications) which one is obliged to remain compatible with, or to maintain (**DP** types call this *legacy code*, a term hackers consider smarmy and excessively reverent). The term implies that the software in question is a holdover from card-punch days. Used esp. when referring to old scientific and **number-crunching** software, much of which was written in FORTRAN and very poorly documented but is believed to be too expensive to replace. See **fossil**; compare **crawling horror**.

DWIM */dwim/* [acronym, 'Do What I Mean'] 1. adj. Able to guess, sometimes even correctly, the result intended when bogus input was provided. 2. n.,obs. The BBNLISP/INTERLISP function that attempted to accomplish this feat by correcting many of the more common errors. See **hairy**. 3. Occasionally, an interjection hurled at a balky computer, esp. when one senses one might be tripping over legalisms (see **legalese**).

Warren Teitelman originally wrote DWIM to fix his typos and spelling errors, so it was somewhat idiosyncratic to his style, and would often make hash of anyone else's typos if they were stylistically different. Some victims of DWIM thus claimed that the acronym stood for 'Damn Warren's Infernal Machine!'.

In one notorious incident, Warren added a DWIM feature to the command interpreter used at Xerox PARC. One day another hacker there typed `delete *$` to free up some disk space. (The editor there named backup files by appending `$` to the original file name, so he was trying to delete any backup files left over from old editing sessions.) It happened that there weren't any editor backup files, so DWIM helpfully reported `*$ not found, assuming you meant 'delete *'`. It then started to delete all the files on the disk! The hacker managed to stop it with a **Vulcan nerve pinch** after only a half dozen or so files were lost.

The disgruntled victim later said he had been sorely tempted to go to Warren's office, tie Warren down in his chair in front of his workstation, and then type `delete *$` twice.

DWIM is often suggested in jest as a desired feature for a complex program; it is also occasionally described as the single instruction the ideal computer would have. Back when proofs of program correctness were in vogue, there were also jokes about *DWIMC* (Do What I Mean, Correctly). A related term, more often seen as a verb, is DTRT (Do The Right Thing); see **Right Thing**.

dynner */din´r/* 32 bits, by analogy with **nybble** and **byte**. Usage: rare and extremely silly. See also **playte, tayste, crumb**.

= E =

earthquake [IBM] n. The ultimate real-world shock test for computer hardware. Hackish sources at IBM deny the rumor that the Bay Area quake of 1989 was initiated by the company to test quality-assurance procedures at its California plants.

Easter egg [from the custom of the Easter Egg hunt observed in the U.S. and many parts of Europe] n. 1. A message hidden in the object code of a program as a joke, intended to be found by persons disassembling or browsing the code. 2. A message, graphic, or sound effect emitted by a program (or, on a PC, the BIOS ROM) in response to some undocumented set of commands or keystrokes, intended as a joke or to display program credits. One well-known early Easter egg found in a couple of OSes caused them to respond to the command `make love` with `not war?`. Many personal computers have much more elaborate eggs hidden in ROM, including lists of the developers' names, political exhortations, snatches of music, and (in one case) graphics images of the entire development team.

Easter egging [IBM] n. The act of replacing unrelated components more or less at random in hopes that a malfunction will go away. Hackers consider this the normal operating mode of **field circus** techs and do not love them for it. See also the jokes under **field circus**. Compare **shotgun debugging**.

eat flaming death imp. A construction popularized among hackers by the infamous **CPU Wars** comic; supposedly derive from a famously turgid line in a WWII-era anti-Nazi propaganda comic that ran "Eat flaming death, non-Aryan mongrels!" or something of the sort (however, it is also reported that the Firesign Theater's 1975 album "In The Next World, You're On Your Own" included the phrase "Eat flaming death, fascist media pigs"; this may have been an influence). Used in humorously overblown expressions of hostility. "Eat flaming death, **EBCDIC** users!"

EBCDIC */eb´sə-dik/*, */eb´see`dik/*, or */eb´kə-dik/* [abbreviation, Extended Binary Coded Decimal Interchange Code] n. An alleged character set used on IBM **dinosaurs**. It exists in at least six mutually incompatible versions, all

IPM tells us to **eat flaming death**

featuring such delights as non-contiguous letter sequences and the absence of several ASCII punctuation characters fairly important for modern computer languages (exactly which characters are absent varies according to which version of EBCDIC you're looking at). IBM adapted EBCDIC from **punched card** code in the early 1960s and promulgated it as a customer-control tactic (see **connector conspiracy**), spurning the already established ASCII standard. Today, IBM claims to be an open-systems company, but IBM's own description of the EBCDIC variants and how to convert between them is still internally classified top-secret, burn-before-reading. Hackers blanch at the very *name* of EBCDIC and consider it a manifestation of purest **evil**. See also **fear and loathing**.

echo [FidoNet] n. A **topic group** on **FidoNet**'s echomail system. Compare **newsgroup**.

eighty-column mind [IBM] n. The sort said to be possessed by persons for whom the transition from **punched card** to tape was traumatic (nobody has dared tell them about disks yet). It is said that these people, including (according to an old joke) the founder of IBM, will be buried 'face down, 9-edge first' (the 9-edge being the bottom of the card). This directive is inscribed on IBM's 1402 and 1622 card readers and is referenced in a famous bit of doggerel called "The Last Bug", the climactic lines of which are as follows:

> He died at the console
> Of hunger and thirst.
> Next day he was buried,
> Face down, 9-edge first.

The eighty-column mind is thought by most hackers to dominate IBM's customer base and its thinking. See **IBM**, **fear and loathing**, **card walloper**.

El Camino Bignum */el′ kə-mee′noh big′nuhm/* n. The road mundanely called El Camino Real, a road through the San Francisco peninsula that originally extended all the way down to Mexico City and many portions of which are still intact. Navigation on the San Francisco peninsula is usually done relative to El Camino Real, which defines **logical** north and south even though it isn't really north-south many places. El Camino Real runs right past Stanford University and so is familiar to hackers.

The Spanish word 'real' (which has two syllables: */ray-ol′/*) means 'royal'; El Camino Real is 'the royal road'. In the FORTRAN language, a 'real' quantity is a number typically precise to seven significant digits, and a 'double precision' quantity is a larger floating-point number, precise to perhaps fourteen significant digits (other languages have similar 'real' types).

When a hacker from MIT visited Stanford in 1976, he remarked what a long road El Camino Real was. Making a pun on 'real', he started calling it 'El Camino Double Precision' — but when the hacker was told that the road was hundreds of miles long, he renamed it 'El Camino Bignum', and that name has stuck. (See **bignum**.)

elder days n. The heroic age of hackerdom (roughly, pre-1980); the era of the **PDP-10**, **TECO**, **ITS**, and the ARPANET. This term has been rather consciously adopted from J. R. R. Tolkien's fantasy epic *The Lord of the Rings*. Compare **Iron Age**; see also **elvish** and **Great Worm, the**.

elegant [from mathematical usage] adj. Combining simplicity, power, and a certain ineffable grace of design. Higher praise than 'clever', 'winning', or even **cuspy**.

The French aviator, adventurer, and author Antoine de Saint-Exupéry, probably best known for his classic children's book *The Little Prince*, was also an aircraft designer. He gave us perhaps the best definition of engineering elegance when he said "A designer knows he has achieved perfection not when there is nothing left to add, but when there is nothing left to take away."

elephantine adj. Used of programs or systems that are both conspicuous **hogs** (owing perhaps to poor design founded on **brute force and ignorance**) and exceedingly **hairy** in source form. An elephantine program may be functional and even friendly, but (as in the old joke about being in bed with an elephant) it's tough to have around all the same (and, like a pachyderm, difficult to maintain). In extreme cases, hackers have been known to make trumpeting sounds or perform expressive proboscatory mime at the mention of the offending program. Usage: semi-humorous. Compare 'has the elephant nature' and the somewhat more pejorative **monstrosity**. See also **second-system effect** and **baroque**.

elevator controller n. An archetypal dumb embedded-systems application, like **toaster** (which superseded it). During one period (1983–84) in the deliberations of ANSI X3J11 (the C standardization committee) this was the canonical example of a really stupid, memory-limited computation environment. "You can't require `printf(3)` to be part of the default runtime library — what if you're targeting an elevator controller?" Elevator controllers became important rhetorical weapons on both sides of several **holy wars**.

ELIZA effect */ə-li:´zə ə-fekt´/* [AI community] n. The tendency of humans to attach associations to terms from prior experience. For example, there is nothing magic about the symbol '+' that makes it well-suited to indicate addition; it's just that people associate it with addition. Using '+' or 'plus' to mean addition in a computer language is taking advantage of the ELIZA effect.

This term comes from the famous ELIZA program by Joseph Weizenbaum, which simulated a Rogerian psychoanalyst by rephrasing many of the patient's statements as questions and posing them to the patient. It worked by simple pattern recognition and substitution of key words into canned phrases. It was so convincing, however, that there are many anecdotes about people becoming very emotionally caught up in dealing with ELIZA. All this was due to people's tendency to attach to words meanings which the computer never put there. The ELIZA effect is a **Good Thing** when writing a programming language, but it can blind you to serious shortcomings when analyzing an Artificial Intelligence system. Compare **ad-hockery**; see also **AI-complete**.

elvish n. 1. The Tengwar of Feanor, a table of letterforms resembling the beautiful Celtic half-uncial hand of the *Book of Kells.* Invented and described by J. R. R. Tolkien in *The Lord of The Rings* as an orthography for his fictional 'elvish' languages, this system (which is both visually and phonetically **elegant**) has long fascinated hackers (who tend to be intrigued by artificial languages in general). It is traditional for graphics printers, plotters, window systems, and the like to support a Feanorian typeface as one of their demo items. See also **elder days**. 2. By extension, any odd or unreadable typeface produced by a graphics device. 3. The typeface mundanely called 'Böcklin', an art-decoish display font.

EMACS */ee´maks/* [from Editing MACroS] n. The ne plus ultra of hacker editors, a programmable text editor with an entire LISP system inside it. It was originally written by Richard Stallman in **TECO** under **ITS** at the MIT AI lab; AI Memo 554 described it as "an advanced, self-documenting, customizable, extensible real-time display editor". It has since been reimplemented any number of times, by various hackers, and versions exist that run under most major operating systems. Perhaps the most widely used version, also written by Stallman and now called "**GNU** EMACS" or **GNUMACS**, runs principally under UNIX. It includes facilities to run compilation subprocesses and send and receive mail; many hackers spend up to 80% of their **tube time** inside it. Other variants include **GOSMACS**, CCA EMACS, UniPress EMACS, Montgomery EMACS, jove, epsilon, and MicroEMACS.

Some EMACS versions running under window managers iconify as an overflowing kitchen sink, perhaps to suggest the one feature the editor does not (yet) include. Indeed, some hackers find EMACS too **heavyweight** and **baroque** for their taste, and expand the name as 'Escape Meta Alt Control Shift' to spoof its heavy reliance on keystrokes decorated with **bucky bits**. Other spoof expansions include 'Eight Megabytes And Constantly Swapping', 'Eventually `malloc()`s All Computer Storage', and 'EMACS Makes A Computer Slow' (see **recursive acronym**). See also **vi**.

email */ee´mayl/* (also written 'e-mail') 1. n. Electronic mail automatically passed through computer networks and/or via modems over common-carrier lines. Contrast **snail-mail**, **paper-net**, **voice-net**. See **network address**. 2. vt. To send electronic mail.

Oddly enough, the word *emailed* is actually listed in the OED; it means "embossed (with a raised pattern) or arranged in a net work". A use from 1480 is given. The word is derived from French *emmailleure*, network.

emoticon */ee-moh´ti-kon/* n. An ASCII glyph used to indicate an emotional state in email or news. Although originally intended mostly as jokes, emoticons (or some other explicit humor indication) are virtually required under certain circumstances in high-volume text-only communication forums such as USENET; the lack of verbal and visual cues can otherwise cause what were intended to be humorous, sarcastic, ironic, or otherwise non-100%-serious comments to be badly misinterpreted (not always even by **newbies**), resulting in arguments and **flame wars**.

Hundreds of emoticons have been proposed, but only a few are in common use. These include:

`:-)`	'smiley face' (for humor, laughter, friendliness, occasionally sarcasm)
`:-(`	'frowney face' (for sadness, anger, or upset)
`;-)`	'half-smiley' (**ha ha only serious**); also known as *semi-smiley* or *winkey face*.
`:-/`	'wry face'

(These may become more comprehensible if you tilt your head sideways, to the left.)

The first two listed are by far the most frequently encountered. Hyphenless forms of them are common on CompuServe, GEnie, and BIX; see also **bixie**. On **USENET**, *smiley* is often used as a generic term synonymous with **emoticon**, as well as specifically for the happy-face emoticon.

It appears that the emoticon was invented by one Scott Fahlman on the CMU **bboard** systems around 1980. He later wrote: "I wish I had saved the original post, or at least recorded the date for posterity, but I had no idea that I was starting something that would soon pollute all the world's communication channels." [GLS confirms that he remembers this original posting].

Note for the **newbie**: Overuse of the smiley is a mark of loserhood! More than one per paragraph is a fairly sure sign that you've gone over the line.

empire n. Any of a family of military simulations derived from a game written by Peter Langston many years ago. Five or six multi-player variants of varying degrees of sophistication exist, and one single-player version implemented for both UNIX and VMS; the latter is even available as MS-DOS freeware. All are notoriously addictive.

engine n. 1. A piece of hardware that encapsulates some function but can't be used without some kind of **front end**. Today we have, especially, *print engine*: the guts of a laser printer. 2. An analogous piece of software; notionally, one that does a lot of noisy crunching, such as a *database engine*.

The hackish senses of *engine* are actually close to its original, pre-Industrial-Revolution sense of a skill, clever device, or instrument (the word is cognate to 'ingenuity'). This sense had not been completely eclipsed by the modern connotation of power-transducing machinery in Charles Babbage's time, which explains why he named the stored-program computer that he designed in 1844 the *Analytical Engine*.

English 1. n.,obs. The source code for a program, which may be in any language, as opposed to the linkable or executable binary produced from it by a compiler. The idea behind the term is that to a real hacker, a program written in his favorite programming language is at least as readable as English. Usage: mostly by old-time hackers, though recognizable in context. 2. The official name of the database language used by the Pick Operating System, actually a sort of crufty, brain-damaged SQL with delusions of grandeur. The name permits **marketroid**s to say "Yes, and you can program our computers in English!" to ignorant **suit**s without quite running afoul of the truth-in-advertising laws.

enhancement n. **Marketroid**-speak for a bug **fix**. This abuse of language is a popular and time-tested way to turn incompetence into increased revenue. A hacker being ironic would instead call the fix a **feature** — or perhaps save some effort by declaring the bug itself to be a feature.

ENQ */enkw/* or */enk/* [from the ASCII mnemonic ENQuire for 0000101] An on-line convention for querying someone's availability. After opening a **talk mode** connection to someone apparently in heavy hack mode, one might type `SYN SYN ENQ?` (the SYNs representing notional synchronization bytes), and expect a return of **ACK** or **NAK** depending on whether or not the person felt interruptible. Compare **ping**, **finger**, and the usage of `FOO?` listed under **talk mode**.

EOF */E-O-F/* [abbreviation, 'End Of File'] n. 1. [techspeak] The **out-of-band** value returned by C's sequential character-input functions (and their equivalents in other environments) when end of file has been reached. This value is −1 under C libraries postdating V6 UNIX, but was originally 0. 2. [UNIX] The keyboard character (usually control-D, the ASCII EOT (End Of Transmission) character) that is mapped by the terminal driver into an end-of-file condition. 3. Used by extension in non-computer contexts when a human is doing something that can be modeled as a sequential read and can't go further. "Yeah, I looked for a list of 360 mnemonics to post as a joke, but I hit EOF pretty fast; all the library had was a **JCL** manual." See also **EOL**.

EOL */E-O-L/* [End Of Line] n. Syn. for **newline**, derived perhaps from the original CDC6600 Pascal. Now rare, but widely recognized and occasionally used for brevity. Used in the example entry under **BNF**. See also **EOF**.

EOU */E-O-U/* n. The mnemonic of a mythical ASCII control character (End Of User) that would make an ASR-33 Teletype explode on receipt. This construction parodies the numerous obscure delimiter and control characters left in ASCII from the days when it was associated more with wire-service teletypes than computers (e.g., FS, GS, RS, US, EM, SUB, ETX, and esp. EOT). It is worth remembering that ASR-33s were big, noisy mechanical beasts with a lot of clattering parts; the notion that one might explode was nowhere near as ridiculous as it might seem to someone sitting in front of a **tube** or flatscreen today.

epoch [UNIX: prob. from astronomical timekeeping] n. The time and date corresponding to 0 in an operating system's clock and timestamp values. Under most UNIX versions the epoch is 00:00:00 GMT, January 1, 1970; under VMS, it's 00:00:00 of November 17, 1858 (base date of the U.S. Naval Observatory's ephemerides). System time is measured in seconds or **tick**s past the epoch. Weird problems may ensue when the clock wraps around (see

wrap around), which is not necessarily a rare event; on systems counting 10 ticks per second, a signed 32-bit count of ticks is good only for 6.8 years. The 1-tick-per-second clock of UNIX is good only until January 18, 2038, assuming at least some software continues to consider it signed and that word lengths don't increase by then. See also **wall time**.

epsilon [see **delta**] 1. n. A small quantity of anything. "The cost is epsilon." 2. adj. Very small, negligible; less than **marginal**. "We can get this feature for epsilon cost." 3. *within epsilon of*: close enough to be indistinguishable for all practical purposes, even closer than being *within delta of*. "That's not what I asked for, but it's within epsilon of what I wanted." Alternatively, it may mean not close enough, but very little is required to get it there: "My program is within epsilon of working."

epsilon squared n. A quantity even smaller than **epsilon**, as small in comparison to epsilon as epsilon is to something normal; completely negligible. If you buy a supercomputer for a million dollars, the cost of the thousand-dollar terminal to go with it is **epsilon**, and the cost of the ten-dollar cable to connect them is epsilon squared. Compare **lost in the underflow**, **lost in the noise**.

era, the Syn. **epoch**. Webster's Unabridged makes these words almost synonymous, but *era* usually connotes a span of time rather than a point in time. The **epoch** usage is recommended.

Eric Conspiracy n. A shadowy group of mustachioed hackers named Eric first pinpointed as a sinister conspiracy by an infamous *talk.bizarre* posting ca. 1986; this was doubtless influenced by the numerous 'Eric' jokes in the Monty Python oeuvre. There do indeed seem to be considerably more mustachioed Erics in hackerdom than the frequency of these three traits can account for unless they are correlated in some arcane way. Well-known examples include Eric Allman (he of the 'Allman style' described under **indent style**) and Erik Fair (co-author of NNTP); your editor has heard from about fifteen others by email, and the organization line 'Eric Conspiracy Secret Laboratories' now emanates regularly from more than one site.

Eris */e´ris/* n. The Greek goddess of Chaos, Discord, Confusion, and Things You Know Not Of; her name was latinized to Discordia and she was worshiped by that name in Rome. Not a very friendly deity in the Classical original, she was reinvented as a more benign personification of creative anarchy starting in 1959 by the adherents of **Discordianism** and has since been a semi-serious subject of veneration in several 'fringe' cultures, including hackerdom. See **Discordianism**, **Church of the SubGenius**.

erotics */ee-ro´tiks/* n. [Helsinki University of Technology, Finland] n. English-language university slang for electronics. Often used by hackers in Helsinki, maybe because good electronics excites them and makes them warm.

error 33 [XEROX PARC] n. 1. Predicating one research effort upon the success of another. 2. Allowing your own research effort to be placed on the critical path of some other project (be it a research effort or not).

evil adj. As used by hackers, implies that some system, program, person, or institution is sufficiently maldesigned as to be not worth the bother of dealing with. Unlike the adjectives in the **cretinous/losing/brain-damaged** series, *evil* does not imply incompetence or bad design, but rather a set of goals or design criteria fatally incompatible with the speaker's. This usage is more an esthetic and engineering judgment than a moral one in the mainstream sense. "We thought about adding a **Blue Glue** interface but decided it was too evil to deal with." "**TECO** is neat, but it can be pretty evil if you're prone to typos." Often pronounced with the first syllable lengthened, as */eeee´vil/*. Compare **evil and rude**.

evil and rude adj. Both **evil** and **rude**, but with the additional connotation that the rudeness was due to malice rather than incompetence. Thus, for example: Microsoft's Windows NT is *evil* because it's a competent implementation of a bad design; it's *rude* because it's gratuitously incompatible with UNIX in places where compatibility would have been as easy and effective to do; but it's *evil and rude* because the incompatiblities are apparently there not to fix design bugs in UNIX but rather to lock hapless customers and developers into the Microsoft way. Hackish *evil and rude* is close to the mainstream sense of 'evil'.

exa- */ek´sə/* [SI] pref. See **quantifiers**.

examining the entrails n. The process of **grovel**ling through a **core dump** or hex image in an attempt to discover the bug that brought a program or system down. The reference is to divination from the entrails of a sacrified animal. Compare **runes**, **incantation**, **black art**, **desk check**.

EXCH */eks´chə/* or */eksch/* vt. To exchange two things, each for the other;

to swap places. If you point to two people sitting down and say "Exch!", you are asking them to trade places. EXCH, meaning EXCHange, was originally the name of a PDP-10 instruction that exchanged the contents of a register and a memory location. Many newer hackers are probably thinking instead of the **PostScript** exchange operator (which is usually written in lowercase).

excl */eks´kl/* n. Abbreviation for 'exclamation point'. See **bang**, **shriek**, **ASCII**.

EXE */eks´ee/* or */eek´see/* or */E-X-E/* n. An executable binary file. Some operating systems (notably MS-DOS, VMS, and TWENEX) use the extension .EXE to mark such files. This usage is also occasionally found among UNIX programmers even though UNIX executables don't have any required suffix.

exec */eg-zek´/* vt., n. 1. [UNIX: from 'execute'] Synonym for **chain**, derives from the `exec(2)` call. 2. [from 'executive'] obs. The command interpreter for an **OS** (see **shell**); term esp. used around mainframes, and prob. derived from UNIVAC's archaic EXEC 2 and EXEC 8 operating systems. 3. At IBM and VM/CMS shops, the equivalent of a shell command file (among VM/CMS users).

The mainstream 'exec' as an abbreviation for (human) executive is *not* used. To a hacker, an 'exec' is a always a program, never a person.

exercise, left as an [from technical books] Used to complete a proof when one doesn't mind a **handwave**, or to avoid one entirely. The complete phrase is: "The proof [or 'the rest'] is left as an exercise for the reader." This comment *has* occasionally been attached to unsolved research problems by authors possessed of either an evil sense of humor or a vast faith in the capabilities of their audiences.

external memory n. A memo pad or written notes. "Hold on while I write that to external memory". The analogy is with store or DRAM versus nonvolatile disk storage on computers.

eyeball search n.,v. To look for something in a mass of code or data with one's own native optical sensors, as opposed to using some sort of pattern matching software like **grep** or any other automated search tool. Also called a **vgrep**; compare **vdiff**, **desk check**.

= F =

face time n. Time spent interacting with somebody face-to-face (as opposed to via electronic links). "Oh, yeah, I spent some face time with him at the last Usenix."

factor n. See **coefficient of X**.

fall over [IBM] vi. Yet another synonym for **crash** or **lose**. 'Fall over hard' equates to **crash and burn**.

fall through v. (n. *fallthrough*, var. *fall-through*) 1. To exit a loop by exhaustion, i.e., by having fulfilled its exit condition rather than via a break or exception condition that exits from the middle of it. This usage appears to be *really* old, dating from the 1940s and 1950s. 2. To fail a test that would have passed control to a subroutine or some other distant portion of code. 3. In C, 'fall-through' occurs when the flow of execution in a switch statement reaches a `case` label other than by jumping there from the switch header, passing a point where one would normally expect to find a `break`. A trivial example:

```
switch (color)
{
case GREEN:
   do_green();
   break;
case PINK:
   do_pink();
   /* FALL THROUGH */
case RED:
   do_red();
   break;
default:
   do_blue();
   break;
}
```

The variant spelling `/* FALL THRU */` is also common.

The effect of the above code is to `do_green()` when color is `GREEN`, `do_red()` when color is `RED`, `do_blue()` on any other color other than `PINK`, and (and this is the important part) `do_pink()` *and then* `do_red()` when color is `PINK`. Fall-through is **considered harmful** by some, though there are contexts (such as the coding of state machines) in which it is natural; it is generally considered good practice to include a comment highlighting the fall-through where one would normally expect a break.

fan n. Without qualification, indicates a fan of science fiction, especially one who goes to **cons** and tends to hang out with other fans. Many hackers are fans, so this term has been imported from fannish slang; however, unlike much fannish slang it is recognized by most non-fannish hackers. Among SF fans the plural is correctly *fen*, but this usage is not automatic to hackers. "Laura reads the stuff occasionally but isn't really a fan."

fandango on core [UNIX/C hackers, from the Mexican dance] n. In C, a wild pointer that runs out of bounds, causing a **core dump**, or corrupts the `malloc(3)` **arena** in such a way as to cause mysterious failures later on, is sometimes said to have 'done a fandango on core'. On low-end personal machines without an MMU, this can corrupt the OS itself, causing massive lossage. Other frenetic dances such as the rhumba, cha-cha, or watusi, may be substituted. See **aliasing bug**, **precedence lossage**, **smash the stack**, **memory leak**, **memory smash**, **overrun screw**, **core**.

FAQ */F-A-Q/* or */fak/* [USENET] n. 1. A Frequently Asked Question. 2. A compendium of accumulated lore, posted periodically to high-volume newsgroups in an attempt to forestall such questions. Some people prefer the term 'FAQ list' or 'FAQL' */fa´kl/*, reserving 'FAQ' for sense 1.

This lexicon itself serves as a good example of a collection of one kind of lore, although it is far too big for a regular FAQ posting. Examples: "What is the proper type of NULL?" and "What's that funny name for the '#' character?" are both Frequently Asked Questions. Several FAQs refer readers to the Jargon File (the on-line version of this lexicon).

FAQ list */F-A-Q list/* or */fak list/* [USENET] n. Syn **FAQ**, sense 2.

FAQL */fa´kl/* n. Syn. **FAQ list**.

faradize */far´ə-di:z/* [US Geological Survey] v. To start any hyper-addictive process or trend, or to continue adding current to such a trend. Telling one user about a new octo-tetris game you compiled would be a faradizing act — in two weeks you might find your entire department playing the faradic game.

farkled */far´kld/* [DeVry Institute of Technology, Atlanta] adj. Syn. **hosed**.

Poss. owes something to Yiddish 'farblondjet' and/or the 'Farkle Family' skits on Saturday Nite Live.

farming [Adelaide University, Australia] n. What the heads of a disk drive are said to do when they plow little furrows in the magnetic media. Associated with a **crash**. Typically used as follows: "Oh no, the machine has just crashed; I hope the hard drive hasn't gone **farming** again."

fascist adj. 1. Said of a computer system with excessive or annoying security barriers, usage limits, or access policies. The implication is that said policies are preventing hackers from getting interesting work done. The variant *fascistic* seems to have been preferred at MIT, poss. by analogy with *touristic* (see **tourist**). 2. In the design of languages and other software tools, *the fascist alternative* is the most restrictive and structured way of capturing a particular function; the implication is that this may be desirable in order to simplify the implementation or provide tighter error checking. Compare **bondage-and-discipline language**, although that term is global rather than local.

fat electrons n. Old-time hacker David Cargill's theory on the causation of computer glitches. Your typical electric utility draws its line current out of the big generators with a pair of coil taps located near the top of the dynamo. When the normal tap brushes get dirty, they take them off line to clean them up, and use special auxiliary taps on the *bottom* of the coil. Now, this is a problem, because when they do that they get not ordinary or 'thin' electrons, but the fat'n'sloppy electrons that are heavier and so settle to the bottom of the generator. These flow down ordinary wires just fine, but when they have to turn a sharp corner (as in an integrated-circuit via), they're apt to get stuck. This is what causes computer glitches. [Fascinating. Obviously, fat electrons must gain mass by **bogon** absorption — ESR] Compare **bogon**, **magic smoke**.

faulty adj. Non-functional; buggy. Same denotation as **bletcherous**, **losing**, q.v., but the connotation is much milder.

fd leak */F-D leek/* n. A kind of programming bug analogous to a **core leak**, in which a program fails to close file descriptors ('fd's) after file operations are completed, and thus eventually runs out of them. See **leak**.

fear and loathing [from Hunter S. Thompson] n. A state inspired by the prospect of dealing with certain real-world systems and standards that

Fascist security strikes again.

The next cartoon in the Crunchly saga is 05-28-73, page 58.

are totally **brain-damaged** but ubiquitous — Intel 8086s, or **COBOL**, or **EBCDIC**, or any **IBM** machine except the Rios (a.k.a. the RS/6000). "Ack! They want PCs to be able to talk to the AI machine. Fear and loathing time!"

feature n. 1. A good property or behavior (as of a program). Whether it was intended or not is immaterial. 2. An intended property or behavior (as of a program). Whether it is good or not is immaterial (but if bad, it is also a **misfeature**). 3. A surprising property or behavior; in particular, one that is purposely inconsistent because it works better that way — such an inconsistency is therefore a **feature** and not a **bug**. This kind of feature is sometimes called a **miswart**; see that entry for a classic example. 4. A property or behavior that is gratuitous or unnecessary, though perhaps also impressive or cute. For example, one feature of Common LISP's `format` function is the ability to print numbers in two different Roman-numeral formats (see **bells, whistles, and gongs**). 5. A property or behavior that was put in to help someone else but that happens to be in your way. 6. A bug that has been documented. To call something a feature sometimes means the author of the program did not consider the particular case, and that the program responded in a way that was unexpected but not strictly incorrect. A standard joke is that a bug can be turned into a **feature** simply by documenting it (then theoretically no one can complain about it because it's in the manual), or even by simply declaring it to be good. "That's not a bug, that's a feature!" is a common catchphrase. See also **feetch feetch**, **creeping featurism**, **wart**, **green lightning**.

The relationship among bugs, features, misfeatures, warts, and miswarts might be clarified by the following hypothetical exchange between two hackers on an airliner:

A: "This seat doesn't recline."

B: "That's not a bug, that's a feature. There is an emergency exit door built around the window behind you, and the route has to be kept clear."

A: "Oh. Then it's a misfeature; they should have increased the spacing between rows here."

B: "Yes. But if they'd increased spacing in only one section it would have been a wart — they would've had to make nonstandard-length ceiling panels to fit over the displaced seats."

A: "A miswart, actually. If they increased spacing throughout they'd lose several rows and a chunk out of the profit margin. So unequal spacing would actually be the Right Thing."

B: "Indeed."

Undocumented feature is a common, allegedly humorous euphemism for a **bug**.

feature creature [poss. fr. slang 'creature feature' for a horror movie] n. 1. One who loves to add features to designs or programs, perhaps at the expense of coherence, concision, or **taste**. 2. Alternately, a mythical being that induces otherwise rational programmers to perpetrate such crocks. See also **feeping creaturism**, **creeping featurism**.

feature key n. The Macintosh key with the cloverleaf graphic on its keytop; sometimes referred to as *flower, pretzel, clover, propeller, beanie* (an apparent reference to the major feature of a propeller beanie), **splat**, or the *command key*. The Mac's equivalent of an **alt** key (and so labeled on on some Mac II keyboards). The proliferation of terms for this creature may illustrate one subtle peril of iconic interfaces.

Many people have been mystified by the cloverleaf-like symbol that appears on the feature key. Its oldest name is 'cross of St. Hannes', but it occurs in pre-Christian Viking art as a decorative motif. Throughout Scandinavia today the road agencies use it to mark sites of historical interest. Apple picked up the symbol from an early Mac developer who happened to be Swedish. Apple documentation gives the translation "interesting feature"!

There is some dispute as to the proper (Swedish) name of this symbol. It technically stands for the word 'sevärdhet' (interesting feature) many of these are old churches. Some Swedes report as an idiom for it the word *kyrka*, cognate to English 'church' and Scots-dialect 'kirk' but pronounced */shir´kə/* in modern Swedish. Others say this is nonsense.

feature shock [from Alvin Toffler's book title *Future Shock*] n. A user's (or programmer's!) confusion when confronted with a package that has too many features and poor introductory material.

featurectomy */fee`chər-ek´tə-mee/* n. The act of removing a feature from a program. Featurectomies come in two flavors, the *righteous* and the *reluctant*. Righteous featurectomies are performed because the remover believes the program would be more elegant without the feature, or there is already an equivalent and better way to achieve the same end. (Doing so is not quite the same thing as removing a **misfeature**.) Reluctant featurectomies are performed to satisfy some external constraint such as code size or execution speed.

feep */feep/* 1. n. The soft electronic 'bell' sound of a display terminal (except for a VT-52); a beep (in fact, the microcomputer world seems to prefer **beep**). 2. vi. To cause the display to make a feep sound. ASR-33s (the original TTYs) do not feep; they have mechanical bells that ring. Alternate forms: **beep**, 'bleep', or just about anything suitably onomatopoeic. (Jeff MacNelly, in his comic strip "Shoe", uses the word 'eep' for sounds made by computer terminals and video games; this is perhaps the closest written approximation yet.) The term 'breedle' was sometimes heard at SAIL, where the terminal bleepers are not particularly soft (they sound more like the musical equivalent of a raspberry or Bronx cheer; for a close approximation, imagine the sound of a Star Trek communicator's beep lasting for five seconds). The 'feeper' on a VT-52 has been compared to the sound of a '52 Chevy stripping its gears. See also **ding**.

feeper */fee´pr/* n. The device in a terminal or workstation (usually a loudspeaker of some kind) that makes the **feep** sound.

feeping creature [from **feeping creaturism**] n. An unnecessary feature; a bit of **chrome** that, in the speaker's judgment, is the camel's nose for a whole horde of new features.

feeping creaturism */fee´ping kree`chər-izm/* n. A deliberate spoonerism for **creeping featurism**, meant to imply that the system or program in question has become a misshapen creature of hacks. This term isn't really well defined, but it sounds so neat that most hackers have said or heard it. It is probably reinforced by an image of terminals prowling about in the dark making their customary noises.

feetch feetch */feech feech/* interj. If someone tells you about some new improvement to a program, you might respond: "Feetch, feetch!" The meaning of this depends critically on vocal inflection. With enthusiasm, it means something like "Boy, that's great! What a great hack!" Grudgingly or with obvious doubt, it means "I don't know; it sounds like just one more unnecessary and complicated thing". With a tone of resignation, it means, "Well, I'd rather keep it simple, but I suppose it has to be done".

fence n. 1. A sequence of one or more distinguished (**out-of-band**) characters (or other data items), used to delimit a piece of data intended to be treated as a unit (the computer-science literature calls this a 'sentinel'). The NUL (ASCII 0000000) character that terminates strings in C is a fence. Hex FF is also (though slightly less frequently) used this way. See **zigamorph**. 2. An extra data value inserted in an array or other data structure in order to allow some normal test on the array's contents also to function as a termination test. For example, a highly optimized routine for finding a value in an array might artificially place a copy of the value to be searched for after the last slot of the array, thus allowing the main search loop to search for the value without having to check at each pass whether the end of the array had been reached. 3. [among users of optimizing compilers] Any technique, usually exploiting knowledge about the compiler, that blocks certain optimizations. Used when explicit mechanisms are not available or are overkill. Typically a hack: "I call a dummy procedure there to force a flush of the optimizer's register-coloring info" can be expressed by the shorter "That's a fence procedure".

fencepost error n. 1. A problem with the discrete equivalent of a boundary condition, often exhibited in programs by iterative loops. From the following problem: "If you build a fence 100 feet long with posts 10 feet apart, how many posts do you need?" (Either 9 or 11 is a better answer than the obvious 10.) For example, suppose you have a long list or array of items, and want to process items m through n; how many items are there? The obvious answer is $n-m$, but that is off by one; the right answer is $n-m+1$. A program that used the 'obvious' formula would have a fencepost error in it. See also **zeroth** and **off-by-one error**, and note that not all off-by-one errors are fencepost errors. The game of Musical Chairs involves a catastrophic off-by-one error where N people try to sit in $N-1$ chairs, but it's not a fencepost error. Fencepost errors come from counting things rather than the spaces between them, or vice versa, or by neglecting to consider whether one should count one or both ends of a row. 2. [rare] An error induced by unexpected regularities in input values, which can (for instance) completely thwart a theoretically efficient binary tree or hash table implementation. (The error here involves the difference between expected and worst case behaviors of an algorithm.)

fepped out */fept owt/* adj. The Symbolics 3600 LISP Machine has a Front-End Processor called a 'FEP' (compare sense 2 of **box**). When the main processor gets **wedged**, the FEP takes control of the keyboard and screen. Such a machine is said to have *fepped out* or *dropped into the fep.*

FidoNet n. A worldwide hobbyist network of personal computers which exchanges mail, discussion groups, and files. Founded in 1984 and originally consisting only of IBM PCs and compatibles, FidoNet now includes such diverse machines as Apple][s, Ataris, Amigas, and UNIX systems. Though it is much younger than **USENET**, FidoNet is already (in early 1991) a significant fraction of USENET's size at some 8000 systems.

field circus [a derogatory pun on 'field service'] n. The field service organization of any hardware manufacturer, but especially DEC. There is an entire genre of jokes about DEC field circus engineers:

> Q: How can you recognize a DEC field circus engineer with a flat tire?
> A: He's changing one tire at a time to see which one is flat.
>
> Q: How can you recognize a DEC field circus engineer who is out of gas?
> A: He's changing one tire at a time to see which one is flat.

[See **Easter egging** for additional insight on these jokes.]

There is also the 'Field Circus Cheer' (from the **plan file** for DEC on MIT-AI):

> Maynard! Maynard!
> Don't mess with us!
> We're mean and we're tough!
> If you get us confused
> We'll screw up your stuff.

(DEC's service HQ is located in Maynard, Massachusetts.)

field servoid [play on 'android'] */fee´ld ser´voyd/* n. Representative of a field service organization (see **field circus**). This has many of the implications of **droid**.

Fight-o-net [FidoNet] n. Deliberate distortion of **FidoNet**, often applied after a flurry of **flamage** in a particular **echo**, especially the SYSOP echo or Fidonews (see **'Snooze**).

File Attach [FidoNet] 1. n. A file sent along with a mail message from one BBS to another. 2. vt. Sending someone a file by using the File Attach option in a BBS mailer.

File Request [FidoNet] 1. n. The **FidoNet** equivalent of **FTP**, in which one BBS system automatically dials another and **snarf**s one or more files. Often abbreviated *FReq*; files are often announced as being "available for FReq" in the same way that files are announced as being "available for/by anonymous FTP" on the Internet. 2. vt. The act of getting a copy of a file by using the File Request option of the BBS mailer.

file signature n. A **magic number**, sense 3.

filk */filk/* [from SF fandom, where a typo for 'folk' was adopted as a new word] n.,v. A popular or folk song with lyrics revised or completely new lyrics, intended for humorous effect when read, and/or to be sung late at night at SF conventions. There is a flourishing subgenre of these called *computer filks*, written by hackers and often containing rather sophisticated technical humor. See **double bucky** for an example. Compare **grilf**, **hing** and **newsfroup**.

film at 11 [MIT: in parody of TV newscasters] 1. Used in conversation to announce ordinary events, with a sarcastic implication that these events are earth-shattering. "**ITS** crashes; film at 11." "Bug found in scheduler; film at 11." 2. Also widely used outside MIT to indicate that additional information will be available at some future time, *without* the implication of anything particularly ordinary about the referenced event. For example, "The mail file server died this morning; we found garbage all over the root directory. Film at 11." would indicate that a major failure had occurred but that the people working on it have no additional information about it as yet; use of the phrase in this way suggests gently that the problem is liable to be fixed more quickly if the people doing the fixing can spend time doing the fixing rather than responding to questions, the answers to which will appear on the normal "11:00 news", if people will just be patient.

filter [orig. **UNIX**, now also in **MS-DOS**] n. A program that processes an input data stream into an output data stream in some well-defined way, and does no I/O to anywhere else except possibly on error conditions; one designed to be used as a stage in a *pipeline* (see **plumbing**). Compare **sponge**.

Finagle's Law n. The generalized or 'folk' version of **Murphy's Law**, fully named "Finagle's Law of Dynamic Negatives" and usually rendered "Anything that can go wrong, will". One variant favored among hackers is "The perversity of the Universe tends towards a maximum" (but see also **Hanlon's**

Razor). The label 'Finagle's Law' was popularized by SF author Larry Niven in several stories depicting a frontier culture of asteroid miners; this 'Belter' culture professed a religion and/or running joke involving the worship of the dread god Finagle and his mad prophet Murphy.

fine [WPI] adj. Good, but not good enough to be **cuspy**. The word *fine* is used elsewhere, of course, but without the implicit comparison to the higher level implied by **cuspy**.

finger [WAITS, via BSD UNIX] 1. n. A program that displays information about a particular user or all users logged on the system, or a remote system. Typically shows full name, last login time, idle time, terminal line, and terminal location (where applicable). May also display a **plan file** left by the user (see also **Hacking X for Y**). 2. vt. To apply finger to a username. 3. vt. By extension, to check a human's current state by any means. "Foodp?" "T!" "OK, finger Lisa and see if she's idle." 4. Any picture (composed of ASCII characters) depicting 'the finger'. Originally a humorous component of one's plan file to deter the curious fingerer (sense 2), it has entered the arsenal of some **flamers**.

finger-pointing syndrome n. All-too-frequent result of bugs, esp. in new or experimental configurations. The hardware vendor points a finger at the software. The software vendor points a finger at the hardware. All the poor users get is the finger.

finn [IRC] v. To pull rank on somebody based on the amount of time one has spent on **IRC**. The term derives from the fact that IRC was originally written in Finland in 1987.

firebottle n. A large, primitive, power-hungry active electrical device, similar in function to a FET but constructed out of glass, metal, and vacuum. Characterized by high cost, low density, low reliability, high-temperature operation, and high power dissipation. Sometimes mistakenly called a *tube* in the U.S. or a *valve* in England; another hackish term is **glassfet**.

firefighting n. 1. What sysadmins have to do to correct sudden operational problems. An opposite of hacking. "Been hacking your new newsreader?" "No, a power glitch hosed the network and I spent the whole afternoon fighting fires." 2. The act of throwing lots of manpower and late nights at a project, esp. to get it out before deadline. See also **gang bang**, **Mongolian**

Hordes technique; however, the term *firefighting* connotes that the effort is going into chasing bugs rather than adding features.

firehose syndrome n. In mainstream folklore it is observed that trying to drink from a firehose can be a good way to rip your lips off. On computer networks, the absence or failure of flow control mechanisms can lead to situations in which the sending system sprays a massive flood of packets at an unfortunate receiving system, more than it can handle. Compare **overrun**, **buffer overflow**.

firewall code n. 1. The code you put in a system (say, a telephone switch) to make sure that the users can't do any damage. Since users always want to be able to do everything but never want to suffer for any mistakes, the construction of a firewall is a question not only of defensive coding but also of interface presentation, so that users don't even get curious about those corners of a system where they can burn themselves. 2. Any sanity check inserted to catch a **can't happen** error. Wise programmers often change code to fix a bug twice: once to fix the bug, and once to insert a firewall which would have arrested the bug before it did quite as much damage.

firewall machine n. A dedicated gateway machine with special security precautions on it, used to service outside network connections and dial-in lines. The idea is to protect a cluster of more loosely administered machines hidden behind it from **crackers**. The typical firewall is an inexpensive micro-based UNIX box kept clean of critical data, with a bunch of modems and public network ports on it but just one carefully watched connection back to the rest of the cluster. The special precautions may include threat monitoring, callback, and even a complete **iron box** keyable to particular incoming IDs or activity patterns. Syn. **flytrap**, **Venus flytrap**.

fireworks mode n. The mode a machine is sometimes said to be in when it is performing a **crash and burn** operation.

firmy */fer´mee/* Syn. **stiffy** (a 3.5-inch floppy disk).

fish [Adelaide University, Australia] n. 1. Another **metasyntactic variable**. See **foo**. Derived originally from the Monty Python skit in the middle of "The Meaning of Life" entitled "Find the Fish". 2. A pun for *microfiche*. A microfiche file cabinet may be referred to as a *fish tank*.

FISH queue [acronym, by analogy with FIFO (First In, First Out)] n. 'First

In, Still Here'. A joking way of pointing out that processing of a particular sequence of events or requests has stopped dead. Also *FISH mode* and *FISH-net*; the latter may be applied to any network that is running really slowly or exhibiting extreme flakiness.

FITNR // [Thinking Machines, Inc.] Fixed In the Next Release. A written-only notation attached to bug reports. Often wishful thinking.

fix n.,v. What one does when a problem has been reported too many times to be ignored.

FIXME imp. A standard tag often put in C comments near a piece of code that needs work. The point of doing so is that a `grep` or a similar pattern-matching tool can find all such places quickly.

`FIXME: note this is common in` **GNU** `code.`

Compare **XXX**.

flag n. A variable or quantity that can take on one of two values; a bit, particularly one that is used to indicate one of two outcomes or is used to control which of two things is to be done. "This flag controls whether to clear the screen before printing the message." "The program status word contains several flag bits." Used of humans analogously to **bit**. See also **hidden flag**, **mode bit**.

flag day n. A software change that is neither forward- nor backward-compatible, and which is costly to make and costly to reverse. "Can we install that without causing a flag day for all users?" This term has nothing to do with the use of the word **flag** to mean a variable that has two values. It came into use when a massive change was made to the **Multics** timesharing system to convert from the old ASCII code to the new one; this was scheduled for Flag Day (a U.S. holiday), June 14, 1966. See also **backward combatability**.

flaky adj. (var sp. *flakey*) Subject to frequent **lossage**. This use is of course related to the common slang use of the word to describe a person as eccentric, crazy, or just unreliable. A system that is flaky is working, sort of — enough that you are tempted to try to use it — but fails frequently enough that the odds in favor of finishing what you start are low. Commonwealth hackish prefers **dodgy** or **wonky**.

flamage */flay´məj/* n. Flaming verbiage, esp. high-noise, low-signal postings to **USENET** or other electronic **fora**. Often in the phrase *the usual flamage. Flaming* is the act itself; *flamage* the content; a *flame* is a single flaming message. See **flame**.

flame 1. vi. To post an email message intended to insult and provoke. 2. vi. To speak incessantly and/or rabidly on some relatively uninteresting subject or with a patently ridiculous attitude. 3. vt. Either of senses 1 or 2, directed with hostility at a particular person or people. 4. n. An instance of flaming. When a discussion degenerates into useless controversy, one might tell the participants "Now you're just flaming" or "Stop all that flamage!" to try to get them to cool down (so to speak).

USENETter Marc Ramsey, who was at WPI from 1972 to 1976, adds: "I am 99% certain that the use of *flame* originated at WPI. Those who made a nuisance of themselves insisting that they needed to use a TTY for 'real work' came to be known as *flaming asshole lusers.* Other particularly annoying people became *flaming asshole ravers,* which shortened to *flaming ravers,* and ultimately *flamers.* I remember someone picking up on the Human Torch pun, but I don't think 'flame on/off' was ever much used at WPI." See also **asbestos**.

The term may have been independently invented at several different places; it is also reported that *flaming* was in use to mean something like 'interminably drawn-out semi-serious discussions' (late-night bull sessions) at Carleton College during 1968–1971.

It is possible that the hackish sense of 'flame' is much older than that. The poet Chaucer was also what passed for a wizard hacker in his time; he wrote a treatise on the astrolabe, the most advanced computing device of the day. In Chaucer's *Troilus and Cressida,* Cressida laments her inability to grasp the proof of a particular mathematical theorem; her uncle Pandarus then observes that it's called "the fleminge of wrecches." This phrase seems to have been intended in context as "that which puts the wretches to flight" but was probably just as ambiguous in Middle English as "the flaming of wretches" would be today. One suspects that Chaucer would feel right at home on USENET.

flame bait n. A posting intended to trigger a **flame war**, or one that invites flames in reply.

flame on vi.,interj. 1. To begin to **flame**. The punning reference to Marvel

Comics's Human Torch is no longer widely recognized. 2. To continue to flame. See **rave, burble**.

flame war n. (var. *flamewar*) An acrimonious dispute, especially when conducted on a public electronic forum such as **USENET**.

flamer n. One who habitually **flames**. Said esp. of obnoxious **USENET** personalities.

flap vt. 1. To unload a DECtape (so it goes flap, flap, flap . . .). Old-time hackers at MIT tell of the days when the disk was device 0 and **microtapes** were 1, 2, . . . and attempting to flap device 0 would instead start a motor banging inside a cabinet near the disk. 2. By extension, to unload any magnetic tape. See also **macrotape**. Modern cartridge tapes no longer actually flap, but the usage has remained. (The term could well be re-applied to DEC's TK50 cartridge tape drive, a spectacularly misengineered contraption which makes a loud flapping sound, almost like an old reel-type lawnmower, in one of its many tape-eating failure modes.)

flarp */flarp/* [Rutgers University] n. Yet another **metasyntactic variable** (see **foo**). Among those who use it, it is associated with a legend that any program not containing the word *flarp* somewhere will not work. The legend is discreetly silent on the reliability of programs which *do* contain the magic word.

flat adj. 1. Lacking any complex internal structure. "That **bitty box** has only a flat filesystem, not a hierarchical one." The verb form is **flatten**. 2. Said of a memory architecture (like that of the VAX or 680x0) that is one big linear address space (typically with each possible value of a processor register corresponding to a unique core address), as opposed to a *segmented* architecture (like that of the 80x86) in which addresses are composed from a base-register/offset pair (segmented designs are generally considered **cretinous**).

Note that sense 1 (at least with respect to filesystems) is usually used pejoratively, while sense 2 is a **Good Thing**.

flat-ASCII adj. Said of a text file that contains only 7-bit ASCII characters and uses only ASCII-standard control characters (that is, has no embedded codes specific to a particular text formatter markup language, or output device, and no **meta**-characters). Syn. **plain-ASCII**. Compare **flat-file**.

flat-file adj. A **flatten**ed representation of some database or tree or network structure as a single file from which the structure could implicitly be rebuilt, esp. one in **flat-ASCII** form. See also **sharchive**.

flatten vt. To remove structural information, esp. to filter something with an implicit tree structure into a simple sequence of leaves; also tends to imply mapping to **flat-ASCII**. "This code flattens an expression with parentheses into an equivalent **canonical** form."

flavor n. 1. Variety, type, kind. "DDT commands come in two flavors." "These lights come in two flavors, big red ones and small green ones." See **vanilla**. 2. The attribute that causes something to be **flavorful**. Usually used in the phrase "yields additional flavor". "This convention yields additional flavor by allowing one to print text either right-side-up or upside-down." See **vanilla**. This usage was certainly reinforced by the terminology of quantum chromodynamics, in which quarks (the constituents of, e.g., protons) come in six flavors (up, down, strange, charm, top, bottom) and three colors (red, blue, green) — however, hackish use of *flavor* at MIT predated QCD. 3. The term for 'class' (in the object-oriented sense) in the LISP Machine Flavors system. Though the Flavors design has been superseded (notably by the Common LISP CLOS facility), the term *flavor* is still used as a general synonym for 'class' by some LISP hackers.

flavorful adj. Full of **flavor** (sense 2); esthetically pleasing. See **random** and **losing** for antonyms. See also the entries for **taste** and **elegant**.

flippy */flip´ee/* n. A single-sided floppy disk altered for double-sided use by addition of a second write-notch, so called because it must be flipped over for the second side to be accessible. No longer common.

flood [IRC] v. To dump large amounts of text onto an **IRC** channel. This is especially rude when the text is uninteresting and the other users are trying to carry on a serious conversation.

flowchart [techspeak] n. An archaic form of visual control-flow specification employing arrows and 'speech balloons' of various shapes. Hackers never use flowcharts, consider them extremely silly, and associate them with **COBOL** programmers, **card walloper**s, and other lower forms of life. This attitude follows from the observations that flowcharts (at least from a hacker's point of view) are no easier to read than code, are less precise, and tend to fall out of sync with the code (so that they either obfuscate it rather than explaining it, or require extra maintenance effort that doesn't improve the code). See also **pdl**, sense 3.

flower key [Mac users] n. See **feature key**.

flush v. 1. To delete something, usually superfluous, or to abort an operation. "All that nonsense has been flushed." 2. [UNIX/C] To force buffered I/O to disk, as with an `fflush(3)` call. This is *not* an abort or deletion as in sense 1, but a demand for early completion! 3. To leave at the end of a day's work (as opposed to leaving for a meal). "I'm going to flush now." "Time to flush." 4. To exclude someone from an activity, or to ignore a person.

'Flush' was standard ITS terminology for aborting an output operation; one spoke of the text that would have been printed, but was not, as having been flushed. It is speculated that this term arose from a vivid image of flushing unwanted characters by hosing down the internal output buffer, washing the characters away before they could be printed. The UNIX/C usage, on the other hand, was propagated by the `fflush(3)` call in C's standard I/O library (though it is reported to have been in use among BLISS programmers at DEC and on Honeywell and IBM machines as far back as 1965). UNIX/C hackers find the ITS usage confusing, and vice versa.

flypage */fli:´payj/* n. (alt. *fly page*) A **banner**, sense 1.

Flyspeck 3 n. Standard name for any font that is so tiny as to be unreadable (by analogy with names like 'Helvetica 10' for 10-point Helvetica). Legal boilerplate is usually printed in Flyspeck 3.

flytrap n. See **firewall machine**.

FM n. *Not* 'Frequency Modulation' but rather an abbreviation for 'Fucking Manual', the back-formation from **RTFM**. Used to refer to the manual itself in the **RTFM**. "Have you seen the Networking FM lately?"

fnord [from the *Illuminatus Trilogy*] n. 1. A word used in email and news postings to tag utterances as surrealist mind-play or humor, esp. in connection with **Discordianism** and elaborate conspiracy theories. "I heard that David Koresh is sharing an apartment in Argentina with Hitler. (Fnord.)" "Where can I fnord get the Principia Discordia from?" 2. A **metasyntactic variable**, commonly used by hackers with ties to **Discordianism** or the **Church of the SubGenius**.

Crunchly gets **flush**ed.
The next cartoon in the Crunchly saga is 05-01-76, page 395.

FOAF // [USENET] n. Acronym for 'Friend Of A Friend'. The source of an unverified, possibly untrue story. This term was not originated by hackers (it is used in Jan Brunvand's books on urban folklore), but is much better recognized on USENET and elsewhere than in mainstream English.

FOD */fod/* v. [Abbreviation for 'Finger of Death', originally a spell-name from fantasy gaming] To terminate with extreme prejudice and with no regard for other people. From **MUD**s where the wizard command 'FOD <player>' results in the immediate and total death of <player>, usually as punishment for obnoxious behavior. This usage migrated to other circumstances, such as "I'm going to fod the process that is burning all the cycles." Compare **gun**.

In aviation, FOD means Foreign Object Damage, e.g., what happens when a jet engine sucks up a rock on the runway or a bird in flight. Finger of Death is a distressingly apt description of what this generally does to the engine.

fold case v. See **smash case**. This term tends to be used more by people who don't mind that their tools smash case. It also connotes that case is ignored but case distinctions in data processed by the tool in question aren't destroyed.

followup n. On USENET, a **posting** generated in response to another posting (as opposed to a **reply**, which goes by email rather than being broadcast). Followups include the ID of the **parent message** in their headers; smart news-readers can use this information to present USENET news in 'conversation' sequence rather than order-of-arrival. See **thread**.

fontology [XEROX PARC] n. The body of knowledge dealing with the construction and use of new fonts (e.g., for window systems and typesetting software). It has been said that fontology recapitulates file-ogeny.

[Unfortunately, this reference to the embryological dictum that "Ontogeny recapitulates phylogeny" is not merely a joke. On the Macintosh, for example, System 7 has to go through contortions to compensate for an earlier design error that created a whole different set of abstractions for fonts parallel to 'files' and 'folders' — ESR]

foo */foo/* 1. interj. Term of disgust. 2. Used very generally as a sample name for absolutely anything, esp. programs and files (esp. scratch files). 3. First on the standard list of **metasyntactic variable**s used in syntax examples. See also **bar**, **baz**, **qux**, **quux**, **corge**, **grault**, **garply**, **waldo**, **fred**, **plugh**, **xyzzy**, **thud**.

The etymology of hackish 'foo' is obscure. When used in connection with 'bar' it is generally traced to the WWII-era Army slang acronym FUBAR ('Fucked Up Beyond All Repair'), later bowdlerized to **foobar**. (See also **FUBAR**).

However, the use of the word 'foo' itself has more complicated antecedents, including a long history in comic strips and cartoons. The old "Smokey Stover" comic strips by Bill Holman often included the word 'FOO', in particular on license plates of cars; allegedly, 'FOO' and 'BAR' also occurred in Walt Kelly's "Pogo" strips. In the 1938 cartoon "The Daffy Doc", a very early version of Daffy Duck holds up a sign saying "SILENCE IS FOO!"; oddly, this seems to refer to some approving or positive affirmative use of foo. It has been suggested that this might be related to the Chinese word 'fu' (sometimes transliterated 'foo'), which can mean "happiness" when spoken with the proper tone (the lion-dog guardians flanking the steps of many Chinese restaurants are properly called "fu dogs").

Earlier versions of this entry suggested the possibility that hacker usage actually sprang from *FOO, Lampoons and Parody*, the title of a comic book first issued in September 1958, a joint project of Charles and Robert Crumb. Though Robert Crumb (then in his mid-teens) later became one of the most important and influential artists in underground comics, this venture was hardly a success; indeed, the brothers later burned most of the existing copies in disgust. The title FOO was featured in large letters on the front cover. However, very few copies of this comic actually circulated, and students of Crumb's 'oeuvre' have established that this title was a reference to the earlier Smokey Stover comics.

An old-time member reports that in the 1959 *Dictionary of the TMRC Language*, compiled at **TMRC** there was an entry that went something like this:

> FOO: The first syllable of the sacred chant phrase "FOO MANE PADME HUM." Our first obligation is to keep the foo counters turning.

For more about the legendary foo counters, see **TMRC**. Almost the entire staff of what became the MIT AI LAB was involved with TMRC, and probably picked the word up there.

Very probably, hackish 'foo' had no single origin and derives through all these channels from Yiddish 'feh' and/or English 'fooey'.

foobar n. Another common **metasyntactic variable**; see **foo**. Hackers do *not* generally use this to mean **FUBAR** in either the slang or jargon sense.

fool n. As used by hackers, specifically describes a person who habitually reasons from obviously or demonstrably incorrect premises and cannot be persuaded by evidence to do otherwise; it is not generally used in its other senses, i.e., to describe a person with a native incapacity to reason correctly, or a clown. Indeed, in hackish experience many fools are capable of reasoning all too effectively in executing their errors. See also **cretin**, **loser**, **fool file, the**.

fool file, the [USENET] n. A notional repository of all the most dramatically and abysmally stupid utterances ever. An entire subgenre of **sig block**s consists of the header "From the fool file:" followed by some quote the poster wishes to represent as an immortal gem of dimwittery; for this usage to be really effective, the quote has to be so obviously wrong as to be laughable. More than one USENETter has achieved an unwanted notoriety by being quoted in this way.

Foonly n. 1. The **PDP-10** successor that was to have been built by the Super Foonly project at the Stanford Artificial Intelligence Laboratory along with a new operating system. The intention was to leapfrog from the old DEC timesharing system SAIL was then running to a new generation, bypassing TENEX which at that time was the ARPANET standard. ARPA funding for both the Super Foonly and the new operating system was cut in 1974. Most of the design team went to DEC and contributed greatly to the design of the PDP-10 model KL10. 2. The name of the company formed by Dave Poole, one of the principal Super Foonly designers, and one of hackerdom's more colorful personalities. Many people remember the parrot which sat on Poole's shoulder and was a regular companion. 3. Any of the machines built by Poole's company. The first was the F-1 (a.k.a. Super Foonly), which was the computational engine used to create the graphics in the movie "TRON". The F-1 was the fastest PDP-10 ever built, but only one was ever made. The effort drained Foonly of its financial resources, and the company turned towards building smaller, slower, and much less expensive machines. Unfortunately, these ran not the popular **TOPS-20** but a TENEX variant called Foonex; this seriously limited their market. Also, the machines shipped were actually wire-wrapped engineering prototypes requiring individual attention from more than usually competent site personnel, and thus had significant reliability problems. Poole's legendary temper and unwillingness to suffer fools gladly did not help matters. By the time of the Jupiter project cancellation in 1983, Foonly's proposal to build another F-1 was eclipsed by the **Mars**, and the company never quite recovered. See the **Mars** entry for the continuation and moral of this story.

footprint n. 1. The floor or desk area taken up by a piece of hardware. 2. [IBM] The audit trail (if any) left by a crashed program (often in plural, *footprints*). See also **toeprint**.

for free adj. Said of a capability of a programming language or hardware equipment that is available by its design without needing cleverness to implement: "In APL, we get the matrix operations for free." "And owing to the way revisions are stored in this system, you get revision trees for free." The term usually refers to a serendipitous feature of doing things a certain way (compare **big win**), but it may refer to an intentional but secondary feature.

for the rest of us [from the Mac slogan "The computer for the rest of us"] adj. 1. Used to describe a **spiffy** product whose affordability shames other comparable products, or (more often) used sarcastically to describe **spiffy** but very overpriced products. 2. Describes a program with a limited interface, deliberately limited capabilities, non-orthogonality, inability to compose primitives, or any other limitation designed to not 'confuse' a naive user. This places an upper bound on how far that user can go before the program begins to get in the way of the task instead of helping accomplish it. Used in reference to Macintosh software which doesn't provide obvious capabilities because it is thought that the poor lusers might not be able to handle them. Becomes 'the rest of *them*' when used in third-party reference; thus, "Yes, it is an attractive program, but it's designed for The Rest Of Them" means a program that superficially looks neat but has no depth beyond the surface flash. See also **WIMP environment**, **Macintrash**, **point-and-drool interface**, **user-friendly**.

for values of [MIT] A common rhetorical maneuver at MIT is to use any of the canonical **random numbers** as placeholders for variables. "The max function takes 42 arguments, for arbitrary values of 42." "There are 69 ways to leave your lover, for 69 = 50." This is especially likely when the speaker has uttered a random number and realizes that it was not recognized as such, but even 'non-random' numbers are occasionally used in this fashion. A related joke is that π equals 3 — for small values of π and large values of 3.

Historical note: this usage probably derives from the programming language MAD (Michigan Algorithm Decoder), an Algol-like language that was the most common choice among mainstream (non-hacker) users at MIT in the mid-60s. It had a control structure FOR VALUES OF X = 3, 7, 99 DO ... that would repeat the indicated instructions for each value in the list (unlike the usual FOR that only works for arithmetic sequences of values). MAD is long extinct, but similar for-constructs still flourish (e.g., in UNIX's shell languages).

fora pl.n. Plural of **forum**.

foreground [UNIX] vt. To bring a task to the top of one's **stack** for immediate processing, and hackers often use it in this sense for non-computer tasks. "If your presentation is due next week, I guess I'd better foreground writing up the design document."

Technically, on a time-sharing system, a task executing in foreground is one able to accept input from and return output to the user; oppose **background**. Nowadays this term is primarily associated with **UNIX**, but it appears first to have been used in this sense on OS/360. Normally, there is only one foreground task per terminal (or terminal window); having multiple processes simultaneously reading the keyboard is a good way to **lose**.

fork bomb [UNIX] n. A particular species of **wabbit** that can be written in one line of C (`main() for(;;)fork();`) or shell (`$0 & $0 &`) on any UNIX system, or occasionally created by an egregious coding bug. A fork bomb process 'explodes' by recursively spawning copies of itself (using the UNIX system call `fork(2)`). Eventually it eats all the process table entries and effectively wedges the system. Fortunately, fork bombs are relatively easy to spot and kill, so creating one deliberately seldom accomplishes more than to bring the just wrath of the gods down upon the perpetrator. See also **logic bomb**.

forked [UNIX; prob. influenced by a mainstream expletive] adj. Terminally slow, or dead. Originated when one system was slowed to a snail's pace by an inadvertent **fork bomb**.

Fortrash */for´trash/* n. Hackerism for the FORTRAN (FORmula TRANslator) language, referring to its primitive design, gross and irregular syntax, limited control constructs, and slippery, exception-filled semantics.

fortune cookie [WAITS, via UNIX] n. A random quote, item of trivia, joke, or maxim printed to the user's tty at login time or (less commonly) at logout time. Items from this lexicon have often been used as fortune cookies. See **cookie file**.

forum n. [USENET, GEnie, CI$; pl. *fora* or *forums*] Any discussion group accessible through a dial-in **BBS**, a **mailing list**, or a **newsgroup** (see **network, the**). A forum functions much like a bulletin board; users submit **postings** for all to read and discussion ensues. Contrast real-time chat via **talk mode** or point-to-point personal **email**.

fossil n. 1. In software, a misfeature that becomes understandable only in historical context, as a remnant of times past retained so as not to break compatibility. Example: the retention of octal as default base for string escapes in **C**, in spite of the better match of hexadecimal to ASCII and modern byte-addressable architectures. See **dusty deck**. 2. More restrictively, a feature with past but no present utility. Example: the force-all-caps (LCASE) bits in the V7 and **BSD** UNIX tty driver, designed for use with monocase terminals. (In a perversion of the usual backward-compatibility goal, this functionality has actually been expanded and renamed in some later **USG UNIX** releases as the IUCLC and OLCUC bits.) 3. The FOSSIL (Fido/Opus/Seadog Standard Interface Level) driver specification for serial-port access to replace the **brain-dead** routines in the IBM PC ROMs. Fossils are used by most MS-DOS **BBS** software in preference to the 'supported' ROM routines, which do not support interrupt-driven operation or setting speeds above 9600; the use of a semistandard FOSSIL library is preferable to the **bare metal** serial port programming otherwise required. Since the FOSSIL specification allows additional functionality to be hooked in, drivers that use the **hook** but do not provide serial-port access themselves are named with a modifier, as in 'video fossil'.

four-color glossies 1. Literature created by **marketroid**s that allegedly contains technical specs but which is in fact as superficial as possible without being totally **content-free**. "Forget the four-color glossies, give me the tech ref manuals." Often applied as an indication of superficiality even when the material is printed on ordinary paper in black and white. Four-color-glossy manuals are *never* useful for finding a problem. 2. [rare] Applied by extension to manual pages that don't contain enough information to diagnose why the program doesn't produce the expected or desired output.

fragile adj. Syn **brittle**.

fred n. 1. The personal name most frequently used as a **metasyntactic variable** (see **foo**). Allegedly popular because it's easy for a non-touch-typist to type on a standard QWERTY keyboard. Unlike **J. Random Hacker** or *J. Random Loser*, this name has no positive or negative loading (but see **Mbogo, Dr. Fred**). See also **barney**. 2. An acronym for 'Flipping Ridiculous Electronic Device'; other F-verbs may be substituted for 'flipping'.

frednet */fred´net/* n. Used to refer to some **random** and uncommon protocol encountered on a network. "We're implementing bridging in our router to solve the frednet problem."

freeware n. Free software, often written by enthusiasts and distributed by users' groups, or via electronic mail, local bulletin boards, **USENET**, or other electronic media. At one time, *freeware* was a trademark of Andrew Fluegelman, the author of the well-known MS-DOS comm program PC-TALK III. It wasn't enforced after his mysterious disappearance and presumed death in 1984. See **shareware**.

freeze v. To lock an evolving software distribution or document against changes so it can be released with some hope of stability. Carries the strong implication that the item in question will 'unfreeze' at some future date. "OK, fix that bug and we'll freeze for release."

There are more specific constructions on this term. A *feature freeze*, for example, locks out modifications intended to introduce new features but still allows bugfixes and completion of existing features; a *code freeze* connotes no more changes at all. At Sun Microsystems and elsewhere, one may also hear references to *code slush* — that is, an almost-but-not-quite frozen state.

fried adj. 1. Non-working due to hardware failure; burnt out. Especially used of hardware brought down by a *power glitch* (see **glitch**), **drop-outs**, a short, or some other electrical event. (Sometimes this literally happens to electronic circuits! In particular, resistors can burn out and transformers can melt down, emitting noxious smoke — see **friode**, **SED** and **LER**. However, this term is also used metaphorically.) Compare **frotzed**. 2. Of people, exhausted. Said particularly of those who continue to work in such a state. Often used as an explanation or excuse. "Yeah, I know that fix destroyed the file system, but I was fried when I put it in." Esp. common in conjunction with *brain*: "My brain is fried today, I'm very short on sleep."

frink */frink/* v. The unknown ur-verb, fill in your own meaning. Found esp.

on the USENET newsgroup *alt.fan.lemurs*, where it is said that the lemurs know what 'frink' means, but they aren't telling. Compare **gorets**.

friode */fri:´ohd/* [TMRC] n. A reversible (that is, fused or blown) diode. Compare **fried**; see also **SED**, **LER**.

fritterware n. An excess of capability that serves no productive end. The canonical example is font-diddling software on the Mac (see **macdink**); the term describes anything that eats huge amounts of time for quite marginal gains in function but seduces people into using it anyway. See also **window shopping**.

frob */frob/* 1. n. [MIT] The **TMRC** definition was "FROB = a protruding arm or trunnion"; by metaphoric extension, a *frob* is any random small thing; an object that you can comfortably hold in one hand; something you can frob (sense 2). See **frobnitz**. 2. vt. Abbreviated form of **frobnicate**. 3. [from the **MUD** world] A command on some MUDs that changes a player's experience level (this can be used to make wizards); also, to request **wizard** privileges on the 'professional courtesy' grounds that one is a wizard elsewhere. The command is actually 'frobnicate' but is universally abbreviated to the shorter form.

frobnicate */frob´ni-kayt/* vt. [Poss. derived from **frobnitz**, and usually abbreviated to **frob**, but *frobnicate* is recognized as the official full form.] To manipulate or adjust, to tweak. One frequently frobs bits or other 2-state devices. Thus: "Please frob the light switch" (that is, flip it), but also "Stop frobbing that clasp; you'll break it". One also sees the construction *to frob a frob*. See **tweak** and **twiddle**.

Usage: frob, twiddle, and tweak sometimes connote points along a continuum. 'Frob' connotes aimless manipulation; *twiddle* connotes gross manipulation, often a coarse search for a proper setting; *tweak* connotes fine-tuning. If someone is turning a knob on an oscilloscope, then if he's carefully adjusting it, he is probably tweaking it; if he is just turning it but looking at the screen, he is probably twiddling it; but if he's just doing it because turning a knob is fun, he's frobbing it. The variant *frobnosticate* has been recently reported.

frobnitz */frob´nits/*, plural *frobnitzem /frob´nit-zm/* or *frobni /frob´ni:/* [TMRC] n. An unspecified physical object, a widget. Also refers to electronic black boxes. This rare form is usually abbreviated to *frotz*, or more commonly to **frob**. Also used are *frobnule* (*/frob´n[y]ool/*) and *frobule* (*/frob´yool/*).

Starting perhaps in 1979, *frobozz /frə-boz'/* (plural: *frobbotzim /frə-bot'zm/*) has also become very popular, largely through its exposure as a name via **Zork**. These variants can also be applied to nonphysical objects, such as data structures.

Pete Samson, compiler of the original **TMRC** lexicon, adds, "Under the TMRC [railroad] layout were many storage boxes, managed (in 1958) by David R. Sawyer. Several had fanciful designations written on them, such as 'Frobnitz Coil Oil'. Perhaps DRS intended Frobnitz to be a proper name, but the name was quickly taken for the thing". This was almost certainly the origin of the term.

frog alt. *phrog* 1. interj. Term of disgust (we seem to have a lot of them). 2. Used as a name for just about anything. See **foo**. 3. n. Of things, a crock. 4. n. Of people, somewhere in between a turkey and a toad. 5. *froggy*: adj. Similar to **bagbiting**, but milder. "This froggy program is taking forever to run!"

frogging [University of Waterloo] v. 1. Partial corruption of a text file or input stream by some bug or consistent glitch, as opposed to random events like line noise or media failures. Might occur, for example, if one bit of each incoming character on a tty were stuck, so that some characters were correct and others were not. See **terminak** for a historical example. 2. By extension, accidental display of text in a mode where the output device emits special symbols or mnemonics rather than conventional ASCII. This often happens, for example, when using a terminal or comm program on a device like an IBM PC with a special 'high-half' character set and with the bit-parity assumption wrong. A hacker sufficiently familiar with ASCII bit patterns might be able to read the display anyway.

front end n. 1. An intermediary computer that does set-up and filtering for another (usually more powerful but less friendly) machine (a *back end*). 2. What you're talking to when you have a conversation with someone who is making replies without paying attention. "Look at the dancing elephants!" "Uh-huh." "Do you know what I just said?" "Sorry, you were talking to the front end." See also **fepped out**. 3. Software that provides an interface to another program 'behind' it, which may not be as user-friendly. Probably from analogy with hardware front-ends (see sense 1) that interfaced with mainframes.

frotz */frots/* 1. n. See **frobnitz**. 2. *mumble frotz*: An interjection of mildest disgust.

frotzed */frotst/* adj. **down** because of hardware problems. Compare **fried**. A machine that is merely frotzed may be fixable without replacing parts, but a fried machine is more seriously damaged.

frowney n. (alt. *frowney face*) See **emoticon**.

fry 1. vi. To fail. Said especially of smoke-producing hardware failures. More generally, to become non-working. Usage: never said of software, only of hardware and humans. See **fried**, **magic smoke**. 2. vt. To cause to fail; to **roach**, **toast**, or **hose** a piece of hardware. Never used of software or humans, but compare **fried**.

FTP */F-T-P/, not /fit´ip/* 1. [techspeak] n. The File Transfer Protocol for transmitting files between systems on the Internet. 2. vt. To **beam** a file using the File Transfer Protocol. 3. Sometimes used as a generic even for file transfers not using **FTP**. "Lemme get a copy of *Wuthering Heights* ftp'd from uunet."

FUBAR n. The Failed UniBus Address Register in a VAX. A good example of how jargon can occasionally be snuck past the **suits**; see **foobar**, and **foo** for a fuller etymology.

fuck me harder excl. Sometimes uttered in response to egregious misbehavior, esp. in software, and esp. of misbehaviors which seem unfairly persistent (as though designed in by the imp of the perverse). Often theatrically elaborated: "Aiighhh! Fuck me with a piledriver and 16 feet of curare-tipped wrought-iron fence *and no lubricants*!" The phrase is sometimes heard abbreviated *FMH* in polite company.

[This entry is an extreme example of the hackish habit of coining elaborate and evocative terms for lossage. Here we see a quite self-conscious parody of mainstream expletives that has become a running gag in part of the hacker culture; it illustrates the hackish tendency to turn any situation, even one of extreme frustration, into an intellectual game (the point being, in this case, to creatively produce a long-winded description of the most anatomically absurd mental image possible — the short forms implicitly allude to all the ridiculous long forms ever spoken). Scatological language is actually relatively uncommon among hackers, and there was some controversy over whether this entry ought to be included at all. As it reflects a live usage recognizably peculiar to the hacker culture, we feel it is in the hackish spirit of truthfulness and opposition to all forms of censorship to record it here. — ESR & GLS]

FUD */fuhd/* n. Defined by Gene Amdahl after he left IBM to found his own company: "FUD is the fear, uncertainty, and doubt that IBM sales people instill in the minds of potential customers who might be considering [Amdahl] products." The idea, of course, was to persuade them to go with safe IBM gear rather than with competitors' equipment. This implicit coercion was traditionally accomplished by promising that Good Things would happen to people who stuck with IBM, but Dark Shadows loomed over the future of competitors' equipment or software. See **IBM**.

FUD wars */fuhd worz/* n. [from **FUD**] Political posturing engaged in by hardware and software vendors ostensibly committed to standardization but actually willing to fragment the market to protect their own shares. The UNIX International vs. OSF conflict is but one outstanding example.

fudge 1. vt. To perform in an incomplete but marginally acceptable way, particularly with respect to the writing of a program. "I didn't feel like going through that pain and suffering, so I fudged it — I'll fix it later." 2. n. The resulting code.

fudge factor n. A value or parameter that is varied in an ad hoc way to produce the desired result. The terms *tolerance* and **slop** are also used, though these usually indicate a one-sided leeway, such as a buffer that is made larger than necessary because one isn't sure exactly how large it needs to be, and it is better to waste a little space than to lose completely for not having enough. A fudge factor, on the other hand, can often be tweaked in more than one direction. A good example is the 'fuzz' typically allowed in floating-point calculations: two numbers being compared for equality must be allowed to differ by a small amount; if that amount is too small, a computation may never terminate, while if it is too large, results will be needlessly inaccurate. Fudge factors are frequently adjusted incorrectly by programmers who don't fully understand their import. See also **coefficient of X**.

fuel up vi. To eat or drink hurriedly in order to get back to hacking. "Food-p?" "Yeah, let's fuel up." "Time for a **great-wall**!" See also **oriental food**.

fum [XEROX PARC] n. At PARC, often the third of the standard **meta-syntactic variables** (after **foo** and **bar**). Competes with **baz**, which is more common outside PARC.

funky adj. Said of something that functions, but in a slightly strange, klugey way. It does the job and would be difficult to change, so its obvious non-optimality is left alone. Often used to describe interfaces. The more bugs something has that nobody has bothered to fix because workarounds are easier, the funkier it is. **TECO** and UUCP are funky. The Intel i860's exception handling is extraordinarily funky. Most standards acquire funkiness as they age. "The new mailer is installed, but is still somewhat funky; if it bounces your mail for no reason, try resubmitting it." "This UART is pretty funky. The data ready line is active-high in interrupt mode and active-low in DMA mode."

funny money n. 1. Notional 'dollar' units of computing time and/or storage handed to students at the beginning of a computer course; also called *play money* or *purple money* (in implicit opposition to real or *green* money). In New Zealand and Germany the odd usage *paper money* has been recorded; in Germany, the particularly amusing synonym *transfer ruble* commemmorates the funny money used for trade between COMECON countries back when the Soviet Bloc still existed. When your funny money ran out, your account froze and you needed to go to a professor to get more. Fortunately, the plunging cost of timesharing cycles has made this less common. The amounts allocated were almost invariably too small, even for the non-hackers who wanted to slide by with minimum work. In extreme cases, the practice led to small-scale black markets in bootlegged computer accounts. 2. By extension, phantom money or quantity tickets of any kind used as a resource-allocation hack within a system. Antonym: *real money*.

furrfu // [USENET] excl. Written-only equivalent of "Sheesh!"; it is, in fact, "sheesh" modified by **rot13**. Evolved in mid-1992 as a response to notably silly postings repeating urban myths on the USENET newsgroup *alt.folklore.urban*. See also **FOAF**.

fuzzball [TCP/IP hackers] n. A DEC LSI-11 running a particular suite of homebrewed software written by Dave Mills and assorted co-conspirators, used in the early 1980s for Internet protocol testbedding and experimentation. These were used as NSFnet backbone sites in its early 56KB-line days; a few are still active on the Internet as of early 1991, doing odd jobs such as network time service.

= G =

G [SI] pref.,suff. See **quantifiers**.

gabriel */gay'bree-əl/* [for Dick Gabriel, SAIL LISP hacker and volleyball fanatic] n. An unnecessary (in the opinion of the opponent) stalling tactic, e.g., tying one's shoelaces or combing one's hair repeatedly, asking the time, etc. Also used to refer to the perpetrator of such tactics. Also, *pulling a Gabriel, Gabriel mode.*

gag vi. Equivalent to **choke**, but connotes more disgust. "Hey, this is FORTRAN code. No wonder the C compiler gagged." See also **barf**.

gang bang n. The use of large numbers of loosely coupled programmers in an attempt to wedge a great many features into a product in a short time. Though there have been memorable gang bangs (e.g., that over-the-weekend assembler port mentioned in Steven Levy's *Hackers*), most are perpetrated by large companies trying to meet deadlines; the inevitable result is enormous buggy masses of code entirely lacking in **orthogonal**ity. When market-driven managers make a list of all the features the competition has and assign one programmer to implement each, the probability of maintaining a coherent (or even functional) design goes infinitesimal. See also **firefighting**, **Mongolian Hordes technique**, **Conway's Law**.

garbage collect vi. (also *garbage collection*, n.) See **GC**.

garply */gar'plee/* [Stanford] n. Another metasyntactic variable (see **foo**); once popular among SAIL hackers.

gas [as in 'gas chamber'] 1. interj. A term of disgust and hatred, implying that gas should be dispensed in generous quantities, thereby exterminating the source of irritation. "Some loser just reloaded the system for no reason! Gas!" 2. interj. A suggestion that someone or something ought to be flushed out of mercy. "The system's getting **wedged** every few minutes. Gas!" 3. vt. To **flush** (sense 1). "You should gas that old crufty software." 4. [IBM] n. Dead space in nonsequentially organized files that was occupied by data that has since been deleted; the compression operation that removes it is called 'degassing' (by analogy, perhaps, with the use of the same term in vacuum technology). 5. [IBM] n. Empty space on a disk that has been clandestinely allocated against future need.

gaseous adj. Deserving of being **gass**ed. Disseminated by Geoff Goodfellow while at SRI; became particularly popular after the Moscone-Milk killings in San Francisco, when it was learned that the defendant Dan White (a politician who had supported Proposition 7) would get the gas chamber under Proposition 7 if convicted of first-degree murder (he was eventually convicted of manslaughter).

GC */G-C/* [from LISP terminology; 'Garbage Collect'] 1. vt. To clean up and throw away useless things. "I think I'll GC the top of my desk today." When said of files, this is equivalent to **GFR**. 2. vt. To recycle, reclaim, or put to another use. 3. n. An instantiation of the garbage collector process.

'Garbage collection' is computer-science techspeak for a particular class of strategies for dynamically but transparently reallocating computer memory (i.e., without requiring explicit allocation and deallocation by higher-level software). One such strategy involves periodically scanning all the data in memory and determining what is no longer accessible; useless data items are then discarded so that the memory they occupy can be recycled and used for another purpose. Implementations of the LISP language usually use garbage collection.

In jargon, the full phrase is sometimes heard but the **abbrev** is more frequently used because it is shorter. Note that there is an ambiguity in usage that has to be resolved by context: "I'm going to garbage-collect my desk" usually means to clean out the drawers, but it could also mean to throw away or recycle the desk itself.

GCOS */jee´kohs/* n. A **quick-and-dirty clone** of System/360 DOS that emerged from GE around 1970; originally called GECOS (the General Electric Comprehensive Operating System). Later kluged to support primitive timesharing and transaction processing. After the buyout of GE's computer division by Honeywell, the name was changed to General Comprehensive Operating System (GCOS). Other OS groups at Honeywell began referring to it as 'God's Chosen Operating System', allegedly in reaction to the GCOS crowd's uninformed and snotty attitude about the superiority of their product. All this might be of zero interest, except for two facts: (1) The GCOS people won the political war, and this led in the orphaning and eventual death of Honeywell **Multics**, and (2) GECOS/GCOS left one permanent mark on UNIX. Some early UNIX systems at Bell Labs used GCOS machines for print spooling and various other services; the field added to `/etc/passwd` to carry GCOS ID information was called the 'GECOS field' and survives today as the `pw_gecos` member used for the user's full name and other human-ID information. GCOS later played a major role in keeping Honeywell a dismal also-ran in the mainframe market, and was itself ditched for UNIX in the late 1980s when Honeywell retired its aging **big iron** designs.

GECOS */jee´kohs/* n. See **GCOS**.

gedanken */gə-dahn´kn/* adj. Ungrounded; impractical; not well-thought-out; untried; untested.

'Gedanken' is a German word for 'thought'. A thought experiment is one you carry out in your head. In physics, the term 'gedanken experiment' is used to refer to an experiment that is impractical to carry out, but useful to consider because it can be reasoned about theoretically. (A classic gedanken experiment of relativity theory involves thinking about a man in an elevator accelerating through space.) Gedanken experiments are very useful in physics, but must be used with care. It's too easy to idealize away some important aspect of the real world in constructing the 'apparatus'.

Among hackers, accordingly, the word has a pejorative connotation. It is typically used of a project, especially one in artificial intelligence research, that is written up in grand detail (typically as a Ph.D. thesis) without ever being implemented to any great extent. Such a project is usually perpetrated by people who aren't very good hackers or find programming distasteful or are just in a hurry. A *gedanken thesis* is usually marked by an obvious lack of intuition about what is programmable and what is not, and about what does and does not constitute a clear specification of an algorithm. See also **AI-complete**, **DWIM**.

geef v. [ostensibly from 'gefingerpoken'] vt. Syn. **mung**. See also **blinkenlights**.

geek out vi. To temporarily enter techno-nerd mode while in a non-hackish context, for example at parties held near computer equipment. Especially used when you need to do or say something highly technical and don't have time to explain: "Pardon me while I geek out for a moment." See **computer geek**; see also **propeller head**.

gen */jen/* n.,v. Short for **generate**, used frequently in both spoken and written contexts.

gender mender n. A cable connector shell with either two male or two female connectors on it, used to correct the mismatches that result when some **loser** didn't understand the RS232C specification and the distinction between DTE and DCE. Used esp. for RS-232C parts in either the original D-25 or the IBM PC's bogus D-9 format. Also called *gender bender*, *gender blender*, *sex changer*, and even *homosexual adapter*; however, there appears to be some confusion as to whether a *male homosexual adapter* has pins on both sides (is doubly male) or sockets on both sides (connects two males).

General Public Virus n. Pejorative name for some versions of the **GNU** project **copyleft** or General Public License (GPL), which requires that any tools or **apps** incorporating copylefted code must be source-distributed on the same counter-commercial terms as GNU stuff. Thus it is alleged that the copyleft 'infects' software generated with GNU tools, which may in turn infect other software that reuses any of its code. The Free Software Foundation's official position as of January 1991 is that copyright law limits the scope of the GPL to "programs textually incorporating significant amounts of GNU code", and that the 'infection' is not passed on to third parties unless actual GNU source is transmitted (as in, for example, use of the Bison parser skeleton). Nevertheless, widespread suspicion that the **copyleft** language is 'boobytrapped' has caused many developers to avoid using GNU tools and the GPL. Recent (July 1991) changes in the language of the version 2.00 license may eliminate this problem.

generate vt. To produce something according to an algorithm or program or set of rules, or as a (possibly unintended) side effect of the execution of an algorithm or program. The opposite of **parse**. This term retains its mechanistic connotations (though often humorously) when used of human behavior. "The guy is rational most of the time, but mention nuclear energy around him and he'll generate **infinite** flamage."

gensym */jen´sim/* [from MacLISP for 'generated symbol'] 1. v. To invent a new name for something temporary, in such a way that the name is almost certainly not in conflict with one already in use. 2. n. The resulting name. The canonical form of a gensym is 'Gnnnn' where nnnn represents a number; any LISP hacker would recognize G0093 (for example) as a gensym. 3. A freshly generated data structure with a gensymmed name. Gensymmed names are useful for storing or uniquely identifying crufties (see **cruft**).

Get a life! imp. Hacker-standard way of suggesting that the person to whom it is directed has succumbed to terminal geekdom (see **computer geek**). Often heard on **USENET**, esp. as a way of suggesting that the target is taking some obscure issue of **theology** too seriously. This exhortation was popularized by William Shatner on a "Saturday Night Live" episode in a speech that ended "Get a *life*!", but some respondents believe it to have been in use before then. It was certainly in wide use among hackers for at least five years before achieving mainstream currency in early 1992.

Get a real computer! imp. Typical hacker response to news that somebody is having trouble getting work done on a system that (a) is single-tasking, (b) has no hard disk, or (c) has an address space smaller than 16 megabytes. This is as of mid-1993; note that the threshold for 'real computer' rises with time, and it may well be (for example) that machines with character-only displays will be generally considered 'unreal' in a few years (GLS points out that they already are in some circles). See **essentials**, **bitty box**, and **toy**.

GFR */G-F-R/* vt. [ITS: from 'Grim File Reaper', an ITS and LISP Machine utility] To remove a file or files according to some program-automated or semi-automatic manual procedure, especially one designed to reclaim mass storage space or reduce name-space clutter (the original GFR actually moved files to tape). Often generalized to pieces of data below file level. "I used to have his phone number, but I guess I **GFR**ed it." See also **prowler**, **reaper**. Compare **GC**, which discards only provably worthless stuff.

gig */jig/* or */gig/* [SI] n. See **quantifiers**.

giga- */ji´ga/* or */gi´ga/* [SI] pref. See **quantifiers**.

GIGO */gi:´goh/* [acronym] 1. 'Garbage In, Garbage Out' — usually said in response to **lusers** who complain that a program didn't "do the right thing" when given imperfect input or otherwise mistreated in some way. Also commonly used to describe failures in human decision making due to faulty, incomplete, or imprecise data. 2. *Garbage In, Gospel Out*: this more recent expansion is a sardonic comment on the tendency human beings have to put excessive trust in 'computerized' data.

gilley [USENET] n. The unit of analogical bogosity. According to its originator, the standard for one gilley was "the act of bogotoficiously comparing the shutting down of 1000 machines for a day with the killing of one person". The milligilley has been found to suffice for most normal conversational exchanges.

gillion */gil´yən/* or */jil´yən/* [formed from **giga-** by analogy with mega/million and tera/trillion] n. 10^9. Same as an American billion or a British *milliard*. How one pronounces this depends on whether one speaks **giga-** with a hard or soft 'g'.

GIPS */gips/* or */jips/* [analogy with **MIPS**] n. Giga-Instructions per Second (also possibly 'Gillions of Instructions per Second'; see **gillion**). In 1991, this is used of only a handful of highly parallel machines, but this is expected to change. Compare **KIPS**.

glark */glark/* vt. To figure something out from context. "The System III manuals are pretty poor, but you can generally glark the meaning from context." Interestingly, the word was originally 'glork'; the context was "This gubblick contains many nonsklarkish English flutzpahs, but the overall pluggandisp can be glorked [sic] from context" (David Moser, quoted by Douglas Hofstadter in his "Metamagical Themas" column in the January 1981 *Scientific American*). It is conjectured that hackish usage mutated the verb to 'glark' because **glork** was already an established jargon term. Compare **grok**, **zen**.

glass [IBM] n. Synonym for **silicon**.

glass tty */glas T-T-Y/* or */glas ti´tee/* n. A terminal that has a display screen but which, because of hardware or software limitations, behaves like a teletype or some other printing terminal, thereby combining the disadvantages of both: like a printing terminal, it can't do fancy display hacks, and like a display terminal, it doesn't produce hard copy. An example is the early 'dumb' version of Lear-Siegler ADM 3 (without cursor control). See **tube**, **tty**; compare **dumb terminal**, **smart terminal**. See "TV Typewriters" (appendix A) for an interesting true story about a glass tty.

glassfet */glas´fet/* [by analogy with MOSFET, the acronym for 'Metal-Oxide-Semiconductor Field-Effect Transistor'] n. Syn. **firebottle**, a humorous way to refer to a vacuum tube.

glitch */glich/* [from German 'glitschen' to slip, via Yiddish 'glitshen', to slide or skid] 1. n. A sudden interruption in electric service, sanity, continuity, or program function. Sometimes recoverable. An interruption in electric service is specifically called a *power glitch* (also **power hit**), of grave concern because it usually crashes all the computers. In jargon, though, a hacker who got to the middle of a sentence and then forgot how he or she intended to complete it might say, "Sorry, I just glitched". 2. vi. To commit a glitch. See **gritch**. 3. vt. [Stanford] To scroll a display screen, esp. several lines at a time. **WAITS** terminals used to do this in order to avoid continuous scrolling, which is distracting to the eye. 4. obs. Same as **magic cookie**, sense 2.

All these uses of *glitch* derive from the specific technical meaning the term has in the electronic hardware world, where it is now techspeak. A glitch can occur when the inputs of a circuit change, and the outputs change to some **random** value for some very brief time before they settle down to the correct value. If another circuit inspects the output at just the wrong time, reading the random value, the results can be very wrong and very hard to debug (a glitch is one of many causes of electronic **heisenbug**s).

glob */glob/, not /glohb/* [UNIX] vt.,n. To expand special characters in a wildcarded name, or the act of so doing (the action is also called *globbing*). The UNIX conventions for filename wildcarding have become sufficiently pervasive that many hackers use some of them in written English, especially in email or news on technical topics. Those commonly encountered include the following:

*	wildcard for any string (see also **UN*X**)
?	wildcard for any single character (generally read this way only at the beginning or in the middle of a word)
[]	delimits a wildcard matching any of the enclosed characters
{}	alternation of comma-separated alternatives; thus, 'foo{baz,qux}' would be read as 'foobaz' or 'fooqux'

Some examples: "He said his name was [KC]arl" (expresses ambiguity). "I don't read talk.politics.*" (any of the talk.politics subgroups on **USENET**). Other examples are given under the entry for **X**. Note that glob patterns are similar, but not identical, to those used in **regexp**s.

Historical note: The jargon usage derives from `glob`, the name of a subprogram that expanded wildcards in archaic pre-Bourne versions of the UNIX shell.

glork */glork/* 1. interj. Term of mild surprise, usually tinged with outrage, as when one attempts to save the results of two hours of editing and finds that the system has just crashed. 2. Used as a name for just about anything. See **foo**. 3. vt. Similar to **glitch**, but usually used reflexively. "My program just glorked itself." See also **glark**.

glue n. Generic term for any interface logic or protocol that connects two component blocks. For example, **Blue Glue** is IBM's SNA protocol, and hardware designers call anything used to connect large VLSI's or circuit blocks *glue logic*.

Coping with a hydraulic **glitch**.
The next cartoon in the Crunchly saga is 07-24-73, page 316.

gnarly */nar´lee/* adj. Both **obscure** and **hairy** (sense 1). "**Yow!** — the tuned assembler implementation of BitBlt is really gnarly!" From a similar but less specific usage in surfer slang.

GNU */gnoo/, not /noo/* 1. [acronym: 'GNU's Not UNIX!', see **recursive acronym**] A UNIX-workalike development effort of the Free Software Foundation headed by Richard Stallman *<rms@gnu.ai.mit.edu>*. GNU EMACS and the GNU C compiler, two tools designed for this project, have become very popular in hackerdom and elsewhere. The GNU project was designed partly to proselytize for RMS's position that information is community property and all software source should be shared. One of its slogans is "Help stamp out software hoarding!" Though this remains controversial (because it implicitly denies any right of designers to own, assign, and sell the results of their labors), many hackers who disagree with RMS have nevertheless cooperated to produce large amounts of high-quality software for free redistribution under the Free Software Foundation's imprimatur. See **EMACS**, **copyleft**, **General Public Virus**. 2. Noted UNIX hacker John Gilmore *<gnu@toad.com>*, founder of USENET's anarchic alt.* hierarchy.

GNUMACS */gnoo´maks/* [contraction of 'GNU EMACS'] Often-heard abbreviated name for the **GNU** project's flagship tool, **EMACS**. Used esp. in contrast with **GOSMACS**.

go flatline [from cyberpunk SF, refers to flattening of EEG traces upon brain-death] vi., also adjectival *flatlined*. 1. To **die**, terminate, or fail, esp. irreversibly. In hacker parlance, this is used of machines only, human death being considered somewhat too serious a matter to employ jargon-jokes about. 2. To go completely quiescent; said of machines undergoing controlled shutdown. "You can suffer file damage if you shut down UNIX but power off before the system has gone flatline." 3. Of a video tube, to fail by losing vertical scan, so all one sees is a bright horizontal line bisecting the screen.

go root [UNIX] vi. To temporarily enter **root mode** in order to perform a privileged operation. This use is deprecated in Australia, where v. 'root' refers to animal sex.

go-faster stripes [UK] Syn. **chrome**. Mainstream in some parts of UK. .

gobble vt. 1. To consume, usu. used with 'up'. "The output spy gobbles characters out of a **tty** output buffer." 2. To obtain, usu. used with 'down'.

"I guess I'll gobble down a copy of the documentation tomorrow." See also **snarf**.

Godzillagram */god-zil´ə-gram/* n. [from Japan's national hero] 1. A network packet that in theory is a broadcast to every machine in the universe. The typical case is an IP datagram whose destination IP address is [255.255.255.255]. Fortunately, few gateways are foolish enough to attempt to implement this case! 2. A network packet of maximum size. An IP Godzillagram has 65,536 octets.

golden adj. [prob. from folklore's 'golden egg'] When used to describe a magnetic medium (e.g., *golden disk, golden tape*), describes one containing a tested, up-to-spec, ready-to-ship software version. Compare **platinum-iridium**.

golf-ball printer n. The IBM 2741, a slow but letter-quality printing device and terminal based on the IBM Selectric typewriter. The *golf ball* was a little spherical frob bearing reversed embossed images of 88 different characters arranged on four parallels of latitude; one could change the font by swapping in a different golf ball. This was the technology that enabled APL to use a non-EBCDIC, non-ASCII, and in fact completely non-standard character set. This put it 10 years ahead of its time — where it stayed, firmly rooted, for the next 20, until character displays gave way to programmable bit-mapped devices with the flexibility to support other character sets.

gonk */gonk/* vt.,n. 1. To prevaricate or to embellish the truth beyond any reasonable recognition. In German the term is (mythically) *gonken*; in Spanish the verb becomes *gonkar*. "You're gonking me. That story you just told me is a bunch of gonk." In German, for example, "Du gonkst mir" (You're pulling my leg). See also **gonkulator**. 2. [British] To grab some sleep at an odd time; compare **gronk out**.

gonkulator */gon´kyoo-lay-tr/* [from the old "Hogan's Heroes" TV series] n. A pretentious piece of equipment that actually serves no useful purpose. Usually used to describe one's least favorite piece of computer hardware. See **gonk**.

gonzo */gon´zoh/* [from Hunter S. Thompson] adj. Overwhelming; outrageous; over the top; very large, esp. used of collections of source code, source files, or individual functions. Has some of the connotations of **moby** and **hairy**, but without the implication of obscurity or complexity.

Good Thing n.,adj. Often capitalized; always pronounced as if capitalized. 1. Self-evidently wonderful to anyone in a position to notice: "The Trail-blazer's 19.2Kbaud PEP mode with on-the-fly Lempel-Ziv compression is a Good Thing for sites relaying netnews." 2. Something that can't possibly have any ill side-effects and may save considerable grief later: "Removing the self-modifying code from that shared library would be a Good Thing." 3. When said of software tools or libraries, as in "YACC is a Good Thing", specifically connotes that the thing has drastically reduced a programmer's work load. Oppose **Bad Thing**.

gorets */goh´rets/* n. The unknown ur-noun, fill in your own meaning. Found esp. on the USENET newsgroup *alt.gorets*, which seems to be a running contest to redefine the word by implication in the funniest and most peculiar way, with the understanding that no definition is ever final. [A correspondent from the Former Soviet Union informs me that 'gorets' is Russian for 'mountain dweller' — ESR] Compare **frink**.

gorilla arm n. The side-effect that destroyed touch-screens as a mainstream input technology despite a promising start in the early 1980s. It seems the designers of all those **spiffy** touch-menu systems failed to notice that humans aren't designed to hold their arms in front of their faces making small motions. After more than a very few selections, the arm begins to feel sore, cramped, and oversized — the operator looks like a gorilla while using the touch screen and feels like one afterwards. This is now considered a classic cautionary tale to human-factors designers; "Remember the gorilla arm!" is shorthand for "How is this going to fly in *real* use?".

gorp */gorp/* [CMU: perhaps from the canonical hiker's food, Good Old Raisins and Peanuts] Another **metasyntactic variable**, like **foo** and **bar**.

GOSMACS */goz´maks/* [contraction of 'Gosling EMACS'] n. The first **EMACS**-in-C implementation, predating but now largely eclipsed by **GNU-MACS**. Originally freeware; a commercial version is now modestly popular as 'UniPress EMACS'. The author (James Gosling) went on to invent **NeWS**.

Gosperism */gos´pər-izm/* A hack, invention, or saying due to arch-hacker R. William (Bill) Gosper. This notion merits its own term because there are so many of them. Many of the entries in **HAKMEM** are Gosperisms; see also **life**.

gotcha n. A **misfeature** of a system, especially a programming language or environment, that tends to breed bugs or mistakes because it both enticingly easy to invoke and completely unexpected and/or unreasonable in its outcome. For example, a classic gotcha in **C** is the fact that `if (a=b) {code;}` is syntactically valid and sometimes even correct. It puts the value of `b` into `a` and then executes `code` if `a` is non-zero. What the programmer probably meant was `if (a==b) {code;}`, which executes `code` if `a` and `b` are equal.

GPL */G-P-L/* n. Abbreviation for 'General Public License' in widespread use; see **copyleft**, **General Public Virus**.

GPV */G-P-V/* n. Abbrev. for **General Public Virus** in widespread use.

grault */grawlt/* n. Yet another **metasyntactic variable**, invented by Mike Gallaher and propagated by the **GOSMACS** documentation. See **corge**.

gray goo n. A hypothetical substance composed of **sagan**s of sub-micron-sized self-replicating robots programmed to make copies of themselves out of whatever is available. The image that goes with the term is one of the entire biosphere of Earth being eventually converted to robot goo. This is the simplest of the **nanotechnology** disaster scenarios, easily refuted by arguments from energy requirements and elemental abundances. Compare **blue goo**.

Great Renaming n. The **flag day** in 1985 on which all of the non-local groups on the **USENET** had their names changed from the net.- format to the current multiple-hierarchies scheme. Used esp. in discussing the history of newsgroup names. "The oldest sources group is *comp.sources.misc*; before the Great Renaming, it was *net.sources*."

Great Runes n. Uppercase-only text or display messages. Some archaic operating systems still emit these. See also **runes**, **smash case**, **fold case**.

Decades ago, back in the days when it was the sole supplier of long-distance hardcopy transmittal devices, the Teletype Corporation was faced with a major design choice. To shorten code lengths and cut complexity in the printing mechanism, it had been decided that teletypes would use a monocase font, either ALL UPPER or all lower. The Question Of The Day was therefore, which one to choose. A study was conducted on readability under various conditions of bad ribbon, worn print hammers, etc. Lowercase won; it is less dense and has more distinctive letterforms, and is thus much easier to read both under ideal conditions and when the letters are mangled or partly obscured. The results were filtered up through **management**. The chairman of Teletype killed the proposal because it failed one incredibly important criterion:

> "It would be impossible to spell the name of the Deity correctly."

In this way (or so, at least, hacker folklore has it) superstition triumphed over utility. Teletypes were the major input devices on most early computers, and terminal manufacturers looking for corners to cut naturally followed suit until well into the 1970s. Thus, that one bad call stuck us with Great Runes for thirty years.

Great Worm, the n. The 1988 Internet **worm** perpetrated by **RTM**. This is a play on Tolkien (compare **elvish**, **elder days**). In the fantasy history of his Middle Earth books, there were dragons powerful enough to lay waste to entire regions; two of these (Scatha and Glaurung) were known as "the Great Worms". This usage expresses the connotation that the RTM hack was a sort of devastating watershed event in hackish history; certainly it did more to make non-hackers nervous about the Internet than anything before or since.

great-wall [from SF fandom] vi.,n. A mass expedition to an oriental restaurant, esp. one where food is served family-style and shared. There is a common heuristic about the amount of food to order, expressed as "Get $N-1$ entrees"; the value of N, which is the number of people in the group, can be inferred from context (see **N**). See **oriental food**, **ravs**, **stir-fried random**.

Green Book n. 1. One of the three standard **PostScript** references: *PostScript Language Program Design*, bylined 'Adobe Systems' (Addison-Wesley, 1988; QA76.73.P67P66 ISBN 0-201-14396-8); see also **Red Book**, **Blue Book**, and the **White Book** (sense 2). 2. Informal name for one of the three standard references on SmallTalk: *Smalltalk-80: Bits of History, Words of Advice*, by Glenn Krasner (Addison-Wesley, 1983; QA76.8.S635S58; ISBN 0-201-11669-3) (this, too, is associated with blue and red books). 3. The *X/Open Compatibility Guide*, which defines an international standard **UNIX** environment that is a proper superset of POSIX/SVID; also includes descriptions of a standard utility toolkit, systems administrations features, and the like. This grimoire is taken with particular seriousness in Europe. See **Purple Book**. 4. The IEEE 1003.1 POSIX Operating Systems Interface standard has been dubbed "The Ugly Green Book". 5. Any of the 1992 standards issued by the CCITT's tenth plenary assembly. These include, among other things, the X.400 email standard and the Group 1 through 4 fax standards. See also **book titles**.

green bytes n. (also *green words*) 1. Meta-information embedded in a file, such as the length of the file or its name; as opposed to keeping such information in a separate description file or record. The term comes from an IBM user's group meeting (ca. 1962) at which these two approaches were being debated and the diagram of the file on the blackboard had the *green bytes* drawn in green. 2. By extension, the non-data bits in any self-describing format. "A GIF file contains, among other things, green bytes describing the packing method for the image." Compare **out-of-band**, **zigamorph**, **fence** (sense 1).

green card n. [after the *IBM System/360 Reference Data* card] A summary of an assembly language, even if the color is not green. Less frequently used now because of the decrease in the use of assembly language. "I'll go get my green card so I can check the addressing mode for that instruction." Some green cards are actually booklets.

The original green card became a yellow card when the System/370 was introduced, and later a yellow booklet. An anecdote from IBM refers to a scene that took place in a programmers' terminal room at Yorktown in 1978. A luser overheard one of the programmers ask another "Do you have a green card?" The other grunted and passed the first a thick yellow booklet. At this point the luser turned a delicate shade of olive and rapidly left the room, never to return.

green lightning [IBM] n. 1. Apparently random flashing streaks on the face of 3278-9 terminals while a new symbol set is being downloaded. This hardware bug was left deliberately unfixed, as some genius within IBM suggested it would let the user know that 'something is happening'. That, it certainly does. Later microprocessor-driven IBM color graphics displays were actually *programmed* to produce green lightning! 2. [proposed] Any bug perverted into an alleged feature by adroit rationalization or marketing. "Motorola calls the CISC cruft in the 88000 architecture 'compatibility logic', but I call it green lightning". See also **feature** (sense 6).

green machine n. A computer or peripheral device that has been designed and built to military specifications for field equipment (that is, to withstand mechanical shock, extremes of temperature and humidity, and so forth). Comes from the olive-drab 'uniform' paint used for military equipment.

Green's Theorem [TMRC] prov. For any story, in any group of people there will be at least one person who has not heard the story. A refinement of the theorem states that there will be *exactly* one person (if there were more than one, it wouldn't be as bad to re-tell the story). [The name of this theorem is a play on a fundamental theorem in calculus. — ESR]

grep */grep/* [from the qed/ed editor idiom g/*re*/p , where *re* stands for a regular expression, to Globally search for the Regular Expression and Print the lines containing matches to it, via **UNIX** `grep(1)`] vt. To rapidly scan a file or set of files looking for a particular string or pattern (when browsing through a large set of files, one may speak of *grepping around*). By extension, to look for something by pattern. "Grep the bulletin board for the system backup schedule, would you?" See also **vgrep**.

grilf *//* n. Girl-friend. Like **newsfroup** and **filk**, a typo incarnated as a new word. Seems to have originated sometime in 1992.

grind vt. 1. [MIT and Berkeley] To prettify hardcopy of code, especially LISP code, by reindenting lines, printing keywords and comments in distinct fonts (if available), etc. This usage was associated with the MacLISP community and is now rare; **prettyprint** was and is the generic term for such operations. 2. [UNIX] To generate the formatted version of a document from the **nroff**, **troff**, **TEX**, or Scribe source. 3. To run seemingly interminably, esp. (but not necessarily) if performing some tedious and inherently useless task. Similar to **crunch** or **grovel**. Grinding has a connotation of using a lot of CPU time, but it is possible to grind a disk, network, etc. See also **hog**. 4. To make the whole system slow. "Troff really grinds a PDP-11." 5. *grind grind* excl. Roughly, "Isn't the machine slow today!"

grind crank n. A mythical accessory to a terminal. A crank on the side of a monitor, which when operated makes a zizzing noise and causes the computer to run faster. Usually one does not refer to a grind crank out loud, but merely makes the appropriate gesture and noise. See **grind** and **wugga wugga**.

Historical note: At least one real machine actually had a grind crank — the R1, a research machine built toward the end of the days of the great vacuum tube computers, in 1959. R1 (also known as 'The Rice Institute Computer' (TRIC) and later as 'The Rice University Computer' (TRUC)) had a single-step/free-run switch for use when debugging programs. Since single-stepping through a large program was rather tedious, there was also a crank with a cam and gear arrangement that repeatedly pushed the single-step button. This allowed one to 'crank' through a lot of code, then slow down to single-step for a bit when you got near the code of interest, poke at some registers using the console typewriter, and then keep on cranking.

gripenet [IBM] n. A wry (and thoroughly unofficial) name for IBM's internal VNET system, deriving from its common use by IBMers to voice pointed criticism of IBM management that would be taboo in more formal channels.

gritch */grich/* 1. n. A complaint (often caused by a **glitch**). 2. vi. To complain. Often verb-doubled: "Gritch gritch". 3. A synonym for **glitch** (as verb or noun).

grok */grok/*, var. */grohk/* [from the novel *Stranger in a Strange Land*, by Robert A. Heinlein, where it is a Martian word meaning literally 'to drink' and metaphorically 'to be one with'] vt. 1. To understand, usually in a global sense. Connotes intimate and exhaustive knowledge. Contrast **zen**, which is similar supernal understanding experienced as a single brief flash. See also **glark**. 2. Used of programs, may connote merely sufficient understanding. "Almost all C compilers grok the `void` type these days."

gronk */gronk/* [popularized by Johnny Hart's comic strip "B.C." but the word apparently predates that] vt. 1. To clear the state of a wedged device and restart it. More severe than 'to **frob**' (sense 2). 2. [TMRC] To cut, sever, smash, or similarly disable. 3. The sound made by many 3.5-inch diskette drives. In particular, the microfloppies on a Commodore Amiga go "grink, gronk".

gronk out vi. To cease functioning. Of people, to go home and go to sleep. "I guess I'll gronk out now; see you all tomorrow."

gronked adj. 1. Broken. "The teletype scanner was gronked, so we took the system down." 2. Of people, the condition of feeling very tired or (less commonly) sick. "I've been chasing that bug for 17 hours now and I am thoroughly gronked!" Compare **broken**, which means about the same as **gronk** used of hardware, but connotes depression or mental/emotional problems in people.

grovel vi. 1. To work interminably and without apparent progress. Often used transitively with 'over' or 'through'. "The file scavenger has been groveling through the /usr directories for 10 minutes now." Compare **grind** and **crunch**. Emphatic form: *grovel obscenely*. 2. To examine minutely or in complete detail. “The compiler grovels over the entire source program before beginning to translate it.” “I grovelled through all the documentation, but I still couldn’t find the command I wanted.”

grunge */gruhnj/* n. 1. That which is grungy, or that which makes it so. 2. [Cambridge] Code which is inaccessible due to changes in other parts of the program. The preferred term in North America is **dead code**.

gubbish */guhb´əsh/* [a portmanteau of ‘garbage’ and ‘rubbish’; may have originated with SF author Philip K. Dick] n. Garbage; crap; nonsense. “What is all this gubbish?” The opposite portmanteau ‘rubbage’ is also reported.

guiltware */gilt´weir/* n. 1. A piece of **freeware** decorated with a message telling one how long and hard the author worked on it and intimating that one is a no-good freeloader if one does not immediately send the poor suffering martyr gobs of money. 2. **Shareware** that works.

gumby */guhm´bee/* [from a class of Monty Python characters, poss. with some influence from the 1960s claymation character] n. An act of minor but conspicuous stupidity, often in *gumby maneuver* or *pull a gumby.*

gun [ITS: from the :GUN command] vt. To forcibly terminate a program or job (computer, not career). “Some idiot left a background process running soaking up half the cycles, so I gunned it.” Compare **can**.

gunch */guhnch/* [TMRC] vt. To push, prod, or poke at a device that has almost (but not quite) produced the desired result. Implies a threat to **mung**.

gurfle */ger´fl/* interj. An expression of shocked disbelief. “He said we have to recode this thing in FORTRAN by next week. Gurfle!” Compare **weeble**.

guru n. [UNIX] An expert. Implies not only **wizard** skill but also a history of being a knowledge resource for others. Less often, used (with a qualifier) for other experts on other systems, as in *VMS guru.* See **source of all good bits**.

guru meditation n. Amiga equivalent of ‘panic’ in UNIX (sometimes just called a *guru* or *guru event*). When the system crashes, a cryptic message of the form “GURU MEDITATION #XXXXXXXX.YYYYYYYY” may appear, indicating what the problem was. An Amiga guru can figure things out from the numbers. Generally a **guru** event must be followed by a **Vulcan nerve pinch**.

This term is (no surprise) an in-joke from the earliest days of the Amiga. There used to be a device called a 'Joyboard' which was basically a plastic board built onto a joystick-like device; it was sold with a skiing game cartridge for the Atari game machine. It is said that whenever the prototype OS crashed, the system programmer responsible would calm down by concentrating on a solution while sitting cross-legged on a Joyboard trying to keep the board in balance. This position resembled that of a meditating guru. Sadly, the joke was removed in AmigaOS 2.04.

gweep */gweep/* [WPI] 1. v. To **hack**, usually at night. At WPI, from 1977 onwards, one who gweeped coud often be found at the College Computing Center punching cards or crashing the PDP-10 or, later, the DEC-20. The term has survived the demise of those technologies, however, and is still alive in late 1991. "I'm going to go gweep for a while. See you in the morning." "I gweep from 8 PM till 3 AM during the week." 2. n. One who habitually gweeps in sense 1; a **hacker**. "He's a hard-core gweep, mumbles code in his sleep."

= H =

h [from SF fandom] infix. A method of 'marking' common words, i.e., calling attention to the fact that they are being used in a nonstandard, ironic, or humorous way. Originated in the fannish catchphrase "Bheer is the One True Ghod!" from decades ago. H-infix marking of 'Ghod' and other words spread into the 1960s counterculture via underground comix, and into early hackerdom either from the counterculture or from SF fandom (the three overlapped heavily at the time). More recently, the h infix has become an expected feature of benchmark names (Dhrystone, Rhealstone, etc.); this is prob. patterning on the original Whetstone (the name of a laboratory) but influenced by the fannish/counterculture h infix.

ha ha only serious [from SF fandom, orig. as mutation of HHOK, 'Ha Ha Only Kidding'] A phrase (often seen abbreviated as HHOS) that aptly captures the flavor of much hacker discourse. Applied especially to parodies, absurdities, and ironic jokes that are both intended and perceived to contain a possibly disquieting amount of truth, or truths that are constructed on in-joke and self-parody. This lexicon contains many examples of ha-ha-only-serious in both form and content. Indeed, the entirety of hacker culture is often perceived as ha-ha-only-serious by hackers themselves; to take it either too lightly or too seriously marks a person as an outsider, a **wannabee**, or in **larval stage**. For further enlightenment on this subject, consult any Zen master. See also **Humor, Hacker**, and **AI koans**.

hack 1. n. Originally, a quick job that produces what is needed, but not well. 2. n. An incredibly good, and perhaps very time-consuming, piece of work that produces exactly what is needed. 3. vt. To bear emotionally or physically. "I can't hack this heat!" 4. vt. To work on something (typically a program). In an immediate sense: "What are you doing?" "I'm hacking TECO." In a general (time-extended) sense: "What do you do around here?" "I hack TECO." More generally, "I hack *foo*" is roughly equivalent to "*foo* is my major interest (or project)". "I hack solid-state physics." See **Hacking X for Y**. 5. vt. To pull a prank on. See sense 2 and **hacker** (sense 5). 6. vi. To interact with a computer in a playful and exploratory rather than goal-directed way. "Whatcha up to?" "Oh, just hacking." 7. n. Short for **hacker**. 8. See **nethack**. 9. [MIT] v. To explore the basements, roof ledges, and steam tunnels of a large, institutional building, to the dismay of Physical Plant workers and (since this is usually performed at educational institutions) the Campus Police. This activity has been found to be eerily similar to playing adventure games such as Dungeons and Dragons and **Zork**. See also **vadding**.

Constructions on this term abound. They include *happy hacking* (a farewell), *how's hacking?* (a friendly greeting among hackers) and *hack, hack* (a fairly content-free but friendly comment, often used as a temporary farewell). For more on this totipotent term see "The Meaning of 'Hack'". See also **neat hack, real hack**.

hack attack [poss. by analogy with 'Big Mac Attack' from ads for the McDonald's fast-food chain; the variant *big hack attack* is reported] n. Nearly synonymous with **hacking run**, though the latter more strongly implies an all-nighter.

hack mode n. 1. What one is in when hacking, of course. 2. More specifically, a Zen-like state of total focus on The Problem that may be achieved when one is hacking (this is why every good hacker is part mystic). Ability to enter such concentration at will correlates strongly with wizardliness; it is one of the most important skills learned during **larval stage**. Sometimes amplified as *deep hack mode*.

Being yanked out of hack mode (see **priority interrupt**) may be experienced as a physical shock, and the sensation of being in hack mode is more than a little habituating. The intensity of this experience is probably by itself sufficient explanation for the existence of hackers, and explains why many resist being promoted out of positions where they can code. See also **cyberspace** (sense 2).

Some aspects of hackish etiquette will appear quite odd to an observer unaware of the high value placed on hack mode. For example, if someone appears at your door, it is perfectly okay to hold up a hand (without turning one's eyes away from the screen) to avoid being interrupted. One may read, type, and interact with the computer for quite some time before further acknowledging the other's presence (of course, he or she is reciprocally free to leave without a word). The understanding is that you might be in **hack mode** with a lot of delicate **state** (sense 2) in your head, and you dare not **swap** that context out until you have reached a good point to pause. See also **juggling eggs**.

hack on vt. To **hack**; implies that the subject is some pre-existing hunk of code that one is evolving, as opposed to something one might **hack up**.

hack together vt. To throw something together so it will work. Unlike *kluge together* or **cruft together**, this does not necessarily have negative connotations.

hack up vt. To **hack**, but generally implies that the result is a hack in sense 1 (a quick hack). Contrast this with **hack on**. To *hack up on* implies a **quick-and-dirty** modification to an existing system. Contrast **hacked up**; compare **kluge up**, **monkey up**, **cruft together**.

hack value n. Often adduced as the reason or motivation for expending effort toward a seemingly useless goal, the point being that the accomplished goal is a hack. For example, MacLISP had features for reading and printing Roman numerals, which were installed purely for hack value. See **display hack** for one method of computing hack value, but this cannot really be explained, only experienced. As Louis Armstrong once said when asked to explain jazz: "Man, if you gotta ask you'll never know." (Feminists please note Fats Waller's explanation of rhythm: "Lady, if you got to ask you ain't got it.")

hacked off [analogous to 'pissed off'] adj. Said of system administrators who have become annoyed, upset, or touchy owing to suspicions that their sites have been or are going to be victimized by crackers, or used for inappropriate, technically illegal, or even overtly criminal activities. For example, having unreadable files in your home directory called 'worm', 'lockpick', or 'goroot' would probably be an effective (as well as impressively obvious and stupid) way to get your sysadmin hacked off at you.

hacked up adj. Sufficiently patched, kluged, and tweaked that the surgical scars are beginning to crowd out normal tissue (compare **critical mass**). Not all programs that are hacked become *hacked up*; if modifications are done with some eye to coherence and continued maintainability, the software may emerge better for the experience. Contrast **hack up**.

hacker [originally, someone who makes furniture with an axe] n. 1. A person who enjoys exploring the details of programmable systems and how to stretch their capabilities, as opposed to most users, who prefer to learn only the minimum necessary. 2. One who programs enthusiastically (even obsessively) or who enjoys programming rather than just theorizing about programming. 3. A person capable of appreciating **hack value**. 4. A person who is good at programming quickly. 5. An expert at a particular program, or one who frequently does work using it or on it; as in 'a UNIX hacker'. (Definitions 1 through 5 are correlated, and people who fit them congregate.) 6. An expert or enthusiast of any kind. One might be an astronomy hacker, for example. 7. One who enjoys the intellectual challenge of creatively overcoming or circumventing limitations. 8. [deprecated] A malicious meddler who tries to discover sensitive information by poking around. Hence *password hacker*, *network hacker*. The correct term is **cracker**.

The term 'hacker' also tends to connote membership in the global community defined by the net (see **network, the** and **Internet address**). It also implies that the person described is seen to subscribe to some version of the hacker ethic (see **hacker ethic, the**.

It is better to be described as a hacker by others than to describe oneself that way. Hackers consider themselves something of an elite (a meritocracy based on ability), though one to which new members are gladly welcome. There is thus a certain ego satisfaction to be had in identifying yourself as a hacker (but if you claim to be one and are not, you'll quickly be labeled **bogus**). See also **wannabee**.

hacker ethic, the n. 1. The belief that information-sharing is a powerful positive good, and that it is an ethical duty of hackers to share their expertise by writing free software and facilitating access to information and to computing resources wherever possible. 2. The belief that system-cracking for fun and exploration is ethically OK as long as the cracker commits no theft, vandalism, or breach of confidentiality.

Both of these normative ethical principles are widely, but by no means universally, accepted among hackers. Most hackers subscribe to the hacker ethic in sense 1, and many act on it by writing and giving away free software. A few go further and assert that *all* information should be free and *any* proprietary control of it is bad; this is the philosophy behind the GNU project.

Sense 2 is more controversial: some people consider the act of cracking itself to be unethical, like breaking and entering. But the belief that 'ethical' cracking excludes destruction at least moderates the behavior of people who see themselves as 'benign' crackers (see also **samurai**). On this view, it may be one of the highest forms of hackerly courtesy to (a) break into a system, and then (b) explain to the sysop, preferably by email from a **superuser** account, exactly how it was done and how the hole can be plugged — acting as an unpaid (and unsolicited) **tiger team**.

The most reliable manifestation of either version of the hacker ethic is that almost all hackers are actively willing to share technical tricks, software, and (where possible) computing resources with other hackers. Huge cooperative networks such as **USENET**, **FidoNet** and Internet (see **Internet address**) can function without central control because of this trait; they both rely on and reinforce a sense of community that may be hackerdom's most valuable intangible asset.

hacking run [analogy with 'bombing run' or 'speed run'] n. A hack session extended long outside normal working times, especially one longer than 12 hours. May cause you to *change phase the hard way* (see **phase**).

Hacking X for Y [ITS] n. Ritual phrasing of part of the information which ITS made publicly available about each user. This information (the INQUIR record) was a sort of form in which the user could fill out various fields. On display, two of these fields were always combined into a project description of the form "Hacking X for Y" (e.g., `"Hacking perceptrons for Minsky"`). This form of description became traditional and has since been carried over to other systems with more general facilities for self-advertisement (such as UNIX **plan files**).

Hackintosh n. 1. An Apple Lisa that has been hacked into emulating a Macintosh (also called a 'Mac XL'). 2. A Macintosh assembled from parts theoretically belonging to different models in the line.

hackish */hak´ish/* adj. (also **hackishness** n.) 1. Said of something that is or involves a hack. 2. Of or pertaining to hackers or the hacker subculture. See also **true-hacker**.

hackishness n. The quality of being or involving a hack. This term is considered mildly silly. Syn. **hackitude**.

hackitude n. Syn. **hackishness**; this word is considered sillier.

hair [back-formation from **hairy**] n. The complications that make something hairy. "Decoding **TECO** commands requires a certain amount of hair." Often seen in the phrase *infinite hair*, which connotes extreme complexity. Also in *hairiferous* (tending to promote hair growth): "GNUMACS elisp encourages lusers to write complex editing modes." "Yeah, it's pretty hairiferous all right." (or just: "Hair squared!")

hairy adj. 1. Annoyingly complicated. "**DWIM** is incredibly hairy." 2. Incomprehensible. "**DWIM** is incredibly hairy." 3. Of people, high-powered, authoritative, rare, expert, and/or incomprehensible. Hard to explain except in context: "He knows this hairy lawyer who says there's nothing to worry about." See also **hirsute**.

A well-known result in topology called the Brouwer Fixed-Point Theorem states that any continuous transformation of a surface into itself has at least one fixed point. Mathematically literate hackers tend to associate the term 'hairy' with the informal version of this theorem; "You can't comb a hairy ball smooth."

The adjective 'long-haired' is well-attested to have been in slang use among scientists and engineers during the early 1950s; it was equivalent to modern *hairy* senses 1 and 2, and was very likely ancestral to the hackish use. In fact the noun 'long-hair' was at the time used to describe a person satisfying sense 3. Both senses probably passed out of use when long hair was adopted as a signature trait by the 1960s counterculture, leaving hackish *hairy* as a sort of stunted mutant relic.

HAKMEM */hak´mem/* n. MIT AI Memo 239 (February 1972). A legendary collection of neat mathematical and programming hacks contributed by many people at MIT and elsewhere. (The title of the memo really is "HAKMEM", which is a 6-letterism for 'hacks memo'.) Some of them are very useful techniques, powerful theorems, or interesting unsolved problems, but most fall into the category of mathematical and computer trivia. Here is a sampling of the entries (with authors), slightly paraphrased:

Item 41 (Gene Salamin): There are exactly 23,000 prime numbers less than 2^{18}.

Item 46 (Rich Schroeppel): The most *probable* suit distribution in bridge hands is 4-4-3-2, as compared to 4-3-3-3, which is the most *evenly* distributed. This is because the world likes to have unequal numbers: a thermodynamic effect saying things will not be in the state of lowest energy, but in the state of lowest disordered energy.

Item 81 (Rich Schroeppel): Count the magic squares of order 5 (that is, all the 5-by-5 arrangements of the numbers from 1 to 25 such that all rows, columns, and diagonals add up to the same number). There are about 320 million, not counting those that differ only by rotation and reflection.

Item 154 (Bill Gosper): The myth that any given programming language is machine independent is easily exploded by computing the sum of powers of 2. If the result loops with period = 1 with sign +, you are on a sign-magnitude machine. If the result loops with period = 1 at -1, you are on a twos-complement machine. If the result loops with period greater than 1, including the beginning, you are on a ones-complement machine. If the result loops with period greater than 1, not including the beginning, your machine isn't binary — the pattern should tell you the base. If you run out of memory, you are on a string or bignum system. If arithmetic overflow is a fatal error, some fascist pig with a read-only mind is trying to enforce machine independence. But the very ability to trap overflow is machine dependent. By this strategy, consider the universe, or, more precisely, algebra: Let X = the sum of many powers of 2 = . . . 111111 (base 2). Now add X to itself: $X + X$ = . . . 111110. Thus, $2X = X - 1$, so $X = -1$. Therefore algebra is run on a machine (the universe) that is two's-complement.

Item 174 (Bill Gosper and Stuart Nelson): 21963283741 is the only number such that if you represent it on the **PDP-10** as both an integer and a floating-point number, the bit patterns of the two representations are identical.

Item 176 (Gosper): The "banana phenomenon" was encountered when processing a character string by taking the last 3 letters typed out, searching for a random occurrence of that sequence in the text, taking the letter following that occurrence, typing it out, and iterating. This ensures that every 4-letter string output occurs in the original. The program typed BANANANANANANANA. . . . We note an ambiguity in the phrase, "the Nth occurrence of." In one sense, there are five 00's in 0000000000; in another, there are nine. The editing program TECO finds five. Thus it finds only the first ANA in BANANA, and is thus obligated to type N next. By Murphy's Law, there is but one NAN, thus forcing A, and thus a loop. An option to find overlapped instances would be useful, although it would require backing up $N - 1$ characters before seeking the next N-character string.

Note: This last item refers to a **Dissociated Press** implementation. See also **banana problem**.

HAKMEM also contains some rather more complicated mathematical and technical items, but these examples show some of its fun flavor.

hakspek */hak´speek/* n. A shorthand method of spelling found on many British academic bulletin boards and **talker system**s. Syllables and whole words in a sentence are replaced by single ASCII characters the names of which are phonetically similar or equivalent, while multiple letters are usually dropped. Hence, 'for' becomes '4'; 'two', 'too', and 'to' become '2'; 'ck' becomes 'k'. "Before I see you tomorrow" becomes "b4 i c u 2moro". First appeared in London about 1986, and was probably caused by the slowness of available talker systems, which operated on archaic machines with outdated operating systems and no standard methods of communication. Has become rarer since. See also **talk mode**.

hammer vt. Commonwealth hackish syn. for **bang on**.

hamster n. 1. [Fairchild] A particularly slick little piece of code that does one thing well; a small, self-contained hack. The image is of a hamster **happily** spinning its exercise wheel. 2. A tailless mouse; that is, one with an infrared link to a receiver on the machine, as opposed to the conventional cable. 3. [UK] Any item of hardware made by Amstrad, a company famous for its cheap plastic PC-almost-compatibles.

hand cruft [pun on 'hand craft'] vt. See **cruft**, sense 3.

hand-hacking n. 1. The practice of translating **hot spot**s from an **HLL** into hand-tuned assembler, as opposed to trying to coerce the compiler into generating better code. Both the term and the practice are becoming uncommon. See **tune**, **bum**, **by hand**; syn. with v. **cruft**. 2. More generally, manual construction or patching of data sets that would normally be generated by a translation utility and interpreted by another program, and aren't really designed to be read or modified by humans.

handle n. 1. [from CB slang] An electronic pseudonym; a 'nom de guerre' intended to conceal the user's true identity. Network and BBS handles function as the same sort of simultaneous concealment and display one finds on Citizen's Band radio, from which the term was adopted. Use of grandiose handles is characteristic of **crackers**, **weenies**, **spods**, and other lower forms of network life; true hackers travel on their own reputations rather than invented legendry. Compare **nick**. 2. [Mac] A pointer to a pointer to dynamically-allocated memory; the extra level of indirection allows on-the-fly memory compaction (to cut down on fragmentation) or aging out of unused resources, with minimal impact on the (possibly multiple) parts of the larger program containing references to the allocated memory. Compare **snap** (to snap a handle would defeat its purpose); see also **aliasing bug**, **dangling pointer**.

hand-roll [from obs. mainstream slang *hand-rolled* in opposition to *ready-made*, referring to cigarettes] v. To perform a normally automated software installation or configuration process **by hand**; implies that the normal process failed due to bugs in the configurator or was defeated by something exceptional in the local environment. "The worst thing about being a gateway between four different nets is having to hand-roll a new sendmail configuration every time any of them upgrades."

handshaking n. Hardware or software activity designed to start or keep two machines or programs in synchronization as they **do protocol**. Often applied to human activity; thus, a hacker might watch two people in conversation nodding their heads to indicate that they have heard each others' points and say "Oh, they're handshaking!". See also **protocol**.

handwave [poss. from gestures characteristic of stage magicians] 1. v. To gloss over a complex point; to distract a listener; to support a (possibly actually valid) point with blatantly faulty logic. 2. n. The act of handwaving. "Boy, what a handwave!"

If someone starts a sentence with "Clearly . . . " or "Obviously . . . " or "It is self-evident that . . . ", it is a good bet he is about to handwave (alternatively, use of these constructions in a sarcastic tone before a paraphrase of someone else's argument suggests that it is a handwave). The theory behind this term is that if you wave your hands at the right moment, the listener may be sufficiently distracted to not notice that what you have said is **bogus**. Failing that, if a listener does object, you might try to dismiss the objection with a wave of your hand.

The use of this word is often accompanied by gestures: both hands up, palms forward, swinging the hands in a vertical plane pivoting at the elbows and/or shoulders (depending on the magnitude of the handwave); alternatively, holding the forearms in one position while rotating the hands at the wrist to make them flutter. In context, the gestures alone can suffice as a remark; if a speaker makes an outrageously unsupported assumption, you might simply wave your hands in this way, as an accusation, far more eloquent than words could express, that his logic is faulty.

hang v. 1. To wait for an event that will never occur. "The system is hanging because it can't read from the crashed drive". See **wedged**, **hung**. 2. To wait for some event to occur; to hang around until something happens. "The program displays a menu and then hangs until you type a character." Compare **block**. 3. To attach a peripheral device, esp. in the construction 'hang off': "We're going to hang another tape drive off the file server." Implies a device attached with cables, rather than something that is strictly inside the machine's chassis.

Hanlon's Razor prov. A corollary of **Finagle's Law**, similar to Occam's Razor, that reads "Never attribute to malice that which can be adequately explained by stupidity." The derivation of the common title Hanlon's Razor is unknown; a similar epigram has been attributed to William James. Quoted here because it seems to be a particular favorite of hackers, often showing up in **sig blocks**, **fortune cookie** files and the login banners of BBS systems and commercial networks. This probably reflects the hacker's daily experience of environments created by well-intentioned but short-sighted people. Compare **Sturgeon's Law**.

happily adv. Of software, used to emphasize that a program is unaware of some important fact about its environment, either because it has been fooled into believing a lie, or because it doesn't care. The sense of 'happy' here is not that of elation, but rather that of blissful ignorance. "The program continues to run, happily unaware that its output is going to /dev/null."

haque */hak/* [USENET] n. Variant spelling of **hack**, used only for the noun form and connoting an **elegant** hack. that is a **hack** in sense 2.

hard boot n. See **boot**.

hardcoded adj. 1. Said of data inserted directly into a program, where it cannot be easily modified, as opposed to data in some **profile**, resource (see **de-rezz** sense 2), or environment variable that a **user** or hacker can easily modify. 2. In C, this is esp. applied to use of a literal instead of a `#define` macro (see **magic number**).

hardwarily */hard-weir´ə-lee/* adv. In a way pertaining to hardware. "The system is hardwarily unreliable." The adjective 'hardwary' is *not* traditionally used, though it has recently been reported from the U.K. See **softwarily**.

hardwired adj. 1. In software, syn. for **hardcoded**. 2. By extension, anything that is not modifiable, especially in the sense of customizable to one's particular needs or tastes.

has the X nature [seems to derive from Zen Buddhist koans of the form "Does an X have the Buddha-nature?"] adj. Common hacker construction for 'is an X', used for humorous emphasis. "Anyone who can't even use a program with on-screen help embedded in it truly has the **loser** nature!" See also **the X that can be Y is not the true X**.

hash bucket n. A notional receptacle, a set of which might be used to apportion data items for sorting or lookup purposes. When you look up a name in the phone book (for example), you typically hash it by extracting its first letter; the hash buckets are the alphabetically ordered letter sections. This term is used as techspeak with respect to code that uses actual hash functions; in jargon, it is used for human associative memory as well. Thus, two things 'in the same hash bucket' are more difficult to discriminate, and may be confused. "If you hash English words only by length, you get too many common grammar words in the first couple of hash buckets." Compare **hash collision**.

hash collision [from the technical usage] n. (var. *hash clash*) When used of people, signifies a confusion in associative memory or imagination, especially a persistent one (see **thinko**). True story: One of us [ESR] was once on the phone with a friend about to move out to Berkeley. When asked what he expected Berkeley to be like, the friend replied: "Well, I have this mental picture of naked women throwing Molotov cocktails, but I think that's just a collision in my hash tables." Compare **hash bucket**.

hat n. Common (spoken) name for the circumflex ('^', ASCII 1011110) character. See **ASCII** for other synonyms.

HCF */H-C-F/* n. Mnemonic for 'Halt and Catch Fire', any of several undocumented and semi-mythical machine instructions with destructive side-effects, supposedly included for test purposes on several well-known architectures going as far back as the IBM 360. The MC6800 microprocessor was the first for which an HCF opcode became widely known. This instruction caused the processor to **toggle** a subset of the bus lines as rapidly as it could; in some configurations this could actually cause lines to burn up.

heads down [Sun] adj. Concentrating, usually so heavily and for so long that everything outside the focus area is missed. See also **hack mode** and **larval stage**, although this mode is hardly confined to fledgling hackers.

heartbeat n. 1. The signal emitted by a Level 2 Ethernet transceiver at the end of every packet to show that the collision-detection circuit is still connected. 2. A periodic synchronization signal used by software or hardware, such as a bus clock or a periodic interrupt. 3. The 'natural' oscillation frequency of a computer's clock crystal, before frequency division down to the machine's clock rate. 4. A signal emitted at regular intervals by software to demonstrate that it is still alive. Sometimes hardware is designed to reboot the machine if it stops hearing a heartbeat. See also **breath-of-life packet**.

heatseeker [IBM] n. A customer who can be relied upon to buy, without fail, the latest version of an existing product (not quite the same as a member of the **lunatic fringe**). A 1993 example of a heatseeker is someone who, owning a 286 PC and Windows 3.0, goes out and buys Windows 3.1 (which offers no worthwhile benefits unless you have a 386). If all customers were heatseekers, vast amounts of money could be made by just fixing the bugs in each release (n) and selling it to them as release (n+1).

heavy metal [Cambridge] n. Syn. **big iron**.

heavy wizardry n. Code or designs that trade on a particularly intimate knowledge or experience of a particular operating system or language or complex application interface. Distinguished from **deep magic**, which trades more on arcane *theoretical* knowledge. Writing device drivers is heavy wizardry; so is interfacing to **X** (sense 2) without a toolkit. Esp. found in source-code comments of the form "Heavy wizardry begins here". Compare **voodoo programming**.

heavyweight adj. High-overhead; **baroque**; code-intensive; featureful, but costly. Esp. used of communication protocols, language designs, and any sort of implementation in which maximum generality and/or ease of implementation has been pushed at the expense of mundane considerations such as speed, memory utilization, and startup time. **EMACS** is a heavyweight editor; **X** is an *extremely* heavyweight window system. This term isn't pejorative, but one hacker's heavyweight is another's **elephantine** and a third's **monstrosity**. Oppose *lightweight.* Usage: now borders on techspeak, especially in the compound 'heavyweight process'.

heisenbug */hi:´zen-buhg/* [from Heisenberg's Uncertainty Principle in quantum physics] n. A bug that disappears or alters its behavior when one attempts to probe or isolate it. (This usage is not even particularly fanciful; the use of a debugger sometimes alters a program's operating environment significantly enough that buggy code, such as that which relies on the values of uninitialized memory, behaves quite differently.) Antonym of **Bohr bug**; see also **mandelbug**, **schroedinbug**. In C, nine out of ten heisenbugs result from uninitialized auto variables, **fandango on core** phenomena (esp. lossage related to corruption of the malloc **arena**) or errors that **smash the stack**.

Helen Keller mode n. 1. State of a hardware or software system that is deaf, dumb, and blind, i.e., accepting no input and generating no output, usually due to an infinite loop or some other excursion into **deep space**. (Unfair to the real Helen Keller, whose success at learning speech was triumphant.) See also **go flatline**, **catatonic**. 2. On IBM PCs under DOS, refers to a specific failure mode in which a screen saver has kicked in over an **ill-behaved** application which bypasses the very interrupts the screen saver watches for activity. Your choices are to try to get from the program's current state through a successful save-and-exit without being able to see what you're doing, or to re-boot the machine. This isn't (strictly speaking) a crash.

hello, sailor! interj. Occasional West Coast equivalent of **hello, world**; seems to have originated at SAIL, later associated with the game **Zork** (which also included "hello, aviator" and "hello, implementor"). Originally from the traditional hooker's greeting to a swabbie fresh off the boat, of course.

hello, wall! excl. See **wall**.

hello, world interj. 1. The canonical minimal test message in the C/UNIX universe. 2. Any of the minimal programs that emit this message. Traditionally, the first program a C coder is supposed to write in a new environment is one that just prints "hello, world" to standard output (and indeed it is the first example program in **K&R**). Environments that generate an unreasonably large executable for this trivial test or which require a **hairy** compiler-linker invocation to generate it are considered to **lose** (see **X**). 3. Greeting uttered by a hacker making an entrance or requesting information from anyone present. "Hello, world! Is the **VAX** back up yet?"

hex n. 1. Short for **hexadecimal**, base 16. 2. A 6-pack of anything (compare **quad**, sense 2). Neither usage has anything to do with **magic** or **black art**, though the pun is appreciated and occasionally used by hackers. True story: As a joke, some hackers once offered some surplus ICs for sale to be worn as protective amulets against hostile magic. The chips were, of course, hex inverters.

hexadecimal n. Base 16. Coined in the early 1960s to replace earlier 'sexadecimal', which was too racy and amusing for stuffy IBM, and later adopted by the rest of the industry.

Actually, neither term is etymologically pure. If we take 'binary' to be paradigmatic, the most etymologically correct term for base 10, for example, is 'denary', which comes from 'deni' (ten at a time, ten each), a Latin 'distributive' number; the corresponding term for base-16 would be something like 'sendenary'. 'Decimal' is from an ordinal number; the corresponding prefix for 6 would imply something like 'sextidecimal'. The 'sexa-' prefix is Latin but incorrect in this context, and 'hexa-' is Greek. The word 'octal' is similarly incorrect; a correct form would be 'octaval' (to go with decimal), or 'octonary' (to go with binary). If anyone ever implements a base-3 computer, computer scientists will be faced with the unprecedented dilemma of a choice between two *correct* forms; both 'ternary' and 'trinary' have a claim to this throne.

hexit */hek´sit/* n. A hexadecimal digit (0–9, and A–F or a–f). Used by people who claim that there are only *ten* digits, dammit; sixteen-fingered human beings are rather rare, despite what some keyboard designs might seem to imply (see **space-cadet keyboard**).

HHOK See **ha ha only serious**.

HHOS See **ha ha only serious**.

hidden flag [scientific computation] n. An extra option added to a routine without changing the calling sequence. For example, instead of adding an explicit input variable to instruct a routine to give extra diagnostic output, the programmer might just add a test for some otherwise meaningless feature of the existing inputs, such as a negative mass. The use of hidden flags can make a program very hard to debug and understand, but is all too common wherever programs are hacked on in a hurry.

high bit [from 'high-order bit'] n. 1. The most significant bit in a byte. 2. By extension, the most significant part of something other than a data byte: "Spare me the whole **saga**, just give me the high bit." See also **meta bit**, **hobbit**, **dread high-bit disease**, and compare the mainstream slang *bottom line*.

high moby */hi:´ mohb´ee/* n. The high half of a 512K **PDP-10**'s physical address space; the other half was of course the low moby. This usage has been generalized in a way that has outlasted the **PDP-10**; for example, at the 1990 Washington D.C. Area Science Fiction Conclave (Disclave), when a miscommunication resulted in two separate wakes being held in commemoration of the shutdown of MIT's last **ITS** machines, the one on the upper floor was dubbed the 'high moby' and the other the 'low moby'. All parties involved **grok**ked this instantly. See **moby**.

highly [scientific computation] adv. The preferred modifier for overstating an understatement. As in: *highly nonoptimal*, the worst possible way to do something; *highly nontrivial*, either impossible or requiring a major research project; *highly nonlinear*, completely erratic and unpredictable; *highly nontechnical*, drivel written for **lusers**, oversimplified to the point of being misleading or incorrect (compare **drool-proof paper**). In other computing cultures, postfixing of **in the extreme** might be preferred.

hing *//* [IRC] n. Fortuitous typo for 'hint', now in wide intentional use among players of **initgame**. Compare **newsfroup**, **filk**.

hirsute adj. Occasionally used humorously as a synonym for **hairy**.

HLL */H-L-L/* n. [High-Level Language (as opposed to assembler)] Found primarily in email and news rather than speech. Rarely, the variants 'VHLL' and 'MLL' are found. VHLL stands for 'Very-High-Level Language' and is used to describe a **bondage-and-discipline language** that the speaker happens to like; Prolog and Backus's FP are often called VHLLs. 'MLL' stands for 'Medium-Level Language' and is sometimes used half-jokingly to describe **C**, alluding to its 'structured-assembler' image. See also **languages of choice**.

hobbit n. 1. The High Order Bit of a byte; same as the **meta bit** or **high bit**. 2. The non-ITS name of *vad@ai.mit.edu* (*Hobbit*), master of lasers.

hog n.,vt. 1. Favored term to describe programs or hardware that seem to eat far more than their share of a system's resources, esp. those which noticeably degrade interactive response. *Not* used of programs that are simply extremely large or complex or that are merely painfully slow themselves (see **pig, run like a**). More often than not encountered in qualified forms, e.g., *memory hog, core hog, hog the processor, hog the disk.* "A controller that never gives up the I/O bus gets killed after the bus-hog timer expires." 2. Also said of *people* who use more than their fair share of resources (particularly disk, where it seems that 10% of the people use 90% of the disk, no matter how big the disk is or how many people use it). Of course, once disk hogs fill up one filesystem, they typically find some other new one to infect, claiming to the sysadmin that they have an important new project to complete.

holy wars [from **USENET**, but may predate it] n. **flame wars** over **religious issues**. The paper by Danny Cohen that popularized the terms **big-endian** and **little-endian** in connection with the LSB-first/MSB-first controversy was entitled "On Holy Wars and a Plea for Peace". Other perennial Holy Wars have included **EMACS** vs. **vi**, my personal computer vs. everyone else's personal computer, **ITS** vs. **UNIX**, **UNIX** vs. **VMS**, **BSD** UNIX vs. **USG UNIX**, **C** vs. **Pascal**, **C** vs. FORTRAN, etc., ad nauseam. The characteristic that distinguishes holy wars from normal technical disputes is that in a holy wars most of the participants spend their time trying to pass off personal value choices and cultural attachments as objective technical evaluations. See also **theology**.

home box n. A hacker's personal machine, especially one he or she owns. "Yeah? Well, *my* home box runs a full 4.2 BSD, so there!"

home machine n. 1. Syn. **home box**. 2. The machine that receives your email. These senses might be distinct, for example, for a hacker who owns one computer at home, but reads email at work.

hook n. A software or hardware feature included in order to simplify later additions or changes by a user. For example, a simple program that prints numbers might always print them in base 10, but a more flexible version would let a variable determine what base to use; setting the variable to 5 would make the program print numbers in base 5. The variable is a simple hook. An even more flexible program might examine the variable and treat a value of 16 or less as the base to use, but treat any other number as the address of a user-supplied routine for printing a number. This is a **hairy** but powerful hook; one can then write a routine to print numbers as Roman numerals, say, or as Hebrew characters, and plug it into the program through the hook. Often the difference between a good program and a superb one is that the latter has useful hooks in judiciously chosen places. Both may do the original job about equally well, but the one with the hooks is much more flexible for future expansion of capabilities (**EMACS**, for example, is *all* hooks). The term 'user exit' is synonymous but much more formal and less hackish.

hop 1. n. One file transmission in a series required to get a file from point A to point B on a store-and-forward network. On such networks (including **UUCPNET** and **FidoNet**), an important inter-machine metric is the number of hops in the shortest path between them, which can be more significant than their geographical separation. See **bang path**. 2. v. To log in to a remote machine, esp. via rlogin or telnet. "I'll hop over to foovax to FTP that."

hose 1. vt. To make non-functional or greatly degraded in performance. "That big ray-tracing program really hoses the system." See **hosed**. 2. n. A narrow channel through which data flows under pressure. Generally denotes data paths that represent performance bottlenecks. 3. n. Cabling, especially thick Ethernet cable. This is sometimes called *bit hose* or *hosery* (play on 'hosiery') or 'etherhose'. See also **washing machine**.

hosed adj. Same as **down**. Used primarily by UNIX hackers. Humorous: also implies a condition thought to be relatively easy to reverse. Probably derived from the Canadian slang 'hoser' popularized by the Bob and Doug Mackenzie skits on SCTV, but this usage predated SCTV by years in hackerdom (it was certainly already live at CMU in the 1970s). See **hose**. It is also widely used of people in the mainstream sense of 'in an extremely unfortunate situation'.

Once upon a time, a Cray that had been experiencing periodic difficulties crashed, and it was announced to have been hosed. It was discovered that the crash was due to the disconnection of some coolant hoses. The problem was corrected, and users were then assured that everything was OK because the system had been rehosed. See also **dehose**.

hot spot n. 1. [primarily used by C/UNIX programmers, but spreading] It is received wisdom that in most programs, less than 10% of the code eats 90% of the execution time; if one were to graph instruction visits versus code addresses, one would typically see a few huge spikes amidst a lot of low-level noise. Such spikes are called *hot spots* and are good candidates for heavy optimization or **hand-hacking**. The term is especially used of tight loops and recursions in the code's central algorithm, as opposed to (say) initial set-up costs or large but infrequent I/O operations. See **tune**, **bum**, **hand-hacking**. 2. The active location of a cursor on a bit-map display. "Put the mouse's hot spot on the 'ON' widget and click the left button." 3. A screen region that is sensitive to mouse clicks, which trigger some action. Hypertext help screens are an example, in which a hot spot exists in the vicinity of any word for which additional material is available. 4. In a massively parallel computer with shared memory, the one location that all 10,000 processors are trying to read or write at once (perhaps because they are all doing a **busy-wait** on the same lock). 5. More generally, any place in a hardware design that turns into a performance bottleneck due to resource contention.

house wizard [prob. from ad-agency tradetalk, 'house freak'] n. A hacker occupying a technical-specialist, R&D, or systems position at a commercial shop. A really effective house wizard can have influence out of all proportion to his/her ostensible rank and still not have to wear a suit. Used esp. of UNIX wizards. The term *house guru* is equivalent.

HP-SUX */H-P suhks/* n. Unflattering hackerism for HP-UX, Hewlett-Packard's UNIX port, which features some truly unique bogosities in the filesystem internals and elsewhere (these occasionally create portability problems). HP-UX is often referred to as 'hockey-pux' inside HP, and one respondent claims that the proper pronunciation is */H-P ukkkhhhh/* as though one were about to spit. Another such alternate spelling and pronunciation is "H-PUX" */H-puhks/*. Hackers at HP/Apollo (the former Apollo Computers which was swallowed by HP in 1989) have been heard to complain that Mr. Packard should have pushed to have his name first, if for no other reason than the greater eloquence of the resulting acronym. Compare **AIDX**, **buglix**. See also **Nominal Semidestructor**, **Telerat**, **Open DeathTrap**, **ScumOS**, **sun-stools**.

huff v. To compress data using a Huffman code. Various programs that use such methods have been called 'HUFF' or some variant thereof. Oppose **puff**. Compare **crunch**, **compress**.

humma // excl. A filler word used on various 'chat' and 'talk' programs when you had nothing to say but felt that it was important to say something. The word apparently originated (at least with this definition) on the MECC Timeshare System (MTS, a now-defunct educational time-sharing system running in Minnesota during the 1970s and the early 1980s) but was later sighted on early UNIX systems.

Humor, Hacker n. A distinctive style of shared intellectual humor found among hackers, having the following marked characteristics:

1. Fascination with form-vs.-content jokes, paradoxes, and humor having to do with confusion of metalevels (see **meta**). One way to make a hacker laugh: hold a red index card in front of him/her with "GREEN" written on it, or vice-versa (note, however, that this is funny only the first time).
2. Elaborate deadpan parodies of large intellectual constructs, such as specifications (see **write-only memory**), standards documents, language descriptions (see **INTERCAL**), and even entire scientific theories (see **quantum bogodynamics, computron**).
3. Jokes that involve screwily precise reasoning from bizarre, ludicrous, or just grossly counter-intuitive premises.
4. Fascination with puns and wordplay.
5. A fondness for apparently mindless humor with subversive currents of intelligence in it — for example, old Warner Brothers and Rocky & Bullwinkle cartoons, the Marx brothers, the early B-52s, and Monty Python's Flying Circus. Humor that combines this trait with elements of high camp and slapstick is especially favored.
6. References to the symbol-object antinomies and associated ideas in Zen Buddhism and (less often) Taoism. See **has the X nature**, **Discordianism**, **zen**, **ha ha only serious**, **AI koans**.

   See also **filk**, **retrocomputing**, and Appendix B. If you have an itchy feeling that all 6 of these traits are really aspects of one thing that is incredibly difficult to talk about exactly, you are (a) correct and (b) responding like a hacker. These traits are also recognizable (though in a less marked form) throughout **science-fiction fandom**.

hung [from 'hung up'] adj. Equivalent to **wedged**, but more common at UNIX/C sites. Not generally used of people. Syn. with **locked up**, **wedged**; compare **hosed**. See also **hang**. A hung state is distinguished from **crash**ed or **down**, where the program or system is also unusable but because it is not running rather than because it is waiting for something. However, the recovery from both situations is often the same.

hungry puppy n. Syn. **slopsucker**.

hungus */huhng´gəs/* [perhaps related to slang 'humongous'] adj. Large, unwieldy, usually unmanageable. "TCP is a hungus piece of code." "This is a hungus set of modifications."

hyperspace */hi:´per-spays/* n. A memory location that is *far* away from where the program counter should be pointing, often inaccessible because it is not even mapped in. "Another core dump — looks like the program jumped off to hyperspace somehow." (Compare **jump off into never-never land**.) This usage is from the SF notion of a spaceship jumping *into hyperspace*, that is, taking a shortcut through higher-dimensional space — in other words, bypassing this universe. The variant *east hyperspace* is recorded among CMU and Bliss hackers.

hysterical reasons (also *hysterical raisins*) n. A variant on the stock phrase "for historical reasons", indicating specifically that something must be done in some stupid way for backwards compatibility, and moreover that the feature it must be compatible with was the result of a bad design in the first place. "All IBM PC video adapters have to support MDA text mode for hysterical reasons." Compare **bug-for-bug compatible**.

= I =

I didn't change anything! interj. An aggrieved cry often heard as bugs manifest during a regression test. The **canonical** reply to this assertion is "Then it works just the same as it did before, doesn't it?" See also **one-line fix**. This is also heard from applications programmers trying to blame an obvious applications problem on an unrelated systems software change, for example a divide-by-0 fault after terminals were added to a network. Usually, their statement is found to be false. Upon close questioning, they will admit some major restructuring of the program that shouldn't have broken anything, in their opinion, but which actually **hosed** the code completely.

I see no X here. Hackers (and the interactive computer games they write) traditionally favor this slightly marked usage over other possible equivalents such as "There's no X here!" or "X is missing." or "Where's the X?". This goes back to the original PDP-10 **ADVENT**, which would respond in this wise if you asked it to do something involving an object not present at your location in the game.

IBM */I-B-M/* Inferior But Marketable; It's Better Manually; Insidious Black

Magic; It's Been Malfunctioning; Incontinent Bowel Movement; and a near-**infinite** number of even less complimentary expansions, including 'International Business Machines'. See **TLA**. These abbreviations illustrate the considerable antipathy most hackers have long felt toward the 'industry leader' (see **fear and loathing**).

What galls hackers about most IBM machines above the PC level isn't so much that they are underpowered and overpriced (though that does count against them), but that the designs are incredibly archaic, **crufty**, and **elephantine** . . . and you can't *fix* them — source code is locked up tight, and programming tools are expensive, hard to find, and bletcherous to use once you've found them. With the release of the UNIX-based RIOS family this may have begun to change — but then, we thought that when the PC-RT came out, too.

In the spirit of universal peace and brotherhood, this lexicon now includes a number of entries attributed to 'IBM'; these derive from some rampantly unofficial jargon lists circulated within IBM's own beleaguered hacker underground.

IBM discount n. A price increase. Outside IBM, this derives from the common perception that IBM products are generally overpriced (see **clone**); inside, it is said to spring from a belief that large numbers of IBM employees living in an area cause prices to rise.

ICBM address n. (Also *missile address*) The form used to register a site with the USENET mapping project includes a blank for longitude and latitude, preferably to seconds-of-arc accuracy. This is actually used for generating geographically-correct maps of USENET links on a plotter; however, it has become traditional to refer to this as one's *ICBM address* or *missile address*, and many people include it in their **sig block** with that name. (A real missile address would include target altitude.)

ice [coined by USENETter Tom Maddox, popularized by William Gibson's cyberpunk SF novels: a contrived acronym for 'Intrusion Countermeasure Electronics'] Security software (in Gibson's novels, software that responds to intrusion by attempting to literally kill the intruder). Also, *icebreaker*: a program designed for cracking security on a system.

Neither term is in serious use yet as of mid-1993, but many hackers find the metaphor attractive, and each may develop a denotation in the future. In the meantime, the speculative usage could be confused with 'ICE', an acronym for “in-circuit emulator”.

idempotent [from mathematical techspeak] adj. Acting as if used only once, even if used multiple times. This term is often used with respect to **C** header files, which contain common definitions and declarations to be included by several source files. If a header file is ever included twice during the same compilation (perhaps due to nested #include files), compilation errors can result unless the header file has protected itself against multiple inclusion; a header file so protected is said to be idempotent. The term can also be used to describe an initialization subroutine that is arranged to perform some critical action exactly once, even if the routine is called several times.

If you want X, you know where to find it. There is a legend that Dennis Ritchie, inventor of **C**, once responded to demands for features resembling those of what at the time was a much more popular language by observing “If you want PL/I, you know where to find it.” Ever since, this has been hackish standard form for fending off requests to alter a new design to mimic some older (and, by implication, inferior and **baroque**) one. The case X = **Pascal** manifests semi-regularly on USENET’s *comp.lang.c* newsgroup. Indeed, the case X = X has been reported in discussions of graphics software (see **X**).

ifdef out */if´def owt/* v. Syn. for **condition out**, specific to **C**.

ill-behaved adj. 1. [numerical analysis] Said of an algorithm or computational method that tends to blow up because of accumulated roundoff error or poor convergence properties. 2. Software that bypasses the defined **OS** interfaces to do things (like screen, keyboard, and disk I/O) itself, often in a way that depends on the hardware of the machine it is running on or which is nonportable or incompatible with other pieces of software. In the IBM PC/MS-DOS world, there is a folk theorem (nearly true) to the effect that (owing to gross inadequacies and performance penalties in the OS interface) all interesting applications are ill-behaved. See also **bare metal**. Oppose **well-behaved**, compare **PC-ism**. See **mess-dos**.

IMHO // [from SF fandom via USENET; abbreviation for ‘In My Humble Opinion’] “IMHO, mixed-case C names should be avoided, as mistyping something in the wrong case can cause hard-to-detect errors — and they look too Pascalish anyhow.” Also seen in variant forms such as IMNSHO (In My Not-So-Humble Opinion) and IMAO (In My Arrogant Opinion).

Imminent Death Of The Net Predicted! [USENET] prov. Since **USENET** first got off the ground in 1980–81, it has grown exponentially, approximately doubling in size every year. On the other hand, most people feel the **signal-to-noise ratio** of USENET has dropped steadily. These trends led, as far back as mid-1983, to predictions of the imminent collapse (or death) of the net. Ten years and numerous doublings later, enough of these gloomy prognostications have been confounded that the phrase "Imminent Death Of The Net Predicted!" has become a running joke, hauled out any time someone grumbles about the **S/N ratio** or the huge and steadily increasing volume, or the possible loss of a key node or link, or the potential for lawsuits when ignoramuses post copyrighted material, etc., etc., etc.

in the extreme adj. A preferred superlative suffix for many hackish terms. See, for example, *obscure in the extreme* under **obscure**, and compare **highly**.

inc */ink/* v. Verbal (and only rarely written) shorthand for *increment*, i.e. 'increase by one'. Especially used by assembly programmers, as many assembly languages have an `inc` mnemonic. Antonym: **dec**.

incantation n. Any particularly arbitrary or obscure command that one must mutter at a system to attain a desired result. Not used of passwords or other explicit security features. Especially used of tricks that are so poorly documented that they must be learned from a **wizard**. "This compiler normally locates initialized data in the data segment, but if you **mutter** the right incantation they will be forced into text space."

include vt. [USENET] 1. To duplicate a portion (or whole) of another's message (typically with attribution to the source) in a reply or followup, for clarifying the context of one's response. See the discussion of inclusion styles under "Hacker Writing Style". 2. [from **C**] `#include <disclaimer.h>` has appeared in **sig blocks** to refer to a notional *standard* **disclaimer** *file*.

include war n. Excessive multi-leveled including within a discussion **thread**, a practice that tends to annoy readers. In a forum with high-traffic newsgroups, such as USENET, this can lead to **flames** and the urge to start a **kill file**.

indent style [C programmers] n. The rules one uses to indent code in a readable fashion. There are four major C indent styles, described below; all have the aim of making it easier for the reader to visually track the scope of control constructs. The significant variable is the placement of '`{`' and '`}`' with respect to the statement(s) they enclose and to the guard or controlling statement (`if`, `else`, `for`, `while`, or `do`) on the block, if any.

K&R style — Named after Kernighan & Ritchie, because the examples in **K&R** are formatted this way. Also called *kernel style* because the UNIX kernel is written in it, and the 'One True Brace Style' (abbrev. 1TBS) by its partisans. The basic indent shown here is eight spaces (or one tab) per level; four spaces are occasionally seen, but are much less common.

```
if (cond) {
        <body>
}
```

Allman style — Named for Eric Allman, a Berkeley hacker who wrote a lot of the BSD utilities in it (it is sometimes called *BSD style*). Resembles normal indent style in Pascal and Algol. Basic indent per level shown here is eight spaces, but four spaces are just as common (esp. in C++ code).

```
if (cond)
{
        <body>
}
```

Whitesmiths style — popularized by the examples that came with Whitesmiths C, an early commercial C compiler. Basic indent per level shown here is eight spaces, but four spaces are occasionally seen.

```
if (cond)
        {
        <body>
        }
```

GNU style — Used throughout GNU EMACS and the Free Software Foundation code, and just about nowhere else. Indents are always four spaces per level, with `{` and `}` halfway between the outer and inner indent levels.

```
if (cond)
  {
    <body>
  }
```

Surveys have shown the Allman and Whitesmiths styles to be the most common, with about equal mind shares. K&R/1TBS used to be nearly universal, but is now much less common (the opening brace tends to get lost against the right paren of the guard part in an `if` or `while`, which is a **Bad Thing**). Defenders of 1TBS argue that any putative gain in readability is less important than their style's relative economy with vertical space, which enables one to see more code on one's screen at once. Doubtless these issues will continue to be the subject of **holy wars**.

index n. See **coefficient of X**.

infant mortality n. It is common lore among hackers (and in the electronics industry at large; this term is possibly techspeak by now) that the chances of sudden hardware failure drop off exponentially with a machine's time since first use (that is, until the relatively distant time at which enough mechanical wear in I/O devices and thermal-cycling stress in components has accumulated for the machine to start going senile). Up to half of all chip and wire failures happen within a new system's first few weeks; such failures are often referred to as *infant mortality* problems (or, occasionally, as *sudden infant death syndrome*). See **bathtub curve**, **burn-in period**.

infinite adj. Consisting of a large number of objects; extreme. Used very loosely as in: "This program produces infinite garbage." "He is an infinite loser." The word most likely to follow *infinite*, though, is **hair**. (It has been pointed out that fractals are an excellent example of infinite hair.) These uses are abuses of the word's mathematical meaning. The term *semi-infinite*, denoting an immoderately large amount of some resource, is also heard. "This compiler is taking a semi-infinite amount of time to optimize my program." See also **semi**.

infinite loop n. One that never terminates (that is, the machine **spin**s or **buzz**es forever and goes **catatonic**). There is a standard joke that has been made about each generation's exemplar of the ultra-fast machine: "The Cray-3 is so fast it can execute an infinite loop in under 2 seconds!"

Infinite-Monkey Theorem n. "If you put an **infinite** number of monkeys at typewriters, eventually one will bash out the script for Hamlet." (One may also hypothesize a small number of monkeys and a very long period of time.) This theorem asserts nothing about the intelligence of the one **random** monkey that eventually comes up with the script (and note that the mob will also type out all the possible *incorrect* versions of Hamlet). It may be referred to semi-seriously when justifying a **brute force** method; the implication is that, with enough resources thrown at it, any technical challenge becomes a **one-banana problem**.

This theorem was first popularized by the classic SF short story "Inflexible Logic" by Russell Maloney, many younger hackers know it through a reference in Douglas Adams's *Hitchhiker's Guide to the Galaxy.*

infinity n. 1. The largest value that can be represented in a particular type of variable (register, memory location, data type, whatever). 2. *minus infinity*: The smallest such value, not necessarily or even usually the simple negation of plus infinity. In N-bit twos-complement arithmetic, infinity is $2^{N-1} - 1$ but minus infinity is $-(2^{N-1})$, not $-(2^{N-1} - 1)$. Note also that this is different from *time T equals minus infinity*, which is closer to a mathematician's usage of infinity.

initgame */in-it´gaym/* [IRC] n. An **IRC** version of the venerable trivia game "20 questions", in which one user changes his **nick** to the initials of a famous person or other named entity, and the others on the channel ask yes or no questions, with the one to guess the person getting to be "it" next. As a courtesy, the one picking the initials starts by providing a 4-letter hint of the form sex, nationality, life-status, reality-status. For example, MAAR means "Male, American, Alive, Real" (as opposed to "fictional"). Initgame can be surprisingly addictive. See also **hing**.

insanely great adj. [Mac community, from Steve Jobs; also BSD UNIX people via Bill Joy] Something so incredibly **elegant** that it is imaginable only to someone possessing the most puissant of **hacker**-natures.

INTERCAL */in´tər-kal/* [said by the authors to stand for *Compiler Language With No Pronounceable Acronym*] n. A computer language designed by Don Woods and James Lyons in 1972. INTERCAL is purposely different from all other computer languages in all ways but one; it is purely a written language, being totally unspeakable. An excerpt from the INTERCAL Reference Manual will make the style of the language clear:

> It is a well-known and oft-demonstrated fact that a person whose work is incomprehensible is held in high esteem. For example, if one were to state that the simplest way to store a value of 65536 in a 32-bit INTERCAL variable is:
>
> ```
> DO :1 <- #0$#256
> ```
>
> any sensible programmer would say that that was absurd. Since this is indeed the simplest method, the programmer would be made to look foolish in front of his boss, who would of course have happened to turn up, as bosses are wont to do. The effect would be no less devastating for the programmer having been correct.

INTERCAL has many other peculiar features designed to make it even more unspeakable. The Woods-Lyons implementation was actually used by many (well, at least several) people at Princeton. The language has been recently reimplemented as C-INTERCAL and is consequently enjoying an unprecedented level of unpopularity; there is even an *alt.lang.intercal* newsgroup devoted to the study and . . . appreciation of the language on USENET.

interesting adj. In hacker parlance, this word has strong connotations of 'annoying', or 'difficult', or both. Hackers relish a challenge, and enjoy wringing all the irony possible out of the ancient Chinese curse "May you live in interesting times". Oppose **trivial, uninteresting**.

Internet address n. 1. [techspeak] An absolute network address of the form *foo@bar.baz,* where foo is a user name, bar is a **sitename**, and baz is a *domain* name, possibly including periods itself. Contrast with **bang path**; see also **network, the** and **network address**. All Internet machines and most UUCP sites can now resolve these addresses, thanks to a large amount of behind-the-scenes magic and PD software written since 1980 or so. See also **bang path, domainist**. 2. More loosely, any network address reachable through Internet; this includes **bang path** addresses and some internal corporate and government networks.

Reading Internet addresses is something of an art. Here are the four most important top-level functional Internet domains followed by a selection of geographical domains:

com	commercial organizations
edu	educational institutions
gov	U.S. government civilian sites
mil	U.S. military sites

Note that most of the sites in the *com* and *edu* domains are in the U.S. or Canada.

us	sites in the U.S. outside the functional domains
su	sites in the ex-Soviet Union (see **kremvax**).
uk	sites in the United Kingdom

Within the *us* domain, there are subdomains for the fifty states, each generally with a name identical to the state's postal abbreviation. Within the *uk* domain, there is an *ac* subdomain for academic sites and a *co* domain for commercial ones. Other top-level domains may be divided up in similar ways.

interrupt 1. [techspeak] n. On a computer, an event that interrupts normal processing and temporarily diverts flow-of-control through an "interrupt handler" routine. See also **trap**. 2. interj. A request for attention from a hacker. Often explicitly spoken. "Interrupt — have you seen Joe recently?" See **priority interrupt**. 3. Under MS-DOS, nearly synonymous with 'system call', because the OS and BIOS routines are both called using the INT instruction (see **interrupt list, the**) and because programmers so often have to bypass the OS (going directly to a BIOS interrupt) to get reasonable performance.

interrupt list, the [MS-DOS] n. The list of all known software interrupt calls (both documented and undocumented) for IBM PCs and compatibles, maintained and made available for free redistribution by Ralf Brown *<ralf@cs.cmu.edu>*. As of late 1992, it had grown to approximately two megabytes in length.

interrupts locked out adj. When someone is ignoring you. In a restaurant, after several fruitless attempts to get the waitress's attention, a hacker might well observe "She must have interrupts locked out". The synonym *interrupts disabled* is also common. Variations abound; "to have one's interrupt mask bit set" and "interrupts masked out" are also heard. See also **spl**.

IRC */I-R-C/* [Internet Relay Chat] n. A worldwide "party line" network that allows one to converse with others in real time. IRC is structured as a network of Internet servers, each of which accepts connections from client programs, one per user. The IRC community and the **USENET** and **MUD** communities overlap to some extent, including both hackers and regular folks who have discovered the wonders of computer networks. Some USENET jargon has been adopted on IRC, as have some conventions such as **emoticons**. There is also a vigorous native jargon, represented in this lexicon by entries marked '[IRC]'. See also **talk mode**.

iron n. Hardware, especially older and larger hardware of **mainframe** class with big metal cabinets housing relatively low-density electronics (but the term is also used of modern supercomputers). Often in the phrase **big iron**. Oppose **silicon**. See also **dinosaur**.

Iron Age n. In the history of computing, 1961–1971 — the formative era of commercial **mainframe** technology, when ferrite-core **dinosaurs** ruled the earth. The Iron Age began, ironically enough, with the delivery of the first minicomputer (the PDP-1) and ended with the introduction of the first commercial microprocessor (the Intel 4004) in 1971. See also **Stone Age**; compare **elder days**.

iron box [UNIX/Internet] n. A special environment set up to trap a **cracker** logging in over remote connections long enough to be traced. May include a modified **shell** restricting the cracker's movements in unobvious ways, and 'bait' files designed to keep him interested and logged on. See also **back door**, **firewall machine**, **Venus flytrap**, and Clifford Stoll's account in *The Cuckoo's Egg* of how he made and used one (see the Bibliography in appendix C). Compare **padded cell**.

ironmonger [IBM] n. A hardware specialist (derogatory). Compare **sandbender**, **polygon pusher**.

ITS */I-T-S/* n. 1. Incompatible Time-sharing System, an influential but highly idiosyncratic operating system written for PDP-6s and PDP-10s at MIT and long used at the MIT AI Lab. Much AI-hacker jargon derives from ITS folklore, and to have been 'an ITS hacker' qualifies one instantly as an old-timer of the most venerable sort. ITS pioneered many important innovations, including transparent file sharing between machines and terminal-independent I/O. After about 1982, most actual work was shifted to newer machines, with the remaining ITS boxes run essentially as a hobby and service to the hacker community. The shutdown of the lab's last ITS machine in May 1990 marked the end of an era and sent old-time hackers into mourning nationwide (see **high moby**). The Royal Institute of Technology in Sweden is maintaining one 'live' ITS site at its computer museum (right next to the only TOPS-10 system still on the Internet), so ITS is still alleged to hold the record for OS in longest continuous use (however, **WAITS** is a credible rival for this palm). See Appendix A. 2. A mythical image of operating-system perfection worshiped by a bizarre, fervent retro-cult of old-time hackers and ex-users (see **troglodyte**, sense 2). ITS worshipers manage somehow to continue believing that an OS maintained by assembly-language hand-hacking that supported only monocase 6-character filenames in one directory per account remains superior to today's state of commercial art (their venom against UNIX is particularly intense). See also **holy wars**, **Weenix**.

IWBNI *//* [abbreviation] 'It Would Be Nice If'. Compare **WIBNI**.

IYFEG // [USENET] Abbreviation for 'Insert Your Favorite Ethnic Group'. Used as a meta-name when telling ethnic jokes on the net to avoid offending anyone. See **JEDR**.

= J =

J. Random */J rand´m/* n. [generalized from **J. Random Hacker**] Arbitrary; ordinary; any one; any old. 'J. Random' is often prefixed to a noun to make a name out of it. It means roughly *some particular* or *any specific one.* "Would you let J. Random Loser marry your daughter?" The most common uses are 'J. Random Hacker', 'J. Random Loser', and 'J. Random Nerd' ("Should J. Random Loser be allowed to **gun** down other people?"), but it can be used simply as an elaborate version of **random** in any sense.

J. Random Hacker [MIT] */J rand´m hak´r/* n. A mythical figure like the Unknown Soldier; the archetypal hacker nerd. See **random**, **Suzie COBOL**. This may originally have been inspired by 'J. Fred Muggs', a show-biz chimpanzee whose name was a household word back in the early days of **TMRC**, and was probably influenced by 'J. Presper Eckert' (one of the co-inventors of the electronic computer).

jack in v. To log on to a machine or connect to a network or **BBS**, esp. for purposes of entering a **virtual reality** simulation such as a **MUD** or **IRC** (leaving is "jacking out"). This term derives from **cyberpunk** SF, in which it was used for the act of plugging an electrode set into neural sockets in order to interface the brain directly to a virtual reality. It is primarily used by MUD and IRC fans and younger hackers on BBS systems.

jaggies */jag´eez/* n. The 'stairstep' effect observable when an edge (esp. a linear edge of very shallow or steep slope) is rendered on a pixel device (as opposed to a vector display).

JCL */J-C-L/* n. 1. IBM's supremely **rude** Job Control Language. JCL is the script language used to control the execution of programs in IBM's batch systems. JCL has a very **fascist** syntax, and some versions will, for example, **barf** if two spaces appear where it expects one. Most programmers confronted with JCL simply copy a working file (or card deck), changing the file names. Someone who actually understands and generates unique JCL is regarded with the mixed respect one gives to someone who memorizes the phone book. It is reported that hackers at IBM itself sometimes sing "Who's the breeder of the crud that mangles you and me? I-B-M, J-C-L, M-o-u-s-e" to the tune of the "Mickey Mouse Club" theme to express their opinion of the beast. 2. A comparative for any very **rude** software that a hacker is expected to use. "That's as bad as JCL." As with **COBOL**, JCL is often used as an archetype of ugliness even by those who haven't experienced it. See also **IBM**, **fear and loathing**.

JEDR // n. Synonymous with **IYFEG**. At one time, people in the USENET newsgroup *rec.humor.funny* tended to use 'JEDR' instead of **IYFEG** or '<ethnic>'; this stemmed from a public attempt to suppress the group once made by a loser with initials JEDR after he was offended by an ethnic joke posted there. (The practice was **retcon**ned by the expanding these initials as 'Joke Ethnic/Denomination/Race'.) After much sound and fury JEDR faded away; this term appears to be doing likewise. JEDR's only permanent effect on the net.culture was to discredit 'sensitivity' arguments for censorship so thoroughly that more recent attempts to raise them have met with immediate and near-universal rejection.

JFCL */jif´kl/, /jaf´kl/, /jə-fi´kl/* vt., obs. (alt. *jfcl*) To cancel or annul something. "Why don't you jfcl that out?" The fastest do-nothing instruction on older models of the PDP-10 happened to be JFCL, which stands for "Jump if Flag set and then CLear the flag"; this does something useful, but is a very fast no-operation if no flag is specified. Geoff Goodfellow, one of the jargon-1 co-authors, had JFCL on the license plate of his BMW for years. Usage: rare except among old-time PDP-10 hackers.

jiffy n. 1. The duration of one tick of the system clock on the computer (see **tick**). Often one AC cycle time (1/60 second in the U.S. and Canada, 1/50 most other places), but more recently 1/100 sec has become common. "The swapper runs every 6 jiffies" means that the virtual memory management routine is executed once for every 6 ticks of the clock, or about ten times a second. 2. Confusingly, the term is sometimes also used for a 1-millisecond **wall time** interval. Even more confusingly, physicists semi-jokingly use 'jiffy' to mean the time required for light to travel one foot in a vacuum, which turns out to be close to one *nanosecond.* 3. Indeterminate time from a few seconds to forever. "I'll do it in a jiffy" means certainly not now and possibly never. This is a bit contrary to the more widespread use of the word. Oppose **nano**. See also **Real Soon Now**.

job security n. When some piece of code is written in a particularly **obscure** fashion, and no good reason (such as time or space optimization) can be discovered, it is often said that the programmer was attempting to increase his job security (i.e., by making himself indispensable for maintenance). This sour joke seldom has to be said in full; if two hackers are looking over some code together and one points at a section and says "job security", the other one may just nod.

jock n. 1. A programmer who is characterized by large and somewhat brute-force programs. See **brute force**. 2. When modified by another noun, describes a specialist in some particular computing area. The compounds *compiler jock* and *systems jock* seem to be the best-established examples.

joe code */joh´ kohd`/* n. 1. Code that is overly **tense** and unmaintainable. "**Perl** may be a handy program, but if you look at the source, it's complete joe code." 2. Badly written, possibly buggy code.

Correspondents wishing to remain anonymous have fingered a particular Joe at the Lawrence Berkeley Laboratory and observed that usage has drifted slightly; the original sobriquet 'Joe code' was intended in sense 1.

jolix n. */joh´liks/* n.,adj. 386BSD, the freeware port of the BSD Net/2 release to the Intel i386 architecture by Bill Jolitz and friends. Used to differentiate from BSDI's port based on the same source tape, which is called BSD/386. See **BSD**.

JR[LN] */J-R-L/, /J-R-N/* n. The names JRL and JRN were sometimes used as example names when discussing a kind of user ID used under **TOPS-10** and **WAITS**; they were understood to be the initials of (fictitious) programmers named 'J. Random Loser' and 'J. Random Nerd' (see **J. Random**). For example, if one said "To log in, type log one comma jay are en" (that is, "log 1,JRN"), the listener would have understood that he should use his own computer ID in place of 'JRN'.

JRST */jerst/* [based on the PDP-10 jump instruction] v.,obs. To suddenly change subjects, with no intention of returning to the previous topic. Usage: rather rare except among PDP-10 diehards, and considered silly. See also **AOS**.

juggling eggs vi. Keeping a lot of **state** in your head while modifying a program. "Don't bother me now, I'm juggling eggs", means that an interrupt is likely to result in the program's being scrambled. In the classic first-contact SF novel *The Mote in God's Eye*, by Larry Niven and Jerry Pournelle, an alien describes a very difficult task by saying "We juggle priceless eggs in variable gravity." See also **hack mode**.

jump off into never-never land [from J. M. Barrie's *Peter Pan*] v. Same as **branch to Fishkill**, but more common in technical cultures associated with non-IBM computers that use the term 'jump' rather than 'branch'. Compare **hyperspace**.

jupiter [IRC] vt. To kill an **IRC robot** or user and then take its place by adopting its **nick** so that it cannot reconnect. Named after a particular IRC user who did this to NickServ, the robot in charge of preventing people from inadvertently using a nick claimed by another user.

= K =

K */K/* [from **kilo-**] n. A kilobyte. Used both as a spoken word and a written suffix (like **meg** and **gig** for megabyte and gigabyte). See **quantifiers**.

K&R [Kernighan and Ritchie] n. Brian Kernighan and Dennis Ritchie's book *The C Programming Language*, esp. the classic and influential first edition (Prentice-Hall 1978; ISBN 0-113-110163-3). Syn. **White Book, Old Testament**. See also **New Testament**.

kahuna */kə-hoo´nə/* [IBM: from the Hawaiian title for a shaman] n. Synonym for **wizard, guru**.

kamikaze packet n. The 'official' jargon for what is more commonly called a **Christmas tree packet**. **RFC**-1025, *TCP and IP Bake Off* says:

> 10 points for correctly being able to process a "Kamikaze" packet (AKA nastygram, christmas tree packet, lamp test segment, et al.). That is, correctly handle a segment with the maximum combination of features at once (e.g., a SYN URG PUSH FIN segment with options and data).

See also **Chernobyl packet**.

kangaroo code n. Syn. **spaghetti code**.

ken */ken/* n. 1. [UNIX] Ken Thompson, principal inventor of UNIX. In the early days he used to hand-cut distribution tapes, often with a note that read "Love, ken". Old-timers still use his first name (sometimes uncapitalized, because it's a login name and mail address) in third-person reference; it is widely understood (on USENET, in particular) that without a last name 'Ken' refers only to Ken Thompson. Similarly, Dennis without last name means Dennis Ritchie (and he is often known as *dmr*). See also **demigod**, **UNIX**. 2. A flaming user. This was originated by the Software Support group at Symbolics because the two greatest flamers in the user community were both named Ken.

kgbvax */K-G-B´vaks/* n. See **kremvax**.

KIBO */ki:´boh/* 1. [acronym] Knowledge In, Bullshit Out. A summary of what happens whenever valid data is passed through an organization (or person) that deliberately or accidentally disregards or ignores its significance. Consider, for example, what an advertising campaign can do with a product's actual specifications. Compare **GIGO**; see also **SNAFU principle**. 2. James Parry <kibo@world.std.com>, a USENETter infamous for various surrealist net.pranks and an uncanny, machine-assisted knack for joining any thread in which his nom de guerre is mentioned.

kiboze [USENET] v. To grep the USENET news for a string, especially with the intention of posting a follow-up. This activity was popularised by Kibo (see **KIBO**, sense 2).

kick [IRC] v. To cause somebody to be removed from a **IRC** channel, an option only available to **CHOP**s. This is an extreme measure, often used to combat extreme **flamage** or **flood**ing, but sometimes used at the chop's whim. Compare **gun**.

kill file [USENET] n. (alt. *KILL file*) Per-user file(s) used by some **USENET** reading programs (originally Larry Wall's `rn(1)`) to discard summarily (without presenting for reading) articles matching some particularly uninteresting (or unwanted) patterns of subject, author, or other header lines. Thus to add a person (or subject) to one's kill file is to arrange for that person to be ignored by one's newsreader in future. By extension, it may be used for a decision to ignore the person or subject in other media. See also **plonk**.

killer micro [popularized by Eugene Brooks] n. A microprocessor-based machine that infringes on mini, mainframe, or supercomputer performance turf. Often heard in "No one will survive the attack of the killer micros!", the battle cry of the downsizers. Used esp. of RISC architectures.

The popularity of the phrase 'attack of the killer micros' is doubtless reinforced by the movie title "Attack Of The Killer Tomatoes" (one of the **canonical** examples of so-bad-it's-wonderful among hackers). This has even more flavor now that killer micros have gone on the offensive not just individually (in workstations) but in hordes (within massively parallel computers).

killer poke n. A recipe for inducing hardware damage on a machine via insertion of invalid values (see **poke**) into a memory-mapped control register; used esp. of various fairly well-known tricks on **bitty box**es without hardware memory management (such as the IBM PC and Commodore PET) that can overload and trash analog electronics in the monitor. See also **HCF**.

kilo- [SI] pref. See **quantifiers**.

KIPS */kips/* [abbreviation, by analogy with **MIPS** using **K**] n. Thousands (*not* 1024s) of Instructions Per Second. Usage: rare.

KISS Principle */kis´ prin´si-pl/* n. "Keep It Simple, Stupid". A maxim often invoked when discussing design to fend off **creeping featurism** and control development complexity. Possibly related to the **marketroid** maxim on sales presentations, "Keep It Short and Simple".

kit [USENET; poss. fr. DEC slang for a full software distribution, as opposed to a patch or upgrade] n. A source software distribution that has been packaged in such a way that it can (theoretically) be unpacked and installed according to a series of steps using only standard UNIX tools, and entirely documented by some reasonable chain of references from the top-level **README file**. The more general term **distribution** may imply that special tools or more stringent conditions on the host environment are required.

klone */klohn/* n. See **clone**, sense 4.

kludge */klooj/* or */kluhj/* n. Common (but incorrect) variant of **kluge**, q.v.

kluge */klooj/* [from the German 'klug', clever] 1. n. A Rube Goldberg (or Heath Robinson) device, whether in hardware or software. (A long-ago *Data-*

mation article by Jackson Granholme said: "An ill-assorted collection of poorly matching parts, forming a distressing whole.") 2. n. A clever programming trick intended to solve a particular nasty case in an expedient, if not clear, manner. Often used to repair bugs. Often involves **ad-hockery** and verges on being a **crock**. In fact, the TMRC Dictionary defined 'kludge' as "a crock that works". 3. n. Something that works for the wrong reason. 4. vt. To insert a kluge into a program. "I've kluged this routine to get around that weird bug, but there's probably a better way." 5. [WPI] n. A feature that is implemented in a **rude** manner.

Nowadays this term is often encountered in the variant spelling 'kludge'. Reports from **old fart**s are consistent that 'kluge' was the original spelling, reported around computers as far back as the mid-1950s and, at that time, used exclusively of *hardware* kluges. In 1947, the *New York Folklore Quarterly* reported a classic shaggy-dog story 'Murgatroyd the Kluge Maker' then current in the Armed Forces, in which a 'kluge' was a complex and puzzling artifact with a trivial function. Other sources report that 'kluge' was common Navy slang in the WWII era for any piece of electronics that worked well on shore but consistently failed at sea.

However, there is reason to believe this slang use may be a decade older. Several respondents have connected it to the brand name of a device called a "Kluge paper feeder" dating back at least to 1935, an adjunct to mechanical printing presses. The Kluge feeder was designed before small, cheap electric motors and control electronics; it relied on a fiendishly complex assortment of cams, belts, and linkages to both power and synchronize all its operations from one motive driveshaft. It was accordingly tempermental, subject to frequent breakdowns, and devilishly difficult to repair — but oh, so clever! One traditional folk etymology of 'kluge' makes it the name of a design engineer; in fact, 'Kluge' is a surname in German, and the designer of the Kluge feeder may well have been the man behind this myth.

TMRC and the MIT hacker culture of the early '60s seems to have developed in a milieu that remembered and still used some WWII military slang (see also **foobar**). It seems likely that 'kluge' came to MIT via alumni of the many military electronics projects that had been located in Cambridge (many in MIT's venerable Building 20, in which **TMRC** is also located) during the war.

The variant 'kludge' was apparently popularized by the **Datamation** article mentioned above; it was titled "How to Design a Kludge" (February 1962, pp. 30, 31). Some people who encountered the word first in print or on-line jumped to the reasonable but incorrect conclusion that the word should be pronounced */kluhj/* (rhyming with 'sludge'). The result of this tangled history is a mess; in 1993, many (perhaps even most) hackers pronounce the word correctly as */klooj/* but spell it incorrectly as 'kludge' (compare the pronunciation drift of **mung**). Some observers consider this appropriate in view of its meaning.

kluge around vt. To avoid a bug or difficult condition by inserting a **kluge**. Compare **workaround**.

kluge up vt. To lash together a quick hack to perform a task; this is milder than **cruft together** and has some of the connotations of **hack up** (note, however, that the construction *kluge on* corresponding to **hack on** is never used). "I've kluged up this routine to dump the buffer contents to a safe place."

Knights of the Lambda Calculus n. A semi-mythical organization of wizardly LISP and Scheme hackers. The name refers to a mathematical formalism invented by Alonzo Church, with which LISP is intimately connected. There is no enrollment list and the criteria for induction are unclear, but one well-known LISPer has been known to give out buttons and, in general, the *members* know who they are. . . .

Knuth */knooth/* [Donald E. Knuth's *The Art of Computer Programming*] n. Mythically, the reference that answers all questions about data structures or algorithms. A safe answer when you do not know: "I think you can find that in Knuth." Contrast **literature, the**. See also **bible**.

kremvax */krem-vaks/* [from the then large number of **USENET VAXen** with names of the form *foovax*] n. Originally, a fictitious USENET site at the Kremlin, announced on April 1, 1984 in a posting ostensibly originated there by Soviet leader Konstantin Chernenko. The posting was actually forged by Piet Beertema as an April Fool's joke. Other fictitious sites mentioned in the hoax were *moskvax* and **kgbvax**. This was probably the funniest of the many April Fool's forgeries perpetrated on USENET (which has negligible security against them), because the notion that USENET might ever penetrate the Iron Curtain seemed so totally absurd at the time.

In fact, it was only six years later that the first genuine site in Moscow, *demos.su*, joined USENET. Some readers needed convincing that the postings from it weren't just another prank. Vadim Antonov, senior programmer at Demos and the major poster from there up to mid-1991, was quite aware of all this, referred to it frequently in his own postings, and at one point twitted some credulous readers by blandly asserting that he *was* a hoax!

Eventually he even arranged to have the domain's gateway site *named kremvax*, thus neatly turning fiction into truth and demonstrating that the hackish sense of humor transcends cultural barriers. [Mr. Antonov also contributed the Russian-language material for this lexicon. — ESR]

In an even more ironic historical footnote, *kremvax* became an electronic center of the anti-communist resistance during the bungled hard-line coup of August 1991. During those three days the Soviet UUCP network centered on *kremvax* became the only trustworthy news source for many places within the USSR. Though the sysops were concentrating on internal communications, cross-border postings included immediate transliterations of Boris Yeltsin's decrees condemning the coup and eyewitness reports of the demonstrations in Moscow's streets. In those hours, years of speculation that totalitarianism would prove unable to maintain its grip on politically-loaded information in the age of computer networking were proved devastatingly accurate — and the original *kremvax* joke became a reality as Yeltsin and the new Russian revolutionaries of *glasnost* and *perestroika* made *kremvax* one of the timeliest means of their outreach to the West.

kyrka */shir´kə/* [Swedish] n. See **feature key**.

= L =

lace card n. obs. A **punched card** with all holes punched (also called a *whoopee card* or *ventilator card*). Card readers tended to jam when they got to one of these, as the resulting card had too little structural strength to avoid buckling inside the mechanism. Card punches could also jam trying to produce these things owing to power-supply problems. When some practical joker fed a lace card through the reader, you needed to clear the jam with a *card knife* — which you used on the joker first.

language lawyer n. A person, usually an experienced or senior software engineer, who is intimately familiar with many or most of the numerous restrictions and features (both useful and esoteric) applicable to one or more computer programming languages. A language lawyer is distinguished by the ability to show you the five sentences scattered through a 200-plus-page manual that together imply the answer to your question "if only you had thought to look there". Compare **wizard**, **legal**, **legalese**.

languages of choice n. **C** and **LISP**. Nearly every hacker knows one of these, and most good ones are fluent in both. Smalltalk and Prolog are also popular in small but influential communities.

There is also a rapidly dwindling category of older hackers with FORTRAN, or even assembler, as their language of choice. They often prefer to be known as **Real Programmers**, and other hackers consider them a bit odd (see "The Story of Mel, a Real Programmer" in Appendix A). Assembler is generally no longer considered interesting or appropriate for anything but **HLL** implementation, **glue**, and a few time-critical and hardware-specific uses in systems programs. FORTRAN occupies a shrinking niche in scientific programming.

Most hackers tend to frown on languages like **Pascal** and **Ada**, which don't give them the near-total freedom considered necessary for hacking (see **bondage-and-discipline language**), and to regard everything even remotely connected with **COBOL** or other traditional **card walloper** languages as a total and unmitigated **loss**.

larval stage n. Describes a period of monomaniacal concentration on coding apparently passed through by all fledgling hackers. Common symptoms include the perpetration of more than one 36-hour **hacking run** in a given week; neglect of all other activities including usual basics like food, sleep, and personal hygiene; and a chronic case of advanced bleary-eye. Can last from 6 months to 2 years, the apparent median being around 18 months. A few so afflicted never resume a more 'normal' life, but the ordeal seems to be necessary to produce really wizardly (as opposed to merely competent) programmers. See also **wannabee**. A less protracted and intense version of larval stage (typically lasting about a month) may recur when one is learning a new **OS** or programming language.

lase */layz/* vt. To print a given document via a laser printer. "OK, let's lase that sucker and see if all those graphics-macro calls did the right things."

laser chicken n. Kung Pao Chicken, a standard Chinese dish containing chicken, peanuts, and hot red peppers in a spicy pepper-oil sauce. Many hackers call it *laser chicken* for two reasons: It can **zap** you just like a laser, and the sauce has a red color reminiscent of some laser beams.

In a variation on this theme, it is reported that some Australian hackers have redesignated the common dish 'lemon chicken' as *Chernobyl Chicken.*

The name is derived from the color of the sauce, which is considered bright enough to glow in the dark (as, mythically, do some of the inhabitants of Chernobyl).

Lasherism [Harvard] n. A program that solves a standard problem (such as the Eight Queens puzzle or implementing the **life** algorithm) in a deliberately nonstandard way. Distinguished from a **crock** or **kluge** by the fact that the programmer did it on purpose as a mental exercise. Such constructions are quite popular in exercises such as the **Obfuscated C contest**, and occasionally in **retrocomputing**. Lew Lasher was a student at Harvard around 1980 who became notorious for such behavior.

laundromat n. Syn. **disk farm**; see **washing machine**.

LDB */lə´dəb/* [from the PDP-10 instruction set] vt. To extract from the middle. "LDB me a slice of cake, please." This usage has been kept alive by Common LISP's function of the same name. Considered silly. See also **DPB**.

leaf site n. A machine that merely originates and reads USENET news or mail, and does not relay any third-party traffic. Often uttered in a critical tone; when the ratio of leaf sites to backbone, rib, and other relay sites gets too high, the network tends to develop bottlenecks. Compare **backbone site**, **rib site**.

leak n. With qualifier, one of a class of resource-management bugs that occur when resources are not freed properly after operations on them are finished, so they effectively disappear (leak out). This leads to eventual exhaustion as new allocation requests come in. **memory leak** and **fd leak** have their own entries; one might also refer, to, say, a *window handle leak* in a window system.

leaky heap [Cambridge] n. An **arena** with a **memory leak**.

leapfrog attack n. Use of userid and password information obtained illicitly from one host (e.g., downloading a file of account IDs and passwords, tapping TELNET, etc.) to compromise another host. Also, to TELNET through one or more hosts in order to confuse a trace (a standard cracker procedure).

legal adj. Loosely used to mean 'in accordance with all the relevant rules', esp. in connection with some set of constraints defined by software. "The older =+ alternate for += is no longer legal syntax in ANSI C." "This parser processes each line of legal input the moment it sees the trailing linefeed." Hackers often model their work as a sort of game played with the environment in which the objective is to maneuver through the thicket of 'natural laws' to achieve a desired objective. Their use of *legal* is flavored as much by this game-playing sense as by the more conventional one having to do with courts and lawyers. Compare **language lawyer**, **legalese**.

legalese n. Dense, pedantic verbiage in a language description, product specification, or interface standard; text that seems designed to obfuscate and requires a **language lawyer** to **parse** it. Though hackers are not afraid of high information density and complexity in language (indeed, they rather enjoy both), they share a deep and abiding loathing for legalese; they associate it with deception, **suits**, and situations in which hackers generally get the short end of the stick.

LER */L-E-R/* [TMRC, from 'Light-Emitting Diode'] n. A light-emitting resistor (that is, one in the process of burning up). Ohm's law was broken. See also **SED**.

LERP */lerp/* vi.,n. Quasi-acronym for Linear Interpolation, used as a verb or noun for the operation. "Bresenham's algorithm lerps incrementally between the two endpoints of the line."

let the smoke out v. To fry hardware (see **fried**). See **magic smoke** for a discussion of the underlying mythology.

letterbomb 1. n. A piece of **email** containing **live data** intended to do nefarious things to the recipient's machine or terminal. It is possible, for example, to send letterbombs that will lock up some specific kinds of terminals when they are viewed, so thoroughly that the user must cycle power (see **cycle**, sense 3) to unwedge them. Under UNIX, a letterbomb can also try to get part of its contents interpreted as a shell command to the mailer. The results of this could range from silly to tragic. See also **Trojan horse**; compare **nastygram**. 2. Loosely, a **mailbomb**.

lexer */lek´sr/* n. Common hacker shorthand for 'lexical analyzer', the input-tokenizing stage in the parser for a language (the part that breaks it into word-like pieces). "Some C lexers get confused by the old-style compound ops like =-."

lexiphage */lek´si-fayj`/* n. A notorious word **chomper** on ITS. See **bagbiter**.

This program would draw on a selected victim's bitmapped terminal the words "THE BAG" in ornate letters, followed a pair of jaws biting pieces of it off.

life n. 1. A cellular-automata game invented by John Horton Conway and first introduced publicly by Martin Gardner (*Scientific American*, October 1970); the game's popularity had to wait a few years for computers on which it could reasonably be played, as it's no fun to simulate the cells by hand. Many hackers pass through a stage of fascination with it, and hackers at various places contributed heavily to the mathematical analysis of this game (most notably Bill Gosper at MIT, who even implemented life in **TECO**!; see **Gosperism**). When a hacker mentions 'life', he is much more likely to mean this game than the magazine, the breakfast cereal, or the human state of existence. 2. The opposite of **USENET**. As in "**Get a life!**"

Life is hard [XEROX PARC] prov. This phrase has two possible interpretations: (1) "While your suggestion may have some merit, I will behave as though I hadn't heard it." (2) "While your suggestion has obvious merit, equally obvious circumstances prevent it from being seriously considered." The charm of the phrase lies precisely in this subtle but important ambiguity.

light pipe n. Fiber optic cable. Oppose **copper**.

lightweight adj. Opposite of **heavyweight**; usually found in combining forms such as 'lightweight process'.

like kicking dead whales down the beach adj. Describes a slow, difficult, and disgusting process. First popularized by a famous quote about the difficulty of getting work done under one of IBM's mainframe OSes. "Well, you *could* write a C compiler in COBOL, but it would be like kicking dead whales down the beach." See also **fear and loathing**.

like nailing jelly to a tree adj. Used to describe a task thought to be impossible, esp. one in which the difficulty arises from poor specification or inherent slipperiness in the problem domain. "Trying to display the 'prettiest' arrangement of nodes and arcs that diagrams a given graph is like nailing jelly to a tree, because nobody's sure what 'prettiest' means algorithmically."

line 666 [from Christian eschatological myth] n. The notional line of source at which a program fails for obscure reasons, implying either that *somebody* is out to get it (when you are the programmer), or that it richly deserves to be so gotten (when you are not). "It works when I trace through it, but seems to crash on line 666 when I run it." "What happens is that whenever a large batch comes through, mmdf dies on the Line of the Beast. Probably some twit hardcoded a buffer size."

line eater, the [USENET] n. 1. A bug in some now-obsolete versions of the netnews software that used to eat up to BUFSIZ bytes of the article text. The bug was triggered by having the text of the article start with a space or tab. This bug was quickly personified as a mythical creature called the *line eater*, and postings often included a dummy line of *line eater food*. Ironically, line eater 'food' not beginning with a space or tab wasn't actually eaten, since the bug was avoided; but if there *was* a space or tab before it, then the line eater would eat the food *and* the beginning of the text it was supposed to be protecting. The practice of *sacrificing to the line eater* continued for some time after the bug had been **nailed to the wall**, and is still humorously referred to. The bug itself is still (in mid-1991) occasionally reported to be lurking in some mail-to-netnews gateways. 2. See **NSA line eater**.

line noise n. 1. [techspeak] Spurious characters due to electrical noise in a communications link, especially an RS-232 serial connection. Line noise may be induced by poor connections, interference or crosstalk from other circuits, electrical storms, **cosmic rays**, or (notionally) birds crapping on the phone wires. 2. Any chunk of data in a file or elsewhere that looks like the results of line noise in sense 1. 3. Text that is theoretically a readable text or program source but employs syntax so bizarre that it looks like line noise in senses 1 or 2. Yes, there are languages this ugly. The canonical example is **TECO**; it is often claimed that "TECO's input syntax is indistinguishable from line noise." Other non-**WYSIWYG** editors, such as Multics `qed` and Unix `ed`, in the hands of a real hacker, also qualify easily, as do deliberately obfuscated languages such as **INTERCAL**.

line starve [MIT] 1. vi. To feed paper through a printer the wrong way by one line (most printers can't do this). On a display terminal, to move the cursor up to the previous line of the screen. "To print 'X squared', you just output 'X', line starve, '2', line feed." (The line starve causes the '2' to appear on the line above the 'X', and the line feed gets back to the original line.) 2. n. A character (or character sequence) that causes a terminal to perform this action. ASCII 0011010, also called SUB or control-Z, was one common line-starve character in the days before microcomputers and the X3.64 terminal standard. Unlike 'line feed', *line starve* is *not* standard **ASCII** terminology. Even among hackers it is considered a bit silly. 3. [proposed] A sequence such as \c (used in System V echo, as well as **nroff** and **troff**) that suppresses a **newline** or other character(s) that would normally be emitted.

link farm [UNIX] n. A directory tree that contains many links to files in a master directory tree of files. Link farms save space when one is maintaining several nearly identical copies of the same source tree — for example, when the only difference is architecture-dependent object files. "Let's freeze the source and then rebuild the FROBOZZ-3 and FROBOZZ-4 link farms." Link farms may also be used to get around restrictions on the number of `-I` (include-file directory) arguments on older C preprocessors. However, they can also get completely out of hand, becoming the filesystem equivalent of **spaghetti code**.

link-dead [MUD] adj. Said of a **MUD** character who has frozen in place because of a dropped Internet connection.

lint [from UNIX's `lint(1)`, named for the bits of fluff it supposedly picks from programs] 1. vt. To examine a program closely for style, language usage, and portability problems, esp. if in C, esp. if via use of automated analysis tools, most esp. if the UNIX utility `lint(1)` is used. This term used to be restricted to use of `lint(1)` itself, but (judging by references on USENET) it has become a shorthand for **desk check** at some non-UNIX shops, even in languages other than C. Also as v. **delint**. 2. n. Excess verbiage in a document, as in "This draft has too much lint".

lion food [IBM] n. Middle management or HQ staff (or, by extension, administrative drones in general). From an old joke about two lions who, escaping from the zoo, split up to increase their chances but agree to meet after 2 months. When they finally meet, one is skinny and the other overweight. The thin one says: "How did you manage? I ate a human just once and they turned out a small army to chase me — guns, nets, it was terrible. Since then I've been reduced to eating mice, insects, even grass." The fat one replies: "Well, *I* hid near an IBM office and ate a manager a day. And nobody even noticed!"

Lions Book n. *Source Code and Commentary on UNIX level 6*, by John Lions. The two parts of this book contained (1) the entire source listing of the UNIX Version 6 kernel, and (2) a commentary on the source discussing the algorithms. These were circulated internally at the University of New South Wales beginning 1976–77, and were, for years after, the *only* detailed kernel documentation available to anyone outside Bell Labs. Because Western Electric wished to maintain trade secret status on the kernel, the Lions book was never formally published and was only supposed to be distributed to affiliates of source licensees (it is still possible to get a Bell Labs reprint of the book by sending a copy of a V6 source license to the right person at Bellcore, but *real* insiders have the UNSW edition). In spite of this, it soon spread by *samizdat* to a good many of the early UNIX hackers.

LISP [from 'LISt Processing language', but mythically from 'Lots of Irritating Superfluous Parentheses'] n. AI's mother tongue, a language based on the ideas of (a) variable-length lists and trees as fundamental data types, and (b) the interpretation of code as data and vice-versa. Invented by John McCarthy at MIT in the late 1950s, it is actually older than any other **HLL** still in use except FORTRAN. Accordingly, it has undergone considerable adaptive radiation over the years; modern variants are quite different in detail from the original LISP 1.5. The dominant HLL among hackers until the early 1980s, LISP now shares the throne with **C**. See **languages of choice**.

All LISP functions and programs are expressions that return values; this, together with the high memory utilization of LISPs, gave rise to Alan Perlis's famous quip (itself a take on an Oscar Wilde quote) that "LISP programmers know the value of everything and the cost of nothing".

One significant application for LISP has been as a proof by example that most newer languages, such as **COBOL** and **Ada**, are full of unnecessary **crocks**. When the **Right Thing** has already been done once, there is no justification for bogosity in newer languages.

literature, the n. Computer-science journals and other publications, vaguely gestured at to answer a question that the speaker believes is **trivial**. Thus, one might answer an annoying question by saying "It's in the literature." Oppose **Knuth**, which has no connotation of triviality.

lithium lick n. [NeXT] n. Steve Jobs. Employees who have gotten too much attention from their esteemed founder are said to have 'lithium lick' when they begin to show signs of Jobsian fervor and repeat the most recent catch phrases in normal conversation — for example, "It just works, right out of the box!"

little-endian adj. Describes a computer architecture in which, within a given

We've got your numbers. . . .

16- or 32-bit word, bytes at lower addresses have lower significance (the word is stored 'little-end-first'). The PDP-11 and VAX families of computers and Intel microprocessors and a lot of communications and networking hardware are little-endian. See **big-endian**, **middle-endian**, **NUXI problem**. The term is sometimes used to describe the ordering of units other than bytes; most often, bits within a byte.

live data n. 1. Data that is written to be interpreted and takes over program flow when triggered by some un-obvious operation, such as viewing it. One use of such hacks is to break security. For example, some smart terminals have commands that allow one to download strings to program keys; this can be used to write live data that, when listed to the terminal, infects it with a security-breaking **virus** that is triggered the next time a hapless user strikes that key. For another, there are some well-known bugs in **vi** that allow certain texts to send arbitrary commands back to the machine when they are simply viewed. 2. In C code, data that includes pointers to function **hooks** (executable code). 3. An object, such as a **trampoline**, that is constructed on the fly by a program and intended to be executed as code. 4. Actual real-world data, as opposed to 'test data'. For example, "I think I have the record deletion module finished." "Have you tried it out on live data?" This usage usually carries the connotation that live data is more fragile and must not be corrupted, or bad things will happen. So a more appropriate response to the above claim might be: "Well, make sure it works perfectly before we throw live data at it." The implication here is that record deletion is something pretty significant, and a haywire record-deletion module running amok on live data would probably cause great harm.

Live Free Or Die! imp. 1. The state motto of New Hampshire, which appears on that state's automobile license plates. 2. A slogan associated with UNIX in the romantic days when UNIX aficionados saw themselves as a tiny, beleaguered underground tilting against the windmills of industry. The "free" referred specifically to freedom from the **fascist** design philosophies and crufty misfeatures common on commercial operating systems. Armando Stettner, one of the early UNIX developers, used to give out fake license plates bearing this motto under a large UNIX, all in New Hampshire colors of green and white. These are now valued collector's items.

livelock */li:v'lok/* n. A situation in which some critical stage of a task is unable to finish because its clients perpetually create more work for it to do after they have been serviced but before it can clear its queue. Differs from **deadlock** in that the process is not blocked or waiting for anything, but has a virtually infinite amount of work to do and can never catch up.

liveware */li:v'weir/* n. 1. Synonym for **wetware**. Less common. 2. [Cambridge] Vermin. "Waiter, there's some liveware in my salad . . . "

lobotomy n. 1. What a hacker subjected to formal management training is said to have undergone. At IBM and elsewhere this term is used by both hackers and low-level management; the latter doubtless intend it as a joke. 2. The act of removing the processor from a microcomputer in order to replace or upgrade it. Some very cheap **clone** systems are sold in *lobotomized* form — everything but the brain.

locals, the pl.n. The users on one's local network (as opposed, say, to people one reaches via public Internet or UUCP connects). The marked thing about this usage is how little it has to do with real-space distance. "I have to do some tweaking on this mail utility before releasing it to the locals."

locked and loaded [from military slang for an M-16 rifle with magazine inserted and prepared for firing] adj. Said of a removable disk volume properly prepared for use — that is, locked into the drive and with the heads loaded.

Ironically, because their heads are 'loaded' whenever the power is up, this description is never used of **Winchester** drives (which are named after a rifle).

locked up adj. Syn. for **hung**, **wedged**.

logic bomb n. Code surreptitiously inserted into an application or OS that causes it to perform some destructive or security-compromising activity whenever specified conditions are met. Compare **back door**.

logical [from the technical term 'logical device', wherein a physical device is referred to by an arbitrary 'logical' name] adj. Having the role of. If a person (say, Les Earnest at SAIL) who had long held a certain post left and were replaced, the replacement would for a while be known as the *logical* Les Earnest. (This does not imply any judgment on the replacement.) Compare **virtual**.

At Stanford, *logical* compass directions denote a coordinate system in which *logical north* is toward San Francisco, *logical west* is toward the ocean, etc., even though logical north varies between physical (true) north near San Francisco and physical west near San Jose. (The best rule of thumb here is that, by definition, El Camino Real always runs logical north-and-south.) In giving directions, one might say: "To get to Rincon Tarasco restaurant, get onto **El Camino Bignum** going logical north." Using the word 'logical' helps to prevent the recipient from worrying about that the fact that the sun is setting almost directly in front of him. The concept is reinforced by North American highways which are almost, but not quite, consistently labeled with logical rather than physical directions. A similar situation exists at MIT: Route 128 (famous for the electronics industry that has grown up along it) is a 3-quarters circle surrounding Boston at a radius of 10 miles, terminating near the coastline at each end. It would be most precise to describe the two directions along this highway as 'clockwise' and 'counterclockwise', but the road signs all say "north" and "south", respectively. A hacker might describe these directions as *logical north* and *logical south*, to indicate that they are conventional directions not corresponding to the usual denotation for those words. (If you went logical south along the entire length of route 128, you would start out going northwest, curve around to the south, and finish headed due east, passing along one infamous stretch of pavement that is simultaneously route 128 south and Interstate 93 north, and is signed as such!)

loop through vt. To process each element of a list of things. "Hold on, I've got to loop through my paper mail." Derives from the computer-language notion of an iterative loop; compare *cdr down* (under **cdr**), which is less common among C and UNIX programmers. ITS hackers used to say *IRP over* after an obscure pseudo-op in the MIDAS PDP-10 assembler.

loose bytes n. Commonwealth hackish term for the padding bytes or **shims** many compilers insert between members of a record or structure to cope with alignment requirements imposed by the machine architecture.

lord high fixer [primarily British, from Gilbert & Sullivan's 'lord high executioner'] n. The person in an organization who knows the most about some aspect of a system. See **wizard**.

lose [MIT] vi. 1. To fail. A program loses when it encounters an exceptional condition or fails to work in the expected manner. 2. To be exceptionally unesthetic or crocky. 3. Of people, to be obnoxious or unusually stupid (as opposed to ignorant). See also **deserves to lose**. 4. n. Refers to something that is **losing**, especially in the phrases "That's a lose!" and "What a lose!"

lose lose interj. A reply to or comment on an undesirable situation. "I accidentally deleted all my files!" "Lose, lose."

loser n. An unexpectedly bad situation, program, programmer, or person. Someone who habitually loses. (Even winners can lose occasionally.) Someone who knows not and knows not that he knows not. Emphatic forms are *real loser, total loser,* and *complete loser* (but not ***moby loser,* which would be a contradiction in terms). See **luser**.

losing adj. Said of anything that is or causes a **lose** or **lossage**.

loss n. Something (not a person) that loses; a situation in which something is losing. Emphatic forms include *moby loss,* and *total loss, complete loss.* Common interjections are "What a loss!" and "What a moby loss!" Note that *moby loss* is OK even though ***moby loser* is not used; applied to an abstract noun, moby is simply a magnifier, whereas when applied to a person it implies substance and has positive connotations. Compare **lossage**.

lossage */los´əj/* n. The result of a bug or malfunction. This is a mass or collective noun. "What a loss!" and "What lossage!" are nearly synonymous. The former is slightly more particular to the speaker's present circumstances;

the latter implies a continuing **lose** of which the speaker is currently a victim. Thus (for example) a temporary hardware failure is a loss, but bugs in an important tool (like a compiler) are serious lossage.

lost in the noise adj. Syn. **lost in the underflow**. This term is from signal processing, where signals of very small amplitude cannot be separated from low-intensity noise in the system. Though popular among hackers, it is not confined to hackerdom; physicists, engineers, astronomers, and statisticians all use it.

lost in the underflow adj. Too small to be worth considering; more specifically, small beyond the limits of accuracy or measurement. This is a reference to *floating underflow*, a condition that can occur when a floating-point arithmetic processor tries to handle quantities smaller than its limit of magnitude. It is also a pun on 'undertow' (a kind of fast, cold current that sometimes runs just offshore and can be dangerous to swimmers). "Well, sure, photon pressure from the stadium lights alters the path of a thrown baseball, but that effect gets lost in the underflow." Compare **epsilon**, **epsilon squared**; see also **overflow bit**.

lots of MIPS but no I/O adj. Used to describe a person who is technically brilliant but can't seem to communicate with human beings effectively. Technically it describes a machine that has lots of processing power but is bottlenecked on input-output (in 1991, the IBM Rios, a.k.a. RS/6000, is a notorious recent example).

low-bandwidth [from communication theory] adj. Used to indicate a talk that, although not **content-free**, was not terribly informative. "That was a low-bandwidth talk, but what can you expect for an audience of **suits**!" Compare **zero-content**, **bandwidth**, **math-out**.

LPT */L-P-T/* or */lip´it/* or */lip-it´/* n. Line printer, of course. Rare under UNIX, more common among hackers who grew up with ITS, MS-DOS, CP/M and other operating systems that were strongly influenced by early DEC conventions.

Lubarsky's Law of Cybernetic Entomology prov. "There is *always* one more bug."

lunatic fringe [IBM] n. Customers who can be relied upon to accept release 1 versions of software.

lurker n. One of the 'silent majority' in a electronic forum; one who posts occasionally or not at all but is known to read the group's postings regularly. This term is not pejorative and indeed is casually used reflexively: "Oh, I'm just lurking." Often used in *the lurkers*, the hypothetical audience for the group's **flamage**-emitting regulars.

luser */loo´zr/* n. A **user**; esp. one who is also a **loser**. (**luser** and **loser** are pronounced identically.) This word was coined around 1975 at MIT. Under ITS, when you first walked up to a terminal at MIT and typed Control-Z to get the computer's attention, it printed out some status information, including how many people were already using the computer; it might print "14 users", for example. Someone thought it would be a great joke to patch the system to print "14 losers" instead. There ensued a great controversy, as some of the users didn't particularly want to be called losers to their faces every time they used the computer. For a while several hackers struggled covertly, each changing the message behind the back of the others; any time you logged into the computer it was even money whether it would say "users" or "losers". Finally, someone tried the compromise "lusers", and it stuck. Later one of the ITS machines supported `luser` as a request-for-help command. ITS died the death in mid-1990, except as a museum piece; the usage lives on, however, and the term *luser* is often seen in program comments.

= M =

M [SI] pref. (on units) suff. (on numbers) See **quantifiers**.

macdink */mak´dink/* [from the Apple Macintosh, which is said to encourage such behavior] vt. To make many incremental and unnecessary cosmetic changes to a program or file. Often the subject of the macdinking would be better off without them. "When I left at 11 P.M. last night, he was still macdinking the slides for his presentation." See also **fritterware**, **window shopping**.

machinable adj. Machine-readable. Having the **softcopy** nature.

machoflops */mach´oh-flops/* [pun on 'megaflops', a coinage for 'millions of FLoating-point Operations Per Second'] n. Refers to artificially inflated performance figures often quoted by computer manufacturers. Real applications are lucky to get half the quoted speed. See **Your mileage may vary**, **benchmark**.

Macintoy */mak'in-toy/* n. The Apple Macintosh, considered as a **toy**. Less pejorative than **Macintrash**.

Macintrash */mak'in-trash`/* n. The Apple Macintosh, as described by a hacker who doesn't appreciate being kept away from the *real computer* by the interface. The term **maggotbox** has been reported in regular use in the Research Triangle area of North Carolina. Compare **Macintoy**. See also **beige toaster**, **WIMP environment**, **point-and-drool interface**, **drool-proof paper**, **user-friendly**.

macro */mak'roh/* [techspeak] n. A name (possibly followed by a formal **arg** list) that is equated to a text or symbolic expression to which it is to be expanded (possibly with the substitution of actual arguments) by a macro expander. This definition can be found in any technical dictionary; what those won't tell you is how the hackish connotations of the term have changed over time.

The term *macro* originated in early assemblers, which encouraged the use of macros as a structuring and information-hiding device. During the early 1970s, macro assemblers became ubiquitous, and sometimes quite as powerful and expensive as **HLLs**, only to fall from favor as improving compiler technology marginalized assembler programming (see **languages of choice**). Nowadays the term is most often used in connection with the C preprocessor, LISP, or one of several special-purpose languages built around a macro-expansion facility (such as TEX or UNIX's [nt]roff suite).

Indeed, the meaning has drifted enough that the collective *macros* is now sometimes used for code in any special-purpose application control language (whether or not the language is actually translated by text expansion), and for macro-like entities such as the 'keyboard macros' supported in some text editors (and PC TSR or Macintosh INIT/CDEV keyboard enhancers).

macro- pref. Large. Opposite of **micro-**. In the mainstream and among other technical cultures (for example, medical people) this competes with the prefix **mega-**, but hackers tend to restrict the latter to quantification.

macrology */mak-rol'ə-jee/* n. 1. Set of usually complex or crufty macros, e.g., as part of a large system written in **LISP**, **TECO**, or (less commonly) assembler. 2. The art and science involved in comprehending a macrology in sense 1. Sometimes studying the macrology of a system is not unlike archeology, ecology, or **theology**, hence the sound-alike construction. See also **boxology**.

macrotape */mak´roh-tayp/* n. An industry-standard reel of tape, as opposed to a **microtape**. See also **round tape**.

maggotbox */mag´ət-boks/* n. See **Macintrash**. This is even more derogatory.

magic adj. 1. As yet unexplained, or too complicated to explain; compare **automagically** and (Arthur C.) Clarke's Third Law: "Any sufficiently advanced technology is indistinguishable from magic." "TTY echoing is controlled by a large number of magic bits." "This routine magically computes the parity of an 8-bit byte in three instructions." 2. Characteristic of something that works although no one really understands why (this is especially called **black magic**). 3. [Stanford] A feature not generally publicized that allows something otherwise impossible, or a feature formerly in that category but now unveiled. Compare **black magic**, **wizardly**, **deep magic**, **heavy wizardry**.

For more about hackish 'magic', see A Story About 'Magic' (in Appendix A).

magic cookie [UNIX] n. 1. Something passed between routines or programs that enables the receiver to perform some operation; a capability ticket or opaque identifier. Especially used of small data objects that contain data encoded in a strange or intrinsically machine-dependent way. E.g., on non-UNIX OSes with a non-byte-stream model of files, the result of `ftell(3)` may be a magic cookie rather than a byte offset; it can be passed to `fseek(3)`, but not operated on in any meaningful way. The phrase *it hands you a magic cookie* means it returns a result whose contents are not defined but which can be passed back to the same or some other program later. 2. An in-band code for changing graphic rendition (e.g., inverse video or underlining) or performing other control functions (see also **cookie**). Some older terminals would leave a blank on the screen corresponding to mode-change magic cookies; this was also called a **glitch** (or occasionally a *turd*; compare **mouse droppings**). See also **cookie**.

magic number [UNIX/C] n. 1. In source code, some non-obvious constant whose value is significant to the operation of a program and that is inserted inconspicuously in-line (**hardcoded**), rather than expanded in by a symbol set by a commented `#define`. Magic numbers in this sense are bad style. 2. A number that encodes critical information used in an algorithm in some opaque way. The classic examples of these are the numbers used in hash or CRC functions, or the coefficients in a linear congruential generator for pseudo-random numbers. This sense actually predates and was ancestral to the more common sense 1. 3. Special data located at the beginning of a binary data file to indicate its type to a utility. Under UNIX, the system and various applications programs (especially the linker) distinguish between types of executable file by looking for a magic number. Once upon a time, these magic numbers were PDP-11 branch instructions that skipped over header data to the start of executable code; 0407, for example, was octal for 'branch 16 bytes relative'. Nowadays only a **wizard** knows the spells to create magic numbers. How do you choose a fresh magic number of your own? Simple — you pick one at random. See? It's magic!

The magic number, on the other hand, is 7 ± 2. See *The magical number seven, plus or minus two: some limits on our capacity for processing information* by George Miller, in the *Psychological Review* 63:81-97 (1956). This classic paper established the number of distinct items (such as numeric digits) that humans can hold in short-term memory. Among other things, this strongly influenced the interface design of the phone system.

magic smoke n. A substance trapped inside IC packages that enables them to function (also called *blue smoke*; this is similar to the archaic 'phlogiston' hypothesis about combustion). Its existence is demonstrated by what happens when a chip burns up — the magic smoke gets let out, so it doesn't work any more. See **smoke test**, **let the smoke out**.

USENETter Jay Maynard tells the following story: "Once, while hacking on a dedicated Z80 system, I was testing code by blowing EPROMs and plugging them in the system, then seeing what happened. One time, I plugged one in backwards. I only discovered that *after* I realized that Intel didn't put power-on lights under the quartz windows on the tops of their EPROMs — the die was glowing white-hot. Amazingly, the EPROM worked fine after I erased it, filled it full of zeros, then erased it again. For all I know, it's still in service. Of course, this is because the magic smoke didn't get let out." Compare the original phrasing of **Murphy's Law**.

mailbomb (also *mail bomb*) [USENET] 1. v. To send, or urge others to send, massive amounts of **email** to a single system or person, as in retaliation for a perceived serious offense. Mailbombing is itself widely regarded as a serious offense — it can disrupt email traffic or other facilities for innocent users on the victim's system, and in extreme cases, even at upstream sites. 2. n. An automatic procedure with a similar effect. 3. n. The mail sent. Compare **letterbomb**, **nastygram**.

mailing list n. (often shortened in context to *list*) 1. An **email** address that is an alias (or **macro**, though that word is never used in this connection) for many other email addresses. Some mailing lists are simple *reflectors*, redirecting mail sent to them to the list of recipients. Others are filtered by humans or programs of varying degrees of sophistication; lists filtered by humans are said to be *moderated.* 2. The people who receive your email when you send it to such an address.

Mailing lists are one of the primary forms of hacker interaction, along with **USENET**. They predate USENET, having originated with the first UUCP and ARPANET connections. They are often used for private information-sharing on topics that would be too specialized for or inappropriate to public USENET groups. Though some of these maintain purely technical content (such as the Internet Engineering Task Force mailing list), others (like the 'sf-lovers' list maintained for many years by Saul Jaffe) are recreational, and others are purely social. Perhaps the most infamous of the social lists was the eccentric *bandykin* distribution; its latter-day progeny, *lectroids* and *tanstaafl*, still include a number of the oddest and most interesting people in hackerdom.

Mailing lists are easy to create and (unlike USENET) don't tie up a significant amount of machine resources (until they get very large, at which point they can become interesting torture tests for mail software). Thus, they are often created temporarily by working groups, the members of which can then collaborate on a project without ever needing to meet face-to-face. Much of the material in this lexicon was criticized and polished on just such a mailing list (called 'jargon-friends'), which included all the co-authors of Steele-1983.

main loop n. The top-level control flow construct in an input- or event-driven program, the one which receives and acts or dispatches on the program's input. See also **driver**.

mainframe n. Term originally referring to the cabinet containing the central processor unit or 'main frame' of a room-filling **Stone Age** batch machine. After the emergence of smaller 'minicomputer' designs in the early 1970s, the traditional **big iron** machines were described as 'mainframe computers' and eventually just as mainframes. The term carries the connotation of a machine designed for batch rather than interactive use, though possibly with an interactive timesharing operating system retrofitted onto it; it is especially used of machines built by IBM, Unisys, and the other great **dinosaur**s surviving from computing's **Stone Age**.

It has been common wisdom among hackers since the late 1980s that the mainframe architectural tradition is essentially dead (outside of the tiny market for **number-crunching** supercomputers (see **cray**)), having been swamped by the recent huge advances in IC technology and low-cost personal computing. As of 1993, corporate America is just beginning to figure this out — the wave of failures, takeovers, and mergers among traditional mainframe makers have certainly provided sufficient omens (see **dinosaurs mating**).

management n. 1. Corporate power elites distinguished primarily by their distance from actual productive work and their chronic failure to manage (see also **suit**). Spoken derisively, as in "*Management* decided that . . . ". 2. Mythically, a vast bureaucracy responsible for all the world's minor irritations. Hackers' satirical public notices are often signed 'The Mgt'; this derives from the *Illuminatus* novels (see the Bibliography in Appendix C).

mandelbug */man´del-buhg/* [from the Mandelbrot set] n. A bug whose underlying causes are so complex and obscure as to make its behavior appear chaotic or even non-deterministic. This term implies that the speaker thinks it is a **Bohr bug**, rather than a **heisenbug**. See also **schroedinbug**.

manged */mahnjd/* [probably from the French 'manger' or Italian 'mangiare', to eat; perhaps influenced by English n. 'mange', 'mangy'] adj. Refers to anything that is mangled or damaged, usually beyond repair. "The disk was manged after the electrical storm." Compare **mung**.

mangle vt. Used similarly to **mung** or **scribble**, but more violent in its connotations; something that is mangled has been irreversibly and totally trashed.

mangler [DEC] n. A manager. Compare **mango**; see also **management**. Note that **system mangler** is somewhat different in connotation.

mango */mang´go/* [orig. in-house jargon at Symbolics] n. A manager. Compare **mangler**. See also **devo** and **doco**.

manularity */man`yoo-la´ri-tee/* [prob. fr. techspeak 'manual' + 'granularity'] n. A notional measure of the manual labor required for some task, particularly one of the sort that automation is supposed to eliminate. "Composing English on paper has much higher manularity than using a text editor, especially in the revising stage." Hackers tend to consider manularity a symptom of primitive methods; in fact, a true hacker confronted with an apparent requirement to do a computing task **by hand** will inevitably seize the opportunity to build another tool (see **toolsmith**).

marbles [from mainstream "lost all his/her marbles"] pl.n. The minimum needed to build your way further up some hierarchy of tools or abstractions. After a bad system crash, you need to determine if the machine has enough marbles to come up on its own, or enough marbles to allow a rebuild from backups, or if you need to rebuild from scratch. "This compiler doesn't even have enough marbles to compile **hello, world**."

marginal adj. 1. Extremely small. "A marginal increase in **core** can decrease **GC** time drastically." In everyday terms, this means that it is a lot easier to clean off your desk if you have a spare place to put some of the junk while you sort through it. 2. Of extremely small merit. "This proposed new feature seems rather marginal to me." 3. Of extremely small probability of **win**ning. "The power supply was rather marginal anyway; no wonder it fried."

Marginal Hacks n. Margaret Jacks Hall, a building into which the Stanford AI Lab was moved near the beginning of the 1980s (from the **D. C. Power Lab**).

marginally adv. Slightly. "The ravs here are only marginally better than at Small Eating Place." See **epsilon**.

marketroid */mar´kə-troyd/* alt. *marketing slime, marketeer, marketing droid, marketdroid.* n. A member of a company's marketing department, esp. one who promises users that the next version of a product will have features that are not actually scheduled for inclusion, are extremely difficult to implement, and/or are in violation of the laws of physics; and/or one who describes existing features (and misfeatures) in ebullient, buzzword-laden adspeak. Derogatory. Compare **droid**.

Mars n. A legendary tragic failure, the archetypal Hacker Dream Gone Wrong. Mars was the code name for a family of PDP-10 compatible computers built by Systems Concepts (now, The SC Group): the multi-processor SC-30M, the small uniprocessor SC-25M, and the never-built superprocessor SC-40M. These machines were marvels of engineering design; although not much slower than the unique **Foonly** F-1, they were physically smaller and consumed less power than the much slower DEC KS10 or Foonly F-2, F-3, or F-4 machines. They were also completely compatible with the DEC KL10, and ran all KL10 binaries (including the operating system) with no modifications at about 2–3 times faster than a KL10.

When DEC cancelled the Jupiter project in 1983, Systems Concepts should have made a bundle selling their machine into shops with a lot of software investment in PDP-10s, and in fact their spring 1984 announcement generated a great deal of excitement in the PDP-10 world. TOPS-10 was running on the Mars by the summer of 1984, and TOPS-20 by early fall. Unfortunately, the hackers running Systems Concepts were much better at designing machines than at mass producing or selling them; the company allowed itself to be sidetracked by a bout of perfectionism into continually improving the design, and lost credibility as delivery dates continued to slip. They also overpriced the product ridiculously; they believed they were competing with the KL10 and VAX 8600 and failed to reckon with the likes of Sun Microsystems and other hungry startups building workstations with power comparable to the KL10 at a fraction of the price. By the time SC shipped the first SC-30M to Stanford in late 1985, most customers had already made the traumatic decision to abandon the PDP-10, usually for VMS or UNIX boxes. Most of the Mars computers built ended up being purchased by CompuServe.

This tale and the related saga of **Foonly** hold a lesson for hackers: if you want to play in the **Real World**, you need to learn Real World moves.

martian n. A packet sent on a TCP/IP network with a source address of the test loopback interface [127.0.0.1]. This means that it will come back labeled with a source address that is clearly not of this earth. “The domain server is getting lots of packets from Mars. Does that gateway have a martian filter?”

massage vt. Vague term used to describe ‘smooth’ transformations of a data set into a different form, esp. transformations that do not lose information. Connotes less pain than **munch** or **crunch**. “He wrote a program that massages X bitmap files into GIF format.” Compare **slurp**.

math-out [poss. from ‘white-out’ (the blizzard variety)] n. A paper or presentation so encrusted with mathematical or other formal notation as to be incomprehensible. This may be a device for concealing the fact that it is actually **content-free**. See also **numbers**, **social science number**.

Matrix [FidoNet] n. 1. What the Opus BBS software and sysops call **Fi-**

A **math-out** approach to history.

The next cartoon in the Crunchly saga is 05-19-73, page 388.

doNet. 2. Fanciful term for a **cyberspace** expected to emerge from current networking experiments (see **network, the**). 3. The totality of present-day computer networks.

maximum Maytag mode What a **washing machine** or, by extension, any hard disk is in when it's being used so heavily that it's shaking like an old Maytag with an unbalanced load. If prolonged for any length of time, can lead to disks becoming **walking drives**.

Mbogo, Dr. Fred */əm-boh´goh, dok´tr fred/* [Stanford] n. The archetypal man you don't want to see about a problem, esp. an incompetent professional; a shyster. "Do you know a good eye doctor?" "Sure, try Mbogo Eye Care and Professional Dry Cleaning." The name comes from synergy between **bogus** and the original Dr. Mbogo, a witch doctor who was Gomez Addams' physician on the old "Addams Family" TV show. Compare **Bloggs Family, the**, see also **fred**.

meatware n. Synonym for **wetware**. Less common.

meeces */mees´əz/* [TMRC] n. Occasional furry visitors who are not **urchins**. [That is, mice. This may no longer be in live use; it clearly derives from the refrain of the early-1960s cartoon character Mr. Jinx: "I hate meeces to *pieces*!" — ESR]

meg */meg/* n. See **quantifiers**.

mega- */me´gə/* [SI] pref. See **quantifiers**.

megapenny */meg´ə-pen`ee/* n. $10,000 (1 cent * 10^6). Used semi-humorously as a unit in comparing computer cost and performance figures.

MEGO */me´goh/* or */mee´goh/* ['My Eyes Glaze Over', often 'Mine Eyes Glazeth (sic) Over', attributed to the futurologist Herman Kahn] Also *MEGO factor*. 1. n. A **handwave** intended to confuse the listener and hopefully induce agreement because the listener does not want to admit to not understanding what is going on. MEGO is usually directed at senior management by engineers and contains a high proportion of **TLA**s. 2. excl. An appropriate response to MEGO tactics. 3. Among non-hackers, often refers not to behavior that causes the eyes to glaze, but to the eye-glazing reaction itself, which may be triggered by the mere threat of technical detail as effectively as by an actual excess of it.

meltdown, network n. See **network meltdown**.

meme */meem/* [coined by analogy with 'gene', by Richard Dawkins] n. An idea considered as a **replicator**, esp. with the connotation that memes parasitize people into propagating them much as viruses do. Used esp. in the phrase *meme complex* denoting a group of mutually supporting memes that form an organized belief system, such as a religion. This lexicon is an (epidemiological) vector of the 'hacker subculture' meme complex; each entry might be considered a meme. However, *meme* is often misused to mean *meme complex*. Use of the term connotes acceptance of the idea that in humans (and presumably other tool- and language-using sophonts) cultural evolution by selection of adaptive ideas has superseded biological evolution by selection of hereditary traits. Hackers find this idea congenial for tolerably obvious reasons.

meme plague n. The spread of a successful but pernicious **meme**, esp. one that parasitizes the victims into giving their all to propagate it. Astrology, BASIC, and the other guy's religion are often considered to be examples. This usage is given point by the historical fact that 'joiner' ideologies like Naziism or various forms of millennarian Christianity have exhibited plague-like cycles of exponential growth followed by collapses to small reservoir populations.

memetics */me-met´iks/* [from **meme**] The study of memes. As of mid-1993, this is still an extremely informal and speculative endeavor, though the first steps towards at least statistical rigor have been made by H. Keith Henson and others. Memetics is a popular topic for speculation among hackers, who like to see themselves as the architects of the new information ecologies in which memes live and replicate.

memory farts n. The flatulent sounds that some DOS box BIOSes (most notably AMI's) make when checking memory on bootup.

memory leak n. An error in a program's dynamic-store allocation logic that causes it to fail to reclaim discarded memory, leading to eventual collapse due to memory exhaustion. Also (esp. at CMU) called **core leak**. These problems were severe on older machines with small, fixed-size address spaces, and special "leak detection" tools were commonly written to root them out. With the advent of virtual memory, it is unfortunately easier to be sloppy about wasting a bit of memory (although when you run out of memory on a VM machine, it means you've got a *real* leak!). See **aliasing bug**, **fandango on core**, **smash the stack**, **precedence lossage**, **overrun screw**, **leaky heap**, **leak**.

memory smash [XEROX PARC] n. Writing through a pointer that doesn't point to what you think it does. This occasionally reduces your machine to a rubble of bits. Note that this is subtly different from (and more general than) related terms such as a **memory leak** or **fandango on core** because it doesn't imply an allocation error or overrun condition.

menuitis */men`yoo-i:´tis/* n. Notional disease suffered by software with an obsessively simple-minded menu interface and no escape. Hackers find this intensely irritating and much prefer the flexibility of command-line or language-style interfaces, especially those customizable via macros or a special-purpose language in which one can encode useful hacks. See **user-obsequious**, **drool-proof paper**, **WIMP environment**, **for the rest of us**.

mess-dos */mes-dos/* n. Derisory term for MS-DOS. Often followed by the ritual banishing "Just say No!" See **MS-DOS**. Most hackers (even many MS-DOS hackers) loathe MS-DOS for its single-tasking nature, its limits on application size, its nasty primitive interface, and its ties to IBMness (see **fear and loathing**). Also *mess-loss*, *messy-dos*, *mess-dog*, *mess-dross*, *mush-dos*, and various combinations thereof. In Ireland and the U.K. it is even sometimes called 'Domestos' after a brand of toilet cleanser.

meta */me´tə/* or */may´tə/* or (Commonwealth) */mee´tə/* [from analytic philosophy] adj.,pref. One level of description up. A metasyntactic variable is a variable in notation used to describe syntax, and meta-language is language used to describe language. This is difficult to explain briefly, but much hacker humor turns on deliberate confusion between meta-levels. See **Humor, Hacker**.

meta bit n. The top bit of an 8-bit character, which is on in character values 128–255. Also called **high bit**, **alt bit**, or **hobbit**. Some terminals and consoles (see **space-cadet keyboard**) have a META shift key. Others (including, *mirabile dictu*, keyboards on IBM PC-class machines) have an ALT key. See also **bucky bits**.

Historical note: although in modern usage shaped by a universe of 8-bit bytes the meta bit is invariably hex 80 (octal 0200), things were different on earlier machines with 36-bit words and 9-bit bytes. The MIT and Stanford keyboards (see **space-cadet keyboard**) generated hex 100 (octal 400) from their meta keys.

metasyntactic variable n. A name used in examples and understood to stand for whatever thing is under discussion, or any random member of a class of things under discussion. The word **foo** is the **canonical** example. To avoid confusion, hackers never (well, hardly ever) use 'foo' or other words like it as permanent names for anything. In filenames, a common convention is that any filename beginning with a metasyntactic-variable name is a **scratch** file that may be deleted at any time.

To some extent, the list of one's preferred metasyntactic variables is a cultural signature. They occur both in series (used for related groups of variables or objects) and as singletons. Here are a few common signatures:

> **foo**, **bar**, **baz**, **quux**, quuux, quuuux...: MIT/Stanford usage, now found everywhere (thanks largely to early versions of this lexicon!). At MIT (but not at Stanford), **baz** dropped out of use for a while in the 1970s and '80s. A common recent mutation of this sequence inserts **qux** before **quux**.
>
> bazola, ztesch: Stanford (from mid-'70s on).
>
> **foo**, **bar**, thud, grunt: This series was popular at CMU. Other CMU-associated variables include **gorp**.
>
> **foo**, **bar**, fum: This series is reported to be common at XEROX PARC.
>
> **fred**, **barney**: See the entry for **fred**. These tend to be Britishisms.
>
> **toto**, titi, tata, tutu: Standard series of metasyntactic variables among francophones.
>
> **corge**, **grault**, **flarp**: Popular at Rutgers University and among **GOSMACS** hackers.
>
> zxc, spqr, **wombat**: Cambridge University (England).
>
> shme: Berkeley, GeoWorks, Ingres. Pronounced */shme/* with a short */e/*.
>
> **foo**, **bar**, zot: Helsinki University of Technology, Finland.
>
> blarg, wibble: New Zealand

Of all these, only *foo* and *bar* are universal (and **baz** nearly so). The compounds **foobar** and *foobaz* also enjoy very wide currency.

Some jargon terms are also used as metasyntactic names; **barf** and **mumble**, for example. See also **Commonwealth Hackish** for discussion of numerous metasyntactic variables found in Great Britain and the Commonwealth.

MFTL */M-F-T-L/* [abbreviation: 'My Favorite Toy Language'] 1. adj. Describes a talk on a programming language design that is heavy on the syntax (with lots of BNF), sometimes even talks about semantics (e.g., type systems), but rarely, if ever, has any content (see **content-free**). More broadly applied to talks — even when the topic is not a programming language — in which the subject matter is gone into in unnecessary and meticulous detail at the sacrifice of any conceptual content. "Well, it was a typical MFTL talk". 2. n. Describes a language about which the developers are passionate (often to the point of prosyletic zeal) but no one else cares about. Applied to the language by those outside the originating group. "He cornered me about type resolution in his MFTL."

The first great goal in the mind of the designer of an MFTL is usually to write a compiler for it, then bootstrap the design away from contamination by lesser languages by writing a compiler for it in itself. Thus, the standard put-down question at an MFTL talk is "Has it been used for anything besides its own compiler?". On the other hand, a language that *cannot* be used to write its own compiler is beneath contempt. See **break-even point**.

(On a related note, Doug McIlroy once proposed a test of the generality and utility of a language and the operating system under which it is compiled: "Is the output of a FORTRAN program acceptable as input to the FORTRAN compiler?" In other words, can you write programs that write programs? (See **toolsmith**.) Alarming numbers of (language, OS) pairs fail this test, particularly when the language is FORTRAN; aficionados are quick to point out that **UNIX** (even using FORTRAN) passes it handily. That the test could ever be failed is only surprising to those who have had the good fortune to have worked only under modern systems which lack OS-supported and -imposed "file types".)

mickey n. The resolution unit of mouse movement. It has been suggested that the *disney* will become a benchmark unit for animation graphics performance.

mickey mouse program n. North American equivalent of a **noddy** (that is, trivial) program. Doesn't necessarily have the belittling connotations of mainstream slang "Oh, that's just mickey mouse stuff!"; sometimes trivial programs can be very useful.

micro- pref. 1. Very small; this is the root of its use as a quantifier prefix. 2. A quantifier prefix, calling for multiplication by 10^{-6} (see **quantifiers**). Neither of these uses is peculiar to hackers, but hackers tend to fling them both around rather more freely than is countenanced in standard English. It is recorded, for example, that one CS professor used to characterize the standard length of his lectures as a microcentury — that is, about 52.6 minutes (see also **attoparsec**, **nanoacre**, and especially **microfortnight**). 3. Personal or human-scale — that is, capable of being maintained or comprehended or manipulated by one human being. This sense is generalized from 'microcomputer', and is esp. used in contrast with *macro-* (the corresponding Greek prefix meaning 'large'). 4. Local as opposed to global (or **macro-**). Thus a hacker might say that buying a smaller car to reduce pollution only solves a microproblem; the macroproblem of getting to work might be better solved by using mass transit, moving to within walking distance, or (best of all) telecommuting.

MicroDroid [USENET] n. A Microsoft employee, esp. one who posts to various operating-system advocacy newsgroups. MicroDroids post follow-ups to any messages critical of Microsoft's operating systems, and often end up sounding like visiting Mormon missionaries.

microfloppies n. 3.5-inch floppies, as opposed to 5.25-inch **vanilla** or mini-floppies and the now-obsolete 8-inch variety. This term may be headed for obsolescence as 5.25-inchers pass out of use, only to be revived if anybody floats a sub-3-inch floppy standard. See **stiffy**, **minifloppies**.

microfortnight n. 1/1000000 of the fundamental unit of time in the Furlong/Firkin/Fortnight system of measurement; 1.2096 sec. (A furlong is 1/8th of a mile; a firkin is 1/4th of a barrel; the mass unit of the system is taken to be a firkin of water). The VMS operating system has a lot of tuning parameters that you can set with the SYSGEN utility, and one of these is TIMEPROMPTWAIT, the time the system will wait for an operator to set the correct date and time at boot if it realizes that the current value is bogus. This time is specified in microfortnights!

Multiple uses of the millifortnight (about 20 minutes) and **nanofortnight** have also been reported.

microLenat */mi:-kroh-len´-ət/* n. See **bogosity**.

microReid */mi:´kroh-reed/* n. See **bogosity**.

Microsloth Windows */mi:'kroh-sloth` win'dohz/* n. Hackerism for 'Microsoft Windows', a windowing system for the IBM-PC which is so limited by bug-for-bug compatibility with **mess-dos** that it is agonizingly slow on anything less than a fast 486. Also just called *Windoze*, with the implication that you can fall asleepm waiting for it to do anything; the latter term is extremely common on USENET. Compare **X**, **sun-stools**.

microtape */mi:'kroh-tayp/* n. Occasionally used to mean a DECtape, as opposed to a **macrotape**. A DECtape is a small reel, about 4 inches in diameter, of magnetic tape about an inch wide. Unlike those for today's **macrotape**s, microtape drivers allowed random access to the data, and therefore could be used to support file systems and even for swapping (this was generally done purely for **hack value**, as they were far too slow for practical use). In their heyday they were used in pretty much the same ways one would now use a floppy disk: as a small, portable way to save and transport files and programs. Apparently the term *microtape* was actually the official term used within DEC for these tapes until someone coined the word 'DECtape', which, of course, sounded sexier to the **marketroid**s; another version of the story holds that someone discovered a conflict with another company's 'microtape' trademark.

middle-endian adj. Not **big-endian** or **little-endian**. Used of perverse byte orders such as 3-4-1-2 or 2-1-4-3, occasionally found in the packed-decimal formats of minicomputer manufacturers who shall remain nameless. See **NUXI problem**.

milliLampson */mil'ə-lamp`sn/* n. A unit of talking speed, abbreviated mL. Most people run about 200 milliLampsons. The eponymous Butler Lampson (a CS theorist and systems implementor highly regarded among hackers) goes at 1000. A few people speak faster. This unit is sometimes used to compare the (sometimes widely disparate) rates at which people can generate ideas and actually emit them in speech. For example, noted computer architect C. Gordon Bell (designer of the PDP-11) is said, with some awe, to think at about 1200 mL but only talk at about 300; he is frequently reduced to fragments of sentences as his mouth tries to keep up with his speeding brain.

minifloppies n. 5.25-inch **vanilla** floppy disks, as opposed to 3.5-inch or **microfloppies** and the now-obsolescent 8-inch variety. At one time, this term was a trademark of Shugart Associates for their SA-400 minifloppy drive. Nobody paid any attention. See **stiffy**.

MIPS */mips/* [abbreviation] n. 1. A measure of computing speed; formally, 'Million Instructions Per Second' (that's 10^6 per second, not 2^{20}!); often rendered by hackers as 'Meaningless Indication of Processor Speed' or in other unflattering ways. This joke expresses a nearly universal attitude about the value of most **benchmark** claims, said attitude being one of the great cultural divides between hackers and **marketroids**. The singular is sometimes '1 MIP' even though this is clearly etymologically wrong. See also **KIPS** and **GIPS**. 2. Computers, especially large computers, considered abstractly as sources of **computrons**. "This is just a workstation; the heavy MIPS are hidden in the basement." 3. The corporate name of a particular RISC-chip company; among other things, they designed the processor chips used in DEC's 3100 workstation series. 4. Acronym for 'Meaningless Information per Second' (a joke, prob. from sense 1).

misbug */mis-buhg/* [MIT] n. An unintended property of a program that turns out to be useful; something that should have been a **bug** but turns out to be a **feature**. Usage: rare. Compare **green lightning**. See **miswart**.

misfeature */mis-fee´chr/* or */mis´fee`chr/* n. A feature that eventually causes lossage, possibly because it is not adequate for a new situation that has evolved. Since it results from a deliberate and properly implemented feature, a misfeature is not a bug. Nor is it a simple unforeseen side effect; the term implies that the feature in question was carefully planned, but its long-term consequences were not accurately or adequately predicted (which is quite different from not having thought ahead at all). A misfeature can be a particularly stubborn problem to resolve, because fixing it usually involves a substantial philosophical change to the structure of the system involved.

Many misfeatures (especially in user-interface design) arise because the designers/implementors mistake their personal tastes for laws of nature. Often a former feature becomes a misfeature because trade-offs were made whose parameters subsequently change (possibly only in the judgment of the implementors). "Well, yeah, it is kind of a misfeature that file names are limited to six characters, but the original implementors wanted to save directory space and we're stuck with it for now."

Missed'em-five n. Pejorative hackerism for AT&T System V UNIX, generally used by **BSD** partisans in a bigoted mood. (The synonym 'SysVile' is also encountered.) See **software bloat**, **Berzerkeley**.

missile address n. See **ICBM address**.

miswart */mis-wort/* [from **wart** by analogy with **misbug**] n. A **feature** that superficially appears to be a **wart** but has been determined to be the **Right Thing**. For example, in some versions of the **EMACS** text editor, the 'transpose characters' command exchanges the character under the cursor with the one before it on the screen, *except* when the cursor is at the end of a line, in which case the two characters before the cursor are exchanged. While this behavior is perhaps surprising, and certainly inconsistent, it has been found through extensive experimentation to be what most users want. This feature is a miswart.

moby */moh´bee/* [MIT: seems to have been in use among model railroad fans years ago. Derived from Melville's *Moby Dick* (some say from 'Moby Pickle').] 1. adj. Large, immense, complex, impressive. "A Saturn V rocket is a truly moby frob." "Some MIT undergrads pulled off a moby hack at the Harvard-Yale game." (See "The Meaning of 'Hack'"). 2. n. obs. The maximum address space of a machine (see below). For a 680[234]0 or VAX or most modern 32-bit architectures, it is 4,294,967,296 8-bit bytes (4 gigabytes). 3. A title of address (never of third-person reference), usually used to show admiration, respect, and/or friendliness to a competent hacker. "Greetings, moby Dave. How's that address-book thing for the Mac going?" 4. adj. In backgammon, doubles on the dice, as in *moby sixes*, *moby ones*, etc. Compare this with **bignum** (sense 3): double sixes are both bignums and moby sixes, but moby ones are not bignums (the use of *moby* to describe double ones is sarcastic). Standard emphatic forms: *Moby foo*, *moby win*, *moby loss*. *Foby moo*: a spoonerism due to Richard Greenblatt. 5. The largest available unit of something which is available in discrete increments. Thus, ordering a "moby Coke" at the local fast-food joint is not just a request for a large Coke, it's an explicit request for the largest size they sell.

This term entered hackerdom with the Fabritek 256K memory added to the MIT AI PDP-6 machine, which was considered unimaginably huge when it was installed in the 1960s (at a time when a more typical memory size for a timesharing system was 72 kilobytes). Thus, a moby is classically 256K 36-bit words, the size of a PDP-6 or PDP-10 moby. Back when address registers were narrow the term was more generally useful, because when a computer had virtual memory mapping, it might actually have more physical memory attached to it than any one program could access directly. One could then say "This computer has 6 mobies" meaning that the ratio of physical memory to address space is 6, without having to say specifically how much memory there actually is. That in turn implied that the computer could timeshare six 'full-sized' programs without having to swap programs between memory and disk.

Nowadays the low cost of processor logic means that address spaces are usually larger than the most physical memory you can cram onto a machine, so most systems have much *less* than one theoretical 'native' moby of **core**. Also, more modern memory-management techniques (esp. paging) make the 'moby count' less significant. However, there is one series of widely-used chips for which the term could stand to be revived — the Intel 8088 and 80286 with their incredibly **brain-damaged** segmented-memory designs. On these, a *moby* would be the 1-megabyte address span of a segment/offset pair (by coincidence, a PDP-10 moby was exactly 1 megabyte of 9-bit bytes).

mockingbird n. Software that intercepts communications (especially login transactions) between users and hosts and provides system-like responses to the users while saving their responses (especially account IDs and passwords). A special case of **Trojan Horse**.

mod vt.,n. 1. Short for 'modify' or 'modification'. Very commonly used — in fact the full terms are considered markers that one is being formal. The plural 'mods' is used esp. with reference to bug fixes or minor design changes in hardware or software, most esp. with respect to **patch** sets or a **diff**. 2. Short for **modulo** but used *only* for its techspeak sense.

mode n. A general state, usually used with an adjective describing the state. Use of the word 'mode' rather than 'state' implies that the state is extended over time, and probably also that some activity characteristic of that state is being carried out. "No time to hack; I'm in thesis mode." In its jargon sense, 'mode' is most often attributed to people, though it is sometimes applied to programs and inanimate objects. In particular, see **hack mode**, **day mode**, **night mode**, **demo mode**, **fireworks mode**, and **yoyo mode**; also **talk mode**.

One also often hears the verbs *enable* and *disable* used in connection with jargon modes. Thus, for example, a sillier way of saying "I'm going to crash" is "I'm going to enable crash mode now". One might also hear a request to "disable flame mode, please".

In a usage much closer to techspeak, a mode is a special state that certain user interfaces must pass into in order to perform certain functions. For example, in order to insert characters into a document in the UNIX editor `vi`, one must type the "i" key, which invokes the "Insert" command. The effect of this command is to put vi into "insert mode", in which typing the "i" key has a quite different effect (to wit, it inserts an "i" into the document). One must then hit another special key, "ESC", in order to leave "insert mode". Nowadays, modeful interfaces are generally considered **losing** but survive in quite a few widely used tools built in less enlightened times.

mode bit n. A **flag**, usually in hardware, that selects between two (usually quite different) modes of operation. The connotations are different from **flag** bit in that mode bits are mainly written during a boot or set-up phase, are seldom explicitly read, and seldom change over the lifetime of an ordinary program. The classic example was the EBCDIC-vs.-ASCII bit (#12) of the Program Status Word of the IBM 360. Another was the bit on a PDP-12 that controlled whether it ran the PDP-8 or the LINC instruction set.

modulo */mod´yu-loh/* prep. Except for. An overgeneralization of mathematical terminology; one can consider saying that 4 equals 22 except for the 9s (4 = 22 mod 9). "Well, LISP seems to work okay now, modulo that **GC** bug." "I feel fine today modulo a slight headache."

molly-guard */mol´ee-gard/* [University of Illinois] n. A shield to prevent tripping of some **Big Red Switch** by clumsy or ignorant hands. Originally used of the plexiglass covers improvised for the BRS on an IBM 4341 after a programmer's toddler daughter (named Molly) frobbed it twice in one day. Later generalized to covers over stop/reset switches on disk drives and networking equipment.

Mongolian Hordes technique [poss. from the Sixties counterculture expression *Mongolian clusterfuck* for a public orgy] n. Development by **gang bang**. Implies that large numbers of inexperienced programmers are being put on a job better performed by a few skilled ones. Also called *Chinese Army technique*; see also **Brooks's Law**.

monkey up vt. To hack together hardware for a particular task, especially a one-shot job. Connotes an extremely **crufty** and consciously temporary solution. Compare **hack up**, **kluge up**, **cruft together**.

monkey, scratch n. See **scratch monkey**.

monstrosity 1. n. A ridiculously **elephantine** program or system, esp. one that is buggy or only marginally functional. 2. The quality of being monstrous (see 'Overgeneralization' in the discussion of jargonification). See also **baroque**.

monty */mon´tee/* [US Geological Survey] n. A program with a ludicrously complex user interface written to perform extremely trivial tasks. An example would be a menu-driven, button clicking, pulldown, pop-up windows program for listing directories. The original monty was an infamous weather-reporting program, Monty the Amazing Weather Man, written at the USGS. Monty had a widget-packed X-window interface with over 200 buttons; and all monty actually *did* was **FTP** files off the network.

Moof */moof/* [MAC users] 1. n. A semi-legendary creature, also called the 'dogcow', that lurks in the depths of the Macintosh Technical Notes Hypercard stack V3.1; specifically, the full story of the dogcow is told in technical note #31 (the particular Moof illustrated is properly named 'Clarus'). Option-shift-click will cause it to emit a characteristic 'Moof!' or '!fooM' sound. *Getting* to tech note 31 is the hard part; to discover how to do that, one must needs examine the stack script with a hackerly eye. Clue: **rot13** is involved. A dogcow also appears if you choose 'Page Setup . . . ' with a LaserWriter selected and click on the 'Options' button. 2. adj. Used to flag software that's a hack, something untested and on the edge. On one Apple CD-ROM, certain folders such as "Tools & Apps (Moof!)" and "Development Platforms (Moof!)", are so marked to indicate that they contain software not fully tested or sanctioned by the powers that be. When you open these folders you cross the boundary into hackerland.

Moore's Law */morz law/* prov. The observation that the logic density of silicon integrated circuits has closely followed the curve (bits per square inch) = $2^{(t-1962)}$ where t is time in years; that is, the amount of information storable on a given amount of silicon has roughly doubled every year since the technology was invented. See also **Parkinson's Law of Data**.

moose call n. See **whalesong**.

moria */mor´ee-ə/* n. Like **nethack** and **rogue**, one of the large PD Dungeons-and-Dragons-like simulation games, available for a wide range of machines and operating systems. The name is from Tolkien's Mines of Moria; compare **elder days, elvish**. The game is extremely addictive and a major consumer of time better used for hacking.

MOTAS */moh-tahz/* [USENET: Member Of The Appropriate Sex, after **MOTOS** and **MOTSS**] n. A potential or (less often) actual sex partner. See also **SO**.

MOTOS */moh-tohs/* [acronym from the 1970 U.S. census forms via USENET: Member Of The Opposite Sex] n. A potential or (less often) actual sex partner. See **MOTAS**, **MOTSS**, **SO**. Less common than MOTSS or **MOTAS**, which have largely displaced it.

MOTSS */mots/* or */M-O-T-S-S/* [from the 1970 U.S. census forms via USENET] n. Member Of The Same Sex, esp. one considered as a possible sexual partner. The gay-issues newsgroup on USENET is called *soc.motss*. See **MOTOS** and **MOTAS**, which derive from it. See also **SO**.

mouse ahead vi. Point-and-click analog of 'type ahead'. To manipulate a computer's pointing device (almost always a mouse in this usage, but not necessarily) and its selection or command buttons before a computer program is ready to accept such input, in anticipation of the program accepting the input. Handling this properly is rare, but it can help make a **WIMP environment** much more usable, assuming the users are familiar with the behavior of the user interface.

mouse around vi. To explore public portions of a large system, esp. a network such as Internet via **FTP** or **TELNET**, looking for interesting stuff to **snarf**.

mouse belt n. See **rat belt**.

mouse droppings [MS-DOS] n. Pixels (usually single) that are not properly restored when the mouse pointer moves away from a particular location on the screen, producing the appearance that the mouse pointer has left droppings behind. The major causes for this problem are programs that write to the screen memory corresponding to the mouse pointer's current location without hiding the mouse pointer first, and mouse drivers that do not quite support the graphics mode in use.

mouse elbow n. A tennis-elbow-like fatigue syndrome resulting from excessive use of a **WIMP environment**. Similarly, *mouse shoulder*; GLS reports that he used to get this a lot before he taught himself to be ambimoustrous.

mouso */mow'soh/* n. [by analogy with 'typo'] An error in mouse usage resulting in an inappropriate selection or graphic garbage on the screen. Compare **thinko**, **braino**.

MS-DOS */M-S-dos/* [MicroSoft Disk Operating System] n. A **clone** of **CP/M** for the 8088 crufted together in 6 weeks by hacker Tim Paterson, who is said to have regretted it ever since. Numerous features, including vaguely UNIX-like but rather broken support for subdirectories, I/O redirection, and pipelines, were hacked into 2.0 and subsequent versions; as a result, there are two or more incompatible versions of many system calls, and MS-DOS programmers can never agree on basic things like what character to use as an option switch or whether to be case-sensitive. The resulting mess is now the highest-unit-volume OS in history. Often known simply as DOS, which annoys people familiar with other similarly abbreviated operating systems (the name goes back to the mid-1960s, when it was attached to IBM's first disk operating system for the 360). The name further annoys those who know what the term **operating system** does (or ought to) connote; DOS is more properly a set of relatively simple interrupt services. Some people like to pronounce DOS like "dose", as in "I don't work on dose, man!", or to compare it to a dose of brain-damaging drugs (a slogan button in wide circulation among hackers exhorts: "MS-DOS: Just say No!"). See **mess-dos**, **ill-behaved**.

mu */moo/* The correct answer to the classic trick question "Have you stopped beating your wife yet?". Assuming that you have no wife or you have never beaten your wife, the answer "yes" is wrong because it implies that you used to beat your wife and then stopped, but "no" is worse because it suggests that you have one and are still beating her. According to various Discordians and Douglas Hofstadter the correct answer is usually "mu", a Japanese word alleged to mean "Your question cannot be answered because it depends on incorrect assumptions". Hackers tend to be sensitive to logical inadequacies in language, and many have adopted this suggestion with enthusiasm. The word 'mu' is actually from Chinese, meaning 'nothing'; it is used in mainstream Japanese in that sense, but native speakers do not recognize the Discordian question-denying use. It almost certainly derives from overgeneralization of the answer in the following well-known Rinzei Zen teaching riddle:

> A monk asked Joshu, "Does a dog have the Buddha nature?" Joshu retorted, "Mu!"

See also **has the X nature**, **AI Koans**, and Douglas Hofstadter's *Gödel, Escher, Bach: An Eternal Golden Braid* (pointer in the Bibliography in **Appendix C**).

MUD */muhd/* [acronym, Multi-User Dungeon; alt. Multi-User Dimension] 1. n. A class of **virtual reality** experiments accessible via the Internet. These are real-time chat forums with structure; they have multiple 'locations' like an adventure game, and may include combat, traps, puzzles, magic, a simple economic system, and the capability for characters to build more structure onto the database that represents the existing world. 2. vi. To play a MUD. The acronym MUD is often lowercased and/or verbed; thus, one may speak of *going mudding*, etc.

Historically, MUDs (and their more recent progeny with names of MU-form) derive from a hack by Richard Bartle and Roy Trubshaw on the University of Essex's DEC-10 in the early 1980s; descendants of that game still exist today and are sometimes generically called *BartleMUDs*. There is a widespread myth (repeated, unfortunately, by earlier versions of this lexicon) that the name MUD was trademarked to the commercial MUD run by Bartle on British Telecom (the motto: "You haven't *lived* 'til you've *died* on MUD!"); however, this is false — Richard Bartle explicitly placed 'MUD' in PD in 1985. BT was upset at this, as they had already printed trademark claims on some maps and posters, which were released and created the myth.

Students on the European academic networks quickly improved on the MUD concept, spawning several new MUDs (VAXMUD, AberMUD, LPMUD). Many of these had associated bulletin-board systems for social interaction. Because these had an image as 'research' they often survived administrative hostility to BBSs in general. This, together with the fact that USENET feeds have been spotty and difficult to get in the U.K., made the MUDs major foci of hackish social interaction there.

AberMUD and other variants crossed the Atlantic around 1988 and quickly gained popularity in the U.S.; they became nuclei for large hacker communities with only loose ties to traditional hackerdom (some observers see parallels with the growth of USENET in the early 1980s). The second wave of MUDs (TinyMUD and variants) tended to emphasize social interaction, puzzles, and cooperative world-building as opposed to combat and competition. In 1991, over 50% of MUD sites are of a third major variety, LPMUD, which synthesizes the combat/puzzle aspects of AberMUD and older systems with the extensibility of TinyMud. The trend toward greater programmability and flexibility will doubtless continue.

The state of the art in MUD design is still moving very rapidly, with new simulation designs appearing (seemingly) every month. There is now (early 1991) a move afoot to deprecate the term **MUD** itself, as newer designs exhibit an exploding variety of names corresponding to the different simulation styles being explored. See also **bonk/oif**, **FOD**, **link-dead**, **mud-head**, **talk mode**.

muddie n. Syn. **mudhead**. More common in Great Britain, possibly because system administrators there like to mutter "bloody muddies" when annoyed at the species.

mudhead n. Commonly used to refer to a **MUD** player who eats, sleeps, and breathes MUD. Mudheads have been known to fail their degrees, drop out, etc., with the consolation, however, that they made wizard level. When encountered in person, on a MUD, or in a chat system, all a mudhead will talk about is three topics: the tactic, character, or wizard that is supposedly always unfairly stopping him/her from becoming a wizard or beating a favorite MUD; why the specific game he/she has experience with is so much better than any other; and the MUD he or she is writing or going to write because his/her design ideas are so much better than in any existing MUD. See also **wannabee**.

To the anthropologically literate, this term may recall the Zuni/Hopi legend of the mudheads or 'koyemshi', mythical half-formed children of an unnatural union. Figures representing them act as clowns in Zuni sacred ceremonies.

multician */muhl-ti´shn/* [coined at Honeywell, ca. 1970] n. Competent user of **Multics**. Perhaps oddly, no one has ever promoted the analogous 'Unician'.

Multics */muhl´tiks/* n. [from "MULTiplexed Information and Computing Service"] An early (late 1960s) timesharing operating system co-designed by a consortium including MIT, GE, and Bell Laboratories. Multics was very innovative for its time — among other things, it introduced the idea of treating all devices uniformly as special files. All the members but GE eventually pulled out after determining that **second-system effect** had bloated Multics to the point of practical unusability (the 'lean' predecessor in question was **CTSS**). Honeywell commercialized Multics after buying out GE's computer group, but it was never very successful (among other things, on some versions one was commonly required to enter a password to log out). One of the developers left in the lurch by the project's breakup was Ken Thompson, a circumstance which led directly to the birth of **UNIX**. For this and other reasons, aspects of the Multics design remain a topic of occasional debate among hackers. See also **brain-damaged** and **GCOS**.

multitask n. Often used of humans in the same meaning it has for computers, to describe a person doing several things at once (but see **thrash**). The term 'multiplex', from communications technology (meaning to handle more than one channel at the same time), is used similarly.

mumblage */muhm´bləj/* n. The topic of one's mumbling (see **mumble**). "All that mumblage" is used like "all that stuff" when it is not quite clear how the subject of discussion works, or like "all that crap" when 'mumble' is being used as an implicit replacement for pejoratives.

mumble interj. 1. Said when the correct response is too complicated to enunciate, or the speaker has not thought it out. Often prefaces a longer answer, or indicates a general reluctance to get into a long discussion. "Don't you think that we could improve LISP performance by using a hybrid reference-count transaction garbage collector, if the cache is big enough and there are some extra cache bits for the microcode to use?" "Well, mumble . . . I'll have to think about it." 2. [MIT] Expression of not-quite-articulated agreement, often used as an informal vote of consensus in a meeting: "So, shall we dike out the COBOL emulation?" "Mumble!" 3. Sometimes used as an expression of disagreement (distinguished from sense 2 by tone of voice and other cues). "I think we should buy a **VAX**." "Mumble!" Common variant: *mumble frotz* (see **frotz**; interestingly, one does not say 'mumble frobnitz' even though 'frotz' is short for 'frobnitz'). 4. Yet another **metasyntactic variable**, like **foo**. 5. When used as a question ("Mumble?") means "I didn't understand you". 6. Sometimes used in 'public' contexts on-line as a placefiller for things one is barred from giving details about. For example, a poster with pre-released hardware in his machine might say "Yup, my machine now has an extra 16M of memory, thanks to the card I'm testing for Mumbleco." 7. A conversational wild card used to designate something one doesn't want to bother spelling out, but which can be **glark**ed from context. Compare **blurgle**. 8. [XEROX PARC] A colloquialism used to suggest that further discussion would be fruitless.

munch [often confused with **mung**, q.v.] vt. To transform information in a serial fashion, often requiring large amounts of computation. To trace down a data structure. Related to **crunch** and nearly synonymous with **grovel**, but connotes less pain.

munching n. Exploration of security holes of someone else's computer for thrills, notoriety, or to annoy the system manager. Compare **cracker**. See also **hacked off**.

munching squares n. A **display hack** dating back to the PDP-1 (ca. 1962, reportedly discovered by Jackson Wright), which employs a trivial computation (repeatedly plotting the graph Y = X XOR T for successive values of T — see **HAKMEM** items 146–148) to produce an impressive display of moving and growing squares that devour the screen. The initial value of T is treated as a parameter, which, when well-chosen, can produce amazing effects. Some of these, later (re)discovered on the LISP machine, have been christened *munching triangles* (try AND for XOR and toggling points instead of plotting them), *munching w's*, and *munching mazes*. More generally, suppose a graphics program produces an impressive and ever-changing display of some basic form, foo, on a display terminal, and does it using a relatively simple program; then the program (or the resulting display) is likely to be referred to as *munching foos*. [This is a good example of the use of the word **foo** as a **metasyntactic variable**.]

munchkin */muhnch´kin/* [from the squeaky-voiced little people in L. Frank Baum's *The Wizard of Oz*] n. A teenage-or-younger micro enthusiast hacking BASIC or something else equally constricted. A term of mild derision — munchkins are annoying but some grow up to be hackers after passing through a **larval stage**. The term **urchin** is also used. See also **wannabee, bitty box**.

mundane [from SF fandom] n. 1. A person who is not in science fiction fandom. 2. A person who is not in the computer industry. In this sense, most often an adjectival modifier as in "in my mundane life. . . ." See also **Real World**.

mung */muhng/* [in 1960 at MIT, 'Mash Until No Good'; sometime after that the derivation from the **recursive acronym** 'Mung Until No Good' became standard] vt. 1. To make changes to a file, esp. large-scale and irrevocable changes. See **BLT**. 2. To destroy, usually accidentally, occasionally maliciously. The system only mungs things maliciously; this is a consequence of **Finagle's Law**. See **scribble, mangle, trash, nuke**. Reports from **USENET** suggest that the pronunciation */muhnj/* is now usual in speech, but the spelling 'mung' is still common in program comments (compare the widespread confusion over the proper spelling of **kluge**). 3. The kind of beans of which the sprouts are used in Chinese food. (That's their real name! Mung beans! Really!)

Like many early hacker terms, this one seems to have originated at **TMRC**; it was already in use there in 1958. Peter Samson (compiler of the original TMRC lexicon) thinks it may originally have been onomatopoeic for the sound of a relay spring (contact) being twanged.

munge */muhnj/* vt. 1. [derogatory] To imperfectly transform information. 2. A comprehensive rewrite of a routine, data structure or the whole program.

This term is often confused with **mung** and may derive from it, or possibly vice-versa.

Murphy's Law prov. The correct, *original* Murphy's Law reads: "If there are two or more ways to do something, and one of those ways can result in a catastrophe, then someone will do it." This is a principle of defensive design, cited here because it is usually given in mutant forms less descriptive of the challenges of design for lusers. For example, you don't make a two-pin plug symmetrical and then label it 'THIS WAY UP'; if it matters which way it is plugged in, then you make the design asymmetrical (see also the anecdote under **magic smoke**).

Edward A. Murphy, Jr. was one of the engineers on the rocket-sled experiments that were done by the U.S. Air Force in 1949 to test human acceleration tolerances (USAF project MX981). One experiment involved a set of 16 accelerometers mounted to different parts of the subject's body. There were two ways each sensor could be glued to its mount, and somebody methodically installed all 16 the wrong way around. Murphy then made the original form of his pronouncement, which the test subject (Major John Paul Stapp) quoted at a news conference a few days later.

Within months 'Murphy's Law' had spread to various technical cultures connected to aerospace engineering. Before too many years had gone by variants had passed into the popular imagination, changing as they went. Most of these are variants on "Anything that can go wrong, will"; this is sometimes referred to as **Finagle's Law**. The memetic drift apparent in these mutants clearly demonstrates Murphy's Law acting on itself!

music n. A common extracurricular interest of hackers (compare **science-fiction fandom**, **oriental food**; see also **filk**). Hackish folklore has long claimed that musical and programming abilities are closely related, and there has been at least one large-scale statistical study that supports this. Hackers, as a rule, like music and often develop musical appreciation in unusual and interesting directions. Folk music is very big in hacker circles; so is electronic music, and the sort of elaborate instrumental jazz/rock that used to be called 'progressive' and isn't recorded much any more. The hacker's musical range tends to be wide; many can listen with equal appreciation to (say) Talking Heads, Yes, Gentle Giant, Pat Metheny, Scott Joplin, Tangerine Dream, King Sunny Ade, The Pretenders, or the Brandenburg Concerti. It is also apparently true that hackerdom includes a much higher concentration of talented amateur musicians than one would expect from a similar-sized control group of **mundane** types.

mutter vt. To quietly enter a command not meant for the ears, eyes, or fingers of ordinary mortals. Often used in 'mutter an **incantation**'. See also **wizard**.

= N =

N */N/* quant. 1. A large and indeterminate number of objects: "There were N bugs in that crock!" Also used in its original sense of a variable name: "This crock has N bugs, as N goes to infinity." (The true number of bugs is always at least $N + 1$; see **Lubarsky's Law of Cybernetic Entomology**.) 2. A variable whose value is inherited from the current context. For example, when a meal is being ordered at a restaurant, N may be understood to mean however many people there are at the table. From the remark "We'd like to order N wonton soups and a family dinner for $N - 1$" you can deduce that one person at the table wants to eat only soup, even though you don't know how many people there are (see **great-wall**). 3. *N th*: adj. The ordinal counterpart of N, senses 1 and 2. "Now for the Nth and last time . . . " In the specific context "Nth-year grad student", N is generally assumed to be at least 4, and is usually 5 or more (see **tenured graduate student**). See also **random numbers**, **two-to-the-N**.

nadger */nad´jr/* [Great Britain] v. Of software or hardware (not people), to twiddle some object in a hidden manner, generally so that it conforms better to some format. For instance, string printing routines on 8-bit processors often take the string text from the instruction stream, thus a print call looks like `jsr print:"Hello world"`. The print routine has to *nadger* the saved instruction pointer so that the processor doesn't try to execute the text as instructions when the subroutine returns.

nagware */nag´weir/* [USENET] n. The variety of **shareware** that displays a large screen at the beginning or end reminding you to register, typically requiring some sort of keystroke to continue so that you can't use the software in batch mode. Compare **crippleware**.

nailed to the wall [like a trophy] adj. Said of a bug finally eliminated after protracted, and even heroic, effort.

nailing jelly vi. See **like nailing jelly to a tree**.

naive adj. Untutored in the perversities of some particular program or system;

one who still tries to do things in an intuitive way, rather than the right way (in really good designs these coincide, but most designs aren't 'really good' in the appropriate sense). This trait is completely unrelated to general maturity or competence, or even competence at any other specific program. It is a sad commentary on the primitive state of computing that the natural opposite of this term is often claimed to be *experienced user* but is really more like *cynical user.*

naive user n. A **luser**. Tends to imply someone who is ignorant mainly owing to inexperience. When this is applied to someone who *has* experience, there is a definite implication of stupidity.

NAK */nak/* [from the ASCII mnemonic for 0010101] interj. 1. On-line joke answer to **ACK**?: "I'm not here." 2. On-line answer to a request for chat: "I'm not available." 3. Used to politely interrupt someone to tell them you don't understand their point or that they have suddenly stopped making sense. See **ACK**, sense 3. "And then, after we recode the project in COBOL. . . ." "Nak, Nak, Nak! I thought I heard you say COBOL!"

nano */nan´oh/* [CMU: from 'nanosecond'] n. A brief period of time. "Be with you in a nano" means you really will be free shortly, i.e., implies what mainstream people mean by "in a jiffy" (whereas the hackish use of 'jiffy' is quite different — see **jiffy**).

nano- [SI: the next quantifier below **micro-**; meaning $*10^{-9}$] pref. Smaller than **micro-**, and used in the same rather loose and connotative way. Thus, one has **nanotechnology** (coined by hacker K. Eric Drexler) by analogy with 'microtechnology'; and a few machine architectures have a *nanocode* level below 'microcode'. Tom Duff at Bell Labs has also pointed out that " seconds is a nanocentury". See also **quantifiers**, **pico-**, **nanoacre**, **nanobot**, **nanocomputer**, **nanofortnight**.

nanoacre */nan´oh-ay`kr/* n. A unit (about 2 mm square) of real estate on a VLSI chip. The term gets its giggle value from the fact that VLSI nanoacres have costs in the same range as real acres once one figures in design and fabrication-setup costs.

nanobot */nan´oh-bot/* n. A robot of microscopic proportions, presumably built by means of **nanotechnology**. As yet, only used informally (and speculatively!). Also called a *nanoagent.*

nanocomputer */nan´oh-kəm-pyoo´tr/* n. A computer with molecular-sized switching elements. Designs for mechanical nanocomputers which use single-molecule sliding rods for their logic have been proposed. The controller for a **nanobot** would be a nanocomputer.

nanofortnight [Adelaide University] n. 1 fortnight $*10^{-}9$, or about 1.2 msec. This unit was used largely by students doing undergraduate practicals. See **microfortnight**, **attoparsec**, and **micro-**.

nanotechnology */nan´-oh-tek-no`lə-jee/* n. A hypothetical fabrication technology in which objects are designed and built with the individual specification and placement of each separate atom. The first unequivocal nanofabrication experiments took place in 1990, for example with the deposition of individual xenon atoms on a nickel substrate to spell the logo of a certain very large computer company. Nanotechnology has been a hot topic in the hacker subculture ever since the term was coined by K. Eric Drexler in his book *Engines of Creation*, where he predicted that nanotechnology could give rise to replicating assemblers, permitting an exponential growth of productivity and personal wealth. See also **blue goo**, **gray goo**, **nanobot**.

nasal demons n. Recognized shorthand on the USENET group *comp.std.c* for any unexpected behavior of a C compiler on encountering an undefined construct. During a discussion on that group in early 1992, a regular remarked "When the compiler encounters [a given undefined construct] it is legal for it to make demons fly out of your nose" (the implication is that the compiler may choose any arbitrarily bizarre way to interpret the code without violating the ANSI C standard). Someone else followed up with a reference to "nasal demons", which quickly became established.

nastygram */nas´tee-gram/* n. 1. A protocol packet or item of email (the latter is also called a **letterbomb**) that takes advantage of misfeatures or security holes on the target system to do untoward things. 2. Disapproving mail, esp. from a **net.god**, pursuant to a violation of **netiquette** or a complaint about failure to correct some mail- or news-transmission problem. Compare **shitogram**, **mailbomb**. 3. A status report from an unhappy, and probably picky, customer. "What'd Corporate say in today's nastygram?" 4. [deprecated] An error reply by mail from a **daemon**; in particular, a **bounce message**.

Nathan Hale n. An asterisk (see also **splat**, **ASCII**). Oh, you want an etymology? Notionally, from "I regret that I have only one asterisk for my country!", a misquote of the famous remark uttered by Nathan Hale just before he was hanged. Hale was a (failed) spy for the rebels in the American War of Independence.

nature n. See **has the X nature**.

neat hack n. 1. A clever technique. 2. A brilliant practical joke, where neatness is correlated with cleverness, harmlessness, and surprise value. Example: the Caltech Rose Bowl card display switch (see "The Meaning of 'Hack'", appendix A). See also **hack**.

neats vs. scruffies n. The label used to refer to one of the continuing **holy wars** in AI research. This conflict tangles together two separate issues. One is the relationship between human reasoning and AI; 'neats' tend to try to build systems that 'reason' in some way identifiably similar to the way humans report themselves as doing, while 'scruffies' profess not to care whether an algorithm resembles human reasoning in the least as long as it works. More importantly, neats tend to believe that logic is king, while scruffies favor looser, more ad-hoc methods driven by empirical knowledge. To a neat, scruffy methods appear promiscuous, successful only by accident, and not productive of insights about how intelligence actually works; to a scruffy, neat methods appear to be hung up on formalism and irrelevant to the hard-to-capture 'common sense' of living intelligences.

neep-neep */neep neep/* [onomatopoeic, from New York SF fandom] n. One who is fascinated by computers. Less specific than **hacker**, as it need not imply more skill than is required to boot games on a PC. The derived noun *neeping* applies specifically to the long conversations about computers that tend to develop in the corners at most SF-convention parties (the term *neepery* is also in wide use). Fandom has a related proverb to the effect that "Hacking is a conversational black hole!".

neophilia */nee`oh-fil´-ee-ə/* n. The trait of being excited and pleased by novelty. Common among most hackers, SF fans, and members of several other connected leading-edge subcultures, including the pro-technology 'Whole Earth' wing of the ecology movement, space activists, many members of Mensa, and the Discordian/neo-pagan underground. All these groups overlap heavily and (where evidence is available) seem to share characteristic hacker tropisms for science fiction, **music**, and **oriental food**. The opposite tendency is *neophobia*.

net.- */net dot/* pref. [USENET] Prefix used to describe people and events related to USENET. From the time before the **Great Renaming**, when most non-local newsgroups had names beginning 'net.'. Includes **net.god**s, *net.goddesses* (various charismatic net.women with circles of on-line admirers), *net.lurkers* (see **lurker**), *net.person, net.parties* (a synonym for **boink**, sense 2), and many similar constructs. See also **net.police**.

net.god */net god/* n. Accolade referring to anyone who satisfies some combination of the following conditions: has been visible on USENET for more than 5 years, ran one of the original backbone sites, moderated an important newsgroup, wrote news software, or knows Gene, Mark, Rick, Mel, Henry, Chuq, and Greg personally. See **demigod**. Net.goddesses such as Rissa or the Slime Sisters have (so far) been distinguished more by personality than by authority.

net.personality */net per`sn-al´-ə-tee/* n. Someone who has made a name for him or herself on **USENET**, through either longevity or attention-getting posts, but doesn't meet the other requirements of **net.god**hood.

net.police */net-pə-lees´/* n. (var. *net.cops*) Those USENET readers who feel it is their responsibility to pounce on and **flame** any posting which they regard as offensive or in violation of their understanding of **netiquette**. Generally used sarcastically or pejoratively. Also spelled 'net police'. See also **net.-**, **code police**.

NetBOLLIX [from bollix: to bungle] n. IBM's NetBIOS, an extremely **brain-damaged** network protocol that, like **Blue Glue**, is used at commercial shops that don't know any better.

netburp [IRC] n. When **netlag** gets really bad, and delays between servers exceed a certain threshhold, the **IRC** network effectively becomes partitioned for a period of time, and large numbers of people seem to be signing off at the same time and then signing back on again when things get better. An instance of this is called a *netburp* (or, sometimes, **netsplit**).

netdead [IRC] n. The state of someone who signs off **IRC**, perhaps during a **netburp**, and doesn't sign back on until later. In the interim, he is "dead to the net".

nethack */net´hak/* [UNIX] n. A dungeon game similar to **rogue** but more elaborate, distributed in C source over **USENET** and very popular at UNIX sites and on PC-class machines (nethack is probably the most widely distributed of the freeware dungeon games). The earliest versions, written by Jay Fenlason and later considerably enhanced by Andries Brouwer, were simply called 'hack'. The name changed when maintenance was taken over by a group of hackers originally organized by Mike Stephenson; the current contact address (as of mid-1993) is *nethack-bugs@linc.cis.upenn.edu.*

netiquette */net´ee-ket/* or */net´i-ket/* [portmanteau from "network etiquette"] n. The conventions of politeness recognized on **USENET**, such as avoidance of cross-posting to inappropriate groups and refraining from commercial pluggery outside the *biz* groups.

netlag [IRC, MUD] n. A condition that occurs when the delays in the **IRC** network or on a **MUD** become severe enough that servers briefly lose and then reestablish contact, causing messages to be delivered in bursts, often with delays of up to a minute. (Note that this term has nothing to do with mainstream "jet lag", a condition which hackers tend not to be much bothered by.)

netnews */net´n[y]ooz/* n. 1. The software that makes **USENET** run. 2. The content of USENET. "I read netnews right after my mail most mornings."

netrock */net´rok/* [IBM] n. A **flame**; used esp. on VNET, IBM's internal corporate network.

netsplit n. Syn. **netburp**.

netter n. 1. Loosely, anyone with a **network address**. 2. More specifically, a **USENET** regular. Most often found in the plural. "If you post *that* in a technical group, you're going to be flamed by angry netters for the rest of time!"

network address n. (also *net address*) As used by hackers, means an address on 'the' network (see **network, the**; this is almost always a **bang path** or **Internet address**). Such an address is essential if one wants to be to be taken seriously by hackers; in particular, persons or organizations that claim to understand, work with, sell to, or recruit from among hackers but *don't* display net addresses are quietly presumed to be clueless poseurs and mentally flushed (see **flush**, sense 4). Hackers often put their net addresses on their business cards and wear them prominently in contexts where they expect to meet other hackers face-to-face (see also **science-fiction fandom**). This is mostly functional, but is also a signal that one identifies with hackerdom (like lodge pins among Masons or tie-dyed T-shirts among Grateful Dead fans). Net addresses are often used in email text as a more concise substitute for personal names; indeed, hackers may come to know each other quite well by network names without ever learning each others' 'legal' monikers. See also **sitename**, **domainist**.

network meltdown n. A state of complete network overload; the network equivalent of **thrash**ing. This may be induced by a **Chernobyl packet**. See also **broadcast storm**, **kamikaze packet**.

network, the n. 1. The union of all the major noncommercial, academic, and hacker-oriented networks, such as Internet, the old ARPANET, NSFnet, **BITNET**, and the virtual UUCP and **USENET** 'networks', plus the corporate in-house networks and commercial time-sharing services (such as CompuServe) that gateway to them. A site is generally considered *on the network* if it can be reached through some combination of Internet-style (@-sign) and UUCP (bang-path) addresses. See **bang path**, **Internet address**, **network address**. 2. A fictional conspiracy of libertarian hacker-subversives and anti-authoritarian monkeywrenchers described in Robert Anton Wilson's novel *Schrödinger's Cat*, to which many hackers have subsequently decided they belong (this is an example of **ha ha only serious**).

In sense 1, *network* is often abbreviated to *net*. "Are you on the net?" is a frequent question when hackers first meet face to face, and "See you on the net!" is a frequent goodbye.

New Jersey [primarily Stanford/Silicon Valley] adj. Brain-damaged or of poor design. This refers to the allegedly wretched quality of such software as C, C++, and UNIX (which originated at Bell Labs in Murray Hill, New Jersey). "This compiler bites the bag, but what can you expect from a compiler designed in New Jersey?" Compare **Berkeley Quality Software**. See also **UNIX conspiracy**.

New Testament n. [C programmers] The second edition of K&R's *The C Programming Language* (Prentice-Hall, 1988; ISBN 0-13-110362-8), describing ANSI Standard C. See **K&R**.

newbie */n[y]oo´bee/* n. [orig. from British public-school and military slang variant of 'new boy'] A USENET neophyte. This term surfaced in the **newsgroup** *talk.bizarre* but is now in wide use. Criteria for being considered a newbie vary wildly; a person can be called a newbie in one newsgroup while remaining a respected regular in another. The label *newbie* is sometimes applied as a serious insult to a person who has been around USENET for a long time but who carefully hides all evidence of having a clue. See **BIFF**.

newgroup wars */n[y]oo´groop worz/* [USENET] n. The salvos of dueling `newgroup` and `rmgroup` messages sometimes exchanged by persons on opposite sides of a dispute over whether a **newsgroup** should be created net-wide, or (even more frequently) whether an obsolete one should be removed. These usually settle out within a week or two as it becomes clear whether the group has a natural constituency (usually, it doesn't). At times, especially in the completely anarchic *alt* hierarchy, the names of newsgroups themselves become a form of comment or humor; e.g., the spinoff of *alt.swedish.chef.bork.bork.bork* from *alt.tv.muppets* in early 1990, or any number of specialized abuse groups named after particularly notorious **flamer**s, e.g., *alt.weemba.*

newline */n[y]oo´li:n/* n. 1. [techspeak, primarily UNIX] The ASCII LF character (0001010), used under **UNIX** as a text line terminator. A Bell-Labs-ism rather than a Berkeleyism; interestingly (and unusually for UNIX jargon), it is said to have originally been an IBM usage. (Though the term 'newline' appears in ASCII standards, it never caught on in the general computing world before UNIX). 2. More generally, any magic character, character sequence, or operation (like Pascal's writeln procedure) required to terminate a text record or separate lines. See **crlf**, **terpri**.

NeWS */nee´wis/*, */n[y]oo´is/* or */n[y]ooz/* [acronym; the 'Network Window System'] n. The road not taken in window systems, an elegant **PostScript**-based environment that would almost certainly have won the standards war with **X** if it hadn't been **proprietary** to Sun Microsystems. There is a lesson here that too many software vendors haven't yet heeded. Many hackers insist on the two-syllable pronunciations above as a way of distinguishing NeWS from **news** (the **netnews** software).

news n. See **netnews**.

newsfroup *//* [USENET] n. Silly synonym for **newsgroup**, originally a typo but now in regular use on USENET's talk.bizarre and other lunatic-fringe groups. Compare **hing**, **grilf**, and **filk**.

newsgroup [USENET] n. One of **USENET**'s huge collection of topic groups or **fora**. Usenet groups can be *unmoderated* (anyone can post) or *moderated* (submissions are automatically directed to a moderator, who edits or filters and then posts the results). Some newsgroups have parallel **mailing lists** for Internet people with no netnews access, with postings to the group automatically propagated to the list and vice versa. Some moderated groups (especially those which are actually gatewayed Internet mailing lists) are distributed as *digests*, with groups of postings periodically collected into a single large posting with an index.

Among the best-known are *comp.lang.c* (the C-language forum), *comp.arch* (on computer architectures), *comp.unix.wizards* (for UNIX wizards), *rec.arts.sf-lovers* (for science-fiction fans), and *talk.politics.misc* (miscellaneous political discussions and **flamage**).

nick [IRC] n. Short for nickname. On **IRC**, every user must pick a nick, which is sometimes the same as the user's real name or login name, but is often more fanciful. Compare **handle**.

nickle */ni´kl/* [from 'nickel', common name for the U.S. 5-cent coin] n. A **nybble** + 1; 5 bits. Reported among developers for Mattel's GI 1600 (the Intellivision games processor), a chip with 16-bit-wide RAM but 10-bit-wide ROM. See also **deckle**.

night mode n. See **phase** (of people).

Nightmare File System n. Pejorative hackerism for Sun's Network File System (NFS). In any nontrivial network of Suns where there is a lot of NFS cross-mounting, when one Sun goes down, the others often freeze up. Some machine tries to access the down one, and (getting no response) repeats indefinitely. This causes it to appear dead to some messages (what is actually happening is that it is locked up in what should have been a brief excursion to a higher **spl** level). Then another machine tries to reach either the down machine or the pseudo-down machine, and itself becomes pseudo-down. The first machine to discover the down one is now trying both to access the down one and to respond to the pseudo-down one, so it is even harder to reach. This situation snowballs very quickly, and soon the entire network of machines is frozen — worst of all, the user can't even abort the file access that started the problem! Many of NFS's problems are excused by partisans as being an inevitable result of its statelessness, which is held to be a great feature (critics, of course, call it a great **misfeature**). (ITS partisans are apt to cite this as proof of UNIX's alleged bogosity; ITS had a working NFS-like shared file system with none of these problems in the early 1970s.) See also **broadcast storm**.

NIL */nil/* No. Used in reply to a question, particularly one asked using the '-P' convention. Most hackers assume this derives simply from LISP terminology for 'false' (see also **T**), but NIL as a negative reply was well-established among radio hams decades before the advent of LISP. The historical connection between early hackerdom and the ham radio world was strong enough that this may have been an influence.

Ninety-Ninety Rule n. "The first 90% of the code accounts for the first 90% of the development time. The remaining 10% of the code accounts for the other 90% of the development time." Attributed to Tom Cargill of Bell Labs, and popularized by Jon Bentley's September 1985 *Bumper-Sticker Computer Science* column in *Communications of the ACM*. It was there called the "Rule of Credibility", a name which seems not to have stuck.

NMI */N-M-I/* n. Non-Maskable Interrupt. An IRQ 7 on the PDP-11 or 680[01234]0; the NMI line on an 80[1234]86. In contrast with a **priority interrupt** (which might be ignored, although that is unlikely), an NMI is *never* ignored.

no-op */noh´op/* alt. NOP */nop/* [no operation] n. 1. (also v.) A machine instruction that does nothing (sometimes used in assembler-level programming as filler for data or patch areas, or to overwrite code to be removed in binaries). See also **JFCL**. 2. A person who contributes nothing to a project, or has nothing going on upstairs, or both. As in "He's a no-op." 3. Any operation or sequence of operations with no effect, such as circling the block without finding a parking space, or putting money into a vending machine and having it fall immediately into the coin-return box, or asking someone for help and being told to go away. "Oh, well, that was a no-op." Hot-and-sour soup (see **great-wall**) that is insufficiently either is *no-op soup*; so is wonton soup if everybody else is having hot-and-sour.

noddy */nod´ee/* [UK: from the children's books] adj. 1. Small and un-useful, but demonstrating a point. Noddy programs are often written by people learning a new language or system. The archetypal noddy program is **hello, world**. Noddy code may be used to demonstrate a feature or bug of a compiler. May be used of real hardware or software to imply that it isn't worth using. "This editor's a bit noddy." 2. A program that is more or less instant to produce. In this use, the term does not necessarily connote uselessness, but describes a **hack** sufficiently trivial that it can be written and debugged while carrying on (and during the space of) a normal conversation. "I'll just throw together a noddy **awk** script to dump all the first fields." In North America this might be called a **mickey mouse program**. See **toy program**.

NOMEX underwear */noh´meks uhn´-der-weir/* [USENET] n. Syn. **asbestos longjohns**, used mostly in auto-related mailing lists and newsgroups. NOMEX underwear is an actual product available on the racing equipment market, used as a fire resistance measure and required in some racing series.

Nominal Semidestructor n. Soundalike slang for 'National Semiconductor', found among other places in the 4.3BSD networking sources. During the late 1970s to mid-1980s this company marketed a series of microprocessors including the NS16000 and NS32000 and several variants. At one point early in the great microprocessor race, the specs on these chips made them look like serious competition for the rising Intel 80x86 and Motorola 680x0 series. Unfortunately, the actual parts were notoriously flaky and never implemented the full instruction set promised in their literature, apparently because the company couldn't get any of the mask steppings to work as designed. They eventually sank without trace, joining the Zilog Z8000 and a few even more obscure also-rans in the graveyard of forgotten microprocessors. Compare **HP-SUX**, **AIDX**, **buglix**, **Macintrash**, **Telerat**, **Open DeathTrap**, **ScumOS**, **sun-stools**.

non-optimal solution n. (also *sub-optimal solution*) An astoundingly stupid way to do something. This term is generally used in deadpan sarcasm, as its impact is greatest when the person speaking looks completely serious. Compare **stunning**. See also **Bad Thing**.

nonlinear adj. [scientific computation] 1. Behaving in an erratic and unpredictable fashion; unstable. When used to describe the behavior of a machine or program, it suggests that said machine or program is being forced to run far outside of design specifications. This behavior may be induced by unreasonable inputs, or may be triggered when a more mundane bug sends the computation far off from its expected course. 2. When describing the behavior of a person, suggests a tantrum or a **flame**. "When you talk to Bob, don't mention the drug problem or he'll go nonlinear for hours." In this context, *go nonlinear* connotes 'blow up out of proportion' (proportion connotes linearity).

nontrivial adj. Requiring real thought or significant computing power. Often used as an understated way of saying that a problem is quite difficult or impractical, or even entirely unsolvable ("Proving P=NP is nontrivial"). The preferred emphatic form is *decidedly nontrivial*. See **trivial**, **uninteresting**, **interesting**.

not ready for prime time adj. Usable, but only just so; not very robust; for internal use only. Said of a program or device. Often connotes that the thing will be made more solid **Real Soon Now**. This term comes from the ensemble name of the original cast of "Saturday Night Live", the "Not Ready for Prime Time Players". It has extra flavor for hackers because of the special (though now semi-obsolescent) meaning of **prime time**. Compare **beta**.

notwork */not´werk/* n. A network, when it is acting **flaky** or is **down**. Compare **nyetwork**. Said at IBM to have originally referred to a particular period of flakiness on IBM's VNET corporate network ca. 1988; but there are independent reports of the term from elsewhere.

NP- */N-P/* pref. Extremely. Used to modify adjectives describing a level or quality of difficulty; the connotation is often 'more so than it should be' (NP-complete problems all seem to be very hard, but so far no one has found a good *a priori* reason that they should be.) "Coding a BitBlt implementation to perform correctly in every case is NP-annoying." This is generalized from the computer-science terms 'NP-hard' and 'NP-complete'. NP is the set of Nondeterministic-Polynomial algorithms, those that can be completed by a nondeterministic Turing machine in an amount of time that is a polynomial function of the size of the input; a solution for one NP-complete problem would solve all the others. Note, however, that the NP- prefix is, from a complexity theorist's point of view, the wrong part of 'NP-complete' to connote extreme difficulty; it is the completeness, not the NP-ness, that puts any problem it describes in the 'hard' category.

nroff */N´rof/* [UNIX, from "new roff" (see **troff**)] n. A companion program to the UNIX typesetter **troff**, accepting identical input but preparing output for terminals and line printers.

NSA line eater n. The National Security Agency trawling program sometimes assumed to be reading the net for the U.S. Government's spooks. Most hackers describe it as a mythical beast, but some believe it actually exists, more aren't sure, and many believe in acting as though it exists just in case. Some netters put loaded phrases like 'KGB', 'Uzi', 'nuclear materials', 'Palestine', 'cocaine', and 'assassination' in their **sig blocks** in a (probably futile) attempt to confuse and overload the creature. The **GNU** version of **EMACS** actually has a command that randomly inserts a bunch of insidious anarcho-verbiage into your edited text.

There is a mainstream variant of this myth involving a 'Trunk Line Monitor', which supposedly used speech recognition to extract words from telephone trunks. This one was making the rounds in the late 1970s, spread by people who had no idea of then-current technology or the storage, signal-processing, or speech recognition needs of such a project. On the basis of mass-storage costs alone it would have been cheaper to hire 50 high-school students and just let them listen in. Speech-recognition technology can't do this job even now (1993), and almost certainly won't in this millennium, either. The peak of silliness came with a letter to an alternative paper in New Haven, Connecticut, laying out the factoids of this Big Brotherly affair. The letter writer then revealed his actual agenda by offering — at an amazing low price, just this once, we take VISA and MasterCard — a scrambler guaranteed to daunt the Trunk Trawler and presumably allowing the would-be Baader-Meinhof gangs of the world to get on with their business.

nude adj. Said of machines delivered without an operating system (compare **bare metal**). "We ordered 50 systems, but they all arrived nude, so we had to spend a an extra weekend with the installation tapes." This usage is a recent innovation reflecting the fact that most PC clones are now delivered with DOS or Microsoft Windows pre-installed at the factory. Other kinds of hardware are still normally delivered without OS, so this term is particular to PC support groups.

nuke */n[y]ook/* vt. 1. To intentionally delete the entire contents of a given directory or storage volume. "On UNIX, `rm -r /usr` will nuke everything in the usr filesystem." Never used for accidental deletion. Oppose **blow away**. 2. Syn. for **dike**, applied to smaller things such as files, features, or code sections. Often used to express a final verdict. "What do you want me to do with that 80-meg **wallpaper** file?" "Nuke it." 3. Used of processes as well as files; nuke is a frequent verbal alias for `kill -9` on UNIX. 4. On IBM PCs, a bug that results in **fandango on core** can trash the operating system, including the FAT (the in-core copy of the disk block chaining information). This can utterly scramble attached disks, which are then said to have been *nuked*. This term is also used of analogous lossages on Macintoshes and other micros without memory protection.

number-crunching n. Computations of a numerical nature, esp. those that make extensive use of floating-point numbers. The only thing **Fortrash** is good for. This term is in widespread informal use outside hackerdom and even in mainstream slang, but has additional hackish connotations: namely, that the computations are mindless and involve massive use of **brute force**. This is not always **evil**, esp. if it involves ray tracing or fractals or some other use that makes **pretty pictures**, esp. if such pictures can be used as **wallpaper**. See also **crunch**.

numbers [scientific computation] n. Output of a computation that may not be significant results but at least indicate that the program is running. May be used to placate management, grant sponsors, etc. *Making numbers* means running a program because output — any output, not necessarily meaningful output — is needed as a demonstration of progress. See **pretty pictures**, **math-out**, **social science number**.

NUXI problem */nuk´see pro´bləm/* n. Refers to the problem of transferring data between machines with differing byte-order. The string 'UNIX' might look like 'NUXI' on a machine with a different *byte sex* (e.g., when transferring data from a **little-endian** to a **big-endian**, or vice-versa). See also **middle-endian**, **swab**, and **bytesexual**.

nybble */nib´l/* (alt. *nibble*) [from v. 'nibble' by analogy with 'bite' ⇒ 'byte'] n. Four bits; one **hex** digit; a half-byte. Though 'byte' is now techspeak, this useful relative is still jargon. Compare **byte**, **crumb**, **tayste**, **dynner**; see also **bit**, **nickle**, **deckle**. Apparently this spelling is uncommon in Commonwealth Hackish, as British orthography suggests the pronunciation */ni:´bl/.*

nyetwork */nyet´werk/* [from Russian 'nyet' = no] n. A network, when it is acting **flaky** or is **down**. Compare **notwork**.

= O =

Ob- */ob/* pref. Obligatory. A piece of **netiquette** acknowledging that the author has been straying from the newsgroup's charter topic. For example, if a posting in alt.sex is a response to a part of someone else's posting that has nothing particularly to do with sex, the author may append 'ObSex' (or 'Obsex') and toss off a question or vignette about some unusual erotic act. It is considered a sign of great **winnitude** when one's Obs are more interesting than other people's whole postings.

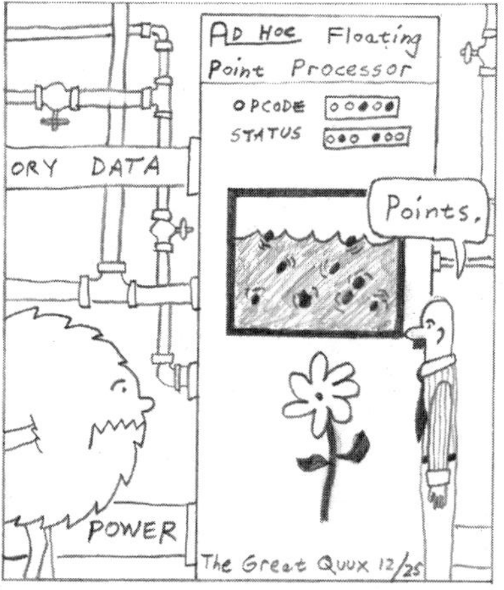

Hydrodynamic **number-crunching**.
The next cartoon in the Crunchly saga is 12-29-74, page 452.

Obfuscated C Contest (in full, the 'International Obfuscated C Code Contest', or IOCCC) n. An annual contest run since 1984 over USENET by Landon Curt Noll and friends. The overall winner is whoever produces the most unreadable, creative, and bizarre (but working) C program; various other prizes are awarded at the judges' whim. C's terse syntax and macro-preprocessor facilities give contestants a lot of maneuvering room. The winning programs often manage to be simultaneously (a) funny, (b) breathtaking works of art, and (c) horrible examples of how *not* to code in C.

This relatively short and sweet entry might help convey the flavor of obfuscated C:

```
/*
 * HELLO WORLD program
 * by Jack Applin and Robert Heckendorn, 1985
 */
main(v,c)
char**c;
{
for(v[c++]="Hello, world!\n)";
(!!c)[*c]&&(v--||--c
&&execlp(*c,*c,c[!!c]+!!c,!c));
**c=!c)
write(!!*c,*c,!!**c);}
```

Here's another good one:

```
/*
 * Program to compute an approximation of pi
 *  by Brian Westley, 1988
 */

#define _ -F<00||--F-OO--;
int F=00,OO=00;
main()
{
F_OO();printf("%1.3f\n",4.*-F/OO/OO);
}
F_OO()
```

```
{
            _-_-_-_
       _-_-_-_-_-_-_-_-_
    _-_-_-_-_-_-_-_-_-_-_-_
  _-_-_-_-_-_-_-_-_-_-_-_-_-_
 _-_-_-_-_-_-_-_-_-_-_-_-_-_-_
 _-_-_-_-_-_-_-_-_-_-_-_-_-_-_
_-_-_-_-_-_-_-_-_-_-_-_-_-_-_-_
_-_-_-_-_-_-_-_-_-_-_-_-_-_-_-_
_-_-_-_-_-_-_-_-_-_-_-_-_-_-_-_
_-_-_-_-_-_-_-_-_-_-_-_-_-_-_-_
 _-_-_-_-_-_-_-_-_-_-_-_-_-_-_
 _-_-_-_-_-_-_-_-_-_-_-_-_-_-_
  _-_-_-_-_-_-_-_-_-_-_-_-_-_
    _-_-_-_-_-_-_-_-_-_-_-_
        _-_-_-_-_-_-_-_
            _-_-_-_
}
```

Note that this program works by computing its own area. For more digits, write a bigger program. See also **hello, world**.

obi-wan error */oh´bee-won` er´ər/* [RPI, from 'off-by-one' and the Obi-Wan Kenobi character in "Star Wars"] n. A loop of some sort in which the index is off by 1. Common when the index should have started from 0 but instead started from 1. A kind of **off-by-one error**. See also **zeroth**.

Objectionable-C n. Hackish take on "Objective-C", the name of an object-oriented dialect of C in competition with the better-known C++ (it is used to write native applications on the NeXT machine). Objectionable-C uses a Smalltalk-like syntax, but lacks the flexibility of Smalltalk method calls, and (like many such efforts) comes frustratingly close to attaining the **Right Thing** without actually doing so.

obscure adj. Used in an exaggeration of its normal meaning, to imply total incomprehensibility. "The reason for that last crash is obscure." "The `find(1)` command's syntax is obscure!" The phrase *moderately obscure* implies that something could be figured out but probably isn't worth the trouble. The construction *obscure in the extreme* is the preferred emphatic form.

octal forty */ok´tl for´tee/* n. Hackish way of saying "I'm drawing a blank."

Octal 40 is the **ASCII** space character, 0100000; by an odd coincidence, **hex** 40 (01000000) is the **EBCDIC** space character. See **wall**.

off the trolley adj. Describes the behavior of a program that malfunctions and goes catatonic, but doesn't actually **crash** or abort. See **glitch**, **bug**, **deep space**.

off-by-one error n. Exceedingly common error induced in many ways, such as by starting at 0 when you should have started at 1 or vice-versa, or by writing < N instead of <= N or vice-versa. Also applied to giving something to the person next to the one who should have gotten it. Often confounded with **fencepost error**, which is properly a particular subtype of it.

offline adv. Not now or not here. "Let's take this discussion offline." Specifically used on **USENET** to suggest that a discussion be moved off a public newsgroup to email.

ogg */awg/* [CMU] v. 1. In the multi-player space combat game Netrek, to execute kamikaze attacks against enemy ships which are carrying armies or occupying strategic positions. Named during a game in which one of the players repeatedly used the tactic while playing Orion ship G, showing up in the player list as "Og". This trick has been roundly denounced by those who would return to the good old days when the tactic of dogfighting was dominant, but as Sun Tzu wrote, "What is of supreme importance in war is to attack the enemy's strategy." However, the traditional answer to the newbie question "What does ogg mean?" is just "Pick up some armies and I'll show you." 2. In other games, to forcefully attack an opponent with the expectation that the resources expended will be renewed faster than the opponent will be able to regain his previous advantage. Taken more seriously as a tactic since it has gained a simple name. 3. To do anything forcefully, possibly without consideration of the drain on future resources. "I guess I'd better go ogg the problem set that's due tomorrow." "Whoops! I looked down at the map for a sec and almost ogged that oncoming car."

old fart n. Tribal elder. A title self-assumed with remarkable frequency by (esp.) USENETters who have been programming for more than about 25 years; often appears in **sig blocks** attached to Jargon File contributions of great archeological significance. This is a term of insult in the second or third person but one of pride in first person.

Old Testament [C programmers] n. The first edition of **K&R**, the sacred text describing **Classic C**.

one-banana problem n. At mainframe shops, where the computers have operators for routine administrivia, the programmers and hardware people tend to look down on the operators and claim that a trained monkey could do their job. It is frequently observed that the incentives that would be offered said monkeys can be used as a scale to describe the difficulty of a task. A one-banana problem is simple; hence, "It's only a one-banana job at the most; what's taking them so long?"

At IBM, folklore divides the world into one-, two-, and three-banana problems. Other cultures have different hierarchies and may divide them more finely; at ICL, for example, five grapes (a bunch) equals a banana. Their upper limit for the in-house **sysapes** is said to be two bananas and three grapes (another source claims it's three bananas and one grape, but observes "However, this is subject to local variations, cosmic rays and ISO"). At a complication level any higher than that, one asks the manufacturers to send someone around to check things.

See also **Infinite-Monkey Theorem**.

one-line fix n. Used (often sarcastically) of a change to a program that is thought to be trivial or insignificant right up to the moment it crashes the system. Usually 'cured' by another one-line fix. See also **I didn't change anything!**

one-liner wars n. A game popular among hackers who code in the language APL (see **write-only language** and **line noise**). The objective is to see who can code the most interesting and/or useful routine in one line of operators chosen from APL's exceedingly **hairy** primitive set. A similar amusement was practiced among **TECO** hackers and is now popular among **Perl** aficionados.

Ken Iverson, the inventor of APL, has been credited with a one-liner that, given a number N, produces a list of the prime numbers from 1 to N inclusive. It looks like this:

$(2 = 0 + . = T \circ . | T)/T \leftarrow \iota N$

ooblick */oo´blik/* [from the Dr. Seuss title *Bartholomew and the Oobleck*] n. A bizarre semi-liquid sludge made from cornstarch and water. Enjoyed among hackers who make batches during playtime at parties for its amusing and extremely non-Newtonian behavior; it pours and splatters, but resists rapid motion like a solid and will even crack when hit by a hammer. Often found near lasers.

Here is a field-tested ooblick recipe contributed by GLS:

$1cupcornstarch$
$1cupbakingsoda$
$3/4cupwater$
$Ndropsoffoodcoloring$

This recipe isn't quite as non-Newtonian as a pure cornstarch ooblick, but has an appropriately slimy feel.

Some, however, insist that the notion of an ooblick *recipe* is far too mechanical, and that it is best to add the water in small increments so that the various mixed states the cornstarch goes through as it *becomes* ooblick can be grokked in fullness by many hands. For optional ingredients of this experience, see the "Ceremonial Chemicals" section of Appendix B.

op */op/* n. 1. In England and Ireland, common verbal abbreviation for 'operator', as in system operator. Less common in the U.S., where **sysop** seems to be preferred. 2. [IRC] Someone who is endowed with privileges on **IRC**, not limited to a particular channel. These are generally people who are in charge of the IRC server at their particular site. Sometimes used interchangeably with **CHOP**. Compare **sysop**.

open n. Abbreviation for 'open (or left) parenthesis' — used when necessary to eliminate oral ambiguity. To read aloud the LISP form (DEFUN FOO (X) (PLUS X 1)) one might say: "Open defun foo, open eks close, open, plus eks one, close close."

Open DeathTrap n. Abusive hackerism for the Santa Cruz Operation's 'Open DeskTop' product, a Motif-based graphical interface over their UNIX. The funniest part is that this was coined by SCO's own developers. . . . Compare **AIDX**, **Macintrash Nominal Semidestructor**, **ScumOS**, **sun-stools**, **HP-SUX**.

open switch [IBM: prob. from railroading] n. An unresolved question, issue, or problem.

operating system [techspeak] n. (Often abbreviated 'OS') The foundation software of a machine, of course; that which schedules tasks, allocates storage, and presents a default interface to the user between applications. The facilities an operating system provides and its general design philosophy exert an extremely strong influence on programming style and on the technical cultures that grow up around its host machines. Hacker folklore has been shaped primarily by the **UNIX**, **ITS**, **TOPS-10**, **TOPS-20/TWENEX**, **WAITS**, **CP/M**, **MS-DOS**, and **Multics** operating systems (most importantly by ITS and UNIX).

optical diff n. See **vdiff**.

optical grep n. See **vgrep**.

optimism n. What a programmer is full of after fixing what is presumably the last bug and just before actually discovering a next last bug. Fred Brooks's book *The Mythical Man-Month* (See *Brooks's Law*) contains the following paragraph that describes this extremely well:

> All programmers are optimists. Perhaps this modern sorcery especially attracts those who believe in happy endings and fairy god-mothers. Perhaps the hundreds of nitty frustrations drive away all but those who habitually focus on the end goal. Perhaps it is merely that computers are young, programmers are younger, and the young are always optimists. But however the selection process works, the result is indisputable: "This time it will surely run," or "I just found the last bug.".

See also **Lubarsky's Law of Cybernetic Entomology**.

Orange Book n. The U.S. Government's standards document *Trusted Computer System Evaluation Criteria, DOD standard 5200.28-STD, December, 1985* which characterize secure computing architectures and defines levels A1 (most secure) through D (least). Stock UNIXes are roughly C1, and can be upgraded to about C2 without excessive pain. See also **crayola books**, **book titles**.

oriental food n. Hackers display an intense tropism towards oriental cuisine, especially Chinese, and especially of the spicier varieties such as Szechuan and Hunan. This phenomenon (which has also been observed in subcultures that overlap heavily with hackerdom, most notably science-fiction fandom) has never been satisfactorily explained, but is sufficiently intense that one can assume the target of a hackish dinner expedition to be the best local Chinese place and be right at least three times out of four. See also **ravs**,

great-wall, **stir-fried random**, **laser chicken**, **Yu-Shiang Whole Fish**. Thai, Indian, Korean, and Vietnamese cuisines are also quite popular.

orphan [UNIX] n. A process whose parent has died; one inherited by `init(1)`. Compare **zombie**.

orphaned i-node */or´fənd i:´nohd/* [UNIX] n. 1. [techspeak] A file that retains storage but no longer appears in the directories of a filesystem. 2. By extension, a pejorative for any person no longer serving a useful function within some organization, esp. **lion food** without subordinates.

orthogonal [from mathematics] adj. Mutually independent; well separated; sometimes, irrelevant to. Used in a generalization of its mathematical meaning to describe sets of primitives or capabilities that, like a vector basis in geometry, span the entire 'capability space' of the system and are in some sense non-overlapping or mutually independent. For example, in architectures such as the PDP-11 or VAX where all or nearly all registers can be used interchangeably in any role with respect to any instruction, the register set is said to be orthogonal. Or, in logic, the set of operators *not* and *or* is orthogonal, but the set *nand*, *or*, and *not* is not (because any one of these can be expressed in terms of the others). Also used in comments on human discourse: "This may be orthogonal to the discussion, but. . . ."

OS */O-S/* 1. [**Operating System**] n. An abbreviation heavily used in email, occasionally in speech. 2. n.,obs. On ITS, an output spy. See "OS and JEDGAR" (in Appendix A).

OS/2 */O S too/* n. The anointed successor to MS-DOS for Intel 286- and 386-based micros; proof that IBM/Microsoft couldn't get it right the second time, either. Often called 'Half-an-OS'. Mentioning it is usually good for a cheap laugh among hackers — the design was so **baroque**, and the implementation of 1.x so bad, that 3 years after introduction you could still count the major **app**s shipping for it on the fingers of two hands — in unary. The 2.x versions are said to have improved somewhat, and informed hackers now rate them superior to Microsoft Windows (an endorsement which, however, could easily be construed as damning with faint praise). See **monstrosity**, **cretinous**, **second-system effect**.

out-of-band [from telecommunications and network theory] adj. 1. In software, describes values of a function which are not in its 'natural' range of return values, but are rather signals that some kind of exception has occurred. Many C functions, for example, return a nonnegative integral value, but indicate failure with an out-of-band return value of −1. Compare **hidden flag**, **green bytes**, **fence**. 2. Also sometimes used to describe what communications people call 'shift characters', such as the ESC that leads control sequences for many terminals, or the level shift indicators in the old 5-bit Baudot codes. 3. In personal communication, using methods other than email, such as telephones or **snail-mail**.

overflow bit n. 1. [techspeak] A **flag** on some processors indicating an attempt to calculate a result too large for a register to hold. 2. More generally, an indication of any kind of capacity overload condition. "Well, the **Ada** description was **baroque** all right, but I could hack it OK until they got to the exception handling . . . that set my overflow bit." 3. The hypothetical bit that will be set if a hacker doesn't get to make a trip to the Room of Porcelain Fixtures: "I'd better process an internal interrupt before the overflow bit gets set".

overflow pdl [MIT] n. The place where you put things when your **pdl** is full. If you don't have one and too many things get pushed, you forget something. The overflow pdl for a person's memory might be a memo pad. This usage inspired the following doggerel:

> Hey, diddle, diddle
> The overflow pdl
> To get a little more stack;
> If that's not enough
> Then you lose it all,
> And have to pop all the way back.
> –The Great Quux

The term **pdl** seems to be primarily an MITism; outside MIT this term is replaced by 'overflow **stack**'.

overrun n. 1. [techspeak] Term for a frequent consequence of data arriving faster than it can be consumed, esp. in serial line communications. For example, at 9600 baud there is almost exactly one character per millisecond, so if a **silo** can hold only two characters and the machine takes longer than 2 msec to get to service the interrupt, at least one character will be lost. 2. Also applied to non-serial-I/O communications. "I forgot to pay my electric bill

Crunchly and the **overflow bit**.
The next cartoon in the Crunchly saga is 07-29-73, page 91.

due to mail overrun." "Sorry, I got four phone calls in 3 minutes last night and lost your message to overrun." When **thrash**ing at tasks, the next person to make a request might be told "Overrun!" Compare **firehose syndrome**. 3. More loosely, may refer to a **buffer overflow** not necessarily related to processing time (as in **overrun screw**).

overrun screw [C programming] n. A variety of **fandango on core** produced by scribbling past the end of an array (C implementations typically have no checks for this error). This is relatively benign and easy to spot if the array is static; if it is auto, the result may be to **smash the stack** — often resulting in **heisenbug**s of the most diabolical subtlety. The term *overrun screw* is used esp. of scribbles beyond the end of arrays allocated with `malloc(3)`; this typically trashes the allocation header for the next block in the **arena**, producing massive lossage within malloc and often a core dump on the next operation to use `stdio(3)` or `malloc(3)` itself. See **spam**, **overrun**; see also **memory leak**, **memory smash**, **aliasing bug**, **precedence lossage**, **fandango on core**, **secondary damage**.

= P =

P-mail n. Physical mail, as opposed to email. Synonymous with **snail-mail**.

P.O.D. */P-O-D/* Acronym for 'Piece Of Data' (as opposed to a code section). Usage: pedantic and rare. See also **pod**.

padded cell n. Where you put **luser**s so they can't hurt anything. A program that limits a luser to a carefully restricted subset of the capabilities of the host system (for example, the `rsh(1)` utility on USG UNIX). Note that this is different from an **iron box** because it is overt and not aimed at enforcing security so much as protecting others (and the luser) from the consequences of the luser's boundless naiveté (see **naive**). Also *padded cell environment*.

page in [MIT] vi. 1. To become aware of one's surroundings again after having paged out (see **page out**). Usually confined to the sarcastic comment: "Eric pages in, **film at 11**!" 2. Syn. *swap in*; see **swap**.

page out [MIT] vi. 1. To become unaware of one's surroundings temporarily, due to daydreaming or preoccupation. "Can you repeat that? I paged out for a minute." See **page in**. Compare **glitch**, **thinko**. 2. Syn. *swap out*; see **swap**.

pain in the net n. A **flamer**.

paper-net n. Hackish way of referring to the postal service, analogizing it to a very slow, low-reliability network. USENET **sig blocks** sometimes include a "Paper-Net:" header just before the sender's postal address; common variants of this are "Papernet" and "P-Net". Note that the standard **netiquette** guidelines discourage this practice as a waste of bandwidth, since netters are quite unlikely to casually use postal addresses. Compare **voice-net**, **snail-mail**, **P-mail**.

param */pə-ram´/* n. Shorthand for 'parameter'. See also **parm**; compare **arg**, **var**.

PARC n. See **XEROX PARC**.

parent message n. What a **followup** follows up.

parity errors pl.n. Little lapses of attention or (in more severe cases) consciousness, usually brought on by having spent all night and most of the next day hacking. "I need to go home and crash; I'm starting to get a lot of parity errors." Derives from a relatively common but nearly always correctable transient error in RAM hardware. Parity errors can also afflict mass storage and serial communication lines; this is more serious because not always correctable.

Parkinson's Law of Data prov. "Data expands to fill the space available for storage"; buying more memory encourages the use of more memory-intensive techniques. It has been observed over the last 10 years that the memory usage of evolving systems tends to double roughly once every 18 months. Fortunately, memory density available for constant dollars also tends to double about once every 12 months (see **Moore's Law**); unfortunately, the laws of physics guarantee that the latter cannot continue indefinitely.

parm */parm/* n. Further-compressed form of **param**. This term is an IBMism, and written use is almost unknown outside IBM shops; spoken */parm/* is more widely distributed, but the synonym **arg** is favored among hackers. Compare **arg**, **var**.

parse [from linguistic terminology] vt. 1. To determine the syntactic structure of a sentence or other utterance (close to the standard English meaning). "That was the one I saw you." "I can't parse that." 2. More generally, to understand or comprehend. "It's very simple; you just kretch the glims and then aos the zotz." "I can't parse that." 3. Of fish, to have to remove the bones yourself. "I object to parsing fish", means "I don't want to get a whole fish, but a sliced one is okay". A *parsed fish* has been deboned. There is some controversy over whether *unparsed* should mean 'bony', or also mean 'deboned'.

Pascal n. An Algol-descended language designed by Niklaus Wirth on the CDC 6600 around 1967–68 as an instructional tool for elementary programming. This language, designed primarily to keep students from shooting themselves in the foot and thus extremely restrictive from a general-purpose-programming point of view, was later promoted as a general-purpose tool and, in fact, became the ancestor of a large family of languages including Modula-2 and **Ada** (see also **bondage-and-discipline language**). The hackish point of view on Pascal was probably best summed up by a devastating (and, in its deadpan way, screamingly funny) 1981 paper by Brian Kernighan (of **K&R** fame) entitled "Why Pascal is Not My Favorite Programming Language", which was turned down by the technical journals but circulated widely via photocopies. It was eventually published in "Comparing and Assessing Programming Languages", edited by Alan Feuer and Narain Gehani (Prentice-Hall, 1984). Part of his discussion is worth repeating here, because its criticisms are still apposite to Pascal itself after ten years of improvement and could also stand as an indictment of many other bondage-and-discipline languages. At the end of a summary of the case against Pascal, Kernighan wrote:

> 9. There is no escape
>
> This last point is perhaps the most important. The language is inadequate but circumscribed, because there is no way to escape its limitations. There are no casts to disable the type-checking when necessary. There is no way to replace the defective run-time environment with a sensible one, unless one controls the compiler that defines the "standard procedures". The language is closed.
>
> People who use Pascal for serious programming fall into a fatal trap. Because the language is impotent, it must be extended. But each group extends Pascal in its own direction, to make it look like whatever language they really want. Extensions for sep-

> arate compilation, FORTRAN-like COMMON, string data types, internal static variables, initialization, octal numbers, bit operators, etc., all add to the utility of the language for one group but destroy its portability to others.
>
> I feel that it is a mistake to use Pascal for anything much beyond its original target. In its pure form, Pascal is a toy language, suitable for teaching but not for real programming.

Pascal has since been almost entirely displaced (by **C**) from the niches it had acquired in serious applications and systems programming, but retains some popularity as a hobbyist language in the MS-DOS and Macintosh worlds.

pastie */pay´stee/* n. An adhesive-backed label designed to be attached to a key on a keyboard to indicate some non-standard character which can be accessed through that key. Pasties are likely to be used in APL environments, where almost every key is associated with a special character. A pastie on the R key, for example, would remind the user that it is used to generate the ρ character. The term properly refers to nipple-concealing devices formerly worn by strippers in concession to indecent-exposure laws; compare **tits on a keyboard**.

patch 1. n. A temporary addition to a piece of code, usually as a **quick-and-dirty** remedy to an existing bug or misfeature. A patch may or may not work, and may or may not eventually be incorporated permanently into the program. Distinguished from a **diff** or **mod** by the fact that a patch is generated by more primitive means than the rest of the program; the classical examples are instructions modified by using the front panel switches, and changes made directly to the binary executable of a program originally written in an **HLL**. Compare **one-line fix**. 2. vt. To insert a patch into a piece of code. 3. [in the UNIX world] n. A **diff** (sense 2). 4. A set of modifications to binaries to be applied by a patching program. IBM operating systems often receive updates to the operating system in the form of absolute hexadecimal patches. If you have modified your OS, you have to disassemble these back to the source. The patches might later be corrected by other patches on top of them (patches were said to "grow scar tissue"). The result was often a convoluted **patch space** and headaches galore. 5. [UNIX] the `patch(1)` program, written by Larry Wall, which automatically applies a patch (sense 3) to a set of source code.

There is a classic story of a **tiger team** penetrating a secure military computer that illustrates the danger inherent in binary patches (or, indeed, any patches that you can't — or don't — inspect and examine before installing). They couldn't find any **trap doors** or any way to penetrate security of IBM's OS, so they made a site visit to an IBM office (remember, these were official military types who were purportedly on official business), swiped some IBM stationery, and created a fake patch. The patch was actually the trapdoor they needed. The patch was distributed at about the right time for an IBM patch, had official stationery and all accompanying documentation, and was dutifully installed. The installation manager very shortly thereafter learned something about proper procedures.

patch space n. An unused block of bits left in a binary so that it can later be modified by insertion of machine-language instructions there (typically, the patch space is modified to contain new code, and the superseded code is patched to contain a jump or call to the patch space). The widening use of HLLs has made this term rare; it is now primarily historical outside IBM shops. See **patch** (sense 4), **zap** (sense 4), **hook**.

path n. 1. A **bang path** or explicitly routed **Internet address**; a node-by-node specification of a link between two machines. 2. [UNIX] A filename, fully specified relative to the root directory (as opposed to relative to the current directory; the latter is sometimes called a *relative path*). This is also called a *pathname*. 3. [UNIX and MS-DOS] The *search path*, an environment variable specifying the directories in which the **shell** (COMMAND.COM, under MS-DOS) should look for commands. Other, similar constructs abound under UNIX (for example, the C preprocessor has a 'search path' it uses in looking for `#include` files).

pathological adj. 1. [scientific computation] Used of a data set that is grossly atypical of normal expected input, esp. one that exposes a weakness or bug in whatever algorithm one is using. An algorithm that can be broken by pathological inputs may still be useful if such inputs are very unlikely to occur in practice. 2. When used of test input, implies that it was purposefully engineered as a worst case. The implication in both senses is that the data is spectacularly ill-conditioned or that someone had to explicitly set out to break the algorithm in order to come up with such a crazy example. 3. Also said of an unlikely collection of circumstances. "If the network is down and comes up halfway through the execution of that command by root, the system may just crash." "Yes, but that's a pathological case." Often used to dismiss the case from discussion, with the implication that the consequences are acceptable, since they will happen so infrequently (if at all) that it doesn't seem worth going to the extra trouble to handle that case (see sense 1).

payware */pay´weir/* n. Commercial software. Oppose **shareware** or **freeware**.

PBD */P-B-D/* [abbrev. of 'Programmer Brain Damage'] n. Applied to bug reports revealing places where the program was obviously broken by an incompetent or short-sighted programmer. Compare **UBD**; see also **brain-damaged**.

PC-ism */P-C-izm/* n. A piece of code or coding technique that takes advantage of the unprotected single-tasking environment in IBM PCs and the like, e.g., by busy-waiting on a hardware register, direct diddling of screen memory, or using hard timing loops. Compare **ill-behaved, vaxism, unixism**. Also, *PC-ware* n., a program full of PC-isms on a machine with a more capable operating system. Pejorative.

PD */P-D/* adj. Common abbreviation for 'public domain', applied to software distributed over **USENET** and from Internet archive sites. Much of this software is not in fact public domain in the legal sense but travels under various copyrights granting reproduction and use rights to anyone who can **snarf** a copy. See **copyleft**.

PDL 1. n. 'Program Design Language'. Any of a large class of formal and profoundly useless pseudo-languages in which **management** forces one to design programs. Too often, management expects PDL descriptions to be maintained in parallel with the code, imposing massive overhead to little or no benefit. See also **flowchart**. 2. v. To design using a program design language. "I've been pdling so long my eyes won't focus beyond 2 feet." 3. n. 'Page Description Language'. Refers to any language which is used to control a graphics device, usually a laserprinter. The most common example is, of course, Adobe's **PostScript** language, but there are many others, such as Xerox InterPress, etc.

pdl */pid´l/* or */puhd´l/* [abbreviation for 'Push Down List'] n. 1. In ITS days, the preferred MITism for **stack**. See **overflow pdl**. 2. Dave Lebling, one of the co-authors of **Zork**; (his **network address** on the ITS machines was at one time pdl@dms). 3. Rarely, any sense of **PDL**, as these are not invariably capitalized.

PDP-10 [Programmed Data Processor model 10] n. The machine that made timesharing real. It looms large in hacker folklore because of its adoption in the mid-1970s by many university computing facilities and research labs, including the MIT AI Lab, Stanford, and CMU. Some aspects of the instruction set (most notably the bit-field instructions) are still considered unsurpassed. The 10 was eventually eclipsed by the VAX machines (descendants of the PDP-11) when DEC recognized that the 10 and VAX product lines were competing with each other and decided to concentrate its software development effort on the more profitable VAX. The machine was finally dropped from DEC's line in 1983, following the failure of the Jupiter Project at DEC to build a viable new model. (Some attempts by other companies to market clones came to nothing; see **Foonly** and **Mars**.) This event spelled the doom of **ITS** and the technical cultures that had spawned the original Jargon File, but by mid-1991 it had become something of a badge of honorable oldtimerhood among hackers to have cut one's teeth on a PDP-10. See **TOPS-10**, **ITS**, **AOS**, **BLT**, **DDT**, **DPB**, **EXCH**, **HAKMEM**, **JFCL**, **LDB**, **pop**, **push**, Appendix A.

PDP-20 n. The most famous computer that never was. **PDP-10** computers running the **TOPS-10** operating system were labeled 'DECsystem-10' as a way of differentiating them from the PDP-11. Later on, those systems running TOPS-20 were labeled 'DECSYSTEM-20' (the block capitals being the result of a lawsuit brought against DEC by Singer, which once made a computer called 'system-10'), but contrary to popular lore there was never a 'PDP-20'; the only difference between a 10 and a 20 was the operating system and the color of the paint. Most (but not all) machines sold to run TOPS-10 were painted 'Basil Blue', whereas most TOPS-20 machines were painted 'Chinese Red' (often mistakenly called orange).

peek n.,vt. (and **poke**) The commands in most microcomputer BASICs for directly accessing memory contents at an absolute address; often extended to mean the corresponding constructs in any **HLL** (peek reads memory, poke modifies it). Much hacking on small, non-MMU micros consists of *peek*ing around memory, more or less at random, to find the location where the system keeps interesting stuff. Long (and variably accurate) lists of such addresses for various computers circulate (see **interrupt list, the**). The results of *poke*s at these addresses may be highly useful, mildly amusing, useless but neat, or (most likely) total **lossage** (see **killer poke**).

Since a **real operating system** provides useful, higher-level services for the tasks commonly performed with peeks and pokes on micros, and real languages tend not to encourage low-level memory groveling, a question like "How do I do a peek in C?" is diagnostic of the newbie. (Of course, OS kernels often have to do exactly this; a real C hacker would unhesitatingly, if unportably, assign an absolute address to a pointer variable and indirect through it.)

pencil and paper n. An archaic information storage and transmission device that works by depositing smears of graphite on bleached wood pulp. More recent developments in paper-based technology include improved 'write-once' update devices which use tiny rolling heads similar to mouse balls to deposit colored pigment. All these devices require an operator skilled at so-called 'handwriting' technique. These technologies are ubiquitous outside hackerdom, but nearly forgotten inside it. Most hackers had terrible handwriting to begin with, and years of keyboarding tend to have encouraged it to degrade further. Perhaps for this reason, hackers deprecate pencil-and-paper technology and often resist using it in any but the most trivial contexts. See also Appendix B.

peon n. A person with no special (**root** or **wheel**) privileges on a computer system. "I can't create an account on *foovax* for you; I'm only a peon there."

percent-S */per-sent´ es´/* [From the code in C's `printf(3)` library function used to insert an arbitrary string argument] n. An unspecified person or object. "I was just talking to some percent-s in administration." Compare **random**.

perf */perf/* n. Syn. **chad** (sense 1). The term *perfory /per´fə-ree/* is also heard. The term **perf** may also refer to the perforations themselves, rather than the chad they produce when torn.

perfect programmer syndrome n. Arrogance; the egotistical conviction that one is above normal human error. Most frequently found among programmers of some native ability but relatively little experience (especially new graduates; their perceptions may be distorted by a history of excellent performance at solving **toy problems**). "Of course my program is correct, there is no need to test it." "Yes, I can see there may be a problem here, but *I'll* never type `rm -r /` while in **root mode**."

Perl */perl/* [Practical Extraction and Report Language, a.k.a Pathologically

Eclectic Rubbish Lister] n. An interpreted language developed by Larry Wall <*lwall@jpl.nasa.gov*>, author of `patch(1)` and `rn(1)`) and distributed over USENET. Superficially resembles `awk(1)`, but is much hairier (see **awk**). UNIX sysadmins, who are almost always incorrigible hackers, increasingly consider it one of the **languages of choice**. Perl has been described, in a parody of a famous remark about `lex(1)`, as the "Swiss-Army chainsaw" of UNIX programming.

person of no account [University of California at Santa Cruz] n. Used when referring to a person with no **network address**, frequently to forestall confusion. Most often as part of an introduction: "This is Bill, a person of no account, but he used to be bill@random.com". Compare **return from the dead**.

pessimal */pes´im-l/* [Latin-based antonym for 'optimal'] adj. Maximally bad. "This is a pessimal situation." Also *pessimize* vt. To make as bad as possible. These words are the obvious Latin-based antonyms for *optimal* and *optimize*, but for some reason they do not appear in most English dictionaries, although 'pessimize' is listed in the OED.

pessimizing compiler */pes´ə-mi:z`ing kəm-pi:l´r/* [antonym of 'optimizing compiler'] n. A compiler that produces object code that is worse than the straightforward or obvious hand translation. The implication is that the compiler is actually trying to optimize the program, but through excessive cleverness is doing the opposite. A few pessimizing compilers have been written on purpose, however, as pranks or burlesques.

peta- */pe´tə/* [SI] pref. See **quantifiers**.

PETSCII */pet´skee/* [abbreviation of PET ASCII] n. The variation (many would say perversion) of the **ASCII** character set used by the Commodore Business Machines PET series of personal computers and the later Commodore C64, C16, and C128 machines. The PETSCII set used left-arrow and up-arrow (as in old-style ASCII) instead of underscore and caret, placed the unshifted alphabet at positions 65–90, put the shifted alphabet at positions 193–218, and added graphics characters.

phage n. A program that modifies other programs or databases in unauthorized ways; esp. one that propagates a **virus** or **Trojan horse**. See also **worm**, **mockingbird**. The analogy, of course, is with phage viruses in biology.

phase 1. n. The offset of one's waking-sleeping schedule with respect to the standard 24-hour cycle; a useful concept among people who often work at night and/or according to no fixed schedule. It is not uncommon to change one's phase by as much as 6 hours per day on a regular basis. "What's your phase?" "I've been getting in about 8 P.M. lately, but I'm going to **wrap around** to the day schedule by Friday." A person who is roughly 12 hours out of phase is sometimes said to be in *night mode*. (The term *day mode* is also (but less frequently) used, meaning you're working 9 to 5 (or, more likely, 10 to 6).) The act of altering one's cycle is called *changing phase*; *phase shifting* has also been recently reported from Caltech. 2. *change phase the hard way*: To stay awake for a very long time in order to get into a different phase. 3. *change phase the easy way*: To stay asleep, etc. However, some claim that either staying awake longer or sleeping longer is easy, and that it is *shortening* your day or night that is really hard (see **wrap around**). The 'jet lag' that afflicts travelers who cross many time-zone boundaries may be attributed to two distinct causes: the strain of travel per se, and the strain of changing phase. Hackers who suddenly find that they must change phase drastically in a short period of time, particularly the hard way, experience something very like jet lag without traveling.

phase of the moon n. Used humorously as a random parameter on which something is said to depend. Sometimes implies unreliability of whatever is dependent, or that reliability seems to be dependent on conditions nobody has been able to determine. "This feature depends on having the channel open in mumble mode, having the foo switch set, and on the phase of the moon." See also **heisenbug**.

True story: Once upon a time there was a bug that really did depend on the phase of the moon. There was a little subroutine that had traditionally been used in various programs at MIT to calculate an approximation to the moon's true phase. GLS incorporated this routine into a LISP program that, when it wrote out a file, would print a timestamp line almost 80 characters long. Very occasionally the first line of the message would be too long and would overflow onto the next line, and when the file was later read back in the program would **barf**. The length of the first line depended on both the precise date and time and the length of the phase specification when the timestamp was printed, and so the bug literally depended on the phase of the moon!

The first paper edition of the Jargon File (Steele-1983) included an example of one of the timestamp lines that exhibited this bug, but the typesetter 'corrected' it. This has since been described as the phase-of-the-moon-bug bug.

phase-wrapping [MIT] n. Syn. **wrap around**, sense 2.

phreaking */freek´ing/* [from 'phone phreak'] n. 1. The art and science of cracking the phone network (so as, for example, to make free long-distance calls). 2. By extension, security-cracking in any other context (especially, but not exclusively, on communications networks) (see **cracking**).

At one time phreaking was a semi-respectable activity among hackers; there was a gentleman's agreement that phreaking as an intellectual game and a form of exploration was OK, but serious theft of services was taboo. There was significant crossover between the hacker community and the hard-core phone phreaks who ran semi-underground networks of their own through such media as the legendary *TAP Newsletter.* This ethos began to break down in the mid-1980s as wider dissemination of the techniques put them in the hands of less responsible phreaks. Around the same time, changes in the phone network made old-style technical ingenuity less effective as a way of hacking it, so phreaking came to depend more on overtly criminal acts such as stealing phone-card numbers. The crimes and punishments of gangs like the '414 group' turned that game very ugly. A few old-time hackers still phreak casually just to keep their hand in, but most these days have hardly even heard of 'blue boxes' or any of the other paraphernalia of the great phreaks of yore.

pico- [SI: a quantifier meaning $\times 10^{-12}$] pref. Smaller than **nano-**; used in the same rather loose connotative way as **nano-** and **micro-**. This usage is not yet common in the way **nano-** and **micro-** are, but should be instantly recognizable to any hacker. See also **quantifiers, micro-**.

pig, run like a v. To run very slowly on given hardware, said of software. Distinct from **hog**.

pilot error [Sun: from aviation] n. A user's misconfiguration or misuse of a piece of software, producing apparently buglike results (compare **UBD**). "Joe Luser reported a bug in sendmail that causes it to generate bogus headers." "That's not a bug, that's pilot error. His `sendmail.cf` is hosed."

ping [from the TCP/IP acronym 'Packet INternet Groper', prob. originally contrived to match the submariners' term for a sonar pulse] 1. n. Slang term for a small network message (ICMP ECHO) sent by a computer to check for the presence and alertness of another (the UNIX command `ping(8)` can be used to do this manually). Occasionally used as a phone greeting. See **ACK**, also **ENQ**. 2. vt. To verify the presence of. 3. vt. To get the attention of. 4. vt. To send a message to all members of a **mailing list** requesting an **ACK** (in order to verify that everybody's addresses are reachable). "We haven't heard much of anything from Geoff, but he did respond with an ACK both times I pinged jargon-friends." 5. n. A quantum packet of happiness. People who are very happy tend to exude pings; furthermore, one can intentionally create pings and aim them at a needy party (e.g., a depressed person). This sense of ping may appear as an exclamation; "Ping!" (I'm happy; I am emitting a quantum of happiness; I have been struck by a quantum of happiness). The form "pingfulness", which is used to describe people who exude pings, also occurs. (In the standard abuse of language, "pingfulness" can also be used as an exclamation, in which case it's a much stronger exclamation than just "ping"!). Oppose **blargh**.

The funniest use of 'ping' to date was described in January 1991 by Steve Hayman on the USENET group *comp.sys.next.* He was trying to isolate a faulty cable segment on a TCP/IP Ethernet hooked up to a NeXT machine, and got tired of having to run back to his console after each cabling tweak to see if the ping packets were getting through. So he used the sound-recording feature on the NeXT, then wrote a script that repeatedly invoked `ping(8)`, listened for an echo, and played back the recording on each returned packet. Result? A program that caused the machine to repeat, over and over, "Ping . . . ping . . . ping . . . " as long as the network was up. He turned the volume to maximum, ferreted through the building with one ear cocked, and found a faulty tee connector in no time.

Pink-Shirt Book *The Peter Norton Programmer's Guide to the IBM PC.* The original cover featured a picture of Peter Norton with a silly smirk on his face, wearing a pink shirt. Perhaps in recognition of this usage, the current edition has a different picture of Norton wearing a pink shirt. See also **book titles**.

PIP */pip/* [Peripheral Interchange Program] vt.,obs. To copy; from the program PIP on CP/M, RSX-11, RSTS/E, TOPS-10, and OS/8 (derived from a utility on the PDP-6) that was used for file copying (and in OS/8 and RT-11 for just about every other file operation you might want to do). It is said that when the program was originated, during the development of the PDP-6 in 1963, it was called ATLATL ('Anything, Lord, to Anything, Lord'; this played on the Nahuatl word 'atlatl' for a spear-thrower, with connotations of utility and primitivity that were no doubt quite intentional). See alao **BLT**, **dd**, **cat**.

pistol [IBM] n. A tool that makes it all too easy for you to shoot yourself in the foot. "UNIX `rm *` makes such a nice pistol!"

pizza box [Sun] n. The largish thin box housing the electronics in (especially Sun) desktop workstations, so named because of its size and shape and the dimpled pattern that looks like air holes.

Two meg single-platter removable disk packs used to be called pizzas, and the huge drive they were stuck into was referred to as a pizza oven. It's an index of progress that in the old days just the disk was pizza-sized, while now the entire computer is.

pizza, ANSI standard */an´see stan´dərd peet´zə/* [CMU] Pepperoni and mushroom pizza. Coined allegedly because most pizzas ordered by CMU hackers during some period leading up to mid-1990 were of that flavor. See also **rotary debugger**; compare **tea, ISO standard cup of**.

plaid screen [XEROX PARC] n. A 'special effect' that occurs when certain kinds of **memory smash**es overwrite the control blocks or image memory of a bit-mapped display. The term "salt and pepper" may refer to a different pattern of similar origin. Though the term as coined at PARC refers to the result of an error, some of the **X** demos induce plaid-screen effects deliberately as a **display hack**.

plain-ASCII */playn-as´kee/* Syn. **flat-ASCII**.

plan file [UNIX] n. On systems that support **finger**, the '.plan' file in a user's home directory is displayed when the user is fingered. This feature was originally intended to be used to keep potential fingerers apprised of one's location and near-future plans, but has been turned almost universally to humorous and self-expressive purposes (like a **sig block**). See also **Hacking X for Y**.

A recent innovation in plan files has been the introduction of "scrolling plan files" which are one-dimensional animations made using only the printable ASCII character set, carriage return and line feed, avoiding terminal specific escape sequences, since the **finger** command will (for security reasons; see **letterbomb**) not pass the escape character.

Scrolling .plan files have become art forms in miniature, and some sites have started competitions to find who can create the longest running, funniest, and most original animations. Various animation characters include:

`Centipede:`	mmmmme
`Lorry/Truck:`	oo-oP
`Andalusian Video Snail:`	_@/

and a compiler (ASP) is available on USENET for producing them. See also **twirling baton**.

platinum-iridium adj. Standard, against which all others of the same category are measured. Usage: silly. The notion is that one of whatever it is has actually been cast in platinum-iridium alloy and placed in the vault beside the Standard Kilogram at the International Bureau of Weights and Measures near Paris. (From 1889 to 1960, the meter was defined to be the distance between two scratches in a platinum-iridium bar kept in that same vault — this replaced an earlier definition as 10^{-7} times the distance between the North Pole and the Equator along a meridian through Paris; unfortunately, this had been based on an inexact value of the circumference of the Earth. From 1960 to 1984 it was defined to be 1650763.73 wavelengths of the orange-red line of krypton-86 propagating in a vacuum. It is now defined as the length of the path traveled by light in a vacuum in the time interval of 1/299,792,458 of a second. The kilogram is now the only unit of measure officially defined in terms of a unique artifact.) "This garbage-collection algorithm has been tested against the platinum-iridium cons cell in Paris." Compare **golden**.

playpen [IBM] n. A room where programmers work. Compare **salt mines**.

playte */playt/* 16 bits, by analogy with **nybble** and **byte**. Usage: rare and extremely silly. See also **dynner** and **crumb**.

plingnet */pling´net/* n. Syn. **UUCPNET**. Also see **Commonwealth Hackish**, which uses 'pling' for **bang** (as in **bang path**).

plokta */plok´tə/* [Acronym for 'Press Lots Of Keys To Abort'] v. To press random keys in an attempt to get some response from the system. One might plokta when the abort procedure for a program is not known, or when trying to figure out if the system is just sluggish or really hung. Plokta can also be used while trying to figure out any unknown key sequence for a particular operation. Someone going into *plokta mode* usually places both hands flat on the keyboard and mashes them down, hoping for some useful response.

A slightly more directed form of plokta can often be seen in mail messages or USENET articles from new users — the text might end with

```
^X^C
q
quit
:q
^C
end
x
exit
ZZ
^D
?
help
```

as the user vainly tries to find the right exit sequence, with the incorrect tries piling up at the end of the message. . . .

plonk [USENET: possibly influenced by British slang 'plonk' for cheap booze, or 'plonker' for someone behaving stupidly] The sound a **newbie** makes as he falls to the bottom of a **kill file**. Used almost exclusively in the **newsgroup** *talk.bizarre*, this term (usually written "*plonk*") is a form of public ridicule.

plugh */ploogh/* [from the **ADVENT** game] v. See **xyzzy**.

plumbing [UNIX] n. Term used for **shell** code, so called because of the prevalence of *pipelines* that feed the output of one program to the input of another. Under UNIX, user utilities can often be implemented or at least prototyped by a suitable collection of pipelines and temp-file grinding encapsulated in a shell script; this is much less effort than writing C every time, and the capability is considered one of UNIX's major winning features. A few other OSs such as IBM's VM/CMS support similar facilities. Esp. used in the construction *hairy plumbing* (see **hairy**). "You can kluge together a basic spell-checker out of `sort(1)`, `comm(1)`, and `tr(1)` with a little plumbing." See also **tee**.

PM */P-M/* 1. v. (from 'preventive maintenance') To bring down a machine for inspection or test purposes. See **provocative maintenance**; see also **scratch monkey**. 2. n. Abbrev. for 'Presentation Manager', an **elephantine** OS/2 graphical user interface.

pnambic */pə-nam´bik/* [Acronym from the scene in the film version of *The Wizard of Oz* in which the true nature of the wizard is first discovered: "Pay no attention to the man behind the curtain."] 1. A stage of development of a process or function that, owing to incomplete implementation or to the complexity of the system, requires human interaction to simulate or replace some or all of the actions, inputs, or outputs of the process or function. 2. Of or pertaining to a process or function whose apparent operations are wholly or partially falsified. 3. Requiring **prestidigitization**.

The ultimate pnambic product was "Dan Bricklin's Demo", a program which supported flashy user-interface design prototyping. There is a related maxim among hackers: "Any sufficiently advanced technology is indistinguishable from a rigged demo." See **magic**, sense 1, for illumination of this point.

pod [allegedly from abbreviation POD for 'Prince Of Darkness'] n. A Diablo 630 (or, latterly, any letter-quality impact printer). From the DEC-10 PODTYPE program used to feed formatted text to it. Not to be confused with **P.O.D.**.

point-and-drool interface n. Parody of the techspeak term 'point-and-shoot interface', describing a windows, icons, and mouse-based interface such as is found on the Macintosh. The implication, of course, is that such an interface is only suitable for idiots. See **for the rest of us**, **WIMP environment**, **Macintrash**, **drool-proof paper**. Also *point-and-grunt interface.*

poke n.,vt. See **peek**.

poll v.,n. 1. [techspeak] The action of checking the status of an input line, sensor, or memory location to see if a particular external event has been registered. 2. To repeatedly call or check with someone: "I keep polling him, but he's not answering his phone; he must be swapped out." 3. To ask. "Lunch? I poll for a takeout order daily."

polygon pusher n. A chip designer who spends most of his or her time at the physical layout level (which requires drawing *lots* of multi-colored polygons). Also *rectangle slinger.*

POM */P-O-M/* n. Common abbreviation for **phase of the moon**. Usage: usually in the phrase *POM-dependent*, which means **flaky**.

pop */pop/* [from the operation that removes the top of a stack, and the fact that procedure return addresses are usually saved on the stack] (also capitalized 'POP') 1. vt. To remove something from a **stack** or **pdl**. If a person says he/she has popped something from his stack, that means he/she has finally finished working on it and can now remove it from the list of things hanging overhead. 2. When a discussion gets to a level of detail so deep that the main point of the discussion is being lost, someone will shout "Pop!", meaning "Get back up to a higher level!" The shout is frequently accompanied by an upthrust arm with a finger pointing to the ceiling.

POPJ */pop´J/* [from a **PDP-10** return-from-subroutine instruction] n.,v. To return from a digression. By verb doubling, "Popj, popj" means roughly "Now let's see, where were we?" See **RTI**.

post v. To send a message to a **mailing list** or **newsgroup**. Distinguished in context from *mail*; one might ask, for example: "Are you going to post the patch or mail it to known users?"

postcardware n. **Shareware** that borders on **freeware**, in that the author requests only that satisfied users send a postcard of their home town or something. (This practice, silly as it might seem, serves to remind users that they are otherwise getting something for nothing, and may also be psychologically related to real estate 'sales' in which $1 changes hands just to keep the transaction from being a gift.)

posting n. Noun corresp. to v. **post** (but note that **post** can be nouned). Distinguished from a 'letter' or ordinary **email** message by the fact that it is broadcast rather than point-to-point. It is not clear whether messages sent to a small mailing list are postings or email; perhaps the best dividing line is that if you don't know the names of all the potential recipients, it is a posting.

postmaster n. The email contact and maintenance person at a site connected to the Internet or UUCPNET. Often, but not always, the same as the **admin**. The Internet standard for electronic mail (**RFC**-822) requires each machine to have a 'postmaster' address; usually it is aliased to this person.

PostScript n. A Page Description Language (**PDL**), based on work originally done by John Gaffney at Evans and Sutherland in 1976, evolving through 'JaM' ('John and Martin', Martin Newell) at **XEROX PARC**, and finally implemented in its current form by John Warnock et al. after he and Chuck Geschke founded Adobe Systems Incorporated in 1982. PostScript gets its leverage by using a full programming language, rather than a series of low-level escape sequences, to describe an image to be printed on a laser printer or other output device (in this it parallels **EMACS**, which exploited a similar insight about editing tasks). It is also noteworthy for implementing on-the fly rasterization, from Bezier curve descriptions, of high-quality fonts at low (e.g. 300 dpi) resolution (it was formerly believed that hand-tuned bitmap fonts were required for this task). Hackers consider PostScript to be among the most elegant hacks of all time, and the combination of technical merits and widespread availability has made PostScript the language of choice for graphical output.

pound on vt. Syn. **bang on**.

power cycle vt. (also, *cycle power* or just *cycle*) To power off a machine and then power it on immediately, with the intention of clearing some kind of **hung** or **gronk**ed state. Syn. **120 reset**; see also **Big Red Switch**. Compare **Vulcan nerve pinch**, **bounce** (sense 4), and **boot**, and see the AI Koan in "A Selection of AI Koans" (in Appendix A) about Tom Knight and the novice.

power hit n. A spike or drop-out in the electricity supplying your machine; a power **glitch**. These can cause crashes and even permanent damage to your machine(s).

PPN */P-P-N/, /pip´n/* [from 'Project-Programmer Number'] n. A user-ID under **TOPS-10** and its various mutant progeny at SAIL, BBN, CompuServe, and elsewhere. Old-time hackers from the PDP-10 era sometimes use this to refer to user IDs on other systems as well.

precedence lossage */pre´sə-dens los´əj/* [C programmers] n. Coding error in an expression due to unexpected grouping of arithmetic or logical operators by the compiler. Used esp. of certain common coding errors in C due to the nonintuitively low precedence levels of `&`, `|`, `^`, `<<`, and `>>` (for this reason, experienced C programmers deliberately forget the language's **baroque** precedence hierarchy and parenthesize defensively). Can always be avoided by suitable use of parentheses. **LISP** fans enjoy pointing out that this can't happen in *their* favorite language, which eschews precedence entirely, requiring one to use explicit parentheses everywhere. See **aliasing bug**, **memory leak**, **memory smash**, **smash the stack**, **fandango on core**, **overrun screw**.

prepend */pree`pend'/* [by analogy with 'append'] vt. To prefix. As with 'append' (but not 'prefix' or 'suffix' as a verb), the direct object is always the thing being added and not the original word (or character string, or whatever). "If you prepend a semicolon to the line, the translation routine will pass it through unaltered."

prestidigitization */pres`tə-di`jə-ti:-zay'shən/* n. 1. The act of putting something into digital notation via sleight of hand. 2. Data entry through legerdemain.

pretty pictures n. [scientific computation] The next step up from **numbers**. Interesting graphical output from a program that may not have any sensible relationship to the system the program is intended to model. Good for showing to **management**.

prettyprint */prit'ee-print/* (alt. *pretty-print*) v. 1. To generate 'pretty' human-readable output from a **hairy** internal representation; esp. used for the process of **grind**ing (sense 1) program code, and most esp. for LISP code. 2. To format in some particularly slick and nontrivial way.

pretzel key [Mac users] n. See **feature key**.

prime time [from TV programming] n. Normal high-usage hours on a timesharing system; the day shift. Avoidance of prime time was traditionally given as a major reason for **night mode** hacking. The rise of the personal workstation has rendered this term, along with timesharing itself, almost obsolete. The hackish tendency to late-night **hacking run**s has changed not a bit.

printing discussion [XEROX PARC] n. A protracted, low-level, time-consuming, generally pointless discussion of something only peripherally interesting to all.

priority interrupt [from the hardware term] n. Describes any stimulus compelling enough to yank one right out of **hack mode**. Classically used to describe being dragged away by an **SO** for immediate sex, but may also refer to more mundane interruptions such as a fire alarm going off in the near vicinity. Also called an **NMI** (non-maskable interrupt), especially in PC-land.

profile n. 1. A control file for a program, esp. a text file automatically read from each user's home directory and intended to be easily modified by the user in order to customize the program's behavior. Used to avoid **hardcoded** choices (see also **dot file, rc file**). 2. [techspeak] A report on the amounts of time spent in each routine of a program, used to find and **tune** away the **hot spot**s in it. This sense is often verbed. Some profiling modes report units other than time (such as call counts) and/or report at granularities other than per-routine, but the idea is similar.

proglet */prog´let/* [UK] n. A short *extempore* program written to meet an immediate, transient need. Often written in BASIC, rarely more than a dozen lines long, and containing no subroutines. The largest amount of code that can be written off the top of one's head, that does not need any editing, and that runs correctly the first time (this amount varies significantly according to one's skill and the language one is using). Compare **toy program, noddy, one-liner wars.**

program n. 1. A magic spell cast over a computer allowing it to turn one's input into error messages. 2. An exercise in experimental epistemology. 3. A form of art, ostensibly intended for the instruction of computers, which is nevertheless almost inevitably a failure if other programmers can't understand it.

Programmer's Cheer "Shift to the left! Shift to the right! Pop up, push down! Byte! Byte! Byte!" A joke so old it has hair on it.

programming n. 1. The art of debugging a blank sheet of paper (or, in these days of on-line editing, the art of debugging an empty file). 2. A pastime similar to banging one's head against a wall, but with fewer opportunities for reward. 3. The most fun you can have with your clothes on (although clothes are not mandatory).

programming fluid n. 1. Coffee. 2. Cola. 3. Any caffeinacious stimulant. Many hackers consider these essential for those all-night hacking runs. See **unleaded, wirewater**.

propeller head n. Used by hackers, this is syn. with **computer geek**. Non-hackers sometimes use it to describe all techies. Prob. derives from SF fandom's tradition (originally invented by old-time fan Ray Faraday Nelson) of propeller beanies as fannish insignia (though nobody actually wears them except as a joke).

propeller key [Mac users] n. See **feature key**.

proprietary adj. 1. In **marketroid**-speak, superior; implies a product imbued with exclusive magic by the unmatched brilliance of the company's own hardware or software designers. 2. In the language of hackers and users, inferior; implies a product not conforming to open-systems standards, and thus one that puts the customer at the mercy of a vendor able to gouge freely on service and upgrade charges after the initial sale has locked the customer in.

protocol n. As used by hackers, this never refers to niceties about the proper form for addressing letters to the Papal Nuncio or the order in which one should use the forks in a Russian-style place setting; hackers don't care about such things. It is used instead to describe any set of rules that allow different machines or pieces of software to coordinate with each other without ambiguity. So, for example, it does include niceties about the proper form for addressing packets on a network or the order in which one should use the forks in the Dining Philosophers Problem. It implies that there is some common message format and an accepted set of primitives or commands that all parties involved understand, and that transactions among them follow predictable logical sequences. See also **handshaking**, **do protocol**.

provocative maintenance [common ironic mutation of 'preventive maintenance'] n. Actions performed upon a machine at regularly scheduled intervals to ensure that the system remains in a usable state. So called because it is all too often performed by a **field servoid** who doesn't know what he is doing; such 'maintenance' often *induces* problems, or otherwise results in the machine's remaining in an *un*usable state for an indeterminate amount of time. See also **scratch monkey**.

prowler [UNIX] n. A **daemon** that is run periodically (typically once a week) to seek out and erase **core** files, truncate administrative logfiles, nuke `lost+found` directories, and otherwise clean up the **cruft** that tends to pile up in the corners of a file system. See also **GFR**, **reaper**, **skulker**.

pseudo */soo´doh/* [USENET: truncation of 'pseudonym'] n. 1. An electronic-mail or **USENET** persona adopted by a human for amusement value or as a means of avoiding negative repercussions of one's net.behavior; a 'nom de USENET', often associated with forged postings designed to conceal message origins. Perhaps the best-known and funniest hoax of this type is **BIFF**. 2. Notionally, a **flamage**-generating AI program simulating a USENET user.

Many flamers have been accused of actually being such entities, despite the fact that no AI program of the required sophistication yet exists. However, in 1989 there was a famous series of forged postings that used a phrase-frequency-based travesty generator to simulate the styles of several well-known flamers; it was based on large samples of their back postings (compare **Dissociated Press**). A significant number of people were fooled by the forgeries, and the debate over their authenticity was settled only when the perpetrator came forward to publicly admit the hoax.

pseudoprime n. A backgammon prime (six consecutive occupied points) with one point missing. This term is an esoteric pun derived from a mathematical method that, rather than determining precisely whether a number is prime (has no divisors), uses a statistical technique to decide whether the number is 'probably' prime. A number that passes this test is called a pseudoprime. The hacker backgammon usage stems from the idea that a pseudoprime is almost as good as a prime: it does the job of a prime until proven otherwise, and that probably won't happen.

pseudosuit */soo´doh-s[y]oot`/* n. A **suit** wannabee; a hacker who has decided that he wants to be in management or administration and begins wearing ties, sport coats, and (shudder!) suits voluntarily. It's his funeral. See also **lobotomy**.

psychedelicware */si:`kə-del´-ik-weir/* [UK] n. Syn. **display hack**. See also **smoking clover**.

psyton */si:´ton/* [TMRC] n. The elementary particle carrying the sinister force. The probability of a process losing is proportional to the number of psytons falling on it. Psytons are generated by observers, which is why demos are more likely to fail when lots of people are watching. [This term appears to have been largely superseded by **bogon**; see also **quantum bogodynamics**. — ESR]

pubic directory [NYU] (also *pube directory /pyoob´ də-rek´tə-ree/*) n. The *pub* (public) directory on a machine that allows **FTP** access. So called because it is the default location for **SEX** (sense 1). "I'll have the source in the pube directory by Friday."

puff vt. To decompress data that has been crunched by Huffman coding. At least one widely distributed Huffman decoder program was actually *named* 'PUFF', but these days it is usually packaged with the encoder. Oppose **huff**.

punched card alt. *punch card* [techspeak] n.obs. The signature medium of computing's **Stone Age**, now obsolescent outside of some IBM shops. The punched card actually predated computers considerably, originating in 1801 as a control device for mechanical looms. The version patented by Hollerith and used with mechanical tabulating machines in the 1890 U.S. Census was a piece of cardboard about 90 mm by 215 mm. There is a widespread myth that it was designed to fit in the currency trays used for that era's larger dollar bills, but recent investigations have falsified this.

IBM (which originated as a tabulating-machine manufacturer) married the punched card to computers, encoding binary information as patterns of small rectangular holes; one character per column, 80 columns per card. Other coding schemes, sizes of card, and hole shapes were tried at various times.

The 80-column width of most character terminals is a legacy of the IBM punched card; so is the size of the quick-reference cards distributed with many varieties of computers even today. See **chad**, **chad box**, **eighty-column mind**, **green card**, **dusty deck**, **lace card**, **card walloper**.

punt [from the punch line of an old joke referring to American football: "Drop back 15 yards and punt!"] v. 1. To give up, typically without any intention of retrying. "Let's punt the movie tonight." "I was going to hack all night to get this feature in, but I decided to punt" may mean that you've decided not to stay up all night, and may also mean you're not ever even going to put in the feature. 2. More specifically, to give up on figuring out what the **Right Thing** is and resort to an inefficient hack. 3. A design decision to defer solving a problem, typically because one cannot define what is desirable sufficiently well to frame an algorithmic solution. "No way to know what the right form to dump the graph in is — we'll punt that for now." 4. To hand a tricky implementation problem off to some other section of the design. "It's too hard to get the compiler to do that; let's punt to the runtime system."

Purple Book n. 1. The *System V Interface Definition.* The covers of the first editions were an amazingly nauseating shade of off-lavender. 2. Syn. **Wizard Book**. See also **book titles**.

purple wire [IBM] n. Wire installed by Field Engineers to work around problems discovered during testing or debugging. These are called 'purple wires' even when (as is frequently the case) their actual physical color is yellow. . . . Compare **blue wire**, **yellow wire**, and **red wire**.

push [from the operation that puts the current information on a stack, and the fact that procedure return addresses are saved on a stack] (Also PUSH */push/* or PUSHJ */push´J/*, the latter based on the PDP-10 procedure call instruction.) 1. To put something onto a **stack** or **pdl**. If one says that something has been pushed onto one's stack, it means that the Damoclean list of things hanging over ones's head has grown longer and heavier yet. This may also imply that one will deal with it *before* other pending items; otherwise one might say that the thing was 'added to my queue'. 2. vi. To enter upon a digression, to save the current discussion for later. Antonym of **pop**; see also **stack, pdl**.

= Q =

quad n. 1. Two bits; syn. for **quarter, crumb, tayste**. 2. A four-pack of anything (compare **hex**, sense 2). 3. The rectangle or box glyph used in the APL language for various arcane purposes mostly related to I/O. Former Ivy-Leaguers and Oxford types are said to associate it with nostalgic memories of dear old University.

quadruple bucky n., obs. 1. On an MIT **space-cadet keyboard**, use of all four of the shifting keys (control, meta, hyper, and super) while typing a character key. 2. On a Stanford or MIT keyboard in **raw mode**, use of four shift keys while typing a fifth character, where the four shift keys are the control and meta keys on *both* sides of the keyboard. This was very difficult to do! One accepted technique was to press the left-control and left-meta keys with your left hand, the right-control and right-meta keys with your right hand, and the fifth key with your nose.

Quadruple-bucky combinations were very seldom used in practice, because when one invented a new command one usually assigned it to some character that was easier to type. If you want to imply that a program has ridiculously many commands or features, you can say something like: "Oh, the command that makes it spin the tapes while whistling Beethoven's Fifth Symphony is quadruple-bucky-cokebottle." See **double bucky, bucky bits, cokebottle**.

quantifiers In techspeak and jargon, the standard metric prefixes used in the SI (Système International) conventions for scientific measurement have dual uses. With units of time or things that come in powers of 10, such as money, they retain their usual meanings of multiplication by powers of $1000 = 10^3$.

But when used with bytes or other things that naturally come in powers of 2, they usually denote multiplication by powers of $1024 = 2^{10}$.

Here are the SI magnifying prefixes, along with the corresponding binary interpretations in common use:

prefix	decimal	binary
kilo-	1000^1	$1024^1 = 2^{10} = 1,024$
mega-	1000^2	$1024^2 = 2^{20} = 1,048,576$
giga-	1000^3	$1024^3 = 2^{30} = 1,073,741,824$
tera-	1000^4	$1024^4 = 2^{40} = 1,099,511,627,776$
peta-	1000^5	$1024^5 = 2^{50} = 1,125,899,906,842,624$
exa-	1000^6	$1024^6 = 2^{60} = 1,152,921,504,606,846,976$
zetta-	1000^7	$1024^7 = 2^{70} = 1,180,591,620,717,411,303,424$
yotta-	1000^8	$1024^8 = 2^{80} = 1,208,925,819,614,629,174,706,176$

Here are the SI fractional prefixes:

prefix	decimal	jargon usage
milli-	1000^{-1}	(seldom used in jargon)
micro-	1000^{-2}	small or human-scale (see **micro-**)
nano-	1000^{-3}	even smaller (see **nano-**)
pico-	1000^{-4}	even smaller yet (see **pico-**)
femto-	1000^{-5}	(not used in jargon — yet)
atto-	1000^{-6}	(not used in jargon — yet)
zepto-	1000^{-7}	(not used in jargon — yet)
yocto-	1000^{-8}	(not used in jargon — yet)

The prefixes zetta-, yotta-, zepto-, and yocto- have been included in these tables purely for completeness and giggle value; they were adopted in 1990 by the '19th Conference Generale des Poids et Mesures'. The binary peta- and exa- loadings, though well established, are not in jargon use either — yet. The prefix milli-, denoting multiplication by 1000^{-1}, has always been rare in jargon (there is, however, a standard joke about the *millihelen* — notionally, the amount of beauty required to launch one ship). See the entries on **micro-**, **pico-**, and **nano-** for more information on connotative jargon use of these terms. 'Femto' and 'atto' (which, interestingly, derive not from Greek but from Danish) have not yet acquired jargon loadings, though it is easy to predict what those will be once computing technology enters the required realms of magnitude (however, see **attoparsec**).

There are, of course, some standard unit prefixes for powers of 10. In the following table, the 'prefix' column is the international standard suffix for the appropriate power of ten; the 'binary' column lists jargon abbreviations and words for the corresponding power of 2. The B-suffixed forms are commonly used for byte quantities; the words 'meg' and 'gig' are nouns that may (but do not always) pluralize with 's'.

prefix	decimal	binary suffixes and words	pronunciation
kilo-	k	K, KB,	*/kay/*
mega-	M	M, MB, meg	*/meg/*
giga-	G	G, GB, gig	*/gig/, /jig/*

Confusingly, hackers often use K or M as though they were suffix or numeric multipliers rather than a prefix; thus "2K dollars", "2M of disk space". This is also true (though less commonly) of G.

Note that the formal SI metric prefix for 1000 is 'k'; some use this strictly, reserving 'K' for multiplication by 1024 (KB is thus 'kilobytes').

K, M, and G used alone refer to quantities of bytes; thus, 64G is 64 gigabytes and 'a K' is a kilobyte (compare mainstream use of 'a G' as short for 'a grand', that is, $1000). Whether one pronounces 'gig' with hard or soft 'g' depends on what one thinks the proper pronunciation of 'giga-' is.

Confusing 1000 and 1024 (or other powers of 2 and 10 close in magnitude) — for example, describing a memory in units of 500K or 524K instead of 512K — is a sure sign of the **marketroid**. One example of this: it is common to refer to the capacity of 3.5" microfloppies as '1.44 MB' In fact, this is a completely **bogus** number. The correct size is 1440 KB, that is, 1440 * 1024 = 1474560 bytes. So the 'mega' in '1.44 MB' is compounded of two 'kilos', one of which is 1024 and the other of which is 1000. The correct number of megabytes would of course be 1440 / 1024 = 1.40625. Alas, this fine point is probably lost on the world forever.

[1993 update: hacker Morgan Burke has proposed, to general approval on USENET, the following additional prefixes:

groucho	10^-30
harpo	10^-27
harpi	10^27
grouchi	10^30

We observe that this would leave the prefixes zeppo-, gummo-, and chico- available for future expansion. Sadly, there is little immediate prospect that Mr. Burke's eminently sensible proposal will be ratified.]

quantum bogodynamics */kwon´tm boh`goh-di:-nam´iks/* n. A theory that characterizes the universe in terms of bogon sources (such as politicians, used-car salesmen, TV evangelists, and **suits** in general), bogon sinks (such as taxpayers and computers), and bogosity potential fields. Bogon absorption, of course, causes human beings to behave mindlessly and machines to fail (and may also cause both to emit secondary bogons); however, the precise mechanics of the bogon-computron interaction are not yet understood and remain to be elucidated. Quantum bogodynamics is most often invoked to explain the sharp increase in hardware and software failures in the presence of suits; the latter emit bogons, which the former absorb. See **bogon, computron, suit, psyton**.

quarter n. Two bits. This in turn comes from the 'pieces of eight' famed in pirate movies — Spanish silver crowns that could be broken into eight pie-slice-shaped 'bits' to make change. Early in American history the Spanish coin was considered equal to a dollar, so each of these 'bits' was considered worth 12.5 cents. Syn. **tayste**, **crumb**, **quad**. Usage: rare. See also **nickle**, **nybble**, **byte**, **dynner**.

ques */kwes/* 1. n. The question mark character ('`?`', ASCII 0111111). 2. interj. What? Also frequently verb-doubled as "Ques ques?" See **wall**.

quick-and-dirty adj. Describes a **crock** put together under time or user pressure. Used esp. when you want to convey that you think the fast way might lead to trouble further down the road. "I can have a quick-and-dirty fix in place tonight, but I'll have to rewrite the whole module to solve the underlying design problem." See also **kluge**.

quine */kwi:n/* [from the name of the logician Willard V. Quine, via Douglas Hofstadter] n. A program that generates a copy of its own source text as its complete output. Devising the shortest possible quine in some given programming language is a common hackish amusement. Here is one classic quine:

```
((lambda (x)
  (list x (list (quote quote) x)))
 (quote
    (lambda (x)
      (list x (list (quote quote) x)))))
```

This one works in LISP or Scheme. It's relatively easy to write quines in other languages such as Postscript which readily handle programs as data; much harder (and thus more challenging!) in languages like C which do not. Here is a classic C quine for ASCII machines:

```
char*f="char*f=%c%s%c;main()
printf(f,34,f,34,10);%c";
main()printf(f,34,f,34,10);
```

For excruciatingly exact quinishness, remove the interior line breaks. Some infamous **Obfuscated C Contest** entries have been quines that reproduced in exotic ways.

quote chapter and verse [by analogy with the mainstream phrase] v. To cite a relevant excerpt from an appropriate **bible**. "I don't care if `rn` gets it wrong; 'Followup-To: poster' is explicitly permitted by **RFC**-1036. I'll quote chapter and verse if you don't believe me." See also **legalese**, **language lawyer**, **RTFS** (sense 2).

quotient n. See **coefficient of X**.

quux */kwuhks/* [Mythically, from the Latin semi-deponent verb quuxo, quuxare, quuxandum iri; noun form variously 'quux' (plural 'quuces', anglicized to 'quuxes') and 'quuxu' (genitive plural is 'quuxuum', for four u-letters out of seven in all, using up all the 'u' letters in Scrabble).] 1. Originally, a **metasyntactic variable** like **foo** and **foobar**. Invented by Guy Steele for precisely this purpose when he was young and naive and not yet interacting with the real computing community. Many people invent such words; this one seems simply to have been lucky enough to have spread a little. In an eloquent display of poetic justice, it has returned to the originator in the form of a nickname. 2. interj. See **foo**; however, denotes very little disgust, and is uttered mostly for the sake of the sound of it. 3. Guy Steele in his persona as 'The Great Quux', which is somewhat infamous for light verse and for the 'Crunchly' cartoons. 4. In some circles, used as a punning opposite of 'crux'. "Ah, that's the quux of the matter!" implies that the point is *not* crucial (compare **tip of the ice-cube**). 5. quuxy: adj. Of or pertaining to a quux.

qux */kwuhks/* The fourth of the standard **metasyntactic variable**, after **baz** and before the quu(u . . .)x series. See **foo**, **bar**, **baz**, **quux**. This appears to be a recent mutation from **quux**, and many versions (especially older versions) of the standard series just run **foo**, **bar**, **baz**, **quux**,. . . .

QWERTY */kwer´tee/* [from the keycaps at the upper left] adj. Pertaining to a standard English-language typewriter keyboard (sometimes called the Sholes keyboard after its inventor), as opposed to Dvorak or foreign-language layouts or a **space-cadet keyboard** or APL keyboard.

Historical note: The QWERTY layout is a fine example of a **fossil**. It is sometimes said that it was designed to slow down the typist, but this is wrong; it was designed to allow *faster* typing — under a constraint now long obsolete. In early typewriters, fast typing using nearby type-bars jammed the mechanism. So Sholes fiddled the layout to separate the letters of many common digraphs (he did a far from perfect job, though; 'th', 'tr', 'ed', and 'er', for example, each use two nearby keys). Also, putting the letters of 'typewriter' on one line allowed it to be typed with particular speed and accuracy for **demos**. The jamming problem was essentially solved soon afterward by a suitable use of springs, but the keyboard layout lives on.

= R =

rabbit job [Cambridge] n. A batch job that does little, if any, real work, but creates one or more copies of itself, breeding like rabbits. Compare **wabbit**, **fork bomb**.

rain dance n. 1. Any ceremonial action taken to correct a hardware problem, with the expectation that nothing will be accomplished. This especially applies to reseating printed circuit boards, reconnecting cables, etc. "I can't boot up the machine. We'll have to wait for Greg to do his rain dance." 2. Any arcane sequence of actions performed with computers or software in order to achieve some goal; the term is usually restricted to rituals that include both an **incantation** or two and physical activity or motion. Compare **magic**, **voodoo programming**, **black art**, **cargo-cult programming**, **wave a dead chicken**.

rainbow series n. Any of several series of technical manuals distinguished by cover color. The original rainbow series was the NCSC security manuals (see **Orange Book**, **crayola books**); the term has also been commonly applied to the PostScript reference set (see **Red Book**, **Green Book**, **Blue Book**, **White Book**). Which books are meant by "*the* rainbow series" unqualified is thus dependent on one's local technical culture.

random adj. 1. Unpredictable (closest to mathematical definition); weird.

"The system's been behaving pretty randomly." 2. Assorted; undistinguished. "Who was at the conference?" "Just a bunch of random business types." 3. (pejorative) Frivolous; unproductive; undirected. "He's just a random loser." 4. Incoherent or inelegant; poorly chosen; not well organized. "The program has a random set of misfeatures." "That's a random name for that function." "Well, all the names were chosen pretty randomly." 5. In no particular order, though deterministic. "The I/O channels are in a pool, and when a file is opened one is chosen randomly." 6. Arbitrary. "It generates a random name for the scratch file." 7. Gratuitously wrong, i.e., poorly done and for no good apparent reason. For example, a program that handles file name defaulting in a particularly useless way, or an assembler routine that could easily have been coded using only three registers, but redundantly uses seven for values with non-overlapping lifetimes, so that no one else can invoke it without first saving four extra registers. What **randomness**! 8. n. A random hacker; used particularly of high-school students who soak up computer time and generally get in the way. 9. n. Anyone who is not a hacker (or, sometimes, anyone not known to the hacker speaking); the noun form of sense 2. "I went to the talk, but the audience was full of randoms asking bogus questions". 10. n. (occasional MIT usage) One who lives at Random Hall. See also **J. Random**, **some random X**.

random numbers n. When one wishes to specify a large but random number of things, and the context is inappropriate for **N**, certain numbers are preferred by hacker tradition (that is, easily recognized as placeholders). These include the following:

17	Long described at MIT as 'the least random number'; see 23.
23	Sacred number of Eris, Goddess of Discord (along with 17 and 5).
42	The Answer to the Ultimate Question of Life, the Universe, and Everything. (Note that this answer is completely fortuitous. :-))
69	From the sexual act. This one was favored in MIT's ITS culture.
105	69 hex = 105 decimal, and 69 decimal = 105 octal.
666	The Number of the Beast.

For further enlightenment, study the *Principia Discordia*, *The Hitchhiker's*

Guide to the Galaxy, *The Joy of Sex*, and the Christian Bible (Revelation 13:18). See also **Discordianism** or consult your pineal gland. See also **for values of**.

randomness n. 1. An inexplicable misfeature; gratuitous inelegance. 2. A **hack** or **crock** that depends on a complex combination of coincidences (or, possibly, the combination upon which the crock depends for its accidental failure to malfunction). "This hack can output characters 40–57 by putting the character in the four-bit accumulator field of an XCT and then extracting six bits — the low 2 bits of the XCT opcode are the right thing." "What randomness!" 3. Of people, synonymous with *flakiness*. The connotation is that the person so described is behaving weirdly, incompetently, or inappropriately for reasons which are (a) too tiresome to bother inquiring into, (b) are probably as inscrutable as quantum phenomena anyway, and (c) are likely to pass with time. "Maybe he has a real complaint, or maybe it's just randomness. See if he calls back."

rape vt. 1. To **screw** someone or something, violently; in particular, to destroy a program or information irrecoverably. Often used in describing file-system damage. "So-and-so was running a program that did absolute disk I/O and ended up raping the master directory." 2. To strip a piece of hardware for parts. 3. [CMU/Pitt] To mass-copy files from an anonymous ftp site. "Last night I raped Simtel's dskutl directory."

rare mode [UNIX] adj. CBREAK mode (character-by-character with interrupts enabled). Distinguished from **raw mode** and **cooked mode**; the phrase "a sort of half-cooked (rare?) mode" is used in the V7/BSD manuals to describe the mode. Usage: rare.

raster blaster n. [Cambridge] Specialized hardware for **bitblt** operations (a **blitter**). Allegedly inspired by 'Rasta Blasta', British slang for the sort of portable stereo Americans call a 'boom box' or 'ghetto blaster'.

raster burn n. Eyestrain brought on by too many hours of looking at low-res, poorly tuned, or glare-ridden monitors, esp. graphics monitors. See **terminal illness**.

rat belt n. A cable tie, esp. the sawtoothed, self-locking plastic kind that you can remove only by cutting (as opposed to a random twist of wire or a twist tie or one of those humongous metal clip frobs). Small cable ties are *mouse belts*.

rave [WPI] vi. 1. To persist in discussing a specific subject. 2. To speak authoritatively on a subject about which one knows very little. 3. To complain to a person who is not in a position to correct the difficulty. 4. To purposely annoy another person verbally. 5. To evangelize. See **flame**. 6. Also used to describe a less negative form of blather, such as friendly bullshitting. 'Rave' differs slightly from **flame** in that *rave* implies that it is the persistence or obliviousness of the person speaking that is annoying, while **flame** implies somewhat more strongly that the tone or content is offensive as well.

rave on! imp. Sarcastic invitation to continue a **rave**, often by someone who wishes the raver would get a clue but realizes this is unlikely.

ravs */ravz/*, also *Chinese ravs* n. Jiao-zi (steamed or boiled) or Guo-tie (pan-fried). A Chinese appetizer, known variously in the plural as dumplings, pot stickers (the literal translation of guo-tie), and (around Boston) 'Peking Ravioli'. The term *rav* is short for 'ravioli', which among hackers always means the Chinese kind rather than the Italian kind. Both consist of a filling in a pasta shell, but the Chinese kind includes no cheese, uses a thinner pasta, has a pork-vegetable filling (good ones include Chinese chives), and is cooked differently, either by steaming or frying. A rav or dumpling can be cooked any way, but a potsticker is always the fried kind (so called because it sticks to the frying pot and has to be scraped off). "Let's get hot-and-sour soup and three orders of ravs." See also **oriental food**.

raw mode n. A mode that allows a program to transfer bits directly to or from an I/O device (or, under **bogus** systems that make a distinction, a disk file) without any processing, abstraction, or interpretation by the operating system. Compare **rare mode**, **cooked mode**. This is techspeak under UNIX, jargon elsewhere.

rc file */R-C fi:l/* [UNIX: from the startup script `/etc/rc`, but this is commonly believed to have been named after older scripts to 'run commands'] n. Script file containing startup instructions for an application program (or an entire operating system), usually a text file containing commands of the sort that might have been invoked manually once the system was running but are to be executed automatically each time the system starts up. See also **dot file**, **profile** (sense 1).

RE */R-E/* n. Common spoken and written shorthand for **regexp**.

read-only user n. Describes a **luser** who uses computers almost exclusively for reading USENET, bulletin boards, and/or email, rather than writing code or purveying useful information. See **twink**, **terminal junkie**, **lurker**.

README file n. Hacker's-eye introduction traditionally included in the top-level directory of a UNIX source distribution, containing a pointer to more detailed documentation, credits, miscellaneous revision history, notes, etc. (The file may be named README, or READ.ME, or rarely ReadMe or readme.txt or some other variant.) In the Mac and PC worlds, software is not usually distributed in source form, and the README is more likely to contain user-oriented material like last-minute documentation changes, error workarounds, and restrictions. When asked, hackers invariably relate the README convention to the famous scene in Lewis Carroll's *Alice's Adventures In Wonderland* in which Alice confronts magic munchies labeled "Eat Me" and "Drink Me".

real adj. Not simulated. Often used as a specific antonym to **virtual** in any of its jargon senses.

real estate n. May be used for any critical resource measured in units of area. Most frequently used of *chip real estate*, the area available for logic on the surface of an integrated circuit (see also **nanoacre**). May also be used of floor space in a **dinosaur pen**, or even space on a crowded desktop (whether physical or electronic).

real hack n. A **crock**. This is sometimes used affectionately; see **hack**.

real operating system n. The sort the speaker is used to. People from the BSDophilic academic community are likely to issue comments like "System V? Why don't you use a *real* operating system?", people from the commercial/industrial UNIX sector are known to complain "BSD? Why don't you use a *real* operating system?", and people from IBM object "UNIX? Why don't you use a *real* operating system?" See **holy wars**, **religious issues**, **proprietary**, **Get a real computer!**

Real Programmer [indirectly, from the book *Real Men Don't Eat Quiche*] n. A particular sub-variety of hacker: one possessed of a flippant attitude toward complexity that is arrogant even when justified by experience. The archetypal *Real Programmer* likes to program on the **bare metal** and is very good at same, remembers the binary opcodes for every machine he has ever programmed, thinks that HLLs are sissy, and uses a debugger to edit his code because full-screen editors are for wimps. Real Programmers aren't satisfied with code that hasn't been **bum**med into a state of **tense**ness just short of rupture. Real Programmers never use comments or write documentation: "If it was hard to write", says the Real Programmer, "it should be hard to understand." Real Programmers can make machines do things that were never in their spec sheets; in fact, they are seldom really happy unless doing so. A Real Programmer's code can awe with its fiendish brilliance, even as its crockishness appalls. Real Programmers live on junk food and coffee, hang line-printer art on their walls, and terrify the crap out of other programmers — because someday, somebody else might have to try to understand their code in order to change it. Their successors generally consider it a **Good Thing** that there aren't many Real Programmers around any more. For a famous (and somewhat more positive) portrait of a Real Programmer, see "The Story of Mel, a Real Programmer" in Appendix A. The term itself was popularized by a 1983 Datamation article "Real Programmers Don't Use Pascal" by Ed Post, still circulating on USENET and Internet in on-line form.

Real Soon Now [orig. from SF's fanzine community, popularized by Jerry Pournelle's column in *BYTE*] adv. 1. Supposed to be available (or fixed, or cheap, or whatever) real soon now according to somebody, but the speaker is quite skeptical. 2. When one's gods, fates, or other time commitments permit one to get to it (in other words, don't hold your breath). Often abbreviated RSN.

real time 1. [techspeak] adj. Describes an application which requires a program to respond to stimuli within some small upper limit of response time (typically milli- or microseconds). Process control at a chemical plant is the classic example. Such applications often require special operating systems (because everything else must take a back seat to response time) and speed-tuned hardware. 2. adv. In jargon, refers to doing something while people are watching or waiting. "I asked her how to find the calling procedure's program counter on the stack and she came up with an algorithm in real time."

real user n. 1. A commercial user. One who is paying *real* money for his computer usage. 2. A non-hacker. Someone using the system for an explicit purpose (a research project, a course, etc.) other than pure exploration. See **user**. Hackers who are also students may also be real users. "I need this fixed so I can do a problem set. I'm not complaining out of randomness, but as a real user." See also **luser**.

Real World n. 1. Those institutions at which 'programming' may be used in the same sentence as 'FORTRAN', '**COBOL**', 'RPG', '**IBM**', 'DBASE', etc. Places where programs do such commercially necessary but intellectually uninspiring things as generating payroll checks and invoices. 2. The location of non-programmers and activities not related to programming. 3. A bizarre dimension in which the standard dress is shirt and tie and in which a person's working hours are defined as 9 to 5 (see **code grinder**). 4. Anywhere outside a university. "Poor fellow, he's left MIT and gone into the Real World." Used pejoratively by those not in residence there. In conversation, talking of someone who has entered the Real World is not unlike speaking of a deceased person. It is also noteworthy that on the campus of Cambridge University in England, there is a gaily-painted lamp-post which bears the label 'REALITY CHECKPOINT'. It marks the boundary between university and the Real World; check your notions of reality before passing. This joke is funnier because the Cambridge 'campus' is actually coextensive with the center of Cambridge. See also **fear and loathing**, **mundane**, and **uninteresting**.

Life in the Real World

reality check n. 1. The simplest kind of test of software or hardware; doing the equivalent of asking it what 2+2 is and seeing if you get 4. The software equivalent of a **smoke test**. 2. The act of letting a **real user** try out prototype software. Compare **sanity check**.

reaper n. A **prowler** that **GFR**s files. A file removed in this way is said to have been *reaped.*

rectangle slinger n. See **polygon pusher**.

recursion n. See **recursion**. See also **tail recursion**.

recursive acronym pl.n. A hackish (and especially MIT) tradition is to choose acronyms/abbreviations that refer humorously to themselves or to other acronyms/abbreviations. The classic examples were two MIT editors called EINE ("EINE Is Not EMACS") and ZWEI ("ZWEI Was EINE Initially"). More recently, there is a Scheme compiler called LIAR (Liar Imitates Apply Recursively), and **GNU** (q.v., sense 1) stands for "GNU's Not UNIX!" — and a company with the name CYGNUS, which expands to "Cygnus, Your GNU Support". See also **mung**, **EMACS**.

Red Book n. 1. Informal name for one of the three standard references on **PostScript** (*PostScript Language Reference Manual*, Adobe Systems (Addison-Wesley, 1985; QA76.73.P67P67; ISBN 0-201-10174-2, or the 1990 second edition ISBN 0-201-18127-4); the others are known as the **Green Book**, the **Blue Book**, and the **White Book** (sense 2). 2. Informal name for one of the 3 standard references on Smalltalk (*Smalltalk-80: The Interactive Programming Environment* by Adele Goldberg (Addison-Wesley, 1984; QA76.8.S635G638; ISBN 0-201-11372-4); this too is associated with blue and green books). 3. Any of the 1984 standards issued by the CCITT eighth plenary assembly. These include, among other things, the X.400 email spec and the Group 1 through 4 fax standards. 4. The new version of the **Green Book** (sense 4) — IEEE 1003.1-1990, a.k.a ISO 9945-1 — is (because of the color and the fact that it is printed on A4 paper) known in the U.S.A. as "the Ugly Red Book That Won't Fit On The Shelf" and in Europe as "the Ugly Red Book That's A Sensible Size". 5. The NSA *Trusted Network Interpretation* companion to the **Orange Book**. See also **book titles**.

red wire [IBM] n. Patch wires installed by programmers who have no business mucking with the hardware. It is said that the only thing more dangerous than a hardware guy with a code patch is a **softy** with a soldering iron. . . . Compare **blue wire**, **yellow wire**, **purple wire**.

regexp */reg´eksp/* [UNIX] n. (alt. *regex* or *reg-ex*) 1. Common written and spoken abbreviation for 'regular expression', one of the wildcard patterns used, e.g., by UNIX utilities such as `grep(1)`, `sed(1)`, and `awk(1)`. These use conventions similar to but more elaborate than those described under **glob**. For purposes of this lexicon, it is sufficient to note that regexps also allow complemented character sets using '^'; thus, one can specify 'any non-alphabetic character' with `[^A-Za-z]`. 2. Name of a well-known PD regexp-handling package in portable C, written by revered USENETter Henry Spencer <*henry@zoo.toronto.edu*>.

register dancing n. Many older processor architectures suffer from a serious shortage of general-purpose registers. This is especially a problem for compiler-writers, because their generated code needs places to store temporaries for things like intermediate values in expression evaluation. Some designs with this problem, like the Intel 80x86, do have a handful of special-purpose registers that can be pressed into service, providing suitable care is taken to avoid unpleasant side effects on the state of the processor: while the special-purpose register is being used to hold an intermediate value, a delicate minuet is required in which the previous value of the register is saved and then restored just before the official function (and value) of the special-purpose register is again needed.

reincarnation, cycle of n. See **cycle of reincarnation**.

reinvent the wheel v. To design or implement a tool equivalent to an existing one or part of one, with the implication that doing so is silly or a waste of time. This is often a valid criticism. On the other hand, automobiles don't use wooden rollers, and some kinds of wheel have to be reinvented many times before you get them right. On the third hand, people reinventing the wheel do tend to come up with the moral equivalent of a trapezoid with an offset axle.

religion of CHI n. */ki:/* [Case Western Reserve University] n. Yet another hackish parody religion (see also **Church of the SubGenius**, **Discordianism**). In the mid-70s, the canonical "Introduction to Programming" courses at CWRU were taught in Algol, and student exercises were punched on cards and run on a Univac 1108 system using a homebrew operating system named CHI. The religion had no doctrines and but one ritual: whenever the worshipper noted that a digital clock read 11:08, he or she would recite the phrase "It is 11:08; ABS, ALPHABETIC, ARCSIN, ARCCOS, ARCTAN." The last five words were the first five functions in the appropriate chapter of the Algol manual; note the special pronunciations */obz/* and */ark´sin/* rather than the more common */abz/* and */ark´si:n/*. Using an alarm clock to warn of 11:08's arrival was **considered harmful**.

religious issues n. Questions which seemingly cannot be raised without touching off **holy wars**, such as "What is the best operating system (or editor, language, architecture, shell, mail reader, news reader)?", "What about that Heinlein guy, eh?", "What should we add to the new Jargon File?" See **holy wars**; see also **theology**, **bigot**.

This term is a prime example of **ha ha only serious**. People actually develop the most amazing and religiously intense attachments to their tools, even when the tools are intangible. The most constructive thing one can do when one stumbles into the crossfire is mumble **Get a life!** and leave — unless, of course, one's *own* unassailably rational and obviously correct choices are being slammed.

replicator n. Any construct that acts to produce copies of itself; this could be a living organism, an idea (see **meme**), a program (see **quine**, **worm**, **wabbit**, **fork bomb**, and **virus**), a pattern in a cellular automaton (see **life**, sense 1), or (speculatively) a robot or **nanobot**. It is even claimed by some that **UNIX** and **C** are the symbiotic halves of an extremely successful replicator; see **UNIX conspiracy**.

reply n. See **followup**.

restriction n. A **bug** or design error that limits a program's capabilities, and which is sufficiently egregious that nobody can quite work up enough nerve to describe it as a **feature**. Often used (esp. by **marketroid** types) to make it sound as though some crippling bogosity had been intended by the designers all along, or was forced upon them by arcane technical constraints of a nature no mere user could possibly comprehend (these claims are almost invariably false).

Old-time hacker Joseph M. Newcomer advises that whenever choosing a quantifiable but arbitrary restriction, you should make it either a power of 2 or a power of 2 minus 1. If you impose a limit of 17 items in a list, everyone will know it is a random number — on the other hand, a limit of 15 or 16 suggests some deep reason (involving 0- or 1-based indexing in binary) and you will get less **flamage** for it. Limits which are round numbers in base 10 are always especially suspect.

retcon */ret´kon/* [short for 'retroactive continuity', from the USENET newsgroup *rec.arts.comics*] 1. n. The common situation in pulp fiction (esp. comics or soap operas) where a new story 'reveals' things about events in previous stories, usually leaving the 'facts' the same (thus preserving continuity) while completely changing their interpretation. For example, revealing that a whole season of "Dallas" was a dream was a retcon. 2. vt. To write such a story about a character or fictitious object. "Byrne has retconned Superman's cape so that it is no longer unbreakable." "Marvelman's old adventures were retconned into synthetic dreams." "Swamp Thing was retconned from a transformed person into a sentient vegetable." "Darth Vader was retconned into Luke Skywalker's father in "The Empire Strikes Back".

[This term is included because it is a good example of hackish linguistic innovation in a field completely unrelated to computers. The word *retcon* will probably spread through comics fandom and lose its association with hackerdom within a couple of years; for the record, it started here. — ESR]

[1993 update: some comics fans on the net now claim that retcon was independently in use in comics fandom before *rec.arts.comics*. In lexicography, nothing is ever simple. — ESR]

RETI v. Syn. **RTI**

retrocomputing */ret´-roh-kəm-pyoo´ting/* n. Refers to emulations of way-behind-the-state-of-the-art hardware or software, or implementations of never-was-state-of-the-art; esp. if such implementations are elaborate practical jokes and/or parodies, written mostly for **hack value**, of more 'serious' designs. Perhaps the most widely distributed retrocomputing utility was the `pnch(6)` or `bcd(6)` program on V7 and other early UNIX versions, which would accept up to 80 characters of text argument and display the corresponding pattern in **punched card** code. Other well-known retrocomputing hacks have included the programming language **INTERCAL**, a **JCL**-emulating shell for UNIX, the card-punch-emulating editor named 029, and various elaborate PDP-11 hardware emulators and RT-11 OS emulators written just to keep an old, sourceless **Zork** binary running.

return from the dead v. To regain access to the net after a long absence. Compare **person of no account**.

RFC */R-F-C/* [Request For Comment] n. One of a long-established series of numbered Internet standards widely followed by commercial software and freeware in the Internet and UNIX communities. Perhaps the single most influential one has been RFC-822 (the Internet mail-format standard). The

RFCs are unusual in that they are floated by technical experts acting on their own initiative and reviewed by the Internet at large, rather than formally promulgated through an institution such as ANSI. For this reason, they remain known as RFCs even once adopted.

The RFC tradition of pragmatic, experience-driven, after-the-fact standard writing done by individuals or small working groups has important advantages over the more formal, committee-driven process typical of ANSI or ISO. Emblematic of some of these advantages is the existence of a flourishing tradition of 'joke' RFCs; usually at least one a year is published, usually on April 1st. Well-known joke RFCs have included 527 ("ARPAWOCKY", R. Merryman, UCSD; 22 June 1973), 748 ("Telnet Randomly-Lose Option", Mark R. Crispin; 1 April 1978), and 1149 ("A Standard for the Transmission of IP Datagrams on Avian Carriers", D. Waitzman, BBN STC; 1 April 1990). The first was a Lewis Carroll pastiche; the second a parody of the TCP-IP documentation style, and the third a deadpan skewering of standards-document legalese, describing protocols for transmitting Internet data packets by carrier pigeon.

The RFCs are most remarkable for how well they work — they manage to have neither the ambiguities that are usually rife in informal specifications, nor the committee-perpetrated misfeatures that often haunt formal standards, and they define a network that has grown to truly worldwide proportions.

RFE */R-F-E/* n. 1. [techspeak] Request For Enhancement (compare **RFC**). 2. [from 'Radio Free Europe', Bellcore and Sun] Radio Free Ethernet, a system (originated by Peter Langston) for broadcasting audio among Sun SPARCstations over the ethernet.

rib site [by analogy with **backbone site**] n. A machine that has an on-demand high-speed link to a **backbone site** and serves as a regional distribution point for lots of third-party traffic in email and USENET news. Compare **leaf site**, **backbone site**.

rice box [from ham radio slang] n. Any Asian-made commodity computer, esp. an 80x86-based machine built to IBM PC-compatible ISA or EISA-bus standards.

Right Thing n. That which is *compellingly* the correct or appropriate thing to use, do, say, etc. Often capitalized, always emphasized in speech as though capitalized. Use of this term often implies that in fact reasonable people may disagree. "What's the right thing for LISP to do when it sees `(mod a 0)`? Should it return `a`, or give a divide-by-0 error?" Oppose **Wrong Thing**.

RL // [MUD community] n. Real Life. "Firiss laughs in RL" means that Firiss's player is laughing. Oppose **VR**.

roach [Bell Labs] vt. To destroy, esp. of a data structure. Hardware gets **toast**ed or **fried**, software gets roached.

robot [IRC, MUD] n. An **IRC** or **MUD** user who is actually a program. On IRC, typically the robot provides some useful service. Examples are NickServ, which tries to prevent random users from adopting **nick**s already claimed by others, and MsgServ, which allows one to send asynchronous messages to be delivered when the recipient signs on. Also common are 'annoybots', such as KissServ, which perform no useful function except to send cute messages to other people. Service robots are less common on MUDs; but some others, such as the 'Julia' robot active in 1990–91, have been remarkably impressive Turing-test experiments, able to pass as human for as long as ten or fifteen minutes of conversation.

robust adj. Said of a system that has demonstrated an ability to recover gracefully from the whole range of exceptional inputs and situations in a given environment. One step below **bulletproof**. Carries the additional connotation of elegance in addition to just careful attention to detail. Compare **smart**, oppose **brittle**.

rococo adj. **Baroque** in the extreme. Used to imply that a program has become so encrusted with the software equivalent of gold leaf and curlicues that they have completely swamped the underlying design. Called after the later and more extreme forms of Baroque architecture and decoration prevalent during the mid-1700s in Europe. Alan Perlis said: "Every program eventually becomes rococo, and then rubble." Compare **critical mass**.

rogue [UNIX] n. A Dungeons-and-Dragons-like game using character graphics, written under BSD UNIX and subsequently ported to other UNIX systems. The original BSD `curses(3)` screen-handling package was hacked together by Ken Arnold to support `rogue(6)` and has since become one of UNIX's most important and heavily used application libraries. Nethack, Omega, Larn, and an entire subgenre of computer dungeon games all took off from the inspiration provided by `rogue(6)`. See also **nethack**.

room-temperature IQ [IBM] quant. 80 or below. Used in describing the expected intelligence range of the **luser**. "Well, but how's this interface going to play with the room-temperature IQ crowd?" See **drool-proof paper**. This is a much more insulting phrase in countries that use Celsius thermometers.

root [UNIX] n. 1. The **superuser** account (with user name 'root') that ignores permission bits, user number 0 on a UNIX system. The term **avatar** is also used. 2. The top node of the system directory structure (home directory of the root user). 3. By extension, the privileged system-maintenance login on any OS. See **root mode**, **go root**, see also **wheel**.

root mode n. Syn. with **wizard mode** or *wheel mode*. Like these, it is often generalized to describe privileged states in systems other than OSes.

rot13 */rot ther´teen/* [USENET: from 'rotate alphabet 13 places'] n., v. The simple Caesar-cypher encryption that replaces each English letter with the one 13 places forward or back along the alphabet, so that "The butler did it!" becomes "Gur ohgyre qvq vg!" Most USENET news reading and posting programs include a rot13 feature. It is used to enclose the text in a sealed wrapper that the reader must choose to open — e.g., for posting things that might offend some readers, or **spoilers**. A major advantage of rot13 over rot(N) for other N is that it is self-inverse, so the same code can be used for encoding and decoding.

rotary debugger [Commodore] n. Essential equipment for those late-night or early-morning debugging sessions. Mainly used as sustenance for the hacker. Comes in many decorator colors, such as Sausage, Pepperoni, and Garbage. See **pizza, ANSI standard**.

round tape n. Industry-standard 1/2-inch magnetic tape (7- or 9-track) on traditional circular reels. See **macrotape**, oppose **square tape**.

RSN */R-S-N/* adj. See **Real Soon Now**.

RTBM */R-T-B-M/* [UNIX] imp. Commonwealth Hackish variant of **RTFM**; expands to 'Read The Bloody Manual'. RTBM is often the entire text of the first reply to a question from a **newbie**; the *second* would escalate to "RTFM".

RTFAQ */R-T-F-A-Q/* [USENET: primarily written, by analogy with **RTFM**] imp. Abbrev. for 'Read the FAQ!', an exhortation that the person addressed ought to read the newsgroup's **FAQ list** before posting questions.

RTFB */R-T-F-B/* [UNIX] imp. Acronym for 'Read The Fucking Binary'. Used when neither documentation nor source for the problem at hand exists, and the only thing to do is use some debugger or monitor and directly analyze the assembler or even the machine code. "No source for the buggy port driver? Aaargh! I *hate* proprietary operating systems. Time to RTFB."

Of the various RTF? forms, 'RTFB' is the least pejorative against anyone asking a question for which RTFB is the answer; the anger here is directed at the absence of both source *and* adequate documentation.

RTFM */R-T-F-M/* [UNIX] imp. Acronym for 'Read The Fucking Manual'. 1. Used by **gurus** to brush off questions they consider trivial or annoying. Compare **Don't do that, then!**. 2. Used when reporting a problem to indicate that you aren't just asking out of **randomness**. "No, I can't figure out how to interface UNIX to my toaster, and yes, I have RTFM." Unlike sense 1, this use is considered polite. See also **FM**, **RTFAQ**, **RTFB**, **RTFS**, **RTM**, all of which mutated from RTFM, and compare **UTSL**.

RTFS */R-T-F-S/* [UNIX] 1. imp. Acronym for 'Read The Fucking Source'. Variant form of **RTFM**, used when the problem at hand is not necessarily obvious and not answerable from the manuals — or the manuals are not yet written and maybe never will be. For even trickier situations, see **RTFB**. Unlike RTFM, the anger inherent in RTFS is not usually directed at the person asking the question, but rather at the people who failed to provide adequate documentation. 2. imp. 'Read The Fucking Standard'; this oath can only be used when the problem area (e.g., a language or operating system interface) has actually been codified in a ratified standards document. The existence of these standards documents (and the technically inappropriate but politically mandated compromises that they inevitably contain, and the impenetrable **legalese** in which they are invariably written, and the unbelievably tedious bureaucratic process by which they are produced) can be unnerving to hackers, who are used to a certain amount of ambiguity in the specifications of the systems they use. (Hackers feel that such ambiguities are acceptable as long as the **Right Thing** to do is obvious to any thinking observer; sadly, this casual attitude towards specifications becomes unworkable when a system becomes popular in the **Real World**.) Since a hacker is likely to feel that a standards document is both unnecessary and technically deficient, the deprecation inherent in this term may be directed as much against the standard as against the person who ought to read it.

RTI */R-T-I/* interj. The mnemonic for the 'return from interrupt' instruction on many computers including the 6502 and 6800. The variant *RETI* is found among former Z80 hackers (almost nobody programs these things in assembler anymore). Equivalent to "Now, where was I?" or used to end a conversational digression. See **pop**; see also **POPJ**.

RTM */R-T-M/* [USENET: abbreviation for 'Read The Manual'] 1. Politer variant of **RTFM**. 2. Robert T. Morris Jr., perpetrator of the great Internet worm of 1988 (see **Great Worm, the**); villain to many, naive hacker gone wrong to a few. Morris claimed that the worm that brought the Internet to its knees was a benign experiment that got out of control as the result of a coding error. After the storm of negative publicity that followed this blunder, Morris's username on ITS was hacked from RTM to **RTFM**.

rude [WPI] adj. 1. (of a program) Badly written. 2. Functionally poor, e.g., a program that is very difficult to use because of gratuitously poor (random?) design decisions. Oppose **cuspy**. 3. Anything that manipulates a shared resource without regard for its other users in such a way as to cause a (non-fatal) problem. Examples: programs that change tty modes without resetting them on exit, or windowing programs that keep forcing themselves to the top of the window stack. Compare **all-elbows**.

runes pl.n. 1. Anything that requires **heavy wizardry** or **black art** to **parse**: core dumps, JCL commands, APL, or code in a language you haven't a clue how to read. Not quite as bad as **line noise**, but close. Compare **casting the runes**, **Great Runes**. 2. Special display characters (for example, the high-half graphics on an IBM PC).

runic adj. Syn. **obscure**. VMS fans sometimes refer to UNIX as 'Runix'; UNIX fans return the compliment by expanding VMS to 'Very Messy Syntax' or 'Vachement Mauvais Système' (French; lit. "Cowlike Bad System", idiomatically "Bitchy Bad System").

rusty iron n. Syn. **tired iron**. It has been claimed that this is the inevitable fate of **water MIPS**.

rusty memory n. Mass-storage that uses iron-oxide-based magnetic media (esp. tape and the pre-Winchester removable disk packs used in **washing machines**). Compare **donuts**.

= S =

S/N ratio // n. (also *s/n ratio, s:n ratio*). Syn. **signal-to-noise ratio**. Often abbreviated *SNR*.

sacred adj. Reserved for the exclusive use of something (an extension of the standard meaning). Often means that anyone may look at the sacred object, but clobbering it will screw whatever it is sacred to. The comment "Register 7 is sacred to the interrupt handler" appearing in a program would be interpreted by a hacker to mean that if any *other* part of the program changes the contents of register 7, dire consequences are likely to ensue.

saga [WPI] n. A cuspy but bogus raving story about *N* random broken people.

Here is a classic example of the saga form, as told by Guy L. Steele:

> Jon L. White (login name JONL) and I (GLS) were office mates at MIT for many years. One April, we both flew from Boston to California for a week on research business, to consult face-to-face with some people at Stanford, particularly our mutual friend Richard P. Gabriel (RPG; see **Gabriel**).
>
> RPG picked us up at the San Francisco airport and drove us back to Palo Alto (going **logical** south on route 101, parallel to **El Camino Bignum**). Palo Alto is adjacent to Stanford University and about 40 miles south of San Francisco. We ate at The Good Earth, a 'health food' restaurant, very popular, the sort whose milkshakes all contain honey and protein powder. JONL ordered such a shake — the waitress claimed the flavor of the day was "lalaberry". I still have no idea what that might be, but it became a running joke. It was the color of raspberry, and JONL said it tasted rather bitter. I ate a better tostada there than I have ever had in a Mexican restaurant.
>
> After this we went to the local Uncle Gaylord's Old Fashioned Ice Cream Parlor. They make ice cream fresh daily, in a variety of intriguing flavors. It's a chain, and they have a slogan: "If you don't live near an Uncle Gaylord's — MOVE!" Also, Uncle Gaylord (a real person) wages a constant battle to force big-name ice cream makers to print their ingredients on the package (like air and plastic and other non-natural garbage). JONL and I had first discovered Uncle Gaylord's the previous August, when we had

flown to a computer-science conference in Berkeley, California, the first time either of us had been on the West Coast. When not in the conference sessions, we had spent our time wandering the length of Telegraph Avenue, which (like Harvard Square in Cambridge) was lined with picturesque street vendors and interesting little shops. On that street we discovered Uncle Gaylord's Berkeley store. The ice cream there was very good. During that August visit JONL went absolutely bananas (so to speak) over one particular flavor, ginger honey.

Therefore, after eating at The Good Earth — indeed, after every lunch and dinner and before bed during our April visit — a trip to Uncle Gaylord's (the one in Palo Alto) was mandatory. We had arrived on a Wednesday, and by Thursday evening we had been there at least four times. Each time, JONL would get ginger honey ice cream, and proclaim to all bystanders that "Ginger was the spice that drove the Europeans mad! That's why they sought a route to the East! They used it to preserve their otherwise off-taste meat." After the third or fourth repetition RPG and I were getting a little tired of this spiel, and began to paraphrase him: "Wow! Ginger! The spice that makes rotten meat taste good!" "Say! Why don't we find some dog that's been run over and sat in the sun for a week and put some *ginger* on it for dinner?!" "Right! With a lalaberry shake!" And so on. This failed to faze JONL; he took it in good humor, as long as we kept returning to Uncle Gaylord's. He loves ginger honey ice cream.

Now RPG and his then-wife KBT (Kathy Tracy) were putting us up (putting up with us?) in their home for our visit, so to thank them JONL and I took them out to a nice French restaurant of their choosing. I unadventurously chose the filet mignon, and KBT had *je ne sais quoi du jour*, but RPG and JONL had *lapin* (rabbit). (Waitress: "*Oui*, we have fresh rabbit, fresh today." RPG: "Well, JONL, I guess we won't need any *ginger*!")

We finished the meal late, about 11 P.M., which is 2 A.M Boston time, so JONL and I were rather droopy. But it wasn't yet midnight. Off to Uncle Gaylord's!

Now the French restaurant was in Redwood City, north of Palo Alto. In leaving Redwood City, we somehow got onto route 101 going north instead of south. JONL and I wouldn't have known the difference had RPG not mentioned it. We still knew very little of the local geography. I did figure out, however, that we were headed in the direction of Berkeley, and half-jokingly suggested that we continue north and go to Uncle Gaylord's in Berkeley.

RPG said "Fine!" and we drove on for a while and talked. I was drowsy, and JONL actually dropped off to sleep for 5 minutes. When he awoke, RPG said, "Gee, JONL, you must have slept all the way over the bridge!", referring to the one spanning San Francisco Bay. Just then we came to a sign that said "University Avenue". I mumbled something about working our way over to Telegraph Avenue; RPG said "Right!" and maneuvered some more. Eventually we pulled up in front of an Uncle Gaylord's.

Now, I hadn't really been paying attention because I was so sleepy, and I didn't really understand what was happening until RPG let me in on it a few moments later, but I was just alert enough to notice that we had somehow come to the Palo Alto Uncle Gaylord's after all.

JONL noticed the resemblance to the Palo Alto store, but hadn't caught on. (The place is lit with red and yellow lights at night, and looks much different from the way it does in daylight.) He said, "This isn't the Uncle Gaylord's I went to in Berkeley! It looked like a barn! But this place looks *just like* the one back in Palo Alto!"

RPG deadpanned, "Well, this is the one *I* always come to when I'm in Berkeley. They've got two in San Francisco, too. Remember, they're a chain."

JONL accepted this bit of wisdom. And he was not totally ignorant — he knew perfectly well that University Avenue was in Berkeley, not far from Telegraph Avenue. What he didn't know was that there is a completely different University Avenue in Palo Alto.

JONL went up to the counter and asked for ginger honey. The guy at the counter asked whether JONL would like to taste it first, evidently their standard procedure with that flavor, as not too many people like it.

JONL said, "I'm sure I like it. Just give me a cone." The guy behind the counter insisted that JONL try just a taste first. "Some people think it tastes like soap." JONL insisted, "Look, I *love* ginger. I eat Chinese food. I eat raw ginger roots. I already went through this hassle with the guy back in Palo Alto. I *know* I like that flavor!"

At the words "back in Palo Alto" the guy behind the counter got a very strange look on his face, but said nothing. KBT caught his eye and winked. Through my stupor I still hadn't quite grasped what was going on, and thought RPG was rolling on the floor laughing and clutching his stomach just because JONL had launched into his spiel ("makes rotten meat a dish for princes") for the forty-third time. At this point, RPG clued me in fully.

RPG, KBT, and I retreated to a table, trying to stifle our chuckles. JONL remained at the counter, talking about ice cream with the guy b.t.c., comparing Uncle Gaylord's to other ice cream shops and generally having a good old time.

At length the g.b.t.c. said, "How's the ginger honey?" JONL said, "Fine! I wonder what exactly is in it?" Now Uncle Gaylord publishes all his recipes and even teaches classes on how to make his ice cream at home. So the g.b.t.c. got out the recipe, and he and JONL pored over it for a while. But the g.b.t.c. could contain his curiosity no longer, and asked again, "You really like that stuff, huh?" JONL said, "Yeah, I've been eating it constantly back in Palo Alto for the past two days. In fact, I think this batch is about as good as the cones I got back in Palo Alto!"

G.b.t.c. looked him straight in the eye and said, "You're *in* Palo Alto!"

JONL turned slowly around, and saw the three of us collapse in a fit of giggles. He clapped a hand to his forehead and exclaimed, "I've been hacked!"

[My spies on the West Coast inform me that there is a close relative of the raspberry found out there called an 'ollalieberry' — ESR]

[Ironic footnote: it appears that the **meme** about ginger vs. rotting meat may be an urban legend. It's not borne out by an examination of medieval recipes or period purchase records for spices, and appears full-blown in the works of Samuel Pegge, a gourmand and notorious flake case who originated numerous food myths. — ESR]

sagan */say´gn/* [from Carl Sagan's TV series "Cosmos"; think "billions and billions"] n. A large quantity of anything. "There's a sagan different ways to tweak EMACS." "The U.S. Government spends sagans on bombs and welfare — hard to say which is more destructive."

SAIL */sayl/*, not */S-A-I-L/* n. 1. The Stanford Artificial Intelligence Lab. An important site in the early development of LISP; with the MIT AI Lab, BBN, CMU, XEROX PARC, and the UNIX community, one of the major well-springs of technical innovation and hacker-culture traditions (see the **WAITS** entry for details). The SAIL machines were shut down in late May 1990, scant weeks after the MIT AI Lab's ITS cluster was officially decommissioned. 2. The Stanford Artificial Intelligence Language used at SAIL (sense 1). It was an Algol-60 derivative with a coroutining facility and some new data types intended for building search trees and association lists.

salescritter */sayls´kri`tr/* n. Pejorative hackerism for a computer salesperson. Hackers tell the following joke:

> Q. What's the difference between a used-car dealer and a computer salesman?
> A. The used-car dealer knows he's lying. [Some versions add: ...and probably knows how to drive.]

This reflects the widespread hacker belief that salescritters are self-selected for stupidity (after all, if they had brains and the inclination to use them, they'd be in programming). The terms *salesthing* and *salesdroid* are also common. Compare **marketroid**, **suit**, **droid**.

salt n. A tiny bit of near-random data inserted where too much regularity would be undesirable; a data **frob** (sense 1). For example, the Unix crypt(3) man page mentions that "the salt string is used to perturb the DES algorithm in one of 4096 different ways."

salt mines n. Dense quarters housing large numbers of programmers working long hours on grungy projects, with some hope of seeing the end of the tunnel in *N* years. Noted for their absence of sunshine. Compare **playpen**, **sandbox**.

salt substrate [MIT] n. Collective noun used to refer to potato chips, pretzels, saltines, or any other form of snack food designed primarily as a carrier for sodium chloride. From the technical term 'chip substrate', used to refer to the silicon on the top of which the active parts of integrated circuits are deposited.

same-day service n. Ironic term used to describe long response time, particularly with respect to **MS-DOS** system calls (which ought to require only a tiny fraction of a second to execute). Such response time is a major incentive for programmers to write programs that are not **well-behaved**. See also **PC-ism**.

samizdat [Russian, literally "self publishing"] n. The process of disseminating documentation via underground channels. Originally referred to photocopy duplication and distribution of banned books in the former Soviet Union; now refers by obvious extension to any less-than-official promulgation of textual material, esp. rare, obsolete, or never-formally-published computer documentation. Samizdat is obviously much easier when one has access to high-bandwidth networks and high-quality laser printers. Note that samizdat is properly used only with respect to documents which contain needed information (see also **hacker ethic, the**) but which are for some reason otherwise unavailable, but *not* in the context of documents which are available through normal channels, for which unauthorized duplication would be unethical copyright violation. See **Lions Book** for a historical example.

samurai n. A hacker who hires out for legal cracking jobs, snooping for factions in corporate political fights, lawyers pursuing privacy-rights and First Amendment cases, and other parties with legitimate reasons to need an electronic locksmith. In 1991, mainstream media reported the existence of a loose-knit culture of samurai that meets electronically on BBS systems, mostly bright teenagers with personal micros; they have modeled themselves explicitly on the historical samurai of Japan and on the "net cowboys" of William Gibson's **cyberpunk** novels. Those interviewed claim to adhere to a rigid ethic of loyalty to their employers and to disdain the vandalism and theft practiced by criminal crackers as beneath them and contrary to the hacker ethic; some quote Miyamoto Musashi's *Book of Five Rings*, a classic of historical samurai doctrine, in support of these principles. See also **Stupids**, **social engineering**, **cracker**, **hacker ethic, the**, and **dark-side hacker**.

sandbender [IBM] n. A person involved with silicon lithography and the physical design of chips. Compare **ironmonger**, **polygon pusher**.

sandbox n. 1. (also 'sandbox, the') Common term for the R&D department at many software and computer companies (where hackers in commercial environments are likely to be found). Half-derisive, but reflects the truth that research is a form of creative play. Compare **playpen**. 2. Syn. **link farm**.

sanity check n. 1. The act of checking a piece of code (or anything else, e.g., a USENET posting) for completely stupid mistakes. Implies that the check is to make sure the author was sane when it was written; e.g., if a piece of scientific software relied on a particular formula and was giving unexpected results, one might first look at the nesting of parentheses or the coding of the formula, as a *sanity check*, before looking at the more complex I/O or data structure manipulation routines, much less the algorithm itself. Compare **reality check**. 2. A run-time test, either validating input or ensuring that the program hasn't screwed up internally (producing an inconsistent value or state).

Saturday-night special [from police slang for a cheap handgun] n. A **quick-and-dirty** program or feature kluged together during off hours, under a deadline, and in response to pressure from a **salescritter**. Such hacks are dangerously unreliable, but all too often sneak into a production release after insufficient review.

say vt. 1. To type to a terminal. "To list a directory verbosely, you have to say `ls -l`." Tends to imply a **newline**-terminated command (a 'sentence'). 2. A computer may also be said to 'say' things to you, even if it doesn't have a speech synthesizer, by displaying them on a terminal in response to your commands. Hackers find it odd that this usage confuses **mundanes**.

scag vt. To destroy the data on a disk, either by corrupting the filesystem or by causing media damage. "That last power hit scagged the system disk." Compare **scrog**, **roach**.

scanno */skan´oh/* n. An error in a document caused by a scanner glitch, analogous to a typo or **thinko**.

schroedinbug */shroh´din-buhg/* [MIT: from the Schroedinger's Cat thought-experiment in quantum physics] n. A design or implementation bug in a program that doesn't manifest until someone reading source or using the program in an unusual way notices that it never should have worked, at which point the program promptly stops working for everybody until fixed. Though (like **bit rot**) this sounds impossible, it happens; some programs have harbored latent schroedinbugs for years. Compare **heisenbug**, **Bohr bug**, **mandelbug**.

science-fiction fandom n. Another voluntary subculture having a very heavy overlap with hackerdom; most hackers read SF and/or fantasy fiction avidly, and many go to 'cons' (SF conventions) or are involved in fandom-connected activities such as the Society for Creative Anachronism. Some hacker jargon originated in SF fandom; see **defenestration**, **great-wall**, **cyberpunk**, **h**, **ha ha only serious**, **IMHO**, **mundane**, **neep-neep**, **Real Soon Now**. Additionally, the jargon terms **cowboy**, **cyberspace**, **de-rezz**, **go flatline**, **ice**, **phage**, **virus**, **wetware**, **wirehead**, and **worm** originated in SF stories.

scram switch [from the nuclear power industry] n. An emergency-power-off switch (see **Big Red Switch**), esp. one positioned to be easily hit by evacuating personnel. In general, this is *not* something you **frob** lightly; these often initiate expensive events (such as Halon dumps) and are installed in a **dinosaur pen** for use in case of electrical fire or in case some luckless **field servoid** should put 120 volts across himself while **Easter egging**. (See also molly-guard.)

scratch 1. [from 'scratchpad'] adj. Describes a data structure or recording medium attached to a machine for testing or temporary-use purposes; one that can be **scribbled** on without loss. Usually in the combining forms *scratch memory*, *scratch register*, *scratch disk*, *scratch tape*, *scratch volume*. See also **scratch monkey**. 2. [primarily IBM] vt. To delete (as in a file).

scratch monkey n. As in "Before testing or reconfiguring, always mount a **scratch monkey**", a proverb used to advise caution when dealing with irreplaceable data or devices. Used to refer to any scratch volume hooked to a computer during any risky operation as a replacement for some precious resource or data that might otherwise get trashed.

This term preserves the memory of Mabel, the Swimming Wonder Monkey, star of a biological research program at the University of Toronto. Mabel was not (so the legend goes) your ordinary monkey; the university had spent years teaching her how to swim, breathing through a regulator, in order to study the effects of different gas mixtures on her physiology. Mabel suffered an untimely demise one day when a DEC engineer troubleshooting a crash on the program's VAX inadvertently interfered with some custom hardware that was wired to Mabel.

It is reported that, after calming down an understandably irate customer sufficiently to ascertain the facts of the matter, a DEC troubleshooter called up the **field circus** manager responsible and asked him sweetly, "Can you swim?"

Not all the consequences to humans were so amusing; the sysop of the machine in question was nearly thrown in jail at the behest of certain clueless droids at the local 'humane' society. The moral is clear: When in doubt, always mount a scratch monkey.

[There is a version of this story, complete with reported dialogue between one of the project people and DEC field service, that has been circulating on Internet since 1986. It is hilarious and mythic, but gets some facts wrong. For example, it reports the machine as a PDP-11 and alleges that Mabel's demise occurred when DEC **PM**ed the machine. Earlier versions of this entry were based on that story; this one has been corrected from an interview with the hapless sysop. — ESR]

scream and die v. Syn. **cough and die**, but connotes that an error message was printed or displayed before the program crashed.

screaming tty [UNIX] n. A terminal line which spews an infinite number of random characters at the operating system. This can happen if the terminal is either disconnected or connected to a powered-off terminal but still enabled for login; misconfiguration, misimplementation, or simple bad luck can start such a terminal screaming. A screaming tty or two can seriously degrade the performance of a vanilla UNIX system; the arriving "characters" are treated as userid/password pairs and tested as such. The UNIX password encryption algorithm is designed to be computationally intensive in order to foil brute-force crack attacks, so although none of the logins succeeds; the overhead of rejecting them all can be substantial.

screw [MIT] n. A **lose**, usually in software. Especially used for user-visible misbehavior caused by a bug or misfeature. This use has become quite widespread outside MIT.

screwage */skroo´əj/* n. Like **lossage** but connotes that the failure is due to a designed-in misfeature rather than a simple inadequacy or a mere bug.

scribble n. To modify a data structure in a random and unintentionally destructive way. "Bletch! Somebody's disk-compactor program went berserk and scribbled on the i-node table." "It was working fine until one of the allocation routines scribbled on low core." Synonymous with **trash**; compare **mung**, which conveys a bit more intention, and **mangle**, which is more violent and final.

scrog */skrog/* [Bell Labs] vt. To damage, trash, or corrupt a data structure. "The list header got scrogged." Also reported as *skrog*, and ascribed to the comic strip “The Wizard of Id”. Compare **scag**; possibly the two are related. Equivalent to **scribble** or **mangle**.

scrool */skrool/* [from the pioneering Roundtable chat system in Houston ca. 1984; prob. originated as a typo for ‘scroll’] n. The log of old messages, available for later perusal or to help one get back in synch with the conversation. It was originally called the *scrool monster*, because an early version of the roundtable software had a bug where it would dump all 8K of scrool on a user’s terminal.

scrozzle */skroz´l/* vt. Used when a self-modifying code segment runs incorrectly and corrupts the running program or vital data. “The damn compiler scrozzled itself again!”

scruffies n. See **neats vs. scruffies**.

SCSI [Small Computer System Interface] n. A bus-independent standard for system-level interfacing between a computer and intelligent devices. Typically annotated in literature with ‘sexy’ (*/sek´see/*), ‘sissy’ (*/sis´ee/*), and ‘scuzzy’ (*/skuh´zee/*) as pronunciation guides — the last being the overwhelmingly predominant form, much to the dismay of the designers and their marketing people. One can usually assume that a person who pronounces it */S-C-S-I/* is clueless.

ScumOS */skuhm´os/* or */skuhm´O-S/* n. Unflattering hackerism for SunOS, the UNIX variant supported on Sun Microsystems’s UNIX workstations (see also **sun-stools**), and compare **AIDX**, **Macintrash**, **Nominal Semidestructor**, **Open DeathTrap**, **HP-SUX**. Despite what this term might suggest, Sun was founded by hackers and still enjoys excellent relations with hackerdom; usage is more often in exasperation than outright loathing.

search-and-destroy mode n. Hackerism for a noninteractive search-and-replace facility in an editor, so called because an incautiously chosen match pattern can cause **infinite** damage.

second-system effect n. (sometimes, more euphoniously, *second-system syndrome*) When one is designing the successor to a relatively small, elegant, and successful system, there is a tendency to become grandiose in one’s success and design an **elephantine** feature-laden monstrosity. The term was first used by Fred Brooks in his classic *The Mythical Man-Month: Essays on Software Engineering* (Addison-Wesley, 1975; ISBN 0-201-00650-2). It described the jump from a set of nice, simple operating systems on the IBM 70xx series to OS/360 on the 360 series. A similar effect can also happen in an evolving system; see **Brooks's Law**, **creeping elegance**, **creeping featurism**. See also **Multics**, **OS/2**, **X**, **software bloat**.

This version of the jargon lexicon has been described (with altogether too much truth for comfort) as an example of second-system effect run amok on jargon-1. . . .

secondary damage n. When a fatal error occurs (esp. a **segfault**) the immediate cause may be that a pointer has been trashed due to a previous **fandango on core**. However, this fandango may have been due to an *earlier* fandango, so no amount of analysis will reveal (directly) how the damage occurred. "The data structure was clobbered, but it was secondary damage."

By extension, the corruption resulting from N cascaded fandangoes on core is 'Nth-level damage'. There is at least one case on record in which 17 hours of **grovel**ling with `adb` actually dug up the underlying bug behind an instance of seventh-level damage! The hacker who accomplished this near-superhuman feat was presented with an award by his fellows.

security through obscurity alt. *security by obscurity* n. A term applied by hackers to most OS vendors' favorite way of coping with security holes — namely, ignoring them, documenting neither any known holes nor the underlying security algorithms, trusting that nobody will find out about them and that people who do find out about them won't exploit them. This "strategy" never works for long and occasionally sets the world up for debacles like the **RTM** worm of 1988 (see **Great Worm, the**), but once the brief moments of panic created by such events subside most vendors are all too willing to turn over and go back to sleep. After all, actually fixing the bugs would siphon off the resources needed to implement the next user-interface frill on marketing's wish list — and besides, if they started fixing security bugs customers might begin to *expect* it and imagine that their warranties of merchantability gave them some sort of *right* to a system with fewer holes in it than a shotgunned Swiss cheese, and *then* where would we be?

Historical note: There are conflicting stories about the origin of this term. It has been claimed that it was first used in the USENET newsgroup in *comp.sys.apollo* during a campaign to get HP/Apollo to fix security problems in its UNIX-**clone** Aegis/DomainOS (they didn't change a thing). **ITS** fans, on the other hand, say it was coined years earlier in opposition to the incredibly paranoid **Multics** people down the hall, for whom security was everything. In the ITS culture it referred to (1) the fact that that by the time a tourist figured out how to make trouble he'd generally gotten over the urge to make it, because he felt part of the community; and (2) (self-mockingly) the poor coverage of the documentation and obscurity of many commands. One instance of *deliberate* security through obscurity is recorded; the command to allow patching the running ITS system (**altmode** altmode control-R) echoed as $$^D. If you actually typed alt alt ^D, that set a flag that would prevent patching the system even if you later got it right.

SED [TMRC, from 'Light-Emitting Diode'] */S-E-D/* n. Smoke-emitting diode. A **friode** that lost the war. See also **LER**.

segfault n.,vi. Syn. **segment, segmentation fault**.

seggie */seg´ee/* [UNIX] n. Shorthand for **segmentation fault** reported from Britain.

segment */seg´ment/* vi. To experience a **segmentation fault**. Confusingly, this is often pronounced more like the noun 'segment' than like mainstream v. segment; this is because it is actually a noun shorthand that has been verbed.

segmentation fault n. [UNIX] 1. An error in which a running program attempts to access memory not allocated to it and **core dump**s with a segmentation violation error. 2. To lose a train of thought or a line of reasoning. Also uttered as an exclamation at the point of befuddlement.

segv */seg´vee/* n.,vi. Yet another synonym for **segmentation fault** (actually, in this case, 'segmentation violation').

self-reference n. See **self-reference**.

selvage */sel´vəj/* [from sewing and weaving] n. See **chad** (sense 1).

semi */se´mee/* or */se´mi:/* 1. n. Abbreviation for 'semicolon', when speaking. "Commands to **grind** are prefixed by semi-semi-star" means that the prefix is ' ; ; * ', not 1/4 of a star. 2. A prefix used with words such as 'immediately' as a qualifier. "When is the system coming up?" "Semi-immediately." (That is, maybe not for an hour.) "We did consider that possibility semi-seriously." See also **infinite**.

semi-infinite n. See **infinite**.

senior bit [IBM] n. Syn. **meta bit**.

server n. A kind of **daemon** that performs a service for the requester and which often runs on a computer other than the one on which the server runs. A particularly common term on the Internet, which is rife with *name servers, domain servers,* 'news servers', *finger servers,* and the like.

SEX */seks/* [Sun Users' Group & elsewhere] n. 1. Software EXchange. A technique invented by the blue-green algae hundreds of millions of years ago to speed up their evolution, which had been terribly slow up until then. Today, SEX parties are popular among hackers and others (of course, these are no longer limited to exchanges of genetic software). In general, SEX parties are a **Good Thing**, but unprotected SEX can propagate a **virus**. See also **pubic directory**. 2. The rather Freudian mnemonic often used for Sign EXtend, a machine instruction found in the PDP-11 and many other architectures. The RCA 1802 chip used in the early Elf and SuperElf personal computers had a 'SEt X register' SEX instruction, but this seems to have had little folkloric impact.

DEC's engineers nearly got a PDP-11 assembler that used the `SEX` mnemonic out the door at one time, but (for once) marketing wasn't asleep and forced a change. That wasn't the last time this happened, either. The author of *The Intel 8086 Primer,* who was one of the original designers of the 8086, noted that there was originally a `SEX` instruction on that processor, too. He says that Intel management got cold feet and decreed that it be changed, and thus the instruction was renamed `CBW` and `CWD` (depending on what was being extended). Amusingly, the Intel 8048 (the microcontroller used in IBM PC keyboards) is also missing straight `SEX` but has logical-or and logical-and instructions `ORL` and `ANL`.

The Motorola 6809, used in the U.K.'s 'Dragon 32' personal computer, actually had an official `SEX` instruction; the 6502 in the Apple II with which it competed did not. British hackers thought this made perfect mythic sense; after all, it was commonly observed, you could (on some theoretical level) have sex with a dragon, but you can't have sex with an apple.

sex changer n. Syn. **gender mender**.

shambolic link */sham-bol'ik link/* n. A UNIX symbolic link, particularly when it confuses you, points to nothing at all, or results in your ending up in some completely unexpected part of the filesystem. . . .

sharchive [UNIX and USENET; from /bin/sh archive] n. A **flatten**ed representation of a set of one or more files, with the unique property that it can be unflattened (the original files restored) by feeding it through a standard UNIX shell; thus, a sharchive can be distributed to anyone running UNIX, and no special unpacking software is required. Sharchives are also intriguing in that they are typically created by shell scripts; the script that produces sharchives is thus a script which produces self-unpacking scripts, which may themselves contain scripts. (The downsides of sharchives are that they are an ideal venue for **Trojan horse** attacks and that, for recipients not running UNIX, no simple un-sharchiving program is possible; sharchives can and do make use of arbitrarily-powerful shell features.)

Share and enjoy! imp. 1. Commonly found at the end of software release announcements and **README files**, this phrase indicates allegiance to the hacker ethic of free information sharing (see **hacker ethic, the**, sense 1). 2. The motto of the Sirius Cybernetics Corporation (the ultimate gaggle of incompetent **suits**) in Douglas Adams's *Hitch Hiker's Guide to the Galaxy.* The irony of using this as a cultural recognition signal appeals to freeware hackers.

shareware */sheir´weir/* n. **Freeware** (sense 1) for which the author requests some payment, usually in the accompanying documentation files or in an announcement made by the software itself. Such payment may or may not buy additional support or functionality. See also **careware**, **charityware**, **crippleware**, **guiltware**, **postcardware**, and **-ware**; compare **payware**.

shelfware */shelfweir/* n. Software purchased on a whim (by an individual user) or in accordance with policy (by a corporation or government agency), but not actually required for any particular use. Therefore, it often ends up on some shelf.

shell [orig. **Multics** techspeak, widely propagated via UNIX] n. 1. [techspeak] The command interpreter used to pass commands to an operating system; so called because it is the part of the operating system that interfaces with the outside world. 2. More generally, any interface program that mediates access to a special resource or **server** for convenience, efficiency, or security reasons; for this meaning, the usage is usually *a shell around* whatever. This sort of program is also called a *wrapper.*

shell out [UNIX] n. To spawn an interactive subshell from within a program (e.g., a mailer or editor). "Bang foo runs foo in a subshell, while bang alone shells out."

shift left (or right) logical [from any of various machines' instruction sets] 1. vi. To move oneself to the left (right). To move out of the way. 2. imper. "Get out of that (my) seat! You can shift to that empty one to the left (right)." Often used without the *logical*, or as *left shift* instead of *shift left*. Sometimes heard as LSH */lish/*, from the **PDP-10** instruction set. See **Programmer's Cheer**.

shim n. A small piece of data inserted in order to achieve a desired memory alignment or other addressing property. For example, the PDP-11 UNIX linker, in split I&D (instructions and data) mode, inserts a two-byte shim at location 0 in data space so that no data object will have an address of 0 (and be confused with the C null pointer). See also **loose bytes**.

shitogram */shit´oh-gram/* n. A *really* nasty piece of email. Compare **nastygram**, **flame**.

short card n. A half-length IBM PC expansion card or adapter that will fit in one of the two short slots located towards the right rear of a standard chassis (tucked behind the floppy disk drives). See also **tall card**.

shotgun debugging n. The software equivalent of **Easter egging**; the making of relatively undirected changes to software in the hope that a bug will be perturbed out of existence. This almost never works, and usually introduces more bugs.

shovelware n. Extra software dumped onto a CD-ROM or tape to fill up the remaining space on the medium after the software distribution it's intended to carry, but not integrated with the distribution.

showstopper n. A hardware or (especially) software bug that makes an implementation effectively unusable; one that absolutely has to be fixed before development can go on. Opposite in connotation from its original theatrical use, which refers to something stunningly *good*.

shriek n. See **excl**. Occasional CMU usage, also in common use among APL fans and mathematicians, especially category theorists.

Shub-Internet */shuhb in´tər-net/* [MUD: from H. P. Lovecraft's evil fictional deity 'Shub-Niggurath', the Black Goat with a Thousand Young] n. The harsh personification of the Internet, Beast of a Thousand Processes, Eater of Characters, Avatar of Line Noise, and Imp of Call Waiting; the hideous multi-tendriled entity formed of all the manifold connections of the net. A sect of MUDders worships Shub-Internet, sacrificing objects and praying for good connections. To no avail — its purpose is malign and evil, and is the cause of all network slowdown. Often heard as in "Freela casts a tac nuke at Shub-Internet for slowing her down." (A forged response often follows along the lines of: "Shub-Internet gulps down the tac nuke and burps happily.") Also cursed by users of **FTP** and **telnet** when the system slows down. The dread name of Shub-Internet is seldom spoken aloud, as it is said that repeating it three times will cause the being to wake, deep within its lair beneath the Pentagon.

sidecar n. 1. Syn. **slap on the side**. Esp. used of add-ons for the late and unlamented IBM PCjr. 2. The IBM PC compatibility box that could be bolted onto the side of an Amiga. Designed and produced by Commodore, it broke all of the company's own design rules. If it worked with any other peripherals, it was by **magic**.

SIG */sig/* n. (also common as a prefix in combining forms) A Special Interest Group, in one of several technical areas, sponsored by the Association for Computing Machinery; well-known ones include SIGPLAN (the Special Interest Group on Programming Languages), SIGARCH (the Special Interest Group for Computer Architecture) and SIGGRAPH (the Special Interest Group for Computer Graphics). Hackers, not surprisingly, like to overextend this naming convention to less formal associations like SIGBEER (at ACM conferences) and SIGFOOD (at University of Illinois).

sig block */sig blok/* [UNIX; often written '.sig' there] n. Short for 'signature', used specifically to refer to the electronic signature block that most UNIX mail- and news-posting software will **automagically** append to outgoing mail and news. The composition of one's sig can be quite an art form, including an ASCII logo or one's choice of witty sayings (see **sig quote**, **fool file, the**); but many consider large sigs a waste of **bandwidth**, and it has been observed that the size of one's sig block is usually inversely proportional to one's longevity and level of prestige on the net. See also **doubled sig**.

sig quote */sig kwoht/* [USENET] n. A maxim, quote, proverb, joke, or slogan embedded in one's **sig block** and intended to convey something of one's philosophical stance, pet peeves, or sense of humor. “Calm down, it’s only ones and zeroes.”

sig virus n. A parasitic **meme** embedded in a **sig block**. There was a **meme plague** or fad for these on USENET in late 1991. Most were equivalents of “I am a .sig virus. Please reproduce me in your .sig block.”. Of course, the .sig virus’s memetic hook is the giggle value of going along with the gag; this, however, was a self-limiting phenomenon as more and more people picked up on the idea. There were creative variants on it; some people stuck ‘sig virus antibody’ texts in their sigs, and there was at least one instance of a sig virus eater.

signal-to-noise ratio [from analog electronics] n. Used by hackers in a generalization of its technical meaning. ‘Signal’ refers to useful information conveyed by some communications medium, and ‘noise’ to anything else on that medium. Hence a low ratio implies that it is not worth paying attention to the medium in question. Figures for such metaphorical ratios are never given. The term is most often applied to **USENET** newsgroups during **flame wars**. Compare **bandwidth**. See also **coefficient of X**, **lost in the noise**.

silicon n. Hardware, esp. ICs or microprocessor-based computer systems (compare **iron**). Contrasted with software. See also **sandbender**.

silly walk [from Monty Python’s Flying Circus] vi. 1. A ridiculous procedure required to accomplish a task. Like **grovel**, but more **random** and humorous. “I had to silly-walk through half the /usr directories to find the maps file.” 2. Syn. **fandango on core**.

silo n. The FIFO input-character buffer in an RS-232 line card. So called from DEC terminology used on DH and DZ line cards for the VAX and PDP-11, presumably because it was a storage space for fungible stuff that went in at the top and came out at the bottom.

Silver Book n. Jensen and Wirth’s infamous *Pascal User Manual and Report*, so called because of the silver cover of the widely distributed Springer-Verlag second edition of 1978 (ISBN 0-387-90144-2). See **book titles**, **Pascal**.

since time T equals minus infinity adv. A long time ago; for as long as anyone can remember; at the time that some particular frob was first designed. Usually the word ‘time’ is omitted. See also **time T**; contrast **epoch**.

sitename */si:t'naym/* [UNIX/Internet] n. The unique electronic name of a computer system, used to identify it in UUCP mail, USENET, or other forms of electronic information interchange. The folklore interest of sitenames stems from the creativity and humor they often display. Interpreting a sitename is not unlike interpreting a vanity license plate; one has to mentally unpack it, allowing for mono-case and length restrictions and the lack of whitespace. Hacker tradition deprecates dull, institutional-sounding names in favor of punchy, humorous, and clever coinages (except that it is considered appropriate for the official public gateway machine of an organization to bear the organization's name or acronym). Mythological references, cartoon characters, animal names, and allusions to SF or fantasy literature are probably the most popular sources for sitenames (in roughly descending order). The obligatory comment when discussing these is Harris's Lament: "All the good ones are taken!" See also **network address**.

skrog v. Syn. **scrog**.

skulker n. Syn. **prowler**.

slack n. 1. Space allocated to a disk file but not actually used to store useful information. The techspeak equivalent is 'internal fragmentation'. 2. In the theology of the **Church of the SubGenius**, a mystical substance or quality that is the prerequisite of all human happiness.

Since UNIX files are stored compactly, except for the unavoidable wastage in the last block or fragment, it might be said that "Unix has no slack". See **ha ha only serious**.

slap on the side n. (also called a **sidecar**, or abbreviated *SOTS*.) A type of external expansion hardware marketed by computer manufacturers (e.g., Commodore for the Amiga 500/1000 series and IBM for the hideous failure called 'PCjr'). Various SOTS boxes provided necessities such as memory, hard drive controllers, and conventional expansion slots.

slash n. Common name for the slant ('/', ASCII 0101111) character. See **ASCII** for other synonyms.

sleep vi. 1. [techspeak] To relinquish a claim (of a process on a multitasking system) for service; to indicate to the scheduler that a process may be deactivated until some given event occurs or a specified time delay elapses. 2. In jargon, used very similarly to v. **block**; also in *sleep on*, syn. with *block* *on*. Often used to indicate that the speaker has relinquished a demand for resources until some (possibly unspecified) external event: "They can't get the fix I've been asking for into the next release, so I'm going to sleep on it until the release, then start hassling them again."

slim n. A small, derivative change (e.g., to code).

slop n. 1. A one-sided **fudge factor**, that is, an allowance for error but in only one of two directions. For example, if you need a piece of wire 10 feet long and have to guess when you cut it, you make very sure to cut it too long, by a large amount if necessary, rather than too short by even a little bit, because you can always cut off the slop but you can't paste it back on again. When discrete quantities are involved, slop is often introduced to avoid the possibility of being on the losing side of a **fencepost error**. 2. The percentage of 'extra' code generated by a compiler over the size of equivalent assembler code produced by **hand-hacking**; i.e., the space (or maybe time) you lose because you didn't do it yourself. This number is often used as a measure of the goodness of a compiler; slop below 5% is very good, and 10% is usually acceptable. With modern compiler technology, esp. on RISC machines, the compiler's slop may actually be *negative*; that is, humans may be unable to generate code as good. This is one of the reasons assembler programming is no longer common.

slopsucker */slop´suhk-r/* n. A lowest-priority task that waits around until everything else has 'had its fill' of machine resources. Only when the machine would otherwise be idle is the task allowed to 'suck up the slop'. Also called a *hungry puppy* or *bottom feeder*. One common variety of slopsucker hunts for large prime numbers. Compare **background**.

slurp vt. To read a large data file entirely into **core** before working on it. This may be contrasted with the strategy of reading a small piece at a time, processing it, and then reading the next piece. "This program slurps in a 1K-by-1K matrix and does an FFT." See also **sponge**.

smart adj. Said of a program that does the **Right Thing** in a wide variety of complicated circumstances. There is a difference between calling a program smart and calling it intelligent; in particular, there do not exist any intelligent programs (yet — see **AI-complete**). Compare **robust** (smart programs can be **brittle**).

smart terminal n. 1. A terminal that has enough computing capability to render graphics or to offload some kind of front-end processing from the computer it talks to. The development of workstations and personal computers has made this term and the product it describes semi-obsolescent, but one may still hear variants of the phrase *act like a smart terminal* used to describe the behavior of workstations or PCs with respect to programs that execute almost entirely out of a remote **server**'s storage, using said devices as displays. 2. obs. Any terminal with an addressable cursor; the opposite of a **glass tty**. Today, a terminal with merely an addressable cursor, but with none of the more-powerful features mentioned in sense 1, is called a **dumb terminal**.

There is a classic quote from Rob Pike (inventor of the **blit** terminal): "A smart terminal is not a smart*ass* terminal, but rather a terminal you can educate." This illustrates a common design problem: The attempt to make peripherals (or anything else) intelligent sometimes results in finicky, rigid 'special features' that become just so much dead weight if you try to use the device in any way the designer didn't anticipate. Flexibility and programmability, on the other hand, are *really* smart. Compare **hook**.

smash case vi. To lose or obliterate the uppercase/lowercase distinction in text input. "MS-DOS will automatically smash case in the names of all the files you create." Compare **fold case**.

smash the stack [C programming] n. To corrupt the execution stack by writing past the end of a local array or other data structure. Code that smashes the stack can cause a return from the routine to jump to a random address, resulting in some of the most insidious data-dependent bugs known to mankind. Variants include *trash* the stack, **scribble** the stack, **mangle** the stack; the term ****mung** the stack is not used, as this is never done intentionally. See **spam**; see also **aliasing bug**, **fandango on core**, **memory leak**, **memory smash**, **precedence lossage**, **overrun screw**.

smiley n. See **emoticon**.

smoke vi. 1. To crash or blow up, usually spectacularly. "The new version smoked, just like the last one." Used for both hardware (where it often describes an actual physical event), and software (where it's merely colorful). 2. [from automotive slang] To be conspicuously fast. "That processor really smokes." Compare **magic smoke**.

smoke and mirrors n. Marketing deceptions. The term is mainstream in this general sense. Among hackers it's strongly associated with bogus demos and crocked **benchmarks** (see also **MIPS**, **machoflops**). "They claim their new box cranks 50 MIPS for under $5000, but didn't specify the instruction mix — sounds like smoke and mirrors to me." The phrase has been said to derive from carnie slang for magic acts and 'freak show' displays that depend on 'trompe l'oeil' effects, but also calls to mind the fierce Aztec god Tezcatlipoca (lit. "Smoking Mirror") for whom the hearts of huge numbers of human sacrificial victims were regularly cut out. Upon hearing about a rigged demo or yet another round of fantasy-based marketing promises, hackers often feel analogously disheartened.

smoke test n. 1. A rudimentary form of testing applied to electronic equipment following repair or reconfiguration, in which power is applied and the tester checks for sparks, smoke, or other dramatic signs of fundamental failure. See **magic smoke**. 2. By extension, the first run of a piece of software after construction or a critical change. See and compare **reality check**.

There is an interesting semi-parallel to this term among typographers and printers: When new typefaces are being punch-cut by hand, a *smoke test* (hold the letter in candle smoke, then press it onto paper) is used to check out new dies.

smoking clover [ITS] n. A **display hack** originally due to Bill Gosper. Many convergent lines are drawn on a color monitor in **AOS** mode (so that every pixel struck has its color incremented). The lines all have one endpoint in the middle of the screen; the other endpoints are spaced one pixel apart around the perimeter of a large square. The color map is then repeatedly rotated. This results in a striking, rainbow-hued, shimmering four-leaf clover. Gosper joked about keeping it hidden from the FDA (the U.S.'s Food and Drug Administration) lest its hallucinogenic properties cause it to be banned.

SMOP */S-M-O-P/* [Simple (or Small) Matter of Programming] n. 1. A piece of code, not yet written, whose anticipated length is significantly greater than its complexity. Used to refer to a program that could obviously be written, but is not worth the trouble. Also used ironically to imply that a difficult problem can be easily solved because a program can be written to do it; the irony is that it is very clear that writing such a program will be a great deal of work. "It's easy to enhance a FORTRAN compiler to compile COBOL as well; it's just an SMOP." 2. Often used ironically by the intended victim when a suggestion for a program is made which seems easy to the suggester, but is obviously (to the victim) a lot of work.

smurf */smerf/* [from the *soc.motss* newsgroup on USENET, after some obnoxiously gooey cartoon characters] n. A newsgroup regular with a habitual style that is irreverent, silly, and *cute*. Like many other hackish terms for people, this one may be praise or insult depending on who uses it. In general, being referred to as a smurf is probably not going to make your day unless you've previously adopted the label yourself in a spirit of irony. Compare **old fart**.

SNAFU principle */sna´foo prin´si-pl/* [from a WWII Army acronym for 'Situation Normal, All Fucked Up'] n. "True communication is possible only between equals, because inferiors are more consistently rewarded for telling their superiors pleasant lies than for telling the truth." — a central tenet of **Discordianism**, often invoked by hackers to explain why authoritarian hierarchies screw up so reliably and systematically. The effect of the SNAFU principle is a progressive disconnection of decision-makers from reality. This lightly adapted version of a fable dating back to the early 1960s illustrates the phenomenon perfectly:

> In the beginning was the plan, and then the specification; And the plan was without form, and the specification was void.
>
> And darkness was on the faces of the implementors thereof; And they spake unto their leader, saying: "It is a crock of shit, and smells as of a sewer."
>
> And the leader took pity on them, and spoke to the project leader: "It is a crock of excrement, and none may abide the odor thereof."
>
> And the project leader spake unto his section head, saying: "It is a container of excrement, and it is very strong, such that none may abide it."
>
> The section head then hurried to his department manager, and informed him thus: "It is a vessel of fertilizer, and none may abide its strength."
>
> The department manager carried these words to his general manager, and spoke unto him saying: "It containeth that which aideth the growth of plants, and it is very strong."
>
> And so it was that the general manager rejoiced and delivered the good news unto the Vice President. "It promoteth growth, and it is very powerful."

> The Vice President rushed to the President's side, and joyously exclaimed: "This powerful new software product will promote the growth of the company!"
>
> And the President looked upon the product, and saw that it was very good.

After the subsequent disaster, the **suits** protect themselves by saying "I was misinformed!", and the implementors are demoted or fired.

snail vt. To **snail-mail** something. "Snail me a copy of those graphics, will you?"

snail-mail n. Paper mail, as opposed to electronic. Sometimes written as the single word 'SnailMail'. One's postal address is, correspondingly, a *snail address.* Derives from earlier coinage 'USnail' (from 'U.S. Mail'), for which there have even been parody posters and stamps made. Oppose **email.**

snap v. To replace a pointer to a pointer with a direct pointer; to replace an old address with the forwarding address found there. If you telephone the main number for an institution and ask for a particular person by name, the operator may tell you that person's extension before connecting you, in the hopes that you will *snap your pointer* and dial direct next time. The underlying metaphor may be that of a rubber band stretched through a number of intermediate points; if you remove all the thumbtacks in the middle, it snaps into a straight line from first to last. See **chase pointers**.

Often, the behavior of a **trampoline** is to perform an error check once and then snap the pointer that invoked it so as henceforth to bypass the trampoline (and its one-shot error check). In this context one also speaks of *snapping links.* For example, in a LISP implementation, a function interface trampoline might check to make sure that the caller is passing the correct number of arguments; if it is, and if the caller and the callee are both compiled, then snapping the link allows that particular path to use a direct procedure-call instruction with no further overhead.

snarf */snarf/* vt. 1. To grab, esp. to grab a large document or file for the purpose of using it with or without the author's permission. See also **BLT**. 2. [in the UNIX community] To fetch a file or set of files across a network. See also **blast**. This term was mainstream in the late 1960s, meaning 'to eat piggishly'. It may still have this connotation in context. "He's in the snarfing phase of hacking — **FTP**ing megs of stuff a day." 3. To acquire, with little

concern for legal forms or *politesse* (but not quite by stealing). "They were giving away samples, so I snarfed a bunch of them." 4. Syn. for **slurp**. "This program starts by snarfing the entire database into core, then. . . ." 5. [GEnie] To spray food or **programming fluid**s due to laughing at the wrong moment. "I was drinking coffee, and when I read your post I snarfed all over my desk." "If I keep reading this topic, I think I'll have to snarf-proof my computer with a keyboard **condom**." [This sense appears to be widespread among mundane teenagers — ESR]

snarf & barf */snarf´n-barf´/* n. Under a **WIMP environment**, the act of grabbing a region of text and then stuffing the contents of that region into another region (or the same one) to avoid retyping a command line. In the late 1960s, this was a mainstream expression for an 'eat now, regret it later' cheap-restaurant expedition.

snarf down v. To **snarf**, with the connotation of absorbing, processing, or understanding. "I'll snarf down the latest version of the **nethack** user's guide — it's been a while since I played last and I don't know what's changed recently."

snark [Lewis Carroll, via the Michigan Terminal System] n. 1. A system failure. When a user's process bombed, the operator would get the message "Help, Help, Snark in MTS!" 2. More generally, any kind of unexplained or threatening event on a computer (especially if it might be a boojum). Often used to refer to an event or a log file entry that might indicate an attempted security violation. See **snivitz**. 3. UUCP name of *snark.thyrsus.com*, home site of the Jargon File 2.*.* versions (i.e., this lexicon).

sneakernet */snee´ker-net/* n. Term used (generally with ironic intent) for transfer of electronic information by physically carrying tape, disks, or some other media from one machine to another. "Never underestimate the bandwidth of a station wagon filled with magtape, or a 747 filled with CD-ROMs." Also called 'Tennis-Net', 'Armpit-Net', 'Floppy-Net' or 'Shoenet'.

sniff v.,n. Synonym for **poll**.

snivitz */sniv´itz/* n. A hiccup in hardware or software; a small, transient problem of unknown origin (less serious than a **snark**). Compare **glitch**.

SO */S-O/* n. 1. (also *S.O.*) Abbrev. for Significant Other, almost invariably written abbreviated and pronounced */S-O/* by hackers. Used to refer to one's

primary relationship, esp. a live-in to whom one is not married. See **MOTAS**, **MOTOS**, **MOTSS**. 2. The Shift Out control character in ASCII (Control-N, 0001110).

social engineering n. Term used among **crackers** and **samurai** for cracking techniques that rely on weaknesses in **wetware** rather than software; the aim is to trick people into revealing passwords or other information that compromises a target system's security. Classic scams include phoning up a mark who has the required information and posing as a field service tech or a fellow employee with an urgent access problem. See also the **tiger team** story in the **patch** entry.

social science number [IBM] n. A statistic that is **content-free**, or nearly so. A measure derived via methods of questionable validity from data of a dubious and vague nature. Predictively, having a social science number in hand is seldom much better than nothing, and can be considerably worse. **Management** loves them. See also **numbers**, **math-out**, **pretty pictures**.

soft boot n. See **boot**.

softcopy */soft´kop-ee/* n. [by analogy with 'hardcopy'] A machine-readable form of corresponding hardcopy. See **bits**, **machinable**.

software bloat n. The results of **second-system effect** or **creeping featuritis**. Commonly cited examples include `ls(1)`, **X**, **BSD**, **Missed'em-five**, and **OS/2**.

software laser n. An optical laser works by bouncing photons back and forth between two mirrors, one totally reflective and one partially reflective. If the lasing material (usually a crystal) has the right properties, photons scattering off the atoms in the crystal will excite cascades of more photons, all in lockstep. Eventually the beam will escape through the partially-reflective mirror. One kind of **sorcerer's apprentice mode** involving bounce messages can produce closely analogous results, with a **cascade** of messages escaping to flood nearby systems. By mid-1993 there had been at least two publicized incidents of this kind.

software rot n. Term used to describe the tendency of software that has not been used in a while to **lose**; such failure may be semi-humorously ascribed to **bit rot**. More commonly, *software rot* strikes when a program's assumptions become out of date. If the design was insufficiently **robust**, this may cause it to fail in mysterious ways.

For example, owing to endemic shortsightedness in the design of COBOL programs, most will succumb to software rot when their 2-digit year counters **wrap around** at the beginning of the year 2000. Actually, related lossages often afflict centenarians who have to deal with computer software designed by unimaginative clods. One such incident became the focus of a minor public flap in 1990, when a gentleman born in 1889 applied for a driver's license renewal in Raleigh, North Carolina. The new system refused to issue the card, probably because with 2-digit years the ages 101 and 1 cannot be distinguished.

Historical note: Software rot in an even funnier sense than the mythical one was a real problem on early research computers (e.g., the R1; see **grind crank**). If a program that depended on a peculiar instruction hadn't been run in quite a while, the user might discover that the opcodes no longer did the same things they once did. ("Hey, so-and-so needs an instruction to do such-and-such. We can **snarf** this opcode, right? No one uses it.")

Another classic example of this sprang from the time an MIT hacker found a simple way to double the speed of the unconditional jump instruction on a PDP-6, so he patched the hardware. Unfortunately, this broke some fragile timing software in a music-playing program, throwing its output out of tune. This was fixed by adding a defensive initialization routine to compare the speed of a timing loop with the real-time clock; in other words, it figured out how fast the PDP-6 was that day, and corrected appropriately.

Compare **bit rot**.

softwarily */soft-weir´i-lee/* adv. In a way pertaining to software. "The system is softwarily unreliable." The adjective **'softwary' is *not* used. See **hardwarily**.

softy [IBM] n. Hardware hackers' term for a software expert who is largely ignorant of the mysteries of hardware.

some random X adj. Used to indicate a member of class X, with the implication that Xs are interchangeable. "I think some random cracker tripped over the guest timeout last night." See also **J. Random**.

sorcerer's apprentice mode [from Friedrich Schiller's *Der Zauberlehrling* via the film "Fantasia"] n. A bug in a protocol where, under some circumstances, the receipt of a message causes multiple messages to be sent, each of which, when received, triggers the same bug. Used esp. of such behavior caused by **bounce message** loops in **email** software. Compare **broadcast storm**, **network meltdown**, **software laser**, **ARMM**.

SOS n.,obs. */S-O-S/* 1. An infamously **losing** text editor. Once, back in the 1960s, when a text editor was needed for the PDP-6, a hacker crufted together a **quick-and-dirty** 'stopgap editor' to be used until a better one was written. Unfortunately, the old one was never really discarded when new ones (in particular, **TECO**) came along. SOS is a descendant ('Son of Stopgap') of that editor, and many PDP-10 users gained the dubious pleasure of its acquaintance. Since then other programs similar in style to SOS have been written, notably the early font editor BILOS */bye´lohs/*, the Brother-In-Law Of Stopgap (the alternate expansion 'Bastard Issue, Loins of Stopgap' has been proposed). 2. */sos/* vt. To decrease; inverse of **AOS**, from the PDP-10 instruction set.

source of all good bits n. A person from whom (or a place from which) useful information may be obtained. If you need to know about a program, a **guru** might be the source of all good bits. The title is often applied to a particularly competent secretary.

space-cadet keyboard n. A now-legendary device used on MIT LISP machines, which inspired several still-current jargon terms and influenced the design of **EMACS**. It was equipped with no fewer than *seven* shift keys: four keys for **bucky bits** ('control', 'meta', 'hyper', and 'super') and three like regular shift keys, called 'shift', 'top', and 'front'. Many keys had three symbols on them: a letter and a symbol on the top, and a Greek letter on the front. For example, the 'L' key had an 'L' and a two-way arrow on the top, and the Greek letter lambda on the front. By pressing this key with the right hand while playing an appropriate 'chord' with the left hand on the shift keys, you could get the following results:

L	lowercase l
shift-L	uppercase L
front-L	lowercase lambda λ
front-shift-L	uppercase lambda
top-L	two-way arrow $\leftrightarrow$ (front and shift are ignored)

And of course each of these might also be typed with any combination of the control, meta, hyper, and super keys. On this keyboard, you could

An early **space-cadet keyboard**
The next cartoon in the Crunchly saga is 05-20-73, page 153.

type over 8000 different characters! This allowed the user to type very complicated mathematical text, and also to have thousands of single-character commands at his disposal. Many hackers were actually willing to memorize the command meanings of that many characters if it reduced typing time (this attitude obviously shaped the interface of EMACS). Other hackers, however, thought having that many bucky bits was overkill, and objected that such a keyboard can require three or four hands to operate. See **bucky bits**, **cokebottle**, **double bucky**, **meta bit**, **quadruple bucky**.

Note: early versions of this entry incorrectly identified the space-cadet keyboard with the *Knight keyboard*. Though both were designed by Tom Knight, the latter term was properly applied only to a keyboard used for ITS on the PDP-10 and modeled on the Stanford keyboard (as described under **bucky bits**). The true space-cadet keyboard evolved from the Knight keyboard.

SPACEWAR n. A space-combat simulation game, inspired by E. E. "Doc" Smith's "Lensman" books, in which two spaceships duel around a central sun, shooting torpedoes at each other and jumping through hyperspace. This game was first implemented on the PDP-1 at MIT in 1960–61. SPACEWAR aficionados formed the core of the early hacker culture at MIT. Nine years later, a descendant of the game motivated Ken Thompson to build, in his spare time on a scavenged PDP-7, the operating system that became **UNIX**. Less than nine years after that, SPACEWAR was commercialized as one of the first video games; descendants are still **feep**ing in video arcades everywhere.

spaghetti code n. Code with a complex and tangled control structure, esp. one using many GOTOs, exceptions, or other 'unstructured' branching constructs. Pejorative. The synonym *kangaroo code* has been reported, doubtless because such code has so many jumps in it.

spaghetti inheritance n. [encountered among users of object-oriented languages that use inheritance, such as Smalltalk] A convoluted class-subclass graph, often resulting from carelessly deriving subclasses from other classes just for the sake of reusing their code. Coined in a (successful) attempt to discourage such practice, through guilt-by-association with **spaghetti code**.

spam [from the **MUD** community] vt. To crash a program by overrunning a fixed-size buffer with excessively large input data. See also **buffer overflow**, **overrun screw**, **smash the stack**.

special-case vt. To write unique code to handle input to or situations arising in a program that are somehow distinguished from normal processing. This would be used for processing of mode switches or interrupt characters in an interactive interface (as opposed, say, to text entry or normal commands), or for processing of **hidden flags** in the input of a batch program or **filter**.

speedometer n. A pattern of lights displayed on a linear set of LEDs (today) or nixie tubes (yesterday, on ancient mainframes). The pattern is shifted left every N times the operating system goes through its **main loop**. A swiftly moving pattern indicates that the system is mostly idle; the speedometer slows down as the system becomes overloaded. The speedometer on Sun Microsystems hardware bounces back and forth like the eyes on one of the Cylons from the wretched "Battlestar Galactica" TV series.

Historical note: One computer, the GE 600 (later Honeywell 6000) actually had an *analog* speedometer on the front panel, calibrated in instructions executed per second.

spell n. Syn. **incantation**.

spelling flame [USENET] n. A posting ostentatiously correcting a previous article's spelling as a way of casting scorn on the point the article was trying to make, instead of actually responding to that point (compare **dictionary flame**). Of course, people who are more than usually slovenly spellers are prone to think *any* correction is a spelling flame.

spiffy */spi´fee/* adj. 1. Said of programs having a pretty, clever, or exceptionally well-designed interface. "Have you seen the spiffy **X** version of **empire** yet?" 2. Said sarcastically of a program that is perceived to have little more than a flashy interface going for it. Which meaning should be drawn depends delicately on tone of voice and context. This word was common mainstream slang during the 1940s, in a sense close to 1.

spike v. To defeat a selection mechanism by introducing a (sometimes temporary) device that forces a specific result. The word is used in several industries; telephone engineers refer to spiking a relay by inserting a pin to hold the relay in either the closed or open state, and railroaders refer to spiking a track switch so that it cannot be moved. In programming environments it normally refers to a temporary change, usually for testing purposes (as opposed to a permanent change, which would be called **hardwired**).

spin vi. Equivalent to **buzz**. More common among C and UNIX programmers.

spl */S-P-L/* [abbrev, from Set Priority Level] The way traditional UNIX kernels implement mutual exclusion by running code at high interrupt levels. Used in jargon to describe the act of tuning in or tuning out ordinary communication. Classically, spl levels run from 1 to 7; "Fred's at spl 6 today" would mean that he is very hard to interrupt. "Wait till I finish this; I'll spl down then." See also **interrupts locked out**.

splash screen [Mac] n. Syn. **banner**, sense 3.

splat n. 1. Name used in many places (DEC, IBM, and others) for the asterisk ('*') character (ASCII 0101010). This may derive from the 'squashed-bug' appearance of the asterisk on many early line printers. 2. [MIT] Name used by some people for the '#' character (ASCII 0100011). 3. [Rochester Institute of Technology] The **feature key** on a Mac (same as **alt**, sense 2). 4. [Stanford] Name used by some people for the Stanford/ITS extended ASCII $\otimes$, the 'circle-x' character. This character is also called *blobby* and *frob*, among other names; it is sometimes used by mathematicians as a notation for 'tensor product'. 5. [Stanford] Name for the semi-mythical extended ASCII $\oplus$, the 'circle-plus' character. 6. Canonical name for an output routine that outputs whatever the local interpretation of *splat* is.

With ITS and WAITS gone, senses 4–6 are now nearly obsolete. See also **ASCII**.

spod [Great Britain] n. A lower form of life found on **talker systems** and **MUDs**. The spod has few friends in **RL** and uses talkers instead, finding communication easier and preferable over the net. He has all the negative traits of the **computer geek** without having any interest in computers per se. Lacking any knowledge of or interest in how networks work, and considering his access a God-given right, he is a major irritant to sysadmins, clogging up lines in order to reach new MUDs, following passed-on instructions on how to sneak his way onto Internet ("Wow! It's in America!") and complaining when he is not allowed to use busy routes. A true spod will start any conversation with "Are you male or female?" (and follow it up with "Got any good numbers/IDs/passwords?") and will not talk to someone physically present in the same terminal room until they log onto the same machine that he is using and enter talk mode. Compare **newbie**, **tourist**, **weenie**, **twink**, **terminal junkie**.

spoiler [USENET] n. 1. A remark which reveals important plot elements from books or movies, thus denying the reader (of the article) the proper suspense when reading the book or watching the movie. 2. Any remark which telegraphs the solution of a problem or puzzle, thus denying the reader the pleasure of working out the correct answer (see also **interesting**). Either sense readily forms compounds like *total spoiler*, *quasi-spoiler* and even *pseudo-spoiler*.

By convention, articles which are spoilers in either sense should contain the word 'spoiler' in the Subject: line, or guarantee via various tricks that the answer appears only after several screensful of warning, or conceal the sensitive information via **rot13**, or some combination of these techniques.

sponge [UNIX] n. A special case of a **filter** that reads its entire input before writing any output; the canonical example is a sort utility. Unlike most filters, a sponge can conveniently overwrite the input file with the output data stream. If a file system has versioning (as ITS did and VMS does now) the sponge/filter distinction loses its usefulness, because directing filter output would just write a new version. See also **slurp**.

spoo n. Variant of **spooge**, sense 1.

spooge */spooj/* 1. n. Inexplicable or arcane code, or random and probably incorrect output from a computer program. 2. vi. To generate spooge (sense 1).

spool [from early IBM 'Simultaneous Peripheral Operation On-Line', but this acronym is widely thought to have been contrived for effect] vt. To send files to some device or program (a *spooler*) that queues them up and does something useful with them later. Without qualification, the spooler is the *print spooler* controlling output of jobs to a printer; but the term has been used in connection with other peripherals (especially plotters and graphics devices) and occasionally even for input devices. See also **demon**.

spool file n. Any file to which data is **spool**ed to await the next stage of processing. Especially used in circumstances where spooling the data copes with a mismatch between speeds in two devices or pieces of software. For example, when you send mail under UNIX, it's typically copied to a spool file to await a transport **demon**'s attentions. This is borderline techspeak.

square tape n. Mainframe magnetic tape cartridges for use with IBM 3480 or compatible tape drives; or QIC tapes used on workstations and micros. The term comes from the square (actually rectangular) shape of the cartridges; contrast **round tape**.

stack n. The set of things a person has to do in the future. One speaks of the next project to be attacked as having risen to the top of the stack. "I'm afraid I've got real work to do, so this'll have to be pushed way down on my stack." "I haven't done it yet because every time I pop my stack something new gets pushed." If you are interrupted several times in the middle of a conversation, "My stack overflowed" means "I forget what we were talking about." The implication is that more items were pushed onto the stack than could be remembered, so the least recent items were lost. The usual physical example of a stack is to be found in a cafeteria: a pile of plates or trays sitting on a spring in a well, so that when you put one on the top they all sink down, and when you take one off the top the rest spring up a bit. See also **push** and **pop**.

At MIT, **pdl** used to be a more common synonym for **stack** in all these contexts, and this may still be true. Everywhere else **stack** seems to be the preferred term. **Knuth** (*The Art of Computer Programming*, second edition, vol. 1, p. 236) says:

> Many people who realized the importance of stacks and queues independently have given other names to these structures: stacks have been called push-down lists, reversion storages, cellars, nesting stores, piles, last-in-first-out ("LIFO") lists, and even yo-yo lists!

stack puke n. Some processor architectures are said to 'puke their guts onto the stack' to save their internal state during exception processing. The Motorola 68020, for example, regurgitates up to 92 bytes on a bus fault. On a pipelined machine, this can take a while.

stale pointer bug n. Synonym for **aliasing bug** used esp. among microcomputer hackers.

state n. 1. Condition, situation. "What's the state of your latest hack?" "It's winning away." "The system tried to read and write the disk simultaneously and got into a totally **wedged** state." The standard question "What's your state?" means "What are you doing?" or "What are you about to do?" Typical answers are "about to gronk out", or "hungry". Another standard question is "What's the state of the world?", meaning "What's new?" or "What's going on?". The more terse and humorous way of asking these questions would be "State-p?". Another way of phrasing the first question under sense 1 would be "state-p latest hack?". 2. Information being maintained in non-permanent memory (electronic or human).

steam-powered adj. Old-fashioned or underpowered; archaic. This term does not have a strong negative loading and may even be used semi-affectionately for something that clanks and wheezes a lot but hangs in there doing the job.

stiffy [University of Lowell, Massachusetts.] n. 3.5-inch **microfloppies**, so called because their jackets are more rigid than those of the 5.25-inch and the (now totally obsolete) 8-inch floppy. Elsewhere this might be called a *firmy*.

stir-fried random alt. *stir-fried mumble* n. Term used for the best dish of many of those hackers who can cook. Consists of random fresh veggies and meat wokked with random spices. Tasty and economical. See **random**, **great-wall**, **ravs**, **laser chicken**, **oriental food**; see also **mumble**.

stomp on vt. To inadvertently overwrite something important, usually automatically. "All the work I did this weekend got stomped on last night by the nightly server script." Compare **scribble**, **mangle**, **trash**, **scrog**, **roach**.

Stone Age n., adj. 1. In computer folklore, an ill-defined period from ENIAC (ca. 1943) to the mid-1950s; the great age of electromechanical **dinosaur**s. Sometimes used for the entire period up to 1960–61 (see **Iron Age**); however, it is funnier and more descriptive to characterize the latter period in terms of a 'Bronze Age' era of transistor-logic, pre-ferrite-**core** machines with drum or CRT mass storage (as opposed to just mercury delay lines and/or relays). See also **Iron Age**. 2. More generally, a pejorative for any crufty, ancient piece of hardware or software technology. Note that this is used even by people who were there for the **Stone Age** (sense 1).

stone knives and bearskins [from the Star Trek Classic episode "The City on the Edge of Forever"] n. A term traditionally used to describe (and deprecate) computing environments that are grotesquely primitive in light of what is known about good ways to design things. As in "Don't get too used to the facilities here. Once you leave SAIL it's stone knives and bearskins as far as the eye can see". Compare **steam-powered**.

stoppage */sto´pəj/* n. Extreme **lossage** that renders something (usually something vital) completely unusable. "The recent system stoppage was caused by a **fried** transformer."

How things weren't in the **Stone Age**.

The next cartoon in the Crunchly saga is 07-18-76, page 119.

store [prob. from techspeak 'main store'] n. In some varieties of Commonwealth hackish, the preferred synonym for **core**. Thus, *bringing a program into store* means not that one is returning shrink-wrapped software but that a program is being **swap**ped in.

strided */str:´dəd/* [scientific computing] adj. Said of a sequence of memory reads and writes to addresses, each of which is separated from the last by a constant interval called the *stride length*. These can be a worst-case access pattern for the standard memory-caching schemes when the stride length is a multiple of the cache line size. Strided references are often generated by loops through an array, and (if youre data is large enough that access-time is significant) it can be worthwhile to tune for better locality by inverting double loops or by partially unrolling the outer loop of a loop nest. This usage is borderline techspeak; the related term *memory stride* is definitely techspeak.

stroke n. Common name for the slant ('/', ASCII 0101111) character. See **ASCII** for other synonyms.

strudel n. Common (spoken) name for the at-sign ('@', ASCII 1000000) character. See **ASCII** for other synonyms.

stubroutine */stuhb´roo-teen/* [contraction of 'stub subroutine'] n. Tiny, often vacuous placeholder for a subroutine that is to be written or fleshed out later.

studly adj. Impressive; powerful. Said of code and designs which exhibit both complexity and a virtuoso flair. Has connotations similar to **hairy** but is more positive in tone. Often in the emphatic *most studly* or as noun-form *studliness*. "Smail 3.0's configuration parser is most studly."

studlycaps */stuhd´lee-kaps/* n. A hackish form of silliness similar to **BiCapitalization** for trademarks, but applied randomly and to arbitrary text rather than to trademarks. ThE oRigiN and SigNificaNce of thIs pRacTicE iS oBscuRe.

stunning adj. Mind-bogglingly stupid. Usually used in sarcasm. "You want to code *what* in ADA? That's a . . . stunning idea!"

stupid-sort n. Syn. **bogo-sort**.

Stupids n. Term used by **samurai** for the **suit**s who employ them; succinctly expresses an attitude at least as common, though usually better disguised, among other subcultures of hackers. There may be intended reference here to an SF story originally published in 1952 but much anthologized since, Mark Clifton's *Star, Bright.* In it, a super-genius child classifies humans into a very few 'Brights' like herself, a huge majority of 'Stupids', and a minority of 'Tweens', the merely ordinary geniuses.

Sturgeon's Law prov. "Ninety percent of everything is crap". Derived from a quote by science fiction author Theodore Sturgeon, who once said, "Sure, 90% of science fiction is crud. That's because 90% of everything is crud." Oddly, when Sturgeon's Law is cited, the final word is almost invariably changed to 'crap'. Compare **Hanlon's Razor**, **Ninety-Ninety Rule**. Though this maxim originated in SF fandom, most hackers recognize it and are all too aware of its truth.

sucking mud [Applied Data Research] adj. (also *pumping mud*) Crashed or **wedged**. Usually said of a machine that provides some service to a network, such as a file server. This Dallas regionalism derives from the East Texas oilfield lament, "Shut 'er down, Ma, she's a-suckin' mud". Often used as a query. "We are going to reconfigure the network, are you ready to suck mud?"

sufficiently small adj. Syn. **suitably small**.

suit n. 1. Ugly and uncomfortable 'business clothing' often worn by non-hackers. Invariably worn with a 'tie', a strangulation device that partially cuts off the blood supply to the brain. It is thought that this explains much about the behavior of suit-wearers. Compare **droid**. 2. A person who habitually wears suits, as distinct from a techie or hacker. See **loser**, **burble**, **management**, **Stupids**, **SNAFU principle**, and **brain-damaged**. English, by the way, is relatively kind; our Moscow correspondent informs us that the corresponding idiom in Russian hacker jargon is 'sovok', lit. a tool for grabbing garbage.

suitable win n. See **win**.

suitably small [perverted from mathematical jargon] adj. An expression used ironically to characterize unquantifiable behavior that differs from expected or required behavior. For example, suppose a newly created program came up with a correct full-screen display, and one publicly exclaimed: "It works!"

Then, if the program dumped core on the first mouse click, one might add: "Well, for suitably small values of 'works'." Compare the characterization of π under **random numbers**.

sun lounge [Great Britain] n. The room where all the Sun workstations live. The humor in this term comes from the fact that it's also in mainstream use to describe a solarium, and all those Sun workstations clustered together give off an amazing amount of heat.

sun-stools n. Unflattering hackerism for SunTools, a pre-X windowing environment notorious in its day for size, slowness, and misfeatures. **X**, however, is larger and slower; see **second-system effect**.

sunspots n. 1. Notional cause of an odd error. "Why did the program suddenly turn the screen blue?" "Sunspots, I guess." 2. Also the cause of **bit rot** — from the myth that sunspots will increase **cosmic rays**, which can flip single bits in memory. See also **phase of the moon**.

superprogrammer n. A prolific programmer; one who can code exceedingly well and quickly. Not all hackers are superprogrammers, but many are. (Productivity can vary from one programmer to another by three orders of magnitude. For example, one programmer might be able to write an average of 3 lines of working code in one day, while another, with the proper tools, might be able to write 3,000. This range is astonishing; it is matched in very few other areas of human endeavor.) The term *superprogrammer* is more commonly used within such places as IBM than in the hacker community. It tends to stress naive measures of productivity and to underweight creativity, ingenuity, and getting the job *done* — and to sidestep the question of whether the 3,000 lines of code do more or less useful work than three lines that do the **Right Thing**. Hackers tend to prefer the terms **hacker** and **wizard**.

superuser [UNIX] n. Syn. **root, avatar**. This usage has spread to non-UNIX environments; the superuser is any account with all **wheel** bits on. A more specific term than **wheel**.

support n. After-sale handholding; something many software vendors promise but few deliver. To hackers, most support people are useless — because by the time a hacker calls support he or she will usually know the software and the relevant manuals better than the support people (sadly, this is *not* a joke or exaggeration). A hacker's idea of 'support' is a tête-à-tête with the software's designer.

Suzie COBOL */soo´zee koh´bol/* 1. [IBM: prob. from Frank Zappa's 'Suzy Creamcheese'] n. A coder straight out of training school who knows everything except the value of comments in plain English. Also (fashionable among personkind wishing to avoid accusations of sexism) 'Sammy Cobol' or (in some non-IBM circles) 'Cobol Charlie'. 2. [proposed] Meta-name for any **code grinder**, analogous to **J. Random Hacker**.

swab */swob/* [From the mnemonic for the PDP-11 'SWAp Byte' instruction, as immortalized in the `dd(1)` option `conv=swab` (see **dd**)] 1. vt. To solve the **NUXI problem** by swapping bytes in a file. 2. n. The program in V7 UNIX used to perform this action, or anything functionally equivalent to it. See also **big-endian**, **little-endian**, **middle-endian**, **bytesexual**.

swap vt. 1. [techspeak] To move information from a fast-access memory to a slow-access memory (*swap out*), or vice versa (*swap in*). Often refers specifically to the use of disks as 'virtual memory'. As pieces of data or program are needed, they are swapped into **core** for processing; when they are no longer needed they may be swapped out again. 2. The jargon use of these terms analogizes people's short-term memories with core. Cramming for an exam might be spoken of as swapping in. If you temporarily forget someone's name, but then remember it, your excuse is that it was swapped out. To *keep something swapped in* means to keep it fresh in your memory: "I reread the TECO manual every few months to keep it swapped in." If someone interrupts you just as you got a good idea, you might say "Wait a moment while I swap this out", implying that a piece of paper is your extra-somatic memory and that if you don't swap the idea out by writing it down it will get overwritten and lost as you talk. Compare **page in**, **page out**.

swap space n. Storage space, especially temporary storage space used during a move or reconfiguration. "I'm just using that corner of the machine room for swap space."

swapped in n. See **swap**. See also **page in**.

swapped out n. See **swap**. See also **page out**.

swizzle v. To convert external names, array indices, or references within a data structure into address pointers when the data structure is brought into main memory from external storage (also called *pointer swizzling*); this may be done for speed in chasing references or to simplify code (e.g., by turning lots of name lookups into pointer dereferences). The converse operation is sometimes termed *unswizzling*. See also **snap**.

sync */sink/* (var. *synch*) n., vi. 1. To synchronize, to bring into synchronization. 2. [techspeak] To force all pending I/O to the disk; see **flush**, sense 2. 3. More generally, to force a number of competing processes or agents to a state that would be 'safe' if the system were to crash; thus, to checkpoint (in the database-theory sense).

syntactic salt n. The opposite of **syntactic sugar**, a feature designed to make it harder to write bad code. Specifically, syntactic salt is a hoop the programmer must jump through just to prove that he knows what's going on, rather than to express a program action. Some programmers consider required type declarations to be syntactic salt. A requirement to write `end if`, `end while`, `end do`, etc. to terminate the last block controlled by a control construct (as opposed to just `end`) would definitely be syntactic salt. Syntactic salt is like the real thing in that it tends to raise hackers' blood pressures in an unhealthy way. Compare **candygrammar**. .

syntactic sugar [coined by Peter Landin] n. Features added to a language or other formalism to make it 'sweeter' for humans, features which do not affect the expressiveness of the formalism (compare **chrome**). Used esp. when there is an obvious and trivial translation of the 'sugar' feature into other constructs already present in the notation. C's `a[i]` notation is syntactic sugar for `*(a + i)`. "Syntactic sugar causes cancer of the semicolon." — Alan Perlis.

The variants *syntactic saccharin* and *syntactic syrup* are also recorded. These denote something even more gratuitous, in that syntactic sugar serves a purpose (making something more acceptable to humans), but syntactic saccharin or syrup serve no purpose at all. Compare **candygrammar**, **syntactic salt**.

sys-frog */sis´frog/* [the PLATO system] n. Playful variant of *sysprog*, which is in turn short for 'systems programmer'.

sysadmin */sis´ad-min/* n. Common contraction of 'system admin'; see **admin**.

sysape */sys´ayp/* n. A rather derogatory term for a computer operator; a play on **sysop** common at sites that use the banana hierarchy of problem complexity (see **one-banana problem**).

sysop */sis'op/* n. [esp. in the BBS world] The operator (and usually the owner) of a bulletin-board system. A common neophyte mistake on **FidoNet** is to address a message to *sysop* in an international **echo**, thus sending it to hundreds of sysops around the world.

system n. 1. The supervisor program or OS on a computer. 2. The entire computer system, including input/output devices, the supervisor program or OS, and possibly other software. 3. Any large-scale program. 4. Any method or algorithm. 5. *System hacker*: one who hacks the system (in senses 1 and 2 only; for sense 3 one mentions the particular program: e.g., *LISP hacker*)

systems jock n. See **jock**, sense 2.

system mangler n. Humorous synonym for 'system manager', poss. from the fact that one major IBM OS had a **root** account called SYSMANGR. Refers specifically to a systems programmer in charge of administration, software maintenance, and updates at some site. Unlike **admin**, this term emphasizes the technical end of the skills involved.

SysVile */sis-vi:l'/* n. See **Missed'em-five**.

= T =

T */T/* 1. [from LISP terminology for 'true'] Yes. Used in reply to a question (particularly one asked using **The '-P' convention**). In LISP, the constant T means 'true', among other things. Some hackers use 'T' and 'NIL' instead of 'Yes' and 'No' almost reflexively. This sometimes causes misunderstandings. When a waiter or flight attendant asks whether a hacker wants coffee, he may well respond 'T', meaning that he wants coffee; but of course he will be brought a cup of tea instead. As it happens, most hackers (particularly those who frequent Chinese restaurants) like tea at least as well as coffee — so it is not that big a problem. 2. See **time T** (also **since time T equals minus infinity**). 3. [techspeak] In transaction-processing circles, an abbreviation for the noun 'transaction'. 4. [Purdue] Alternate spelling of **tee**. 5. A dialect of **LISP** developed at Yale.

tail recursion n. If you aren't sick of it already, see **tail recursion**.

talk mode n. A feature supported by UNIX, ITS, and some other OSes that allows two or more logged-in users to set up a real-time on-line conversation. It combines the immediacy of talking with all the precision (and verbosity) that written language entails. It is difficult to communicate inflection, though conventions have arisen for some of these (see the section on writing style in the Prependices for details).

Talk mode has a special set of jargon words, used to save typing, which are not used orally. Some of these are identical to (and probably derived from) Morse-code jargon used by ham-radio amateurs since the 1920s.

`BCNU`	be seeing you
`BTW`	by the way
`BYE?`	are you ready to unlink? (this is the standard way to end a talk-mode conversation; the other person types `BYE` to confirm, or else continues the conversation)
`CUL`	see you later
`ENQ?`	are you busy? (expects `ACK` or `NAK` in return)
`FOO?`	are you there? (often used on unexpected links, meaning also "Sorry if I butted in . . . " (linker) or "What's up?" (linkee))
`FWIW`	for what it's worth
`FYI`	for your information
`FYA`	for your amusement
`GA`	go ahead (used when two people have tried to type simultaneously; this cedes the right to type to the other)
`GRMBL`	grumble (expresses disquiet or disagreement)
`HELLOP`	hello? (an instance of the '-P' convention)
`JAM`	just a minute (equivalent to `SEC....`)
`MIN`	same as `JAM`
`NIL`	no (see **NIL**)
`O`	over to you
`OO`	over and out
`/`	another form of "over to you" (from x/y as "x over y")
`\`	lambda (used in discussing LISPy things)
`OBTW`	oh, by the way
`R U THERE?`	are you there?
`SEC`	wait a second (sometimes written `SEC...`)
`T`	yes (see the main entry for **T**)

TNX	thanks
TNX 1.0E6	thanks a million (humorous)
TNXE6	another form of "thanks a million"
WRT	with regard to, or with respect to.
WTF	the universal interrogative particle; WTF knows what it means?
WTH	what the hell?
<double newline>	When the typing party has finished, he/she types two newlines to signal that he/she is done; this leaves a blank line between 'speeches' in the conversation, making it easier to reread the preceding text.
<name>:	When three or more terminals are linked, it is conventional for each typist to **prepend** his/her login name or handle and a colon (or a hyphen) to each line to indicate who is typing (some conferencing facilities do this automatically). The login name is often shortened to a unique prefix (possibly a single letter) during a very long conversation.
/\/\/\	A giggle or chuckle. On a MUD, this usually means 'earthquake fault'.

Most of the above sub-jargon is used at both Stanford and MIT. Several of these expressions are also common in **email**, esp. FYI, FYA, BTW, BCNU, WTF, and CUL. A few other abbreviations have been reported from commercial networks, such as GEnie and CompuServe, where on-line 'live' chat including more than two people is common and usually involves a more 'social' context, notably the following:

<g>	grin
<gr&d>	grinning, running, and ducking
BBL	be back later
BRB	be right back
HHOJ	ha ha only joking
HHOK	ha ha only kidding
HHOS	**ha ha only serious**
IMHO	in my humble opinion (see **IMHO**)
LOL	laughing out loud

`NHOH`	Never Heard of Him/Her (often used in **initgame**)
`ROTF`	rolling on the floor
`ROTFL`	rolling on the floor laughing
`AFK`	away from keyboard
`b4`	before
`CU l8tr`	see you later
`MORF`	male or female?
`TTFN`	ta-ta for now
`TTYL`	talk to you later
`OIC`	oh, I see
`rehi`	hello again

Most of these are not used at universities or in the UNIX world, though ROTF and TTFN have gained some currency there and IMHO is common; conversely, most of the people who know these are unfamiliar with FOO?, BCNU, HELLOP, **NIL**, and **T**.

The **MUD** community uses a mixture of USENET/Internet emoticons, a few of the more natural of the old-style talk-mode abbrevs, and some of the 'social' list above; specifically, MUD respondents report use of BBL, BRB, LOL, b4, BTW, WTF, TTFN, and WTH. The use of *rehi* is also common; in fact, mudders are fond of re- compounds and will frequently *rehug* or *rebonk* (see **bonk/oif**) people. The word *re* by itself is taken as 'regreet'. In general, though, MUDders express a preference for typing things out in full rather than using abbreviations; this may be due to the relative youth of the MUD cultures, which tend to include many touch typists and to assume high-speed links. The following uses specific to MUDs are reported:

`CU l8er`	see you later (mutant of `CU l8tr`)
`FOAD`	fuck off and die (use of this is generally OTT)
`OTT`	over the top (excessive, uncalled for)
`ppl`	abbrev for "people"
`THX`	thanks (mutant of `TNX`; clearly this comes in batches of 1138 (the Lucasian K)).
`UOK?`	are you OK?

Some **BIFF**isms (notably the variant spelling `d00d`) appear to be passing into wider use among some subgroups of MUDders.

One final note on talk mode style: neophytes, when in talk mode, often seem to think they must produce letter-perfect prose because they are typing rather than speaking. This is not the best approach. It can be very frustrating to wait while your partner pauses to think of a word, or repeatedly makes the same spelling error and backs up to fix it. It is usually best just to leave typographical errors behind and plunge forward, unless severe confusion may result; in that case it is often fastest just to type "xxx" and start over from before the mistake.

See also **hakspek**, **emoticon**.

talker system n. British hackerism for software that enables real-time chat or **talk mode**.

tall card n. A PC/AT-size expansion card (these can be larger than IBM PC or XT cards because the AT case is bigger). See also **short card**. When IBM introduced the PS/2 model 30 (its last gasp at supporting the ISA) they made the case lower and many industry-standard tall cards wouldn't fit; this was felt to be a reincarnation of the **connector conspiracy**, done with less style.

tanked adj. Same as **down**, used primarily by UNIX hackers. See also **hosed**. Popularized as a synonym for 'drunk' by Steve Dallas in the late lamented "Bloom County" comic strip.

TANSTAAFL */tan´stah-fl/* [acronym, from Robert Heinlein's classic *The Moon is a Harsh Mistress.*] "There Ain't No Such Thing As A Free Lunch", often invoked when someone is balking at the prospect of using an unpleasantly **heavyweight** technique, or at the poor quality of some piece of free software, or at the **signal-to-noise ratio** of unmoderated USENET newsgroups. "What? Don't tell me I have to implement a database back end to get my address book program to work!" "Well, TANSTAAFL you know." This phrase owes some of its popularity to the high concentration of science-fiction fans and political libertarians in hackerdom (see **Appendix B**).

tar and feather [from UNIX `tar(1)`] vt. To create a transportable archive from a group of files by first sticking them together with `tar(1)` (the Tape ARchiver) and then compressing the result (see **compress**). The latter action is dubbed *feathering* partly for euphony and (if only for contrived effect) by analogy to what you do with an airplane propeller to decrease wind resistance, or with an oar to reduce water resistance; smaller files, after all, slip through comm links more easily.

taste [primarily MIT] n. 1. The quality in a program that tends to be inversely proportional to the number of features, hacks, and kluges programmed into it. Also *tasty, tasteful, tastefulness.* "This feature comes in N tasty flavors." Although *tasteful* and *flavorful* are essentially synonyms, *taste* and **flavor** are not. Taste refers to sound judgment on the part of the creator; a program or feature can *exhibit* taste but cannot *have* taste. On the other hand, a feature can have **flavor**. Also, **flavor** has the additional meaning of 'kind' or 'variety' not shared by *taste.* **Flavor** is a more popular word than *taste,* though both are used. See also **elegant**. 2. Alt. sp. of **tayste**.

tayste */tayst/* n. Two bits; also as **taste**. Syn. **crumb**, **quarter**. Compare **byte**, **dynner**, **playte**, **nybble**, **quad**.

TCB */T-C-B/* [IBM] n. 1. Trouble Came Back. An intermittent or difficult-to-reproduce problem that has failed to respond to neglect or **shotgun debugging**. Compare **heisenbug**. Not to be confused with: 2. Trusted Computing Base, an 'official' jargon term from the **Orange Book**.

tea, ISO standard cup of [South Africa] n. A cup of tea with milk and one teaspoon of sugar, where the milk is poured into the cup before the tea. Variations are ISO 0, with no sugar; ISO 2, with two spoons of sugar; and so on.

Like many ISO standards, this one has a faintly alien ring in North America, where hackers generally shun the decadent British practice of adulterating perfectly good tea with dairy products and prefer instead to add a wedge of lemon, if anything. If one were feeling extremely silly, one might hypothesize an analogous *ANSI standard cup of tea* and wind up with a political situation distressingly similar to several that arise in much more serious technical contexts. Milk and lemon don't mix very well.

TechRef */tek´ref/* [MS-DOS] n. The original *IBM PC Technical Reference Manual,* including the BIOS listing and complete schematics for the PC. The only PC documentation in the issue package that's considered serious by real hackers.

TECO */tee´koh/* obs. 1. [originally an acronym for '[paper] Tape Editor and COrrector'; later, 'Text Editor and COrrector'] n. A text editor developed at MIT and modified by just about everybody. With all the dialects included, TECO may have been the most prolific editor in use before **EMACS**, to which it was directly ancestral. Noted for its powerful programming-language-like features and its unspeakably hairy syntax. It is literally the case that every string of characters is a valid TECO program (though probably not a useful one); one common game used to be mentally working out what the TECO commands corresponding to human names did. 2. vt. Originally, to edit using the TECO editor in one of its infinite variations (see below). 3. vt.,obs. To edit even when TECO is *not* the editor being used! This usage is rare and now primarily historical.

As an example of TECO's obscurity, here is a TECO program that takes a list of names such as:

```
Loser, J. Random
Quux, The Great
Dick, Moby
```

sorts them alphabetically according to surname, and then puts the surname last, removing the comma, to produce the following:

```
Moby Dick
J. Random Loser
The Great Quux
```

The program is

```
[1 J^P$L$$
J <.-Z; .,(S,$ -D .)FX1 @F^B $K :L I $ G1 L>$$
```

(where ^B means 'Control-B' (ASCII 0000010) and $ is actually an **alt** or escape (ASCII 0011011) character).

In fact, this very program was used to produce the second, sorted list from the first list. The first hack at it had a **bug**: GLS (the author) had accidentally omitted the `@` in front of `F^B`, which as anyone can see is clearly the **Wrong Thing**. It worked fine the second time. There is no space to describe all the features of TECO, but it may be of interest that `^P` means 'sort' and `J<.-Z; . . . L>` is an idiomatic series of commands for 'do once for every line'.

In mid-1991, TECO is pretty much one with the dust of history, having been replaced in the affections of hackerdom by **EMACS**. Descendants of an early (and somewhat lobotomized) version adopted by DEC can still be found lurking on VMS and a couple of crufty PDP-11 operating systems, however, and ports of the more advanced MIT versions remain the focus of some antiquarian interest. See also **retrocomputing**, **write-only language**.

tee n.,vt. [Purdue] A carbon copy of an electronic transmission. "Oh, you're sending him the **bits** to that? Slap on a tee for me." From the UNIX command `tee(1)`, itself named after a pipe fitting (see **plumbing**). Can also mean 'save one for me', as in "Tee a slice for me!" Also spelled 'T'.

teledildonics */tel`ə-dil-do´-niks/* n. Sex in a computer simulated virtual reality, esp. computer-mediated sexual interaction between the **VR** presences of two humans. This practice is not yet possible except in the rather limited form of erotic conversation on **MUD**s and the like. The term, however, is widely recognized in the VR community as a **ha ha only serious** projection of things to come. "When we can sustain a multi-sensory surround good enough for teledildonics, *then* we'll know we're getting somewhere."

Telerat */tel´ə-rat/* n. Unflattering hackerism for 'Teleray', a line of extremely losing terminals. Compare **AIDX**, **Macintrash Nominal Semidestructor**, **Open DeathTrap**, **ScumOS**, **sun-stools**, **HP-SUX**.

TELNET */tel´net/* vt. To communicate with another Internet host using the TELNET (**RFC** 854) protocol (usually using a program of the same name). TOPS-10 people used the word IMPCOM, since that was the program name for them. Sometimes abbreviated to TN */T-N/*. "I usually TN over to SAIL just to read the AP News."

ten-finger interface n. The interface between two networks that cannot be directly connected for security reasons; refers to the practice of placing two terminals side by side and having an operator read from one and type into the other.

tense adj. Of programs, very clever and efficient. A tense piece of code often got that way because it was highly **bum**med, but sometimes it was just based on a great idea. A comment in a clever routine by Mike Kazar, once a grad-student hacker at CMU: "This routine is so tense it will bring tears to your eyes." A tense programmer is one who produces tense code.

tenured graduate student n. One who has been in graduate school for 10 years (the usual maximum is 5 or 6): a 'ten-yeared' student (get it?). Actually, this term may be used of any grad student beginning in his seventh year. Students don't really get tenure, of course, the way professors do, but a tenth-year graduate student has probably been around the university longer than any untenured professor.

tera- */te´rə/* [SI] pref. See **quantifiers**.

teraflop club */te´rə-flop kluhb/* [FLOP = Floating Point Operation] n. A mythical association of people who consume outrageous amounts of computer time in order to produce a few simple pictures of glass balls with intricate ray-tracing techniques. Caltech professor James Kajiya is said to have been the founder.

terminak */ter´mi-nak`/* [Caltech, ca. 1979] n. Any malfunctioning computer terminal. A common failure mode of Lear-Siegler ADM 3a terminals caused the 'L' key to produce the 'K' code instead; complaints about this tended to look like "Terminak #3 has a bad keyboard. Pkease fix." See **AIDX**, **Nominal Semidestructor**, **Open DeathTrap**, **ScumOS**, **sun-stools**, **Telerat**, **HP-SUX**.

terminal brain death n. The extreme form of **terminal illness** (sense 1). What someone who has obviously been hacking continuously for far too long is said to be suffering from.

terminal illness n. 1. Syn. **raster burn**. 2. The 'burn-in' condition your CRT tends to get if you don't have a screen saver.

terminal junkie [UK] n. A **wannabee** or early **larval stage** hacker who spends most of his or her time wandering the directory tree and writing **noddy** programs just to get a fix of computer time. Variants include *terminal jockey*, *console junkie*, and **console jockey**. The term *console jockey* seems to imply more expertise than the other three (possibly because of the exalted status of the **console** relative to an ordinary terminal). See also **twink**, **read-only user**.

terpri */ter´pree/* [from LISP 1.5 (and later, MacLISP)] vi. To output a **newline**. Now rare as jargon, though still used as techspeak in Common LISP. It is a contraction of 'TERminate PRInt line', named for the fact that, on some early OSes and hardware, no characters would be printed until a complete line was formed, so this operation terminated the line and emitted the output.

test n. 1. Real users bashing on a prototype long enough to get thoroughly acquainted with it, with careful monitoring and followup of the results. 2. Some bored random user trying a couple of the simpler features with a developer looking over his or her shoulder, ready to pounce on mistakes. Judging by the quality of most software, the second definition is far more prevalent. See also **demo**.

TEX */tekh/* n. An extremely powerful **macro**-based text formatter written by Donald E. **Knuth**, very popular in the computer-science community (it is good enough to have displaced UNIX **troff**, the other favored formatter, even at many UNIX installations). TEX fans insist on the correct (guttural) pronunciation, and the correct spelling (all caps, squished together, with the E depressed below the baseline; the mixed-case 'TeX' is considered an acceptable kluge on ASCII-only devices). Fans like to proliferate names from the word 'TEX' — such as TEXnician (TEX user), TEXhacker (TEX programmer), TEXmaster (competent TEX programmer), TEXhax, and TEXnique. [This book was typeset in TEX. — ESR]

Knuth began TEX because he had become annoyed at the declining quality of the typesetting in volumes I–III of his monumental *Art of Computer Programming* (see **Knuth**, also **bible**). In a manifestation of the typical hackish urge to solve the problem at hand once and for all, he began to design his own typesetting language. He thought he would finish it on his sabbatical in 1978; he was wrong by only about 8 years. The language was finally frozen around 1985, but volume IV of *The Art of Computer Programming* has yet to appear as of mid-1993. The impact and influence of TEX's design has been such that nobody minds this very much. Many grand hackish projects have started as a bit of **toolsmith**ing on the way to something else; Knuth's diversion was simply on a grander scale than most.

TEX has also been a noteworthy example of free, shared, but high-quality software. Knuth used to offer monetary awards to people who found and reported bugs in it; as the years wore on and the few remaining bugs were fixed (and new ones even harder to find), the bribe went up. Though well-written, TEX is so large (and so full of cutting edge technique) that it is said to have unearthed at least one bug in every Pascal system it has been compiled with.

text n. 1. [techspeak] Executable code, esp. a 'pure code' portion shared between multiple instances of a program running in a multitasking OS. Compare **English**. 2. Textual material in the mainstream sense; data in ordinary **ASCII** or **EBCDIC** representation (see **flat-ASCII**). "Those are text files; you can review them using the editor." These two contradictory senses confuse hackers, too.

thanks in advance [USENET] Conventional net.politeness ending a posted request for information or assistance. Sometimes written 'advTHANKSance' or 'aTdHvAaNnKcSe' or abbreviated 'TIA'. See **net.-**, **netiquette**.

That's not a bug, that's a feature! The **canonical** first parry in a debate about a purported bug. The complainant, if unconvinced, is likely to retort that the bug is then at best a **misfeature**. See also **feature**.

the X that can be Y is not the true X Yet another instance of hackerdom's peculiar attraction to mystical references — a common humorous way of making exclusive statements about a class of things. The template is from the *Tao te Ching*: "The Tao which can be spoken of is not the true Tao." The implication is often that the X is a mystery accessible only to the enlightened. See the **trampoline** entry for an example, and compare **has the X nature**.

theology n. 1. Ironically or humorously used to refer to **religious issues**. 2. Technical fine points of an abstruse nature, esp. those where the resolution is of theoretical interest but is relatively **marginal** with respect to actual use of a design or system. Used esp. around software issues with a heavy AI or language-design component, such as the smart-data vs. smart-programs dispute in AI.

theory n. The consensus, idea, plan, story, or set of rules that is currently being used to inform a behavior. This usage is a generalization and (deliberate) abuse of the technical meaning. "What's the theory on fixing this TECO loss?" "What's the theory on dinner tonight?" ("Chinatown, I guess.") "What's the current theory on letting lusers on during the day?" "The theory behind this change is to fix the following well-known screw. . . ."

thinko */thing´koh/* [by analogy with 'typo'] n. A momentary, correctable glitch in mental processing, especially one involving recall of information learned by rote; a bubble in the stream of consciousness. Syn. **braino**; see also **brain fart**. Compare **mouso**.

This can't happen Less clipped variant of **can't happen**.

This time, for sure! excl. Ritual affirmation frequently uttered during protracted debugging sessions involving numerous small obstacles (e.g., attempts to bring up a UUCP connection). For the proper effect, this must be uttered in a fruity imitation of Bullwinkle J. Moose. Also heard: "Hey, Rocky! Watch me pull a rabbit out of my hat!" The **canonical** response is, of course, "But that trick *never* works!" See **Humor, Hacker**.

thrash vi. To move wildly or violently, without accomplishing anything useful. Paging or swapping systems that are overloaded waste most of their time moving data into and out of core (rather than performing useful computation) and are therefore said to thrash. Someone who keeps changing his mind (esp. about what to work on next) is said to be thrashing. A person frantically trying to execute too many tasks at once (and not spending enough time on any single task) may also be described as thrashing. Compare **multitask.**

thread n. [USENET, GEnie, CompuServe] Common abbreviation of *topic thread*, a more or less continuous chain of postings on a single topic. To *follow a thread* is to read a series of USENET postings sharing a common subject or (more correctly) which are connected by Reference headers. The better newsreaders can present news in thread order automatically.

three-finger salute n. Syn. **Vulcan nerve pinch**.

thud n. 1. Yet another **metasyntactic variable** (see **foo**). It is reported that at CMU from the mid-1970s the canonical series of these was 'foo', 'bar', 'thud', 'blat'. 2. Rare term for the hash character, '#' (ASCII 0100011). See **ASCII** for other synonyms.

thumb n. The slider on a window-system scrollbar. So called because moving it allows you to browse through the contents of a text window in a way analogous to thumbing through a book.

thunk */thuhnk/* n. 1. "A piece of coding which provides an address", according to P. Z. Ingerman, who invented thunks in 1961 as a way of binding actual parameters to their formal definitions in Algol-60 procedure calls. If a procedure is called with an expression in the place of a formal parameter, the compiler generates a thunk which computes the expression and leaves the address of the result in some standard location. 2. Later generalized into: an expression, frozen together with its environment, for later evaluation if and when needed (similar to what in techspeak is called a 'closure'). The process of unfreezing these thunks is called 'forcing'. 3. A **stubroutine**, in an overlay programming environment, that loads and jumps to the correct overlay. Compare **trampoline**. 4. People and activities scheduled in a thunklike manner. "It occurred to me the other day that I am rather accurately modeled by a thunk — I frequently need to be forced to completion." — paraphrased from a **plan file**.

Historical note: There are a couple of onomatopoeic myths circulating about the origin of this term. The most common is that it is the sound made by data hitting the stack; another holds that the sound is that of the data hitting an accumulator. Yet another suggests that it is the sound of the expression being unfrozen at argument-evaluation time. In fact, according to the inventors, it was coined after they realized (in the wee hours after hours of discussion) that the type of an argument in Algol-60 could be figured out in advance with a little compile-time thought, simplifying the evaluation machinery. In other words, it had 'already been thought of'; thus it was christened a *thunk*, which is "the past tense of 'think' at two in the morning".

tick n. 1. A **jiffy** (sense 1). 2. In simulations, the discrete unit of time that passes between iterations of the simulation mechanism. In AI applications, this amount of time is often left unspecified, since the only constraint of interest is the ordering of events. This sort of AI simulation is often pejoratively referred to as *tick-tick-tick* simulation, especially when the issue of simultaneity of events with long, independent chains of causes is **handwaved**. 3. In the FORTH language, a single quote character.

tick-list features [Acorn Computers] n. Features in software or hardware that customers insist on but never use (calculators in desktop TSRs and that sort of thing). The American equivalent would be *checklist features*, but this jargon sense of the phrase has not been reported.

tickle a bug vt. To cause a normally hidden bug to manifest itself through some known series of inputs or operations. "You can tickle the bug in the Paradise VGA card's highlight handling by trying to set bright yellow reverse video."

tiger team [U.S. military jargon] n. 1. Originally, a team whose purpose is to penetrate security, and thus test security measures. These people are paid professionals who do hacker-type tricks, e.g., leave cardboard signs saying "bomb" in critical defense installations, hand-lettered notes saying "Your codebooks have been stolen" (they usually haven't been) inside safes, etc. After a successful penetration, some high-ranking security type shows up the next morning for a 'security review' and finds the sign, note, etc., and all hell breaks loose. Serious successes of tiger teams sometimes lead to early retirement for base commanders and security officers (see the **patch** entry for an example). 2. Recently, and more generally, any official inspection team or special **firefighting** group called in to look at a problem.

A subset of tiger teams are professional **crackers**, testing the security of military computer installations by attempting remote attacks via networks or supposedly 'secure' comm channels. Some of their escapades, if declassified, would probably rank among the greatest hacks of all times. The term has been adopted in commercial computer-security circles in this more specific sense.

time bomb n. A subspecies of **logic bomb** that is triggered by reaching some preset time, either once or periodically. There are numerous legends about time bombs set up by programmers in their employers' machines, to go off if the programmer is fired or laid off and is not present to perform the appropriate suppressing action periodically.

Interestingly, the only such incident for which we have been pointed to documentary evidence took place in the Soviet Union in 1986! A disgruntled programmer at the Volga Automobile Plant (where the Fiat clones called Ladas were manufactured) planted a time bomb which, a week after he'd left on vacation, stopped the entire main assembly line for a day. The case attracted lots of attention in the Soviet Union because it was the first cracking case to make it to court there. The perpetrator got 3 years in jail.

time sink [poss. by analogy with 'heat sink' or 'current sink'] n. A project that consumes unbounded amounts of time.

time T */ti:m T/* n. 1. An unspecified but usually well-understood time, often used in conjunction with a later time $T + 1$. "We'll meet on campus at time T or at Louie's at time $T + 1$" means, in the context of going out for dinner: "We can meet on campus and go to Louie's, or we can meet at Louie's itself a bit later." (Louie's was a Chinese restaurant in Palo Alto that was a favorite with hackers.) Had the number 30 been used instead of the number 1, it would have implied that the travel time from campus to Louie's is 30 minutes; whatever time T is (and that hasn't been decided on yet), you can meet half an hour later at Louie's than you could on campus and end up eating at the same time. See also **since time T equals minus infinity**.

times-or-divided-by [by analogy with 'plus-or-minus'] quant. Term occasionally used when describing the uncertainty associated with a scheduling estimate, for either humorous or brutally honest effect. For a software project, the scheduling uncertainty factor is usually at least 2.

tip of the ice-cube [IBM] n. The visible part of something small and insignificant. Used as an ironic comment in situations where 'tip of the iceberg' might be appropriate if the subject were at all important.

tired iron [IBM] n. Hardware that is perfectly functional but far enough behind the state of the art to have been superseded by new products, presumably with sufficient improvement in bang-per-buck that the old stuff is starting to look a bit like a **dinosaur**.

tits on a keyboard n. Small bumps on certain keycaps to keep touch-typists registered (usually on the '`5`' of a numeric keypad, and on the '`F`' and '`J`' of a **QWERTY** keyboard; but the Mac, perverse as usual, has them on the '`D`' and '`K`' keys).

TLA */T-L-A/* [Three-Letter Acronym] n. 1. Self-describing abbreviation for a species with which computing terminology is infested. 2. Any confusing acronym. Examples include MCA, FTP, SNA, CPU, MMU, SCCS, DMU, FPU, NNTP, TLA. People who like this looser usage argue that not all TLAs have three letters, just as not all four-letter words have four letters. One also hears of 'ETLA' (Extended Three-Letter Acronym, pronounced */ee tee el ay/*) being used to describe four-letter acronyms. The term 'SFLA' (Stupid Four-Letter Acronym) has also been reported. See also **YABA**.

The self-effacing phrase "TDM TLA" (Too Damn Many . . .) is often used to bemoan the plethora of TLAs in use. In 1989, a random of the journalistic persuasion asked hacker Paul Boutin "What do you think will be the biggest problem in computing in the 90s?" Paul's straight-faced response: "There are only 17,000 three-letter acronyms." (To be exact, there are $26^3 = 17{,}576$.)

TMRC */tmerk'/* n. The Tech Model Railroad Club at MIT, one of the well-springs of hacker culture. The 1959 *Dictionary of the TMRC Language* compiled by Peter Samson included several terms that became basics of the hackish vocabulary (see esp. **foo**, **mung**, and **frob**).

By 1962, TMRC's legendary layout was already a marvel of complexity (and has grown in the thirty years since; all the features described here are still present). The control system alone featured about 1200 relays. There were **scram switch**es located at numerous places around the room that could be thwacked if something undesirable was about to occur, such as a train going full-bore at an obstruction. Another feature of the system was a digital clock on the dispatch board, which was itself something of a wonder in those bygone days before cheap LEDS and seven-segment displays. When someone hit a scram switch the clock stopped and the display was replaced with the word 'FOO'; at TMRC the scram switches are therefore called *foo switches*.

Steven Levy, in his book *Hackers* (see the Bibliography in Appendix C), gives a stimulating account of those early years. TMRC's Power and Signals group included most of the early PDP-1 hackers and the people who later bacame the core of the MIT AI Lab staff. Thirty years later that connection is still very much alive, and this lexicon accordingly includes a number of entries from a recent revision of the TMRC dictionary.

TMRCie */tmerk´ee/,* [MIT] n. A denizen of **TMRC**.

to a first approximation 1. [techspeak] When one is doing certain numerical computations, an approximate solution may be computed by any of several heuristic methods, then refined to a final value. By using the starting point of a first approximation of the answer, one can write an algorithm that converges more quickly to the correct result. 2. In jargon, a preface to any comment that indicates that the comment is only approximately true. The remark "To a first approximation, I feel good" might indicate that deeper questioning would reveal that not all is perfect (e.g., a nagging cough still remains after an illness).

to a zeroth approximation [from 'to a first approximation'] A *really* sloppy approximation; a wild guess. Compare **social science number**.

toast 1. n. Any completely inoperable system or component, esp. one that has just crashed and burned: "Uh, oh . . . I think the serial board is toast." 2. vt. To cause a system to crash accidentally, especially in a manner that requires manual rebooting. "Rick just toasted the **firewall machine** again." Compare **frie**.

toaster n. 1. The archetypal really stupid application for an embedded microprocessor controller; often used in comments that imply that a scheme is inappropriate technology (but see **elevator controller**). "**DWIM** for an assembler? That'd be as silly as running UNIX on your toaster!" 2. A very, very dumb computer. "You could run this program on any dumb toaster." See **bitty box**, **Get a real computer!**, **toy**, **beige toaster**. 3. A Macintosh, esp. the Classic Mac. Some hold that this is implied by sense 2. 4. A peripheral device. "I bought my box without toasters, but since then I've added two boards and a second disk drive."

toeprint n. A **footprint** of especially small size.

toggle vt. To change a **bit** from whatever state it is in to the other state;

to change from 1 to 0 or from 0 to 1. This comes from 'toggle switches', such as standard light switches, though the word *toggle* actually refers to the mechanism that keeps the switch in the position to which it is flipped rather than to the fact that the switch has two positions. There are four things you can do to a bit: set it (force it to be 1), clear (or zero) it, leave it alone, or toggle it. (Mathematically, one would say that there are four distinct boolean-valued functions of one boolean argument, but saying that is much less fun than talking about toggling bits.)

tool 1. n. A program used primarily to create, manipulate, modify, or analyze other programs, such as a compiler or an editor or a cross-referencing program. Oppose **app, operating system**. 2. [UNIX] An application program with a simple, 'transparent' (typically text-stream) interface designed specifically to be used in programmed combination with other tools (see **filter**, **plumbing**). 3. [MIT: general to students there] vi. To work; to study (connotes tedium). The TMRC Dictionary defined this as "to set one's brain to the grindstone". See **hack**. 4. [MIT] n. A student who studies too much and hacks too little. (MIT's student humor magazine rejoices in the name *Tool and Die*.)

toolsmith n. The software equivalent of a tool-and-die specialist; one who specializes in making the **tool**s with which other programmers create applications. Many hackers consider this more fun than applications per se; to understand why, see **uninteresting**. Jon Bentley, in the "Bumper-Sticker Computer Science" chapter of his book *More Programming Pearls*, quotes Dick Sites from DEC as saying "I'd rather write programs to write programs than write programs".

topic drift n. Term used on GEnie, USENET and other electronic fora to describe the tendency of a **thread** to drift away from the original subject of discussion (and thus, from the Subject header of the originating message), or the results of that tendency. Often used in gentle reminders that the discussion has strayed off any useful track. "I think we started with a question about Niven's last book, but we've ended up discussing the sexual habits of the common marmoset. Now *that's* topic drift!"

topic group n. Syn. **forum**.

TOPS-10 */tops-ten/* n. DEC's proprietary OS for the fabled **PDP-10** machines, long a favorite of hackers but now effectively extinct. A fountain of hacker folklore; see Appendix A. See also **ITS**, **TOPS-20**, **TWENEX**, **VMS**, **operating system**. TOPS-10 was sometimes called BOTS-10 (from 'bottoms-ten') as a comment on the inappropriateness of describing it as the top of anything.

TOPS-20 */tops-twen´tee/* n. See **TWENEX**.

toto */toh-toh´/* n. Reportedy the default scratch file name among French-speaking programmers — in other words, a francophone **foo**. It is reported that the phonetic mutations "titi", "tata", and "tutu" canonically follow *toto*, analogously to **bar**, **baz** and **quux** in English.

tourist [ITS] n. A guest on the system, especially one who generally logs in over a network from a remote location for **comm mode**, email, games, and other trivial purposes. One step below **luser**. Hackers often spell this **turist**, perhaps by some sort of tenuous analogy with **luser** (this also expresses the ITS culture's penchant for six-letterisms). Compare **twink**, **read-only user**.

tourist information n. Information in an on-line display that is not immediately useful, but contributes to a viewer's gestalt of what's going on with the software or hardware behind it. Whether a given piece of info falls in this category depends partly on what the user is looking for at any given time. The 'bytes free' information at the bottom of an MS-DOS `dir` display is tourist information; so (most of the time) is the TIME information in a UNIX `ps(1)` display.

touristic adj. Having the quality of a **tourist**. Often used as a pejorative, as in 'losing touristic scum'. Often spelled 'turistic' or 'turistik', so that phrase might be more properly rendered 'lusing turistic scum'.

toy n. A computer system; always used with qualifiers. 1. *nice toy*: One that supports the speaker's hacking style adequately. 2. *just a toy*: A machine that yields insufficient **computron**s for the speaker's preferred uses. This is not condemnatory, as is **bitty box**; toys can at least be fun. It is also strongly conditioned by one's expectations; Cray XMP users sometimes consider the Cray-1 a *toy*, and certainly all RISC boxes and mainframes are toys by their standards. See also **Get a real computer!**.

toy language n. A language useful for instructional purposes or as a proof-of-concept for some aspect of computer-science theory, but inadequate for general-purpose programming. **Bad Thing**s can result when a toy language is promoted as a general purpose solution for programming (see **bondage-and-discipline language**); the classic example is **Pascal**. Several moderately well-known formalisms for conceptual tasks such as programming Turing machines also qualify as toy languages in a less negative sense. See also **MFTL**.

toy problem [AI] n. A deliberately oversimplified case of a challenging problem used to investigate, prototype, or test algorithms for a real problem. Sometimes used pejoratively. See also **gedanken**, **toy program**.

toy program n. 1. One that can be readily comprehended; hence, a trivial program (compare **noddy**). 2. One for which the effort of initial coding dominates the costs through its life cycle. See also **noddy**.

trampoline n. An incredibly **hairy** technique, found in some **HLL** and program-overlay implementations (e.g., on the Macintosh), that involves on-the-fly generation of small executable (and, likely as not, self-modifying) code objects to do indirection between code sections. These pieces of **live data** are called *trampolines*. Trampolines are notoriously difficult to understand in action; in fact, it is said by those who use this term that the trampoline that doesn't bend your brain is not the true trampoline. See also **snap**.

trap 1. n. A program interrupt, usually an interrupt caused by some exceptional situation in the user program. In most cases, the OS performs some action, then returns control to the program. 2. vi. To cause a trap. "These instructions trap to the monitor." Also used transitively to indicate the cause of the trap. "The monitor traps all input/output instructions."

This term is associated with assembler programming ('interrupt' or 'exception' is more common among **HLL** programmers) and appears to be fading into history among programmers as the role of assembler continues to shrink. However, it is still important to computer architects and systems hackers (see **system**, sense 1), who use it to distinguish deterministically repeatable exceptions from timing-dependent ones (such as I/O interrupts).

trap door alt. *trapdoor* n. 1. Syn. **back door** — a **Bad Thing**. 2. [techspeak] A *trap-door function* is one which is easy to compute but very difficult to compute the inverse of. Such functions are **Good Thing**s with important applications in cryptography, specifically in the construction of public-key cryptosystems.

trash vt. To destroy the contents of (said of a data structure). The most common of the family of near-synonyms including **mung**, **mangle**, and **scribble**.

trawl v. To sift through large volumes of data (e.g., USENET postings, FTP archives, or the Jargon File) looking for something of interest.

tree-killer [Sun] n. 1. A printer. 2. A person who wastes paper. This epithet should be interpreted in a broad sense; 'wasting paper' includes the production of **spiffy** but **content-free** documents. Thus, most **suits** are tree-killers. The negative loading of this term may reflect the epithet 'tree-killer' applied by Treebeard the Ent to the Orcs in J.R.R. Tolkien's *Lord of the Rings* (see also **elvish**, **elder days**).

treeware n. Printouts, books, and other information media made from pulped dead trees. Compare **tree-killer**, see **documentation**.

trit */trit/* [by analogy with 'bit'] n. One base-3 digit; the amount of information conveyed by a selection among one of three equally likely outcomes (see also **bit**). Trits arise, for example, in the context of a **flag** that should actually be able to assume *three* values — such as yes, no, or unknown. Trits are sometimes jokingly called *3-state bits*. A trit may be semi-seriously referred to as *a bit and a half*, although it is linearly equivalent to 1.5849625 bits (that is, $\log_2(3)$ bits).

trivial adj. 1. Too simple to bother detailing. 2. Not worth the speaker's time. 3. Complex, but solvable by methods so well known that anyone not utterly **cretinous** would have thought of them already. 4. Any problem one has already solved (some claim that hackish *trivial* usually evaluates to 'I've seen it before'). Hackers' notions of triviality may be quite at variance with those of non-hackers. See **nontrivial**, **uninteresting**.

troff */T´rof/* or */trof/* [UNIX] n. The gray eminence of UNIX text processing; a formatting and phototypesetting program, written originally in PDP-11 assembler and then in barely-structured early C by the late Joseph Ossanna, modeled after the earlier ROFF which was in turn modeled after Multics' RUNOFF by Jerome Saltzer (*that* name came from the expression "to run off a copy"). A companion program, **nroff**, formats output for terminals and line printers.

In 1979, Brian Kernighan modified `troff` so that it could drive phototypesetters other than the Graphic Systems CAT. His paper describing that work ("A Typesetter-independent troff," AT&T CSTR #97) explains troff's durability. After discussing the program's "obvious deficiencies — a rebarbative input syntax, mysterious and undocumented properties in some areas, and a voracious appetite for computer resources" and noting the ugliness and extreme hairiness of the code and internals, Kernighan concludes:

> None of these remarks should be taken as denigrating Ossanna's accomplishment with TROFF. It has proven a remarkably robust tool, taking unbelievable abuse from a variety of preprocessors and being forced into uses that were never conceived of in the original design, all with considerable grace under fire.

The success of **TEX** and desktop publishing systems have reduced `troff`'s relative importance, but this tribute perfectly captures the strengths that secured `troff` a place in hacker folklore; indeed, it could be taken more generally as an indication of those qualities of good programs that, in the long run, hackers most admire.

troglodyte [Commodore] n. 1. A hacker who never leaves his cubicle. The term *Gnoll* (from Dungeons & Dragons) is also reported. 2. A curmudgeon attached to an obsolescent computing environment. The combination *ITS troglodyte* was flung around some during the USENET and email wringle-wrangle attending the 2.x.x revision of the Jargon File; at least one of the people it was intended to describe adopted it with pride.

troglodyte mode [Rice University] n. Programming with the lights turned off, sunglasses on, and the terminal inverted (black on white) because you've been up for so many days straight that your eyes hurt (see **raster burn**). Loud music blaring from a stereo stacked in the corner is optional but recommended. See **larval stage**, **hack mode**.

Trojan horse [coined by MIT-hacker-turned-NSA-spook Dan Edwards] n. A malicious, security-breaking program that is disguised as something benign, such as a directory lister, archiver, game, or (in one notorious 1990 case on the Mac) a program to find and destroy viruses! See **back door**, **virus**, **worm**, **phage**, **mockingbird**.

tron [NRL, CMU; prob. fr. the movie *Tron*] v. To become inaccessible except via email or `talk(1)`, especially when one is normally available via telephone or in person. Frequently used in the past tense, as in: "Ran seems to have tronned on us this week" or "Gee, Ran, glad you were able to un-tron yourself". One may also speak of *tron mode*; compare **spod**.

true-hacker [analogy with 'trufan' from SF fandom] n. One who exemplifies the primary values of hacker culture, esp. competence and helpfulness to other hackers. A high compliment. "He spent 6 hours helping me bring up UUCP and netnews on my FOOBAR 4000 last week — manifestly the act of a true-hacker." Compare **demigod**, oppose **munchkin**.

tty */T-T-Y/* [UNIX], */tit'ee/* [ITS, but some UNIX people say it this way as well; this pronunciation is not considered to have sexual undertones] n. 1. A terminal of the teletype variety, characterized by a noisy mechanical printer, a very limited character set, and poor print quality. Usage: antiquated (like the TTYs themselves). See also **bit-paired keyboard**. 2. [especially UNIX] Any terminal at all; sometimes used to refer to the particular terminal controlling a given job. 3. [UNIX] Any serial port, whether or not the device connected to it is a terminal; so called because under UNIX such devices have names of the form tty*. Ambiguity between senses 2 and 3 is common but seldom bothersome.

tube 1. n. A CRT terminal. Never used in the mainstream sense of TV; real hackers don't watch TV, except for Loony Toons, Rocky & Bullwinkle, Trek Classic, the Simpsons, and the occasional cheesy old swashbuckler movie (see Appendix B). 2. [IBM] To send a copy of something to someone else's terminal. "Tube me that note?"

tube time n. Time spent at a terminal or console. More inclusive than hacking time; commonly used in discussions of what parts of one's environment one uses most heavily. "I find I'm spending too much of my tube time reading mail since I started this revision."

tunafish n. In hackish lore, refers to the mutated punchline of an age-old joke to be found at the bottom of the manual pages of `tunefs(8)` in the original **BSD** 4.2 distribution. The joke was removed in later releases once commercial sites started using 4.2. Tunefs relates to the 'tuning' of file-system parameters for optimum performance, and at the bottom of a few pages of wizardly inscriptions was a 'BUGS' section consisting of the line "You can tune a file system, but you can't tunafish". Variants of this can be seen in other BSD versions, though it has been excised from some versions by humorless management **droid**s. The [nt]roff source for SunOS 4.1.1 contains a comment apparently designed to prevent this: "Take this out and a Unix Demon will dog your steps from now until the `time_t`'s wrap around."

tune [from automotive or musical usage] vt. To optimize a program or system for a particular environment, esp. by adjusting numerical parameters designed as **hooks** for tuning, e.g., by changing `#define` lines in C. One may *tune for time* (fastest execution), *tune for space* (least memory use), or *tune for configuration* (most efficient use of hardware). See **bum**, **hot spot**, **hand-hacking**.

turbo nerd n. See **computer geek**.

Turing tar-pit n. 1. A place where anything is possible but nothing of interest is practical. Alan Turing helped lay the foundations of computer science by showing that all machines and languages capable of expressing a certain very primitive set of operations are logically equivalent in the kinds of computations they can carry out, and in principle have capabilities that differ only in speed from those of the most powerful and elegantly designed computers. However, no machine or language exactly matching Turing's primitive set has ever been built (other than possibly as a classroom exercise), because it would be horribly slow and far too painful to use. A *Turing tar-pit* is any computer language or other tool that shares this property. That is, it's theoretically universal — but in practice, the harder you struggle to get any real work done, the deeper its inadequacies suck you in. Compare **bondage-and-discipline language**. 2. The perennial **holy wars** over whether language A or B is the "most powerful".

turist */too´rist/* n. Var. sp. of **tourist**, q.v. Also in adjectival form, 'turistic'. Poss. influenced by **luser** and 'Turing'.

tweak vt. 1. To change slightly, usually in reference to a value. Also used synonymously with **twiddle**. If a program is almost correct, rather than figure out the precise problem you might just keep tweaking it until it works. See **frobnicate** and **fudge factor**; also see **shotgun debugging**. 2. To **tune** or **bum** a program; preferred usage in the U.K.

tweeter [University of Waterloo] n. Syn. **perf**, **chad** (sense 1). This term (like **woofer**) has been in use at Waterloo since 1972 but is elsewhere unknown. In audio jargon, the word refers to the treble speaker(s) on a hi-fi.

TWENEX */twe´neks/* n. The TOPS-20 operating system by DEC — the second proprietary OS for the PDP-10 — preferred by most PDP-10 hackers over TOPS-10 (that is, by those who were not **ITS** or **WAITS** partisans).

TOPS-20 began in 1969 as Bolt, Beranek & Newman's TENEX operating system using special paging hardware. By the early 1970s, almost all of the systems on the ARPANET ran TENEX. DEC purchased the rights to TENEX from BBN and began work to make it their own. The first in-house code name for the operating system was VIROS (VIRtual memory Operating System); when customers started asking questions, the name was changed to SNARK so DEC could truthfully deny that there was any project called VIROS. When the name SNARK became known, the name was briefly reversed to become KRANS; this was quickly abandoned when someone objected that *krans* meant 'funeral wreath' in Swedish (though some Swedish speakers have since said it means simply 'wreath'; this part of the story may be apocryphal). Ultimately DEC picked TOPS-20 as the name of the operating system, and it was as TOPS-20 that it was marketed. The hacker community, mindful of its origins, quickly dubbed it TWENEX (a contraction of 'twenty TENEX'), even though by this point very little of the original TENEX code remained (analogously to the differences between AT&T V6 UNIX and BSD). DEC people cringed when they heard "TWENEX", but the term caught on nevertheless (the written abbreviation '20x' was also used). TWENEX was successful and very popular; in fact, there was a period in the early 1980s when it commanded as fervent a culture of partisans as UNIX or ITS — but DEC's decision to scrap all the internal rivals to the VAX architecture and its relatively stodgy VMS OS killed the DEC-20 and put a sad end to TWENEX's brief day in the sun. DEC attempted to convince TOPS-20 users to convert to **VMS**, but instead, by the late 1980s, most of the TOPS-20 hackers had migrated to UNIX.

twiddle n. 1. Tilde (ASCII 1111110, '~'). Also called *squiggle*, *sqiggle* (sic — pronounced */skig´l/*), and *twaddle*, but twiddle is the most common term. 2. A small and insignificant change to a program. Usually fixes one bug and generates several new ones (see also **shotgun debugging**). 3. vt. To change something in a small way. Bits, for example, are often twiddled. Twiddling a switch or knob implies much less sense of purpose than toggling or tweaking it; see **frobnicate**. To speak of twiddling a bit connotes aimlessness, and at best doesn't specify what you're doing to the bit; 'toggling a bit' has a more specific meaning (see **bit twiddling**, **toggle**).

twilight zone [IRC] n. Notionally, the area of cyberspace where **IRC** operators live. An **op** is said to have a "connection to the twilight zone".

twink */twink/* [UCSC] n. Equivalent to **read-only user**. Also reported on the USENET group *soc.motss*; may derive from gay slang for a cute young thing with nothing upstairs (compare mainstream 'chick').

twirling baton [PLATO] n. The overstrike sequence -/|\-/|\- which produces an animated twirling baton. If you output it with a single backspace between characters, the baton spins in place. If you output the sequence BS SP between characters, the baton spins from left to right. If you output BS SP BS BS between characters, the batton spins from right to left.

The twirling baton was a popular component of animated signature files on the pioneering PLATO educational timesharing system. The `archie` Internet service is perhaps the best-known baton program today; it uses the twirling baton as an idler indicating that the program is working on a query.

two pi quant. The number of years it takes to finish one's thesis. Occurs in stories in the following form: "He started on his thesis; 2 pi years later . . . "

two-to-the-N quant. An amount much larger than **N** but smaller than **infinity**. "I have 2-to-the-*N* things to do before I can go out for lunch" means you probably won't show up.

twonkie */twon´kee/* n. The software equivalent of a Twinkie (a variety of sugar-loaded junk food, or (in gay slang) the male equivalent of 'chick'); a useless 'feature' added to look sexy and placate a **marketroid** (compare **Saturday-night special**). The term may also be related to "The Twonky", title menace of a classic SF short story by Lewis Padgett (Henry Kuttner and C. L. Moore), first published in the September 1942 *Astounding Science Fiction* and subsequently much anthologized.

= U =

UBD */U-B-D/* [abbreviation for 'User Brain Damage'] An abbreviation used to close out trouble reports obviously due to utter cluelessness on the user's part. Compare **pilot error**; oppose **PBD**; see also **brain-damaged**.

UN*X n. Used to refer to the UNIX operating system (a trademark of AT&T) in writing, but avoiding the need for the ugly (TM) typography (see also **(TM)**). Also used to refer to any or all varieties of Unixoid operating systems. Ironically, lawyers now say that the requirement for the TM-postfix has no legal force, but the asterisk usage is entrenched anyhow. It has been suggested that there may be a psychological connection to practice in certain religions (especially Judaism) in which the name of the deity is never written out in full, e.g., 'YHWH' or 'G–d' is used. See also **glob**.

undefined external reference excl. [UNIX] A message from UNIX's linker. Used in speech to flag loose ends or dangling references in an argument or discussion.

under the hood [hot-rodder talk] prep. 1. Used to introduce the underlying implementation of a product (hardware, software, or idea). Implies that the implementation is not intuitively obvious from the appearance, but the speaker is about to enable the listener to **grok** it. "Let's now look under the hood to see how. . . ." 2. Can also imply that the implementation is much simpler than the appearance would indicate: "Under the hood, we are just fork/execing the shell." 3. Inside a chassis, as in "Under the hood, this baby has a 40MHz 68030!"

undocumented feature n. See **feature**.

uninteresting adj. 1. Said of a problem that, although **nontrivial**, can be solved simply by throwing sufficient resources at it. 2. Also said of problems for which a solution would neither advance the state of the art nor be fun to design and code.

Hackers regard uninteresting problems as intolerable wastes of time, to be solved (if at all) by lesser mortals. *Real* hackers (see **toolsmith**) generalize uninteresting problems enough to make them interesting and solve them — thus solving the original problem as a special case (and, it must be admitted, occasionally turning a molehill into a mountain, or a mountain into a tectonic plate). See **WOMBAT**, **SMOP**; compare **toy problem**, oppose **interesting**.

UNIX */yoo´niks/* [In the authors' words, "A weak pun on Multics"] n. (also 'Unix') An interactive time-sharing system invented in 1969 by Ken Thompson after Bell Labs left the Multics project, originally so he could play games on his scavenged PDP-7. Dennis Ritchie, the inventor of C, is considered a co-author of the system. The turning point in UNIX's history came when it was reimplemented almost entirely in C during 1972–1974, making it the first source-portable OS. UNIX subsequently underwent mutations and expansions at the hands of many different people, resulting in a uniquely flexible and developer-friendly environment. By 1991, UNIX had become the most widely used multiuser general-purpose operating system in the world. Many people consider this the most important victory yet of hackerdom over industry opposition (but see **UNIX weenie** and **UNIX conspiracy** for an opposing point of view). See **Version 7**, **BSD**, **USG UNIX**.

UNIX brain damage n. Something that has to be done to break a network program (typically a mailer) on a non-UNIX system so that it will interoperate with UNIX systems. The hack may qualify as *UNIX brain damage* if the program conforms to published standards and the UNIX program in question does not. UNIX brain damage happens because it is much easier for other (minority) systems to change their ways to match non-conforming behavior than it is to change all the hundreds of thousands of UNIX systems out there.

An example of UNIX brain damage is a **kluge** in a mail server to recognize bare line feed (the UNIX newline) as an equivalent form to the Internet standard newline, which is a carriage return followed by a line feed. Such things can make even a hardened **jock** weep.

UNIX conspiracy [ITS] n. According to a conspiracy theory long popular among **ITS** and **TOPS-20** fans, UNIX's growth is the result of a plot, hatched during the 1970s at Bell Labs, whose intent was to hobble AT&T's competitors by making them dependent upon a system whose future evolution was to be under AT&T's control. This would be accomplished by disseminating an operating system that is apparently inexpensive and easily portable, but also relatively unreliable and insecure (so as to require continuing upgrades from AT&T). This theory was lent a substantial impetus in 1984 by the paper referenced in the **back door** entry.

In this view, UNIX was designed to be one of the first computer viruses (see **virus**) — but a virus spread to computers indirectly by people and market forces, rather than directly through disks and networks. Adherents of this 'UNIX virus' theory like to cite the fact that the well-known quotation "UNIX is snake oil" was uttered by DEC president Kenneth Olsen shortly before DEC began actively promoting its own family of UNIX workstations. (Olsen now claims to have been misquoted.)

UNIX weenie [ITS] n. 1. A derogatory play on 'UNIX wizard', common among hackers who use UNIX by necessity but would prefer alternatives. The implication is that although the person in question may consider mastery of UNIX arcana to be a wizardly skill, the only real skill involved is the ability to tolerate (and the bad taste to wallow in) the incoherence and needless complexity that is alleged to infest many UNIX programs. "This shell script tries to parse its arguments in 69 bletcherous ways. It must have been written by a real UNIX weenie." 2. A derogatory term for anyone who engages in uncritical praise of UNIX. Often appearing in the context "stupid UNIX weenie". See **Weenix**, **UNIX conspiracy**. See also **weenie**.

unixism n. A piece of code or a coding technique that depends on the protected multi-tasking environment with relatively low process-spawn overhead that exists on virtual-memory UNIX systems. Common **unixisms** include: gratuitous use of `fork(2)`; the assumption that certain undocumented but well-known features of UNIX libraries such as `stdio(3)` are supported elsewhere; reliance on **obscure** side-effects of system calls (use of `sleep(2)` with a 0 argument to clue the scheduler that you're willing to give up your time-slice, for example); the assumption that freshly allocated memory is zeroed; and the assumption that fragmentation problems won't arise from never `free()`ing memory. Compare **vaxocentrism**; see also **New Jersey**.

unleaded adj. Said of decaffeinated coffee, Diet Coke, and other imitation **programming fluids**. "Do you want regular or unleaded?" Appears to be widespread among programmers associated with the oil industry in Texas (and probably elsewhere). Usage: silly, and probably unintelligible to the next generation of hackers.

unswizzle v. See **swizzle**.

unwind the stack vi. 1. [techspeak] During the execution of a procedural language, one is said to *unwind the stack* from a called procedure up to a caller when one discards the stack frame and any number of frames above it, popping back up to the level of the given caller. In C this is done with `longjmp/setjmp`, in LISP with `throw/catch`. See also **smash the stack**. 2. People can unwind the stack as well, by quickly dealing with a bunch of problems: "Oh heck, let's do lunch. Just a second while I unwind my stack."

unwind-protect [MIT: from the name of a LISP operator] n. A task you must remember to perform before you leave a place or finish a project. "I have an unwind-protect to call my advisor."

up adj. 1. Working, in order. "The down escalator is up." Oppose **down**.

2. *bring up*: vt. To create a working version and start it. "They brought up a down system." 3. *come up* vi. To become ready for production use.

upload */uhp´lohd/* v. 1. [techspeak] To transfer programs or data over a digital communications link from a smaller or peripheral 'client' system to a larger or central 'host' one. A transfer in the other direction is, of course, called a **download** (but see the note about ground-to-space comm under that entry). 2. [speculatively] To move the essential patterns and algorithms that make up one's mind from one's brain into a computer. Those who are convinced that such patterns and algorithms capture the complete essence of the self view this prospect with pleasant anticipation.

upthread adv. Earlier in the discussion (see **thread**), i.e., 'above'. "As Joe pointed out upthread, . . . " See also **followup**.

urchin n. See **munchkin**.

USENET */yoos´net/* or */yooz´net/* [from 'Users' Network'] n. A distributed **bboard** (bulletin board) system supported mainly by UNIX machines. Originally implemented in 1979–1980 by Steve Bellovin, Jim Ellis, Tom Truscott, and Steve Daniel at Duke University, it has swiftly grown to become international in scope and is now probably the largest decentralized information utility in existence. As of early 1993, it hosts well over 1200 **newsgroup**s and an average of 40 megabytes (the equivalent of several thousand paper pages) of new technical articles, news, discussion, chatter, and **flamage** every day.

user n. 1. Someone doing 'real work' with the computer, using it as a means rather than an end. Someone who pays to use a computer. See **real user**. 2. A programmer who will believe anything you tell him. One who asks silly questions. [GLS observes: This is slightly unfair. It is true that users ask questions (of necessity). Sometimes they are thoughtful or deep. Very often they are annoying or downright stupid, apparently because the user failed to think for two seconds or look in the documentation before bothering the maintainer.] See **luser**. 3. Someone who uses a program from the outside, however skillfully, without getting into the internals of the program. One who reports bugs instead of just going ahead and fixing them.

The general theory behind this term is that there are two classes of people who work with a program: there are implementors (hackers) and **luser**s. The users are looked down on by hackers to some extent because they don't understand the full ramifications of the system in all its glory. (The few users who do are known as *real winners*.) The term is a relative one: a skilled hacker may be a user with respect to some program he himself does not hack. A LISP hacker might be one who maintains LISP or one who uses LISP (but with the skill of a hacker). A LISP user is one who uses LISP, whether skillfully or not. Thus there is some overlap between the two terms; the subtle distinctions must be resolved by context.

user-friendly adj. Programmer-hostile. Generally used by hackers in a critical tone, to describe systems that hold the user's hand so obsessively that they make it painful for the more experienced and knowledgeable to get any work done. See **menuitis**, **drool-proof paper**, **Macintrash**, **user-obsequious**.

user-obsequious adj. Emphatic form of **user-friendly**. Connotes a system so verbose, inflexible, and determinedly simple-minded that it is nearly unusable. "Design a system any fool can use and only a fool will want to use it." See **WIMP environment**, **Macintrash**.

USG UNIX */U-S-G yoo´niks/* n. Refers to AT&T UNIX commercial versions after **Version 7**, especially System III and System V releases 1, 2, and 3. So called because during most of the lifespan of those versions AT&T's support crew was called the 'UNIX Support Group'. See **BSD**, **UNIX**.

UTSL // [UNIX] n. On-line acronym for 'Use the Source, Luke' (a pun on Obi-Wan Kenobi's "Use the Force, Luke!" in *Star Wars*) — analogous to **RTFS** (sense 1), but more polite. This is a common way of suggesting that someone would be better off reading the source code that supports whatever feature is causing confusion, rather than making yet another futile pass through the manuals, or broadcasting questions on USENET that haven't attracted **wizard**s to answer them.

Once upon a time in **Elder Days**, everyone running UNIX had source. After 1978, AT&T's policy tightened up, so this objurgation was in theory appropriately directed only at associates of some outfit with a UNIX source license. In practice, bootlegs of UNIX source code (made precisely for reference purposes) were so ubiquitous that one could utter it at almost anyone on the network without concern.

Nowadays, free UNIX clones are becoming common enough that almost anyone can read source legally. The most widely distributed is probably Linux, with 386BSD (aka **jolix**) running second. Cheap commercial UNIXes with source such as BSD/386 are accelerating this trend.

UUCPNET n. The store-and-forward network consisting of all the world's connected UNIX machines (and others running some clone of the UUCP (UNIX-to-UNIX CoPy) software). Any machine reachable only via a **bang path** is on UUCPNET. See **network address**.

= V =

vadding */vad´ing/* [from VAD, a permutation of ADV (i.e., **ADVENT**), used to avoid a particular **admin**'s continual search-and-destroy sweeps for the game] n. A leisure-time activity of certain hackers involving the covert exploration of the 'secret' parts of large buildings — basements, roofs, freight elevators, maintenance crawlways, steam tunnels, and the like. A few go so far as to learn locksmithing in order to synthesize vadding keys. The verb is *to vad* (compare **phreaking**; see also **hack**, sense 9). This term dates from the late 1970s, before which such activity was simply called 'hacking'; the older usage is still prevalent at MIT.

The most extreme and dangerous form of vadding is *elevator rodeo*, a.k.a. *elevator surfing*, a sport played by wrasslin' down a thousand-pound elevator car with a 3-foot piece of string, and then exploiting this mastery in various stimulating ways (such as elevator hopping, shaft exploration, rat-racing, and the ever-popular drop experiments). Kids, don't try this at home! See also **hobbit** (sense 2).

vanilla [from the default flavor of ice cream in the U.S.] adj. Ordinary **flavor**, standard. When used of food, very often does not mean that the food is flavored with vanilla extract! For example, *vanilla wonton soup* means ordinary wonton soup, as opposed to hot-and-sour wonton soup. Applied to hardware and software, as in "Vanilla Version 7 UNIX can't run on a vanilla 11/34." Also used to orthogonalize chip nomenclature; for instance, a 74V00 means what TI calls a 7400, as distinct from a 74LS00, etc. This word differs from **canonical** in that the latter means 'default', whereas vanilla simply means 'ordinary'. For example, when hackers go on a **great-wall**, hot-and-sour wonton soup is the **canonical** wonton soup to get (because that is what most of them usually order) even though it isn't the vanilla wonton soup.

vannevar */van´ə-var/* n. A bogus technological prediction or a foredoomed engineering concept, esp. one that fails by implicitly assuming that technologies develop linearly, incrementally, and in isolation from one another when in fact the learning curve tends to be highly nonlinear, revolutions are common, and competition is the rule. The prototype was Vannevar Bush's prediction of 'electronic brains' the size of the Empire State Building with a Niagara-Falls-equivalent cooling system for their tubes and relays, a prediction made at a time when the semiconductor effect had already been demonstrated. Other famous vannevars have included magnetic-bubble memory, LISP machines, **videotex**, and a paper from the late 1970s that computed a purported ultimate limit on areal density for ICs that was in fact less than the routine densities of 5 years later.

vaporware */vay´pr-weir/* n. Products announced far in advance of any release (which may or may not actually take place). See also **brochureware**.

var */veir/* or */var/* n. Short for 'variable'. Compare **arg**, **param**.

VAX */vaks/* n. 1. [from Virtual Address eXtension] The most successful minicomputer design in industry history, possibly excepting its immediate ancestor, the PDP-11. Between its release in 1978 and its eclipse by **killer micros** after about 1986, the VAX was probably the hacker's favorite machine of them all, esp. after the 1982 release of 4.2 BSD UNIX (see **BSD**). Esp. noted for its large, assembler-programmer-friendly instruction set — an asset that became a liability after the RISC revolution. 2. A major brand of vacuum cleaner in Britain. Cited here because its alleged sales pitch, "Nothing sucks like a VAX!" became a sort of battle-cry of RISC partisans. It is even sometimes claimed that DEC actually entered a cross-licensing deal with the vacuum-Vax people that allowed them to market VAX computers in the U.K. in return for not challenging the vacuum cleaner trademark in the U.S.

It is sometimes claimed that this slogan was *not* actually used by the Vax vacuum-cleaner people, but was actually that of a rival brand called Electrolux (as in "Nothing sucks like . . . "). It has been reliably confirmed that Electrolux (a Swedish company) actually did use this slogan in the late 1960s; it has apparently become a classic example (used in textbooks) of the perils of not knowing the local idiom.

It appears, however, that the Vax people thought the slogan a sufficiently good idea to copy it. Several British hackers report that their promotions used it in 1986–1987, and we have one report from a New Zealander that the infamous slogan surfaced there in TV ads for the product as recently as 1992!

VAXectomy */vak-sek´tə-mee/* [by analogy with 'vasectomy'] n. A VAX removal. DEC's Microvaxen, especially, are much slower than newer RISC-based workstations such as the SPARC. Thus, if one knows one has a replacement coming, VAX removal can be cause for celebration.

VAXen */vak´sn/* [from 'oxen', perhaps influenced by 'vixen'] n. (alt. *vaxen*) The plural canonically used among hackers for the DEC VAX computers. "Our installation has four PDP-10s and twenty vaxen." See **boxen**.

vaxherd n. */vaks´herd/* [from 'oxherd'] A VAX operator.

vaxism */vak´sizm/* n. A piece of code that exhibits **vaxocentrism** in critical areas. Compare **PC-ism**, **unixism**.

vaxocentrism */vak`soh-sen´trizm/* [analogy with 'ethnocentrism'] n. A notional disease said to afflict C programmers who persist in coding according to certain assumptions that are valid (esp. under UNIX) on **VAXen** but false elsewhere. Among these are:

1. The assumption that dereferencing a null pointer is safe because it is all bits 0, and location 0 is readable and 0. Problem: this may instead cause an illegal-address trap on non-VAXen, and even on VAXen under OSes other than BSD UNIX. Usually this is an implicit assumption of sloppy code (forgetting to check the pointer before using it), rather than deliberate exploitation of a misfeature.
2. The assumption that characters are signed.
3. The assumption that a pointer to any one type can freely be cast into a pointer to any other type. A stronger form of this is the assumption that all pointers are the same size and format, which means you don't have to worry about getting the casts or types correct in calls. Problem: this fails on word-oriented machines or others with multiple pointer formats.
4. The assumption that the parameters of a routine are stored in memory, on a stack, contiguously, and in strictly ascending or descending order. Problem: this fails on many RISC architectures.
5. The assumption that pointer and integer types are the same size, and that pointers can be stuffed into integer variables (and vice-versa) and drawn back out without being truncated or mangled. Problem: this fails on segmented architectures or word-oriented machines with funny pointer formats.

6. The assumption that a data type of any size may begin at any byte address in memory (for example, that you can freely construct and dereference a pointer to a word- or greater-sized object at an odd char address). Problem: this fails on many (esp. RISC) architectures better optimized for **HLL** execution speed, and can cause an illegal address fault or bus error.
7. The (related) assumption that there is no padding at the end of types and that in an array you can thus step right from the last byte of a previous component to the first byte of the next one. This is not only machine- but compiler-dependent.
8. The assumption that memory address space is globally flat and that the array reference `foo[-1]` is necessarily valid. Problem: this fails at 0, or other places on segment-addressed machines like Intel chips (yes, segmentation is universally considered a **brain-damaged** way to design machines (see **moby**), but that is a separate issue).
9. The assumption that objects can be arbitrarily large with no special considerations. Problem: this fails on segmented architectures and under non-virtual-addressing environments.
10. The assumption that the stack can be as large as memory. Problem: this fails on segmented architectures or almost anything else without virtual addressing and a paged stack.
11. The assumption that bits and addressable units within an object are ordered in the same way and that this order is a constant of nature. Problem: this fails on **big-endian** machines.
12. The assumption that it is meaningful to compare pointers to different objects not located within the same array, or to objects of different types. Problem: the former fails on segmented architectures, the latter on word-oriented machines or others with multiple pointer formats.
13. The assumption that an `int` is 32 bits, or (nearly equivalently) the assumption that `sizeof(int) == sizeof(long)`. Problem: this fails on PDP-11s, 286-based systems and even on 386 and 68000 systems under some compilers.
14. The assumption that `argv[]` is writable. Problem: this fails in many embedded-systems C environments and even under a few flavors of UNIX.

Note that a programmer can validly be accused of vaxocentrism even if he or she has never seen a VAX. Some of these assumptions (esp. 2–5) were valid on the PDP-11, the original C machine, and became endemic years before the VAX. The terms *vaxocentricity* and *all-the-world's-a-VAX syndrome* have been used synonymously.

vdiff */vee´dif/* v.,n. Visual diff. The operation of finding differences between two files by **eyeball search**. The term *optical diff* has also been reported, and is sometimes more specifically used for the act of superimposing two nearly identical printouts on one another and holding them up to a light to spot differences. Though this method is poor for detecting omissions in the 'rear' file, it can also be used with printouts of graphics, a claim few if any diff programs can make. See **diff**.

veeblefester */vee´bəl-fes`tr/* [from the "Born Loser" comix via Commodore; prob. originally from *Mad* Magazine's 'Veeblefeetzer' parodies ca. 1960] n. Any obnoxious person engaged in the (alleged) professions of marketing or management. Antonym of **hacker**. Compare **suit**, **marketroid**.

ventilator card n. Syn. **lace card**.

Venus flytrap [after the insect-eating plant] n. See **firewall machine**.

verbage */ver´bəj/* n. A deliberate misspelling and mispronunciation of **verbiage** that assimilates it to the word 'garbage'. Compare **content-free**. More pejorative than 'verbiage'.

verbiage n. When the context involves a software or hardware system, this refers to **documentation**. This term borrows the connotations of mainstream 'verbiage' to suggest that the documentation is of marginal utility and that the motives behind its production have little to do with the ostensible subject.

Version 7 alt. V7 */vee´ se´vn/* n. The 1978 unsupported release of **UNIX** ancestral to all current commercial versions. Before the release of the POSIX/SVID standards, V7's features were often treated as a UNIX portability baseline. See **BSD**, **USG UNIX**, **UNIX**. Some old-timers impatient with commercialization and kernel bloat still maintain that V7 was the Last True UNIX.

vgrep */vee´grep/* v.,n. Visual grep. The operation of finding patterns in a file optically rather than digitally (also called an *optical grep*). See **grep**; compare **vdiff**.

vi */V-I/, not /vi:/* and *never /siks/* [from 'Visual Interface'] n. A screen editor crufted together by Bill Joy for an early **BSD** release. Became the *de facto* standard UNIX editor and a nearly undisputed hacker favorite outside of MIT until the rise of **EMACS** after about 1984. Tends to frustrate new users no end, as it will neither take commands while expecting input text nor vice versa, and the default setup provides no indication of which mode the editor is in (one correspondent accordingly reports that he has often heard the editor's name pronounced */vi:l/*). Nevertheless it is still widely used (about half the respondents in a 1991 USENET poll preferred it), and even EMACS fans often resort to it as a mail editor and for small editing jobs (mainly because it starts up faster than the bulkier versions of EMACS). See **holy wars**.

videotex n. obs. An electronic service offering people the privilege of paying to read the weather on their television screens instead of having somebody read it to them for free while they brush their teeth. The idea bombed everywhere it wasn't government-subsidized, because by the time videotex was practical the installed base of personal computers could hook up to timesharing services and do the things for which videotex might have been worthwhile better and cheaper. Videotex planners badly overestimated both the appeal of getting information from a computer and the cost of local intelligence at the user's end. Like the **gorilla arm** effect, this has been a cautionary tale to hackers ever since. See also **vannevar**.

virgin adj. Unused; pristine; in a known initial state. "Let's bring up a virgin system and see if it crashes again." (Esp. useful after contracting a **virus** through **SEX**.) Also, by extension, buffers and the like within a program that have not yet been used.

virtual [via the technical term 'virtual memory', prob. from the term 'virtual image' in optics] adj. 1. Common alternative to **logical**; often used to refer to the artificial objects (like addressable virtual memory larger than physical memory) created by a computer system to help the system control access to shared resources. 2. Simulated; performing the functions of something that isn't really there. An imaginative child's doll may be a virtual playmate. Oppose **real**.

virtual Friday n. (also *logical Friday*) The last day before an extended weekend, if that day is not a 'real' Friday. For example, the U.S. holiday Thanksgiving is always on a Thursday. The next day is often also a holiday or taken as an extra day off, in which case Wednesday of that week is a virtual Friday (and Thursday is a virtual Saturday, as is Friday). There are also *virtual Mondays* that are actually Tuesdays, after the three-day weekends associated with many national holidays in the U.S.

virtual reality n. 1. Computer simulations that use 3-D graphics and devices such as the Dataglove to allow the user to interact with the simulation. See **cyberspace**. 2. A form of network interaction incorporating aspects of role-playing games, interactive theater, improvisational comedy, and 'true confessions' magazines. In a virtual reality forum (such as USENET's *alt.callahans* newsgroup or the **MUD** experiments on Internet), interaction between the participants is written like a shared novel complete with scenery, *foreground characters* that may be personae utterly unlike the people who write them, and common *background characters* manipulable by all parties. The one iron law is that you may not write irreversible changes to a character without the consent of the person who 'owns' it. Otherwise anything goes. See **bamf**, **cyberspace**.

virtual shredder n. The jargonic equivalent of the **bit bucket** at shops using IBM's VM/CMS operating system. VM/CMS officially supports a whole bestiary of virtual card readers, virtual printers, and other phantom devices; these are used to supply some of the same capabilities UNIX gets from pipes and I/O redirection.

virus [from the obvious analogy with biological viruses, via SF] n. A cracker program that searches out other programs and 'infects' them by embedding a copy of itself in them, so that they become **Trojan horse**s. When these programs are executed, the embedded virus is executed too, thus propagating the 'infection'. This normally happens invisibly to the user. Unlike a **worm**, a virus cannot infect other computers without assistance. It is propagated by vectors such as humans trading programs with their friends (see **SEX**). The virus may do nothing but propagate itself and then allow the program to run normally. Usually, however, after propagating silently for a while, it starts doing things like writing cute messages on the terminal or playing strange tricks with the display (some viruses include nice **display hack**s). Many nasty viruses, written by particularly perversely minded **cracker**s, do irreversible damage, like nuking all the user's files.

In the 1990s, viruses have become a serious problem, especially among IBM PC and Macintosh users (the lack of security on these machines enables viruses to spread easily, even infecting the operating system). The production of special anti-virus software has become an industry, and a number of exaggerated media reports have caused outbreaks of near hysteria among users; many **lusers** tend to blame *everything* that doesn't work as they had expected on virus attacks. Accordingly, this sense of *virus* has passed not only into techspeak but into also popular usage (where it is often incorrectly used to denote a **worm** or even a **Trojan horse**). See **phage**; compare **back door**; see also **UNIX conspiracy**.

visionary n. 1. One who hacks vision, in the sense of an Artificial Intelligence researcher working on the problem of getting computers to 'see' things using TV cameras. (There isn't any problem in sending information from a TV camera to a computer. The problem is, how can the computer be programmed to make use of the camera information? See **SMOP**, **AI-complete**.) 2. [IBM] One who reads the outside literature. At IBM, apparently, such a penchant is viewed with awe and wonder.

VMS */V-M-S/* n. DEC's proprietary operating system for its VAX minicomputer; one of the seven or so environments that loom largest in hacker folklore. Many UNIX fans generously concede that VMS would probably be the hacker's favorite commercial OS if UNIX didn't exist; though true, this makes VMS fans furious. One major hacker gripe with VMS concerns its slowness — thus the following limerick:

> There once was a system called VMS
> Of cycles by no means abstemious.
> It's chock-full of hacks
> And runs on a VAX
> And makes my poor stomach all squeamious.
> — The Great Quux

See also **VAX**, **TOPS-10**, **TOPS-20**, **UNIX**, **runic**.

voice vt. To phone someone, as opposed to emailing them or connecting in **talk mode**. "I'm busy now; I'll voice you later."

voice-net n. Hackish way of referring to the telephone system, analogizing it to a digital network. USENET **sig blocks** not uncommonly include the sender's phone next to a "Voice:" or "Voice-Net:" header; common variants of this are "Voicenet" and "V-Net". Compare **paper-net**, **snail-mail**.

voodoo programming [from George Bush's "voodoo economics"] n. The use by guess or cookbook of an **obscure** or **hairy** system, feature, or algorithm that one does not truly understand. The implication is that the technique may not work, and if it doesn't, one will never know why. Almost synonymous with **black magic**, except that black magic typically isn't documented and *nobody* understands it. Compare **magic**, **deep magic**, **heavy wizardry**, **rain dance**, **cargo cult programming**, **wave a dead chicken**.

VR // [MUD] n. On-line abbrev for **virtual reality**, as opposed to **RL**.

Vulcan nerve pinch n. [from the old "Star Trek" TV series via Commodore Amiga hackers] The keyboard combination that forces a soft-boot or jump to ROM monitor (on machines that support such a feature). On many micros this is Ctrl-Alt-Del; on Suns, L1-A; on some Macintoshes, it is <Cmd>-<Power switch>! Also called **three-finger salute**. Compare **quadruple bucky**.

vulture capitalist n. Pejorative hackerism for 'venture capitalist', deriving from the common practice of pushing contracts that deprive inventors of control over their own innovations and most of the money they ought to have made from them.

= W =

wabbit */wab´it/* [almost certainly from Elmer Fudd's immortal line "You wascawwy wabbit!"] n. 1. A legendary early hack reported on a System/360 at RPI and elsewhere around 1978; this may have descended (if only by inspiration) from hack called RABBITS reported from 1969 on a Burroughs 55000 at the University of Washington Computer Center. The program would make two copies of itself every time it was run, eventually crashing the system. 2. By extension, any hack that includes infinite self-replication but is not a **virus** or **worm**. See **fork bomb** and **rabbit job**, see also **cookie monster**.

WAITS */wayts/* n. The mutant cousin of **TOPS-10** used on a handful of systems at **SAIL** up to 1990. There was never an 'official' expansion of WAITS (the name itself having been arrived at by a rather sideways process), but it was frequently glossed as 'West-coast Alternative to ITS'. Though WAITS was less visible than ITS, there was frequent exchange of people and ideas between the two communities, and innovations pioneered at WAITS exerted enormous indirect influence. The early screen modes of **EMACS**, for example, were directly inspired by WAITS's 'E' editor — one of a family of editors that were the first to do 'real-time editing', in which the editing commands were invisible and where one typed text at the point of insertion/overwriting. The modern style of multi-region windowing is said to have originated there, and WAITS alumni at XEROX PARC and elsewhere played major roles in the developments that led to the XEROX Star, the Macintosh, and the Sun workstations. **Bucky bits** were also invented there — thus, the ALT key on every IBM PC is a WAITS legacy. One notable WAITS feature seldom duplicated elsewhere was a news-wire interface that allowed WAITS hackers to read, store, and filter AP and UPI dispatches from their terminals; the system also featured a still-unusual level of support for what is now called 'multimedia' computing, allowing analog audio and video signals to be switched to programming terminals.

waldo */wol´doh/* [From Robert A. Heinlein's story "Waldo"] 1. A mechanical agent, such as a gripper arm, controlled by a human limb. When these were developed for the nuclear industry in the mid-1940s they were named after the invention described by Heinlein in the story, which he wrote in 1942. Now known by the more generic term 'telefactoring', this technology is of intense interest to NASA for tasks like space station maintenance. 2. At Harvard (particularly by Tom Cheatham and students), this is used instead of **foobar** as a metasyntactic variable and general nonsense word. See **foo**, **bar**, **foobar**, **quux**.

walk n.,vt. Traversal of a data structure, especially an array or linked-list data structure in **core**. See also **codewalker**, **silly walk**, **clobber**.

walk off the end of vt. To run past the end of an array, list, or medium after stepping through it — a good way to land in trouble. Often the result of an **off-by-one error**. Compare **clobber**, **roach**, **smash the stack**.

walking drives n. An occasional failure mode of magnetic-disk drives back in the days when they were huge, clunky **washing machines**. Those old **dinosaur** parts carried terrific angular momentum; the combination of a misaligned spindle or worn bearings and stick-slip interactions with the floor could cause them to 'walk' across a room, lurching alternate corners forward a couple of millimeters at a time. There is a legend about a drive that walked over to the only door to the computer room and jammed it shut; the staff had to cut a hole in the wall in order to get at it! Walking could also be induced by certain patterns of drive access (a fast seek across the whole width of the disk, followed by a slow seek in the other direction). Some bands of old-time hackers figured out how to induce disk-accessing patterns that would do this to particular drive models and held disk-drive races.

wall [WPI] interj. 1. An indication of confusion, usually spoken with a quizzical tone: "Wall??" 2. A request for further explication. Compare **octal forty**. 3. [UNIX] v. To send a message to everyone currently logged in, esp. with the wall(8) utility.

It is said that sense 1 came from the idiom 'like talking to a blank wall'. It was originally used in situations where, after you had carefully answered a question, the questioner stared at you blankly, clearly having understood nothing that was explained. You would then throw out a "Hello, wall?" to elicit some sort of response from the questioner. Later, confused questioners began voicing "Wall?" themselves.

wall follower n. A person or algorithm that compensates for lack of sophistication or native stupidity by efficiently following some simple procedure shown to have been effective in the past. Used of an algorithm, this is not necessarily pejorative; it recalls 'Harvey Wallbanger', the winning robot in an early AI contest (named, of course, after the cocktail). Harvey successfully solved mazes by keeping a 'finger' on one wall and running till it came out the other end. This was inelegant, but it was mathematically guaranteed to work on simply-connected mazes — and, in fact, Harvey outperformed more sophisticated robots that tried to 'learn' each maze by building an internal representation of it. Used of humans, the term *is* pejorative and implies an uncreative, bureaucratic, by-the-book mentality. See also **code grinder**, **droid**.

wall time n. (also *wall clock time*) 1. 'Real world' time (what the clock on the wall shows), as opposed to the system clock's idea of time. 2. The real running time of a program, as opposed to the number of **tick**s required to execute it (on a timesharing system these always differ, as no one program gets all the ticks, and on multiprocessor systems with good thread support one may get more processor time than real time).

wallpaper n. 1. A file containing a listing (e.g., assembly listing) or a transcript, esp. a file containing a transcript of all or part of a login session. (The idea was that the paper for such listings was essentially good only for wallpaper, as evidenced at Stanford, where it was used to cover windows.) Now rare, esp. since other systems have developed other terms for it (e.g., PHOTO on TWENEX). However, the UNIX world doesn't have an equivalent term, so perhaps **wallpaper** will take hold there. The term probably originated on ITS, where the commands to begin and end transcript files were `:WALBEG` and `:WALEND`, with default file `WALL PAPER` (the space was a path delimiter). 2. The background pattern used on graphical workstations (this is techspeak under the 'Windows' graphical user interface to MS-DOS). 3. *wallpaper file* n. The file that contains the wallpaper information before it is actually printed on paper. (Even if you don't intend ever to produce a real paper copy of the file, it is still called a wallpaper file.)

wango */wang´goh/* n. Random bit-level **grovel**ling going on in a system during some unspecified operation. Often used in combination with **mumble**. For example: "You start with the '.o' file, run it through this postprocessor that does mumble-wango — and it comes out a snazzy object-oriented executable."

wank */wangk/* [Columbia University: prob. by mutation from Commonwealth slang v. *wank*, to masturbate] n.,v. Used much as **hack** is elsewhere, as a noun denoting a clever technique or person or the result of such cleverness. May describe (negatively) the act of hacking for hacking's sake ("Quit wanking, let's go get supper!") or (more positively) a **wizard**. Adj. *wanky* describes something particularly clever (a person, program, or algorithm). Conversations can also get wanky when there are too many wanks involved. This excess wankiness is signalled by an overload of the *wankometer* (compare **bogometer**). When the wankometer overloads, the conversation's subject must be changed, or all non-wanks will leave. Compare *neep-neeping* (under **neep-neep**). Usage: U.S. only. In Britain and the Commonwealth this word is *extremely* rude and is best avoided unless one intends to give offense.

wannabee */won´ə-bee/* (also, more plausibly, spelled *wannabe*) [from a term recently used to describe Madonna fans who dress, talk, and act like their idol; prob. originally from biker slang] n. A would-be **hacker**. The connotations of this term differ sharply depending on the age and exposure of the subject. Used of a person who is in or might be entering **larval stage**, it is semi-approving; such wannabees can be annoying but most hackers remember that they, too, were once such creatures. When used of any professional programmer, CS academic, writer, or **suit**, it is derogatory, implying that said person is trying to cuddle up to the hacker mystique but doesn't, fundamentally, have a prayer of understanding what it is all about. Overuse of terms from this lexicon is often an indication of the **wannabee** nature. Compare **newbie**.

Historical note: The wannabee phenomenon has a slightly different flavor now (1993) than it did ten or fifteen years ago. When the people who are now hackerdom's tribal elders were in **larval stage**, the process of becoming a hacker was largely unconscious and unaffected by models known in popular culture — communities formed spontaneously around people who, *as individuals*, felt irresistibly drawn to do hackerly things, and what wannabees experienced was a fairly pure, skill-focused desire to become similarly wizardly. Those days of innocence are gone forever; society's adaptation to the advent of the microcomputer after 1980 included the elevation of the hacker as a new kind of folk hero, and the result is that some people semi-consciously set out to *be hackers* and borrow hackish prestige by fitting the popular image of hackers. Fortunately, to do this really well, one has to actually become a wizard. Nevertheless, old-time hackers tend to share a poorly articulated disquiet about the change; among other things, it gives them mixed feelings about the effects of public compendia of lore like this one.

warlording [from the USENET group *alt.fan.warlord*] v. The act of excoriating a bloated, ugly, or derivative **sig block**. Common grounds for warlording include the presence of a signature rendered in a **BUAF**, over-used or cliched **sig quote**s, ugly **ASCII art**, or simply excessive size. The original 'Warlord' was a **BIFF**-like **newbie** c.1991 who featured in his sig a particularly large and obnoxious ASCII graphic resembling the sword of Conan the Barbarian in the 1981 John Milius movie; the group name *alt.fan.warlord* was sarcasm, and the characteristic mode of warlording is devastatingly sarcastic praise.

warm boot n. See **boot**.

wart n. A small, **crocky feature** that sticks out of an otherwise **clean** design. Something conspicuous for localized ugliness, especially a special-case exception to a general rule. For example, in some versions of `csh(1)`, single quotes literalize every character inside them except '`!`'. In ANSI C, the '`??`' syntax used for obtaining ASCII characters in a foreign environment is a wart. See also **miswart**.

washing machine n. Old-style 14-inch hard disks in floor-standing cabinets. So called because of the size of the cabinet and the 'top-loading' access to the media packs — and, of course, they were always set on 'spin cycle'. The washing-machine idiom transcends language barriers; it is even used in Russian hacker jargon. See also **walking drives**. The thick channel cables connecting these were called *bit hoses* (see **hose**, sense 3).

The next cartoon in the Crunchly saga is 03-17-76:2, page 55.

water MIPS n. (see **MIPS**, sense 2) Large, water-cooled machines of either today's ECL-supercomputer flavor or yesterday's traditional **mainframe** type.

wave a dead chicken v. To perform a ritual in the direction of crashed software or hardware that one believes to be futile but is nevertheless necessary so that others are satisfied that an appropriate degree of effort has been expended. "I'll wave a dead chicken over the source code, but I really think we've run into an OS bug." Compare **voodoo programming**, **rain dance**.

weasel n. [Cambridge] A naive user, one who deliberately or accidentally does things that are stupid or ill-advised. Roughly synonymous with **loser**.

wedged adj. 1. To be stuck, incapable of proceeding without help. This is different from having crashed. If the system has crashed, it has become totally non-functioning. If the system is wedged, it is trying to do something but cannot make progress; it may be capable of doing a few things, but not be fully operational. For example, a process may become wedged if it **deadlock**s with another (but not all instances of wedging are deadlocks). See also **gronk**, **locked up**, **hosed**. 2. Often refers to humans suffering misconceptions. "He's totally wedged — he's convinced that he can levitate through meditation." 3. [UNIX] Specifically used to describe the state of a TTY left in a losing state by abort of a screen-oriented program or one that has messed with the line discipline in some obscure way.

There is some dispute over the origin of this term. It is usually thought to derive from a common description of recto-cranial inversion; however, it may actually have originated with older 'hot-press' printing technology in which physical type elements were locked into type frames with wedges driven in by mallets. Once this had been done, no changes in the typesetting for that page could be made.

wedgie [Fairchild] n. A bug. Prob. related to **wedged**.

wedgitude */wedj´i-t[y]ood/* n. The quality or state of being **wedged**.

weeble */weeb´l/* [Cambridge] interj. Used to denote frustration, usually at amazing stupidity. "I stuck the disk in upside down." "Weeble. . . ." Compare **gurfle**.

weeds n. 1. Refers to development projects or algorithms that have no possible relevance or practical application. Comes from 'off in the weeds'. Used in phrases like "lexical analysis for microcode is serious weeds. . . ." 2. At

A really unusual kind of **water MIPS**.
The next cartoon in the Crunchly saga is 12-25-74, page 307.

CDC/ETA before its demise, the phrase *go off in the weeds* was equivalent to IBM's **branch to Fishkill** and mainstream hackerdom's **jump off into never-never land**.

weenie n. 1. [on BBSes] Any of a species of luser resembling a less amusing version of **BIFF** that infests many **BBS** systems. The typical weenie is a teenage boy with poor social skills travelling under a grandiose **handle** derived from fantasy or heavy-metal rock lyrics. Among sysops, *the weenie problem* refers to the marginally literate and profanity-laden **flamage** weenies tend to spew all over a newly-discovered BBS. Compare **spod**, **computer geek**, **terminal junkie**. 2. [Among hackers] When used with a qualifier (for example, as in **UNIX weenie**, VMS weenie, IBM weenie) this can be either an insult or a term of praise, depending on context, tone of voice, and whether or not it is applied by a person who considers him or herself to be the same sort of weenie. Implies that the weenie has put a major investment of time, effort, and concentration into the area indicated; whether this is good or bad depends on the hearer's judgment of how the speaker feels about that area. See also **bigot**. 3. The semicolon character, '`;`' (ASCII 0111011).

Weenix */wee´niks/* [ITS] n. A derogatory term for **UNIX**, derived from **UNIX weenie**. According to one noted ex-ITSer, it is "the operating system preferred by Unix Weenies: typified by poor modularity, poor reliability, hard file deletion, no file version numbers, case sensitivity everywhere, and users who believe that these are all advantages". Some ITS fans behave as though they believe UNIX stole a future that rightfully belonged to them. See **ITS**, sense 2.

well-behaved adj. 1. [primarily **MS-DOS**] Said of software conforming to system interface guidelines and standards. Well-behaved software uses the operating system to do chores such as keyboard input, allocating memory and drawing graphics. Oppose **ill-behaved**. 2. Software that does its job quietly and without counterintuitive effects. Esp. said of software having an interface spec sufficiently simple and well-defined that it can be used as a **tool** by other software. See **cat**.

well-connected adj. Said of a computer installation, asserts that it has reliable email links with the network and/or that it relays a large fraction of available **USENET** newsgroups. *Well-known* can be almost synonymous, but also implies that the site's name is familiar to many (due perhaps to an archive service or active USENET users).

wetware */wet´weir/* [prob. from the novels of Rudy Rucker] n. 1. The human nervous system, as opposed to computer hardware or software. "Wetware has 7 plus or minus 2 temporary registers." 2. Human beings (programmers, operators, administrators) attached to a computer system, as opposed to the system's hardware or software. See **liveware**, **meatware**.

whack v. According to arch-hacker James Gosling, to "...modify a program with no idea whatsoever how it works." (See **whacker**.) It is actually possible to do this in nontrivial circumstances if the change is small and well-defined and you are very good at **glark**ing things from context. As a trivial example, it is relatively easy to change all `stderr` writes to `stdout` writes in a piece of C filter code which remains otherwise mysterious.

whacker [University of Maryland: from **hacker**] n. 1. A person, similar to a **hacker**, who enjoys exploring the details of programmable systems and how to stretch their capabilities. Whereas a hacker tends to produce great hacks, a whacker only ends up whacking the system or program in question. Whackers are often quite egotistical and eager to claim **wizard** status, regardless of the views of their peers. 2. A person who is good at programming quickly, though rather poorly and ineptly.

whales n. See **like kicking dead whales down the beach**.

whalesong n. The peculiar clicking and whooshing sounds made by a PEP modem such as the Telebit Trailblazer as it tries to synchronize with another PEP modem for their special high-speed mode. This sound isn't anything like the normal two-tone handshake between conventional modems and is instantly recognizable to anyone who has heard it more than once. It sounds, in fact, very much like whale songs. This noise is also called "the moose call" or "moose tones".

What's a spline? [XEROX PARC] This phrase expands to: "You have just used a term that I've heard for a year and a half, and I feel I should know, but don't. My curiosity has finally overcome my guilt." The PARC lexicon adds "Moral: don't hesitate to ask questions, even if they seem obvious."

wheel [from slang 'big wheel' for a powerful person] n. A person who has an active **wheel bit**. "We need to find a wheel to unwedge the hung tape drives." (See **wedged**, sense 1.)

wheel bit n. A privilege bit that allows the possessor to perform some restricted operation on a timesharing system, such as read or write any file on the system regardless of protections, change or look at any address in the running monitor, crash or reload the system, and kill or create jobs and user accounts. The term was invented on the TENEX operating system, and carried over to TOPS-20, XEROX-IFS, and others. The state of being in a privileged logon is sometimes called *wheel mode*. This term entered the UNIX culture from TWENEX in the mid-1980s and has been gaining popularity there (esp. at university sites). See also **root**.

wheel wars [Stanford University] A period in **larval stage** during which student hackers hassle each other by attempting to log each other out of the system, delete each other's files, and otherwise wreak havoc, usually at the expense of the lesser users.

White Book n. 1. Syn. **K&R**. 2. Adobe's fourth book in the PostScript series, describing the previously-secret format of Type 1 fonts; *Adobe Type 1 Font Format, version 1.1*, (Addison-Wesley, 1990, ISBN 0-201-57044-0). See also **Red Book**, **Green Book**, **Blue Book**.

whizzy [Sun] adj. (alt. *wizzy*) Describes a **cuspy** program; one that is feature-rich and well presented.

WIBNI // [Bell Labs: Wouldn't It Be Nice If] n. What most requirements documents and specifications consist entirely of. Compare **IWBNI**.

widget n. 1. A meta-thing. Used to stand for a real object in didactic examples (especially database tutorials). Legend has it that the original widgets were holders for buggy whips. "But suppose the parts list for a widget has 52 entries. . . ." 2. [poss. evoking 'window gadget'] A user interface object in **X** graphical user interfaces.

wiggles n. [scientific computation] In solving partial differential equations by finite difference and similar methods, wiggles are sawtooth (up-down-up-down) oscillations at the shortest wavelength representable on the grid. If an algorithm is unstable, this is often the most unstable waveform, so it grows to dominate the solution. Alternatively, stable (though inaccurate) wiggles can be generated near a discontinuity by a Gibbs phenomenon.

WIMP environment n. [acronym: 'Window, Icon, Menu, Pointing device (or Pull-down menu)'] A graphical-user-interface environment such as **X** or the Macintosh interface, esp. as described by a hacker who prefers command-line interfaces for their superior flexibility and extensibility. However, it is also used without negative connotations; one must pay attention to voice tone and other signals to interpret correctly. See **menuitis, user-obsequious.**

win [MIT] 1. vi. To succeed. A program wins if no unexpected conditions arise, or (especially) if it sufficiently **robust** to take exceptions in stride. 2. n. Success, or a specific instance thereof. A pleasing outcome. "So it turned out I could use a lexer generator instead of hand-coding my own pattern recognizer. What a win!" Emphatic forms: *moby win, super win, hyper-win* (often used interjectively as a reply). For some reason *suitable win* is also common at MIT, usually in reference to a satisfactory solution to a problem. Oppose **lose**; see also **big win**, which isn't quite just an intensification of *win.*

win big vi. To experience serendipity. "I went shopping and won big; there was a 2-for-1 sale." See **big win.**

win win interj. Expresses pleasure at a **win.**

Winchester n. Informal generic term for 'floating-head' magnetic-disk drives in which the read-write head planes over the disk surface on an air cushion. The name arose because the original 1973 engineering prototype for what later became the IBM 3340 featured two 30-megabyte volumes; 30–30 became 'Winchester' when somebody noticed the similarity to the common term for a famous Winchester rifle (in the latter, the first 30 referred to caliber and the second to the grain weight of the charge).

window shopping [US Geological Survey] n. Among users of **WIMP environments** like **X** or the Macintosh, extended experimentation with new window colors, fonts, and icon shapes. This activity can take up hours of what might otherwise have been productive working time. "I spent the afternoon window shopping until I found the coolest shade of green for my active window borders — now they perfectly match my medium slate blue background." Serious window shoppers will spend their days with bitmap editors, creating new and different icons and background patterns for all to see. Also: *window dressing*, the act of applying new fonts, colors, etc. See **fritterware**, compare **macdink.**

Windoze */win´dohz/* n. See **Microsloth Windoze.**

winged comments n. Comments set on the same line as code, as opposed to

boxed comments. In C, for example:

```
d = sqrt(x*x + y*y);   /* distance from origin */
```

Generally these refer only to the action(s) taken on that line.

winkey n. (alt. *winkey face*) See **emoticon**.

winnage */win´əj/* n. The situation when a lossage is corrected, or when something is winning.

winner 1. n. An unexpectedly good situation, program, programmer, or person. 2. *real winner:* Often sarcastic, but also used as high praise (see also the note under **user**). "He's a real winner — never reports a bug till he can duplicate it and send in an example."

winnitude */win´ə-t[y]ood/* n. The quality of winning (as opposed to **winnage**, which is the result of winning). "Guess what? They tweaked the microcode and now the LISP interpreter runs twice as fast as it used to." "That's really great! Boy, what winnitude!" "Yup. I'll probably get a half-hour's winnage on the next run of my program." Perhaps curiously, the obvious antonym 'lossitude' is rare.

wired n. See **hardwired**.

wirehead */wi:r´hed/* n. [prob. from SF slang for an electrical-brain-stimulation addict] 1. A hardware hacker, especially one who concentrates on communications hardware. 2. An expert in local-area networks. A wirehead can be a network software wizard too, but will always have the ability to deal with network hardware, down to the smallest component. Wireheads are known for their ability to lash up an Ethernet terminator from spare resistors, for example.

wirewater n. Syn. **programming fluid**. This melds the mainstream slang adjective 'wired' (stimulated, up, hyperactive) with 'firewater'.

wish list n. A list of desired features or bug fixes that probably won't get done for a long time, usually because the person responsible for the code is too busy or can't think of a clean way to do it. "OK, I'll add automatic filename completion to the wish list for the new interface." Compare **tick-list features**.

The next cartoon in the Crunchly saga is 10-04-75, page 66.

within delta of adj. See **delta**.

within epsilon of adj. See **epsilon**.

wizard n. 1. A person who knows how a complex piece of software or hardware works (that is, who **grok**s it); esp. someone who can find and fix bugs quickly in an emergency. Someone is a **hacker** if he or she has general hacking ability, but is a wizard with respect to something only if he or she has specific detailed knowledge of that thing. A good hacker could become a wizard for something given the time to study it. 2. A person who is permitted to do things forbidden to ordinary people; one who has **wheel** privileges on a system. 3. A UNIX expert, esp. a UNIX systems programmer. This usage is well enough established that 'UNIX Wizard' is a recognized job title at some corporations and to most headhunters. See **guru**, **lord high fixer**. See also **deep magic**, **heavy wizardry**, **incantation**, **magic**, **mutter**, **rain dance**, **voodoo programming**, **wave a dead chicken**.

Wizard Book n. Hal Abelson's, Jerry Sussman's and Julie Sussman's *Structure and Interpretation of Computer Programs* (MIT Press, 1984; ISBN 0-262-01077-1), an excellent computer science text used in introductory courses at MIT. So called because of the wizard on the jacket. One of the **bible**s of the LISP/Scheme world. Also, less commonly, known as the **Purple Book**.

wizard mode [from **rogue**] n. A special access mode of a program or system, usually passworded, that permits some users godlike privileges. Generally not used for operating systems themselves (*root mode* or *wheel mode* would be used instead). This term is often used with respect to games that have editable state.

wizardly adj. Pertaining to wizards. A wizardly **feature** is one that only a wizard could understand or use properly.

womb box n. 1. [TMRC] Storage space for equipment. 2. [proposed] A variety of hard-shell equipment case with heavy interior padding and/or shaped carrier cutouts in a foam-rubber matrix; mundanely called a *flight case*. Used for delicate test equipment, electronics, and musical instruments.

WOMBAT [Waste Of Money, Brains, And Time] adj. Applied to problems which are both profoundly **uninteresting** in themselves and unlikely to benefit anyone interesting even if solved. Often used in fanciful constructions such as *wrestling with a wombat*. See also **crawling horror**, **SMOP**. Also note the rather different usage as a metasyntactic variable in **Commonwealth Hackish**.

wonky */wong´kee/* [from Australian slang] adj. Yet another approximate synonym for **broken**. Specifically connotes a malfunction that produces behavior seen as crazy, humorous, or amusingly perverse. "That was the day the printer's font logic went wonky and everybody's listings came out in Tengwar." Also in *wonked out*. See **funky**, **demented**, **bozotic**.

woofer [University of Waterloo] n. Some varieties of wide paper for printers have a perforation 8.5 inches from the left margin that allows the excess on the right-hand side to be torn off when the print format is 80 columns or less wide. The right-hand excess may be called 'woofer'. This term (like **tweeter**) has been in use at Waterloo since 1972, but is elsewhere unknown. In audio jargon, the word refers to the bass speaker(s) on a hi-fi.

workaround n. 1. A temporary **kluge** used to bypass, mask, or otherwise avoid a **bug** or **misfeature** in some system. Theoretically, workarounds are always replaced by **fixes**; in practice, customers often find themselves living with workarounds for long periods of time. "The code died on NUL characters in the input, so I fixed it to interpret them as spaces." "That's not a fix, that's a workaround!" 2. A procedure to be employed by the user in order to do what some currently non-working feature should do. Hypothetical example: "Using META-F7 crashes the 4.43 build of Weemax, but as a workaround you can type CTRL-R, then SHIFT-F5, and delete the remaining cruft by hand."

working as designed [IBM] adj. 1. In conformance to a wrong or inappropriate specification; useful, but misdesigned. 2. Frequently used as a sardonic comment on a program's utility. 3. Unfortunately also used as a bogus reason for not accepting a criticism or suggestion. At **IBM**, this sense is used in official documents! See **BAD**.

worm [from 'tapeworm' in John Brunner's novel *The Shockwave Rider*, via XEROX PARC] n. A program that propagates itself over a network, reproducing itself as it goes. Compare **virus**. Nowadays the term has negative connotations, as it is assumed that only **cracker**s write worms. Perhaps the best-known example was Robert T. Morris's 'Internet Worm' of 1988, a 'benign' one that got out of control and hogged hundreds of Suns and VAXen across the U.S. See also **cracker**, **RTM**, **Trojan horse**, **ice**, and **Great Worm, the**.

wound around the axle adj. In an infinite loop. Often used by older computer types.

wrap around vi. (also n. *wraparound* and v. shorthand *wrap*) 1. [techspeak] The action of a counter that starts over at zero or at *minus infinity* (see **infinity**) after its maximum value has been reached, and continues incrementing, either because it is programmed to do so or because of an overflow (as when a car's odometer starts over at 0). 2. To change **phase** gradually and continuously by maintaining a steady wake-sleep cycle somewhat longer than 24 hours, e.g., living six long (28-hour) days in a week (or, equivalently, sleeping at the rate of 10 microhertz). This sense is also called **phase-wrapping**.

write-only code [a play on 'read-only memory'] n. Code so arcane, complex, or ill-structured that it cannot be modified or even comprehended by anyone but its author, and possibly not even by him/her. A **Bad Thing**.

write-only language n. A language with syntax (or semantics) sufficiently dense and bizarre that any routine of significant size is automatically **write-only code**. A sobriquet applied occasionally to C and often to APL, though **INTERCAL** and **TECO** certainly deserve it more.

write-only memory n. The obvious antonym to 'read-only memory'. Out of frustration with the long and seemingly useless chain of approvals required of component specifications, during which no actual checking seemed to occur, an engineer at Signetics once created a specification for a write-only memory and included it with a bunch of other specifications to be approved. This inclusion came to the attention of Signetics **management** only when regular customers started calling and asking for pricing information. Signetics published a corrected edition of the data book and requested the return of the 'erroneous' ones. Later, around 1974, Signetics bought a double-page spread in *Electronics* magazine's April issue and used the spec as an April Fools' Day joke. Instead of the more conventional characteristic curves, the 25120 "fully encoded, 9046 x N, Random Access, write-only-memory" data sheet included diagrams of "bit capacity vs. Temp.", "Iff vs. Vff", "Number of pins remaining vs. number of socket insertions", and "AQL vs. selling price". The 25120 required a 6.3 VAC VFF supply, a +10V VCC, and VDD of 0V, ± 2%.

Wrong Thing n. A design, action, or decision that is clearly incorrect or inappropriate. Often capitalized; always emphasized in speech as if capitalized. The opposite of the **Right Thing**; more generally, anything that is not the Right Thing. In cases where 'the good is the enemy of the best', the merely good — although good — is nevertheless the Wrong Thing. "In C, the default is for module-level declarations to be visible everywhere, rather than just within the module. This is clearly the Wrong Thing."

wugga wugga */wuh´gə wuh´gə/* n. Imaginary sound that a computer program makes as it labors with a tedious or difficult task. Compare **cruncha cruncha cruncha**, **grind** (sense 4).

wumpus */wuhm´pəs/* n. The central monster (and, in many versions, the name) of a famous family of very early computer games called "Hunt The Wumpus", dating back at least to 1972 (several years before **ADVENT**) on the Dartmouth Time-Sharing System. The wumpus lived somewhere in a cave with the topology of an dodecahedron's edge/vertex graph (later versions supported other topologies, including an icosahedron and Möbius strip). The player started somewhere at random in the cave with five 'crooked arrows'; these could be shot through up to three connected rooms, and would kill the wumpus on a hit (later versions introduced the wounded wumpus, which got very angry). Unfortunately for players, the movement necessary to map the maze was made hazardous not merely by the wumpus (which would eat you if you stepped on him) but also by bottomless pits and colonies of super bats that would pick you up and drop you at a random location (later versions added 'anaerobic termites' that ate arrows, bat migrations, and earthquakes that randomly changed pit locations).

This game appears to have been the first to use a non-random graph-structured map (as opposed to a rectangular grid like the even older Star Trek games). In this respect, as in the dungeon-like setting and its terse, amusing messages, it prefigured **ADVENT** and **Zork** and was directly ancestral to both (Zork acknowledged this heritage by including a super-bat colony). Today, a port is distributed with SunOS and as freeware for the Mac. A C emulation of the original Basic game is in circulation as freeware on the net.

WYSIAYG */wiz´ee-ayg/* adj. Describes a user interface under which "What You See Is *All* You Get"; an unhappy variant of **WYSIWYG**. Visual, 'point-and-shoot'-style interfaces tend to have easy initial learning curves, but also to lack depth; they often frustrate advanced users who would be better served by a command-style interface. When this happens, the frustrated user has a

WYSIAYG problem. This term is most often used of editors, word processors, and document formatting programs. WYSIWYG 'desktop publishing' programs, for example, are a clear win for creating small documents with lots of fonts and graphics in them, especially things like newsletters and presentation slides. When typesetting book-length manuscripts, on the other hand, scale changes the nature of the task; one quickly runs into WYSIAYG limitations, and the increased power and flexibility of a command-driven formatter like **TEX** or UNIX's **troff** becomes not just desirable but a necessity. Compare **YAFIYGI**.

WYSIWYG */wiz´ee-wig/* adj. Describes a user interface under which "What You See Is What You Get", as opposed to one that uses more-or-less obscure commands that do not result in immediate visual feedback. True WYSIWYG in environments supporting multiple fonts or graphics is a a rarely-attained ideal; there are variants of this term to express real-world manifestations including WYSIAWYG (What You See Is *Almost* What You Get) and WYSIMOLWYG (What You See Is More or Less What You Get). All these can be mildly derogatory, as they are often used to refer to dumbed-down **user-friendly** interfaces targeted at non-programmers; a hacker has no fear of obscure commands (compare **WYSIAYG**). On the other hand, **EMACS** was one of the very first WYSIWYG editors, replacing (actually, at first overlaying) the extremely obscure, command-based **TECO**. See also **WIMP environment**. [Oddly enough, WYSIWYG has already made it into the OED, in lower case yet. — ESR]

= X =

X */X/* n. 1. Used in various speech and writing contexts (also in lowercase) in roughly its algebraic sense of 'unknown within a set defined by context' (compare **N**). Thus, the abbreviation 680x0 stands for 68000, 68010, 68020, 68030, or 68040, and 80x86 stands for 80186, 80286 80386 or 80486 (note that a UNIX hacker might write these as 680[0-4]0 and 80[1-4]86 or 680?0 and 80?86 respectively; see **glob**). 2. [after the name of an earlier window system called 'W'] An over-sized, over-featured, over-engineered and incredibly over-complicated window system developed at MIT and widely used on UNIX systems.

XEROX PARC */zee´roks park´/* The famed Palo Alto Research Center. For more than a decade, from the early 1970s into the mid-1980s, PARC yielded an astonishing volume of groundbreaking hardware and software innovations. The modern mice, windows, and icons style of software interface was invented there. So was the laser printer and the local-area network; and PARC's series of D machines anticipated the powerful personal computers of the 1980s by a decade. Sadly, the prophets at PARC were without honor in their own company, so much so that it became a standard joke to describe PARC as a place that specialized in developing brilliant ideas for everyone else.

The stunning shortsightedness and obtusity of XEROX's top-level **suits** has been well anatomized in *Fumbling The Future: How XEROX Invented, Then Ignored, the First Personal Computer* by Douglas K. Smith and Robert C. Alexander (William Morrow & Co., 1988, ISBN 0-688-09511-9).

XOFF */X-of/* n. Syn. **control-S**.

XON */X-on/* n. Syn. **control-Q**.

xor */X´or/, /kzor/* conj. Exclusive or. 'A xor B' means 'A or B, but not both'. "I want to get cherry pie xor a banana split." This derives from the technical use of the term as a function on truth-values that is true if exactly one of its two arguments is true.

xref */X´ref/* vt., n. Hackish standard abbreviation for 'cross-reference'.

XXX */X-X-X/* n. A marker that attention is needed. Commonly used in program comments to indicate areas that are kluged up or need to be. Some hackers liken 'XXX' to the notional heavy-porn movie rating. Compare **FIXME**.

xyzzy */X-Y-Z-Z-Y/, /X-Y-ziz´ee/, /ziz´ee/*, or */ik-ziz´ee/* [from the ADVENT game] adj. The **canonical** 'magic word'. This comes from **ADVENT**, in which the idea is to explore an underground cave with many rooms and to collect the treasures you find there. If you type *xyzzy* at the appropriate time, you can move instantly between two otherwise distant points. If, therefore, you encounter some bit of **magic**, you might remark on this quite succinctly by saying simply "Xyzzy!" "Ordinarily you can't look at someone else's screen if he has protected it, but if you type quadruple-bucky-clear the system will let you do it anyway." "Xyzzy!" Xyzzy has actually been implemented as an undocumented no-op command on several OSes; in Data General's AOS/VS, for example, it would typically respond "Nothing happens", just as **ADVENT**

did if the magic was invoked at the wrong spot or before a player had performed the action that enabled the word. In more recent 32-bit versions, by the way, AOS/VS responds "Twice as much happens". See also **plugh**.

= Y =

YA- [Yet Another] abbrev. In hackish acronyms this almost invariably expands to **Yet Another**, following the precedent set by UNIX `yacc(1)` (Yet Another Compiler-Compiler). See **YABA**.

YABA */ya´bə/* [Cambridge] n. Yet Another Bloody Acronym. Whenever some program is being named, someone invariably suggests that it be given a name that is acronymic. The response from those with a trace of originality is to remark ironically that the proposed name would then be 'YABA-compatible'. Also used in response to questions like "What is WYSIWYG?" See also **TLA**.

YAFIYGI */yaf´ee-y:-gee/* adj. [coined in response to WYSIWYG] Describes the command-oriented ed/vi/nroff/TEX style of word processing or other user interface, the opposite of **WYSIWYG**. Stands for "You asked for it, you got it", because what you actually asked for is often not apparent until long after it is too late to do anything about it. Used to denote perversity ("Real Programmers use YAFIYGI tools . . . and *like* it!") or, less often, a necessary tradeoff ("Only a YAFIYGI tool can have full programmable flexibility in its interface.").

This precise sense of "You asked for it, you got it" seems to have first appeared in Ed Post's classic parody *Real Programmers don't use Pascal*; the acronym is a more recent (as of 1993) invention.

YAUN */yawn/* [Acronym for 'Yet Another UNIX Nerd'] n. Reported from the San Diego Computer Society (predominantly a microcomputer users' group) as a good-natured punning insult aimed at UNIX zealots.

Yellow Book n. You're holding it. See **book titles**.

yellow wire [IBM] n. Repair wires used when connectors (especially ribbon connectors) got broken due to some schlemiel pinching them, or to reconnect cut traces after the FE mistakenly cut one. Compare **blue wire**, **purple wire**, **red wire**.

Yet Another adj. [From UNIX's `yacc(1)`, 'Yet Another Compiler-Compiler', a LALR parser generator] 1. Of your own work: A humorous allusion often used in titles to acknowledge that the topic is not original, though the content is. As in 'Yet Another AI Group' or 'Yet Another Simulated Annealing Algorithm'. 2. Of others' work: Describes something of which there are already far too many. See also **YA-**, **YABA**, **YAUN**.

YKYBHTL Abbreviation of 'You know you've been hacking too long when...', which became established on the USENET group *alt.folklore.computers* during extended discussion of the indicated entry in the Jargon File.

You are not expected to understand this [UNIX] cav. The canonical comment describing something **magic** or too complicated to bother explaining properly. From an infamous comment in the context-switching code of the V6 UNIX kernel.

You know you've been hacking too long when . . . The set-up line for a genre of one-liners told by hackers about themselves. These include the following:

- not only do you check your email more often than your paper mail, but you remember your **network address** faster than your postal one.
- your **SO** kisses you on the neck and the first thing you think is "Uh, oh, **priority interrupt**."
- you go to balance your checkbook and discover that you're doing it in octal.
- your computers have a higher street value than your car.
- in your universe, 'round numbers' are powers of 2, not 10.
- more than once, you have woken up recalling a dream in some programming language.
- you realize you have never seen half of your best friends.

[An early version of this entry said "All but one of these have been reliably reported as hacker traits (some of them quite often). Even hackers may have trouble spotting the ringer." The ringer was balancing one's checkbook in octal, which I made up out of whole cloth. Although more respondents picked that one out as fiction than any of the others, I also received multiple independent reports of its actually happening, most famously to Grace Hopper while she was working with BINAC in 1949. — ESR]

Your mileage may vary [from the standard disclaimer attached to EPA mileage ratings by American car manufacturers] cav. 1. A ritual warning often found in UNIX freeware distributions. Translates roughly as "Hey, I tried to write this portably, but who *knows* what'll happen on your system?" 2. More generally, a qualifier attached to advice. "I find that sending flowers works well, but your mileage may vary."

Yow! */yow/* [from "Zippy the Pinhead" comix] interj. A favored hacker expression of humorous surprise or emphasis. "Yow! Check out what happens when you twiddle the foo option on this display hack!" Compare **gurfle**.

yoyo mode n. The state in which the system is said to be when it rapidly alternates several times between being up and being down. Interestingly (and perhaps not by coincidence), many hardware vendors give out free yoyos at Usenix exhibits.

Sun Microsystems gave out logoized yoyos at SIGPLAN '88. Tourists staying at one of Atlanta's most respectable hotels were subsequently treated to the sight of 200 of the country's top computer scientists testing yo-yo algorithms in the lobby.

Yu-Shiang Whole Fish */yoo-shyang hohl fish/* n. obs. The character gamma (extended SAIL ASCII 0001001), which with a loop in its tail looks like a little fish swimming down the page. The term is actually the name of a Chinese dish in which a fish is cooked whole (not **parsed**) and covered with Yu-Shiang (or Yu-Hsiang) sauce. Usage: primarily by people on the MIT LISP Machine, which could display this character on the screen. Tends to elicit incredulity from people who hear about it second-hand.

= Z =

zap 1. n. Spiciness. 2. vt. To make food spicy. 3. vt. To make someone 'suffer' by making his food spicy. (Most hackers love spicy food. Hot-and-sour soup is considered wimpy unless it makes you wipe your nose for the rest of the meal.) See **zapped**. 4. vt. To modify, usually to correct; esp. used when the action is performed with a debugger or binary patching tool. Also implies surgical precision. "Zap the debug level to 6 and run it again." In the

IBM mainframe world, binary patches are applied to programs or to the OS with a program called 'superzap', whose file name is 'IMASPZAP' (possibly contrived from I M A SuPerZAP). 5. vt. To erase or reset. 6. To **fry** a chip with static electricity. "Uh oh — I think that lightning strike may have zapped the disk controller."

zapped adj. Spicy. This term is used to distinguish between food that is hot (in temperature) and food that is *spicy*-hot. For example, the Chinese appetizer Bon Bon Chicken is a kind of chicken salad that is cold but zapped; by contrast, **vanilla** wonton soup is hot but not zapped. See also **oriental food**, **laser chicken**. See **zap**, senses 1 and 2.

zen vt. To figure out something by meditation or by a sudden flash of enlightenment. Originally applied to bugs, but occasionally applied to problems of life in general. "How'd you figure out the buffer allocation problem?" "Oh, I zenned it." Contrast **grok**, which connotes a time-extended version of zenning a system. Compare **hack mode**. See also **guru**.

zero vt. 1. To set to 0. Usually said of small pieces of data, such as bits or words (esp. in the construction *zero out*). 2. To erase; to discard all data from. Said of disks and directories, where 'zeroing' need not involve actually writing zeroes throughout the area being zeroed. One may speak of something being *logically zeroed* rather than being *physically zeroed*. See **scribble**.

zero-content adj. Syn. **content-free**.

zeroth */zee´rohth/* adj. First. Among software designers, comes from C's and LISP's 0-based indexing of arrays. Hardware people also tend to start counting at 0 instead of 1; this is natural since, e.g., the 256 states of 8 bits correspond to the binary numbers 0, 1, . . . , 255 and the digital devices known as 'counters' count in this way.

Hackers and computer scientists often like to call the first chapter of a publication 'chapter 0', especially if it is of an introductory nature (one of the classic instances was in the First Edition of **K&R**). In recent years this trait has also been observed among many pure mathematicians (who have an independent tradition of numbering from 0). Zero-based numbering tends to reduce **fencepost errors**, though it cannot eliminate them entirely.

zigamorph */zig´ə-morf/* n. 1. Hex FF (11111111) when used as a delimiter or **fence** character. Usage: primarily at IBM shops. 2. [proposed] n. The

Unicode non-character +UFFFF (1111111111111111), a character code which is not assigned to any character, and so is usable as end-of-string. (Unicode (a subset of ISO 10646) is a 16-bit character code intended to cover all of the world's writing systems, including Roman, Greek, Cyrillic, Chinese, hiragana, katakana, Devanagari, Easter Island 'rongo-rongo', and even **Elvish**.)

zip [primarily MS-DOS] vt. To create a compressed archive from a group of files using PKWare's PKZIP or a compatible archiver. Its use is spreading now that portable implementations of the algorithm have been written. Commonly used as follows: "I'll zip it up and send it to you." See **arc**, **tar and feather**.

zipperhead [IBM] n. A person with a closed mind.

zombie [UNIX] n. A process that has died but has not yet relinquished its process table slot (because the parent process hasn't executed a `wait(2)` for it yet). These can be seen in `ps(1)` listings occasionally. Compare **orphan**.

zorch */zorch/* 1. [TMRC] v. To attack with an inverse heat sink. 2. [TMRC] v. To travel, with v approaching c [that is, with velocity approaching lightspeed — ESR]. 3. [MIT] v. To propel something very quickly. "The new comm software is very fast; it really zorches files through the network." 4. [MIT] n. Influence. Brownie points. Good karma. The intangible and fuzzy currency in which favors are measured. "I'd rather not ask him for that just yet; I think I've used up my quota of zorch with him for the week." 5. [MIT] n. Energy, drive, or ability. "I think I'll **punt** that change for now; I've been up for 30 hours and I've run out of zorch." 6. [MIT] v. To flunk an exam or course.

Zork */zork/* n. The second of the great early experiments in computer fantasy gaming; see **ADVENT**. Originally written on MIT-DM during the late 1970s, later distributed with BSD UNIX (as a patched, sourceless RT-11 FORTRAN binary; see **retrocomputing**) and commercialized as 'The Zork Trilogy' by Infocom. The FORTRAN source was later rewritten for portability and released to USENET under the name "Dungeon". Both FORTRAN "Dungeon" and translated C versions are available at many FTP sites.

zorkmid */zork´mid/* n. The canonical unit of currency in hacker-written games. This originated in **zork** but has spread to **nethack** and is referred to in several other games.

= [^A-Za-z] (see regexp) =

'Snooze */snooz/* [FidoNet] n. Fidonews, the weekly official on-line newsletter of FidoNet. As the editorial policy of Fidonews is "anything that arrives, we print", there are often large articles completely unrelated to FidoNet, which in turn tend to elicit **flamage** in subsequent issues.

(TM) *//* [USENET] ASCII rendition of the trademark-superscript symbol (TM) appended to phrases that the author feels should be recorded for posterity, perhaps in future editions of this lexicon. Sometimes used ironically as a form of protest against the recent spate of software and algorithm patents and 'look and feel' lawsuits. See also **UN*X**.

-oid [from 'android'] suff. 1. Used as in mainstream English to indicate a poor imitation, a counterfeit, or some otherwise slightly bogus resemblance. Hackers will happily use it with all sorts of non-Greco/Latin stem words that wouldn't keep company with it in mainstream English. For example, "He's a nerdoid" means that he superficially resembles a nerd but can't make the grade; a *modemoid* might be a 300-baud box (Real Modems run at 9600 or up); a *computeroid* might be any **bitty box**. The word *keyboid* could be used to describe a **chiclet keyboard**, but would have to be written; spoken, it would confuse the listener as to the speaker's city of origin. 2. More specifically, an indicator for 'resembling an android' which in the past has been confined to science-fiction fans and hackers. It too has recently (in 1991) started to go mainstream (most notably in the term 'trendoid' for victims of terminal hipness). This is probably traceable to the popularization of the term **droid** in "Star Wars" and its sequels.

Coinages in both forms have been common in science fiction for at least fifty years, and hackers (who are often SF fans) have probably been making '-oid' jargon for almost that long [though GLS and I can personally confirm only that they were already common in the mid-1970s — ESR].

-ware [from 'software'] suff. Commonly used to form jargon terms for classes of software. For examples, see **careware**, **crippleware**, **crudware**, **freeware**, **fritterware**, **guiltware**, **liveware**, **meatware**, **payware**, **psychedelicware**, **shareware**, **shelfware**, **vaporware**, **wetware**.

/dev/null */dev-nuhl/* [from the UNIX null device, used as a data sink] n. A notional 'black hole' in any information space being discussed, used, or referred to. A controversial posting, for example, might end "Kudos to rasputin@kremlin.org, flames to /dev/null". See **bit bucket**.

0 Numeric zero, as opposed to the letter 'O' (the 15th letter of the English alphabet). In their unmodified forms they look a lot alike, and various kluges invented to make them visually distinct have compounded the confusion. If your zero is center-dotted and letter-O is not, or if letter-O looks almost rectangular but zero looks more like an American football stood on end (or the reverse), you're probably looking at a modern character display (though the dotted zero seems to have originated as an option on IBM 3270 controllers). If your zero is slashed but letter-O is not, you're probably looking at an old-style ASCII graphic set descended from the default typewheel on the venerable ASR-33 Teletype (Scandinavians, for whom Ø is a letter, curse this arrangement). If letter-O has a slash across it and the zero does not, your display is tuned for a very old convention used at IBM and a few other early mainframe makers (Scandinavians curse *this* arrangement even more, because it means two of their letters collide). Some Burroughs/Unisys equipment displays a zero with a *reversed* slash. And yet another convention common on early line printers left zero unornamented but added a tail or hook to the letter-O so that it resembled an inverted Q or cursive capital letter-O. Are we sufficiently confused yet?

1TBS // n. The "One True Brace Style"; see **indent style**.

120 reset */wuhn-twen´tee ree´set/* [from 120 volts, U.S. wall voltage] n. To cycle power on a machine in order to reset or unjam it. Compare **Big Red Switch**, **power cycle**.

2 infix. In translation software written by hackers, infix 2 often represents the syllable *to* with the connotation 'translate to': as in dvi2ps (DVI to PostScript), int2string (integer to string), and texi2roff (Texinfo to [nt]roff).

@-party */at´par`tee/* [from the @-sign in an Internet address] n. (alt. '@-sign party' */at´si:n par`tee/*) A semi-closed party thrown for hackers at a science-fiction convention (esp. the annual Worldcon); one must have a **network address** to get in, or at least be in company with someone who does. One of the most reliable opportunities for hackers to meet face to face with people who might otherwise be represented by mere phosphor dots on their screens. Compare **boink**.

@Begin // See **\begin**.

\begin // [from the LaTeX command] With \end, used humorously in writing to indicate a context or to remark on the surrounded text. For example:

```
\begin{flame}
Predicate logic is the only good programming
language.  Anyone who would use anything else
is an idiot.  Also, all computers should be
tredecimal instead of binary.
\end{flame}
```

The Scribe users at CMU and elsewhere used to use @Begin/@End in an identical way (LaTeX was built to resemble Scribe). On USENET, this construct would more frequently be rendered as `<FLAME ON>` and `<FLAME OFF>`, or `#ifdef FLAME` and `#endif FLAME'`.

Appendix A Hacker Folklore

This appendix contains several legends and fables that illuminate the meaning of various entries in the lexicon.

The Meaning of 'Hack'

"The word **hack** doesn't really have 69 different meanings", according to MIT hacker Phil Agre. "In fact, **hack** has only one meaning, an extremely subtle and profound one which defies articulation. Which connotation is implied by a given use of the word depends in similarly profound ways on the context. Similar remarks apply to a couple of other hacker words, most notably **random**."

Hacking might be characterized as 'an appropriate application of ingenuity'. Whether the result is a quick-and-dirty patchwork job or a carefully crafted work of art, you have to admire the cleverness that went into it.

An important secondary meaning of **hack** is 'a creative practical joke'. This kind of hack is easier to explain to non-hackers than the programming kind. Of course, some hacks have both natures; see the lexicon entries for **pseudo** and **kgbvax**. But here are some examples of pure practical jokes that illustrate the hacking spirit:

> In 1961, students from Caltech (California Institute of Technology, in Pasadena) hacked the Rose Bowl football game. One student posed as a reporter and 'interviewed' the director of the University of Washington card stunts (such stunts involve people in the stands who hold up colored cards to make pictures). The reporter learned exactly how the stunts were operated, and also that the director would be out to dinner later.
>
> While the director was eating, the students (who called themselves the 'Fiendish Fourteen') picked a lock and stole a blank direction sheet for the card stunts. They then had a printer run off 2300 copies of the blank. The next day they picked the lock again and stole the master plans for the stunts — large sheets of graph paper colored in with the stunt pictures. Using these as a guide, they made new instructions for three of the stunts on the duplicated blanks. Finally, they broke in once more, replacing the stolen master plans and substituting the stack of diddled instruction sheets for the original set.

> The result was that three of the pictures were totally different. Instead of 'WASHINGTON', the word "CALTECH' was flashed. Another stunt showed the word 'HUSKIES', the Washington nickname, but spelled it backwards. And what was supposed to have been a picture of a husky instead showed a beaver. (Both Caltech and MIT use the beaver — nature's engineer — as a mascot.)
>
> After the game, the Washington faculty athletic representative said: "Some thought it ingenious; others were indignant." The Washington student body president remarked: "No hard feelings, but at the time it was unbelievable. We were amazed."

This is now considered a classic hack, particularly because revising the direction sheets constituted a form of programming.

Here is another classic hack:

> On November 20, 1982, MIT hacked the Harvard-Yale football game. Just after Harvard's second touchdown against Yale, in the first quarter, a small black ball popped up out of the ground at the 40-yard line, and grew bigger, and bigger, and bigger. The letters 'MIT' appeared all over the ball. As the players and officials stood around gawking, the ball grew to six feet in diameter and then burst with a bang and a cloud of white smoke.
>
> The *Boston Globe* later reported: "If you want to know the truth, MIT won The Game."
>
> The prank had taken weeks of careful planning by members of MIT's Delta Kappa Epsilon fraternity. The device consisted of a weather balloon, a hydraulic ram powered by Freon gas to lift it out of the ground, and a vacuum-cleaner motor to inflate it. They made eight separate expeditions to Harvard Stadium between 1 and 5 A.M., locating an unused 110-volt circuit in the stadium and running buried wires from the stadium circuit to the 40-yard line, where they buried the balloon device. When the time came to activate the device, two fraternity members had merely to flip a circuit breaker and push a plug into an outlet.
>
> This stunt had all the earmarks of a perfect hack: surprise, publicity, the ingenious use of technology, safety, and harmlessness. The use of manual control allowed the prank to be timed so as not to disrupt the game (it was set off between plays, so the outcome of the game would not be unduly affected). The perpetrators

> had even thoughtfully attached a note to the balloon explaining that the device was not dangerous and contained no explosives.
>
> Harvard president Derek Bok commented: "They have an awful lot of clever people down there at MIT, and they did it again." President Paul E. Gray of MIT said: "There is absolutely no truth to the rumor that I had anything to do with it, but I wish there were."

The hacks above are verifiable history; they can be proved to have happened. Many other classic-hack stories from MIT and elsewhere, though retold as history, have the characteristics of what Jan Brunvand has called 'urban folklore' (see **FOAF**). Perhaps the best known of these is the legend of the infamous trolley-car hack, an alleged incident in which engineering students are said to have welded a trolley car to its tracks with thermite. Numerous versions of this have been recorded from the 1940s to the present, most set at MIT but at least one very detailed version set at CMU.

Brian Leibowitz has researched MIT hacks both real and mythical extensively; the interested reader is referred to his delightful pictorial compendium *The Journal of the Institute for Hacks, Tomfoolery, and Pranks* (MIT Museum, 1990; ISBN 0-917027-03-5).

Finally, here is a story about one of the classic computer hacks.

> Back in the mid-1970s, several of the system support staff at Motorola discovered a relatively simple way to crack system security on the Xerox CP-V timesharing system. Through a simple programming strategy, it was possible for a user program to trick the system into running a portion of the program in 'master mode' (supervisor state), in which memory protection does not apply. The program could then poke a large value into its 'privilege level' byte (normally write-protected) and could then proceed to bypass all levels of security within the file-management system, patch the system monitor, and do numerous other interesting things. In short, the barn door was wide open.
>
> Motorola quite properly reported this problem to Xerox via an official 'level 1 SIDR' (a bug report with an intended urgency of 'needs to be fixed yesterday'). Because the text of each SIDR was entered into a database that could be viewed by quite a number of people, Motorola followed the approved procedure: they simply reported the problem as 'Security SIDR', and attached all of the

necessary documentation, ways-to-reproduce, etc.

The CP-V people at Xerox sat on their thumbs; they either didn't realize the severity of the problem, or didn't assign the necessary operating-system-staff resources to develop and distribute an official patch.

Months passed. The Motorola guys pestered their Xerox field-support rep, to no avail. Finally they decided to take direct action, to demonstrate to Xerox management just how easily the system could be cracked and just how thoroughly the security safeguards could be subverted.

They dug around in the operating-system listings and devised a thoroughly devilish set of patches. These patches were then incorporated into a pair of programs called 'Robin Hood' and 'Friar Tuck'. Robin Hood and Friar Tuck were designed to run as 'ghost jobs' (daemons, in UNIX terminology); they would use the existing loophole to subvert system security, install the necessary patches, and then keep an eye on one another's statuses in order to keep the system operator (in effect, the superuser) from aborting them.

One fine day, the system operator on the main CP-V software development system in El Segundo was surprised by a number of unusual phenomena. These included the following:

- Tape drives would rewind and dismount their tapes in the middle of a job.
- Disk drives would seek back and forth so rapidly that they would attempt to walk across the floor (see **walking drives**).
- The card-punch output device would occasionally start up of itself and punch a **lace card**. These would usually jam in the punch.
- The console would print snide and insulting messages from Robin Hood to Friar Tuck, or vice versa.
- The Xerox card reader had two output stackers; it could be instructed to stack into A, stack into B, or stack into A (unless a card was unreadable, in which case the bad card was placed into stacker B). One of the patches installed by the ghosts added some code to the card-reader driver . . . after reading a card, it would flip over to the opposite stacker. As a result,

card decks would divide themselves in half when they were read, leaving the operator to recollate them manually.

Naturally, the operator called in the operating-system developers. They found the bandit ghost jobs running, and X'ed them . . . and were once again surprised. When Robin Hood was X'ed, the following sequence of events took place:

```
!X id1

id1: Friar Tuck... I am under attack!
     Pray save me!
id1: Off (aborted)

id2: Fear not, friend Robin!  I shall rout
     the Sheriff of Nottingham's men!

id1: Thank you, my good fellow!
```

Each ghost-job would detect the fact that the other had been killed, and would start a new copy of the recently slain program within a few milliseconds. The only way to kill both ghosts was to kill them simultaneously (very difficult) or to deliberately crash the system.

Finally, the system programmers did the latter — only to find that the bandits appeared once again when the system rebooted! It turned out that these two programs had patched the boot-time OS image (the kernel file, in UNIX terms) and had added themselves to the list of programs that were to be started at boot time.

The Robin Hood and Friar Tuck ghosts were finally eradicated when the system staff rebooted the system from a clean boot-tape and reinstalled the monitor. Not long thereafter, Xerox released a patch for this problem.

It is alleged that Xerox filed a complaint with Motorola's management about the merry-prankster actions of the two employees in question. It is not recorded that any serious disciplinary action was taken against either of them.

TV Typewriters: A Tale of Hackish Ingenuity

Here is a true story about a glass tty: One day an MIT hacker was in a motorcycle accident and broke his leg. He had to stay in the hospital quite a while, and got restless because he couldn't **hack**. Two of his friends therefore took a terminal and a modem for it to the hospital, so that he could use the computer by telephone from his hospital bed.

Now this happened some years before the spread of home computers, and computer terminals were not a familiar sight to the average person. When the two friends got to the hospital, a guard stopped them and asked what they were carrying. They explained that they wanted to take a computer terminal to their friend who was a patient.

The guard got out his list of things that patients were permitted to have in their rooms: TV, radio, electric razor, typewriter, tape player, . . . no computer terminals. Computer terminals weren't on the list, so the guard wouldn't let it in. Rules are rules, you know. (This guard was clearly a **droid**.)

Fair enough, said the two friends, and they left again. They were frustrated, of course, because they knew that the terminal was as harmless as a TV or anything else on the list . . . which gave them an idea.

The next day they returned, and the same thing happened: a guard stopped them and asked what they were carrying. They said: "This is a TV typewriter!" The guard was skeptical, so they plugged it in and demonstrated it. "See? You just type on the keyboard and what you type shows up on the TV screen." Now the guard didn't stop to think about how utterly useless a typewriter would be that didn't produce any paper copies of what you typed; but this was clearly a TV typewriter, no doubt about it. So he checked his list: "A TV is all right, a typewriter is all right . . . okay, take it on in!"

[Historical note: Many years ago, *Popular Electronics* published solder-it-yourself plans for a TV typewriter. Despite the essential uselessness of the device, it was an enormously popular project. Steve Ciarcia, the man behind *Byte* magazine's "Circuit Cellar" feature, resurrected this ghost in one of his books of the early 1980s. He ascribed its popularity (no doubt correctly) to the feeling of power the builder could achieve by being able to decide himself what would be shown on the TV. — ESR]

[Antihistorical note: On September 23rd, 1992, the L.A. Times ran the following bit of filler:

> Solomon Waters of Altadena, a 6-year-old first-grader, came home from his first day of school and excitedly told his mother how he had written on "a machine that looks like a computer – but without the TV screen." She asked him if it could have been a "typewriter." "Yeah! Yeah!" he said. "That's what it was called."

I have since investigated this matter and determined that many of today's teenagers have never seen a slide rule, either. . . . — ESR]

A Story About 'Magic' (by GLS)

Some years ago, I was snooping around in the cabinets that housed the MIT AI Lab's PDP-10, and noticed a little switch glued to the frame of one cabinet. It was obviously a homebrew job, added by one of the lab's hardware hackers (no one knows who).

You don't touch an unknown switch on a computer without knowing what it does, because you might crash the computer. The switch was labeled in a most unhelpful way. It had two positions, and scrawled in pencil on the metal switch body were the words 'magic' and 'more magic'. The switch was in the 'more magic' position.

I called another hacker over to look at it. He had never seen the switch before either. Closer examination revealed that the switch had only one wire running to it! The other end of the wire did disappear into the maze of wires inside the computer, but it's a basic fact of electricity that a switch can't do anything unless there are two wires connected to it. This switch had a wire connected on one side and no wire on its other side.

It was clear that this switch was someone's idea of a silly joke. Convinced by our reasoning that the switch was inoperative, we flipped it. The computer instantly crashed.

Imagine our utter astonishment. We wrote it off as coincidence, but nevertheless restored the switch to the 'more magic' position before reviving the computer.

A year later, I told this story to yet another hacker, David Moon as I recall. He clearly doubted my sanity, or suspected me of a supernatural belief in the power of this switch, or perhaps thought I was fooling him with a bogus saga. To prove it to him, I showed him the very switch, still glued to the cabinet frame with only one wire connected to it, still in the 'more magic' position. We scrutinized the switch and its lone connection, and found that the other end of the wire, though connected to the computer wiring, was connected to a ground pin. That clearly made the switch doubly useless: not only was it electrically nonoperative, but it was connected to a place that couldn't affect anything anyway. So we flipped the switch.

The computer promptly crashed.

This time we ran for Richard Greenblatt, a long-time MIT hacker, who was close at hand. He had never noticed the switch before, either. He inspected it, concluded it was useless, got some diagonal cutters and **dike**d it out. We then revived the computer and it has run fine ever since.

We still don't know how the switch crashed the machine. There is a theory that some circuit near the ground pin was marginal, and flipping the switch changed the electrical capacitance enough to upset the circuit as millionth-of-a-second pulses went through it. But we'll never know for sure; all we can really say is that the switch was **magic**.

I still have that switch in my basement. Maybe I'm silly, but I usually keep it set on 'more magic'.

A Selection of AI Koans

These are some of the funniest examples of a genre of jokes told at the MIT AI Lab about various noted hackers. The original koans were composed by Danny Hillis. In reading these, it is at least useful to know that Minsky, Sussman, and Drescher are AI researchers of note, that Tom Knight was one of the Lisp machine's principal designers, and that David Moon wrote much of Lisp machine Lisp.

* * *

A novice was trying to fix a broken Lisp machine by turning the power off and on.

Knight, seeing what the student was doing, spoke sternly: "You cannot fix a machine by just power-cycling it with no understanding of what is going wrong."

Knight turned the machine off and on.

The machine worked.

* * *

One day a student came to Moon and said: "I understand how to make a better garbage collector. We must keep a reference count of the pointers to each cons."

Moon patiently told the student the following story:

> "One day a student came to Moon and said: 'I understand how to make a better garbage collector . . .

[Ed. note: Pure reference-count garbage collectors have problems with circular structures that point to themselves.]

* * *

In the days when Sussman was a novice, Minsky once came to him as he sat hacking at the PDP-6.

"What are you doing?", asked Minsky.

"I am training a randomly wired neural net to play Tic-Tac-Toe" Sussman replied.

"Why is the net wired randomly?", asked Minsky.

"I do not want it to have any preconceptions of how to play", Sussman said.

Minsky then shut his eyes.

"Why do you close your eyes?", Sussman asked his teacher.

"So that the room will be empty."

At that moment, Sussman was enlightened.

* * *

A disciple of another sect once came to Drescher as he was eating his morning meal.

"I would like to give you this personality test", said the outsider, "because I want you to be happy."

Drescher took the paper that was offered him and put it into the toaster, saying: "I wish the toaster to be happy, too."

OS and JEDGAR

This story says a lot about the ITS ethos.

On the ITS system there was a program that allowed you to see what was being printed on someone else's terminal. It spied on the other guy's output by examining the insides of the monitor system. The output spy program was called OS. Throughout the rest of the computer science (and at IBM too) OS means 'operating system', but among old-time ITS hackers it almost always meant 'output spy'.

OS could work because ITS purposely had very little in the way of 'protection' that prevented one user from trespassing on another's areas. Fair is fair, however. There was another program that would automatically notify you if anyone started to spy on your output. It worked in exactly the same way, by looking at the insides of the operating system to see if anyone else was looking at the insides that had to do with your output. This 'counterspy' program was called JEDGAR (a six-letterism pronounced as two syllables: */jed´gr/*), in honor of the former head of the FBI.

But there's more. JEDGAR would ask the user for 'license to kill'. If the user said yes, then JEDGAR would actually **gun** the job of the **luser** who was spying. Unfortunately, people found that this made life too violent, especially when tourists learned about it. One of the systems hackers solved the problem by replacing JEDGAR with another program that only pretended to do its job. It took a long time to do this, because every copy of JEDGAR had to be patched. To this day no one knows how many people never figured out that JEDGAR had been defanged.

The Story of Mel, a Real Programmer

This was posted to USENET by its author, Ed Nather (*utastro!nather*), on May 21, 1983.

> A recent article devoted to the *macho* side of programming
> made the bald and unvarnished statement:
>
> > Real Programmers write in FORTRAN.
>
> Maybe they do now,
> in this decadent era of
> Lite beer, hand calculators, and "user-friendly" software
> but back in the Good Old Days,
> when the term "software" sounded funny
> and Real Computers were made out of drums and vacuum tubes,
> Real Programmers wrote in machine code.
> Not FORTRAN. Not RATFOR. Not, even, assembly language.
> Machine Code.
> Raw, unadorned, inscrutable hexadecimal numbers.
> Directly.
>
> Lest a whole new generation of programmers
> grow up in ignorance of this glorious past,
> I feel duty-bound to describe,
> as best I can through the generation gap,
> how a Real Programmer wrote code.
> I'll call him Mel,
> because that was his name.
>
> I first met Mel when I went to work for Royal McBee Computer Corp.,

a now-defunct subsidiary of the typewriter company.
The firm manufactured the LGP-30,
a small, cheap (by the standards of the day)
drum-memory computer,
and had just started to manufacture
the RPC-4000, a much-improved,
bigger, better, faster — drum-memory computer.
Cores cost too much,
and weren't here to stay, anyway.
(That's why you haven't heard of the company, or the computer.)

I had been hired to write a FORTRAN compiler
for this new marvel and Mel was my guide to its wonders.
Mel didn't approve of compilers.

"If a program can't rewrite its own code",
he asked, "what good is it?"

Mel had written,
in hexadecimal,
the most popular computer program the company owned.
It ran on the LGP-30
and played blackjack with potential customers
at computer shows.
Its effect was always dramatic.
The LGP-30 booth was packed at every show,
and the IBM salesmen stood around
talking to each other.
Whether or not this actually sold computers
was a question we never discussed.

Mel's job was to re-write
the blackjack program for the RPC-4000.
(Port? What does that mean?)
The new computer had a one-plus-one
addressing scheme,
in which each machine instruction,
in addition to the operation code
and the address of the needed operand,
had a second address that indicated where, on the revolving drum,
the next instruction was located.

In modern parlance,

every single instruction was followed by a GO TO!
Put *that* in Pascal's pipe and smoke it.

Mel loved the RPC-4000
because he could optimize his code:
that is, locate instructions on the drum
so that just as one finished its job,
the next would be just arriving at the "read head"
and available for immediate execution.
There was a program to do that job,
an "optimizing assembler",
but Mel refused to use it.

"You never know where it's going to put things",
he explained, "so you'd have to use separate constants".

It was a long time before I understood that remark.
Since Mel knew the numerical value
of every operation code,
and assigned his own drum addresses,
every instruction he wrote could also be considered
a numerical constant.
He could pick up an earlier "add" instruction, say,
and multiply by it,
if it had the right numeric value.
His code was not easy for someone else to modify.

I compared Mel's hand-optimized programs
with the same code massaged by the optimizing assembler program,
and Mel's always ran faster.
That was because the "top-down" method of program design
hadn't been invented yet,
and Mel wouldn't have used it anyway.
He wrote the innermost parts of his program loops first,
so they would get first choice
of the optimum address locations on the drum.
The optimizing assembler wasn't smart enough to do it that way.

Mel never wrote time-delay loops, either,
even when the balky Flexowriter
required a delay between output characters to work right.
He just located instructions on the drum
so each successive one was just *past* the read head

when it was needed;
the drum had to execute another complete revolution
to find the next instruction.
He coined an unforgettable term for this procedure.
Although "optimum" is an absolute term,
like "unique", it became common verbal practice
to make it relative:
"not quite optimum" or "less optimum"
or "not very optimum".
Mel called the maximum time-delay locations
the "most pessimum".

After he finished the blackjack program
and got it to run
("Even the initializer is optimized",
he said proudly),
he got a Change Request from the sales department.
The program used an elegant (optimized)
random number generator
to shuffle the "cards" and deal from the "deck",
and some of the salesmen felt it was too fair,
since sometimes the customers lost.
They wanted Mel to modify the program
so, at the setting of a sense switch on the console,
they could change the odds and let the customer win.

Mel balked.
He felt this was patently dishonest,
which it was,
and that it impinged on his personal integrity as a programmer,
which it did,
so he refused to do it.
The Head Salesman talked to Mel,
as did the Big Boss and, at the boss's urging,
a few Fellow Programmers.
Mel finally gave in and wrote the code,
but he got the test backwards,
and, when the sense switch was turned on,
the program would cheat, winning every time.
Mel was delighted with this,
claiming his subconscious was uncontrollably ethical,
and adamantly refused to fix it.

After Mel had left the company for greener pa$ture$,
the Big Boss asked me to look at the code
and see if I could find the test and reverse it.
Somewhat reluctantly, I agreed to look.
Tracking Mel's code was a real adventure.

I have often felt that programming is an art form,
whose real value can only be appreciated
by another versed in the same arcane art;
there are lovely gems and brilliant coups
hidden from human view and admiration, sometimes forever,
by the very nature of the process.
You can learn a lot about an individual
just by reading through his code,
even in hexadecimal.
Mel was, I think, an unsung genius.

Perhaps my greatest shock came
when I found an innocent loop that had no test in it.
No test. *None.*
Common sense said it had to be a closed loop,
where the program would circle, forever, endlessly.
Program control passed right through it, however,
and safely out the other side.
It took me two weeks to figure it out.

The RPC-4000 computer had a really modern facility
called an index register.
It allowed the programmer to write a program loop
that used an indexed instruction inside;
each time through,
the number in the index register
was added to the address of that instruction,
so it would refer
to the next datum in a series.
He had only to increment the index register
each time through.
Mel never used it.

Instead, he would pull the instruction into a machine register,
add one to its address,
and store it back.
He would then execute the modified instruction

right from the register.
The loop was written so this additional execution time
was taken into account —
just as this instruction finished,
the next one was right under the drum's read head,
ready to go.
But the loop had no test in it.

The vital clue came when I noticed
the index register bit,
the bit that lay between the address
and the operation code in the instruction word,
was turned on —
yet Mel never used the index register,
leaving it zero all the time.
When the light went on it nearly blinded me.

He had located the data he was working on
near the top of memory —
the largest locations the instructions could address —
so, after the last datum was handled,
incrementing the instruction address
would make it overflow.
The carry would add one to the
operation code, changing it to the next one in the instruction set:
a jump instruction.
Sure enough, the next program instruction was
in address location zero,
and the program went happily on its way.

I haven't kept in touch with Mel,
so I don't know if he ever gave in to the flood of
change that has washed over programming techniques
since those long-gone days.
I like to think he didn't.
In any event,
I was impressed enough that I quit looking for the
offending test,
telling the Big Boss I couldn't find it.
He didn't seem surprised.

When I left the company,
the blackjack program would still cheat

if you turned on the right sense switch,
and I think that's how it should be.
I didn't feel comfortable
hacking up the code of a Real Programmer.

This is one of hackerdom's great heroic epics, free verse or no. In a few spare images it captures more about the esthetics and psychology of hacking than all the scholarly volumes on the subject put together. For an opposing point of view, see the entry for **real programmer**.

[1992 postscript — the author writes: "The original submission to the net was not in free verse, nor any approximation to it — it was straight prose style, in non-justified paragraphs. In bouncing around the net it apparently got modified into the 'free verse' form now popular. In other words, it got hacked on the net. That seems appropriate, somehow."]

Appendix B A Portrait of J. Random Hacker

This profile reflects detailed comments on an earlier 'trial balloon' version from about a hundred USENET respondents. Where comparatives are used, the implicit 'other' is a randomly selected segment of the non-hacker population of the same size as hackerdom.

An important point: Except in some relatively minor respects such as slang vocabulary, hackers don't get to be the way they are by imitating each other. Rather, it seems to be the case that the combination of personality traits that makes a hacker so conditions one's outlook on life that one tends to end up being like other hackers whether one wants to or not (much as bizarrely detailed similarities in behavior and preferences are found in genetic twins raised separately).

General Appearance

Intelligent. Scruffy. Intense. Abstracted. Surprisingly for a sedentary profession, more hackers run to skinny than fat; both extremes are more common than elsewhere. Tans are rare.

Dress

Casual, vaguely post-hippie; T-shirts, jeans, running shoes, Birkenstocks (or bare feet). Long hair, beards, and moustaches are common. High incidence of tie-dye and intellectual or humorous 'slogan' T-shirts (only rarely computer related; that would be too obvious).

A substantial minority prefers 'outdoorsy' clothing — hiking boots ("in case a mountain should suddenly spring up in the machine room", as one famous parody put it), khakis, lumberjack or chamois shirts, and the like.

Very few actually fit the *National Lampoon* Nerd stereotype, though it lingers on at MIT and may have been more common before 1975. These days, backpacks are more common than briefcases, and the hacker 'look' is more whole-earth than whole-polyester.

Hackers dress for comfort, function, and minimal maintenance hassles rather than for appearance (some, perhaps unfortunately, take this to extremes and neglect personal hygiene). They have a very low tolerance of suits and other 'business' attire; in fact, it is not uncommon for hackers to quit a job rather than conform to a dress code.

Female hackers almost never wear visible makeup, and many use none at all.

Reading Habits

Omnivorous, but usually includes lots of science and science fiction. The typical hacker household might subscribe to *Analog, Scientific American, Co-Evolution Quarterly*, and *Smithsonian.* Hackers often have a reading range that astonishes liberal arts people but tend not to talk about it as much. Many hackers spend as much of their spare time reading as the average American burns up watching TV, and often keep shelves and shelves of well-thumbed books in their homes.

Other Interests

Some hobbies are widely shared and recognized as going with the culture: science fiction, music, medievalism (in the active form practiced by the Society for Creative Anachronism and similar organizations), chess, go, backgammon, wargames, and intellectual games of all kinds. (Role-playing games such as Dungeons and Dragons used to be extremely popular among hackers but they lost a bit of their luster as they moved into the mainstream and became heavily commercialized.) Logic puzzles. Ham radio. Other interests that seem to correlate less strongly but positively with hackerdom include linguistics and theater teching.

Physical Activity and Sports

Many (perhaps even most) hackers don't follow or do sports at all and are determinedly anti-physical. Among those who do, interest in spectator sports is low to non-existent; sports are something one *does*, not something one watches on TV.

Further, hackers avoid most team sports like the plague (volleyball is a notable exception, perhaps because it's non-contact and relatively friendly). Hacker sports are almost always primarily self-competitive ones involving concentration, stamina, and micromotor skills: martial arts, bicycling, auto racing, kite flying, hiking, rock climbing, aviation, target-shooting, sailing, caving, juggling, skiing, skating (ice and roller). Hackers' delight in techno-toys also tends to draw them towards hobbies with nifty complicated equipment that they can tinker with.

Education

Nearly all hackers past their teens are either college-degreed or self-educated to an equivalent level. The self-taught hacker is often considered (at least by other hackers) to be better-motivated, and may be more respected, than his school-shaped counterpart. Academic areas from which people often gravitate into hackerdom include (besides the obvious computer science and electrical engineering) physics, mathematics, linguistics, and philosophy.

Things Hackers Detest and Avoid

IBM mainframes. Smurfs, Ewoks, and other forms of offensive cuteness. Bureaucracies. Stupid people. Easy listening music. Television (except for cartoons, movies, the old "Star Trek", and the new "Simpsons"). Business suits. Dishonesty. Incompetence. Boredom. COBOL. BASIC. Character-based menu interfaces.

Food

Ethnic. Spicy. Oriental, esp. Chinese and most esp. Szechuan, Hunan, and Mandarin (hackers consider Cantonese vaguely *déclassé*). Hackers prefer the exotic; for example, the Japanese-food fans among them will eat with gusto such delicacies as fugu (poisonous pufferfish) and whale. Thai food has experienced flurries of popularity. Where available, high-quality Jewish delicatessen food is much esteemed. A visible minority of Southwestern and Pacific Coast hackers prefers Mexican.

For those all-night hacks, pizza and microwaved burritos are big. Interestingly, though the mainstream culture has tended to think of hackers as incorrigible junk-food junkies, many have at least mildly health-foodist attitudes and are fairly discriminating about what they eat. This may be generational; anecdotal evidence suggests that the stereotype was more on the mark 10–15 years ago.

Politics

Vaguely left of center, except for the strong libertarian contingent which rejects conventional left-right politics entirely. The only safe generalization is that hackers tend to be rather anti-authoritarian; thus, both conventional conservatism and 'hard' leftism are rare. Hackers are far more likely than most non-hackers to either (a) be aggressively apolitical or (b) entertain peculiar or idiosyncratic political ideas and actually try to live by them day-to-day.

Gender and Ethnicity

Hackerdom is still predominantly male. However, the percentage of women is clearly higher than the low-single-digit range typical for technical professions, and female hackers are generally respected and dealt with as equals.

In the U.S., hackerdom is predominantly Caucasian with strong minorities of Jews (East Coast) and Orientals (West Coast). The Jewish contingent has exerted a particularly pervasive cultural influence (see Food, above, and note that several common jargon terms are obviously mutated Yiddish).

The ethnic distribution of hackers is understood by them to be a function of which ethnic groups tend to seek and value education. Racial and ethnic prejudice is notably uncommon and tends to be met with freezing contempt.

When asked, hackers often ascribe their culture's gender- and color-blindness to a positive effect of text-only network channels, and this is doubtless a powerful influence. Also, the ties many hackers have to AI research and SF literature may have helped them to develop an idea of personhood that is inclusive rather than exclusive — after all, if one's imagination readily grants full human rights to AI programs, robots, dolphins, and extraterrestrial aliens, mere color and gender can't seem very important any more.

Religion

Agnostic. Atheist. Non-observant Jewish. Neo-pagan. Very commonly, three or more of these are combined in the same person. Conventional faith-holding Christianity is rare though not unknown.

Even hackers who identify with a religious affiliation tend to be relaxed about it, hostile to organized religion in general and all forms of religious bigotry in particular. Many enjoy 'parody' religions such as Discordianism and the Church of the SubGenius.

Also, many hackers are influenced to varying degrees by Zen Buddhism or (less commonly) Taoism, and blend them easily with their 'native' religions.

There is a definite strain of mystical, almost Gnostic sensibility that shows up even among those hackers not actively involved with neo-paganism, Discordianism, or Zen. Hacker folklore that pays homage to 'wizards' and speaks of incantations and demons has too much psychological truthfulness about it to be entirely a joke.

Ceremonial Chemicals

Most hackers don't smoke tobacco, and use alcohol in moderation if at all (though there is a visible contingent of exotic-beer fanciers, and a few hackers are serious oenophiles). Limited use of non-addictive psychedelic drugs, such as cannabis, LSD, psilocybin, and nitrous oxide, etc., used to be relatively common and is still regarded with more tolerance than in the mainstream culture. Use of 'downers' and opiates, on the other hand, appears to be particularly rare; hackers seem in general to dislike drugs that 'dumb them down'. On the third hand, many hackers regularly wire up on caffeine and/or sugar for all-night hacking runs.

Communication Style

See the discussions of speech and writing styles near the beginning of this File. Though hackers often have poor person-to-person communication skills, they are as a rule extremely sensitive to nuances of language and very precise in their use of it. They are often better at writing than at speaking.

Geographical Distribution

In the United States, hackerdom revolves on a Bay Area-to-Boston axis; about half of the hard core seems to live within a hundred miles of Cambridge (Massachusetts) or Berkeley (California), although there are significant contingents in Los Angeles, in the Pacific Northwest, and around Washington DC. Hackers tend to cluster around large cities, especially 'university towns' such as the Raleigh-Durham area in North Carolina or Princeton, New Jersey (this may simply reflect the fact that many are students or ex-students living near their alma maters).

Sexual Habits

Hackerdom tolerates a much wider range of sexual and lifestyle variation than the mainstream culture. It includes a relatively large gay and bi contingent. Hackers are somewhat more likely to live in polygynous or polyandrous relationships, practice open marriage, or live in communes or group houses. In this, as in general appearance, hackerdom semi-consciously maintains 'counterculture' values.

Personality Characteristics

The most obvious common 'personality' characteristics of hackers are high intelligence, consuming curiosity, and facility with intellectual abstractions. Also, most hackers are 'neophiles', stimulated by and appreciative of novelty (especially intellectual novelty). Most are also relatively individualistic and anti-conformist.

Although high general intelligence is common among hackers, it is not the *sine qua non* one might expect. Another trait is probably even more important: the ability to mentally absorb, retain, and reference large amounts of 'meaningless' detail, trusting to later experience to give it context and meaning. A person of merely average analytical intelligence who has this trait can become an effective hacker, but a creative genius who lacks it will swiftly find himself outdistanced by people who routinely upload the contents of thick reference manuals into their brains. [During the production of the book version of this document, for example, I learned most of the rather complex typesetting language TEX over about four working days, mainly by inhaling Knuth's 477-page manual. My editor's flabbergasted reaction to this genuinely surprised me, because years of associating with hackers have conditioned me to consider such performances routine and to be expected. — ESR]

Contrary to stereotype, hackers are *not* usually intellectually narrow; they tend to be interested in any subject that can provide mental stimulation, and can often discourse knowledgeably and even interestingly on any number of obscure subjects — if you can get them to talk at all, as opposed to, say, going back to their hacking.

It is noticeable (and contrary to many outsiders' expectations) that the better a hacker is at hacking, the more likely he or she is to have outside interests at which he or she is more than merely competent.

Hackers are 'control freaks' in a way that has nothing to do with the usual coercive or authoritarian connotations of the term. In the same way that children delight in making model trains go forward and back by moving a switch, hackers love making complicated things like computers do nifty stuff for them. But it has to be *their* nifty stuff. They don't like tedium, nondeterminism, or most of the fussy, boring, ill-defined little tasks that go with maintaining a normal existence. Accordingly, they tend to be careful and orderly in their intellectual lives and chaotic elsewhere. Their code will be beautiful, even if their desks are buried in 3 feet of crap.

Hackers are generally only very weakly motivated by conventional rewards such as social approval or money. They tend to be attracted by challenges and excited by interesting toys, and to judge the interest of work or other activities in terms of the challenges offered and the toys they get to play with.

In terms of Myers-Briggs and equivalent psychometric systems, hackerdom appears to concentrate the relatively rare INTJ and INTP types; that is, introverted, intuitive, and thinker types (as opposed to the extroverted-sensate personalities that predominate in the mainstream culture). ENT[JP] types are also concentrated among hackers but are in a minority.

Weaknesses of the Hacker Personality

Hackers have relatively little ability to identify emotionally with other people. This may be because hackers generally aren't much like 'other people'. Unsurprisingly, hackers also tend towards self-absorption, intellectual arrogance, and impatience with people and tasks perceived to be wasting their time.

As cynical as hackers sometimes wax about the amount of idiocy in the world, they tend by reflex to assume that everyone is as rational, 'cool', and imaginative as they consider themselves. This bias often contributes to weakness in communication skills. Hackers tend to be especially poor at confrontation and negotiation.

Because of their passionate embrace of (what they consider to be) the **Right Thing**, hackers can be unfortunately intolerant and bigoted on technical issues, in marked contrast to their general spirit of camaraderie and tolerance of alternative viewpoints otherwise. Old-time **ITS** partisans look down on the ever-growing hordes of **UNIX** hackers; UNIX aficionados despise **VMS** and **MS-DOS**; and hackers who are used to conventional command-line user interfaces loathe mouse-and-menu based systems such as the Macintosh. Hackers who don't indulge in **USENET** consider it a huge waste of time and **bandwidth**; fans of old adventure games such as **ADVENT** and **Zork** consider **MUDs** to be glorified chat systems devoid of atmosphere or interesting puzzles; hackers who are willing to devote endless hours to USENET or MUDs consider **IRC** to be a *real* waste of time; IRCies think MUDs might be okay if there weren't all those silly puzzles in the way. And, of course, there are the perennial **holy wars — EMACS** vs. **vi**, **big-endian** vs. **little-endian**, RISC vs. CISC, etc., etc., etc. As in society at large, the intensity and duration of these debates is usually inversely proportional to the number of objective, factual arguments available to buttress any position.

As a result of all the above traits, many hackers have difficulty maintaining stable relationships. At worst, they can produce the classic **computer geek**: withdrawn, relationally incompetent, sexually frustrated, and desperately unhappy when not submerged in his or her craft. Fortunately, this extreme is far less common than mainstream folklore paints it — but almost all hackers will recognize something of themselves in the unflattering paragraphs above.

Hackers are often monumentally disorganized and sloppy about dealing with the physical world. Bills don't get paid on time, clutter piles up to incredible heights in homes and offices, and minor maintenance tasks get deferred indefinitely.

The sort of person who uses phrases like 'incompletely socialized' usually thinks hackers are. Hackers regard such people with contempt when they notice them at all.

Miscellaneous

Hackers are more likely to have cats than dogs (in fact, it is widely grokked that cats have the hacker nature). Many drive incredibly decrepit heaps and forget to wash them; richer ones drive spiffy Porsches and RX-7s and then forget to have them washed. Almost all hackers have terribly bad handwriting, and often fall into the habit of block-printing everything like junior draftsmen.

Appendix C Bibliography

Here are some other books you can read to help you understand the hacker mindset.

Gödel, Escher, Bach: An Eternal Golden Braid
Douglas Hofstadter
Basic Books, 1979
ISBN 0-394-74502-7

This book reads like an intellectual Grand Tour of hacker preoccupations. Music, mathematical logic, programming, speculations on the nature of intelligence, biology, and Zen are woven into a brilliant tapestry themed on the concept of encoded self-reference. The perfect left-brain companion to *Illuminatus.*

Illuminatus!
I. *The Eye in the Pyramid*
II. *The Golden Apple*
III. *Leviathan.*
Robert Shea and Robert Anton Wilson
Dell, 1988
ISBN 0-440-53981-1

This work of alleged fiction is an incredible berserko-surrealist rollercoaster of world-girdling conspiracies, intelligent dolphins, the fall of Atlantis, who really killed JFK, sex, drugs, rock'n'roll, and the Cosmic Giggle Factor. First published in three volumes, but there is now a one-volume trade paperback, carried by most chain bookstores under SF. The perfect right-brain companion to Hofstadter's *Gödel, Escher, Bach.* See **Eris**, **Discordianism**, **random numbers**, **Church of the SubGenius**.

The Hitchhiker's Guide to the Galaxy
Douglas Adams
Pocket Books, 1981
ISBN 0-671-46149-4

This 'Monty Python in Space' spoof of SF genre traditions has been popular among hackers ever since the original British radio show. Read it if only to learn about Vogons (see **bogon**) and the significance of the number 42 (see **random numbers**) — and why the winningest chess program of 1990 was called 'Deep Thought'.

The Tao of Programming
James Geoffrey
Infobooks, 1987
ISBN 0-931137-07-1

This gentle, funny spoof of the *Tao Te Ching* contains much that is illuminating about the hacker way of thought. "When you have learned to snatch the error code from the trap frame, it will be time for you to leave."

Hackers
Steven Levy
Anchor/Doubleday 1984
ISBN 0-385-19195-2

Levy's book is at its best in describing the early MIT hackers at the Model Railroad Club and the early days of the microcomputer revolution. He never understood UNIX or the networks, though, and his enshrinement of Richard Stallman as "the last true hacker" turns out (thankfully) to have been quite misleading. Numerous minor factual errors also mar the text; for example, Levy's claim that the original Jargon File derived from the TMRC Dictionary (the File originated at Stanford and was brought to MIT in 1976; the co-authors of the first edition had never seen the dictionary in question). There are also numerous misspellings in the book that inflame the passions of old-timers; as Dan Murphy, the author of TECO, once said: "You would have thought he'd take the trouble to spell the name of a winning editor right." Nevertheless, this remains a useful and stimulating book that captures the feel of several important hackish subcultures.

The Devil's DP Dictionary
Stan Kelly-Bootle
McGraw-Hill, 1981
ISBN 0-07-034022-6

This pastiche of Ambrose Bierce's famous work is similar in format to the Jargon File (and quotes several entries from jargon-1) but somewhat different in tone and intent. It is more satirical and less anthropological, and is largely a product of the author's literate and quirky imagination. For example, it defines 'computer science' as "a study akin to numerology and astrology, but lacking the precision of the former and the success of the latter" and "the boring art of coping with a large number of trivialities."

The Devouring Fungus: Tales from the Computer Age
Karla Jennings
Norton, 1990
ISBN 0-393-30732-8

The author of this pioneering compendium knits together a great deal of computer- and hacker-related folklore with good writing and a few well-chosen cartoons. She has a keen eye for the human aspects of the lore and is very good at illuminating the psychology and evolution of hackerdom. Unfortunately, a number of small errors and awkwardnesses suggest that she didn't have the final manuscript checked over by a native speaker; the glossary in the back is particularly embarrassing, and at least one classic tale (the Magic Switch story, retold here under A Story About 'Magic' in appendix A) is given in incomplete and badly mangled form. Nevertheless, this book is a win overall and can be enjoyed by hacker and non-hacker alike.

The Soul of a New Machine
Tracy Kidder
Little, Brown, 1981
(paperback: Avon, 1982
ISBN 0-380-59931-7)

This book (a 1982 Pulitzer Prize winner) documents the adventure of the design of a new Data General computer, the MV-8000 Eagle. It is an amazingly well-done portrait of the hacker mindset — although largely the hardware hacker — done by a complete outsider. It is a bit thin in spots, but with enough technical information to be entertaining to the serious hacker while providing non-technical people a view of what day-to-day life can be like — the fun, the excitement, the disasters. During one period, when the microcode and logic were glitching at the nanosecond level, one of the overworked engineers departed the company, leaving behind a note on his terminal as his letter of resignation: "I am going to a commune in Vermont and will deal with no unit of time shorter than a season."

Life with UNIX: a Guide for Everyone
Don Libes and Sandy Ressler
Prentice-Hall, 1989
ISBN 0-13-536657-7

The authors of this book set out to tell you all the things about UNIX that tutorials and technical books won't. The result is gossipy, funny, opinionated, downright weird in spots, and invaluable. Along the way they expose you to enough of UNIX's history, folklore and humor to qualify as a first-class source for these things. Because so much of today's hackerdom is involved with UNIX, this in turn illuminates many of its in-jokes and preoccupations.

True Names . . . and Other Dangers
Vernor Vinge
Baen Books, 1987
ISBN 0-671-65363-6

Hacker demigod Richard Stallman believes the title story of this book "expresses the spirit of hacking best". This may well be true; it's certainly difficult to recall a better job. The other stories in this collection are also fine work by an author who is perhaps one of today's very best practitioners of hard SF.

Cyberpunk: Outlaws and Hackers on the Computer Frontier
Katie Hafner & John Markoff
Simon & Schuster 1991
ISBN 0-671-68322-5

This book gathers narratives about the careers of three notorious crackers into a clear-eyed but sympathetic portrait of hackerdom's dark side. The principals are Kevin Mitnick, "Pengo" and "Hagbard" of the Chaos Computer Club, and Robert T. Morris (see **RTM**, sense 2) . Markoff and Hafner focus as much on their psychologies and motivations as on the details of their exploits, but don't slight the latter. The result is a balanced and fascinating account, particularly useful when read immediately before or after Cliff Stoll's **The Cuckoo's Egg**. It is especially instructive to compare RTM, a true hacker who blundered, with the sociopathic phone-freak Mitnick and the alienated, drug-addled crackers who made the Chaos Club notorious. The gulf between **wizard** and **wannabee** has seldom been made more obvious.

Technobabble
John Barry
MIT Press 1991
ISBN 0-262-02333-4

Barry's book takes a critical and humorous look at the 'technobabble' of acronyms, neologisms, hyperbole, and metaphor spawned by the computer industry. Though he discusses some of the same mechanisms of jargon formation that occur in hackish, most of what he chronicles is actually suit-speak — the obfuscatory language of press releases, marketroids, and Silicon Valley CEOs rather than the playful jargon of hackers (most of whom wouldn't be caught dead uttering the kind of pompous, passive-voiced word salad he deplores).

The Cuckoo's Egg
Clifford Stoll
Doubleday 1989
ISBN 0-385-24946-2

Clifford Stoll's absorbing tale of how he tracked Markus Hess and the Chaos Club cracking ring nicely illustrates the difference between 'hacker' and 'cracker'. Stoll's portrait of himself, his lady Martha, and his friends at Berkeley and on the Internet paints a marvelously vivid picture of how hackers and the people around them like to live and what they think.

Contributors

This book could never have been without the generally warm and enthusiastic support of the network community. Hundreds of people spent untold thousands of hours putting together submissions and criticizing our drafts; we are deeply grateful. Some of the most dedicated contributors have been cited in the frontmatter; here are the rest. `TNX * 1e6` to you all.

Hobbit <hobbit@ftp.com>, CatWoman <diana@wetware.co
m>, Major <major@pyrmania.oz.au>, Werme <werme@alliant
.com>, mathew <mathew@mantis.co.uk>, Jason Abbott <jas
on@sco.com>, Kathryn Andersen <kat@bacchus.esa.oz.au>,
Dennis Andrews <dsa@uts.amdahl.com>, Dr. T. Andrews <t
anner@cdis-1.compu.com>, Vadim G. Antonov <avg@hq.demo
s.su>, Ken Arromdee <arromdee@server.cs.jhu.edu>, Jame
s Aspnes <asp@cs.cmu.edu>, Ran Atkinson <atkinson@itd.
nrl.navy.mil>, Kristen Axline <kristen@mport.com>, Wil
Baden <wil@sun.com>, Patrick Roger Bahn <prb@digex.acc
ess.com>, Mark S. Bailen <msbailen@msbdcolka.cr.usgs.g
ov>, Bill Barns <barns@gateway.mitre.org>, Olaf Barthe
l <olsen@sourcery>, Richard Bartle <76703.3042@compuse
rve.com>, Richard Basch <probe@uunet!mit.edu>, Samuel
B. Bassett <saml1b@ra-iris.arc.nasa.gov>, Ian G. Batten
<I.G.Batten@fulcrum.bt.co.uk>, Ron Bean <zaphod@madnix
.uucp>, Andrew Beattie <andrew@tug>, Mike Begley <spam
@iastate.edu>, Thomas Bellman <Bellman@Lysator.LiU.SE>
, Steven M. Bellovin <smb@ulysses.att.com>, Randolph B
entson <bentson@grieg.CS.ColoState.edu>, Peter Glen Be
rger <pb1p+@andrew.cmu.edu>, Steve Berlin <stev0@sti.c
om>, Pandora Berman <cent@silver.lcs.mit.edu>, Robert
Biddle <Robert.Biddle@vuw.ac.nz>, James Birdsall <jwbi
rdsa@amc.com>, Eric Black <ericb@Atherton.com>, Paul B
lack <black_pd@darwin.ntu.edu.au>, Matt Blaze <mab@duv
el.princeton.edu>, Earl Boebert <boebert@sctc.com>, Mi
ke Bolotski <mikeb@salmon.ee.ubc.ca>, Bob Bownes <rmb@
coventry.com>, Mark Brader <msb@sq.com>, Eli Brandt <e
brandt@jarthur.claremont.edu>, Kevin Braunsdorf <ksb@n
ostromo.cc.purdue.edu>, Seth Breidbart <sethb@fid.morg
an.com>, David Brooks <dbrooks@osf.org>, Andries Brouw
er <aeb@cwi.nl>, David Brower <daveb@ingres.com>, Ralf
Brown <ralf.brown@b.gp.cs.cmu.edu>, Robert E. Brown <b
rown@grettir.uucp>, Stan Brown <brown@ncoast.org>, Dav

id M. Brumley <dmb@srl01.cacs.usl.edu>, Andrew Bulhak
<ins559n@aurora.cc.monash.edu.au>, Craig Burley <burle
y@ai.mit.edu>, Scott L. Burson <gyro@zeta-soft.com>, L
arry Campbell <campbell@redsox.bsw.com>, Scott Carter
<carters@ajpo.sei.cmu.edu>, Benny the Cat <lebel.demon
@aida.csd.uu.se>, Jonathan A. Chandross <jac@paul.rutg
ers.edu>, Raymond Chen <raymond@math.berkeley.edu>, To
m Christiansen <tchrist@pixel.convex.com>, Lupe Christ
oph <lupe@ukw>, Wayne A. Christopher <faustus!ygdrasil
.berkeley.edu>, John W. St. Clair <jstclair@gmuvax2.gm
u.edu>, Robert E. Van Cleef <vancleef@garg.nas.nasa.go
v>, Nick Clifton <nickc@perisl.uucp>, Shannon D. Cline
<sc19+@andrew.cmu.edu>, Ronald Cole <rjc@devo.unify.co
m>, Forrest Cook <cook@stout.atd.ucar.edu>, Antony Coo
per <csirac@quagga.ru.ac.za>, Bernie Cosell <cosell@bb
n.com>, Michael A. Covington <mcovingt@athena.cs.uga.e
du>, John Cowan <cowan@snark.thyrsus.com>, Alan Cox <a
narchy@tardis.cs.ed.ac.uk>, Mark Crispin <mrc@cac.wash
ington.edu>, Damian Cugley <damian.cugley@prg.oxford.a
c.uk>, Charles Daffinger <cdaf@iuvax.cs.indiana.edu>,
Mike Daly <mtd@ssi>, Eric Davies <edavies@uvicctr.uvic
.ca>, Hugh Davies <Huge.wgc1@rx.xerox.com>, Christophe
r Davis <ckd@eff.org>, Franklin Davis <fad@Think.COM>,
Richard Dawson <rdawson@husky1.stmarys.ca>, Graham Dea
n <psb008@central1.lancaster.ac.uk>, Darragh Delany <d
arragh@maths.tcd.ie>, Mark Delany <mdelany@hbapn1.prim
e.com>, Wolfgang Denk <wd@distel.pcs.com>, Ethan Dicks
<erd@kumiss>, Mark-Jason Dominus <mjd@saul.cis.upenn.e
du>, Jon Doran <jon@ireland.austin.ibm.com>, Doug Douc
ette <stratus!wombat!doug>, Adams Douglas <adams@speed
s01.uucp>, Craig Dowell <dowell@decwrl.dec.com>, Kevin
Draz <kevind@pogo.wv.tek.com>, Shawn Joel Dube <jsd@ow
lnet.rice.edu>, Lars Duening <duening@ibr.cs.tu-bs.de>
, Dick Dunn <rcd@ico.isc.com>, Bryant Durrell <durrell
@umaxc.weeg.uiowa.edu>, Kristin Dyer <quoi@netcom.com>
, David Dyer-Bennet <ddb@anubis.network.com>, Paul Egg
ert <eggert@burns.twinsun.com>, Mark W. Eichin <eichin
@athena.mit.edu>, Per F. Ekman <pfe@csd.uu.se>, James
Ellis <ellis@laura.psc.edu>, P@"ar Emanuelsson <pell@i
sy.liu.se>, Jeremy Epstein <epstein@trwacs.uucp>, Kris
toffer Eriksson <ske@pkmab.se>, Art Evans <Evans@tl-20
b.arpa>, Mikel Evins <mikel@balor>, Scott Fahlman <Sco

tt.Fahlman@sef-pmax.slisp.cs.cmu.edu>, Dan Fain <fain@
icose.msd.anl.gov>, Thomas Farmer <tfarmer@ferrari.dat
amark.co.nz>, Clive Feather <clive@x.co.uk>, Mike Feld
man <feldman@urbana.mcd.mot.com>, Pete Fenellon <pete@
minster.york.ac.uk>, Pete Fenelon <pete@minster.york.a
c.uk>, Dennis Ferguson <dennis@CAnet.CA>, Luis Fernand
es <lfernand@ryelect.uucp>, Jose Fernandez <jaf@Infere
nce.com>, Jonathan R. Ferro <jf41+@andrew.cmu.edu>, Da
vid Fiander <david@sco.com>, Esther Filderman <ef1c+@a
ndrew.cmu.edu>, Gordon Findlay <gordon@chmeds.ac.nz>,
Joel R. Finkel <finkel@orpheo>, Raphael Finkel <raphae
l@ms.uky.edu>, Robert Firth <firth@sei.cmu.edu>, Micha
el Fischbein <mfischbein@east.sun.com>, Mike Fischbein
<mfischbein@East.Sun.com>, Dave Fischer <davefr@idsvax
.ids.com>, Michael J. Flory <mjf@cunixb.cc.columbia.ed
u>, Karl Fogel <kfogel@occs.cs.oberlin.edu>, Wayne Fol
ta <folta@cs.umd.edu>, Scott Forbes <forbes@toolserv.a
tt.com>, Thayne Forbes <Sun.com!unislc!thayne>, Elliot
Frank <esf00@amdahl.com>, Elliott Frank <esf00@juts.cc
c.amdahl.com>, Greg Franks <greg@sce.carleton.ca>, Rob
ert S. French <rfrench@athena.mit.edu>, Terry R. Fried
richsen <venus.sunquest.com>, Eirik Fuller <eirik@elf.
tn.cornell.edu>, Joel Furr <jfurr@nyx.cs.du.edu>, Rich
ard P. Gabriel <rpg@lucid.com>, Keith Gabryelski <ag@a
mix.commodore.com>, Chris Garrigues <7thSon@SLCS.SLB.C
OM>, Larry Gensch <lg@bsw0>, Charlie Gibbs <van-bc!min
dlink!Charlie_Gibbs>, David Gillett <dgil@ipsaint.ipsa
.reuter.com>, John Gilmore <gnu@hop.toad.com>, Brian G
ilstrap <gilstrap@swbatl.SWBT.COM>, Andy Glew <aglew@t
reflan.crhc.uiuc.edu>, Lynn Gold <figmo@mica.berkeley.
edu>, Jacob Gore <jacob@blackbox.gore.com>, Steven Gra
dy <grady@hermes.berkeley.edu>, Alastair Grant <AG129@
phx.cam.ac.uk>, Michael Grant <mgrant@xdr.ncsl.nist.go
v>, Robert J. Granvin <rjg@umnstat.stat.umn.edu>, Bill
Gray <gray@s5000.RSVL.UNISYS.com>, Jimm Griffith <grif
fith@dweeb.fx.com>, Jeremy Grodberg <jgro@apldbio.com>
, Geert Jan de Groot <geertj@ica.philips.nl>, Michael
K. Gschwind <relay.EU.net!vlsivie!mike>, Daniel R. Gui
lderson <ryan%umb.edu@relay.cs.net>, Ronald Guilmette
<rfg@esp.ics.uci.edu>, Arnt Gulbrandsen <agulbra@siri.
unit.no>, Kurt Guntheroth <kurt@tc.fluke.COM>, Scott G
uthery <guthery@acw.com>, Peter Gutmann <Peter_Gutman@

kcbbs.gen.nz>, Telsa Christina Gwynne <tcg8@aberystwyt
h.ac.uk>, Paul Haahr <haahr@cs.Princeton.edu>, Rusty H
addock <rusty@cs.UMD.EDU>, Peter Hahn <hahn@anubis.net
work.com>, Ed Hall <edhall@rand.org>, Josh Hall <josh@
cs.rutgers.edu>, Paul Hardy <ph@ama.caltech.edu>, Mark
Harrison <harrison@csl.dl.nec.com>, Brian Harvey <bh@a
narres.Berkeley.edu>, Larry Hastings <funkstr@ucscb.uc
sc.edu>, Frank Hausman <fhausman@wet.uucp>, Rowan Hawt
horne <rowan@ima.isc.com>, Steve Hayman <sahayman@iuva
x.cs.indiana.edu>, Tom Ivar Helbekkmo <tih@barsoom.nhh
.no>, Edson C. Hendricks <0003698408@mcimail.com>, Rob
ert R. Henry <rrh@tera.com>, Lennart Herlaar <lherlaar
@cs.ruu.nl>, Robert Herndon <rh@craycos.com>, Jarkko H
ietaniemi <jhi@dol-guldur.hut.fi>, Bill Higgins <higgi
ns@dale.fnal.gov>, D. Richard Hipp <drh@cs.duke.edu>,
Charles Hoequist <hoequist@bnr.ca>, Dan Hoey <hoey@aic
.nrl.navy.mil>, Jerry Hollombe <hollombe@ttidcb.tti.co
m>, Andy Holyer <andyh@syma.sussex.ac.uk>, Pete Holzma
nn <pete@Octopus.com>, Berthold K.P. Horn <bkph@mitvma
.mit.edu>, Louis Howell <howell@grover.llnl.gov>, Rola
nd Hutchinson <rhutchin@pilot.njin.net>, Donald E. Eas
tlake III, <dee@ranger.enet.dec.com>, Mark Israel <UAL
TAMTS.bitnet!ugw.utcs.utoronto.ca!USERISRA>, Christoph
er J. Jackson <cjj@east.sun.com>, Donald Jardine <jard
ined@qucis.queensu.ca>, Barr3y Jaspan <bjaspan@athena.
mit.edu>, Barry Jaspan <bjaspan@athena.mit.edu>, Rober
t Jervis <rbj@bjervis>, Dan Johnson <dwj@acd4>, Mark J
ohnson <mhjohnso@us.oracle.com>, Paul Andrew Johnson <
paj@gec-mrc.co.uk>, Arndt Jonasson <arndt@zyx.se>, Bru
ce Jones <bjones@weber.ucsd.edu>, Chris Jones <ksr!clj
@uunet.UU.NET>, Douglas W. Jones <jones@pyrite.cs.uiow
a.edu>, Arthur W. Protin Jr. <protin@pica.army.mil>, R
obert C. White, Jr. <rcw@scicom.alphacdc.com>, Jonatha
n I. Kamens <jik@pit-manager.mit.edu>, Brian Kantor <b
rian@ucsd.edu>, Adam Kao <adam@ip2020>, Michael L. Kau
fman <kaufman@delta.eecs.nwu.edu>, David Keldsen <dak@
sq.com>, Dave Keller <dsac.dla.mil!nha2177>, Michael K
ennett <kennett@maths.uwa.oz.au>, Berry Kercheval <ber
ry@idi>, Phil Kernick <phil@adam.adelaide.edu.au>, Sim
on Kershaw <simon.kershaw@smallworld.co.uk>, Bill Kinn
ersley <kinners@hawk.cs.ukans.edu>, Michael Kirschner
<obnoid@lippy.clipper.ingr.com>, Evan Kirshenbaum <eva

n@hplerk.hpl.hp.com>, Daniel Klein <dvk@sei.cmu.edu>,
Charley Kline <c-kline@uiuc.edu>, Kevin Klop <kevin@cb
mvax.commodore.com>, Thomas Koenig <ig25@rz.uni-karlsr
uhe.de>, Karl-Koenig Koenigsson <kko@asd.tds.philips.s
e>, James J. Koschella <jjk@ghoti.lcs.mit.edu>, Alan T
. Koski <akoski@as.arizona.edu>, David Kra <DACRA@NYCV
MIC1.VNET.IBM>, Jonathan Krueger <jkrueger@dtic.dla.mi
l>, Rich Kulawiec <rsk@oldfield.CS.ColoState.Edu>, Mik
e Kupfer <kupfer@orc.olivetti.com>, Robin C. LaPasha <
ruslan@uncecs.edu>, Joe LaRocque <cbmvax!uunet!eng3.sc
i.com!joe>, Steve Lamont <spl@szechuan.ncsc.org>, Doug
Landauer <landauer@Eng.sun.com>, Nickolas Landsberg <n
pl@mozart.att.com>, Geoff Lane <zzassgl@uk.ac.mcc.uts>
, Bengt Larsson <bengtl@maths.lth.se>, Alex Latzko <la
tzko@dorm.rutgers.edu>, Oliver Laumann <net@tub.cs.tu-
berlin.de>, Merlyn LeRoy <merlyn@digibd.com>, Jeff Lee
<jonah@dgp.toronto.edu>, Doug Lenat <ai.lenat@mcc.com>
, Tim Leonard <Tim.Leonard@computer-lab.cambridge.ac.u
k>, Dan Lester <lester@sapphire.idbsu.edu>, Robert A.
Levene <levene@aplpy.jhuapl.edu>, John R. Levine <john
l@iecc.cambridge.ma.us>, Lewis Levine <levinel@teradyn
e>, James Wilbur Lewis <jwl@garnet.berkeley.edu>, Don
Libes <libes@cme.nist.gov>, Kurt J. Lidl <lidl@eng.umd
.edu>, Per Lindberg <pre@front.se>, Tom Link <tml@unix
.cis.pitt.edu>, Chris Long <clong@remus.rutgers.edu>,
Charles J. Lord <cjl@uncecs.edu>, Mark Lord <mlord@bnr
.ca>, Warner Losh <imp@solbourne.com>, Mark Lottor <mk
l@toad.com>, Pete Lucas <p.lucas@unixa.nerc-swindon.ac
.uk>, John Lupien <lupienj@hpwarq.wal.hp.com>, David J
. MacKenzie <djm@eng.umd.edu>, Stavros Macrakis <macra
kis@gr.osf.org>, Jonathan Magid <magidj@marimba.cellbi
o.duke.edu>, Otto J. Makela <Otto.Makela@jyu.fi>, Sean
Malloy <malloy@nprdc.navy.mil>, Dave Mankins <dm@think
.com>, Bob Manson <manson@cis.ohio-state.edu>, Barry M
argolin <barmar@think.com>, David Matuszek <dave@prc.u
nisys.com>, Paula Matuszek <paula@prc.unisys.com>, Jay
Maynard <jmaynard@thesis1.hsch.utexas.edu>, James E. M
cAdams <jmcadams@casbah.acns.nwu.edu>, Mike McCole <mi
kem@hechcx.hec.harris.com>, Michael McCool <mccool@dgp
.toronto.edu>, Jon McCown <jdm1@eds1.eds.com>, Don McC
ullers <mccullers@msesu4.ENET.DEC.com>, Hugh McGuinnes
s <hughm@tplrd.tpl.oz>, Scott McKay <SWM@SAPSUCKER.SCR

C.Symbolics.com>, Geoff Mccaughan <geoff@equinox.gen.nz>, Michael Meissner <meissner@osf.org>, Rev. Ben A. Mesander <ben@epmooch.UUCP>, David Messer <dave@viper.lynx.mn.org>, Mark Meyer <mmeyer@m2.csc.ti.com>, Peter Miller <pmiller@neccan.oz>, Dave Mills <Mills@udel.edu>, Eugene N. Miya <eugene@wilbur.nas.nasa.gov>, Dave Modiano <needle@athena.mit.edu>, Shamim Zvonko Mohamed <sham@cs.arizona.edu>, Fanya S. Montalvo <montalvo@crl.dec.com>, James Montebello <james@ignatz.bridge.com>, David A. Moon <moon@cambridge.apple.com>, Jim Moore <jmoore@Solbourne.com>, Larry Morandi <larrym@relay.cs.net>, Wes Morgan <morgan@ms.uky.edu>, Joe Morris <jcmorris@mwunix.mitre.org>, Wayne G. Morrison <tewok@tis.com>, Eliot Moss <moss@cs.umass.edu>, der Mouse <mouse@lightning.mcrcim.mcgill.edu>, Scott Hazen Mueller <scott@zorch.SF-Bay.ORG>, Alec Muffett <aem@cs.aber.ac.uk>, Alec D E Muffett <aem@aberystwyth.ac.uk>, Christian Murphy <cpmurphy@vax1.tcd.ie>, M. R. Murphy <mrm@Sceard.com>, John G. Myers <jgm@fed.expres.cs.cmu.edu>, Wayne Myles <ins_wayne@actew.oz.au>, Ed Nather <nather@astro.as.utexas.edu>, Peter Neilson <neilson@osf.org>, Russ Nelson <nelson@image.soe.clarkson.edu>, Thomas Neudecker <tn07+@andrew.cmu.edu>, Joseph M. Newcomer <jn11+@andrew.cmu.edu>, Gerard K. Newman <gkn@sdsc.edu>, Don Nichols <dnichols@ceilidh.beartrack.com>, Jarl Nilsson <jarl@Franz.com>, Michael Niv <niv@linc.cis.upenn.edu>, J. Gregory Noel <greg@relay.cs.net>, Leonard Norrgard <vinsci@brando.uwasa.fi>, Sami Nuwayser <shn@think.com>, Pat O'Connell <oconnell@rye.cs.unm.edu>, Erik O'Shaughnessy <eoshough@dante.nmsu.edu>, John Ockerbloom <John.Ockerbloom@MATHOM.GANDALF.CS.CMU.EDU>, Drew Olbrich <po0o@andrew.cmu.edu>, Paul Andrew Olbrich <po0o+@andrew.cmu.edu>, Mike Oliver <moliver@shadow.pyramid.com>, James Olsen <olsen@masala.lcs.mit.edu>, John Olsen <olsen@hpfcjo.fc.hp.com>, Magnus Olsson <magnus@thep.lu.se>, Stan Osborne <stan@toaster.SFSU.EDU>, David Phillip Oster <oster@well.sf.ca.us>, Lamar Owen <lowen@lorc>, Randolph Pacetti <inel.gov!lph>, Penny Padgett <PADGETT@INTELLICORP.com>, Bob Page <page@eng.sun.com>, Stephen Page <Stephen.Page@prg.oxford.ac.uk>, Anthon Pang <anthon_pang@mindlink.uucp>, Craig Partridge <craig@sics.se>, Jonathan Peatfield <jon@harlqn.co.uk>, Mi ke Van Pelt <mvp@apple.com>, Michael S. Pereckas <msp33327@uxa.cso.uiuc.edu>, John Peterson <jp@apple.com>, Peter Phillips <phillips@ucsd.edu>, Kent M. Pitman <KMP@STONY-BROOK.SCRC.Symbolics.com>, Colin Plumb <ccplumb@lion.waterloo.edu>, Paul Pomes <paul@uxc.cso.uiuc.edu>, Edwin V. Post <Edwin_V_Post@cup.portal.com>, David Potter <potter@csusac.ecs.csus.edu>, Jeff Poulin <poulin@polar.bowdoin.edu>, Craig Presson <craig@jido.ingr.ingr.com>, Ingemar Ragnemalm <ingemar@isy.liu.se>, Marc Ramsey <marc@sunra.uucp>, Anton Rang <rang@cs.wisc.edu>, Heiko Rath <hr@brewhr.swb.de>, Jonathan Rees <jar@altdorf.ai.mit.edu>, George V. Reilly <gvr@cs.brown.edu>, Andy Reiner <reiner@cshl.org>, Liam Relihan <relihanl@ul.ie>, Chris Rende <cfctech.cfc.com!rphroy!trux!car>, Chris Reynolds <chris.reynolds@syd.dit.csiro.au>, William D. Ricker <wdr@world.std.com>, Dennis Ritchie <dmr@research.att.com>, Stephen E. Robbins <stever@ai.mit.edu>, Tim Roberts <Tim_N_Roberts@cup.portal.com>, John Robinson <jr@ksr.com>, David A. Rochberg <dar8808@cec1.wustl.edu>, Frederick G. M. Roeber <roeber@cithe1.cithep.caltech.edu>, Greg Roelofs <roelofs@oddjob.uchicago.edu>, Andrew Rogers <rogers@sud509.ed.ray.com>, John Rogers <johnro@microsoft.com>, Nick Rothwell <nick@lfcs.ed.ac.uk>, Peter Van Roy <vanroy@draco.Berkeley.edu>, Clifton Royston <clifton_r@verifone.com>, Erkki Ruohtula <eru@tele.nokia.fi>, Alan Ruttenberg <alanr@media-lab.media.mit.edu>, Rich Salz <rsalz@bbn.com>, Chip Salzenberg <chip@tct.uucp>, Curt Sampson <curt@cynic.wimsey.bc.ca>, Pete Samson <prs@splunge>, Christopher Samuel <ccs7@uk.ac.aber>, Daan Sandee <sandee@sun16.scri.fsu.edu>, Wayne Sanders <sandy@dev3f.uucp>, Aamod Sane <sane@cs.uiuc.edu>, John Schultz <c491153@umcvmb.missouri.edu>, Richard A. Schumacher <schumach@magnum.convex.com>, Morgan Schweers <mrs@netcom.com>, Eric P. Scott <eps@toaster.sfsu.edu>, Maxwell Scott <maxwell@uxa.cso.uiuc.edu>, Robert E. Seastrom <rs@eddie.mit.edu>, Ryan Sells <t0i@mentor.cc.purdue.edu>, Larry Setlow <pjt@fqyvax.cpac.washington.edu>, Bill Seymour <billsey@agora.rain.com>, Amos Shapir <amos@taux01.nsc.com>, John Shipman <john@jupiter.nmt.edu>, Ken Shirriff <shirriff@sprite.berkeley.edu>, Melinda Shore <shore@mtxinu.com>, Mark Shoulson <shoulson@husc9.harvard.e

du>, Jeff Shrager <shrager@xerox.com>, Nathan Sidwell
<nathan@inmos.com>, Peter da Silva <peter@ficc.ferrant
i.com>, Steve Simmons <scs@iti.org>, Cameron Simpson <
cameron@spectrum.cs.unsw.oz.au>, Ravi Sinnarajah <ravi
@CORNELLC.cit.cornell.edu>, John Sinteur <sinteur@ooc.
uva.nl>, John Sloan <jsloan@niwot.scd.ucar.edu>, Jeff
Slovin <slovin@tdw511.ed.ray.com>, Colin Smiley <ad5@m
entor.cc.purdue.edu>, C. J. Smith <csmith@saber.com>,
James G. Smith <jamie@active-book-co.co.uk>, Joe Smith
<jms@tardis.tymnet.com>, Richard Smith <rss@calstate.b
itnet>, Rick Smith <smith@sctc.com>, Roy Smith <roy@al
anine.phri.nyu.edu>, Sally Smith <sally@tardis.tymnet.
com>, Andrew Solovay <asolovay@bsw.uucp>, Bill Sommerf
eld <wesommer@athena.mit.edu>, Zoltan Somogyi <zs@mull
auna.cs.mu.oz.au>, Don Speck <mangler@csvax.caltech.ed
u>, Walter Spector <wws@sequoia.cray.com>, Tom Spindle
r <u56933@uicvm.uic.edu>, Diomidis Spinellis <dds@cc.i
c.ac.uk>, Charles Spurgeon <spurgeon@sirius.cc.utexas.
edu>, David Stampe <stampe@uhccux.uhcc.hawaii.edu>, Ro
n Stanonik <stanonik@nprdc.navy.mil>, Guy Steele <gls@
think.com>, Brent Sterner <brent@julian.uucp>, Richard
Stevens <stevens@hsi.com>, Bill Stewart <wcs@erebus.at
t.com>, Ken Stewart <kstewart@uk.oracle.com>, William
Clare Stewart <wcs@erebus.att.com>, Anthony J. Stieber
<anthony@csd4.csd.uwm.edu>, Don Stokes <don@gp.co.nz>,
Jorge Stolfi <stolfi@src.dec.com>, Larry Stone <lcs@ic
ad.com>, John Stracke <francis@dogwood>, Steve Strassm
ann <straz@media-lab.media.mit.edu>, Bob Stratton <dsc
3rjs@nmdsc20.nmdsc.nnmc.navy.mil>, Charles Stross <cha
rless@sco.com>, Steve Summit <scs@adam.mit.edu>, Steve
C. Summit <scs@adam.mit.edu>, Julie Sussman <jems@ai.m
it.edu>, Bob Sutterfield <bob@MorningStar.com>, Tony S
weeney <sweeney%ingres.com%mtxinu@uunet.uu.net>, Bruce
Taylor <taylor@solid-earth-physics.uib.no>, Glenn S. T
enney <apple.com!well!tenney>, Scott Terek <sterek@apg
.andersen.com>, Sandra D. Thomas <delores@cis.ohio-sta
te.edu>, Steve Thomas <decwrl.dec.com!garth!sthomas>,
Rich Thomson <thomson@cs.utah.edu>, Bill Thorson <thor
son@typhoon.atmos.colostate.edu>, Wayne Throop <sheol!
throopw@dg-rtp.dg.com>, Eric Tiedemann <est@ollie.acf.
nyu.edu>, Graham Toal <gtoal@ed.ac.uk>, Bennett Todd <
bet@orion.mc.duke.edu>, George Tomasevich <grt@blink.a

tt.com>, Paul Tomblin <pt@geovision.uucp>, Nathan Tork
ington <nathan.torkington@comp.vuw.ac.nz>, J. Eric Tow
nsend <jet@uh.edu>, Paul Traina <pst@ack.Stanford.EDU>
, Gregory Travis <greg@cica.indiana.edu>, Thomas Trusc
ott <trt@rti.rti.org>, Ted Ts'o <tytso@athena.mit.edu>
, Gary Tse <garyt@circle-k.convergent.com>, Scott Turn
er <srt@aerospace.aero.org>, Simon Turner <simon@robot
s.oxford.ac.uk>, Stephen Uitti <suitti@ima.isc.com>, M
atthias Urlichs <urlichs@relay.cs.net>, The Unknown Us
er <gamma967@houston.relay.ucm.org>, Johnathan Vail <v
ail@tegra.com>, Marc-Etienne Vargenau <vargenau@freman
tle.UUCP>, Jay Vassos-Libove <libove@libove.det.dec.co
m>, Jay Vosburgh <fubar@sequent.com>, Keith Waclena <k
eith@gargoyle.uchicago.edu>, David Vinayak Wallace <gu
mby@Gang-of-Four.Stanford.EDU>, Janet Walz <jwalz@rsg1
.er.usgs.gov>, Jeff Wasilko <jjwcmp@ultb.isc.rit.edu>,
William Watson <watson@rhino.uucp>, Allan C. Wechsler
<acw@yukon.scrc.symbolics.com>, Dan Weinreb <dlw@odi.c
om>, Marc Weiser <Mark_Weiser.PARC@xerox.com>, Mike We
lls <3037mpas@hub.ucsb.edu>, Al Wesolowsky <abw@bucrsb
.bu.edu>, Mike Whitaker <mikew@sdl.mdcbbs.com>, Ted Wi
lliams <ted@vms.cis.pitt.edu>, Paul Wilson <wilson@car
coar.Stanford.edu>, Steve Wilson <stevew@wyse.com>, Ph
yllis Winkler <winkler@Sunburn.Stanford.EDU>, Lars Wir
zenius <wirzeniu@cc.helsinki.fi>, Ted Wojcik <wojcik@c
rl.dec.com>, The Grey Wolf <greywolf@autodesk.com>, Ga
rrett Wollman <wollman@griffin.uvm.edu>, Sarah Woodall
<sarah@harlqn.co.uk>, Don Woods <woods@eng.sun.com>, J
eff Woolsey <woolsey@mri>, Paul Christopher Workman <p
w0l+@andrew.cmu.edu>, Mark Wutka <cmrlbmw@prism.gatech
.edu>, Geraldo Xexeo <xexeo@dxcern.cern.ch>, John Yeat
es <johny@syma.sussex.ac.uk>, Ozan S. Yigit <oz@nexus.
yorku.ca>, A. T. Young <aty@ucselx.sdsu.edu>, Doug You
ng <dmy@solbourne.com>, Rayan Zachariassen <rayan@cs.t
oronto.edu>, Mark Zellers <mzellers@starnet>, Seth Zir
in <seth.zirin@att.com>, David D. Zuhn <zoo@aps1.spa.u
mn.edu>, Elizabeth Zwicky <zwicky@itstd.sri.com>, mark
s. bailen <msbailen@msbdcolka.cr.usgs.gov>,

and the USENET community at large.